LESSONS IN LIKENESS

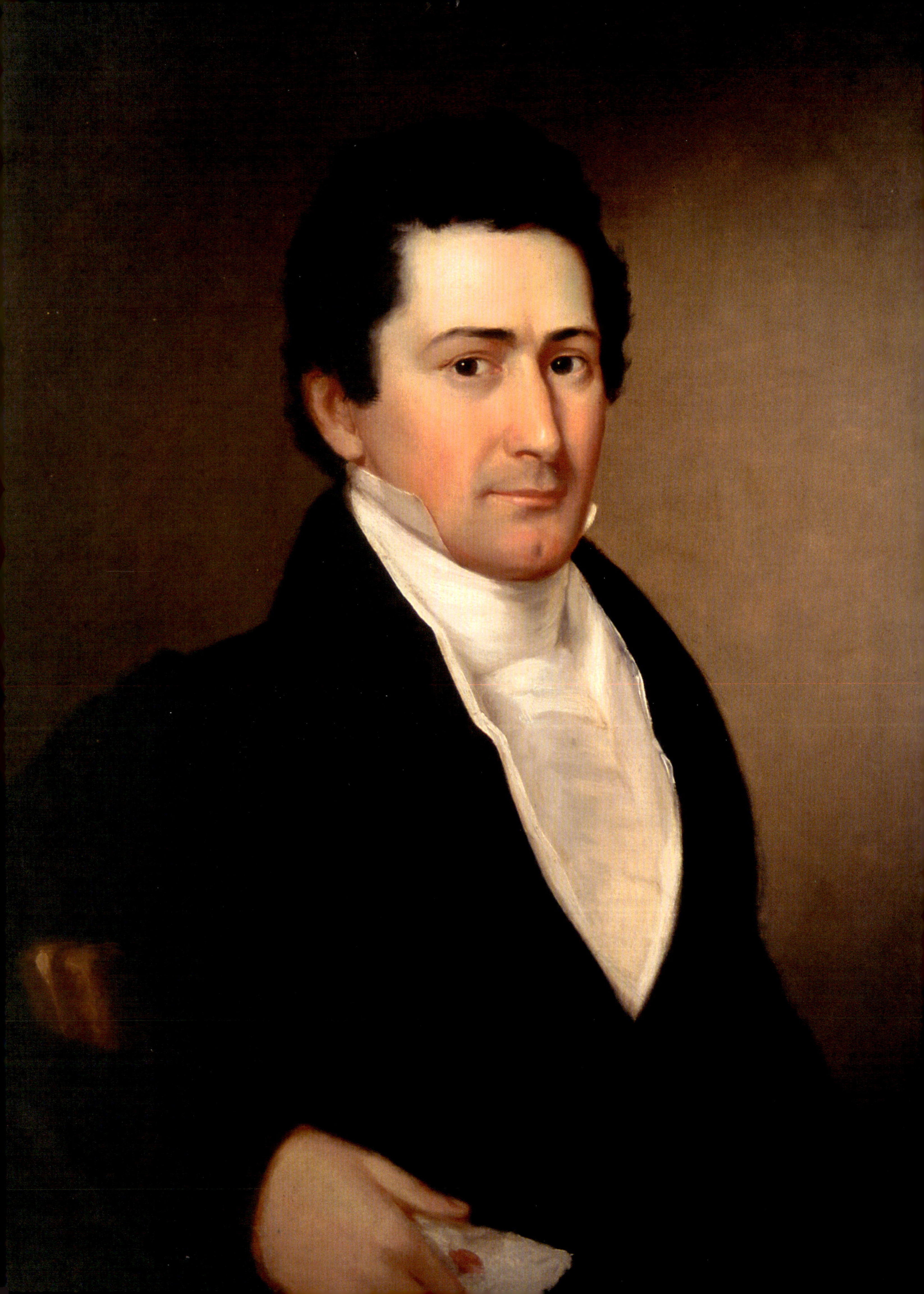

Lessons in Likeness

Portrait Painters in Kentucky and the Ohio River Valley, 1802–1920

ESTILL CURTIS PENNINGTON

Featuring works from The Filson Historical Society

The University Press of Kentucky

Scholarly publisher for the Commonwealth,
serving Bellarmine University, Berea College, Centre College of Kentucky, Eastern Kentucky University, The Filson Historical Society, Georgetown College, Kentucky Historical Society, Kentucky State University, Morehead State University, Murray State University, Northern Kentucky University, Transylvania University, University of Kentucky, University of Louisville, and Western Kentucky University.

Editorial and Sales Offices:
The University Press of Kentucky
663 South Limestone Street
Lexington, Kentucky 40508-4008
www.kentuckypress.com

Frontispiece: Alonzo Douglass, *James C. Morsell,* ca. 1828, oil on canvas, 27¾ × 22¾", The Filson Historical Society, 1989.20.

14 13 12 11 10 5 4 3 2 1

Library of Congress Cataloging-in-Publication Data
Pennington, Estill Curtis.
Lessons in likeness : portrait painters in Kentucky and the Ohio River Valley, 1802–1920 / Estill Curtis Pennington.
p. cm.
Includes bibliographical references and index.
ISBN 978-0-8131-2612-8 (hardcover : alk. paper)
1. Portrait painting, American—Kentucky.
2. Portrait painting, American—Ohio River Region.
3. Portrait painters—Kentucky—Biography.
4. Portrait painters—Ohio River Region—Biography.
I. Title. II. Title: Portrait painters in Kentucky and the Ohio River Valley, 1802–1920.
ND1311.9.K4P46 2011
757.09769'09034—dc22 2010016189

This book is printed on acid-free paper meeting the requirements of the American National Standard for Permanence in Paper for Printed Library Materials.

Manufactured in China.
Design and composition by Julie Allred,
BW&A Books, Inc.

Member of the Association of American University Presses

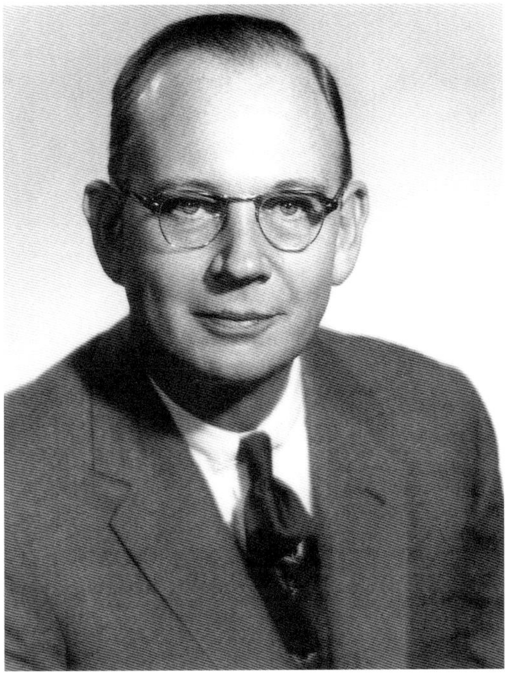

IN MEMORIAM

George Garvin Brown II
(1911–1969)

This book was made possible through
the generous contributions of
G. Garvin Brown III,
Laura Lee Brown,
and Dace Brown Stubbs,
in honor of their father,
George Garvin Brown II.

*There is no limit to the good a man can do
if he doesn't care who gets the credit.*
—Judson Branch

CONTENTS

FOREWORD

Lessons in Likeness, Estill Pennington's study of portrait painting in Kentucky and the Ohio River Valley from about 1800 to the end of the First World War, will delight many readers. In this book he offers a general essay about Kentucky portraiture in that long century and provides a biographical checklist of individual artists, illustrated primarily with portraits in the collection of The Filson Historical Society. The book enriches our knowledge of Kentucky art and history in important ways. The author has been a student of Kentucky portraiture for many years because of his own family history and his strong association with the state and region. Building on earlier sources, including Edna Talbott Whitley's *Kentucky Ante-bellum Portraiture* (1956) and the exhibition catalog *The Kentucky Painter: from the Frontier Era to the Great War* (Arthur F. Jones and Bruce Weber; Lexington: University of Kentucky Art Museum, 1981), Mr. Pennington has developed a wide-ranging knowledge of the history of its portraits through archival research, exhibitions, conferences, and publications. As the most knowledgeable scholar of this region's portraits, he has become the person whom others seek out for clarification of the myriad details of its history. These features of his knowledge, offered in this book, make it a major resource for Kentuckians about their own history.

Lessons in Likeness offers this and more to students of American art in general. It coincides with recent studies of public and private patronage, regionalism in art, itinerancy, and the definitions of styles such as "folk" or "naive" painting. Students of these broader subjects will benefit from Mr. Pennington's close and careful presentation of portraiture in a region with an early history at the time of the expansion of the young American republic westward. The cultural aspects of this growth in other regions have been studied closely by scholars through examination of individual artists and their work, through exhibitions and books on portraiture in regions of the country, and through catalogs of portrait collections at historical societies. After Jules Prown's *John Singleton Copley,* a two-volume study of the work of that colonial American artist (Cambridge, Mass.: Harvard University Press for the National Gallery of Art, 1966), set the standard for studies of the work of individual American portrait painters, numerous major exhibitions and catalogs subsequently helped us understand the individual styles of many important artists, especially before the 1850s. The early focus on portraiture by the Colonial Dames in publications such as the *North Carolina Portrait Index* became the basis for regional surveys, as did studies of portrait collections like the *Catalogue of American Portraits in the New-York Historical Society* (two volumes; New Haven: Yale University Press, 1974) and *American Folk Portraits: Paintings and Drawings from the Abby Aldrich Rockefeller Folk Art Collection* (Boston: New York Graphic Society, 1981) and, more recently, *Portraits in the Collection of the American Antiquarian Society* by Lauren B. Hewes (Worcester, Mass.: American Antiquarian Society, 2004). Previous regional studies have included *Meet Your Neighbors: New England Portraits, Painters, and Society, 1790–1850* (Jack Larkin, Elizabeth Mankin Kornhauser, David Jaffee, and Jessica F. Nicoll; Sturbridge, Mass.: Old Sturbridge Village, 1992), *Painting and Portrait Making in the American Northeast,* a volume in the annual proceedings of the Dublin Seminar for New England Folklife (ed. Peter Benes, assoc. ed. Jane Montague Benes; Boston: Boston University, 1995); *Remembrance of Patria: Dutch Arts and Culture in Colonial America, 1609–1776* (Ruth Piwonka and Roderic H. Blackburn; New York: Albany Institute of History and Art, 1988), *Portrait Painting in Tennessee* (Tennessee Historical Society, 1987), and Pennington's own *Messengers of Style: Itinerancy and Taste in Southern Portraiture, 1784–1867* (Greenville, S.C.: Greenville County Museum of Art, 1993), to mention only a few. And discussions of style have been intelligently addressed by John Michael Vlatch in his *Plain Painters: Making Sense of American Folk Art* (Washington, D.C.: Smithsonian Institution Press, 1988).

In the present study of Kentucky portraiture, Mr. Pennington documents the cultural and artistic transitions that took place in portraiture in the Ohio River Valley region. With *Lessons in Likeness* will come examples that no doubt will vary from assumed norms. By studying the artists of this region, and by being able to see documented examples of their work, scholars and curators can more easily chart the details of the history of American portraiture and its role in the cultural self-consciousness of the young republic. It will be increasingly possible to address key questions, such as: What American cities were considered the important centers for portraiture, at what times? How do regions differ in their patronage? What is the relationship between local artists and itinerant artists? What was the impact of the circulation of prints and the first public exhibitions of art on local portraiture? What was the influence of photography on regional artists after its introduction to the portrait market in 1839? This heartfelt, personal attention to the Kentucky artists and their work thus will enrich the study of American art and American history in important ways.

ELLEN G. MILES
Curator of Painting and Sculpture
Smithsonian National Portrait Gallery

PREFACE

THE MISSION of The Filson Historical Society is to collect, preserve, and tell the significant stories of Kentucky and the Ohio River Valley region's history and culture. The enduring legacy that portrait painters left to our region in the form of portraiture is one of those significant stories. Today, approximately four hundred portraits make up our collection, a number that continues to grow as The Filson reaches its 125th anniversary.

The first documented portrait donation to The Filson was John Wesley Jarvis's likeness of General James Wilkinson, the shady frontier leader and self-promoter, given by the Kentucky historian Richard H. Collins in 1892. The Filson's founder, Reuben T. Durrett, and his associates aggressively pursued other portraits as both donations and purchases. When original works could not be found, Durrett commissioned copies to fill in the gaps in this growing gallery of notables.

Some insight into why portraits mattered to the founders was revealed by Durrett's remarks in 1901, when he accepted on behalf of The Filson a portrait of George M. Davie, one of the institution's founders. Durrett likened portraits to the images uncovered at Pompeii or discovered in Egyptian tombs. He marveled at the "painted likenesses of human beings" that "had lain there for twenty centuries." The portrait painter's work was "magical," Durrett wrote, because it "preserved the form and features of loved ones, and presents them to our eyes as they lived, after death has removed them from us forever."

Lessons in Likeness describes the resident and mostly itinerant artists who crisscrossed the region in search of sitters and a livelihood. By the time the earliest Kentuckian likenesses examined in this study were created, this "western country" that fascinated The Filson's founders had been occupied by Euro-Americans for almost a generation. Early profile painters such as John James Audubon and Samuel H. Dearborn busied themselves capturing for posterity the likenesses of citizens of means and social standing. When the young Patrick Henry Davenport painted Eliza Delaney Rodes, ca. 1818, the frontier south of the Ohio River had moved west. And when the prolific Matthew Harris Jouett died in 1827, the number of people leaving the state for western territories exceeded the number of settlers entering Kentucky from the east.

Thus, these portrait painters lived during times of economic, political, and social upheaval. Over the course of the nineteenth century, they collectively witnessed the dispossession of Indians, the passing of the frontier, the emergence of a prosperous antebellum economy dependent on commercial agriculture and slavery, the Civil War and its aftermath, and the rise of a late nineteenth-century industrial and urban elite. Although the arrival of new technology in the form of studio photography cut into the demand for painted portraits, the region continued to support portrait painting into the twentieth century. Estill Curtis Pennington's *Lessons in Likeness* helps us understand what these changes meant to both painters and sitters and why they mattered, both then and now.

MARK V. WETHERINGTON
Director
The Filson Historical Society

ACKNOWLEDGMENTS

THIS PUBLICATION was made possible by the generosity of Dace Brown Stubbs, Laura Lee Brown, and G. Garvin Brown III, whose contributions were made in memory of their father, George Garvin Brown II. The Filson Historical Society is grateful to them for this opportunity to share a portion of its portrait collection with those who are interested in the study of historical portraiture. The Filson thanks them for their support of this educational endeavor, which continues its mission to be a resource for the study of the history and culture of Kentucky and the Ohio River Valley.

The Director of The Filson Historical Society would also like to thank the following members of his staff for their expertise and assistance: James J. Holmberg, Curator of Special Collections, Jacob F. Lee, Associate Curator of Special Collections, Judy L. Miller, Director of Development and Programs, and Robin L. Wallace, Associate Curator of Special Collections.

The author would like to acknowledge the assistance given and insights offered by the art historical community. Gratitude is offered to Dr. Ellen Gross Miles, Linda Thrift, and Lizanne Garrett, National Portrait Gallery; Cecilia Chinn, National Portrait Gallery/Smithsonian American Art Museum Library; Kurt Ghude and Andrea Fisher, Transylvania University; Kent Whitworth, Marilyn Zoidis, Sarah Elliott, Andy Stupperich, and Julieanne Foster, Kentucky Historical Society; Kevin Grogan, Kelly Woolbright, and Laura Pasche, Morris Museum of Art; Ruth Cloudman, Chuck Pittenger, and Lisa Parrett, Speed Museum; Kathy Walsh-Piper, Barbara Lovejoy, Janie Welker, Dorothy Freeman, and Amy Nelson, University of Kentucky Art Museum; Meg Shaw, Lucille Little Fine Art Library, University of Kentucky; Julie Aronson, Cincinnati Art Museum; Ann Shepherd, Cincinnati Historical Society; Judith Bonner, Historic New Orleans Collection; Dr. Douglas Lewis, National Gallery of Art; David Buchta, Historic Properties Commission, Commonwealth of Kentucky; Mary Nash Cox; and Dr. John Michael Vlach, George Washington University American Studies program. The author is also grateful for hospitality given on research trips by Wayne Amos and Charles Hunnicutt, Clifton Anderson, Edith S. Bingham, Catherine Boardman, Charles and Jessica Burg, Berle Clay, Henry and Barbara Hinkle, William and Mary Morris, and Diane Wachs. Very special thanks go to Kentucky's First Lady, Jane Beshear, and her staff director, Ann Evans.

Additional support for this project has been provided from donors across the commonwealth and beyond. These include Timothy Armstrong, Emily Bingham and Stephen Reily, Edith S. Bingham, Mary C. Bingham, David and Helen Burg, Catesby Clay, Dorothy Lair Clay, Isabel McHenry Clay, Brent Thomas Clements, Thomas Courtenay, Wes Cowan, Joseph and JoAnn Ewalt, Hinkle Contracting Corporation, Sally Spears Hinkle, Susan T. Hinkle, National Society of the Colonial Dames of America in the Commonwealth of Kentucky, Warren and Julie Payne, James Morrow Richards, Lad and Catesby Simpson, James and Mary Stites, and Mr. and Mrs. J. Walker Stites III.

INTRODUCTION

BETWEEN 1802, when the young Kentucky artist William Edward West began to paint portraits while on a downriver journey, and 1920, when the last of Frank Duveneck's students worked in Louisville, a large number of notable portrait artists were active in Kentucky and the Ohio River Valley. The purpose of this study is to identify those artists, illustrate their works, and recall the cultural terrain on which they painted. Within these pages many lessons may be learned: lessons of established masters instructing young apprentices; lessons in likeness by different hands whose similarity indicates a preference for a prevailing style; and more ambiguous lessons from the special appreciation that some of these artists, and some of their works, have attained through oral history, perpetuated social custom, publications, and obscure accounts.

Portraiture involves artists and sitters, and it invokes, if not unites, elements of biography, aesthetics, and sociopolitical history. This study entails brief, but detailed, chronologies of specific artistic activity in Kentucky and the Ohio River Valley, and considers seminal artworks and art-related events that shaped the climate of taste. The region under study has been well explored, but seldom mapped. Part One, "Cultural Chronology," seeks to provide that map, and in so doing makes it clear that the landscape is varied and that its examination requires sensitivity to a depth lacking in previous studies.

Portraiture may well be the most social of painterly pursuits, as it involves sitters with expectations of being well represented and artists, of varied abilities, capturing an interactive moment. The result of this interaction is an object viewed by a responsive audience through all the years of its continued existence. Portraits, especially of ancestors, often accumulate formidable oral histories, which may obscure the context in which they were painted. And as aesthetic objects portraits can also provoke contentious debate about "value" and "style."

Portraits created before the age of photography remain the only likenesses we have of certain individuals, whether they are figures of note or not. Despite specific biblical injunctions against the making of graven images, European painters of the High Renaissance created likenesses of Jesus Christ; of Mary, his mother; and of various saints and a considerable number of sinners. During their original existence these objects served the purpose, if they had not the actual position, of sacred icons—not worshipped in a pagan sense, but certainly venerated for their representational power. None of these works, of course, could claim to be an actual likeness of Jesus or other biblical figures, but they did aspire to *portray* episodes from accounts of their lives and deeds.

Our country's foundations were shaped by the political and popular culture of Western Europe in the seventeenth and eighteenth centuries, a time when portraits in the grand manner, displayed in public buildings and royal palaces, served to affirm the secular authority of the heads of state. "Grand manner," a term for these works, can also be applied to many American portraits of the nineteenth century. Michael Quick, who organized an important exhibition on the style in America art, wrote that the grand manner was "a self-conscious portraiture that reflected Western art historical traditions, particularly those of the Italian High Renaissance." The mission of these painters was to link individuals to an informed social and cultural consciousness; drawing upon "classic works the educated portraitist took the most elevated manner, varied poses, and classical conceits, in effect joining portraiture with the richer, more active and colorful realm of history painting."[1]

From the beginning of the American republic, grand manner portraits "were used . . . to celebrate national achievement and public heroes, as well as the self-aware experiences of private individuals."[2] Not only were portraits *painted* of towering figures such as George Washington, Benjamin Franklin, and, at a later date, Henry Clay and Abraham Lincoln, but they were also reproduced in a variety of printed forms to serve the needs of a public eager to have some idea of their leaders' appearance. Many of these works, such as Gilbert Stuart's "Landsdowne" portrait of George Washington or G. P. A. Healy's seated Lincoln, achieved an iconic status. As material culture, portraits were often the only decorative items in a house. They were hung in places of prominence, gave a sign of affluence, and marked important moments of passage. As an enduring likeness of an ancestor, inherited by subsequent generations, a portrait provided continuity and enhanced family pride.[3] Consider one of the earliest portraits in the Filson Collection. Previously attributed to Jeremiah Theus, who is never known to have worked in Virginia, the portrait of Susannah Smith Preston (Fig. 1) is more likely to be the work of John Wollaston (1710–1775). It is the oldest surviving image of the extended Smith-Preston-Pope-Brown-Davie families. Susannah Preston and her husband, Colonel William Preston, lived in the Blacksburg, Virginia, area, where Wollaston is known to have worked as an itinerant. The portrait has the stiff bodice and sharply defined features characteristic of Wollaston's work in the 1750s.

Studied as objects, portraits provoke questions about "style," defined as qualities specific either to a certain period or to a certain type of portrait. When portraits are considered as objects, however, inevitable questions of "value" also arise, not only their economic value as a commodity for sale or trade but also their aesthetic value as works epitomizing a specific moment in cultural history. Assigning an exemplary status to a work of art opens the question of connoisseurship, a method that compares and contrasts artworks in a judgmental manner, which often raises questions of market value apart from the work's objective historical significance.

The question of "value" also invites a capitalist–Marxist dialogue. Portraits can be viewed as commodities created by workers for a consumer class with sufficient means to commission them. A discussion of the source of those means can overwhelm considerations of a portrait's aesthetic, ethereal, and temporal qualities. Throughout history, patronage has secured production while often victimizing the patronized. Efforts have been made in this study to reference artists whose response to critical social issues of the day confirm that they did not paint in a cultural vacuum. Portraiture often provided the means by which artists could afford to paint more personally expressive works that may not have been as easy to sell, such as landscapes or still lifes. This is a study, however, of varieties of style in the period, not a polemic.

That "the painter had an audience in mind while he worked," as Booth Tarkington said, is a suitable

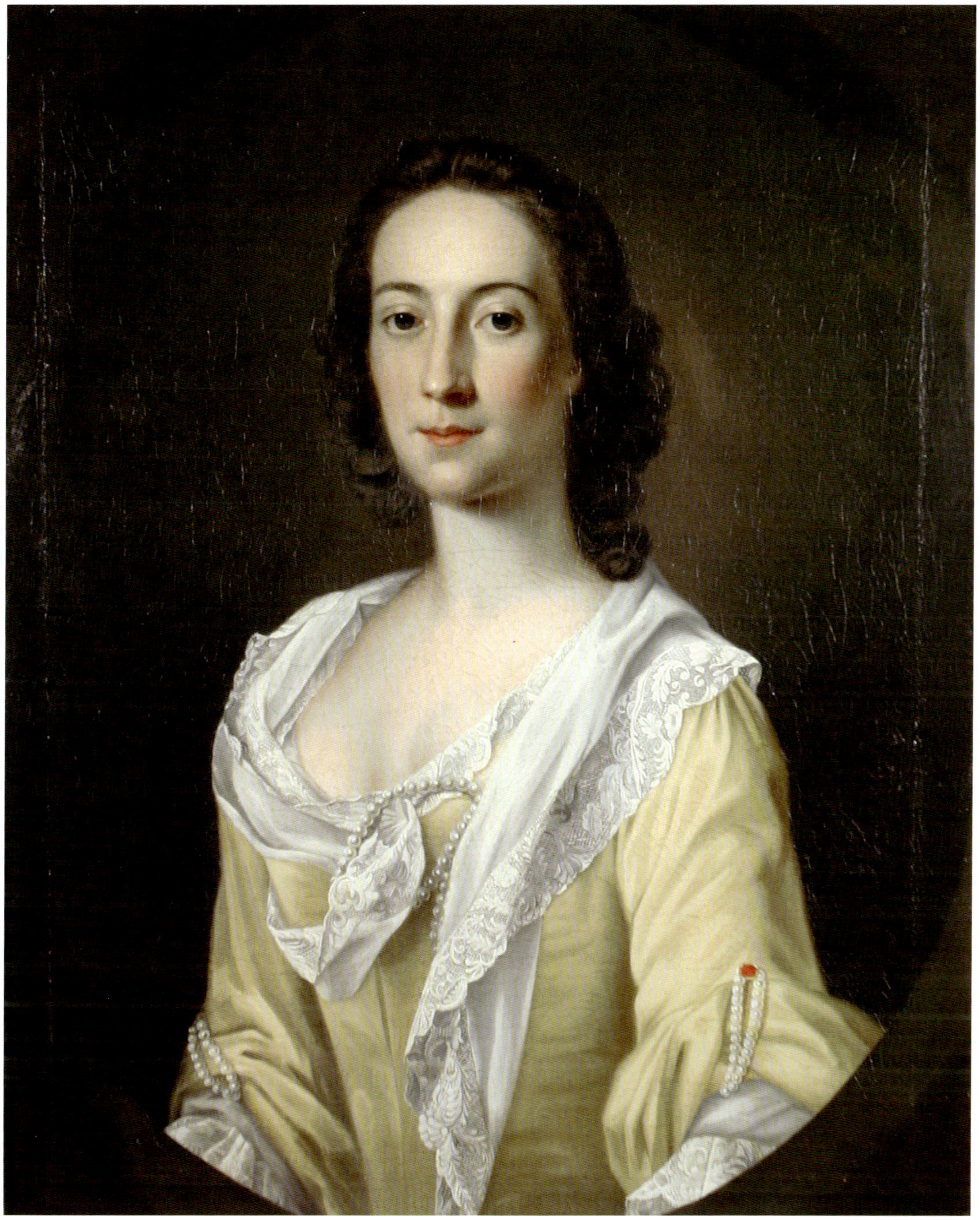

FIGURE 1. John Wollaston (1710–1775), *Susannah Smith Preston* (1739–1823), ca. 1760, oil on canvas, 29 × 24", The Filson Historical Society, 1976.30.18.

introduction to style.[4] Shaped by a wide variety of factors, both practical and intellectual, the vocabulary of style is dictated by the age from which it sprang. It should, however, be kept in mind that the terminology of style is often assigned after the fact, as a sorting device by cultural historians determined to give history a shape and flow that the frantic pace of human activity can scarcely ever be said to have had. Thus it is that "Gothic" became applied to medieval ecclesiastical architecture because later purists found it as barbarian as the Visigoths who descended upon Rome—or, as another example, that "baroque," which can be translated as "an irregularly shaped pearl," came to be applied to the luscious art of the expansive seventeenth century by chaste aesthetes of the eighteenth century.

Two other elements are critical to the study of style, one cautionary and the other phenomenological. First, in our own time, presentism, the imposition of contemporary values upon previous social and artistic constructs, has often resulted in reckless analyses.

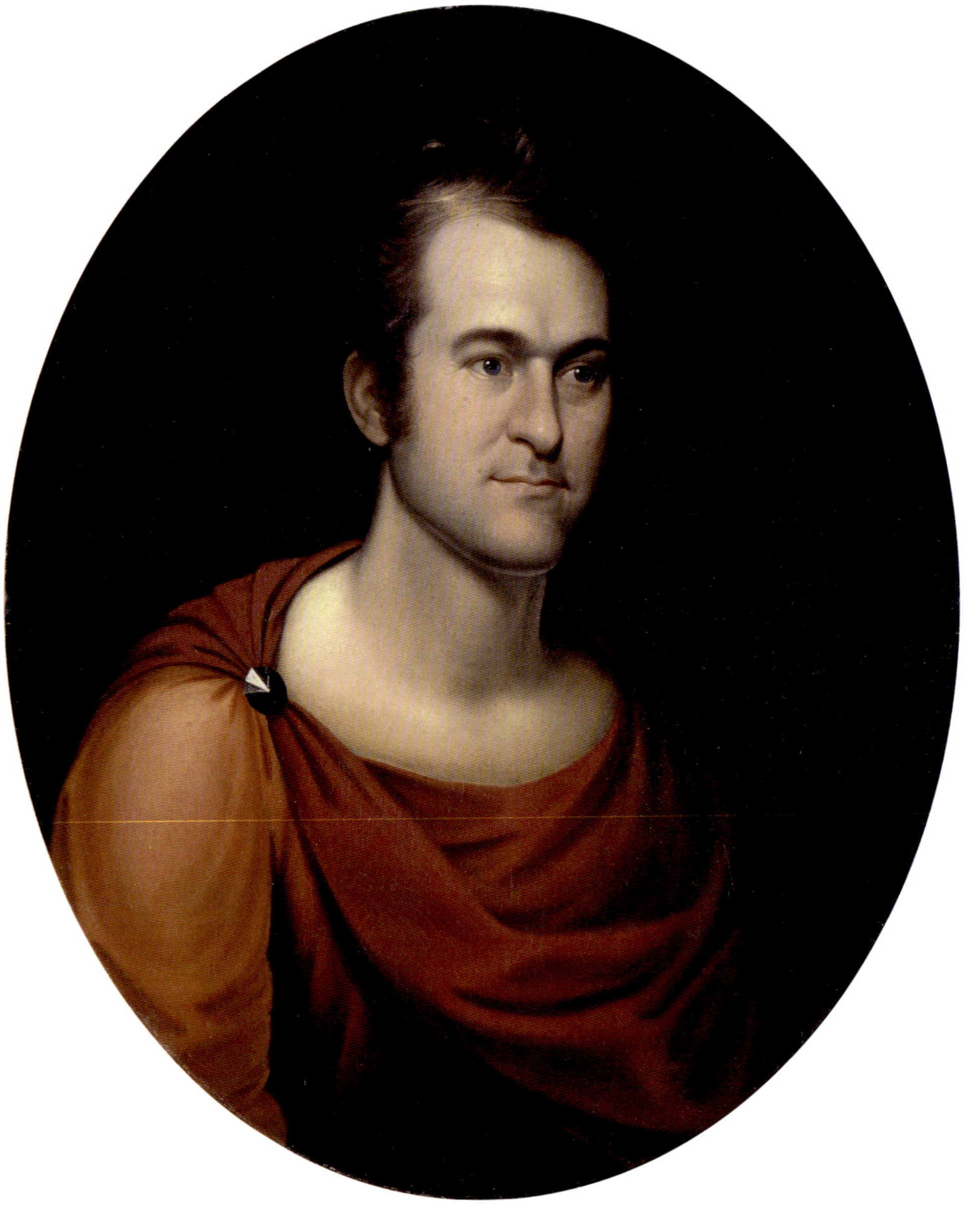

FIGURE 2. Cephas Thompson (1775–1856), *William Wirt* (1733–1834), ca. 1809–1810, oil on canvas, 42⅛ × 35½″, National Portrait Gallery, Smithsonian Institution, NPG 89.11. Greatly admired for his sense of justice, the man who presided at the trial of Aaron Burr and served as Attorney General of the United States from 1817 to 1829 is depicted here as a Roman tribune. Ancient Roman tribunes were to assure that neither patricians nor plebians gained prominence over the people of the republic.

Caution needs to be taken when considering portraits as quaint objects easily dismissed as manifestations of the vanity of a ruling elite or as the simple production of craftsmen whose abilities can be regarded with condescension. To correct that view, we might consider portraiture as a phenomenon to be viewed with a certain spirit of awe and curiosity. Richard Brilliant wrote that "portraits come to the viewer's conscious mind like the magical, unsettling reflections exhibited by the trick mirrors popular in carnivals and circuses. They may reflect an image of the person standing in front of them, often with such distortions . . . that the connection between the image and its source seems uncertain, effectively complicating the relationship between the seeing 'I' and the seen 'You.'"[5]

Ambitious portraitists certainly had an audience in mind when they set to work on the likenesses of a contemporary audience whose patronage was attracted by the popular appeal of their creations. We, subsequent viewers, are a different audience. By gazing at a likeness we are forced to reflect, or "to respond to the artist's interpretation," and establish "the conditions and circumstances" of gazing that shape "the psychological process that implicates the viewer, as a respondent, in answering the question posed by the portraitist, 'Who is the you' that I am looking at and how may I know it?"[6]

In the course of reading the cultural chronology of portrait activity in Kentucky and the Ohio River Valley, certain terms will reoccur, which may be seen as helpful markers in our pursuit of an understanding of style. Grand manner has already been considered in aggrandizing public figures. Other recurring terms used to describe the period under study include *neoclassic, romantic, folk,* and *naturalistic.*

Neoclassicism in America is the style most often associated with the Federal period, from the birth of the republic to the early 1820s. Having revolted against a king and an established church, Americans cherished notions of civic freedom and the civil rights of individuals. The popular culture of the young republic embraced the ideals of Greek democracy and the virtues of Roman republicanism, and reverence for these ideals inspired the construction of civic buildings as temples in the antique style as well as depictions of aspiring political figures in Roman senatorial garb (Fig. 2). Portraiture in this period was dominated by the towering figure of Gilbert Stuart, who was more concerned with capturing individual character than with creating facile, flattering images. In this mode, the role of the neoclassical artist was to observe and portray with care, not to flatter or improve. Matthew Harris Jouett, who studied with Stuart, returned to Kentucky and prospered as the state's first resident portraitist. Jouett's success attracted imitators and competitors, such as Chester Harding, whose works exhibit many similarities of coloration and composition, especially in pendant pairs of male and female couples. Kentuckians retained an affection for this style long after it was vogue in more cosmopolitan, eastern, urban areas, prompting the Kentucky historian Clay Lancaster to call it the "Georgian Survival" style.[7]

Romanticism is an artistic and literary style that characterized U.S. culture during the thirty years before the outbreak of the Civil War. The role of the artist in the society in which he or she works is a central issue of romanticism. For centuries the artist had been seen as a craftsman indebted to society for patronage and the support of what was essentially a peripheral profession. The American and French revolutions, however, challenged long-standing hierarchical notions of the place of creativity and spontaneity in Western culture. During

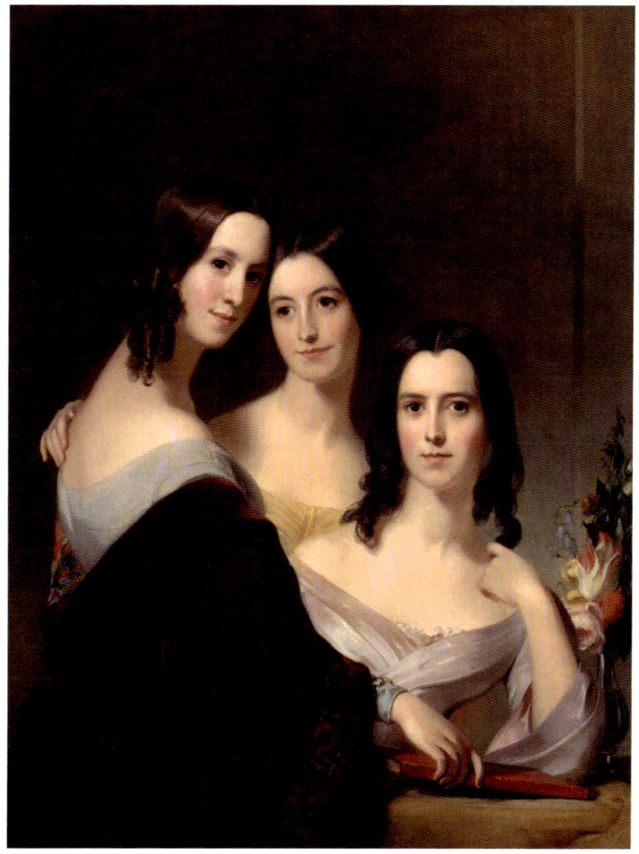

FIGURE 3. Thomas Sully (1783–1872), *The Coleman Sisters,* 1844, oil on canvas, 44 5/16 × 34 7/16", © Board of Trustees, National Gallery of Art, Washington, Gift of William C. Freeman, 1947.9.3.

the romantic era the role of the artist changed to that of a revered insider whose sensitive perceptions offered more than simply art for art's sake. Romanticism also became a line of defense against the surging utilitarian forces of the Industrial Revolution in both Europe and America. Romantic exuberance celebrated the hidden, the magical, and the obviously beautiful features of life, especially as seen in nature and not in things made by man. In this spirit artists moved from an outside role as observers to a central role as interpreters of the age.[8]

Of American romantic portraitists, the most influential figure for artists in Kentucky and the Ohio River Valley was Thomas Sully. Almost as a pilgrimage, many painters from the region made their way to Philadelphia to work in Sully's studio and absorb his approach to the subject and technique of painting. His writings allow us to compare his views with what is known of Gilbert Stuart's approach. Sully's portraits are richly painted

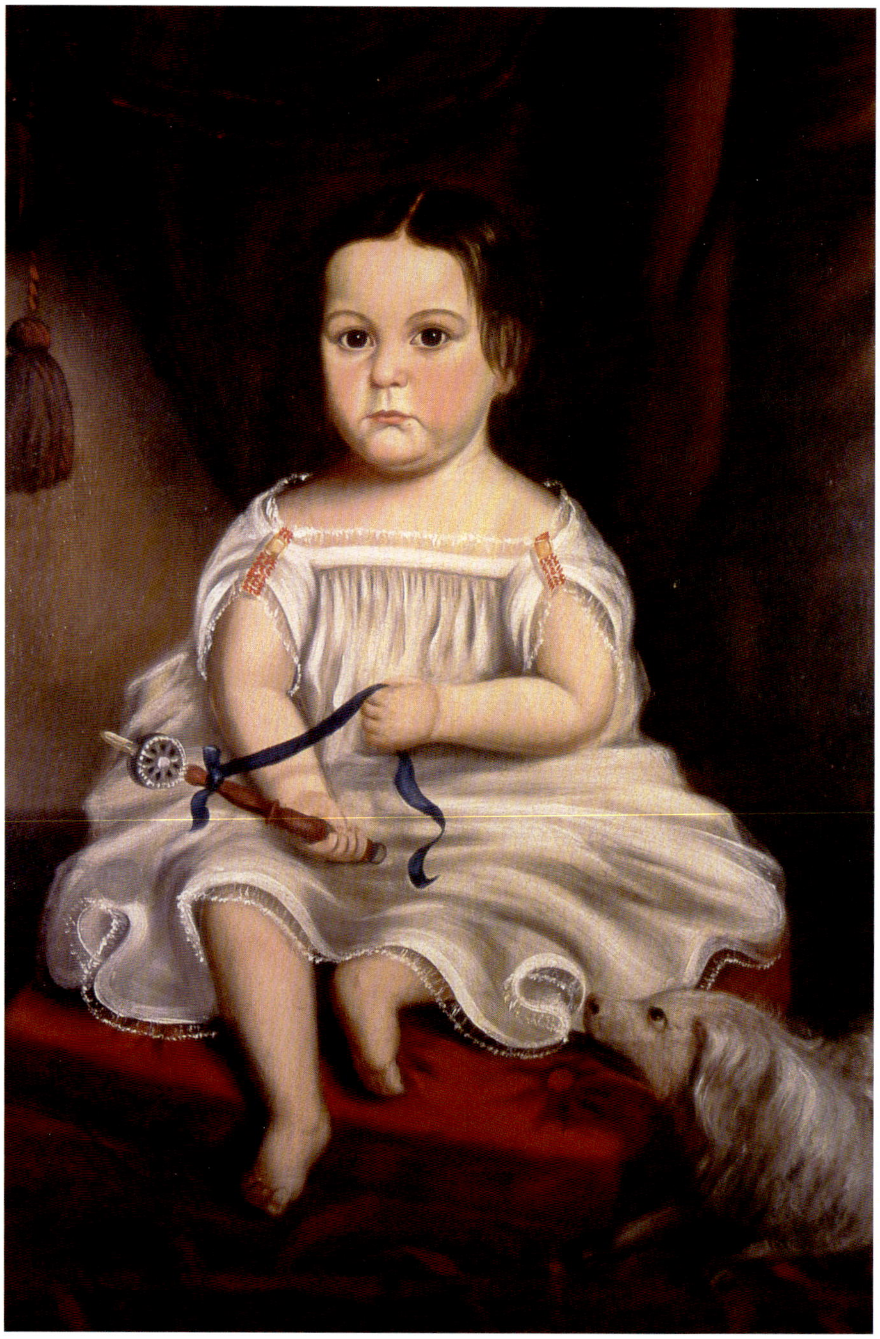

FIGURE 4. James Thomas Poindexter (1832–1891), *Emma Calhoun Noble Clark* (1851–1915), 1853, oil on canvas, 29¼ × 24½", The Filson Historical Society, 1979.17.13.1.

FIGURE 5 *(facing page).* James Thomas Poindexter (1832–1891, *Virginia Franklin Noble,* 1853, oil on canvas, 29¼ × 24½", The Filson Historical Society, 1979.13.2.

and extravagantly posed, and occasionally anatomically challenged (Fig. 3).

Though the terms "neoclassical" and "romantic" would have enjoyed some currency at the time, the term "folk," as applied to portraiture, is an invention of a later time and rife with serious inconsistencies. The Noble girls (Figs. 4, 5) were the daughters of Colonel John C. Noble, a publisher who was editor of the *Paducah Herald.* Virginia is seen with a basket of flowers and coral jewelry holding back the blouson sleeves of her white muslin frock. Coral was frequently used for children's jewelry in the nineteenth century as, according to legend, it warded off illness. James T. Poindexter's ambitions in composition, like those of many self-taught artists, often exceeded his skills as a draftsman and thus render him a candidate for the "folk" misappellation. In his portraits of the two Noble girls, Poindexter has utilized print sources, almost certainly from Italian Renaissance depictions of the Christ child and St. John for the anatomical features. The legs, akimbo, seem awkward, but are meant to suggest animation and to give the picture added depth and perspective.

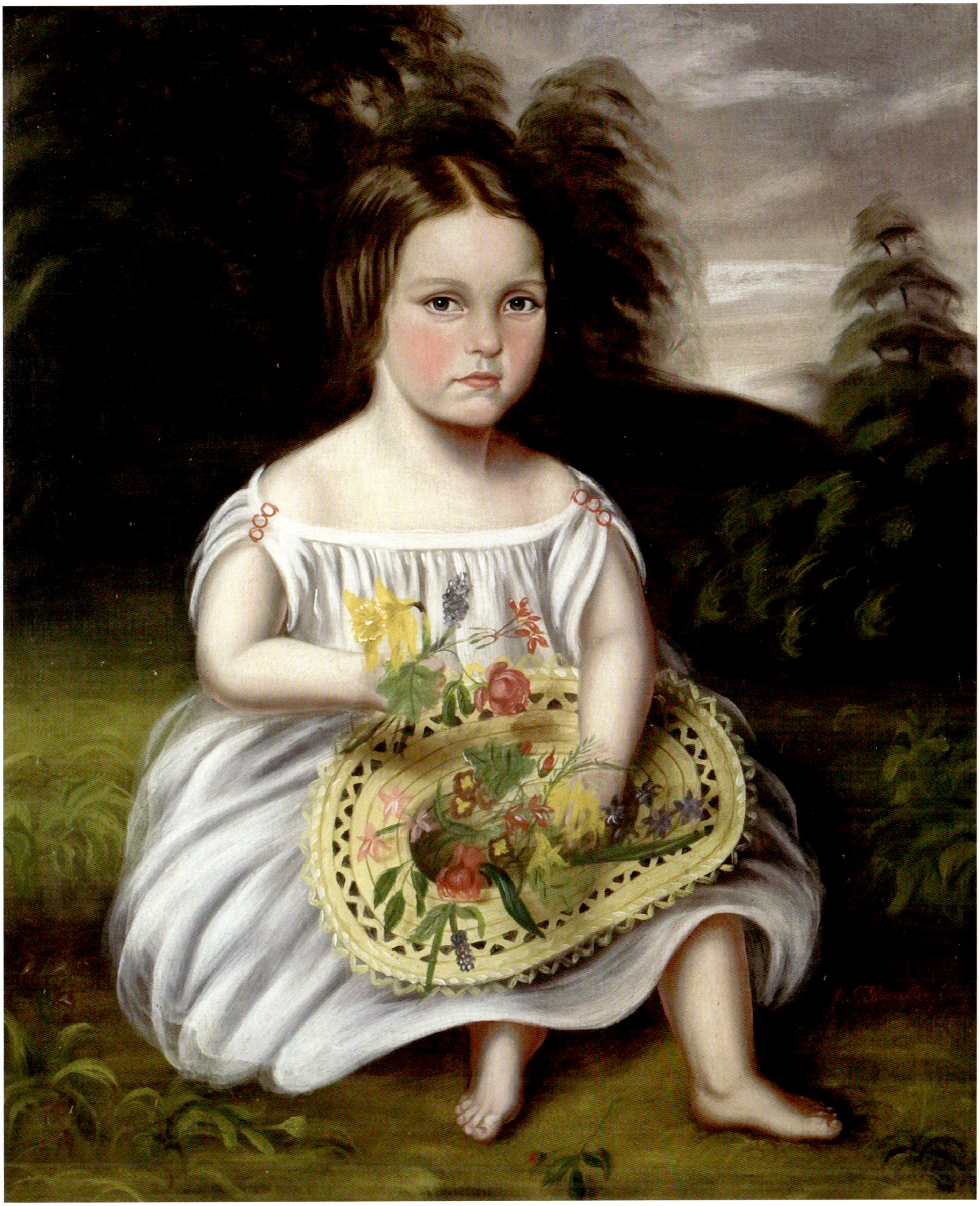

Though now disparaged by many in the academic community, the term "folk" still enjoys a popular currency and so requires explanation. During the late nineteenth century the colonial revival movement in art and architecture inspired a search for homegrown artifacts from early American history. Those artifacts became yet another sign of the eager antiquarian search for a uniquely American past, one that could be verified by extant material culture. Identification of these artifacts as "folk" objects appealed to later generations more infatuated with quaint notions of preindustrial society than with accurate cultural anthropology.

"Folk art" as a topic of study attained gravitas with the founding of the magazine *Antiques* in the 1920s. Alice Winchester, the first editor of the publication, subsequently wrote that connoisseurs of folk "may look for, and find, originality of concept, creativity of design, craftsmanly use of the medium, and flashes of inspiration, even genius. Folk art makes its appeal directly and intimately, even to people quite uninitiated into the mysteries of art."[9]

This search for creative genius untainted by contact with a sophisticated, and corrupt, outside world is part of a persistent fantasy in the Western imagination, most clearly identifiable in Jean-Jacques Rousseau's idea of a noble savage and Daniel Defoe's heroic alter ego in *Robinson Crusoe.* An appreciation for native, self-taught genius was current on the frontier of the Ohio River Valley and is a recurring theme in the fictional and factual literature of the period. Few frontier portraitists had the means or patronage to search for instruction from a master painter. These "self-taught" artists were greatly admired for their plucky individualism. Early portrait artists there painted in a culture that admired self-actualization as a democratic virtue, freed from the sanctions of an established caste, artistic or otherwise. It was a country where, wrote Oliver Larkin, "instead of dwelling on the past and on the signs of pomp and grandeur which have vanished, the mind was filled with images of coming power and splendor."[10]

These general elements of style—the grand manner, the neoclassic, the romantic, and the folk—characterize portrait painting in the sixty years prior to the Civil War, a time when Kentucky moved from being a frontier to a thriving crossroads at the center of American life.

With the conclusion of the war came a shift in the cultural terrain, augmented by the rise of photography and the emergence of academic art centers. Painters who had previously worked with a master painter or learned on their own were now able to take classes at established schools, especially in Cincinnati, which became one of the leading centers for the teaching of art in late nineteenth-century America. Several of the teachers there, Frank Duveneck and Thomas Satterwhite Noble in particular, had firsthand experience with avant-garde European styles, notably the realism and naturalism practiced in Munich and Paris in the last quarter of the nineteenth century and apparent in the art schools of New York and Philadelphia. Perhaps the most defining aspect of naturalism is the attention paid to brushstroke and surface detail. Looking back to certain precedents of the seventeenth century, artists in the naturalistic style created textured works that sought to give the sitter the gravitas appropriate to a generation that had survived war and economic stress. Duveneck's portrait of Leslie Barnum (Fig. 6) utilizes a Van Dyke beard and a Rembrandt collar to transform a late nineteenth-century bon vivant into the very image of a prosperous burgher.

Realism and naturalism embody a textured, nuanced approach to the subject, more expressive of a school than of an individual interpretation. The rise of an academic tradition in art in late nineteenth-century America affects the notion of a cultural chronology. Before the war, portraiture was an enterprise for talented and ambitious individuals whose success often created a cult of personality. Early portrait painting focused on the stylistic impact of noted individuals; the later period, by contrast, was dominated by the expansive nature of academic schools of art. The absence of an established academic setting for the teaching of art in Kentucky was partially offset by the industrial expositions in Louisville, which included large art exhibitions. These exhibitions introduced the local public to prevailing outside trends. They also drew submissions from portrait artists from outside Kentucky, which resulted in commissions that brought those artists to Louisville,

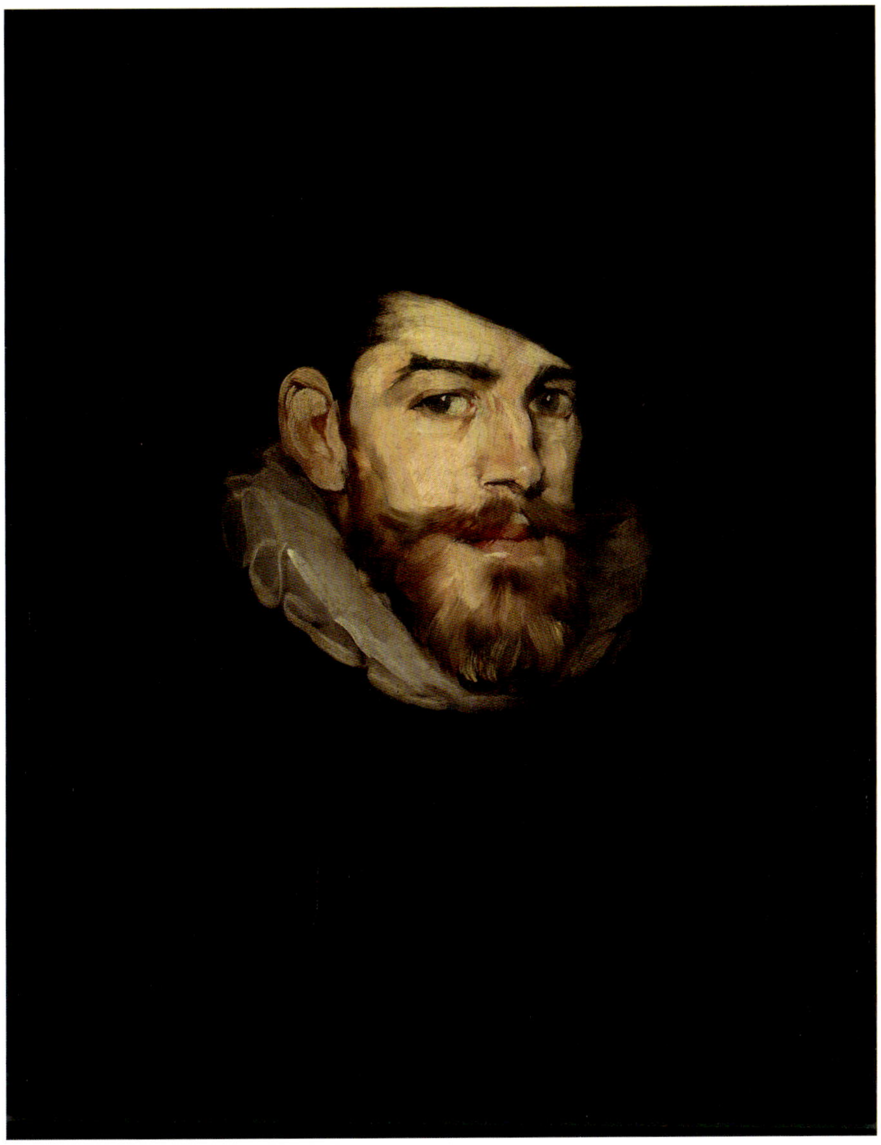

FIGURE 6. Frank Duveneck (1848–1919), *Leslie Pease Barnum,* 1876, oil on canvas, 22 1/16 × 18 1/8", © Board of Trustees, National Gallery of Art, Washington, Andrew W. Mellon Collection, 1942.8.3.

where they became the last itinerant artists to work in the area.

Part One of this book, a cultural chronology, serves as a background to Part Two, which consists of short biographies of portrait artists working in the region in the years from 1802 to 1920. The artists included have appeared in previous art historical literature and have an identifiable body of work that can be found in sufficient quantity in public and private collections to support autograph identification. This book is a study of portrait artists who worked in the traditional bust, half-length, and full-length scale, and does not include miniaturists or sculptors, topics for another, more specialized study. Individual entries in Part Two consist of a brief biography, sources for further study in primary and secondary sources, and locations of works in public collections. The output of each artist is illustrated, when possible, by work from the collection of The Filson Historical Society.

The Filson Historical Society portrait collection includes the widest range of artists within this book's geographical area of study—that is, Kentucky and the neighboring areas of southern Ohio and southern Indiana, the valley through which the Ohio River runs. It is hoped that the illustrations in these pages will provide prototypes to assist in the identification of artists of portraits that are not signed and whose oral history has been lost.

PART ONE

Cultural Chronology

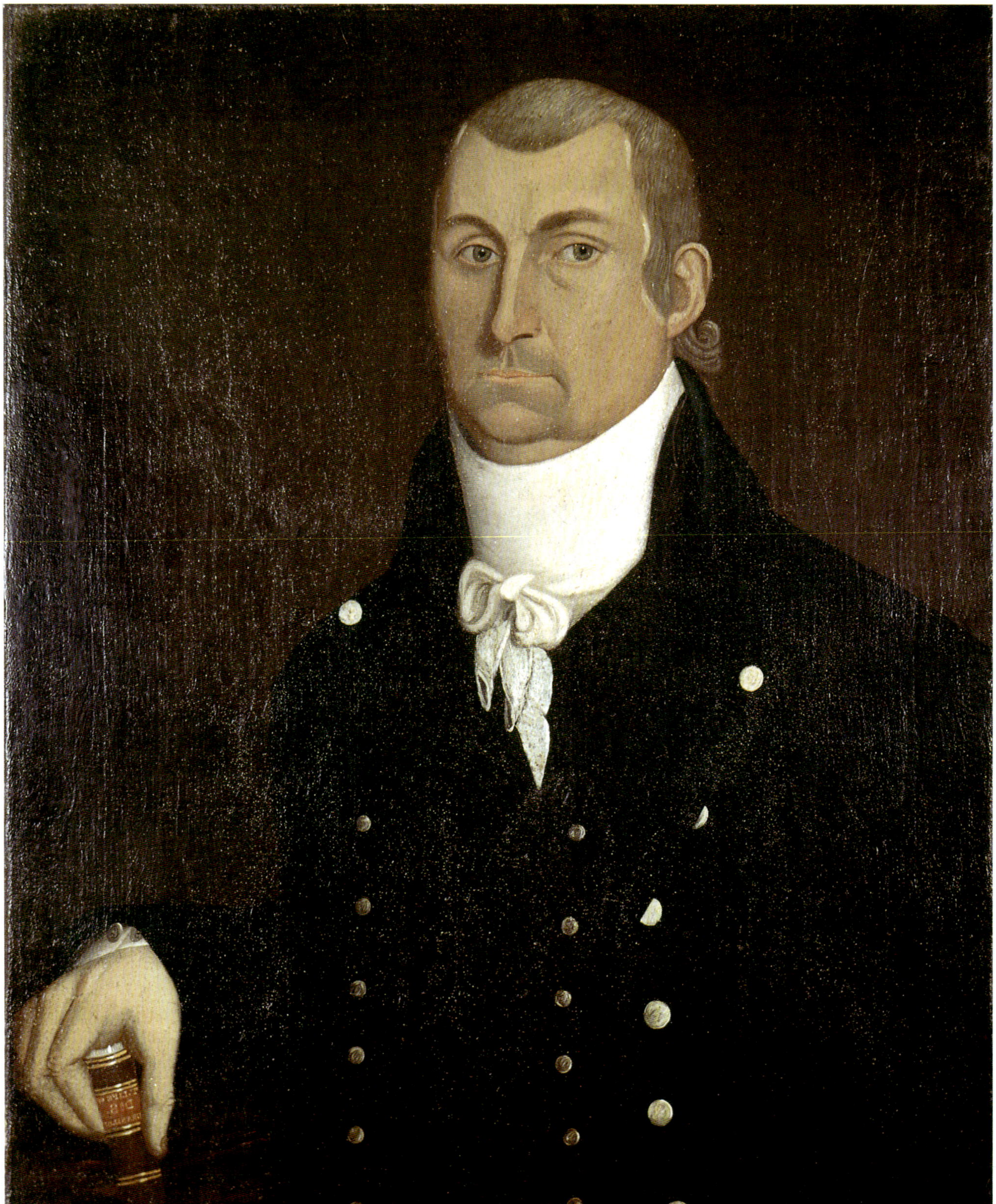

1802–1835

Westward Movement, Eastern Instruction

Reports of early artists and itinerant activity

In 1802 a young William Edward West went downriver to New Orleans with the Bourbon County farmer and distiller Abram Spears and en route painted Spears's portrait in miniature, the first noted instance of Kentucky portraiture.[1] The miniature is still in the possession of Spears descendants. West is known to have painted only one other miniature, that of Margaretta Preston Brown of Frankfort, in whose home he is thought to have first seen the work of Gilbert Stuart, which he imitated in a portrait of Mrs. Brown's brother-in-law, Dr. Samuel Brown, in 1805. During the first decade of the nineteenth century West is known to have begun painting bust-scale portraits in the Lexington area.

Other early portraitists in the Lexington area include Benjamin Trott, George and Mary Beck, and Samuel Dearborn. The first documented itinerant artist to visit Kentucky was the Virginia painter Jacob Frymire, who visited Woodford County in 1806 to paint Marquis Calmes, a Revolutionary War veteran and native of Stafford County, Virginia (Fig. 7).[2] Frymire faced a daunting and lengthy trip to Kentucky, by water and by roads formed from buffalo traces. Once in Lexington he would have had access to the stagecoach line established by John Kennedy and William Dailey, which connected Lexington to Frankfort by way of Offutt's Tavern in Leesburg, a resting and renewal site for horses and a short ride from the Calmes property. Frymire's journey of more than five hundred miles through frontier territory was surely motivated by more than was his previous itinerancy, which had covered a wide territory in the valley of Virginia, western Maryland, and southern Pennsylvania, giving him many extended connections for portrait commissions.[3] In this instance, it seems highly likely that he was called to the scene, rather than undertaking an entrepreneurial expedition.

Samuel Dearborn was often said to have been the first practicing portraitist west of the mountains. A native of Boston, he was known to have worked in Pittsburgh as early as 1804, appearing in Lexington by 1809. Though Dearborn was somewhat competent in oil, his more energetic pursuit was in watercolor profile painting. Advertising his services in the *Kentucky Gazette* on May 1, 1809, he encouraged "those ladies and gentlemen" who wished to have their portraits painted to "apply soon." The price he

FIGURE 7 *(facing page).* Jacob Frymire (1770–1820), *Portrait of Marquis Calmes IV* (1754–1834), 1806, oil on canvas, 29¼ × 24″, Chicago History Museum, 1922.3.

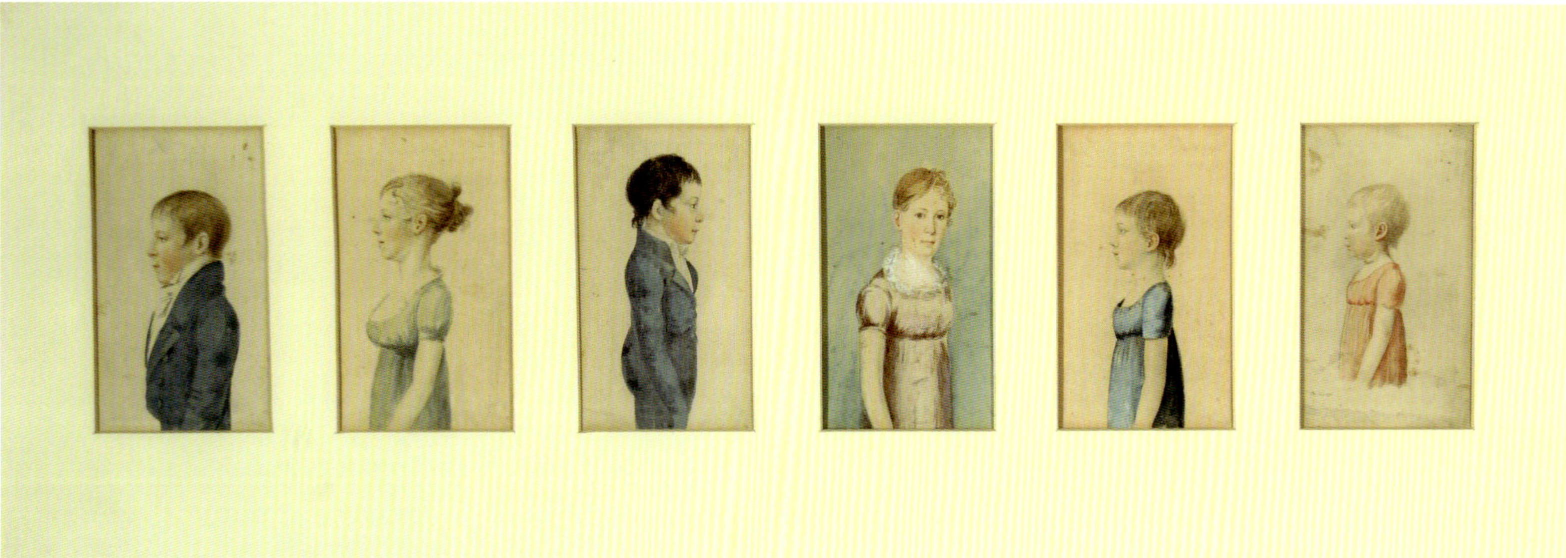

FIGURE 8. Samuel Dearborn (ca. 1786–ca. 1852), *George W. Love, Elizabeth Young Love, James Young Love, Elizabeth Young Love* [a second portrait], *Harriet Love, Mary Brown Love,* ca. 1810, watercolor or gouache on rag paper, 9.9 × 28″, The Filson Historical Society, 1929.5.1.

asked for his small likenesses on paper was low enough that he could expect many to substitute them for "blank profiles," a reference to the art of the silhouette (Fig. 8).

John James Audubon observes wildlife and paints portraits in Kentucky

John James Audubon, the naturalist artist, first came to Kentucky in August 1807 with his business partner and fellow Frenchman, Ferdinand Rozier. His destination was Louisville, where the young—and mismatched—partners opened a general store supplied from the resources of Audubon's future brother-in-law Benjamin Bakewell, a prosperous merchant in Pittsburgh. The venture was a proving ground for the future artist; if he prospered, he could marry Lucy Bakewell. Audubon later wrote poetically of this downriver adventure. He was impressed by the landscape; as night came, it sank in "darkness the broader portions of the river, [and] our minds became affected by strong emotions, and wandered far beyond the present moments."[4] He saw the owls, wild turkeys, grouse, blue-winged teal, and cardinals he would subsequently draw and describe in writing (Fig. 9).

While attempting to establish their mercantile store Audubon made short journeys peddling dry goods to small local communities, such as Shippingport, just downriver from Louisville at the foot of the Falls of the Ohio. There a number of French families, notably the Berthouds, would become subjects for his profile portrait work. He also made the acquaintance at this time of the Clark family: George Rogers, the soldier and settler, and William, the noted explorer. William Galt, an amateur naturalist, provided sympathetic companionship as well. Audubon spent much of his time during store hours working on his renderings of birds; the business failed to survive the depression caused by the congressional embargo of foreign goods, and he was unable to repay the loan of some $3,000 to Bakewell. Regardless, Audubon returned to Pennsylvania in 1808 and married Lucy Bakewell. He then returned to Shippingport with his new wife, where they took up residence.[5]

The years between 1808 and 1818 are well documented as being the most difficult in Audubon's life. None of his business ventures succeeded, and he was eventually forced into bankruptcy. Two sons were born to the marriage; there was also a daughter, who died at the age of two. During the time the Audubon family lived in Henderson, Kentucky, on the Ohio River, he made forays into the woods in search of subjects for his ornithological study. Those woods remained a favorite

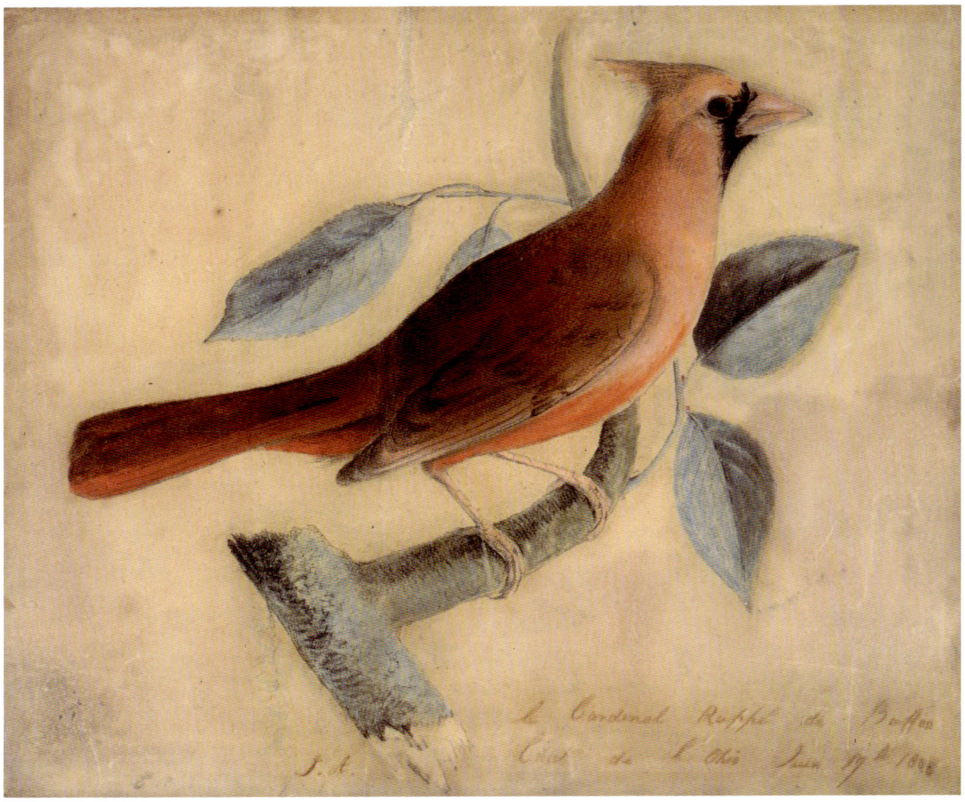

FIGURE 9. John James Audubon (1785–1851), *Cardinal (Grosbeak de Buffon)*, June 19, 1808, pencil and pastel on paper, 7½ × 9½″, The Filson Historical Society, 1946.5.

place throughout his life. Writing of them in later years, he recalled that the "orchards bowed their branches, as if anxious to restore to their mother earth the fruit with which they were laden; the flocks leisurely ruminated as they lay on their grassy beds; and the genial warmth of the season seemed inclined to favor their repose."[6]

Bankruptcy and imprisonment for debt impelled Audubon into an artistic career. Returning to the Louisville area and the company of the Berthoud family, he took up portraiture, creating several portraits of local citizens over the next year (Figs. 10, 11). Most are portraits in profile, a compositional approach he developed from his technique of drawing birds by wiring them to a gridded board. He had taught himself to draw birds, but, noted the Audubon scholar Richard Rhodes, "his portraits . . . were confident from the beginning, implying previous training."[7]

Audubon charged $5 a portrait. "Flat and literal as these profiles are," wrote John Francis McDermott, "they did suggest to the artist a way in which he might earn his living at this time when his enterprises had failed and his capital was exhausted."[8] Once Audubon had depleted the demand for portraits in Louisville, he

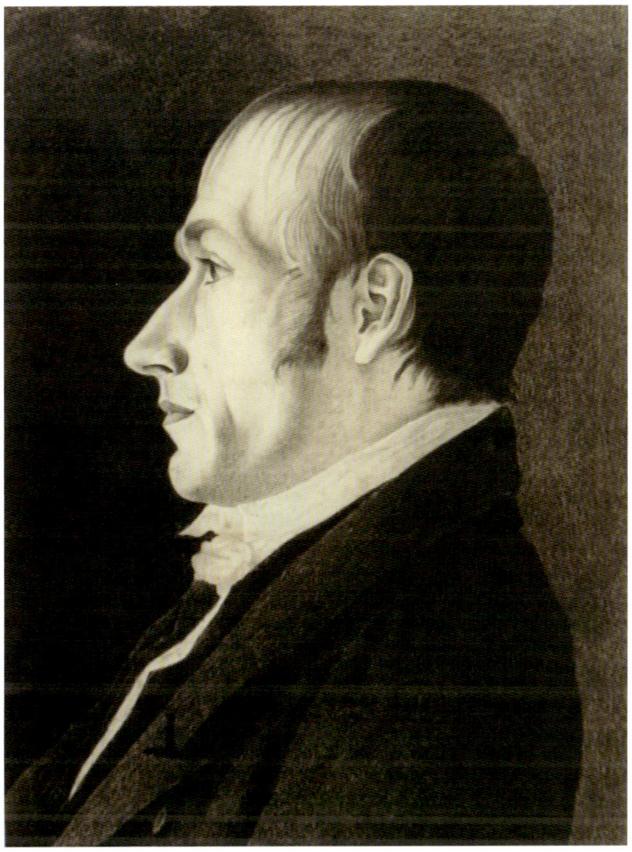

FIGURE 10. John James Audubon (1785–1851), *Reverend Thomas Henderson* (1781–1846), 1819, pencil and charcoal on paper, 20½ × 17″, The Filson Historical Society, 1972.2.

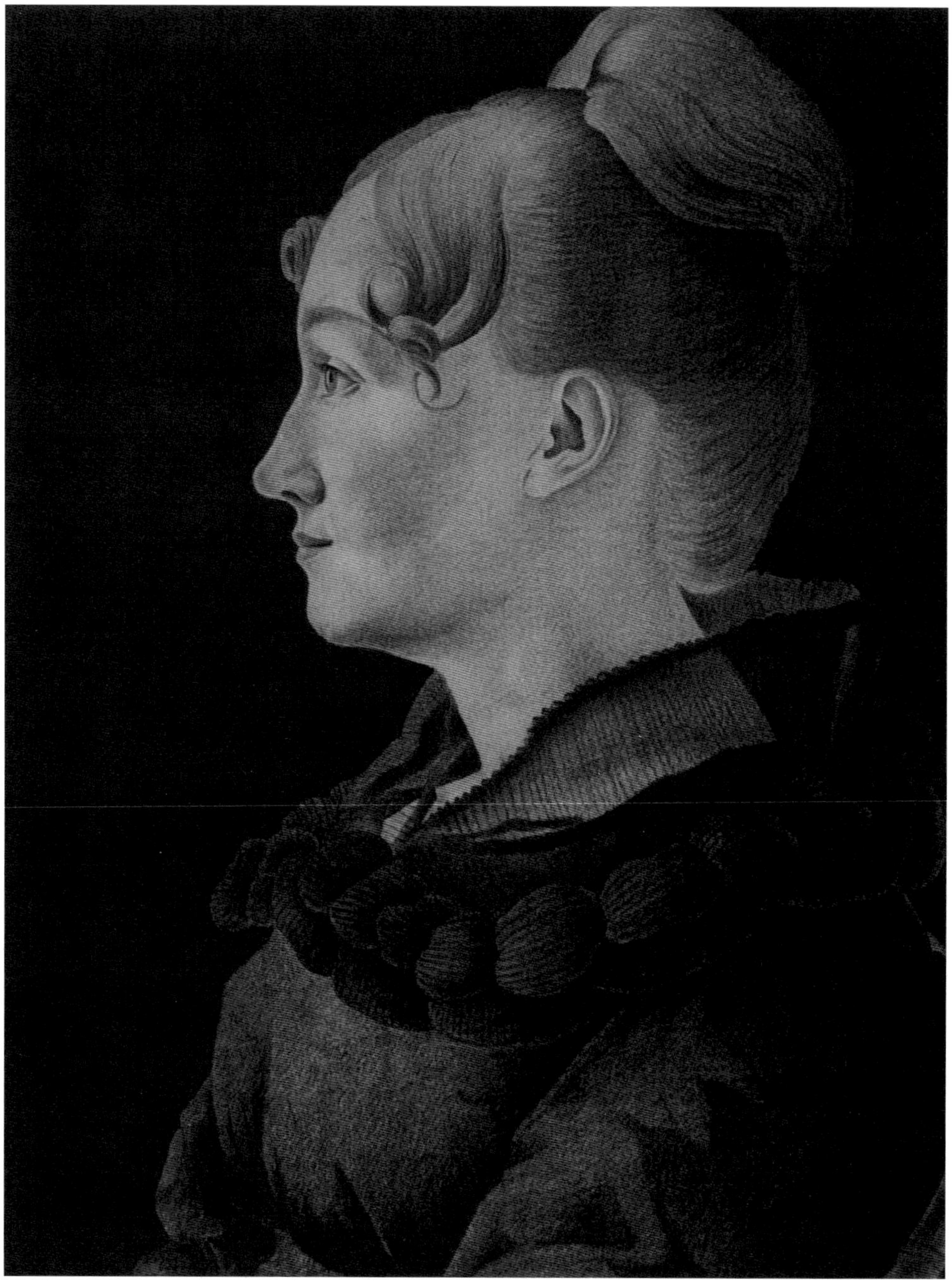

FIGURE 11. John James Audubon (1785–1851), *Barbara Fontaine Cosby Todd,* ca. 1819, charcoal on paper, 10 × 7½″, The Filson Historical Society, 1978.13.1.

moved on to Cincinnati, where he became a drawing master and resident taxidermist at the Western Museum for the rather substantial sum of $125 a month. It was at this time that Audubon made a portrait sketch of the young Aaron Corwine, soon to become Cincinnati's first resident portrait artist.[9]

Following his sojourn in Cincinnati, Audubon passed through Kentucky in 1820 to begin a long trip downriver to New Orleans with a student apprentice, Joseph Mason, aged thirteen. Audubon's legacy to Kentucky does not derive from his portraits and depictions of wildlife alone. He retained a very deep affection for the area, lamenting, as he passed Henderson on a flatboat on November 3, 1820, that he looked on the place "perhaps for the last time, and with thoughts that almost made my blood run cold bade it an eternal farewell."[10] Several essays from his *Ornithological Biography* provide an insight into frontier life that is sensitive to the nuance of the scenery, rare documentary evidence from an artist of an era from which we have few firsthand accounts. Of particular note are Audubon's comments on details of the scenery and of local custom. "The Ohio" describes the "grandeur and beauty" of the "uninhabited shores."[11] His description of the 1811–1812 New Madrid earthquake includes the sound of "a distant rumbling of a violent tornado," after which the "ground rose and fell in successive furrows, like the ruffled waters of a lake."[12] Essays on Kentucky sports and a Fourth of July barbeque recall the "free, single-hearted Kentuckian, bold, erect, and proud of his Virginian descent."[13]

Audubon's recollection of an encounter with Daniel Boone reads like a spellbinding tall tale. He describes the old pioneer as nothing less than a god. "His chest was broad and prominent; his muscular powers displayed themselves in every limb; his countenance gave indication of his great courage, enterprise and perseverance; and when he spoke, the very motion of his lips brought the impression that whatever he uttered could not be otherwise than true."[14] A subsequent encounter with a runaway slave predates Harriet Beecher Stowe in both compassion and emotive narrative.[15]

Matthew Harris Jouett embarks upon a career after instruction from Gilbert Stuart

Matthew Harris Jouett, who would become the most legendary portraitist in the history of Kentucky, was born in Mercer County in central Kentucky. His father had intended him for the law. "I sent Matthew to college," at Transylvania College in Lexington, the elder Jouett was reputed to have said, "to make a gentleman of him, and he has turned out to be nothing but a damned sign painter."[16] Though lacking any formal art training, Jouett had shown a precocious ability to draw, especially likenesses. When his initial efforts proved successful in the Lexington area, he decided to obtain further training. William Edward West, his exact contemporary, was already making a name for himself on an itinerant track from Kentucky to New Orleans by way of Natchez, having spent some time with the painter Thomas Sully in Philadelphia. According to family legend, Jouett set out for Philadelphia in search of the "sons of Edward West"; when unsuccessful, however, he continued to Boston, where he encountered Gilbert Stuart.[17]

Stuart, renowned as the portraitist of famous figures of the Revolution and founders of the young republic, had settled in Boston after fleeing debts in England and Ireland. He constantly dipped snuff and was generally acknowledged as cantankerous, if not outright rude, as evident in his remark to Jouett to get at it "quickly too for I have no time to chat, Kentucky boat man."[18] Stuart always referred to Jouett as "Kentucky," in tribute to the younger artist's abilities as a raconteur, a trait for which Kentuckians of the period were much celebrated.[19]

Jouett kept notes on their encounter, in a document entitled "Rude hints & observations, from repeated Conversations with Gilbert Stuart, Esqr. In the months of July, August, September, & Oct. 1816 under whose patronage and care I was for the time," a rare firsthand account by an impressionable student working with an established master.[20] The young artist so admired Stuart as someone with a "singular facility in conversation and powers of illustration" that he would not defame him by anything except direct quotation. Accordingly, "I hereby so acknowledge that but in two pages have I given his words." Jouett's account is rambling, punctuated with local color and highly charged with an apprentice's deep belief in his master's ability. Stuart's remarks provide "hints" on three general topics: the construction and composition of a portrait, beginning with the placement of the head on the picture plane; the coloration of the facial features and subsequent anatomical and background detail; and, finally, suggestions on how best to capture the character of the sitter.[21]

Stuart informs Jouett that "there are three grand stages in a head as in an argument or plot of any sort: a beginning, middle & end: and to arrive at each of these perfect stages should be the aim of any painter." Stuart was not a practitioner of creating a sketch in chalk or pencil on the canvas and then rendering a colored image. "In his portraits" Jouett saw "all spirited drawing & yet no outline" (Figs. 12–15). Stuart worked *alla prima,* directly from brush to palette to canvas, as he considered drawing "the features distinctly & carefully with chalk loss of time. All studies to be made with brush in hand. Nonsense to think of perfecting oneself in drawing before one begins to paint: When the hand is not able to execute the decisions of the mind in some shape a fastidiousness ensues, and on the heels of that

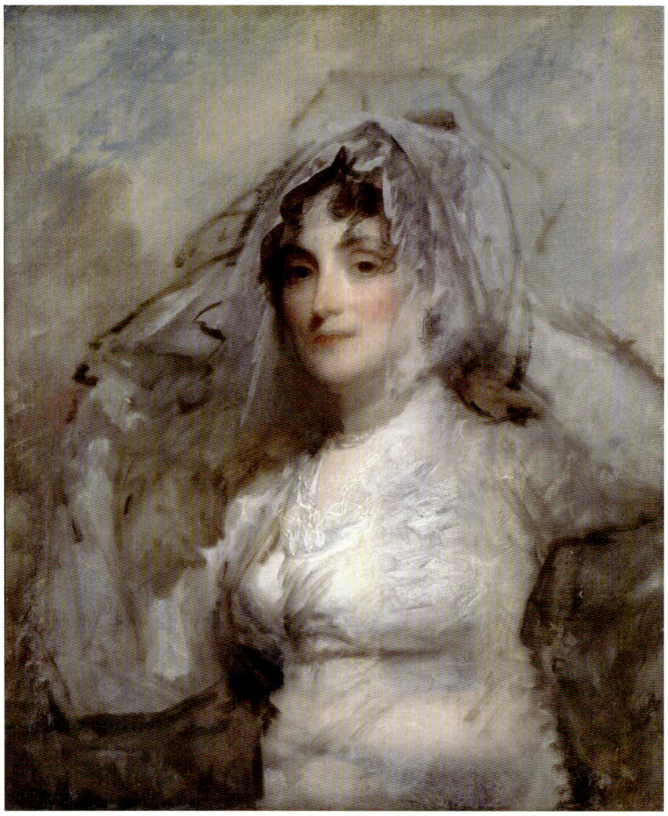

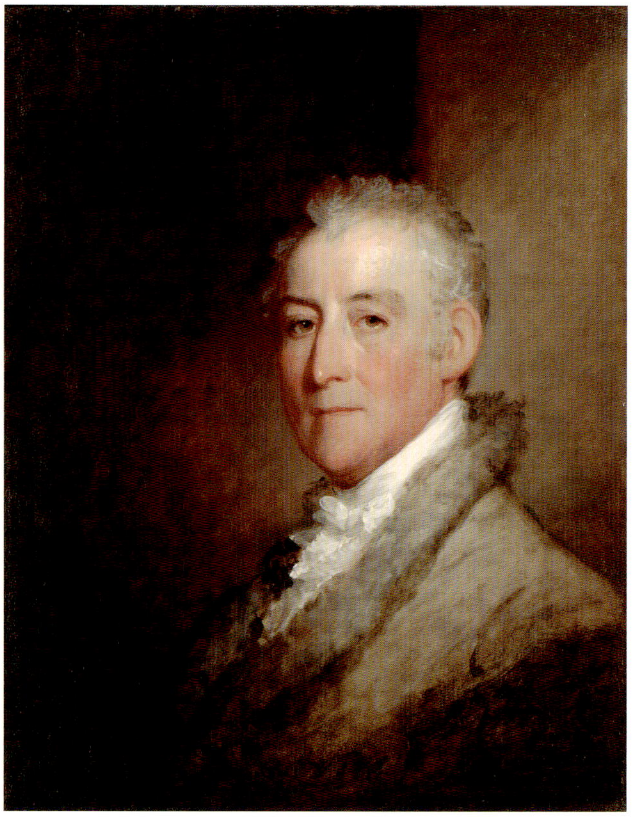

FIGURE 12 *(above left).* Gilbert Stuart (1755–1828), *Mrs. Sarah Wentworth Apthorp Morton* (1759–1846), ca. 1800–1802, oil on canvas, 29⅛ × 24⅛", Worcester Art Museum, Worcester, Massachusetts, 1899.2.

FIGURE 13 *(facing page).* Matthew Harris Jouett (1788–1827), *Peter Grayson* (1788–1838), 1827, oil on canvas, 35 × 29", The Filson Historical Society, 1995.13.2.

FIGURE 14 *(above right).* Gilbert Stuart (1755–1828), *John Trumbull* (1756–1843), 1818, oil on canvas, 26 × 21½", Yale Art Gallery, 1945.238.

FIGURE 15 *(right).* Matthew Harris Jouett (1788–1827), *Peter Grayson* (1788–1838), 1827, oil on canvas, 30 × 25", courtesy of the Pennsylvania Academy of Fine Arts, Philadelphia, gift of Mrs. Sarah B. Menefee, 1897.1.

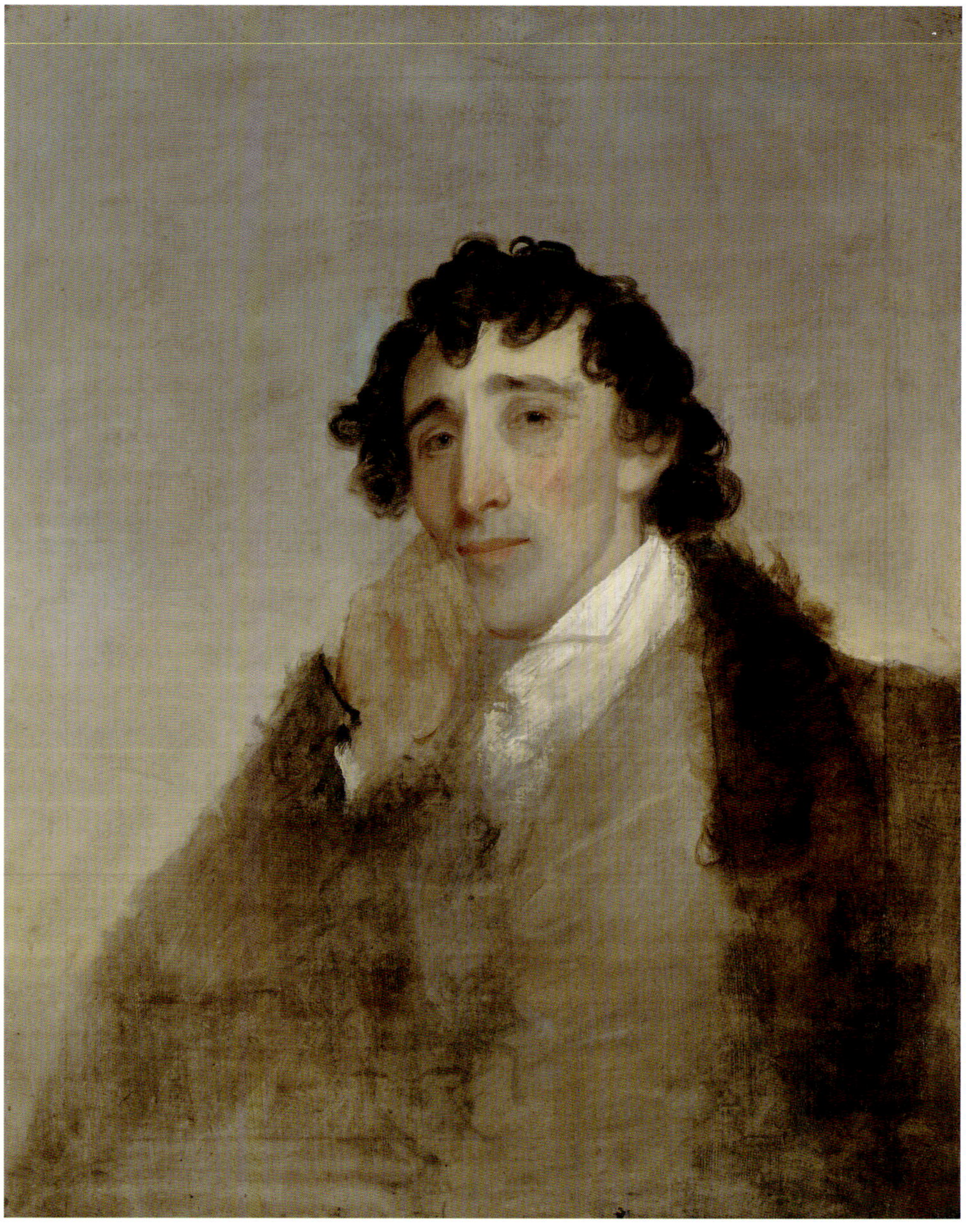

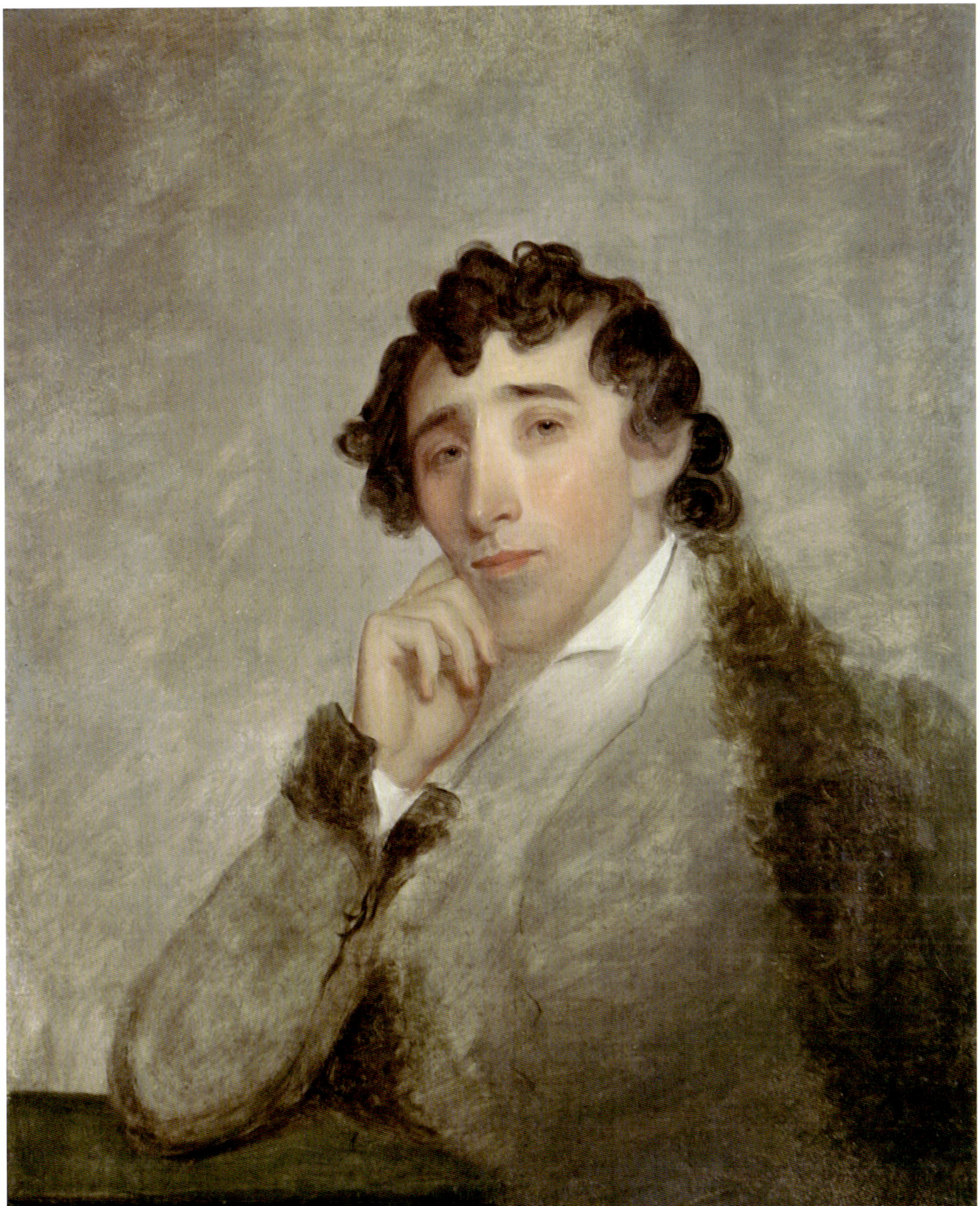

A visual comparison of the portraits of Sarah Morton, John Trumbull, and Peter Grayson demonstrates Stuart's profound influence on Jouett. In her 2004 catalogue entry on the portrait of Mrs. Morton, Ellen Miles writes, "Stuart began as he would with any composition, lightly describing her face, her dark curls, and her jewelry . . . without fully resolving details." The delicate colors and swirling costume details brushed with bravura touches indicate his sure command of light and color as a means of suggesting bodily contour. At the time of his death Jouett was apparently painting Peter Grayson, the original tragic poet of Kentucky, as it was Grayson who wrote the artist's obituary, claiming to have met the funeral procession on the road.

Curiously, there are two extant portraits of Grayson by Jouett, both of which are painted with the same attention to facial likeness and a swirling brushwork suggesting costume detail, although the portrait in the Pennsylvania Academy of Fine Arts (Fig. 15) has a more compressed format. It bears a remarkable resemblance to Stuart's unfinished portrait of his fellow painter John Trumbull, which may have been in progress at the time of Jouett's Boston sojourn. William Barrow Floyd found both Grayson portraits to be a "rare attempt to capture mood and sentiment" on Jouett's part, declaring they bore "a strong resemblance to the unfinished works of the great Bostonian," Stuart.

disappointment & disgust. One reason why the Italians never painted so well as other schools. . . . Preserve as far as practicable the round blunt stroke in preference to the winding flirting wisping manner."[22]

Stuart's disregard for concentric lines, and the mannered parallelisms forcing atmospheric depth and perspective, is oft repeated. "Avoid by all means, parallel lines whether they be parallel straight or parallel curved," for the "eye ought to be accustomed to distances & directions from point to point. More important, to give a prominent admeasurement of distances than a set of mincing curves." Color, not repetitious geometry, is the key to establishing character. "To give great perspective, give great gloom to the foreground," he advised Jouett. Deep, warm flesh tones, which Jouett constantly refers to as "peach," are characteristic of Stuart's portraits. The older artist thought flesh "like no other substance under heaven. It has all the gaiety of a silk mercers shop without the gaudiness or glare and all the soberness of old mahogany without its deadness or sadness." To obtain its special quality he directed Jouett to admit "that the best colorists live in climates with atmospheric change such as Germany or Holland, Venice or Florence as opposed to Rome and Paris where good coloring has never been obtained." An atmospheric evocation of the sitter and not a stultifying exactitude was what made a portrait great, as the "true and perfect image of man is to be seen only in a misty or hazy atmosphere."[23]

Unlike his English contemporaries, especially Thomas Gainsborough, Stuart did not believe in florid, flattering facial coloration. "Equal color upon equal surfaces produce equal effects. That in the commencement of all portraits the first idea is an indistinct mass of light & shadows, or the character of the person as seen in the heel of the evening in the gray of the morning, or at a distance too great to discriminate features with exactness. That in every object there is one light, one shadow & one reflection, and that tis from a judicious entering into & departing from either of them that mark the harmony of a painting." Jouett faithfully records the layout of Stuart's palette and makes a drawing of the artist's board. The best advice Stuart offered to Jouett, it would appear from a review of both artists' work, concerned the final touches. "Always use spirits of turpentine in your white drapery. It assists to evaporate the oil & leaves the white a standing white, & free from the yellowness occasiond by the oil."[24] This practice Jouett brought to Kentucky, giving many of his works a brilliantly delicate quality heightened by the painterly presence of a floating piece of lace or a frothy jabot.

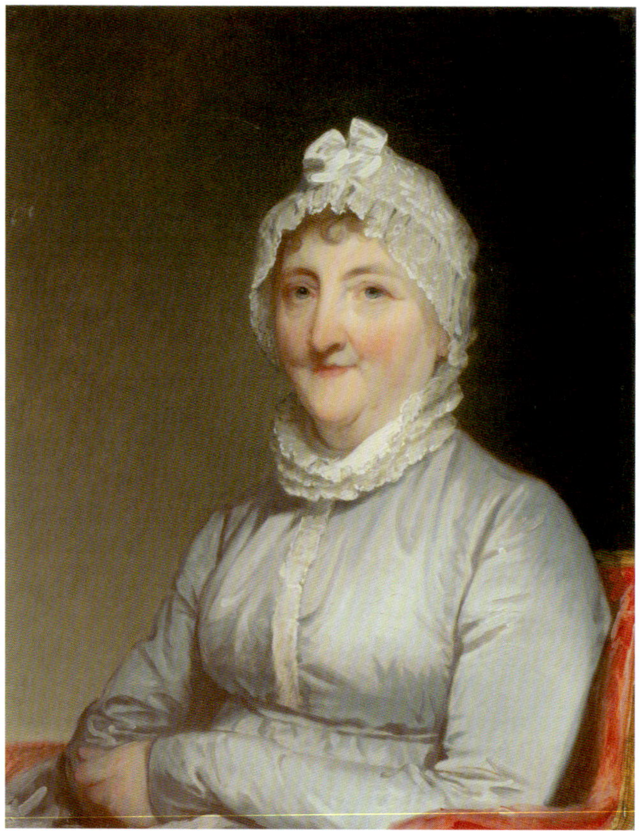

As to character, Stuart advised, "Consult truth rather than fancy; & without reason to systematize & control the fervor of the imagination. . . . That done, our paintings will be like our dreams when they come to be examined coolly & philosophically—fancy without reason & good taste like declamation without sense, or a fine voice and good words & fine gestures without common reason or common arrangement." Never intimidated by a sitter, Stuart advised Jouett to be "decisive in your drawing, seize with firmness your idea and put it down with vigor." The painter should disdain the "folly of attending too closely to the mere mechanical processes of the art" so that "the person should be so portrayd as to be read like the bible without notes."[25]

Thinking that Jouett would return to Kentucky and make his living as a painter of head-and-shoulder

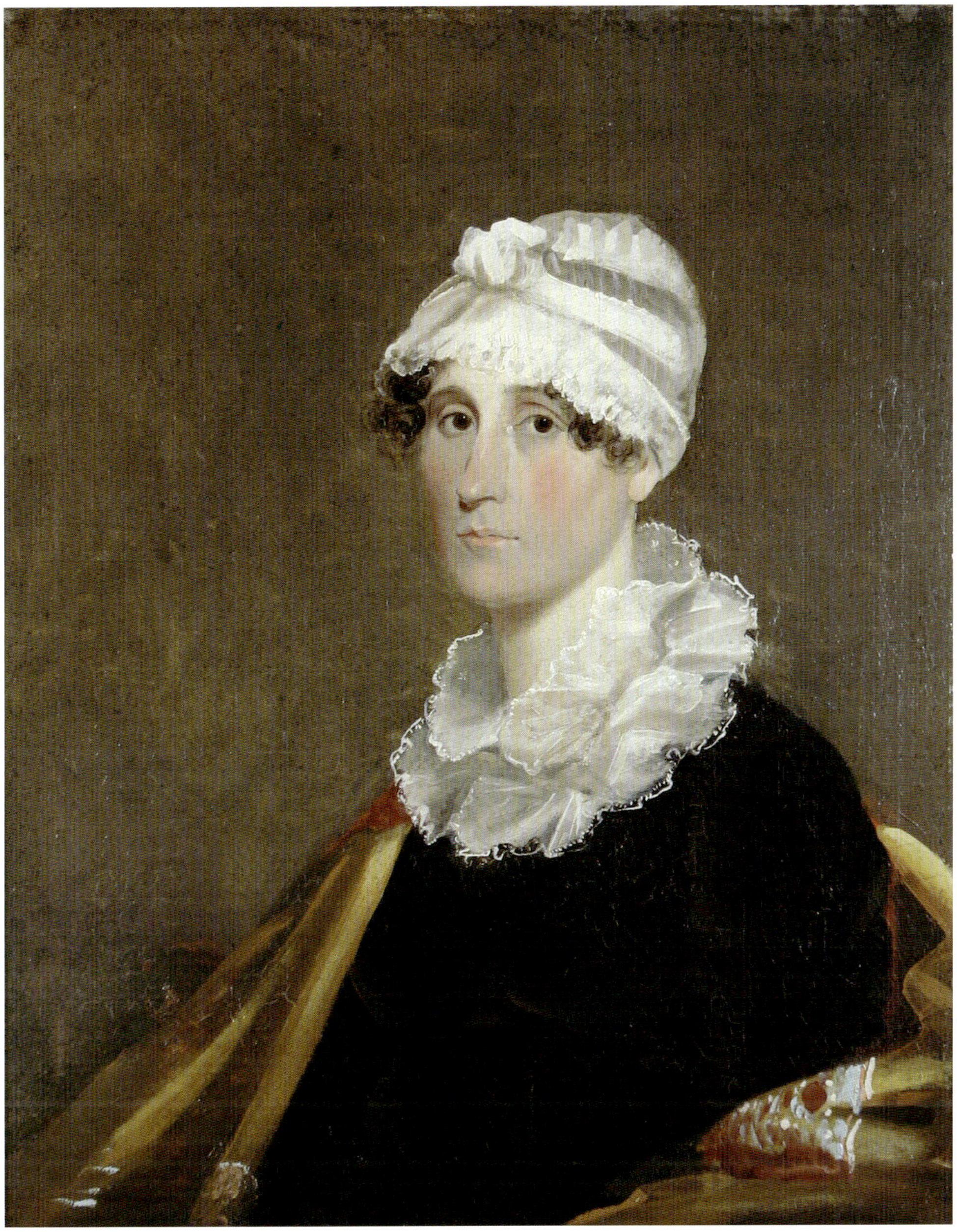

FIGURE 16 *(facing page)*. Gilbert Stuart (1755–1828), *Mrs. Paul Revere (Rachel Walker)* (1745–1813), 1813, oil on panel, 28¼ × 22⅛″, Museum of Fine Arts, Boston, gift of Joseph W. Revere, William B. Revere, and Edward H. R. Revere, 30.783.

FIGURE 17. Matthew Harris Jouett (1788–1827), *Martha Scott Bibb* (?–1829), 1815–1825, oil on canvas, 27½ × 22½″, The Filson Historical Society, 1995.13.1.

The frilly headdress and lace collar worn by Mrs. Paul Revere in Stuart's portrait offer the best source for comparison with Jouett's treatment of a similar costume detail, with its adept application of "standing white" to create a painterly effect. Covering the head with a frilly cap is a convention associated with the depiction of the mature matron and, at an approximate age of thirty-five to forty and having already given birth to ten children, Mrs. Bibb, despite her fresh complexion, might well have considered herself qualified as such. The portraits are approximately the same size, evidence of Jouett's knowledge of Stuart's sense of proportion and scale.

works intended for the home, Stuart warned against "too much attention to background detail," as it "detracts from the establishment of a firm character . . . all background material should serve the purpose of dating." Character derives from close observation, from an awareness of the individual's place in the natural world. "The great danger of a man becoming a mannerist from a too little care to the studies of nature. A blind adherence to any one man's style calculated to fetter the mind & the hand." An artist must learn to look, for in "all nature whether of animate or inanimate there is abundance of character. Or why expands the soul at the sight of old trees & rocks swept over by the raging flood." Stuart insisted that an artist "should never design his picture other than his imagination approves. It often happens that an attitude singularly *necessary & proper* is sacrificed to one that is more easy to the hand. No man can meet his fancy, but tis a good rule not [to] be contented to treat a subject but as it deserves."[26]

Giving a sitter, especially a sitter of note, a proper sense of character depends upon the head's placement on the canvas. Concerning this, Jouett offers a "*reflection of mine:* In painting great public characters be sure to have them elevated above you—this opens the countenance & gives a grandeur to the figure. Another advantage in having your sitters elevated when the

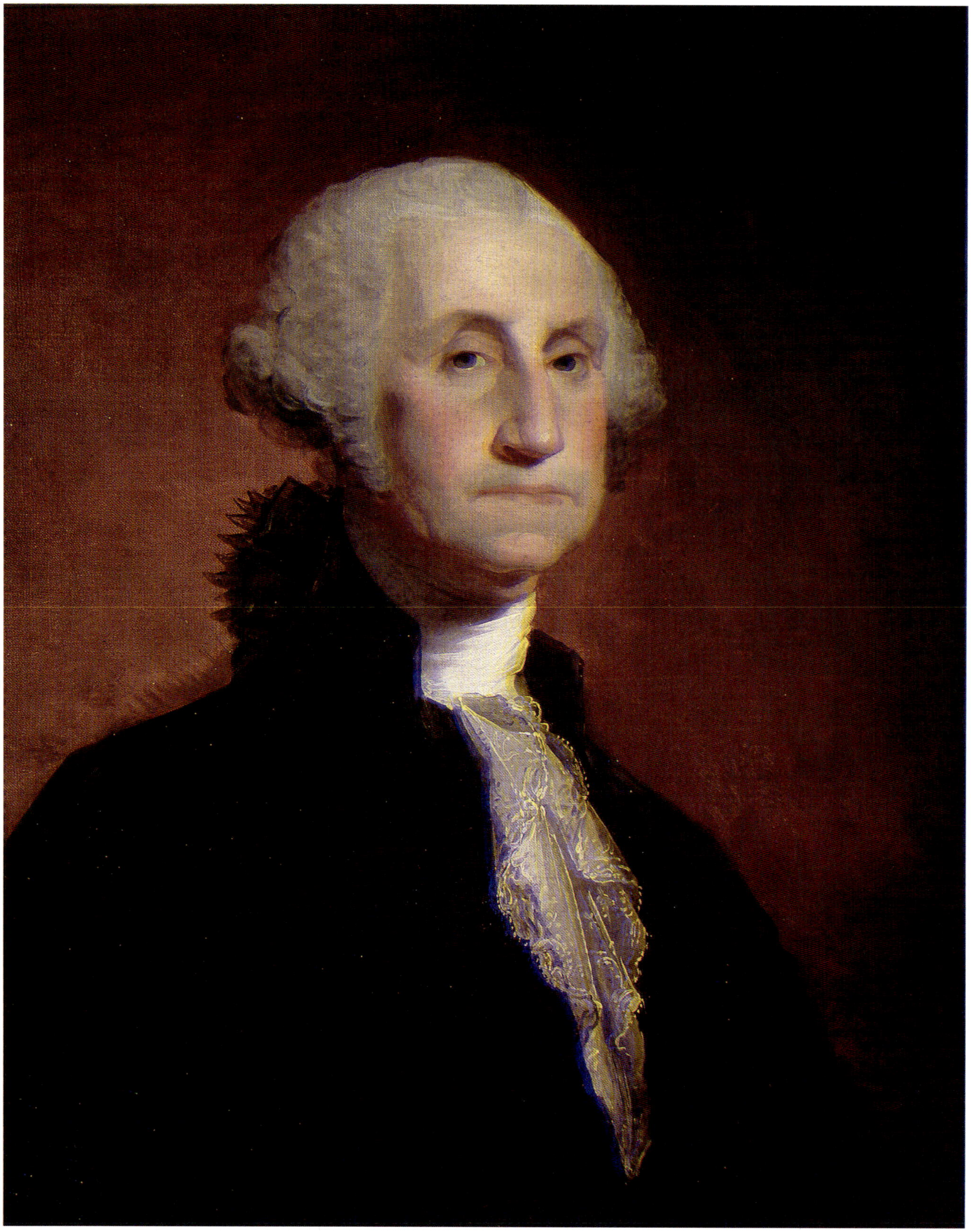

FIGURE 18. Gilbert Stuart (1755–1828), *George Washington* (1732–1799), 1819, oil on canvas, 27 × 22″, courtesy of the Huntington Library, Art Collections, and Botanical Gardens, San Marino, California, 39.1.

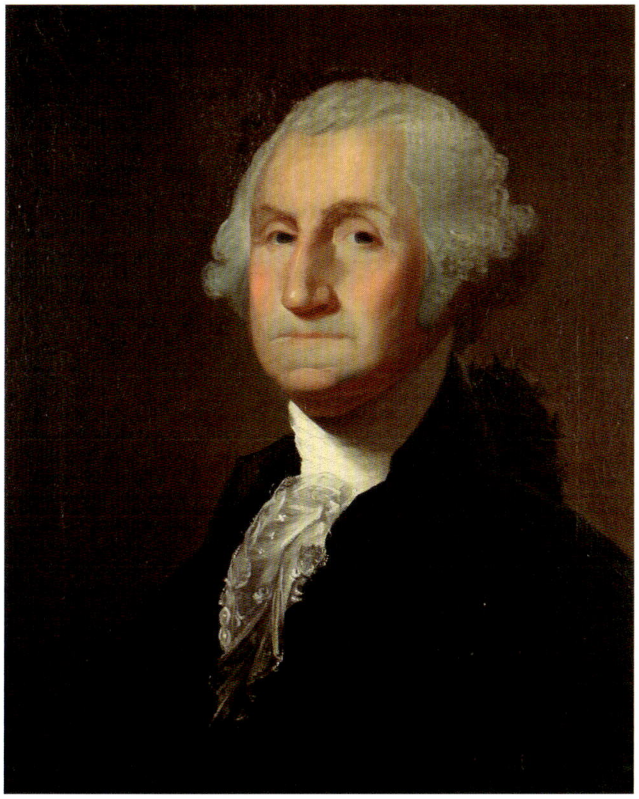

FIGURE 19. Matthew Harris Jouett (1788–1827), *George Washington* (1732–1799), ca. 1827, oil on canvas, 25¼ × 20¾", The Filson Historical Society, 1929.8.62.

Stuart painted at least seventy-five copies of his portrait of George Washington, all based on the unfinished Boston Athenaeum portrait, which he kept in his studio until his death in 1828. Jouett made a copy of this work as well as Stuart's "Edgehill" portrait of Thomas Jefferson, which he took back to Kentucky. There he advertised them for sale, along with a portrait of Isaac Shelby. Like Stuart, Jouett painted copies of these works on demand, several of which are extant. The Filson/Jouett Washington appears to have been reduced in size at some point in restretching, perhaps to accommodate a replacement frame.

pictures are hung the same view seems to be had of them, that is by giving an elevation to the sitter you suit the picture to the height in hanging, and the perspective is agreeable." This advice Stuart also offers himself. "I thus note them that I may not forget to think and act for myself" (Figs. 16, 17).[27]

Stuart's portraits and the compositional format Jouett derived from them have a strong frontality, which places the sitter high on the canvas, close to the picture plane and in a pose directed to engage the viewer. In attitude they reflect the forthright manner of the Neoclassical age. Stuart was not disposed to flattery, nor was Jouett. The art historian James Thomas Flexner has written that although "Stuart never allowed this frank vision to descend to caricature, Jouett produced upon occasion such brutal statements of physical ugliness that it is hard to understand why one of the horse-faced women he recorded did not use the prerogative of the delicately nurtured Southern lady to shoot him straight between the eyes."[28]

There is no doubt that Jouett returned to Kentucky a better painter. Though his career was cut short by his early death, he was indefatigable in his renderings of his fellow Kentuckians. William Barrow Floyd, his most thorough biographer, felt that he "has long been recognized as the most noted painter in the art annals of Kentucky. His ability, his personality, and the large number of portraits he painted have united to create an aura around his name which puts him in a category all alone. The fact that he was the first native son to capture the likenesses of the early settlers has elevated his stature as has the knowledge that he was Gilbert Stuart's favorite pupil" (Figs. 18, 19).[29]

Stuart's naturalistic format, with its even color and strong characterization, remained in favor among Kentucky portrait artists long after northeastern artists had begun to favor the lush coloration and elliptical lines of the romantic movement. In a letter to his son Sidney Payne Clay, a student at Princeton in 1818, General Green Clay advises him to go to Boston and have his portrait painted by Gilbert Stuart. The letter, still in the possession of the Clay family, encourages the young Clay to ask Stuart about the differences between winter and summer light when sitting for a portrait, information he doubtless received from Jouett, who painted him in 1818.[30]

In 1827, not quite forty, Jouett succumbed to "bilious fever" and died. At the time of his death he was the most successful portraitist in the commonwealth, much in demand and highly productive. An effusive early biographer, E. A. Jonas, described Jouett as having "conquered the Bluegrass."[31] His obituary notice in the *Lexington Reporter* of August 17, 1827, described him as "an artist of rare genius and of considerable celebrity. As a father, husband, friend, and citizen his death is deeply lamented, for in all these relations he occupied an elevated and enviable station in our society." His celebrated abilities as a raconteur doubtless entertained his numerous sitters to the last. And his stylistic formulations lived on in the work of Alexander Bradford, John Grimes, Alonzo Douglass, Aaron Houghton Corwine, Joseph Henry Bush, and Oliver Frazer.

Steamboat travel launches Kentucky-Mississippi itinerancy

Following the purchase of the Louisiana territory by the United States in 1803, a large number of Kentucky families migrated to Mississippi, especially to the Natchez region. Those families, including the Turners, Wests, Clays, and Davises, provided an extensive group of contacts for portrait commissions, which ensured the success of Kentucky-Mississippi itinerant portraitists.

The first steamboat to descend the Mississippi was the *New Orleans,* built in Pittsburgh under a commission from Nicholas Roosevelt. On its maiden voyage it was rocked by the violent New Madrid earthquake, survived, and arrived in New Orleans on January 12, 1812. For the following two years the boat provided

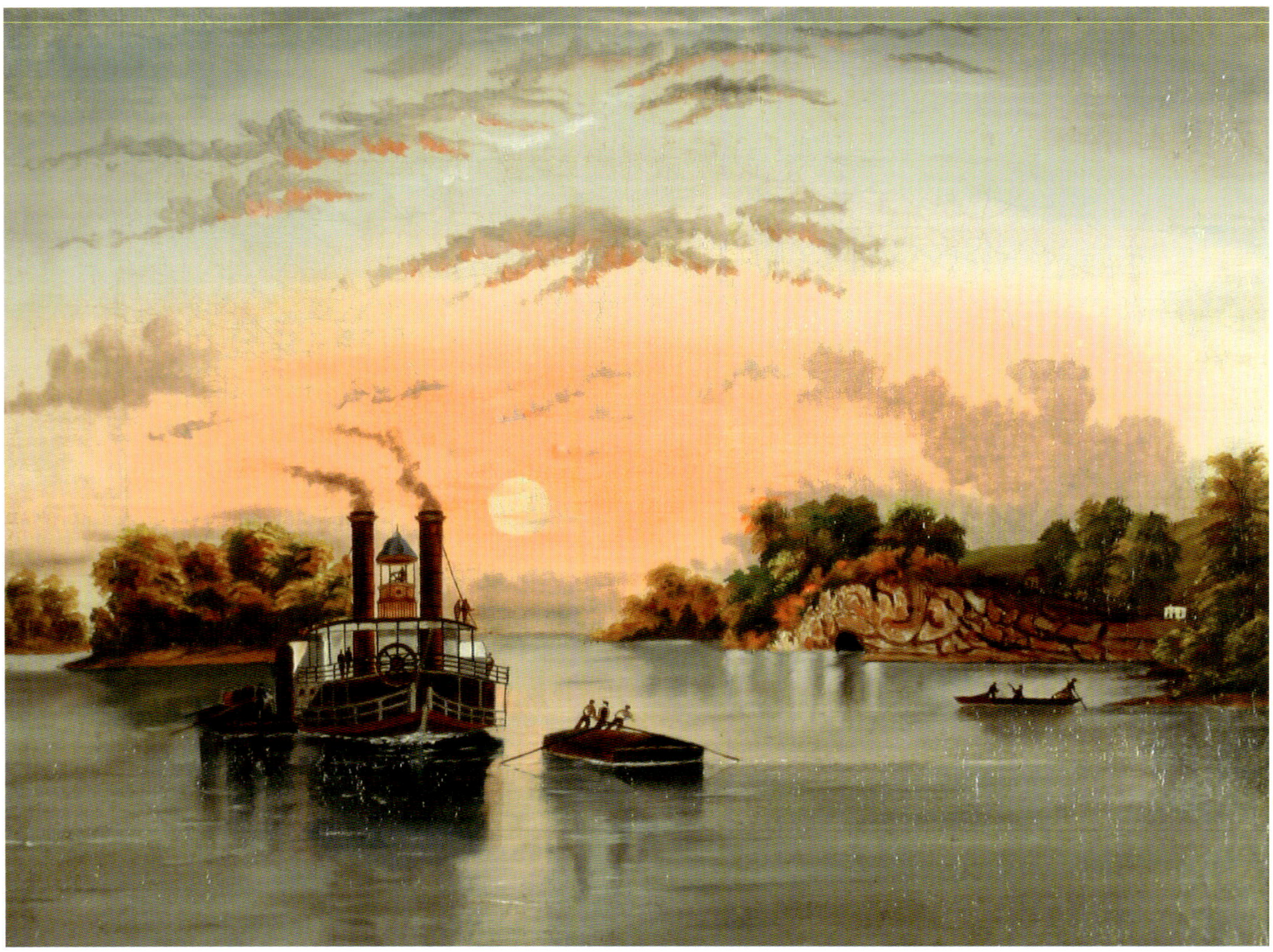

FIGURE 20. George Morrison (1820–1893), *Steamboat and Barge at Sunset,* n.d., oil on canvas, 10½ × 14¾", The Filson Historical Society, 1944.3.16.

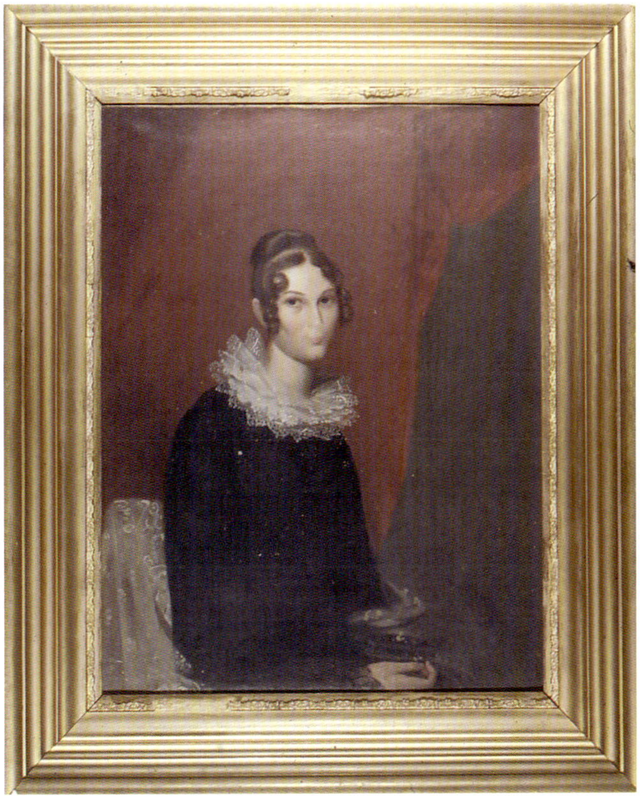

FIGURE 21. William Edward West (1788–1857), *Sarah Buckholtz Richards* (1792–1886), ca. 1818, oil on canvas, 35½ × 27½″, Collection of the Museum of Mississippi History, Mississippi Department of Archives and History.

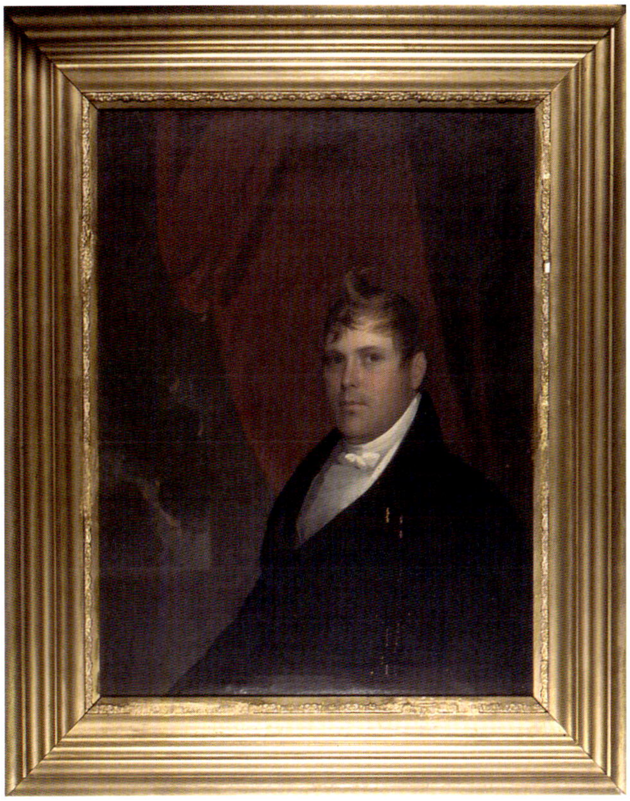

FIGURE 22. William Edward West (1788–1857), *John Richards* (1787–1827), ca. 1818, oil on canvas, 35½ × 27½″, Collection of the Museum of Mississippi History, Mississippi Department of Archives and History.

the first consistent service between New Orleans and Natchez. Henry Shreve's *Washington* pioneered the line between Louisville and New Orleans, commencing with a voyage in 1817. At that time a one-way trip could take up to three weeks; there were only some fourteen boats in service at any time. By 1819 that number had increased to thirty-one. Based on the slave trade, hemp, Bourbon whiskey, and mules, strong social, economic, and cultural bonds between Kentucky and the lower Mississippi River Valley developed, bonds that lasted until the Civil War (Fig. 20).[32]

William Edward West, one of the first itinerants to take advantage of the new mode of travel, went south from Philadelphia to Natchez and New Orleans in 1817. His presence in New Orleans in 1817 is documented by his painting of Julian de Lallande Poydras, a philanthropist who created a fund to endow penniless young brides.[33] West had to flee the city later that year when one of the frequent yellow fever epidemics shut the city down, sending the populace scurrying upriver. He landed in Natchez, where he attracted considerable local attention for his "self-taught" genius. Sophia Maria Michau Robinson, writing to her sister about refugees from New Orleans, noted his presence and found him all the more remarkable "when one considers he owes his talent to nature only."[34] This is not exactly true, as West had been an astute observer in the Philadelphia studio of Thomas Sully, where he had assisted the master by painting background details. Sully's portraits of Jean Terford and Mary Sicard David, with their faint echoes of French neoclassicism, provided the anatomical formula that West deployed in several Natchez works, as can be seen in the pendant portraits of John Richards and his wife, Sarah Buckholtz (Figs. 21, 22). Richards has a vaguely classical drapery behind his head, and his hair is brushed up in the empire style. Mrs. Richards has the same exaggerated torso Sully perfected, but West has also chosen to elongate her arm and place her hand, palm up, resting on the bottom of the picture plane.

After West's departure for Europe, Jouett began to pursue a Southern itinerancy in 1819, taking advantage of the same acquaintances and family connections in the Natchez region. Judge Edward Turner, one of the earliest civic leaders of Mississippi, had been educated at Transylvania and knew Jouett from his days in Kentucky. Jouett painted several members of the extended Turner-Smith-Griffith families. Many of these works were created in Jouett's maturity, during the 1820s, and demonstrate a fine command of style, seen especially in the ambitious compositions in his renderings of mothers with their children. That he found Natchez a profitable location for his trade is evident in a letter he wrote to his closest friend, Lawrence Levy, in 1823. Having landed at Natchez-under-the-Hill and made the long walk up to the city of mansions on the bluff, Jouett took stock of the locals. "This bustle and apparent commercial activity the people [are] conducting under the most insurmountable load of debt," he wrote, "and what adds to the calamity is the low price of cotton. Notwithstanding all this my prospects are fine. . . . had I time I think I could make my visit here a profitable one."[35]

Slightly younger than West and Jouett, Joseph Henry Bush began his itinerancy in 1818. Bush was more truly a wandering itinerant than was either West or Jouett. The latter artists tended to establish "painting rooms" in local hostelries. They steadily painted a group of sitters prearranged by word of mouth of their coming, as is evident by multiple portraits of members of one family. By contrast, Bush was rarely resident in one locale and worked from plantation to plantation, particularly among the extended Chotard families of Natchez and the Flowers family of Vicksburg. In later years, 1831–1848, he gave up this wandering and consistently spent his winters at the St. Charles Hotel in New Orleans. It was at the end of this period that he painted the portrait of General Zachary Taylor that now hangs in the White House (Fig. 23). Taylor's victorious leadership of the Army of the Rio Grande made him a popular candidate for the presidency, and he was nominated by the Whigs in 1848. Bush painted his portrait, in full military regalia, in that same year. Rarely did Bush attempt a work of this size or detail, whose subject's rugged, majestic demeanor embodies the romantic heroic ideal. The gleaming jacket buttons and the upheld sword, gripped by an assertive arm, enhance an atmosphere of authority.[36]

Central Kentucky artists were not the only portraitists to pursue work along the Ohio-Mississippi River trade route. James Reid Lambdin, resident in Louisville after 1832, pursued a seasonal itinerancy in Natchez from 1832 to 1837. Artists from Cincinnati who worked in the deep south included James Henry Beard, intermittently active in New Orleans from 1838 to 1858; Minor Kellogg, who was there in 1840; and Joseph Oriel Eaton, active there in 1855 and 1857. It was not a one-way stream. Painters who came upriver to Kentucky include the team of Theodore Sidney Moïse and Trevor Thomas Fowler, 1840–1854; and C. R. Parker, 1832–1848.[37]

Chester Harding paints in Paris, Kentucky, and pursues Daniel Boone

Abel and Olive Smith Harding of Conway, Massachusetts, had eleven children, four of whom became portrait artists of varying note. Chester, the fourth child, became one of the most celebrated portrait painters of the mid-nineteenth century as a result of his portraits of figures from American public life in the grand manner. His story, however, begins in the same picaresque style as that of Audubon: a trip downriver in search of fortune, followed by a series of misadventures, culminating in success and concluding with a departure for richer fields of activity with an abundant supply of curious anecdotes and reasonable likenesses intact. Prior to 1817, Chester had made his way in the world by various entrepreneurial efforts. He assisted his father and brother in cabinetmaking and tinkering, worked in a tavern, took up sign painting, and played the clarinet. On the side he developed his skills as a self-taught portrait artist, a pursuit also being practiced by his younger brother Horace, who was by then living in Paris, Kentucky, and working as a painter of fancy chairs. It was Horace who brought the demand for portraiture in central Kentucky, generated by Jouett's success, to Chester's attention. That Jouett was receiving $50 a head for his work persuaded

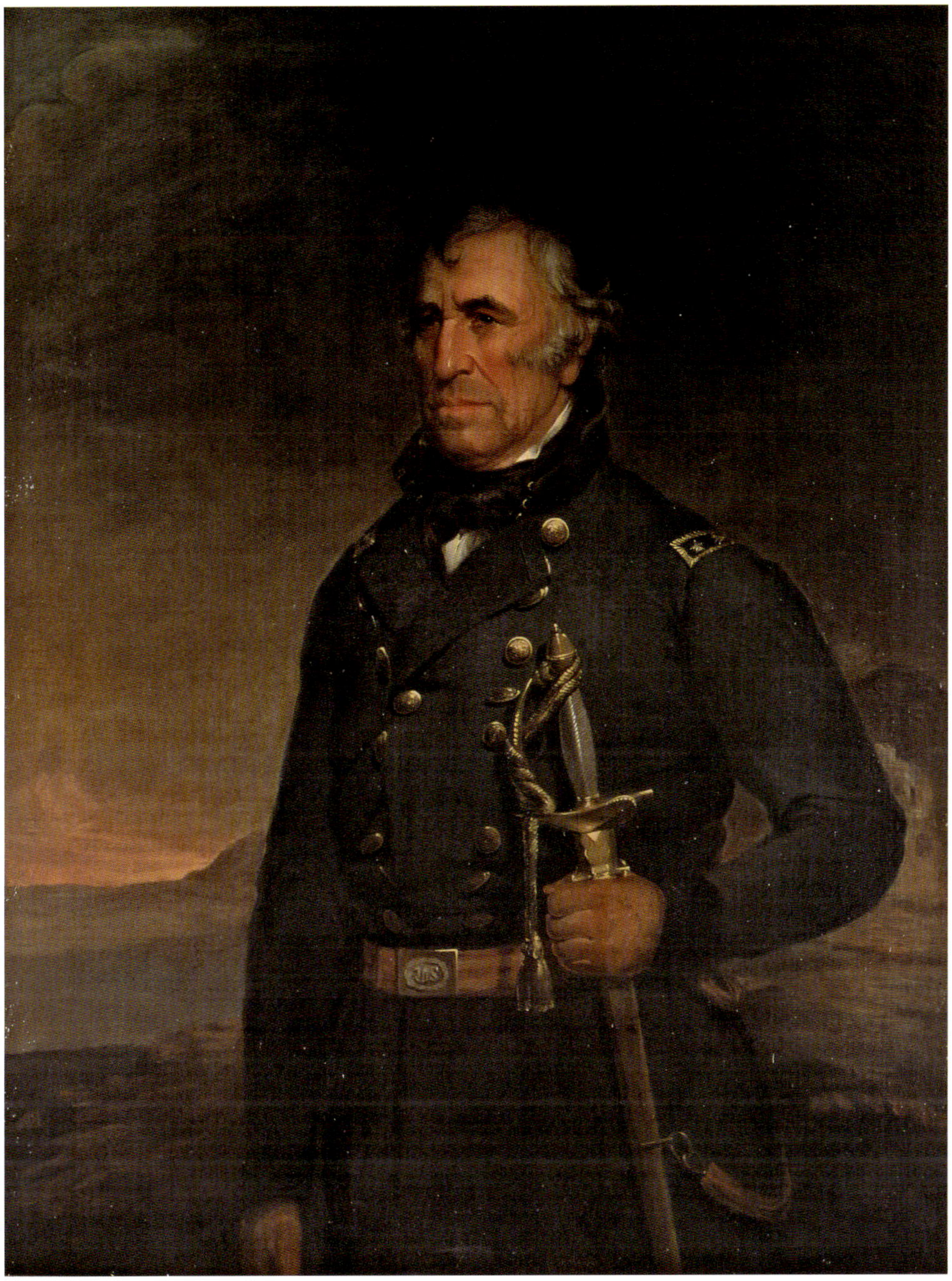

FIGURE 23. Joseph Henry Bush (1794–1865), *General Zachary Taylor* (1784–1850), 1848, oil on canvas, 44⅜ × 35″, The White House Collection, Washington, D.C.

Taylor's strong ties to the Louisville area, where his parents moved in 1785 to establish the Springfield plantation, may have eased Bush's introduction to him. Taylor maintained Kentucky as his official place of residence for voting purposes during his long military career, which saw him move from conflicts in Indiana to Florida to Mexico. In the 1830s he began to buy land in Mississippi and Louisiana, where he eventually resided. His daughter, Sarah Knox Taylor, married Jefferson Davis in Louisville in 1835, extending the interconnection of Kentucky and Mississippi families.

a fledgling artist of little proven ability that he could do the same. Accordingly, Chester Harding and his family, in the company of an itinerant barber named Jarvis and his family, journeyed to Paris and set up shop.[38]

Once there Harding found that his brother was well connected, and after painting a portrait "of a very popular young man," he made a decided hit. After that he claims to have "painted nearly one hundred portraits" in a period of six months, "at twenty-five dollars a head," an amount that "rather disturbed the equanimity of my conscience."[39] No doubt the claim to quantity should also have disturbed his conscience, indicating as it does the production of one portrait almost every other day for the stated period. Harding's boasts may have been induced by more than the tall-tale tradition of his new home. The previously temperate artist notes that at this time it was "the almost universal custom to take a julep before breakfast; and by degrees I fell into the habit of taking *my* julep, and sometimes two."[40] While in Bourbon County and the immediate area, Harding painted several members of the extended family of Governor and Mrs. James Garrard as well as General

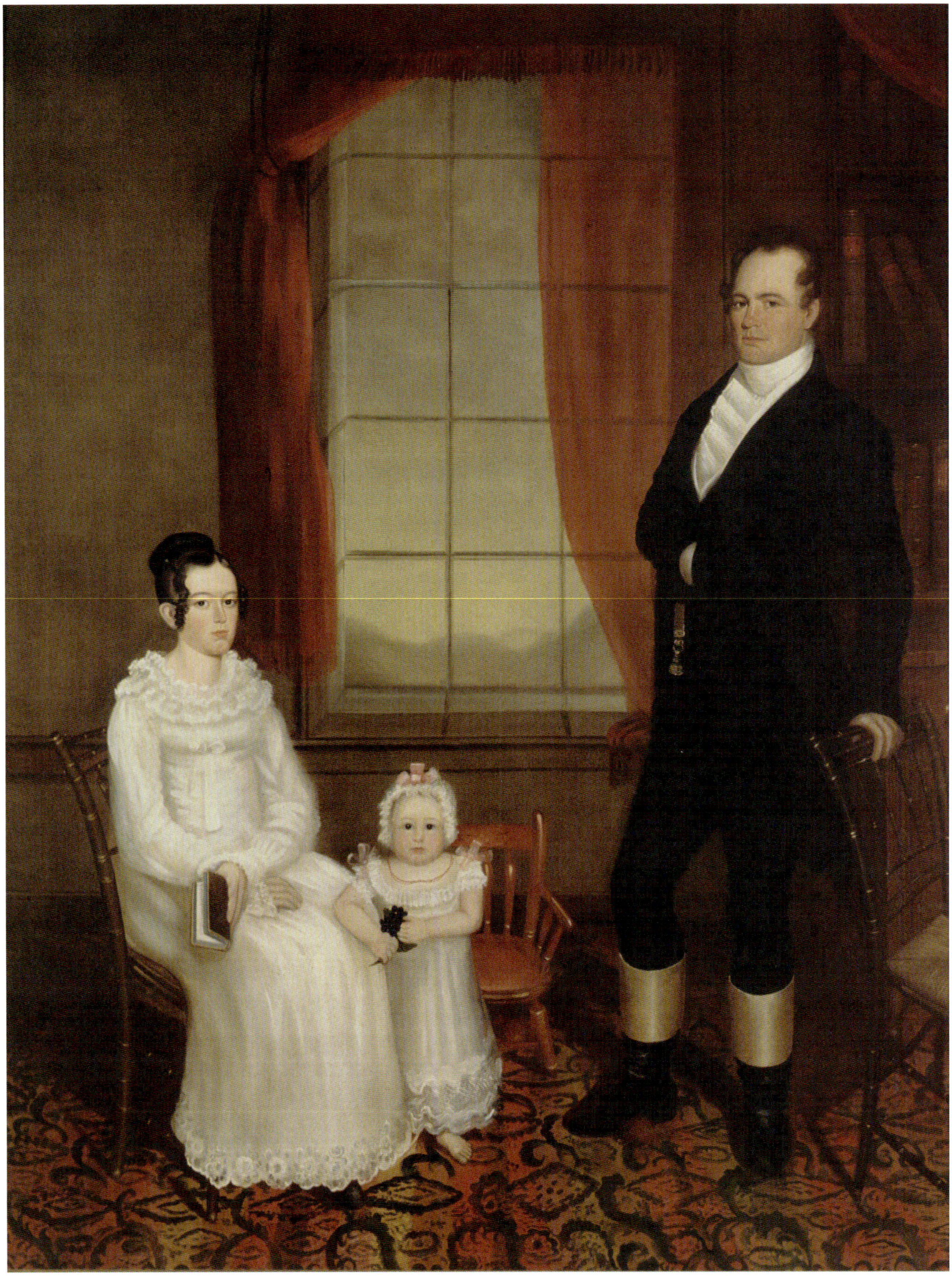

FIGURE 24. Chester Harding (1792–1866), *John Speed Smith Family,* 1819, oil on canvas, 100 × 78″, Speed Art Museum, Louisville, Kentucky.

and Mrs. Green Clay. Garrard had been a farmer and distiller who built an impressive stone house, Mt. Lebanon, in Bourbon County. Green Clay's enormous land claims, starting in 1777, had made him one of the richest men in the commonwealth. He had settled in Madison County, where Harding went to paint him and received a commission to paint the general's daughter Eliza.

The painting was the largest and most ambitious full-length portrait painted in Kentucky to that date and an astonishing achievement for a fledgling portraitist. Colonel and Mrs. John Speed Smith (Eliza Lewis Clay) and their infant daughter Sally Ann were painted life size in the parlor of the house in Richmond that had been Mrs. Smith's dowry (Fig. 24). Details in the work, especially the painted chair and the patterned rug, are rare documents of material culture from the period. The colonel's pose, turned slightly away from the planar field and set apart from the seated figure of his wife, heightens the sense of patrimony graciously laid before the viewer. Little Sally Ann, a stiff witness with wide eyes, recalls the plain painter styles of Harding's native New England. It was during this tenure in Kentucky that Harding "began to entertain more elevated ideas of the art" of portraiture and "to desire some means of improvement." Accordingly, he set out for Philadelphia and "spent two months in that city, devoting my time entirely to drawing in the Academy, and studying the best pictures, practising at the same time with the brush." Humbled by the experience, he became "discouraged as I looked at the works of older artists." Jouett, whom he had previously disparaged, he now thought "really was a good artist" whose "excellence had been beyond my capacity of appreciation."[41]

Upon his return to Kentucky, Harding discovered that portrait commissions had dried up in Paris, so he tried Cincinnati. Having no luck there, he pushed west to St. Louis, with an introduction to the territorial governor, General William Clark, and funds derived from sales "of a dozen silver spoons, and a gold watch and chain" purchased for his wife during "my palmy days in Paris." Governor Clark assisted Harding in getting a "room for a studio, and then offered himself as a sitter" for a work in the head-and-shoulders format. Harding's claim that the life portrait was such a great success that

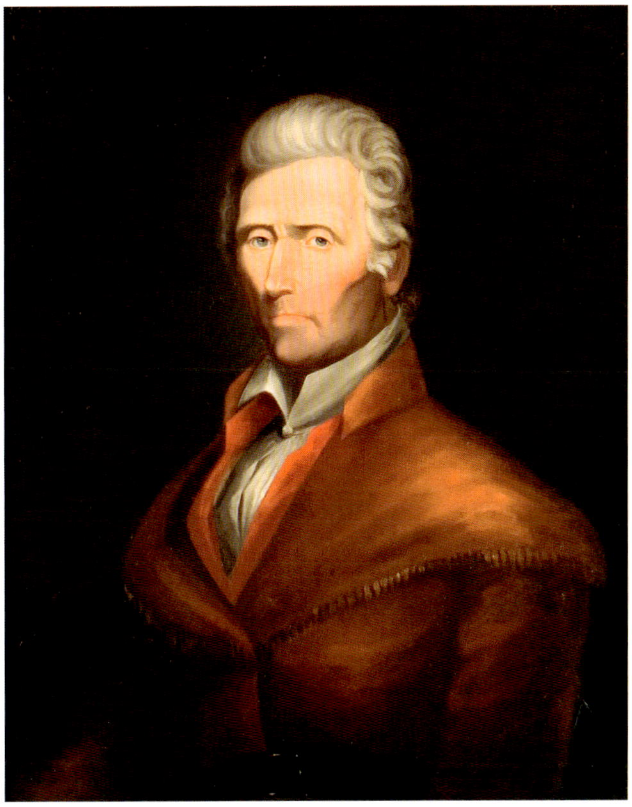

FIGURE 25. Chester Harding (1792–1866), *Daniel Boone* (1734–1820), 1820, oil on canvas, 29 × 24″, The Filson Historical Society, 1929.8.59.

Harding made an oil sketch of Boone in June 1819, a work of robust coloration, lacking background detail, and dominantly centered on the planar field. This work, a gift to the Massachusetts Historical Society by the Harding family, was the basis for several copies Harding subsequently produced, including this Filson version, a gift of R. C. B. Thruston in 1929.

it led to commissions that kept him busy for fifteen months is suspect, owing to that portrait's disappearance.[42] (Harding did make a copy of John Wesley Jarvis's 1810 portrait of Clark, which is now in the Missouri Historical Society's holdings.)

Apparently reluctant to summer in the heat of St. Louis, Harding set out for Franklin, Missouri, with the express purpose of locating Daniel Boone and taking his likeness (Fig. 25). Claiming that the explorer was all but unknown to the locals, the portraitist finally found him "engaged in cooking his dinner" and "lying in his bunk." Harding claimed Boone was then ninety; he was actually eighty-five. In a role reversal it was Boone who entertained Harding during the sitting for a pencil sketch, with "anecdotes of his earlier life." Asked if, lacking a compass, he was ever lost, the white-haired veteran of the frontier replied, "I can't say as ever I was lost, but I was *bewildered* once for three days."[43]

Having accomplished his sketch, Harding returned to Franklin, where the nine-year-old George Caleb Bingham observed him in his studio producing two versions in oil of Boone.[44] These and subsequent copies have achieved prominence as legendary as John Filson's original biography of Boone. One, a full-length work, was left behind in Kentucky in the hopes the state would acquire it for the new state capitol; according to the Harding scholar Leah Lipton, "Because of severe mistreatment later, only the head of this likeness exists today, remounted by Harding on new canvas in 1860."[45]

A second, half-length portrait, showing Boone in a fur-trimmed coat and buckskins, has an even more exotic history. Harding is thought to have given this work to Matthew Harris Jouett in 1821 when he stopped in Kentucky en route to his home in the north. Jouett's estate inventory does indeed record a portrait of Boone, and this work is now in the collection of the Speed Art Museum in Louisville. Sorting fact from fiction at this early stage in Harding's career is as difficult as the passage from wilderness to civilization on the first American frontier. But there is strong evidence that his determination, and much-admired native talent, attracted admiration and recognition.

An Englishwoman traveling abroad gave us an account of the spontaneous expression of that admiration. Frances Trollope began a lengthy journey in America in 1827, writing in her diary the piquant observations on American life that provide firsthand information on the manner of the people she met. During her stay in Cincinnati, an incident she reported indicates that academic training was not especially esteemed on the American frontier. During her travels she had a conversation with an "intelligent and agreeable" gentleman who spoke highly of an American painter who was "perfectly self-taught." As both she and her husband were educators, she was curious why a lack of academic training should be such a pronounced virtue. The gentleman, in turn, expressed "contempt . . . at the idea that study was necessary to the formation of taste, and to the development of genius." When she questioned the value of such lack of training, the man asked, "Can there be higher praise?" Recognizing self-instruction as a virtue in the character of those who attained "individual merit" without "the means of instruction," Trollope failed to understand it as a "praise to his works." The artist in question was Chester Harding.[46] Though he returned to Kentucky in the 1840s as a distinguished and internationally known painter of politicians and English aristocrats, he no longer attracted the tall tales of his youth.

Unsigned portraits and Aaron Houghton Corwine

The large number of extant unsigned and undocumented portraits in the Ohio River Valley poses an enormous challenge to potential detectives of its art history. One case study involves the portraits of Captain and Mrs. Benjamin Bayless and the careers of Aaron Houghton Corwine and Alonzo Douglass. Elizabeth Wood and Benjamin Bayless were married in 1798 and settled in the vicinity of Maysville in the first decade of the nineteenth century. Their portraits, which are well painted, unusually lighted, and rather refined, were preserved by a lateral branch of the family. Although the history of the portraits was preserved in the family's oral tradition, it was never documented on paper. To determine the artist of these portraits, certain facts can be established and specific questions can be asked. The date of the portrait can be approximated by an examination of costume. The gentleman's stock and the lady's lace cap are not unlike attire seen in portraits of the period 1810–1820. If painted in that decade, the appearance of the couple as being in their thirties would be reasonable.

Determining the identity of the artist of these portraits requires a consideration of place and a survey of those painting in the area that time. On June 20, 1817, a John T. Turner of Cincinnati advertised in the *Maysville Eagle* that he had set up at the house of Jacob Boone in Maysville, offering "portrait painting as large as life, and ornamental." Clearly itinerant, Turner advised those wanting portraits that the "sooner the application, the better as they contemplate leaving this place in a few weeks." Thanking any potential sitters in advance, he also noted his gratitude to those who

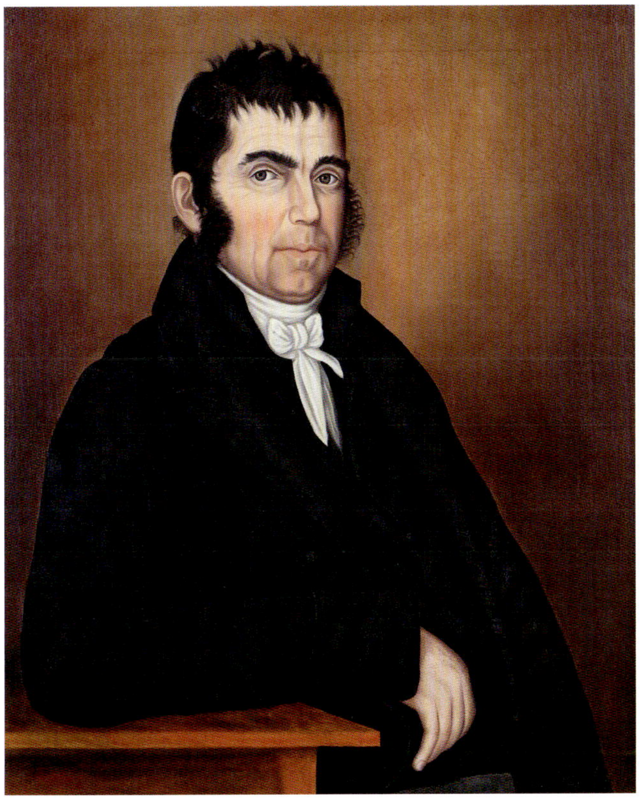

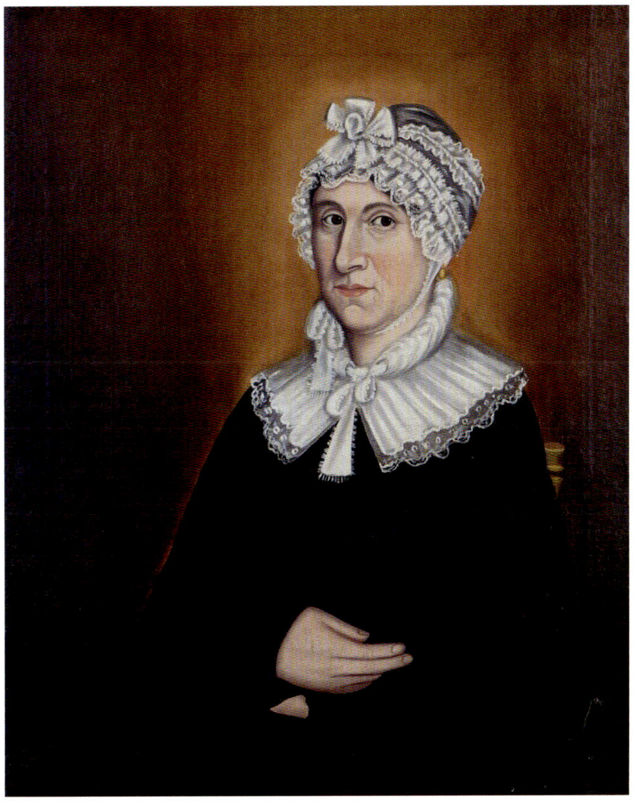

FIGURE 26. John T. Turner (fl. early 1800s), att., *Captain Benjamin Bayless* (1774–1839), ca. 1817, oil on canvas, 29⅞ × 25″, The Filson Historical Society, 2005.23.1.

FIGURE 27. John T. Turner (fl. early 1800s), att., *Elizabeth Wood Bayless* (1780–1867), ca. 1817, oil on canvas, 29⅞ × 25″, The Filson Historical Society, 2005.23.2.

Captain Bayless built a house for his bride, Elizabeth Wood, near Washington, in Mason County, Kentucky, in 1807, which still stands and has long served as the rectory for the local Presbyterian church.

"have already afforded [him] encouragement," from which we can deduce that there was potential work at hand. Like other itinerants, Turner would have been a master of many decorative arts, including sign painting, silhouette cutting, and fancy furniture painting. This type of work requires a sharp attention to detail, which in portraits would set off the subject in a vivid manner so as to attract the eye. Both Bayless subjects are given a strong light behind their heads, providing a golden radiance that adds depth to the background. They are also painted in such intense detail as to invite an attribution of naive realism, that "honesty" so admired in likenesses in that age (Figs. 26, 27).

There is, however, still another, highly intriguing connection to be made between Turner and other artists in the area. Aaron Houghton Corwine was a child prodigy reputed to have had his first instruction from an artist, a Mr. Turner, visiting Maysville from Cincinnati. Taking Turner's advice, Corwine moved to Cincinnati in 1817, where he gained the patronage of Turner's friend Dr. Daniel Drake. Was it from Turner that the younger artist observed the techniques of placing a head, raising color, and applying detail? Corwine's early work is also characterized by a strong light behind the head, which gives high relief and adds a luminous depth to the background, a stylistic conceit he then passed along to his protégé Alonzo Douglass. These lessons in likeness could be called verisimilitude of detail, and though they do not provide empirical evidence in the form of signatures, invoices, or correspondence, they do allow possible artist attributions.

Aaron Houghton Corwine was born in Maysville, Kentucky. Before becoming an artist he was "a plough-boy, for which he never showed much taste," according to the historian Lewis Collins. Collins's mythic history of Corwine includes an episode of painting his father's barns and fences with "grotesque figures," which were so "fanciful and striking" that Amos Corwine determined to give his son "the opportunity to pursue the inclination of his mind." A precocious talent, young Corwine attracted the attention of the *Cincinnati Inquisitor,* which urged its readers to support this "literally self-taught, ingenious and promising youth." His talents soon attracted sufficient sponsors for him to pursue further study in Philadelphia with Thomas Sully, who found him to be "gentle, full of kind sympathy and delicate taste."[47] Sully also noted that the young artist suffered from ill health. Having acquired such knowledge as he needed to establish himself as an artist, Corwine returned to Cincinnati in 1820, becoming that city's first resident portraitist. Over the next five years he painted many of the local grandees, including the seminal patron Nicholas Longworth and his wife, as well as his initial contact, Dr. Drake. In 1825 he painted Andrew Jackson and the Marquis de Lafayette on their visits to the city.

In 1826 Drake and E. D. Mansfield, a local historian and antiquarian, writing of local culture, felt they could "boast of a young artist who has but a single rival in the Western Country" (that being Matthew Harris Jouett).[48] Corwine's work was included in the ill-fated efforts of Frederick Eckstein to organize a local art academy in 1828. Around that time Corwine took on at least one student-apprentice, Alonzo Douglass, who completed several works under Corwine's guidance. By 1829 Corwine's health had seriously deteriorated. Suffering from tuberculosis, he sailed for England in the hope that a sea voyage would improve his condition and that he would profit from further study of art in London. Financial difficulties and ever-worsening health soon forced his return to America, and he died not long after landing in Philadelphia in 1830.[49] That Corwine was remarkably attractive can be seen in portraits of him by his contemporaries and in the generous accounts of his skills in many memoirs. Audubon sketched him in 1820 while visiting Cincinnati, portraying him as a sensitive young scholarly type seen in profile. A young Hiram Powers sculpted his image in wax, showing him "wearing a high collar and a loose cloak," a "delicate image" resembling the portrait medallions of John Flaxman.[50]

Corwine's self-portraits attracted certain legendary, and possibly apocryphal, anecdotes. The earliest was said to have been painted from the artist's reflection in a tub of water, although it shows a strong affinity for the works of Sully at the same time (Fig. 28). A self-portrait painted in England in 1829 is a bravura exercise in the style of Sir Thomas Lawrence. Corwine presented himself with his hallmark curly hair and wearing a fashionable coat trimmed with a fur collar. He looks toward the viewer with a slightly quizzical expression, vulnerable but with an obvious presence. Though Jouett may have a far larger public reputation, owing to the affection he accumulated during the late nineteenth-century colonial revival era, Corwine is certainly his equal. He placed his figures in a bold position, high and forward on the planar field, and deeply modeled with contours suggesting the curvature of face and body. His coloration has an unusual warmth and depth, which make his likenesses highly compelling and immediate. Edward Dwight, a recent admirer, praises his ability to "get a perfect likeness and to capture an expression of vitality." How sadly romantic that galloping consumption should have deprived posterity of more pictures from this artist whose "work, like his character," was

FIGURE 28 *(facing page).* Aaron Houghton Corwine (1802–1830), *Self-Portrait,* ca. 1820, oil on canvas, 25 × 18½", The Filson Historical Society, 2003.6.3.

Though less well known than the dramatically romantic self-portrait in the collection of the Kentucky Gateway Museum Center, Maysville, Kentucky, this work is an interesting document of style and the subject of an elaborate oral history. The frontality and softly focused gaze of the subject is similar to certain Sully works from the same period (see Fig. 3). When the portrait was presented to the Maysville Public Library in 1921, the donor, William R. Corwine, a collateral descendent (i.e., a descendant of one's siblings rather than a direct descendant), perpetuated the oral history that the likeness had been taken from a "reflection in a tub of water." The necessity of the conjunction of pure, clean water, a reflective tub bottom, and the right angle of glancing sunlight to bounce back a recognizable image makes this story probably more charming than factual. At various points in its history the work was damaged in a fire, somewhat reduced in size by restretching, and retired from view. It was rescued by another collateral descendent, Betty Bone Scheiss, who had it extensively restored before presenting it to the Filson.

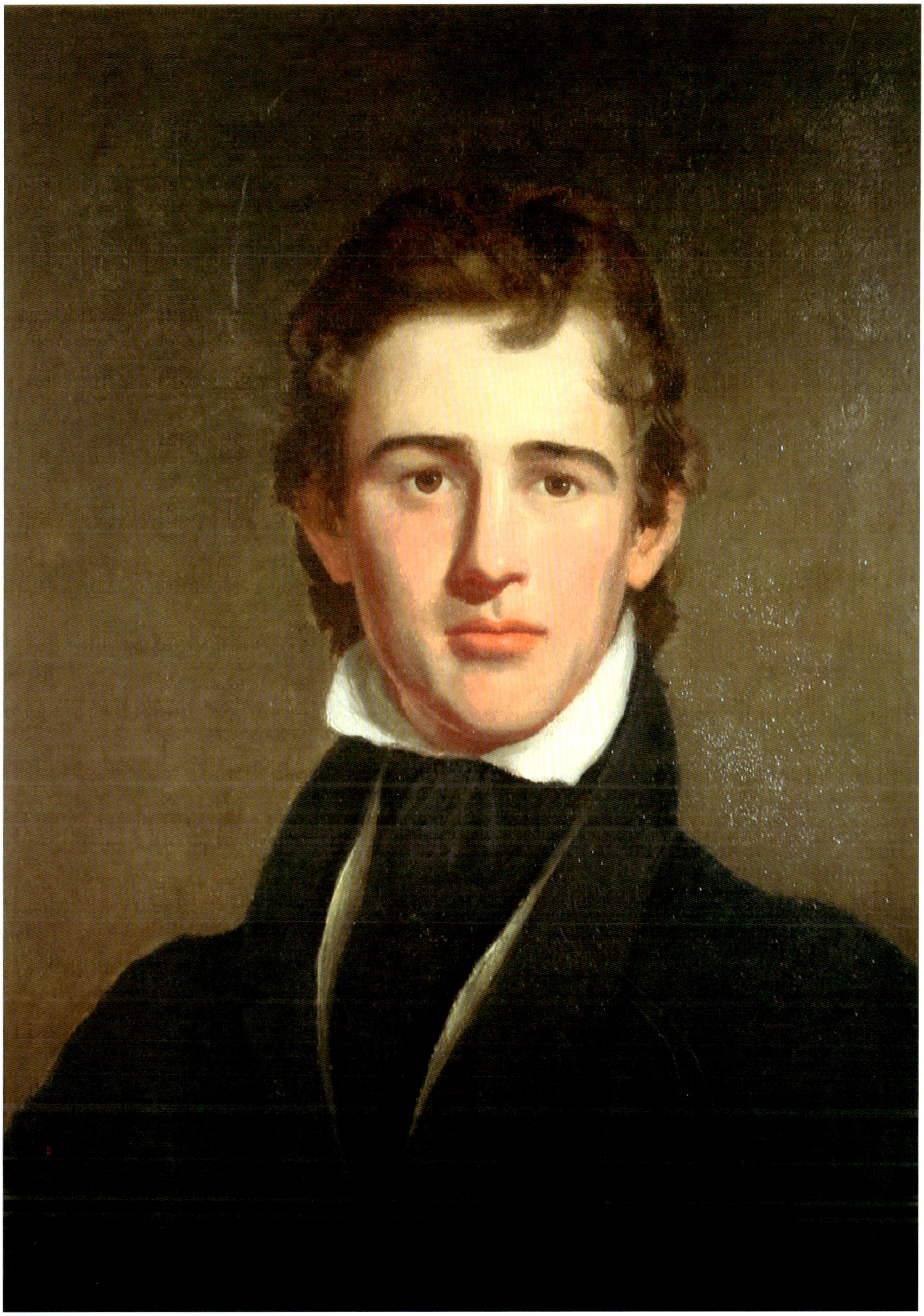

"candid and guileless, modest and unobtrusive."[51] Although Turner and Alonzo Douglass remain largely unknown, Corwine has attracted considerable interest for this accomplished style, as well as his mythic status as one of the region's best early painters.

John Wesley Jarvis visits Louisville and heads south to New Orleans

When John Wesley Jarvis arrived in Louisville in 1820, he was already recognized as one of the most prominent American portrait painters, as well established in New York as was Gilbert Stuart in Boston. He had painted many of the greatest figures of the day, including Washington Irving, Andrew Jackson, the Marquis de Lafayette, and, in a monumental portrait, Oliver Hazard Perry, into the background of which he had inserted a self-portrait. For some years Jarvis had pursued a seasonal itinerancy in the tidewater South, working in Charleston and Baltimore. Having a restless nature, he may have accepted "a standing invitation from the Croghans of Louisville" to make the western journey.[52] Lieutenant Colonel George Croghan was the nephew of George Rogers Clark, the Revolutionary War hero who resided at Locust Grove near the Ohio River in Jefferson County. It is thought that Jarvis took the newly completed national road to Wheeling, West Virginia, where he could book river passage to Louisville.

Jarvis accompanied the young Croghan on the river trip, reaching Louisville in November 1820. There he painted Major William Croghan and Lucy Clark Croghan, and he is said to have painted George Rogers Clark as well, although that episode remains undocumented. On November 9 Jarvis attended a ball at the home of Thomas Bullitt. Jarvis's letter of November 11, 1820, written to his dear friend Richea Etting of Baltimore, provides a rare glimpse of high life on what was still the western frontier. Writing on an early Sunday morning, he wishes "you had seen what a way I was in among the good folks. The frolic was given to me and I assure you the people here know how to enjoy themselves just as well as the folks on the Atlantic. In the first place Mr. Bullet's [*sic*] house is very large and well calculated for company. The ladies were dressed with taste, conversed sensibly, were affable and some, very handsome."[53]

Following descriptions of the women's attire and the men's gruff, petulant behavior, Jarvis offers a bit of doggerel, a poem written to be sung to the tune of "O Poor Robinson Crusoe." The poem celebrates the beauty of the wild terrain he saw on the river journey with Colonel Croghan, as "down the river we glided/ on every hand we saw excellent land/where many good people resided." He found "the rivers are such fine turnpikes," and he greatly admired the energies and customs of the people he met along the way, despite recent episodes of earthquake and the Panic of 1819. "I laughed to think how little they cared about the depreciation of the Kentucky Bank note. I looked at their nimble feet as the flounces of their gowns flew about and fluttered with as much life as if they were determined to be merry in spite of Bank Notes, and their nominal value. The land yields more than they can consume, and while they have health and peace and plenty they will put their wisdom to a bad use if they suffer themselves to be unhappy." He closes with his intent to "go to New Orleans by one of the first . . . boats," but not before he describes a mild earthquake. Apparently the damage from the New Madrid quake had "split . . . Mr. Bullet's house . . . from top to bottom." Then, "we had an earthquake on the ninth about sun down. We were sitting taking wine after dinner. It was rather too gentle. I half wished to have a harder shake but I believe it will do."[54]

Jarvis departed Louisville by steamboat for New Orleans in late November, about the same time as Audubon and Mason were making the journey by keelboat. Both parties arrived the first week in January, in time for the annual celebration of the American victory at the Battle of New Orleans. Audubon noted that he saw "many of the Louisville Gentry," including Colonel George Croghan, who suggested he make the acquaintance of Jarvis and show him his work in progress.[55] Audubon himself writes of encountering Jarvis on the levee at New Orleans (Fig. 29). The naturalist's description of Jarvis as "the original painter" is a scathing caricature that seems to accurately depict a portraitist known for his outlandish attire, propensity to break into song, and fondness for drink. Jarvis was carrying a cage of birds, which Audubon asked to examine. In what is surely the most ironic response in the history of painting in the South, Jarvis replied, "What the devil do you know about birds, Sir?" But the senior artist's rhetoric was not wasted on Audubon, although "it brought a blush into my face," and he acknowledged that the swagger was "not much in discordance with a not unusual mode of granting an answer in the United States."[56]

Audubon's account of his visit to Jarvis's studio provides certain details about how the painter worked. The easel set before the window, the mahl stick in place, the young assistants painting in drapery—all convinced the naturalist that "whoever was the artist, he certainly was possessed of superior talents." After a shocking episode of marksmanship in which Jarvis shot up his own easel, he bade Audubon sit down and observe "how adroitly he transferred the colours from his glistening palet to the canvas before him." The senior artist then proceeded to explain the importance of a cooperative sitter who is willing to engage the artist's attention. He also noted that he "ran the chalk over the canvas to form a rough outline," documentation of underdrawing. Audubon's encounter with Jarvis ended badly. Jarvis roughly criticized Audubon as a "painter of feathers" and dismissed the fledgling bird works without a comment. Nor was he interested in the offer of "assistance to finish his portraits" that Audubon made. They departed under awkward circumstances, as, Audubon recalled, Jarvis "simply told me he could not believe I might help him in the least." Audubon's departing comment, that "no doubt he Looked on Me as I did on him as an Original, and a Craked man," aptly summarizes an encounter in which two very different artistic spirits clashed.[57]

Before Jarvis left New Orleans, he painted a portrait that reconnected him with Kentucky and the earlier history of the Ohio River Valley (Fig. 30). The subject, James Wilkinson, was a native of Calvert County, Maryland, who rose to fame by becoming a brigadier general at the age of twenty during the early days of the American Revolution. From the outset of his career he was prone to reckless behavior and questionable associations, including those with Aaron Burr and Benedict Arnold. Out of favor and distrusted, he spent the last years of the war as quartermaster general of the army's supplies. Having married Ann Biddle, of the influential Biddle family of Philadelphia, Wilkinson went west in 1783 to secure various land warrants he had purchased from Revolutionary War veterans. It was in Kentucky "that his inherent genius for connivance and intrigue would grow and flourish over the next thirty years."[58] He is credited with laying out the town of Frankfort,

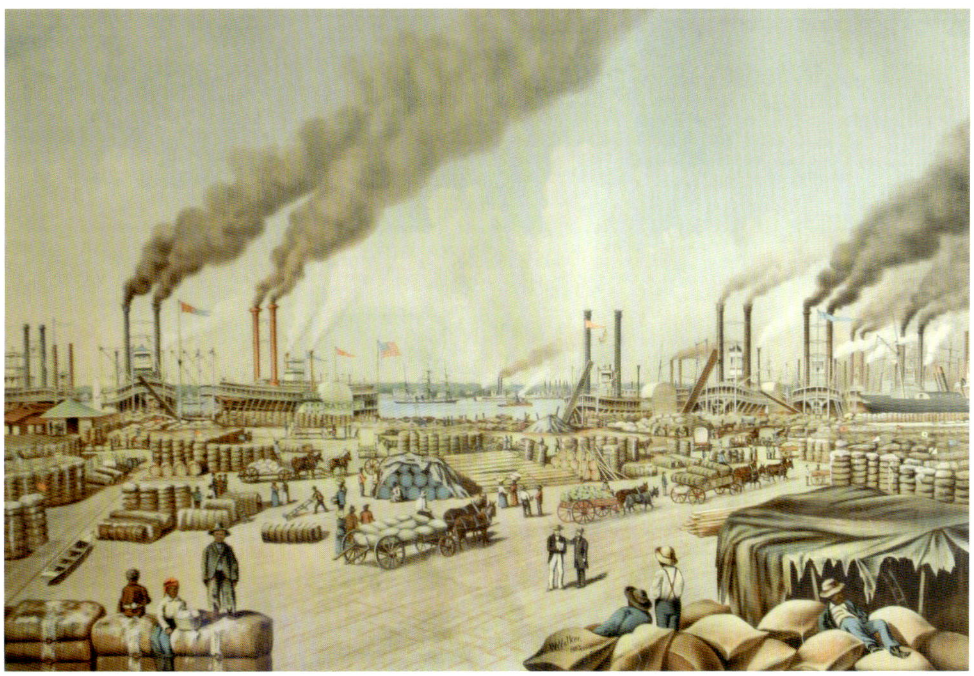

FIGURE 29. Currier and Ives (after W. A. Walker), *The Levee–New Orleans,* 1884, lithograph, 23 × 31″, The Filson Historical Society, 998PR3.

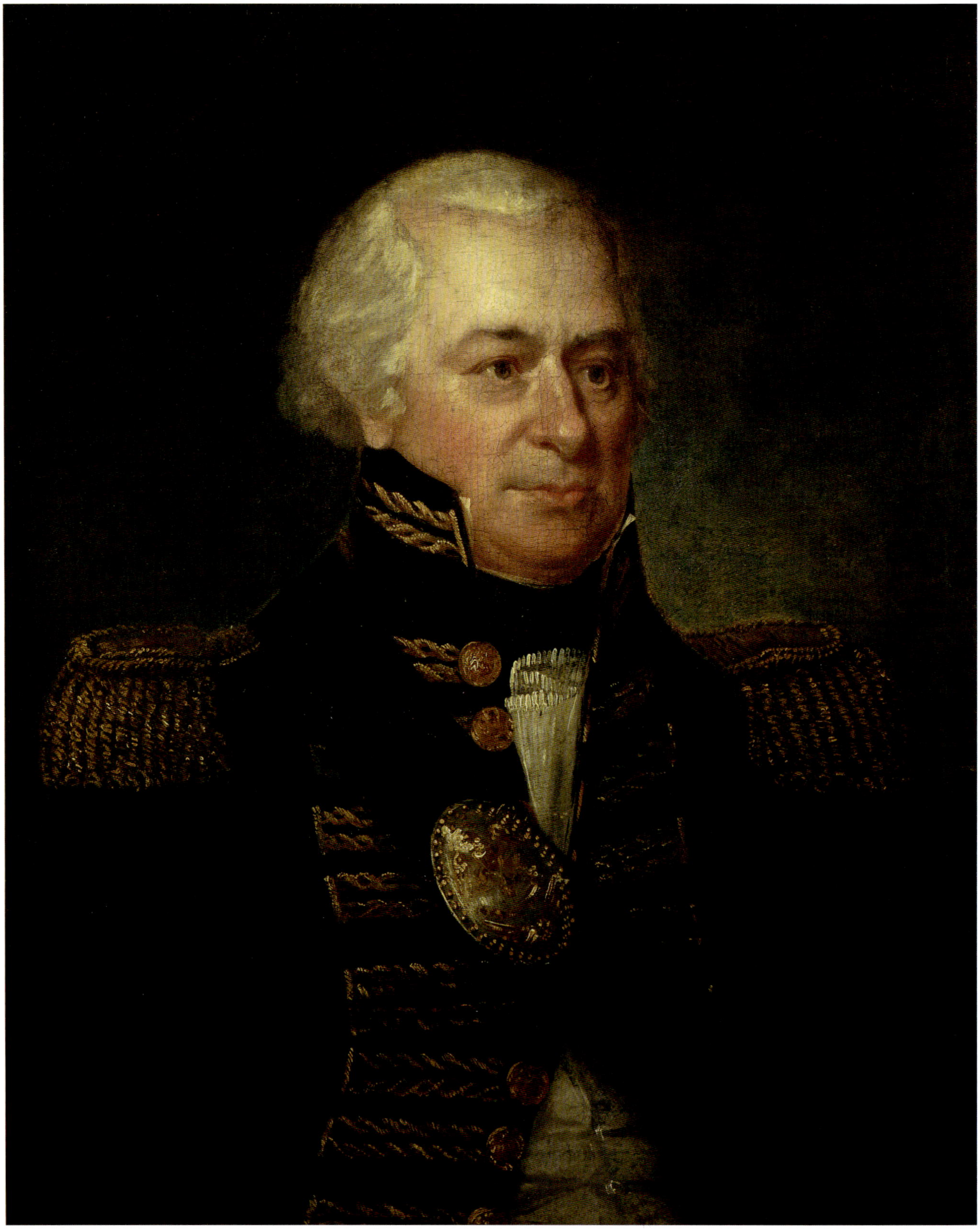

FIGURE 30. John Wesley Jarvis (1780–1840), *General James Wilkinson* (1757–1825), ca. 1820–1825, oil on canvas, 30 × 25¼″, The Filson Historical Society, 1892.1.2.

Wilkinson's portrait was one of the first works acquired by the Filson Club, as it was then known. In a letter to Richard Collins dated November 13, 1882, Ludovic Bigot, the subject's grandson, writes that "this is the only life-size portrait of my said grandfather ever painted." This is not actually true. Wilkinson was painted several times, as documented in the sitter files of the Frick Art Reference Library. James Sharples drew a small pastel of him in 1790, and in 1797 Charles Willson Peale painted his portrait for the Peale Museum in Philadelphia. During one of his visits to New Orleans in 1799 Wilkinson was portrayed wearing his order of the Society of the Cincinnati by Jose de Salazar, the first resident portrait artist in the city. Nor is this version the only one. A variant of this portrait is reproduced as the frontispiece to the 1938 volume *Tarnished Warrior, Major-General James Wilkinson* by James Ripley Jacobs, where it is erroneously attributed to Gilbert Stuart.

and he built a house there, becoming involved in Kentucky politics at a time when separation from Virginia and statehood were the pressing issues of the day.

Ever in need of funds, Wilkinson made a daring trip down the Mississippi River, at that time closed to American traffic and trade by the Spanish; he reached New Orleans in July 1787 with a load of cargo he was able to sell with the patronage of the Spanish governor Don Esteban Miró. Miró extracted from him a pledge of fealty to the Spanish king, and Wilkinson accepted his first bribe as the Spanish "agent 13." He proved to be an enthusiastic accomplice in the scheme to separate Kentucky from the United States, providing a list of many of Kentucky's most prominent political figures and the amounts of money they might be offered as pensions for their cooperation. He would go on to conspire with Aaron Burr and be tried and acquitted. A certain ambiguity about his actions and intentions remains to this day. The old warrior himself protested in his *Memoirs* that he always "demonstrated his respect for the principles and conduct of his predecessors, with whom nor tribunes, nor senates, nor vestal virgins . . . were for a moment" safe from his scorn.[59] In 1820 he settled in Louisiana as a planter with his second wife and their children, and it was at this time that he was painted by Jarvis. By 1825 Wilkinson was impoverished, dependent upon his son James Biddle Wilkinson for support, and soon to die. Devious and self-interested, he remains one of the more controversial figures of the young republic.[60]

"Kentucky" West paints Lord Byron and is himself acclaimed a romantic hero

The career of William Edward West was like a bright ribbon drawn through the fabric of early Kentucky portraiture. A legendary prodigy, he inspired Matthew Harris Jouett and charmed sitters from Philadelphia to Lexington to New Orleans. But nothing he did gained him greater fame than his trip to Italy and his encounter with Lord Byron. Like Jouett, West was also called "Kentucky" for his ability to regale an audience. He left behind a firsthand account of his encounter with one of the defining figures of his age. The meeting with Byron was a fateful one: it proved to be Byron's last life sitting, and it occurred around the time his fellow English Romantic poet Percy Shelley drowned while visiting him.

In his account we can hear West's awe at the encounter as well as his keen self-confidence at being up to the task. "Sometime in the month of July, 1822 my friend Mr. Bruen of New York, who was personally acquainted with Lord Byron, addressed a note to his Lordship requesting the favor of him to sit for me for his portrait stating that it was my wish to send it to America. He immediately returned for an answer that he considered the request a great honor and would sit to me when and where I pleased."[61]

Byron was staying on the Italian coast, some four miles from Livorno at Monte Nero, and had rented the Villa Rossa. He was kept company there by Teresa, the Countess Guiccioli, with whom he was romantically involved. Visiting the Villa Rossa, West struck a modest note.

> Having always had the greatest reverence for genius and talent I felt some diffidence in being introduced to a man so renowned for both. I expected to see a person somewhat thin and swarthy with a high forehead and black curly hair and a countenance severe and stern and manner reserved and lofty. I fancied him in a black mantle with a diamond hilted dagger in his bosom and that to hear the common ideas of conversation attended with the purest eloquence, if not poetry. I was mistaken and much surprised to see almost the reverse of what I had imagined. Altogether he was a larger man than I had fancied, rather fat and apparently effeminate.[62]

Like many portraitists, West had trouble keeping his subject still during the sitting. "I found him a bad sitter," wrote West. "He talked almost all the time and asked me a multitude of questions about America . . . how I liked Italy . . . what I thought of the Italians. . . . When he did not talk he was a worse sitter for he assumed a countenance that did not belong to him." At the first break in the sitting, Byron asked West to share a meal, and after a pleasant conversation, the artist could confess that he "now felt nothing like awe or embarrassment in the company of this great man—he was so

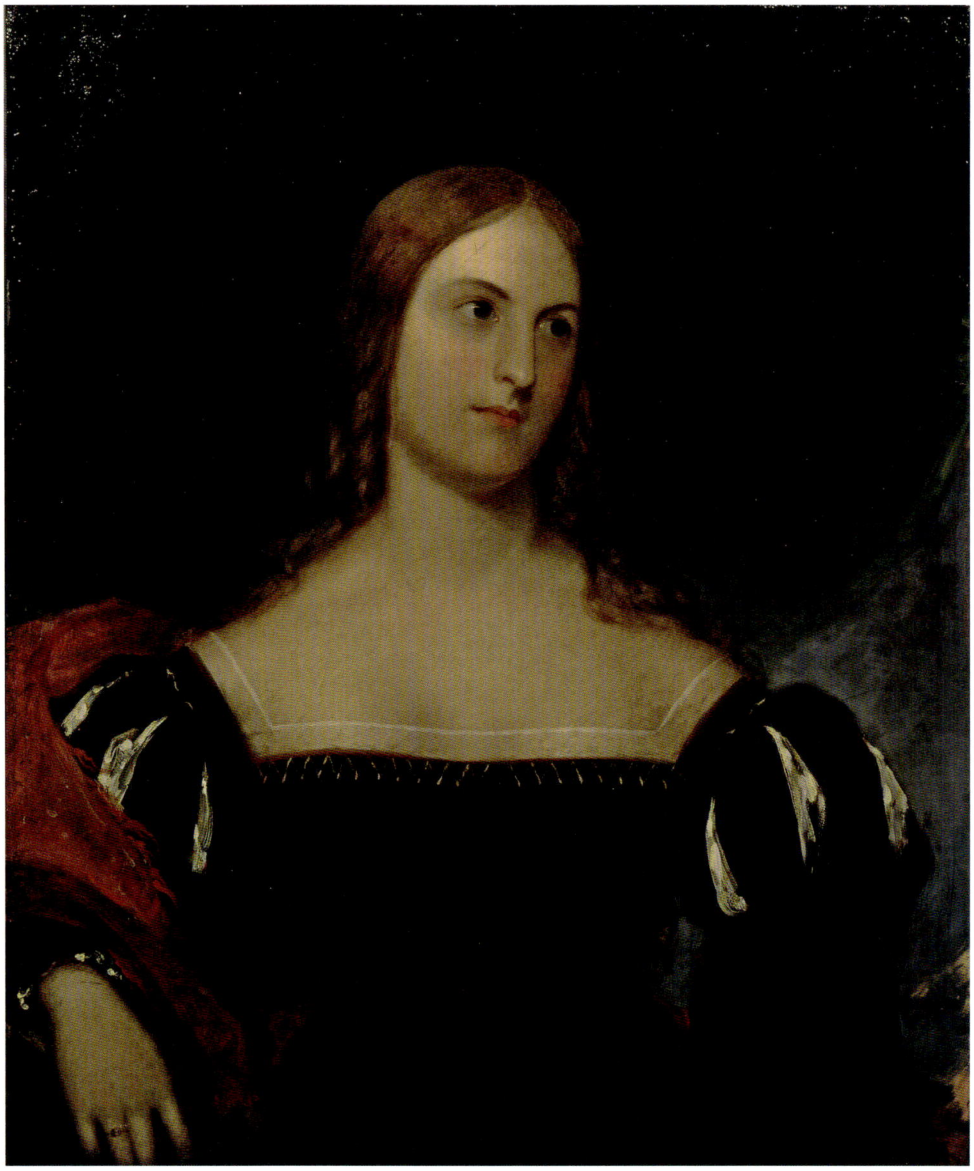

FIGURE 31. William Edward West (1788–1857), *Teresa Gamba, Countess Guiccioli* (1803–1873), 1822, oil on canvas, 31½ × 26½", Miami University Art Museum, Oxford, Ohio, gift of the family of Dr. and Mrs. Robert H. Bishop, 1985.81.

perfectly simple in his manners—so free and easy and even familiar and friendly that I parted with him quite delighted."[63]

At their next encounter Teresa made a spontaneous appearance and declared the portrait in progress to be "troppo bello," too beautiful. For his part, West recalled, "I thought I had never seen a more romantic looking head as it appeared at the window. I was glad she came in for he sat better when she was present." Swept up in the moment, Byron implored West to paint Teresa's portrait as well, which he did, depicting her in Renaissance costume in the style of Titian. "Assented with pleasure and began it the next day. They generally after this, sat alternately until the heads were finished and commonly the Lady Gamba and Lord Byron were present" (Figs. 31, 32). Byron appreciated the work and told West, "I see you are not flattering me." According to West, during the sitting Byron expressed much interest in America.[64] His rather mythic notion of American life and culture seemed to have been inspired by Washington Irving's Knickerbocker tales of old Dutch New York and John Filson's life of Daniel Boone.[65] As a would-be freedom fighter, Byron "could not conceive an American to be a dandy or dangler after the great"; George Washington "he thought was the model of all that was good and great."[66]

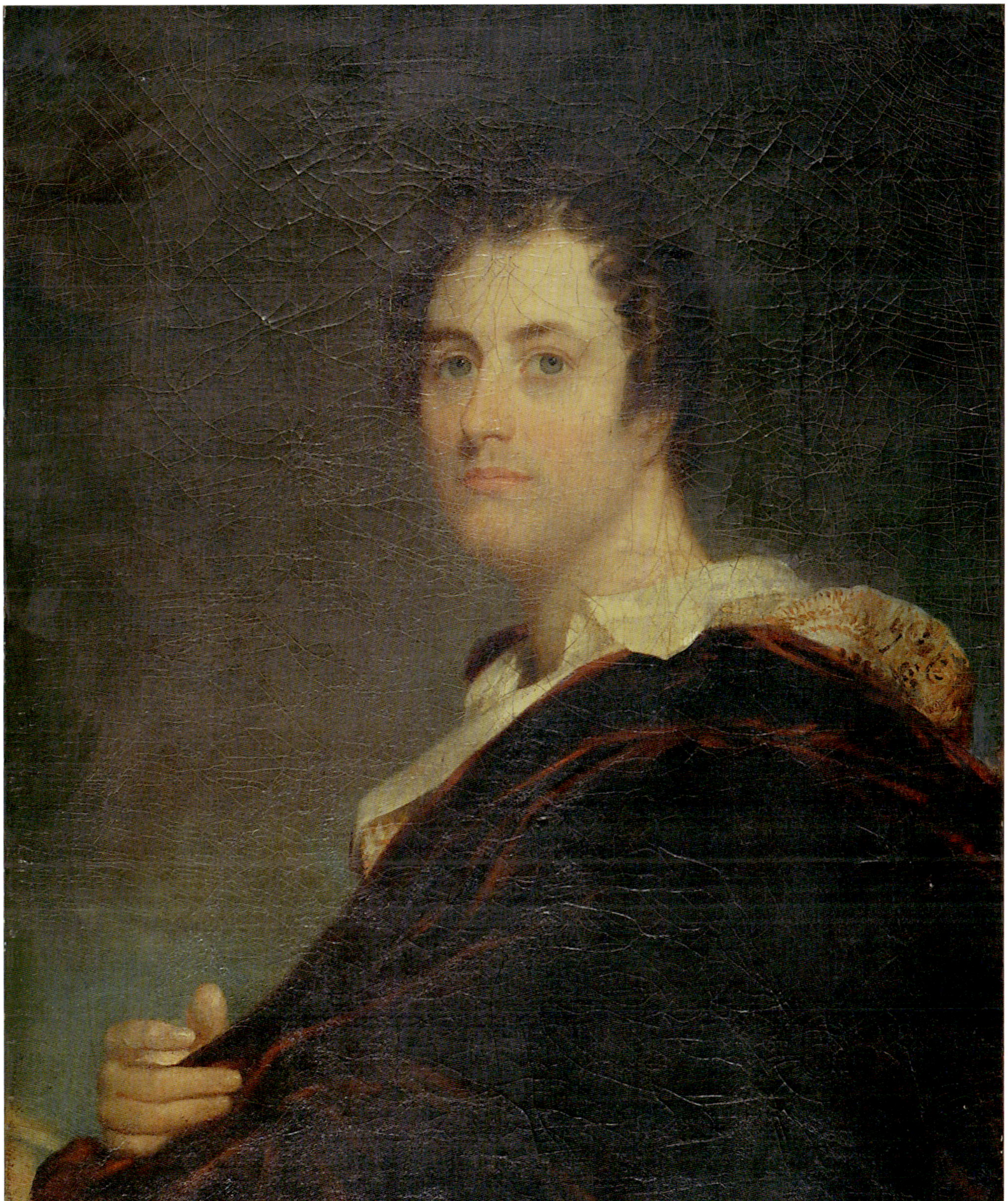

FIGURE 32. William Edward West (1788–1857), *George Noel Gordon, 6th Lord Byron* (1788–1824), 1822, oil on canvas, 30 × 25″, variant of the original, Blue Grass Trust for Historic Preservation, John Hunt Morgan House, Lexington, Kentucky; on extended loan from the National Trust for Historic Preservation, digital image by Julie Payne.

West seemed to follow Stuart's injunction to gauge the character of his sitter and render him accordingly.

> I told him one day notwithstanding his facetious and cheerful manner—I discovered the first hour I saw him that there was grief and sorrow at the bottom of his heart—he seemed very surprised and inquired of me with uncommon eagerness how I came to find it out. I asked him if he had not observed in little children after a paroxysm of grief that they had at intervals a convulsive or tremulous manner of drawing in a long breath—whenever I had observed this in persons of whatever age I had always found it the result of sorrow. He had this habit.

It should come as no surprise that the English master of romantic melancholy had a streak of it himself, although West's satisfaction in finding it lends the experience an air of their being equals, two artists meeting and sharing ideas as well as opportunity. The encounter ends on an equally romantic note of high melodrama. An unidentified local man, angered at Byron's presence, provoked Byron, who rushed to grab a sword and challenge the man; Teresa and West dissuaded him.[67]

The material outcome of this meeting became part of West's European baggage. Although they were supposedly commissioned by Mr. Bruen and Lord Byron, West kept both pictures for the rest of his life, although he did make copies of the Byron portrait at times to keep his creditors at bay. One version of the Byron portrait is on display at the Hunt Morgan House in Lexington, Kentucky, placed in an effort to ensure that one work by the artist is on display in his native city. After twenty years abroad, much of it spent socializing in London, where tales of life in the old South were much in demand, West was forced by a grave financial crisis to return to America in 1837. There, he revived fortune and career by painting a series of portraits in Baltimore and New York. Ironically, though West may have been best known in his lifetime for his painting of Byron and a few bravura genre paintings based on Irving's tales, his subsequent reputation has slowly come to depend upon his portrait of a young army officer passing through Baltimore, Robert E. Lee. West's Byron portrait has faded into the background, outdone by the celebrated portrait of the poet in Greek dress by Thomas Phillips. The portrait of Lee, however, remains one of the icons of painting in the South.[68]

Matthew Harris Jouett precedes Gilbert Stuart in death, leaving Oliver Frazer as sole resident portraitist

Matthew Harris Jouett died in the late summer of 1827, just one year before his old master, Gilbert Stuart, died in Boston. During the last decade of his life, Jouett worked among a group of artists who had settled in Lexington and whose similarity, marked by an affection for the Stuart style and a propensity for depicting their subjects in a curvilinear anatomical composition—what the noted Philadelphia portraitist John Neagle called "spoon fashion"—has led to some confusion of authorship.[69]

Of that group, Asa Park demands the greatest reconsideration. A native of Massachusetts, Park appeared in Lexington in 1816, as documented by an announcement he placed in the November 10, 1816, *Kentucky Reporter,* which reported that he had "taken a room on the corner of Main and Limestone Streets" and "flatters himself [that] by giving satisfaction, which he feels confident of doing, he may not suffer the want of encouragement." The piece went on to state that the artist "is from Boston under the patronage of the celebrated Stuart and Penniman," which meant that Park was almost certainly there at the same time as Jouett, an intriguing coincidence.

John Ritto Penniman (1782–1841) was a painter whose activity in Boston during the first quarter of the nineteenth century assured his reputation as one of the most accomplished and versatile ornamental painters of the era. Though he was well regarded as a portraitist, it was his ability to create panoramas and history paintings that pleased the public; his monumental depiction of the conflagration of the Boston Exchange Coffee House in 1818 was particularly celebrated. From Penniman, Park could have learned the skills required to produce clear, descriptive images, broadly outlined and cast with a visual immediacy that drew even the least discerning eye. Park's advertisement of his services as a sign painter as well as a portraitist documents the need experienced by many early portrait painters to rely upon their abilities as decorative painters to pay the bills between commissions.[70]

As a portraitist Penniman was a classic New England plain painter, an artist whose concern with accuracy resulted in a proto-photographic realism dependent upon a highly linear approach to facial modeling and contouring. It may have been from Penniman that Park learned the technique of placing the subject high on the planar field, usually in the upper left or right quadrant, and very forward toward the picture plane. Penniman's portrait of Henry Nolen, in the Worcester, Massachusetts, Museum of Art, offers an interesting comparison to Park's work: both have a boldness of anatomical detail and a flat, vivid coloration that has more in common with sign painting than with high-art portraiture.

Although Park is not thought to have appeared in Lexington until autumn 1816, he could have met Jouett in Boston during those months. Jouett was known to have bragged that there was good money to be made painting portraits in Kentucky, where the demand for representation far exceeded the pool of talent. Perhaps the acquaintance and the opportunity inspired the move west, although Park's discreet connections to the order of Freemasons may also have been at play.

Park's few known works exhibit the same ability to create a "standing white" in the delicate quality of a piece of white lace or a frothy white jabot that can be seen in Jouett's. Indeed, so similar are some of the works by these artists that misattribution of autograph may have occurred in amateur record keeping, a circumstance further compounded by Jouett's enormous popularity during the colonial revival era of the late nineteenth century. A case in point is two extant portraits attributed to Jouett that may actually be the work of Asa Park. Portraits of Captain Simpson and Major Thomas Howard are both attributed to Jouett, although neither work appears in the inventory prepared by Jouett's grandson Richard Jouett Menefee in the years after the Civil War. The Howard portrait does appear in Elizabeth Martin's list of known Jouett works, published by the Speed Art Museum in 1939. However, as that information was submitted by descendants in the Embry family, who attributed every work they owned to Jouett and who subsequently reattributed several of them to Thomas Sully, it may prove to be more than questionable.

The Simpson and Howard portraits are virtually identical in composition, brushwork, and coloration. Most amazing is the fact that in both portraits the white bow tie is heightened in the exact same standing white technique. Yet they differ from the works of Jouett in two very distinct ways. In both portraits the attenuated anatomical form is separated by a large space between the arm or shoulder and the edge of the planar field. Jouett's portraits in this format do not have that space. Furthermore, Jouett's sitters invariably engage the viewer with their eyes. In the Simpson and Howard portraits both figures seem to be gazing at a distant object, rather than at the viewer, a convention more in keeping with the practice of a well-versed sign painter than with an insightful portraitist striving to be true to Stuart's teachings on character and on equal placement of light and shadow (Figs. 33–35).

While in Lexington, Park became closely associated with the family of the inventor and silversmith Edward West, father of William Edward, who was away working in the deep South. He made several trips to other central Kentucky towns, including Danville. Park seems to have left Lexington for Cincinnati in 1820, but he is again noted in Lexington in 1825. For Lafayette's visit that year he made a large transparency of an eagle rampant, which hung in a prominent archway between the dancing and banqueting halls of the Grand Masonic Lodge. Newspaper accounts indicate that Park closed his Lexington studio on April 1, 1826, and died the following year.[71]

Alexander Bradford, who painted in Kentucky at the same time as Park, was a member of an accomplished family who settled in central Kentucky in the late eighteenth century. His kinsman John Bradford had operated the first printing press in Kentucky. Little is known of Bradford's career except for one remarkable commission. Martha Chandler Prewitt, a widow living on Walnut Hill Road near the Clark-Fayette

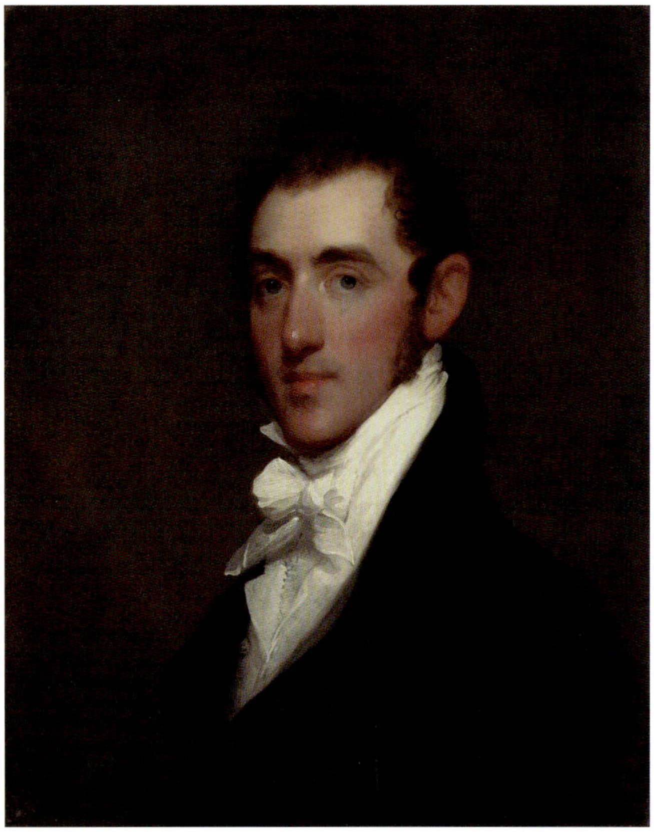

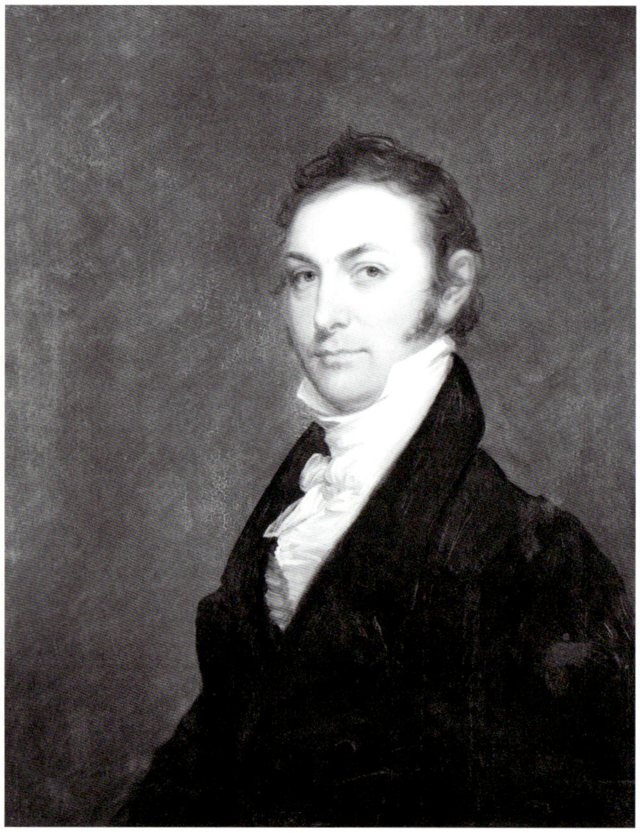

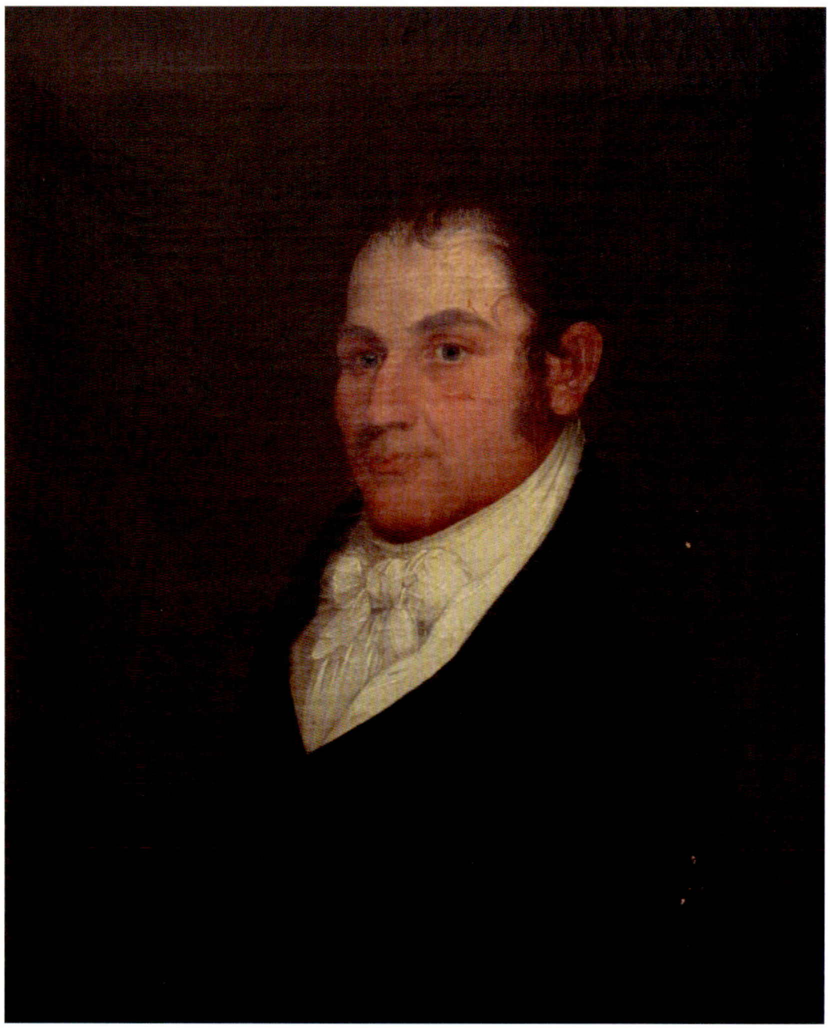

(Clockwise from top left)

FIGURE 33. Gilbert Stuart (1755–1828), *Henry Rice,* ca. 1815, oil on canvas, 26½ × 21½", Metropolitan Museum of Art, 1896 (97.39).

FIGURE 34. Matthew Harris Jouett (1788–1827), *Thomas Smith,* ca. 1820, oil on panel, 30³⁄₁₆ × 24⅛", Brooklyn Museum, Carl H. de Silver Fund, 21.130

FIGURE 35. Asa Park (1790–1827), att., *Major Thomas Howard* (1775–1841), ca. 1817, oil on canvas, 28¾ × 24", Duncan Tavern History Center, Paris, Kentucky.

The juxtaposition of these three portraits clearly demonstrates the appropriation of Stuart's method of pitching the head to the upper right, tapering the anatomical format, and embellishing the high collar and bow-tied stock with "standing white." Jouett's painting is slightly softer in focus, whereas Park's depiction of Howard is marred by eyes that fail to track, giving him a somewhat incoherent, slightly leering expression.

county line, hired him to paint her entire family in 1825, following the death of her husband, of whom she had no likeness. Bradford was to paint her eight sons, a daughter, two daughters-in-law, and the widow herself. He spent an entire year on the project, in residence with Mrs. Prewitt (Fig. 36). These portraits have a bold frontality and strong modeling reminiscent of Aaron Corwine, whom Bradford may have encountered in Cincinnati. His work has often been mistakenly identified as being by Jouett. Edna Talbott Whitley made the observation that "because he was but three years younger than Jouett," Bradford "is not apt to have been his pupil. Since they lived but a few miles apart and their life spans correspond so closely, it is probable that their work has been somewhat confused."[72] Like both Jouett and Park, Bradford also died in 1827.

John Grimes, another painter of the period, was from a Dayton, Ohio, family. He lost both his parents at an early age. When he arrived in Lexington in the early 1820s, he came to the attention of Thomas Grant, the proprietor of a paint and tobacco shop on Cheapside in Lexington, who gave him a job and became a foster father to the young man. It was in that shop that Grimes met Jouett, who was so impressed by the young man's talent at drawing that he took him on as a student (Fig. 37).[73] Grimes assisted Jouett in an ambitious project to paint a monumental *Three Marys* after Annibale Carracci. After Jouett's death Grimes moved to Nashville, where he secured the patronage of Felix Grundy, the local congressman who had also served on the Kentucky Supreme Court. Grimes developed tuberculosis around 1835, and he returned to Lexington to die in the home of his adoptive family, the Thomas Grants, in 1837. Astonishingly, in the space of three years, 1827–1830, four resident Kentucky portraitists of note—Jouett, Park, Bradford, and Grimes—left the central Kentucky stage, with the result that never again would the area have a group of native resident portrait artists who attracted

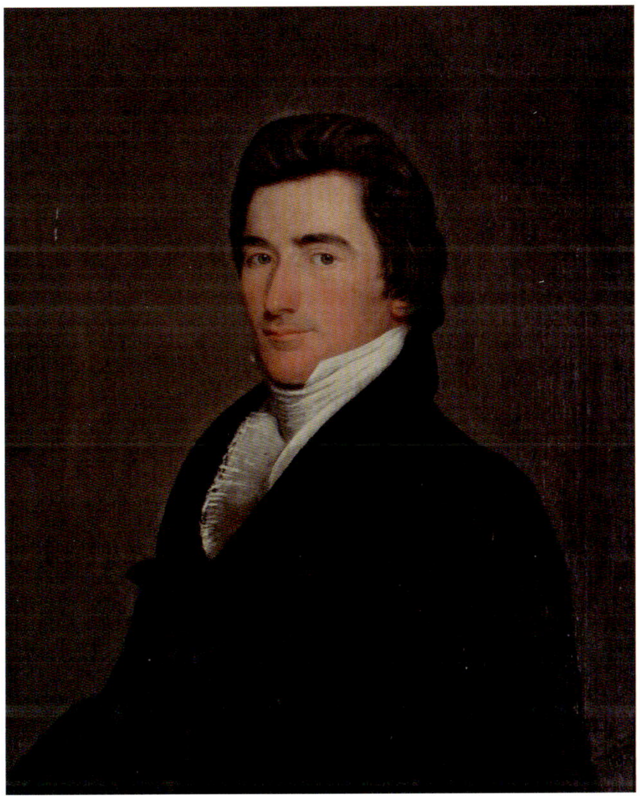

FIGURE 36. Alexander Bradford (1791–1827), *Levi Prewitt* (1799–1880), 1825, oil on canvas, 32 × 27″, collection of Robert Kirkpatrick, Millersburg, Kentucky.

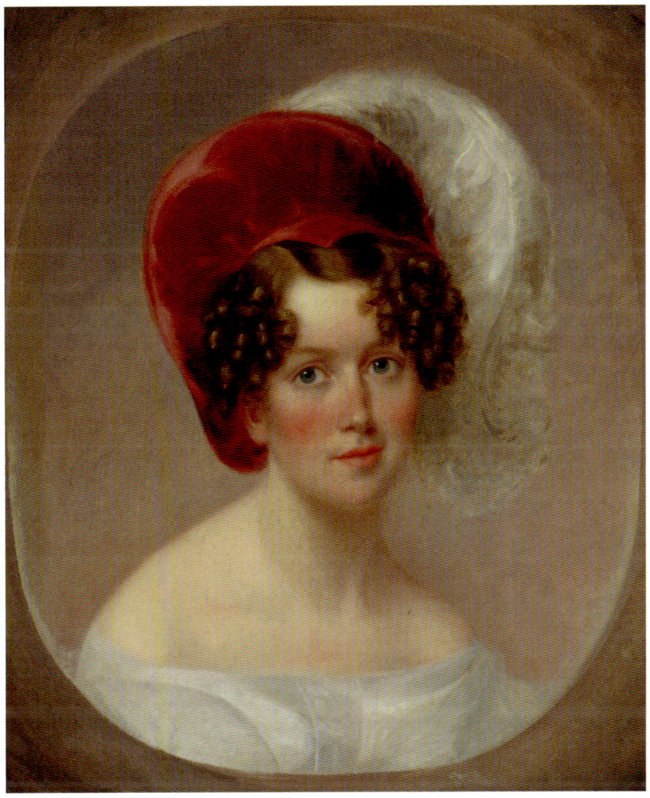

FIGURE 37. John Grimes (1799–1837), *Anna Barrow* (1808–1864), n.d., oil on canvas, 23½ × 21″, Speed Art Museum, Louisville, Kentucky, 1942.1.37.

as much attention as Jouett's generation. By 1830 the field was left almost entirely to Oliver Frazer.

Oliver Frazer was the first Kentucky artist to study abroad. Both Frazer's father and his paternal uncle were successful silversmiths, first in Paris, Kentucky, and then in Lexington. After his father's early death, young Frazer received sufficient support from his uncle to enable him to pursue an artistic career. Following early study with Jouett, he made the obligatory trip to Philadelphia in 1828 to study with Thomas Sully, but he found little joy in the city of brotherly love. "The people are much more selfish than with us," he wrote home; "if you lived here three months you would see the difference between this place and Kentucky; selfishness is handed down from father to son."[74]

Opinions, and strong ones, were always one of Frazer's noted personality traits. While in Philadelphia he saw the works of Washington Allston, which "fell short of my expectations," he wrote, even as they "looked like life in comparison" to early portraits by Benjamin West.[75] Before departing for Europe, he did pay one last homage to early American portraiture by copying Stuart's full-length portrait of Washington for the Kentucky state capitol, with the assistance of William S. Shackleford.

In May 1834 Frazer sailed for France. Upon his arrival in Paris he sought instruction in the ateliers of Baron Gros and Thomas Couture and made the acquaintance of the young artists G. P. A. Healy and James De Veaux, who would become a resident portraitist in Charleston, South Carolina. Though professing no great affection for French portraiture in the neoclassical taste, Frazer did admire the realism of Horace Vernet's battle paintings at the palace of Versailles. He was so moved that he "could scarcely persuade myself that I did not see a real battle."[76] While in Europe Frazer visited museums and galleries in France, Switzerland, Belgium, Germany, and England. Through the auspices of Charles Robert Leslie, the American history painter, he drew copies of old masters' works in English collections. Rembrandt, Titian, and Van Dyck were his noted favorites. His copy of a Titian *Madonna and Child,* commissioned by Richard Higgins of Lexington, is still in the parish hall of Christ Church Cathedral in that city.

Upon his return to Kentucky in 1838, Frazer established a studio in Lexington and became the last permanent resident portraitist in the Kentucky tradition. He married Martha Bell Mitchell, Mrs. Matthew Harris Jouett's niece, in that same year. Well connected, he was soon receiving multiple commissions from the political and social establishment of the inner Bluegrass. He became the house favorite of the Henry Clay family, painting several portraits of the famous politician. His portrait of Nannette Price Smith is one of his most ambitious works (Fig. 38). Painted around 1840, the portrait has always attracted critical attention, as "it may well be the only full-length female likeness ever rendered by Jouett, Bush, or Frazer."[77] It has a very European feel, a reminder that Frazer had spent considerable time copying old master paintings and drawings. The setting—with its quatrefoil balustrade and the large fountain splashing in the background—is quite fanciful for Kentucky. The painting has more in common with the Richmond, Virginia, painter W. J. Hubbard's tradition of the portrait in small than with a monumental full length in the grand manner. The figure is somewhat anatomically challenged; its rather distended right arm and tiny foot sticking out from the dress like a small pet echo Sully.

In later years Frazer's eyesight began to fail, with the result that some of his late works have a slightly dim, murky appearance, giving them a vague, romantic cast. He did continue to paint, however, as is evident

FIGURE 38 *(facing page).* Oliver Frazer (1808–1864), *Nannette Price Smith* (1797–1878), ca. 1840, oil on canvas, 35 × 30″, The Filson Historical Society, 1995.2.2.

Nannette Price Smith was the daughter of Samuel Price and his wife, Susanna Hart, the sister of Henry Clay's wife, Lucretia. She married Thomas Smith, editor and publisher of the *Lexington Reporter,* who was also the president of Kentucky's first railroad, the Lexington and Frankfort line. The couple had no children, but they took in the children of Henry Clay Jr., after his death at Buena Vista during the Mexican War. At some point in the late 1840s the couple moved to Louisville, where, according to Nannette's obituary in the February 4, 1878, *Louisville Courier Journal,* Thomas Smith became "an honored and respected merchant."

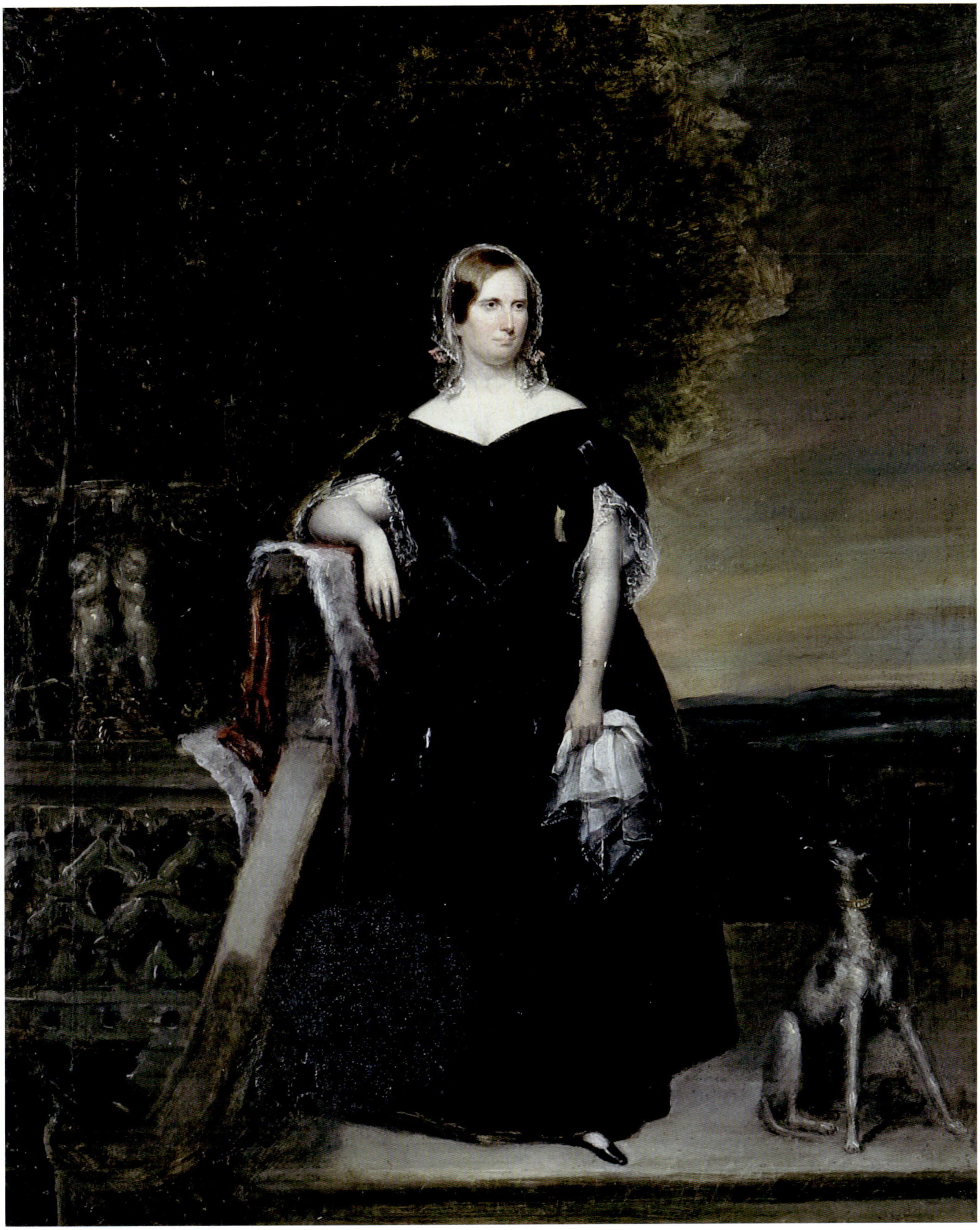

from a letter written by Catherine Waller Carson to her parents, William and Catherine Waller, in January 1851. Writing from Mississippi, Mrs. Carson inquires after her childhood friend Martha Frazer, and then asks, "is Mr. Frazier [*sic*] painting my portraits? I do so hope dearest Mother that you will sit for him and that you will have Father's copied for me." She goes on to request that her mother also have a daguerreotype made of herself, and that she engage Frazer to do so, evidence that portraitists were well aware of the popularity of photographic likenesses and perhaps could sense the death knell of antebellum portraiture.[78]

Cincinnati emerges as an urban center and attracts resident portrait artists

A small publication, *Cincinnati in 1826,* provides a view of that city as an emerging urban culture in a region otherwise dominated by a vast agrarian economy. The comments on art are brief: "Cincinnati is not sufficiently advanced in the Fine Arts, to supply adequate materials for a separate chapter," yet "we have several artists of genius and reputation in the principal branches of this interesting department." But it is in the authors' comments under "State of Society" that there is to be heard the fierce independence that characterized the era of the young republic still free from the bitter regional conflict that would color the two decades leading up to the Civil War. "There is . . . no place in the United States, more favourable for observing the influence of our Republican System upon Society at large, than in Cincinnati." This situation existed because there seems to have been no dominant ethnic group, no "portion of them from any particular district, so numerous, as to cause a general adherence to the peculiar prejudices and manners, in which they have been educated." Specifically, the authors assert that there were none of the societies associated with the internecine conflicts of the British Isles to drive the people apart "in favour of distant lands." Instead, there existed an "entire freedom from political restraint, leaving all at liberty to follow such pursuits as are most agreeable," those being, it is implied, commerce and trade.[79]

Aaron Houghton Corwine is one of the few artists cited at length in *Cincinnati in 1826.* Mention is made of general practitioners in the fields of landscape, ornamental, and scene painting for theaters, including Frederick Eckstein, who attempted, without success, to organize a Cincinnati Academy of Fine Arts in 1828 (Fig. 39). Other efforts succeeded, and by 1830 Cincinnati had attracted one portraitist, James Henry Beard, who not only pursued an itinerancy in Kentucky over the next decade, but proved to be the first insightful genre painter of the Ohio River Valley.

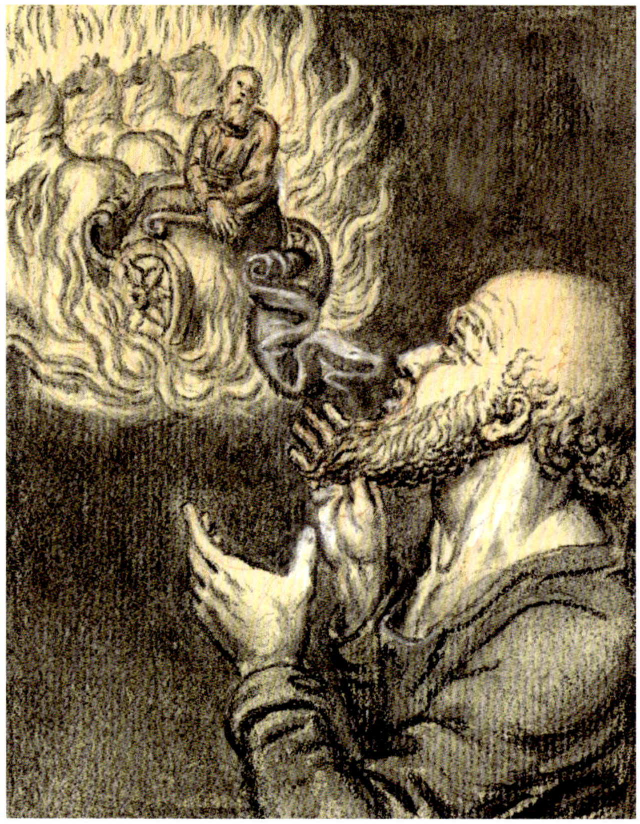

FIGURE 39. Frederick Eckstein (1775–1852), n.d., *Elijah in the Chariot of Fire,* graphite and pastel, 6 × 4¾", The Filson Historical Society.

Beard was a native of Buffalo, New York, who moved to Painesville, Ohio, with his family and began to work as an itinerant painter in 1828, visiting Louisville and central Kentucky. Though qualifying for the era's ultimate compliment of being a largely "self-taught" painter, he honed his skills with periods of study in Pittsburgh and New York, developing in the process a robust, romantic style. He was greatly admired for his ability to paint children and for his atmospheric portraiture, wherein he created rich landscape settings

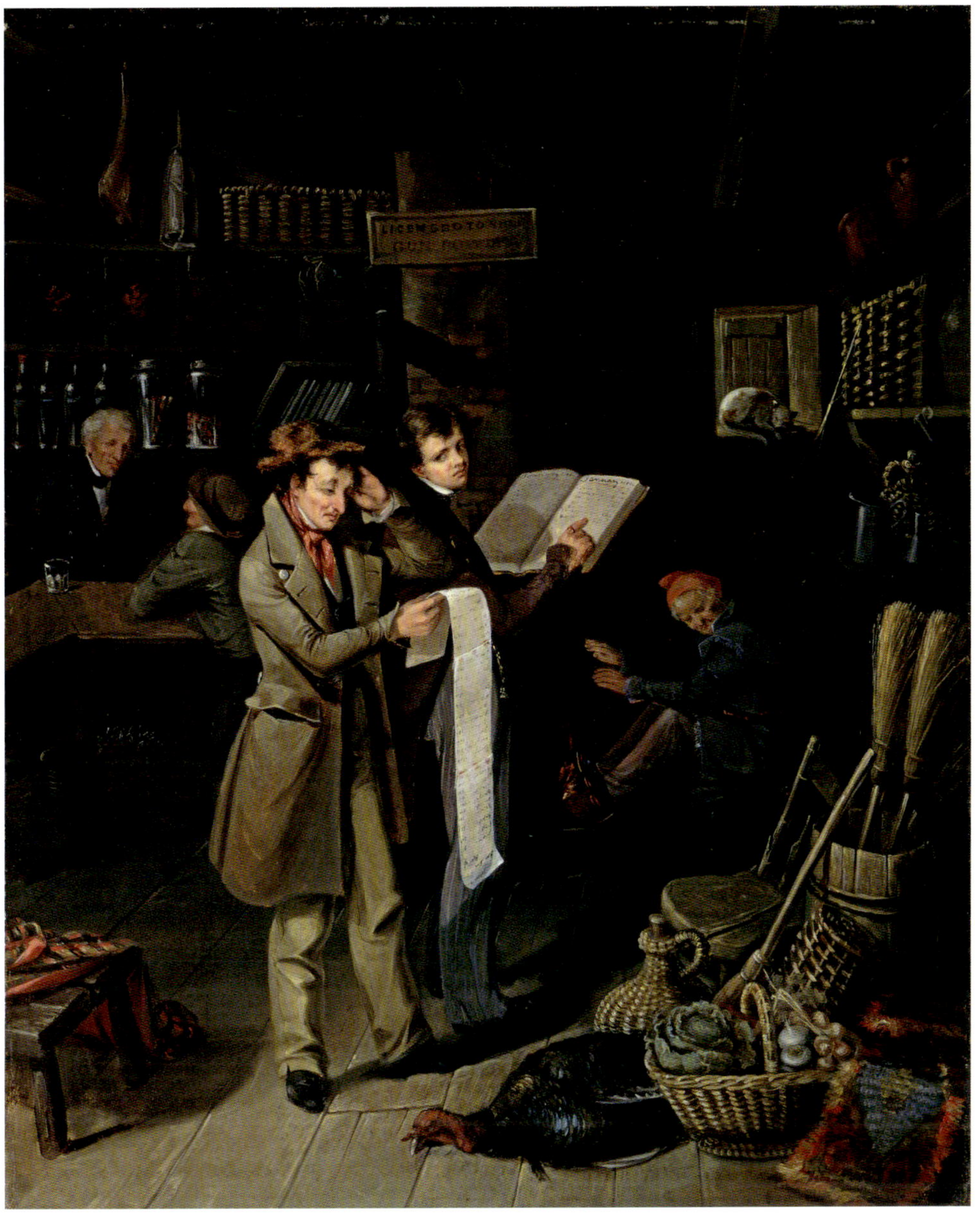

FIGURE 40. James Henry Beard (1812–93), *The Long Bill,* 1840, oil on canvas, 30⅜ × 24⅞″, Cincinnati Art Museum, gift of Mrs. T. E. Houston, 1924.186.

as backdrops for his well-dressed sitters, whose clothing he painted in great detail. But Beard was not only a portraitist. As early as 1834 he began to paint genre works that depicted the inhabitants and socioeconomic concerns of the Ohio River Valley. Jolly flatboatmen, land speculators, merchants in stores whose shelves were stacked with an abundance of goods, and migrant farm laborers were Beard's stock-in-trade. Encouraged by the patronage of local collectors, notably Nicholas Longworth, Peyton Symmes, and Reuben Springer, Beard and several of his contemporaries exhibited genre paintings in seminal exhibitions held in Cincinnati in 1839 and 1841.[80]

One of Beard's more famous works represents a scene in a flourishing general store. *The Long Bill* was painted in 1840 and made its debut at the first annual exhibition of paintings and sculpture organized by the Society for the Promotion of Useful Knowledge (Fig. 40). Beard's characterizations place him in the vanguard of mid-nineteenth-century American genre painters, who observed and depicted the complex vitality of the social construct in which they lived, even as that vitality became increasingly charged with debates on slavery and economic development. Beard's contemporary George Caleb Bingham, from his base in Missouri, was also painting the lively river traffic and trade and the roiling political debate. The contrast between the painters is that central contrast in the Ohio River Valley between an urban culture concerned with the management of supply and demand and a rural culture still dancing, like Bingham's boatmen, atop an abundant agrarian prosperity.

Beard's career in Cincinnati marked the beginning of an era when artists from southern Ohio, whose styles were formed in a teeming urban center and were bolstered by a steady rise in cultural organizations and museums in the "Queen City of the West," began to cross the river in pursuit of itinerancies in Kentucky. In 1838 a new Cincinnati Academy of Fine Arts was organized, which mounted exhibitions and encouraged local artists. By 1840 the Society for the Promotion of Useful Knowledge had been created, which sponsored exhibitions and an attendant sketching club. Artists from Cincinnati who pursued itinerancies in Kentucky include Thomas Campbell, who moved between Cincinnati and Louisville, 1835–1846; John Peter Frankenstein in Louisville, 1839; William Apthorp Adams in central Kentucky, 1840; Sidney J. Lyon in Louisville, 1841–1854; B. W. Jenks in Louisville, 1842; Godfrey Frankenstein in Louisville, 1851; William Penn Brannan in central Kentucky, 1855–1859, Allan Smith in northern Kentucky, 1859–1864; Charles Edward Cridland in Cincinnati, 1860; and Joseph Oriel Eaton in Louisville, 1860.

Godfrey and John Peter Frankenstein were Cincinnati itinerants who left a substantial legacy in Kentucky. The Frankensteins were a talented German family who had settled in Cincinnati by 1831. John Peter was the eldest son, whose early training included some sculpture studies with Frederick Franks and Hiram Powers. As a more practical pursuit he apprenticed to an engraver of maps, an occupation that was to provide his principal income during his attempts as a portrait artist; late in 1838 he opened a studio with his brother Godfrey. The ambitious John Peter possessed a temperament that did not endear him to the local critical establishment; he was said to have "observed towards them the most extreme inconsiderateness."[81] Though he may not have attracted the right attention in Cincinnati, he did secure a major patron during a visit to Louisville in 1839. He painted portraits of Judge John Rowan, whose country estate, Federal Hill in Nelson County, is said to have been the inspiration for Stephen Collins Foster's famous song "My Old Kentucky Home." He also painted the judge's wife and several members of their extended family.

Later that year, while working in New York, Frankenstein used his acquaintance with the Rowan family to secure an introduction to the young politician William Seward, who had just been elected governor of New York. Frankenstein remained on good terms with the Sewards for several years, serving as the governor's private secretary. After 1842 the rest of his family resided in Springfield, Ohio, but John Peter pursued a restless course in the northeast, painting portraits in an effort to fund a study trip abroad to Florence, where he hoped to study sculpture with Joel Tanner Hart, a Kentuckian. He was not successful, and he became increasingly unstable. To vent his spleen he wrote a mock-epic poem, *American Art: Its Awful Altitude,* in which he deplored the state of art patronage in Cincinnati, which others had found so nurturing. He took particular aim at the very generous Nicholas Longworth, whom he called "Nick Littleworth." Feeling greatly wronged, Frankenstein lamented that "Cincinnati is a good place for artists to be born in and to emigrate from."[82] He died in obscurity, apparently alienated from his family, in New York in 1881. A fashionable phrenologist in Cincinnati, Dr. Johann Gaspar Spurzheim, observed that there was a "great deal of impudence and very little reverence in the construction of his skull."[83] Nevertheless, Frankenstein left behind a firsthand account of his frustrations that make an interesting contrast to the enthusiastic recollections of artists such as Jouett and West.

Godfrey Frankenstein seems to have had little of his older brother's troublesome personality. A prodigy, he began painting portraits at the age of fifteen and was elected the president of the fledgling Academy of Fine Arts in 1841. Portraiture, however, was never his greatest interest. He had ambitions to become a monumental landscape painter. A visit to Niagara Falls in 1840 inspired a series of works, engravings of which were created by John Peter and published in *Harper's Magazine* in 1853.[84] Eventually he was to create a

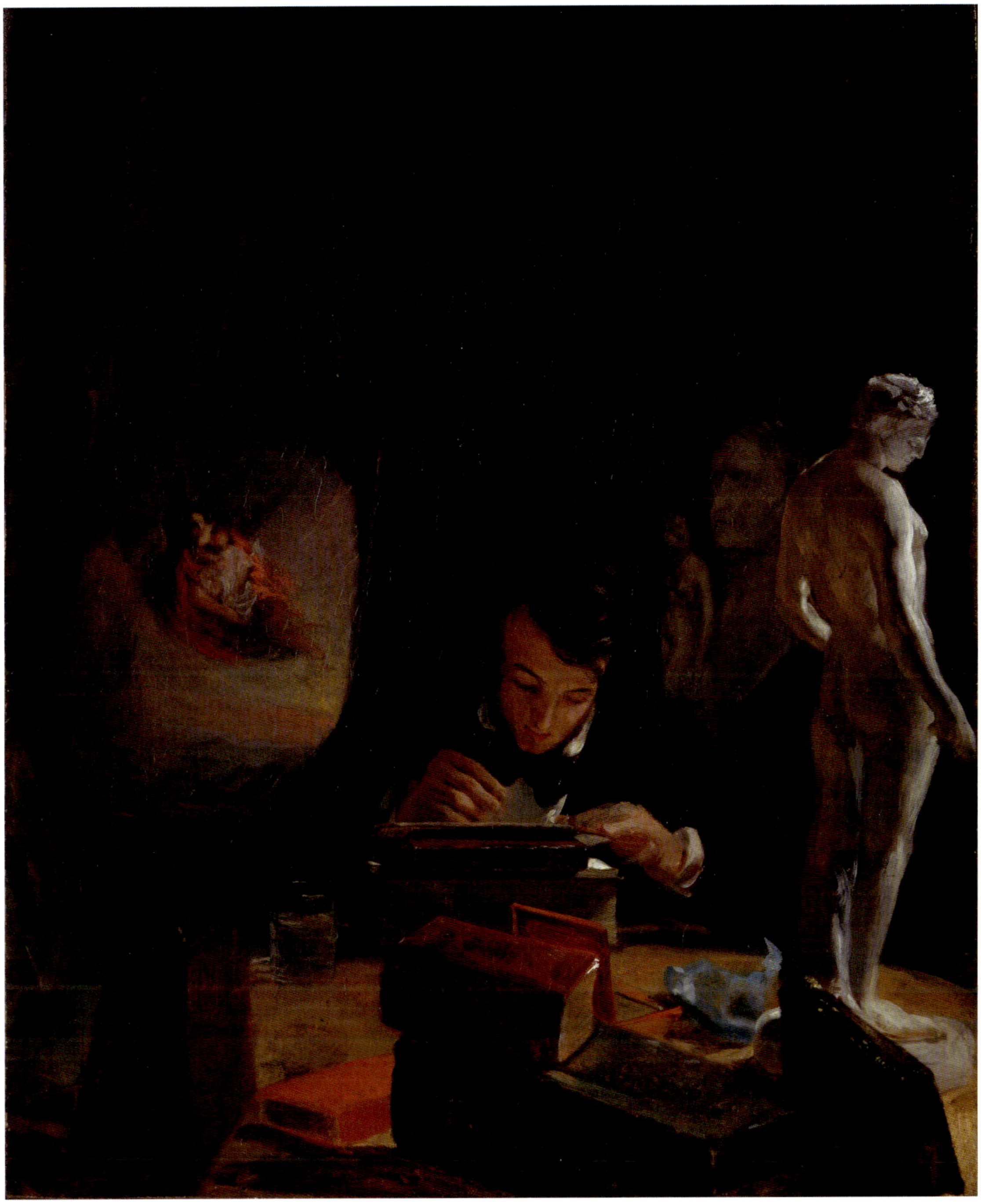

FIGURE 41. John Peter Frankenstein (1817–1881), *Godfrey Frankenstein* (1820–1873), 1840, oil on canvas, 23⅞ × 20″, Smithsonian American Art Museum, 1973.159.

Elisabeth Roark, in her article "John Frankenstein's 'Portrait of Godfrey Frankenstein' and the Aesthetics of Friedrich Schiller" (*American Art,* Spring 2001), suggests that the detailed setting of the portrait implies the artist's strong affinity for the premier German romantic poet, Schiller. Godfrey is at work in "a circle of meticulously placed tools, books, and works of art," evidence of his erudition and discipline. The book in the center foreground has the title *Schiller.* While fervently in favor of widespread political reform in the disparate German states, Schiller, in his writings on the French Revolution, felt that "although based on principles of reason, [it] deteriorated into tyranny." The revolution taught him that "political freedom does not convert people into rational beings." Apparently John Peter Frankenstein extended that philosophy to frontier Ohio. As is evident in his acerbic *American Art: Its Awful Altitude,* he took on the role of the downtrodden artist whose support by a local populace he found to be greedy and unsophisticated was unworthy of the talents he and his brother could possibly lavish upon them.

panorama some one thousand feet long, which he and his siblings George, Gustavus, and Eliza took on tour to great acclaim. His studious nature was well captured by John Peter in an 1840 portrait (Fig. 41). Never married, Godfrey died at home in Springfield, Ohio, after a sudden attack of brain fever.[85]

Thomas Sully attracts students, and sitters, from Kentucky

Though Thomas Sully never visited Kentucky, his portraiture was well known in the commonwealth. Several Kentucky artists made the journey to Philadelphia to study with him, and many Kentuckians were painted there by him (Figs. 42, 43). Precisely what Sully had to offer these young artists is made clear in his later writings. His hints are concerned with techniques of medium and support—preparing the canvas, ordering the palette, mixing colors, gathering and laying out the artist's tools, and varnishing the finished work.[86] They reflect certain ongoing traditions in Western art instruction, dating from the Renaissance, offering in

FIGURE 42 *(below left)*. Thomas Sully (1783–1872), *Benjamin Gratz* (1792–1884), 1831, oil on panel, 19 × 15″, Rosenbach Museum and Library, 1954.1937.

FIGURE 43 *(below right)*. Thomas Sully (1783–1872), *Rebecca Gratz* (1781–1869), 1831, oil on panel, 20 × 17″, Rosenbach Museum and Library, 1954.1936.

Benjamin and Rebecca Gratz were the children of Michael and Miriam Gratz, prominent Jews in Philadelphia. Michael Gratz was a successful entrepreneur who pioneered steamship travel from Pittsburgh to Cincinnati and who had large land holdings in central Kentucky. Rebecca Gratz was a legendary philanthropist in both the Jewish and Christian communities; Sir Walter Scott was inspired to name the heroine of Ivanhoe after her when he learned, through Washington Irving, of her unstinting work in hospitals and orphanages. Benjamin Gratz migrated to Lexington, Kentucky, in 1821 to look after the family interests, taking up residence at Mt. Hope on a green square near Transylvania College, which became known as Gratz Park. Sully painted the siblings' portraits in 1831, not long after Oliver Frazer had returned from studies with him.

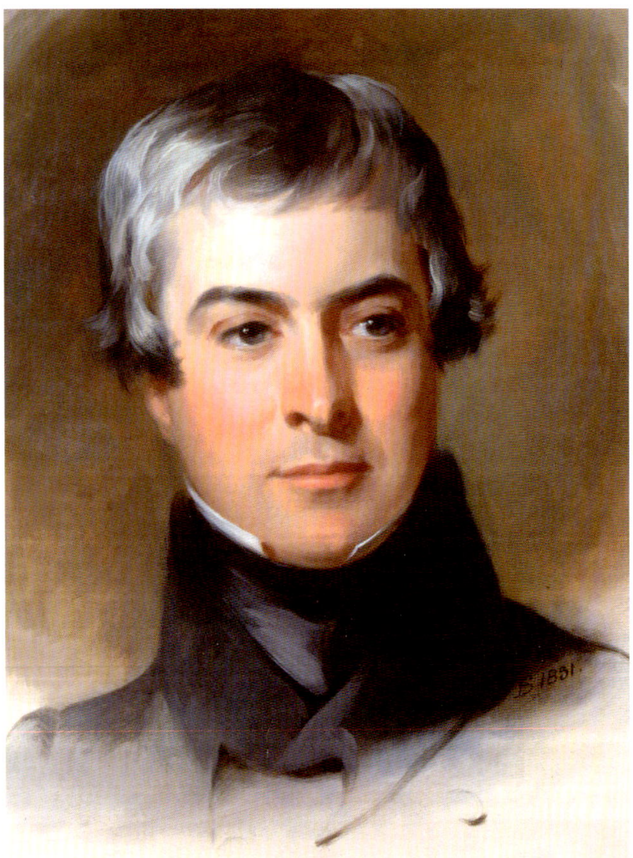

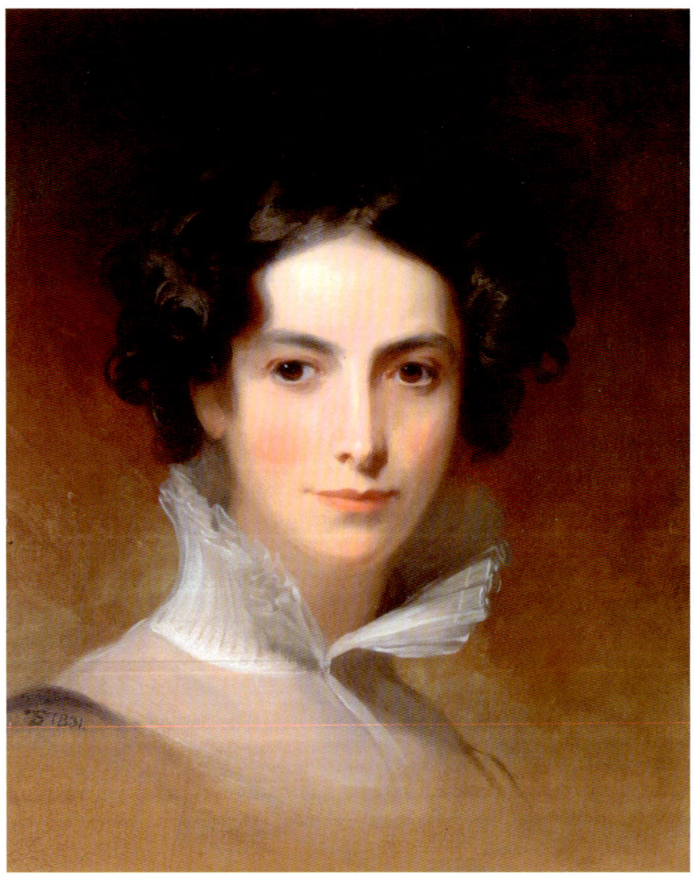

writing what had been an oral tradition disseminated in studios and ateliers. Sully made note of various "receipts" practiced by past masters, as well as particular traits of such English artists as Sir Joshua Reynolds, Thomas Lawrence, and Sir Archer Martin Shee.

Regarding style, Sully's suggestions are spare, linked to observation and the perfection of drawing skills. He writes of the importance of acquiring "the power to draw from memory the human figure in any position. This being attained, painting will be easily acquired; without this power, the painter will be frequently perplexed and liable to error. A knowledge of perspective is requisite." This knowledge, he asserts, is essential to the process of grasping the character of the subject and sympathetically rendering that subject with a technical accuracy that begins at the time of the first sitting. "When the person calls on you to make arrangements for the intended portrait, observe the general manner, etc., so that you may determine the attitude you had best adopt."[87]

Comparing the recorded remarks of Sully and Stuart gives insight into the stylistic shift that was then transforming American portraiture from the forthright perspective of the young republic into the romantic expressionism of a rapidly expanding nation. Whereas Stuart consistently advised his students to work from nature in order to create a painterly foundation for the "equal" application of paint, Sully assumed that his fledgling artists had "acquired the power to draw from memory the human figure in any position." Where Stuart's portraits began with observation, Sully subjected the sitter to anatomical conventions absorbed from the Italian drawing master Pietro Ancora.[88] Stuart encouraged Jouett to begin in paint; Sully began with a study "made in charcoal, with its proper effect of shadow relieved with white chalk."[89] Stuart prompted Jouett to paint from nature, observing character as he went. Sully advised adopting attitudes. Stuart was not interested in flattering his subjects; Sully made his reputation on portraits that did just that, with a masterful warmth of color and painterly detail.

Sully was quite honest about flattering his subjects. "From long experience I know that resemblance in a portrait is essential: but no fault will be found with the artist, at least by the sitter, if he improve the appearance."[90] This advice was well taken by William Edward West, whose early imitations of Sully's compositional formulas matured into the much-demanded, and very lush, romanticism he practiced during his Baltimore period. Though it would be far too simplistic to see the stylistic concerns of portraiture in Kentucky and the Ohio River Valley as rendered between these two dialectics of taste, the currents of style they inspired would linger until the outbreak of the Civil War. The diametric opposition of Stuart's insistence on honesty and truth to nature and of Sully's unabashed willingness to flatter can be revisited in the later careers of Oliver Frazer, Joseph Henry Bush, and G. P. A. Healy in Kentucky, and those of Joseph Oriel Eaton and the Soule family across the river in Ohio.

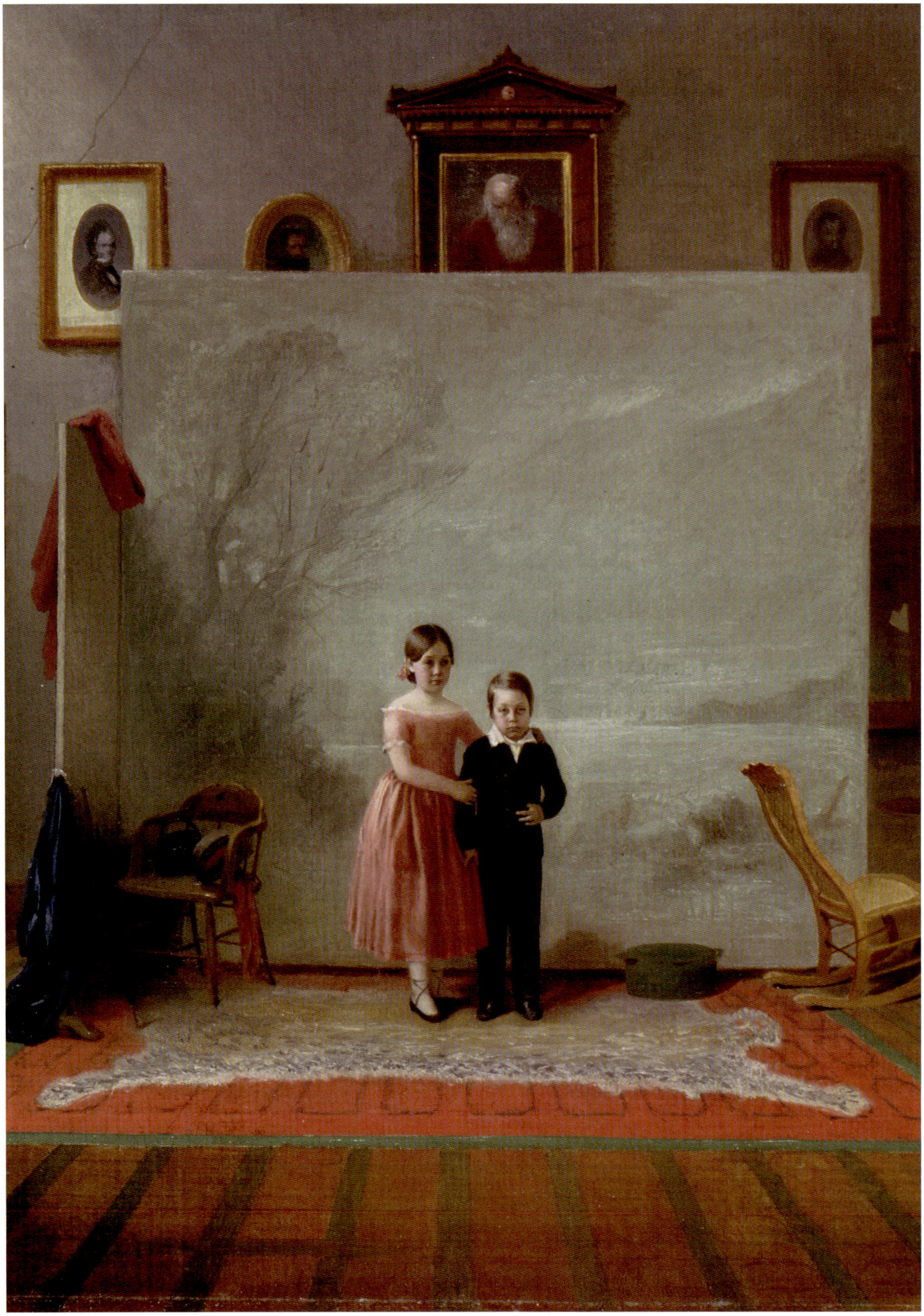

1835–1865

The Invention of Photography and the Coming of War

Itinerant painters, headless bodies, and plain painters

Several types of itinerant artists can be identified in Kentucky and the Ohio River Valley by the trails left behind by their works. Seasonal itinerants from the northern Ohio River Valley worked in the deep South during the warmer winter months. Conversely, painters seeking to escape the intense heat of New Orleans pursued work in Kentucky during its more temperate summer, notably the team of Moïse and Fowler. Several well-established artists from northern, urban centers also pursued itinerancies in Cincinnati and Kentucky, drawn either by the potential for wealthy clients, as in the case of G. P. A. Healy, or by a prestigious subject, as in the works of painters who pursued Henry Clay. Some itinerants, such as Horace and Chester Harding, moved to a certain location and stayed for an extended period. Truly wandering artists attracted the attention of prosperous farm families, who hired them to paint several generations during an extended period, as can be seen in the work of Alexander Bradford for the Prewitt family or E. F. Goddard for the Howard family, all in central Kentucky.

The itinerant portrait artists who have attained the most mythic status in popular culture, however, were those who worked in several different locations with no obvious pattern of visitation and whose works, far flung and created over a prolonged period of time, varied in achievement and had little stylistic relationship to prevailing trends. Some of these artists plied their trade in remote areas, for clients with lesser means than those in urban and more flourishing rural settings. Reson Crafft and James T. Poindexter may be the most intriguing examples of these itinerants, as their somewhat eccentric approach to pose, anatomical modeling, and costume detail has encouraged an exotic oral tradition: the myth of the headless body. Even now, on tours of historic houses, at meetings of local historical societies, and in reports of works of art by portraitists whose works are scarce, that myth still persists. In these stories one hears of itinerant portrait artists who went from door to door with a well-stocked supply of canvases upon which were painted bodies but not heads. These "head hunters" are imagined to have rendered an open invitation to a willing sitter to have his or her likeness placed atop an existing body. It seems most likely that the headless-body theory sprang from amateur critics of a much later day attempting to explain the disparity of proportions in some early works. To many eyes accustomed to photographic accuracy, the frequently disproportionate relationship between a carefully rendered visage and an anatomically vague body seems awkward.

Arguments against the existence of such canvases and the resulting portraits range from the historical to the technical to the psychological. There is neither literary nor physical evidence to verify the headless-body theory. No advertisements have been found announcing empty spaces above the shoulders for willing sitters. Many artists' studios were dismantled and inventoried during the early nineteenth century, and in no instance do the inventories or records kept by the artists themselves note the presence of canvases with headless bodies, although canvases with floating heads, many of them well known and devoid of background detail, do exist, notably Gilbert Stuart's unfinished portraits of George and Martha Washington, now jointly owned by the Boston Museum of Fine Arts and the National Portrait Gallery.

Technically, the addition of a head onto an existing body would have presented several problems. The difference between drying times and medium applications would eventually result in an obvious pentimento (the appearance of earlier brushwork) between the finish of the prototypical body and background and that of the applied head. Gauging the proper proportions between an existing body and an applied head might have been possible for a highly skilled artist with considerable studio experience, but not for the self-taught itinerants.

Consider as well marketing factors. Moving about the countryside with prepainted canvases would have required that they be rolled, and thus rather worn upon arrival, making it still more difficult to imagine any potential sitter longing to have his head stuck atop an untidy, alien body. Furthermore, the psychological implications of a sitter consenting to have his or her head placed atop another body is greatly at odds with that mid-nineteenth-century respect for individuality, one of the era's resounding themes.

The most important visual document relating to this subject may be Charles Bird King's *Itinerant Artist* (Fig. 44). Painted circa 1830, *Itinerant Artist* could be an autobiographical representation of the artist's years as a peripatetic painter, as King pursued an itinerancy in the upper South from 1812 to 1819, notably in Baltimore, Washington, D.C., and Richmond. Andrew Cosentino has written that King "created in the *Itinerant Artist* an imaginary setting and situation that nevertheless effectively convey the story of the itinerant artist triumphing under the most adverse circumstances."[1]

Surrounded by the everyday domestic bustle of a departing huntsman, hovering family members, and cavorting children, the artist is at work. He sits calmly before an easel upon which there is a head-and-shoulders composition under way, not a prepainted body to which he is busily applying a head. Leaning back thoughtfully to consider that likeness, the artist holds a brush aloft, perhaps just before applying a bit of dash to the headdress. His other hand grasps a mahl stick and the palette.

King was known to have been concerned about the proportions of the head as placed on the picture plane and as juxtaposed with suggestive anatomical outline. William Dunlap records that King "has contrived several mechanical machines for facilitating the labor of artists. He uses a slender rod of wire about a foot long, to ascertain certain proportions of his picture compared to the original. It is gauged with white paint, about an inch from the top, which is held upright at such a distance from the subject as to effect one division—the face of a sitter, for example."[2]

One possible defense for the headless-body theory remains. It is known that many artists in the late eighteenth and early nineteenth centuries created portrait compositions based on prints of high-style portraits by renowned European painters. Jeremiah Theus has been documented as using this method in late eighteenth-century Charleston.[3] Intriguingly, the inventory of Matthew Harris Jouett's estate includes a reference to "1 Lot of Engravings" valued at $10.00, a substantial amount compared to evaluations for other objects, such as furnishings and even portraits.[4] It may be that itinerant artists went about with prints with which to impress future sitters, asking if they would like to be painted in that pose, a dialogue that could have been transformed in the oral tradition.

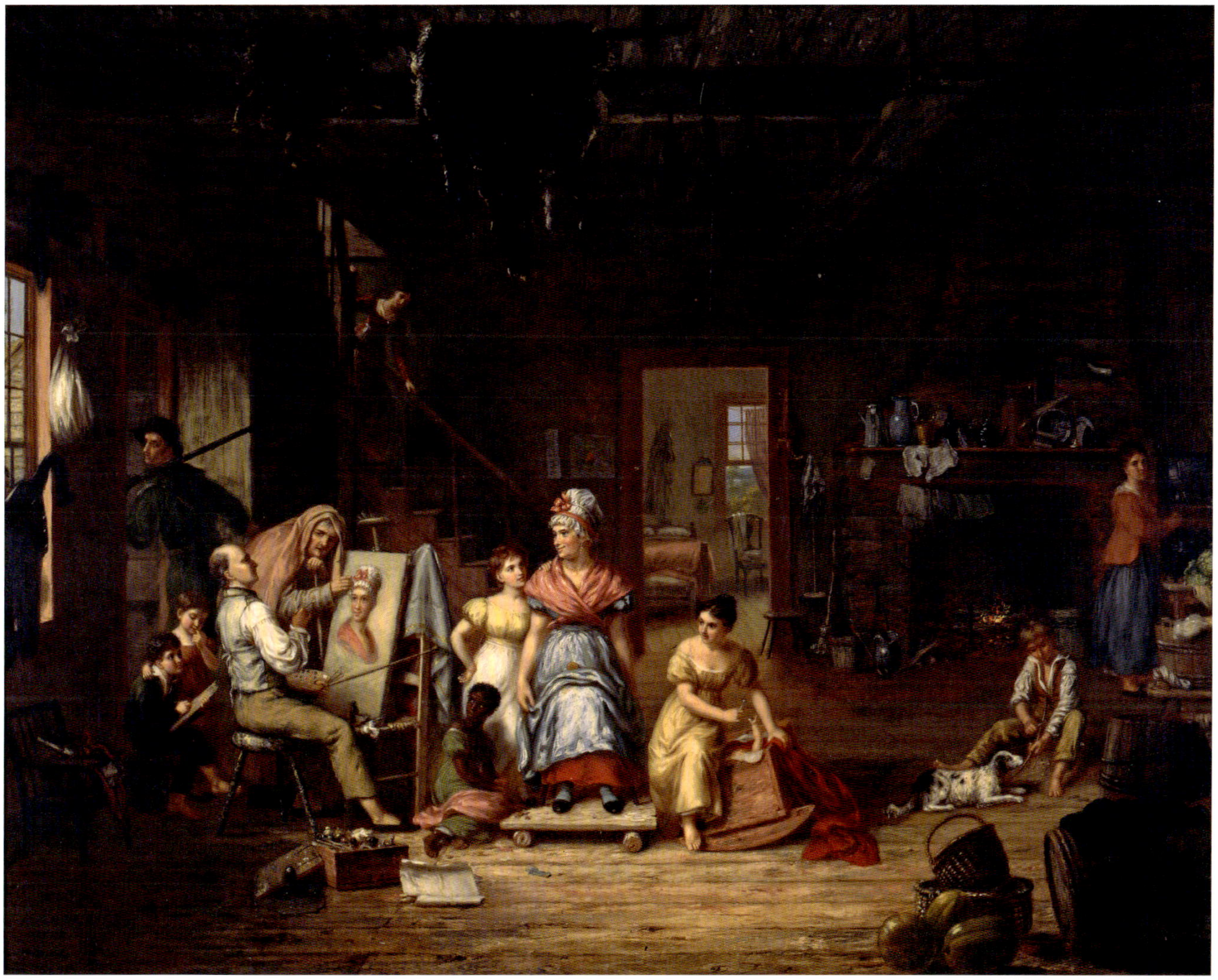

FIGURE 44. Charles Bird King (1785–1862), *Itinerant Artist,* ca. 1830, oil on canvas, 44¾ × 57″, Fenimore Art Museum, Cooperstown, New York, N-537.67.

The artists most suspected of carting canvases of headless bodies about were those whose anatomical arrangements, especially the relationship of the head to the torso, seem most awkward to contemporary eyes and have gathered an oral history of being "folk." Of artists working in Kentucky, Patrick Henry Davenport, James T. Poindexter, Thomas Jefferson Wright, Phillip O. Jenkins, Jacob Frymire, and William Frye have all been criticized for anatomical disparity between head and body. In Davenport's portrait of a woman of the Keller family, for example, the elaborately detailed, highly ambitious hairdo clashes with the attempt at a classic head-and-shoulders pose (Fig. 45).

In the process of attributing a portrait of the Hobbs family to William Frye, an extended correspondence in the 1980s between Bryding Adams, a curator at the Birmingham Museum of Art, and Lyn Renau, a curator at The Filson Historical Society, reveals much about the tradition of "folk" portraits (Fig. 46). Their exchange is also illustrative of the methodological importance of family oral history to portrait attribution. The two curators began with a dialogue on style in anatomical relationships that relates specifically to ideas about plain painters and folk artists. Because of the disparity between the children's head size and their bodies, Renau called them "encephalitic children, although historical records indicate no such illness. That meant that we had a painter with an inability to deal with children, which was compounded by the fact that he chose to turn them on their axis and have them looking over their

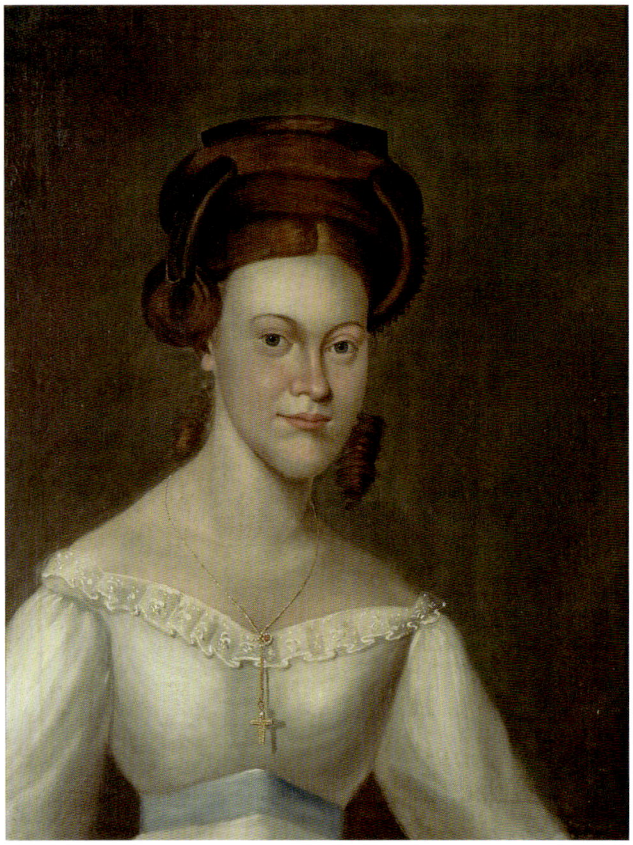

FIGURE 45. Patrick Henry Davenport (1803–1890), *A Woman of the Keller Family,* possibly Mrs. Jacob Keller, née Louisa Caldwell Keller, 1828, oil on canvas, 26¾ × 21″, The Filson Historical Society, 1981.1.2.

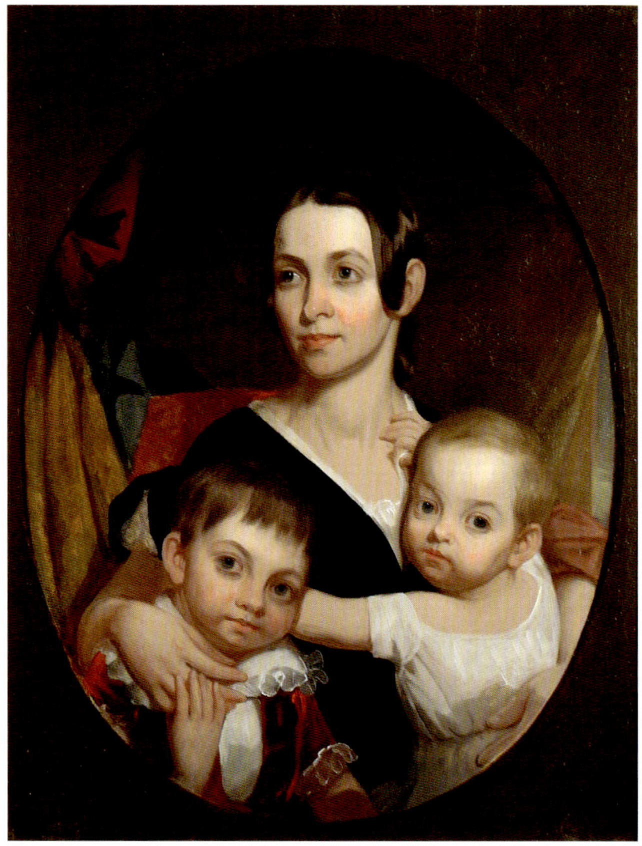

FIGURE 46. William Frye, *Mary Ann Craig Hobbs and Sons, Sidney Johnston and Basil Nicholas,* ca. 1844, oil on canvas, 33¼ × 26¼″, The Filson Historical Society, 1981.8.19.

shoulders, a style which the more accomplished artists of the day handled with a great grace." Renau attributes the work to Frye, and Adams concurs, having previously communicated to Renau her analysis of the artist's style, commenting that the "heads of his children are usually slightly enlarged compared to their bodies. They also seem to have very wide staring eyes," this possibly being the "influence of the daguerreotype." Once this information had been passed along to Nanine Hilliard Greene, a descendent of Edward Dorsey Hobbs's first wife's family, the Hennings, she embraced the stylistic analysis and added a bit of the portrait's social history. Excited to hear about the "two encephalitic children," she writes that her "mother never would hang that portrait of Mary Ann Craig Hobbs and the two boys. She thought they looked like 'idiots' and I suspect . . . so did the rest of the family. All my life the portrait was in the attic," where it had been since the Anchorage house was disbanded.[5]

The composition of the Craig Hobbs portrait would seem to owe more to European print sources featuring Mary and the infants Jesus and John than to a misguided anatomical ability. The fear of later generations that the portrait illustrated severe illness in the children affirms the perception of a likeness as physical evidence and not artistic license. This combination of artistic ability and oral history resounds with the idea of "folk" art. While the works of those artists so labeled lack the sophistication of more academic painters, they often display a charming ambition to transfer a three-dimensional sitter to a two-dimensional plane, with curiously pleasing results. Many artists who did not have exposure to master painters in urban studios developed a personal style, and quite often that style has a flat, literal, descriptive power enlivened by a frequently awkward linearity. However, while "many idealists prefer to believe that the early folk painter sprang from no place, was influenced by nothing, and was simply a creative entity isolated from outside experience," as one scholar put it, this is not true. What was a "seemingly spontaneous creativity often had its origins in early prints, art manuals, and later on, photographs."[6] For that reason, John Vlach's use of the term *plain painter* seems more appropriate. Plain painting is "similar to fine art but at the same time intriguingly different . . . in the paintings generally labeled as folk the conventions of fine art are present but not fully deployed. The net result is a work like fine art but simpler, less ostentatious; it is a plain version of what potentially could have been quite elaborate or complex under different circumstances."[7]

Painting the Sage of Ashland: Itinerants and Henry Clay

In late 1839 financial crises plaguing Martin Van Buren's administration prompted Henry Clay to seek the Whig Party's nomination for the presidency. The party had been formed earlier in the decade in opposition to the policies of Andrew Jackson. While president, Jackson had opposed a national banking system, ignored or defied Supreme Court decisions, and capriciously vetoed congressional legislation. His opposition to public works projects particularly irked Clay, long a champion of an "American System" that promoted improvements to the nation's system of roads, canals, railroads, and harbors, with the aim of fostering better travel and trade routes and an increase in the general prosperity. Whig policies were particularly important to the western movement, whose route originated in Kentucky and the Ohio River Valley.[8] Clay lost the 1840 nomination to William Henry Harrison, who won the presidency over Van Buren but whose early death put John Tyler into office. Tyler proved to be no more receptive to Clay's policies than his predecessors, which prompted Clay to make one of his periodic retirements to his home, Ashland, in Lexington, Kentucky. By 1842, however, he was again ready to run. His strategy this time involved one of the first makeovers in American political history. A series of portraits painted in the 1840s redefined Clay's image, elevating him from the common fray and turning him into the "Sage of Ashland," an eminently electable presidential candidate. The first, and most successful, of those paintings was begun in 1842, when the Whigs of Philadelphia commissioned John Neagle to paint a full-length portrait of Clay.

Neagle, who had visited Kentucky twenty years earlier, went to Ashland in 1842 and made sketches for the work. Completed in 1843, the full-length portrait is one of the most celebrated American works in the grand manner. Clay, immaculate in black suit and tie, stands erect, his head turned slightly left, while his hands graciously gesture down to the right, toward a globe swathed in the folds of the Stars and Stripes. On the globe we see Latin America, a reference to Clay's interest in the extension of U.S. influence in the Western Hemisphere. Foreground details include an anvil and a shuttle, tools of industry. In the background, a cow and a plow stand on a shore, beyond which a distant sailing ship recedes. The "harmonious juxtaposition" of these symbolic elements of Whig prosperity, notes the Neagle scholar Robert Torchia, are "meant to suggest a state of peaceful, productive economic cooperation."[9] The allegorical portrait was well received in Kentucky as well as elsewhere. The engraving made by John Sartain from the portrait in 1843 became the best-known image of Clay as the election of 1844 loomed (Fig. 47). The *Frankfort Commonwealth* of June 6, 1843, called the Neagle portrait "a complete masterpiece, a most perfect likeness, embodying, with the highest and most truthful effect in the full action and animation of debate, the dignity and majesty of the intellectual greatness" of the subject. Clay liked it too, writing to Neagle that it was the "judgment of my family and friends that you have sketched the most perfect likeness of me that has been hitherto made. My opinion coincides with theirs. I think you have happily delineated the character, as well as the physical appearance of your subject." Never mind that Clay had also told Manuel Joachim de Franca, regarding *his* portrait of 1842, that he had "succeeded in some features in respect to which most artists have failed."[10]

Far from grand, but just as critical to the change in image, is the "portrait in small" that the Nashville miniaturist John Wood Dodge created of Clay, an allegorical, intimate rendition in the genteel tradition. Dodge visited Lexington in 1843 and painted

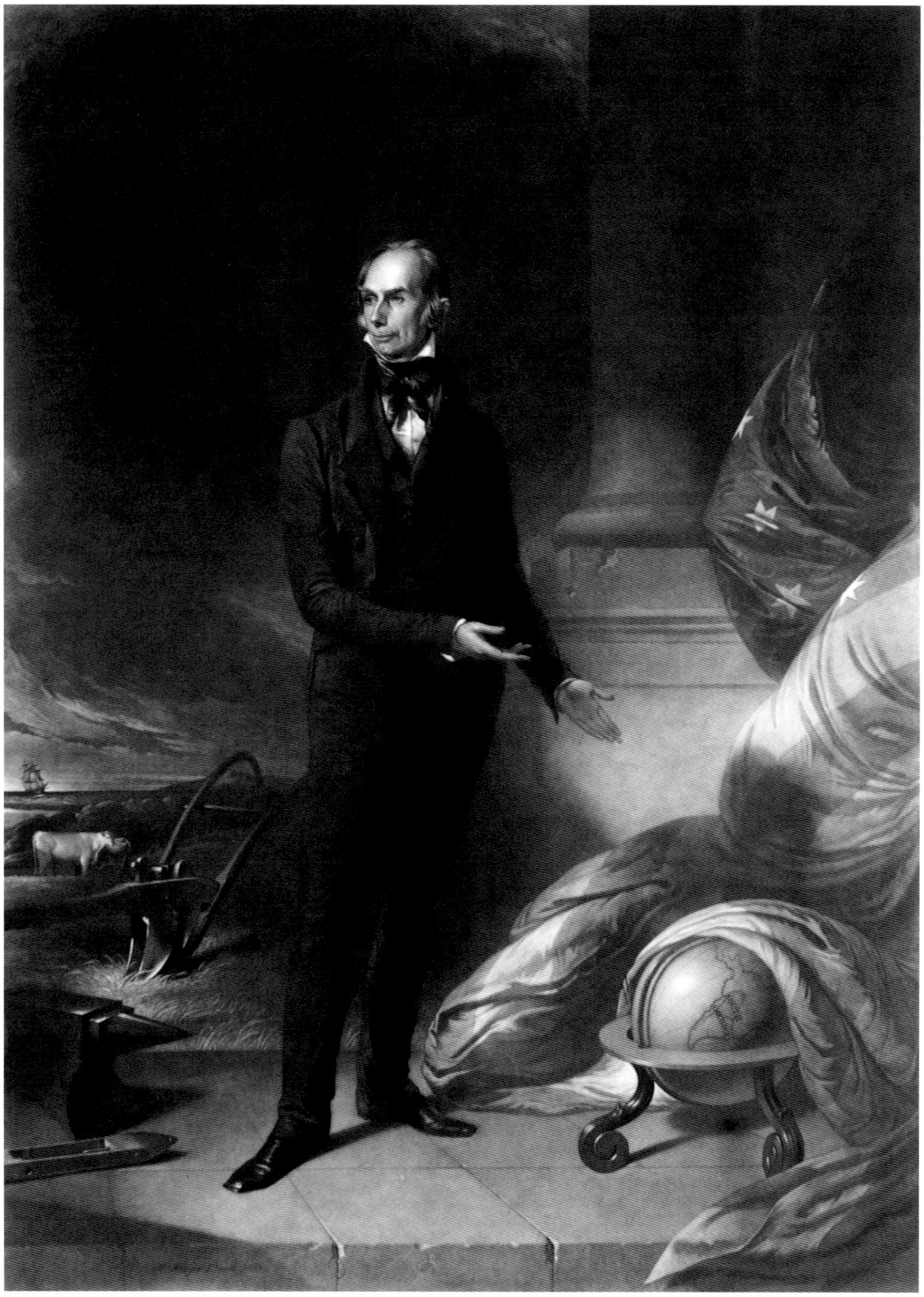

FIGURE 47. John Neagle (1796–1865), *Henry Clay* (1777–1852), 1843, engraved by John Sartain (1808–1897), 1843, distributed by Charles W. Bender & Company, Philadelphia, mezzotint on wove paper, 28 × 19¼″, The Filson Historical Society, 998PR3.

Clay seated beneath a tree at Ashland, with a favorite dog at his feet and a placid, idyllic landscape in the background. Because Dodge was a miniaturist noted for detail it is likely that the work was also intended as the prototype for an engraving (Fig. 48). Indeed, one was issued by H. S. Sadd in 1844, which contributed substantially to the campaign for Clay to be seen as the "Sage of Ashland."[11]

Although Clay successfully pursued the Whig nomination for president in 1844, these works of art in print form may not have redeemed his image. Amos Kendall, a journalist, wrote of him as being "'*the embodiment of Whig principles,*' those immoral principles of aristocrats who seek to increase their natural advantages by manipulating laws and reshaping society to make the government an 'Aristocracy of Wealth.'"[12]

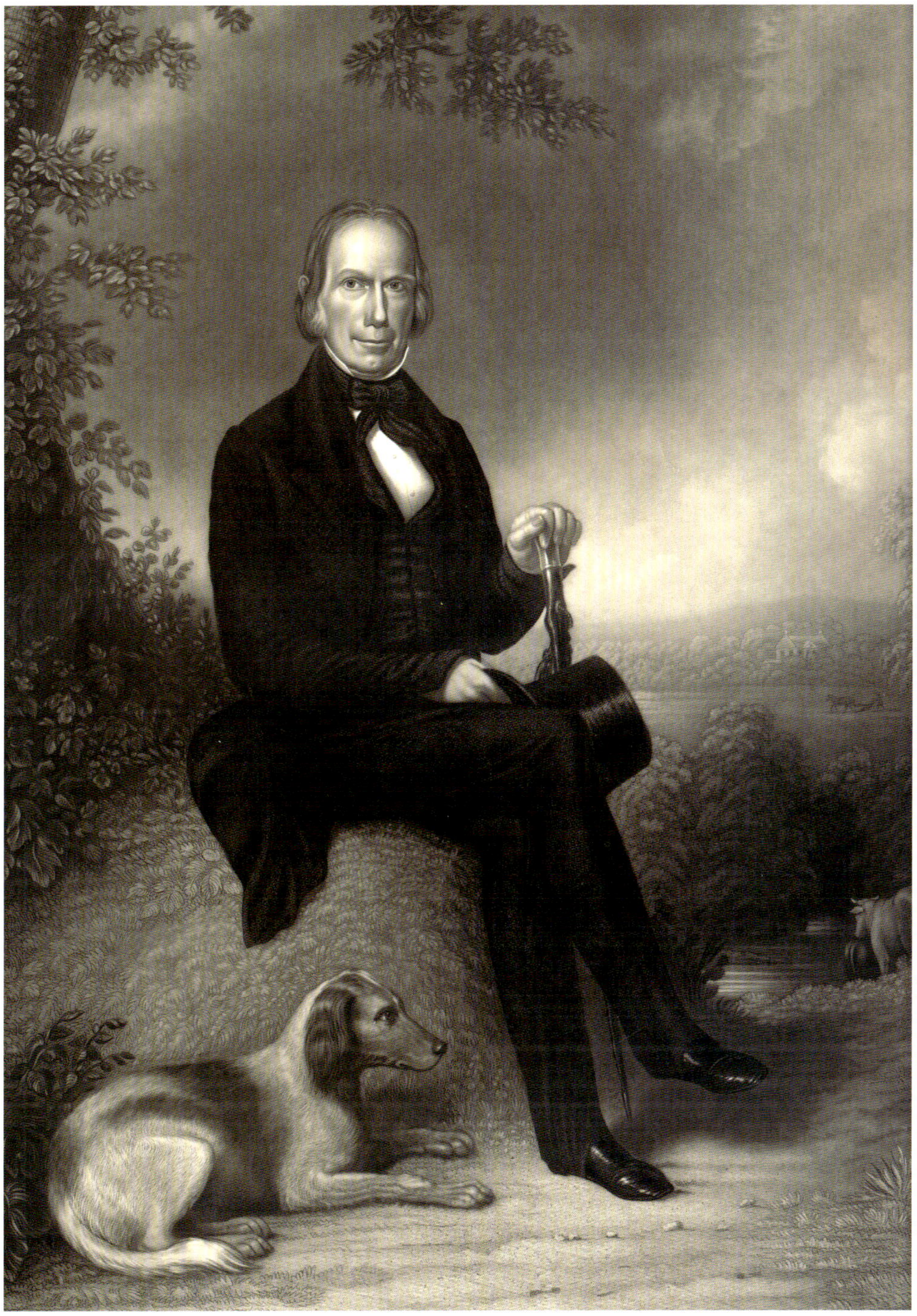

FIGURE 48. John Wood Dodge (1807–1893), *Henry Clay at Ashland* (1777–1852), engraved by H. S. Sadd, 1844, distributed by Coates & Cosine, New York, lithograph on paper, 19¼ × 14¼", The Filson Historical Society, 1984.8.

Other immoralities of Clay's listed by Kendall included drinking, swearing, and card playing, although no mention of dueling seems to have been made: of that Clay had been guilty as well. This time around Clay's opponent was James K. Polk of Tennessee, and the principal political issues were the looming annexation of Texas and a potential war with Mexico. As adding to American territory in the South also raised the question of the expansion of slavery, Clay was again challenged on his position. Attempting to hedge his bets, he issued what became known as the "Alabama letters," announcing that he would welcome Texas annexation if it could be achieved "without dishonor, without war, with the common consent of the union, and upon just and fair terms."[13] This stand alienated New York State, a bastion of the Democratic Party, and he lost the election.

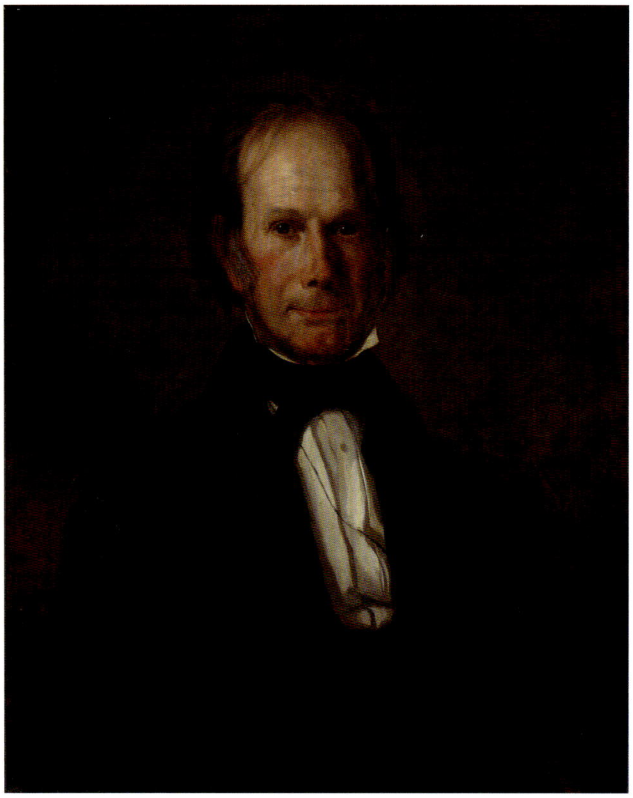

FIGURE 49. George Peter Alexander Healy, 1813–1894, *Henry Clay* (1777–1852), 1845, oil on canvas, 30 × 25″, National Portrait Gallery, Smithsonian Institution, Washington, D.C., NPG.65.44.

Even in defeat Clay remained a figure of national importance and continued to be sought out by ambitious portrait artists as a sitter. In 1845 G. P. A. Healy, a portraitist with a marked flair for the dramatic, found himself in a position truly fraught with drama: he went to Ashland in June to paint Clay, having just left the deathbed of Clay's great nemesis, Andrew Jackson. As Healy later told it in his *Reminiscences,* after his last encounter with the former president the artist, having accomplished all he could do in this final sitting, prepared to take his leave. Yet Old Hickory asked him to stay. "Please come in. I wish it." And so Healy was there to hear Jackson's last words: "Why do you weep for me? I am in the hands of the Lord, who is about to release me. You should rejoice that my sufferings are at an end." With this event behind him, Healy arrived at Ashland, where he found the "contrast was great in every respect. Instead of tears, suffering, of death, I found happiness, luxury and joyous life." Healy had been commissioned by King Louis Philippe of France to paint a series of portraits of famous American men for the Palace of Versailles, a fact of which Clay was aware. Healy's report of his encounter with Clay portrays a sitter far more rustic than the wise sage of the previous years (Fig. 49). The rather worn look Clay wears may have been the result of his having tweaked Healy by saying, "You are an indifferent courtier; though you come to us from the French King's presence, you have not spoken to me of my livestock. Don't you know that I am prouder of my cows and sheep than of my best speeches?"[14]

Implicit in Healy's jovial account is an undercurrent of unease between the two men. Clay challenged Healy on the integrity of Andrew Jackson's faith, and Healy replied that "if General Jackson was not sincere, then I do not know the meaning of the word."[15] The Great Compromiser also exasperated the portraitist by constantly interrupting their sittings for meetings with political cronies who dropped by. But Healy was complimentary about the hospitality, remarking on seeing his first minstrel show and flattering Mrs. Clay on her hospitality and her ability to keep her husband's legendary temper at bay. The portrait proved to be a rather standard head-and-shoulders type. Though the two men parted in peace, Clay had little further interest in sitting for Healy. When the artist visited Washington in later years he presented his card at Clay's office, only to hear him exclaim, "What! Another?" seemingly unaware that Healy was within earshot. But upon Healy's entering, Clay playfully remarked, "I thought you were with the King!" So ended the encounter about which one critic said that Healy "had made of Jackson an old lion" and of Clay "an old fox."[16]

The episode with Healy marks the end of Henry Clay's sittings with itinerant painters at Ashland, though there are three other noteworthy late images of the Great Compromiser. First is a bust portrait of Clay by Manuel Joachim de Franca at Ashland, painted in 1842 on one of the artist's rare trips to Lexington, though there is no verifiable evidence of a sitting. The second is by Chester Harding. More than twenty-five years after Harding left Kentucky, he painted a full-length of Clay from sketches made in Washington in anticipation of the 1848 election. A subscription was taken from Clay's supporters to pay for the work, but when the old politician's chances faded, so did the subscribers, leaving Harding short. He finished the portrait, which the Harding scholar Leah Lipton described as "a rather hard and awkward finished work, especially in the modeling of the head. One might guess that when the financial backing for the portrait evaporated, Harding's interest in it also flagged."[17] The third work, far more curious and certainly more morbid, was Robert W. Weir's painting *The Last Communion of Henry Clay,* which shows the elderly statesman abed by a window through which spills radiant light, an Episcopal priest in attendance with chalice, and a kneeling black figure at prayer. Clay became an Episcopalian after the 1847 death of his son Henry Clay Jr. in the Mexican War, whose pew at Christ Church in Lexington is still memorialized. Weir had only read reports of the scene, which took place on the second floor of the National Hotel in Washington with the Senate chaplain, Dr. Clement Butler of Trinity Parish, present, as well as James G. Marshall, Clay's manservant and companion during his final years.[18]

Robert Scott Duncanson, an African-American artist, responds to Uncle Tom's Cabin

As the twenty-one-year-old, unmarried daughter of Dr. Lyman Beecher, Harriet Beecher accompanied her family to Cincinnati in 1832 when her father was appointed president of Lane Theological Seminary. A devout young woman subject to bouts of depression and religious mania, she spent the next eighteen years of her life in that city. In 1836 she married Calvin E. Stowe, a professor at the seminary, and then gave birth to six children in ten years. Lane Theological Seminary, under Beecher's charismatic direction, was a center for the fervent abolitionist movement that had sprung up in southern Ohio. Both Professor and Mrs. Stowe were fully committed to the cause. Harriet Beecher Stowe's concerns about the salvation of African-American souls, however, were those of a person of deep convictions and transcended any political agenda.[19] When she gave refuge to a fugitive slave girl from Kentucky, she "heard, for the first time in her life, an inquiry which she had not supposed possible to be made in America: 'Who is this Jesus Christ, now, anyhow?'"[20]

Mrs. Stowe's most important firsthand experience with slavery occurred during a visit to the Thomas Kennedy family in Garrard County, Kentucky. Her companion, a Miss Dutton from the Western Female Institute, commented after having read *Uncle Tom's Cabin* that she "recognized scene after scene of that visit portrayed with minute fidelity."[21] Written in Maine, Stowe's novel first appeared as a serial in the *National Era* of June 5, 1851, and concluded on April 1 of the following year.

Teeming with melodramatic subplots of flight and betrayal, *Uncle Tom's Cabin* is ultimately the story of the triumph of faith over adversity, eternal salvation over earthly life. The flight across the Ohio River by one of the central characters is the ultimate symbolic moment of the North-South conflict, immediately witnessed in the conflation of agrarian, slaveholding Kentucky and urban, free Ohio. "Crossing over" is also a theme in many hymns, transporting the mortal to the immortal.

The socioeconomic ties between the two regions, the Bluegrass and Cincinnati, however, were far more complex. Merchants in Cincinnati profited considerably from trade with the South, supplying many of the manufactured goods for a region industrially underdeveloped and increasingly dependent upon the cultivation of cotton. But the myth of a disengagement between the urban north and the rural south persisted in the imagination of popular culture, as is evident in the work of the African-American artist Robert Scott Duncanson. Duncanson's family had been resident in Cincinnati since the early 1840s, and he was acquainted with the abolitionist movement in Ohio and Michigan, where he began to make painting trips in 1852. Duncanson painted portraits of many leading abolitionists, including Robert Bishop, Freeman Cary, and James Birney. He also painted a full-length portrait of his foremost patron, Nicholas Longworth, his most impressive achievement as a portrait artist. But like other socially aware portraitists, Duncanson also had ambitions to paint landscape and genre works, examples of which he began to exhibit in Detroit at the Gallery of Fine Arts of the Fireman's Hall in 1852 and 1853. These

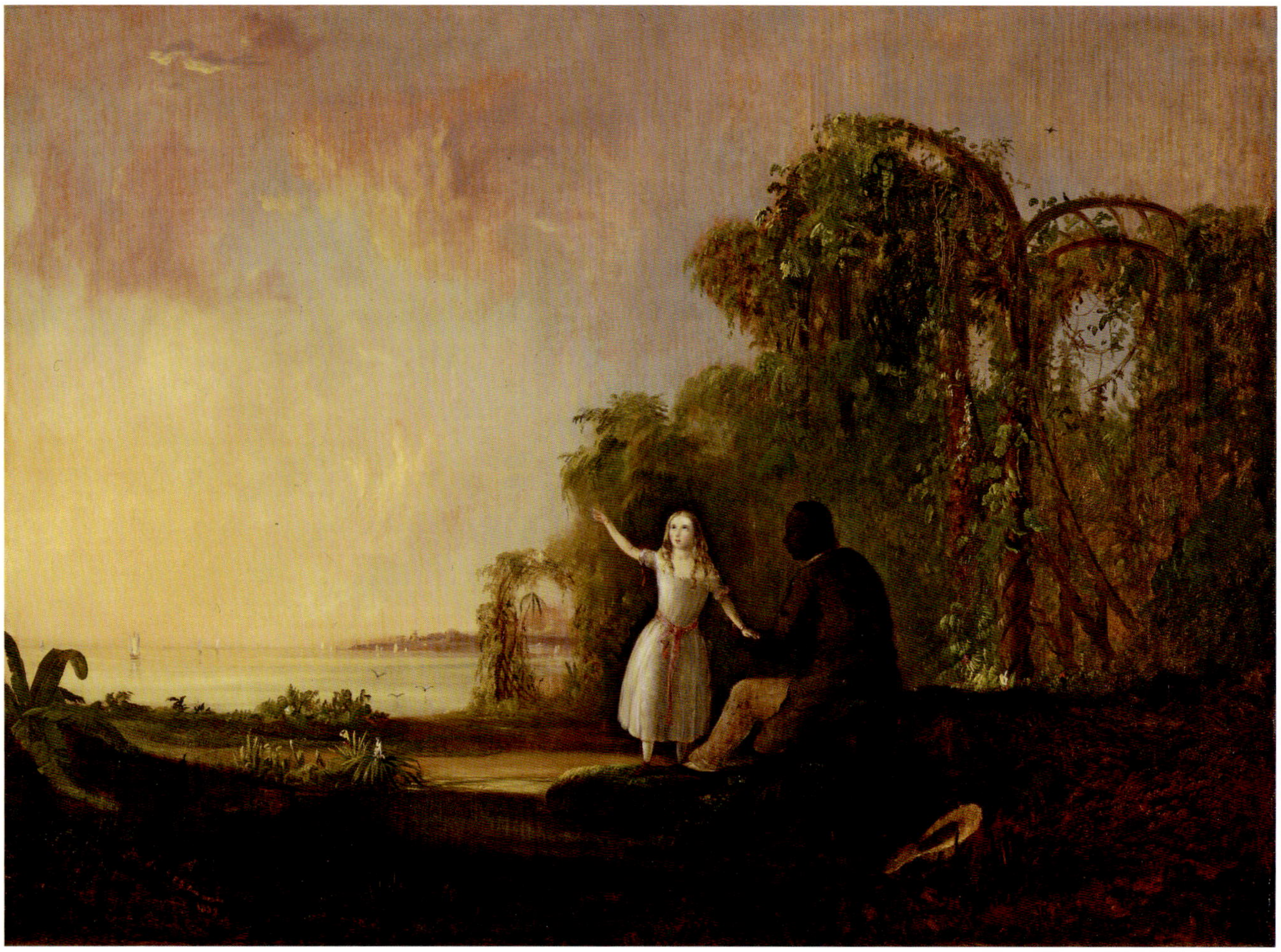

FIGURE 50. Robert Scott Duncanson (1821–1872), *Uncle Tom and Little Eva,* 1853, oil on canvas, 27¼ × 38¼", gift of Mrs. Jefferson Butler and Miss Grace R. Conover, photograph © 2004 The Detroit Institute of Arts, 49.498.

works attracted the attention of the Reverend James Francis Conover, an abolitionist, who commissioned a painting based on a scene from the Stowe novel. As a well-connected African-American and the portraitist of several leading abolitionists, Duncanson was certainly familiar with the novel, as well as the idealistic circles in which Mrs. Stowe had moved while in southern Ohio.[22]

Rather than selecting one of the harsher episodes from the novel, Conover asked Duncanson to paint a scene in which Eva, a white girl, shares a Bible passage with Tom and then points to heaven to indicate an awareness of her own forthcoming demise. An affirmation of enlightenment, the painting represented for African-Americans "the potential for salvation from slavery and oppression through their own religious faith, and the hope that slaveholders would respond to the basic moral tenets of their spiritual beliefs and abolish slavery."[23] In the spirit of American romantic landscape painting, Duncanson invested the glowing sunset with a deistic eminence set in a teeming wilderness (Fig. 50).

Duncanson came to a tragic end. Possibly afflicted by lead poison absorbed over a lifetime, first as a house painter and then as an artist, he became mentally unbalanced in 1872, suffering seizures, paranoia, and dementia. He was dead by the end of the year, mourned in Cincinnati and Detroit for his achievements and his generosity to fellow artists. His discomfort with the patronizing attitudes toward him as a successful free black man should be acknowledged in a larger context. Very light skinned, he was stung by his son's accusation that he tried to pass for white in a country where even a small percentage of black blood dealt a citizen second-class status. Self-liberated, Duncanson reportedly said, "Mark what I say here in black and white I have no color on the brain all I have on the brain is paint."[24]

George Caleb Bingham's Kentucky connections

Although George Caleb Bingham is remembered as a Missouri artist, his connection with Kentucky, where he made many trips and had many close associates, was a source of both nurture and inspiration for his portraiture and political genre painting. Bingham's first contact with a prominent Kentuckian occurred in 1835, when he made the acquaintance of Dr. Anthony Wayne Rollins, a physician from Madison County, Kentucky, who had moved to Columbia, Missouri, to begin a practice and to assist in the establishment of the University of Missouri. Rollins had a classical education, having attended Transylvania College in Lexington and having studied with Dr. Benjamin Rush of Philadelphia. Recognizing the young artist's talent, Rollins became Bingham's first patron and commissioned portraits that enabled Bingham to travel east in 1837 for a brief period of study at the Pennsylvania Academy of Fine Arts. In exchange for this patronage Bingham painted three of his first serious portraits: those of Dr. Rollins; his wife, Sarah Rodes; and their daughter Sarah Helen. All three works display the stiffness of modeling and contouring and the hyperattention to costume detail of the plain painter. The portrait of young Sarah Helen Rollins in particular is an amazing achievement for the twenty-six-year-old artist. In large scale, the work captures the fine clothing of the sitter with geometric precision while placing the figure in a slight counterturn to the picture plane, the left foot splayed out as if in a ballet stance.

Despite the great distance from Madison County, Kentucky, to Boone County, Missouri, the extended families of these two communities maintained close ties. Mrs. Rollins had been a Rodes, with maternal ties to the Estill family. Sarah Helen returned to Richmond to marry Curtis Burnam; her sister also married back into Madison County when she wed Dr. James Bennett. With the Bennett connection came ties to the family of Cassius Clay, whose relatives in Bourbon County, Kentucky, included his brother Brutus Clay and other kin in the Buckner and Wornall families. Bingham would come to paint many members of this vast extended family.[25]

Most of the men in these families were deeply interested in politics of the Whig stripe, and most supported Henry Clay, whom Bingham first painted in Washington at some point during his residency in Washington from 1841 to 1844. Bingham, always interested in partisan politics, was a committed Whig by the time he painted the Rollins portraits. It was an association that, according to the Bingham scholar Nancy Rash, "shaped his ideology and colored his views on the nature of government, on economic and commercial development, and on the interconnectedness of all the states within the Union."[26] James Sidney Rollins, his contemporary and a son of his patron, became a lifelong recipient of Bingham's correspondence on political affairs.

Pursuing Kentucky connections, Bingham returned to Madison County in 1839. Between 1841 and 1844 he was in Washington painting leading political figures of the day, reportedly in a tent he set up on the Mall. Upon his return to Missouri in 1844, he painted three political banners for the Whig Convention held in Boonville in support of Henry Clay's run for the presidency. Among the motifs in the allegorical banners were references to Daniel Boone, welcome in a county that bore his name. For Bingham himself, 1846 was to be a banner year. Having painted a mysteriously evocative scene of fur traders descending the Missouri River, he turned his attention to the jolly flatboatmen of the Western frontier. Popular culture of the Ohio River Valley was rife with stories of the exaggerated abilities and assertive freedom from convention demonstrated by the likes of Daniel Boone, Davy Crockett, and Mike Fink, the original boatman. The region was "saturated with tall tales and comic stories that were laughed at over campfires, aboard rafts floating slowly under the stars, or in villages wherever men gathered."[27] Many who told these tales were proud to pronounce themselves uneducated, and some thought at times that this "lack of education masked a cleverness and common sense which they used to puncture the pretensions of their 'betters.'"[28] Bingham's painting of the jigging boatmen was chosen by the American Art-Union in 1846 for its annual engraving lottery, a selection that brought the artist his first national attention (Fig. 51).

That same year Bingham made his initial foray into politics with a bid for the state legislature, a race that ended in contested ballots and his loss. Boone continued to be a subject of interest to him. The American Art-Union had exhibited William Tylee Ranney's depiction of Boone's first view of Kentucky in 1850. Ranney drew his inspiration from John Filson's account of Boone, when with "joy and wonder" he first beheld the future commonwealth from the promontory of the Cumberland Gap.[29] Ranney's painting features the men of Boone's exploratory party grouped on a rocky ledge, looking, with expressions of biblical awe, as though they were in the company of Moses surveying the Promised Land. Bingham, in his first serious attempt at history painting, depicted instead the families of the settlers who made their way to Boonesborough. Through a yawning gap, exaggerated in density, scale, and degree of threat, Boone leads a horse bearing his wife, serenely cast as an allegorical Renaissance Madonna, her head discreetly covered and her hands demurely folded over the horse's rein. The painting evokes as well the air of a high baroque painting, such as the *Flight into Egypt* by Jacob Jordaens. The settlers pause at a critical juncture, emphasized by the pointing attention of the dog in the lower left. Boone and his tribe are seen passing the gap

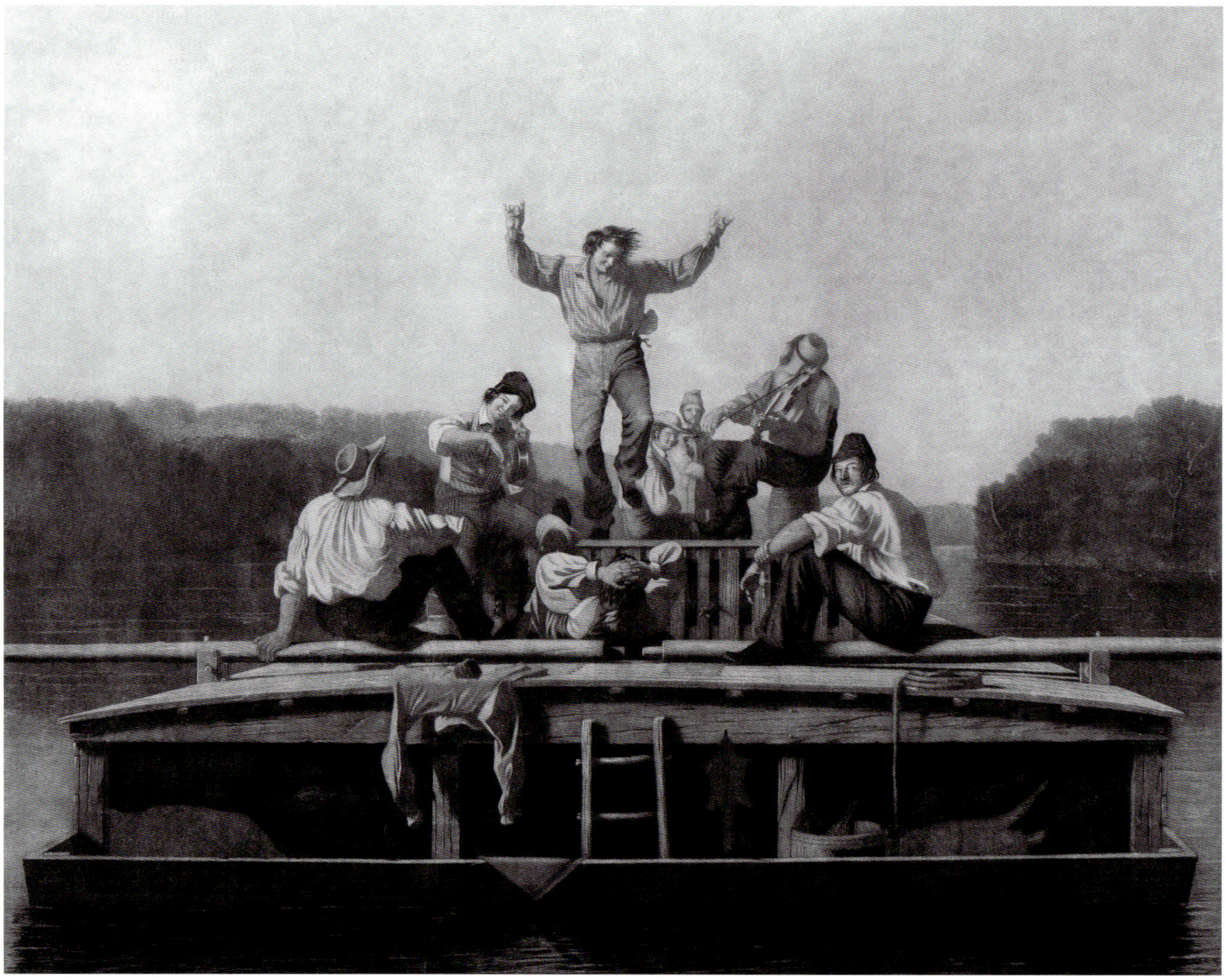

FIGURE 51. George Caleb Bingham (1811–1879), *The Jolly Flatboatmen,* etched by Thomas Doney (active 1844–1849), 1847, distributed by the American Art-Union, New York, mezzotint on paper, 20½ × 25″, The Filson Historical Society, 1929.3.1092.

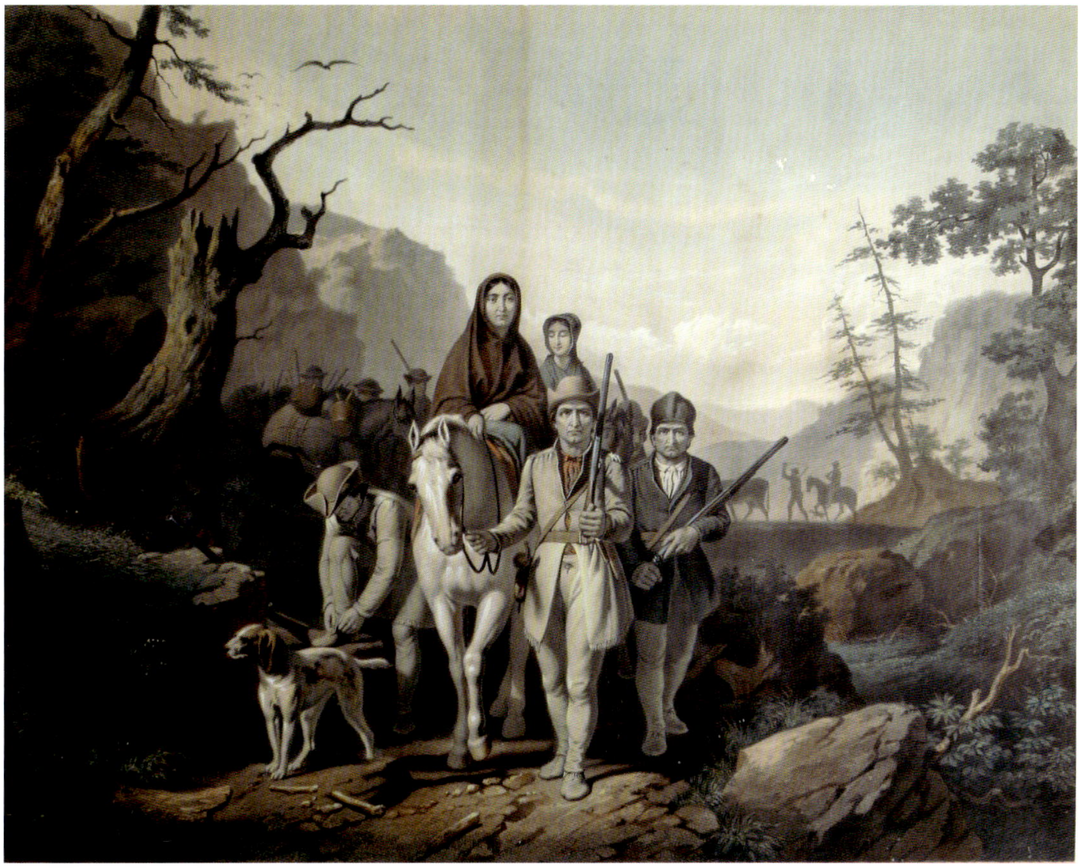

FIGURE 52. George Caleb Bingham (1811–1879), *The Emigration of Daniel Boone with His Family: From North Carolina to Kentucky,* drawn on stone by Claude Regnier (active second quarter of nineteenth century), 1852, impressed by Lemercier, Paris, France, and distributed by Goupil & Company, New York, lithograph on paper, 18¼ × 23⅝″, The Filson Historical Society, 998PR3.

in a dramatically confrontational composition: the figures come straight toward the viewer, as though moving out of the picture plane. Through this device, manifest destiny is richly displayed (Fig. 52).

Although the painting was not accepted by the American Art-Union for the engraving competition, it was engraved by Claude Regnier and enjoyed a wide distribution. Bingham was moving on. Prior to 1850 many of his genre paintings looked back to earlier times, the life of rough-and-ready types on the western frontier. After 1850, with the intensity of the sectional divide heating up, he increasingly turned his attention to contemporary politics. *County Election,* begun in 1851, could be an illustration of the political controversies whose increasing intensity would culminate in the Civil War.

In the most democratic sense it is a painting where the whole is much greater than the sum of the parts, even though great attention to facial detail is given to the scores of voters clustered around a rural polling place. All this stumping was happening in an era dominated by the Compromise of 1850, the death of Henry Clay, the decline of the Whig Party, and the vitriolic issue of slavery (Fig. 53).

To entice subscriptions for the engraving of the painting, Bingham took it on tour from 1852 to 1853. It was well received in Kentucky, where he attracted over a hundred subscribers. The press in Kentucky was also enthusiastic about the work, seeing in it that same diversity of population through the realism of the figures they felt characterized the spirit of the Kentucky electorate. The *Louisville Daily Times* of April 6, 1853, commented on "the sturdy old farmers," the "quiet and intelligent gentlemen," as well as the brawling voters and those being bribed by drink. Robert Ward of Louisville bought the painting for $1,200.[30] Bingham's portraits were said to be "a standard article of furniture in prosperous . . . homes," in Missouri,[31] but there is much about his work that resonates with the spirit of Kentucky in the decade that preceded the Civil War. It was a time when Kentucky could be seen as a microcosm of the national mood—eager for prosperity, torn over

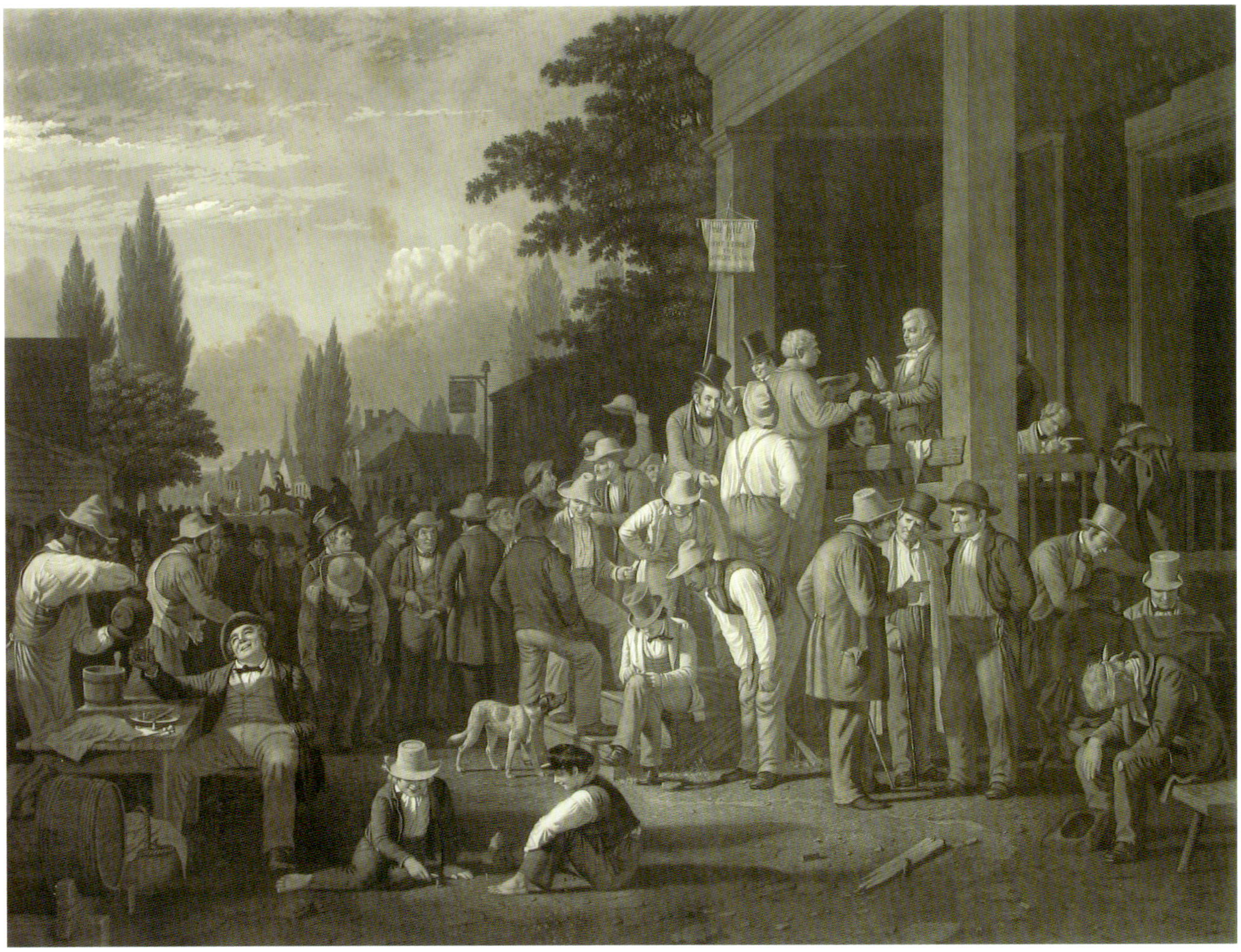

FIGURE 53. George Caleb Bingham (1811–1879), *The County Election,* engraved by John Sartain (1808–1897) at Bingham's request, 1854, printed by James Irwin, Philadelphia, distributed by Goupil & Company, New York, mezzotint on paper, 31½ × 39″, Collection of Warren and Julie Payne.

the issue of slavery, anxious to preserve the Union, and sympathetic to ancient ties of family and trade in the South.

Though often calling himself a southerner in his correspondence with his great friend Major James S. Rollins, Bingham remained a staunch Unionist. In a letter to Rollins written on May 16, 1861, in the aftermath of early Confederate victories, he wrote, "I feel confident that there is a loyal force in the Nation adequate to crush the rebellion impudent arrogant and powerful as it appears." He went on to swear that "upon their heads must rest the fearful responsibility for all the blood which may be shed in this bitter and unnatural contest."[32]

Eastman Johnson creates an enduring portrait of "Old Kentucky"

By the late 1850s Cincinnati, one of the teeming commercial centers for western expansion and trade with the deep South, had become a jumping-off point, attracting a number of creative artists. Of those, Eastman Johnson may have based his enigmatic images of *Negro Life at the South* on the same difficult-to-document exposure to life across the river in Kentucky that Harriet Beecher Stowe had experienced. Johnson was from a prosperous northeastern family that had begun to speculate in land in Ohio and Michigan during the late 1850s. The artist himself had been abroad from 1849 to 1855 studying art in Europe, notably at the Düsseldorf Academy with Emanuel Leutze and at The Hague. Both German and Dutch schools fostered a subcult of atmospheric genre painting, combining detailed historical settings with the nuance of a boisterous working class, whose simple endeavors were held in great esteem as evidence of native intelligence and cunning. While at The Hague, Johnson exhibited his painting *Uncle Tom and Little Eva,* an indication of his familiarity with the melodrama of bondage and betrayal.

Upon his return to America, Johnson pursued a personal itinerancy between Michigan, Minnesota, and Washington, D.C., investing in land with family funds and developing his interest in genre painting of African-American life. From his base in Washington he made trips to George Washington's Mt. Vernon, then suffering from the genteel decay from which it would soon be redeemed by the efforts of Ann Pamela Cunningham between 1853 and 1858. While there, he must have sketched the old kitchen, which he used as a setting for several paintings of slaves sitting before the hearth. Eastman Johnson was not a caricaturist. In the immediate Ohio-Kentucky vicinity he was to visit in the winter of 1858, he would have been familiar, by observation and insight, with the oppressive effect slavery had upon the human spirit, and he pursued a realistic agenda in representing it. During this period he began to paint scenes of "Negro life," sincerely reflecting his experiences in Europe, where emerging realist artists "placed a positive value on the depiction of the low, the humble and commonplace, the socially dispossessed or marginal," thereby giving "importance" to the "social dimension" of the work.[33]

Following the panic of 1857, which devastated the market in land speculation, Johnson spent the winter of 1858 in Cincinnati, where he took a studio in the Bacon Building at Sixth and Walnut and painted several portraits, including one of a prominent local businessman, George Selves. At this time, at the immediate conjunction between slave state and free state, he could have crossed the river and explored the same experiences as had Harriet Beecher Stowe. Returning north and taking up residence in New York, Johnson painted *Negro Life at the South,* which was first exhibited at the National Academy of Design's spring exhibition in April 1859 (Fig. 54). A sensational success, the painting was sold "for the considerable price of $1200" to the noted landscape artist John F. Kensett.[34] Though not specifically sited in Kentucky, the painting was listed as *Old Kentucky Home* when exhibited in Boston that summer. Recent scholarship has established with certainty that the work was based on actual settings in Washington, D.C., near the Johnson family home, where the artist spent the years 1844 to 1848.[35] Knowing of that locale does not diminish the semiotic value of *Old Kentucky Home,* as it came to be known in popular culture, and Johnson never disputed the appellation during a lifetime of profits he received from prints and chromolithographs of the work.

During the decade of the 1850s, the idea of "Kentucky" became synonymous with the border between the pious North and the vituperative South. Kentucky's politicians forged compromises that preserved the Union, even as slavery and the slave trade flourished there. The more patronizing aspects of Stowe's novel clearly present Kentucky as a benign slave state, and that idea, however misguided, became the theme of Stephen Collins Foster's song "Old Kentucky Home, Goodnight." In that lament, a slave, modeled on Uncle Tom, sings for a lost world, a happy home from which he has been sold south. The same themes of seduction, nostalgia, condescension, and the cause of abolition without effect are present in both the novel and the song and can be considered implicit in the painting's ambivalent visual message.

Old Kentucky Home is a highly enigmatic painting that defies stereotype even as it juxtaposes two powerful strata of the social construct. Sitting before the gaping ruin of a back kitchen, a large array of African-Americans are seen pleasantly passing the day even as a white woman steps through a lean-to gate on the far right to gaze upon the scene with a beneficent smile. From a second-floor window an older African-American woman holds a light-skinned baby. Below, on the left, a young man and woman are seen chatting and smiling. The casual presentation of the young lovers of color is a

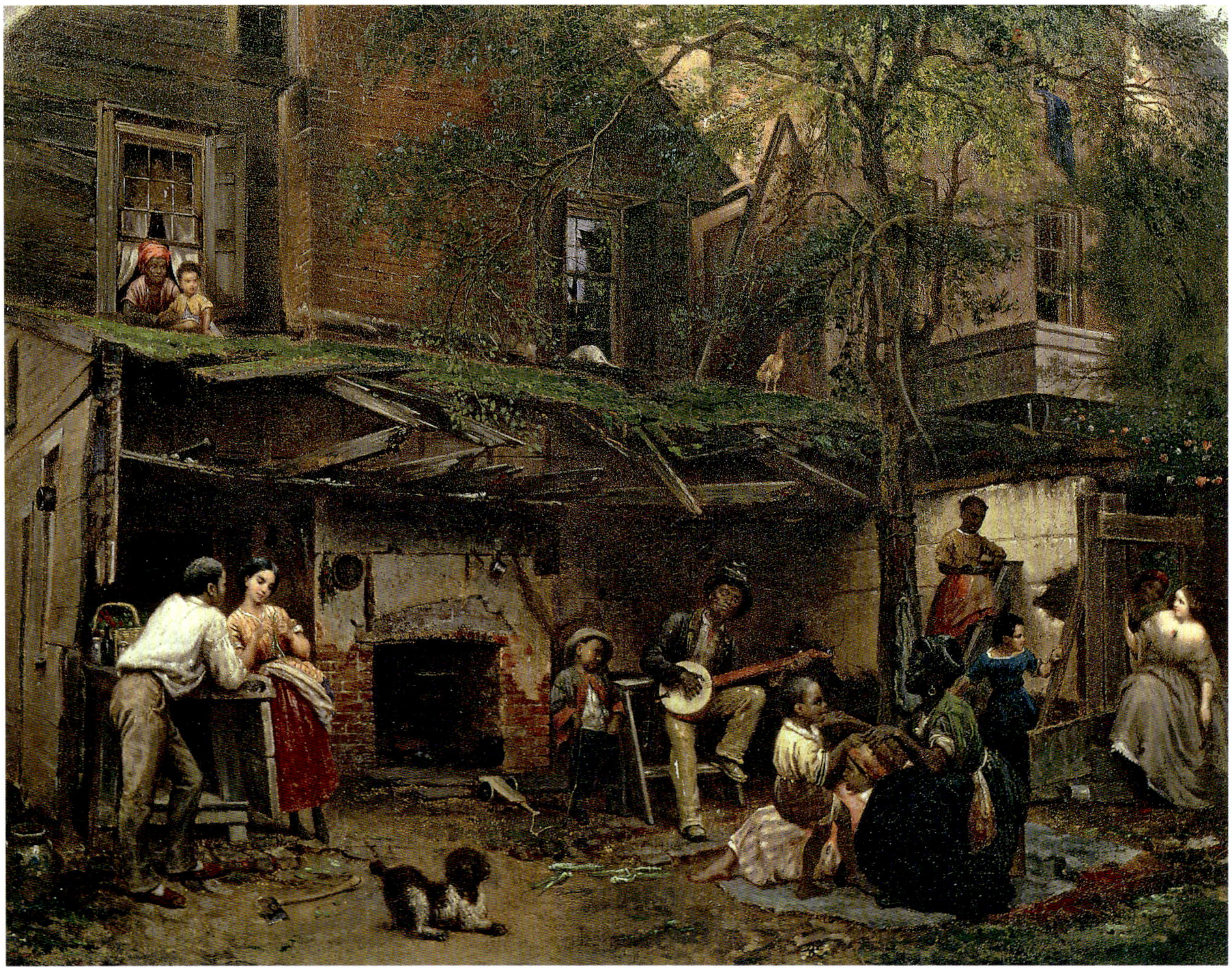

FIGURE 54. Eastman Johnson (1824–1906), *Negro Life at the South,* 1859, oil on linen, 37 × 46″, New-York Historical Society, S-225.

departure from Caucasian subjects, who are seen either as bawdy peasants in the French tradition of François Boucher and Hubert Robert, or as virtuous allegories in the academic tradition of Germany and England at that time. Here the young lovers are of mixed color, she shyly stripping a corn stalk while he leans in attentively to pay court. At least temporarily subdued, his axe rests on the ground before his feet.

In the center an old African-American man plays a banjo while a family group watches and dances. The banjo player is engaging, drawing the attention of several generations, including the admiring youngster to his left and the dancing child before him, a herald of the empowerment African-Americans found in performance. As cast, there is no overt reference to bondage, betrayal, or flight; instead, the various vignettes create an air redolent with the harmony of humans in complex circumstances. The structure of the painting itself quietly suggests a dramatic contrast in historical consciousness. The brown, decayed house with its collapsing roof and yawning fireplace seems to lean against the adjacent, whiter building. The young woman, whose attire suggests a plantation mistress, seems "ready to learn from her slaves and treat them kindly," as Patricia Hills has interpreted the work.[36]

Neither polemic nor caricature, the painting offers a rich, humanized view of life on the fringe, even as we, like the woman on the right, glimpse a great cultural divide. That young white woman is startlingly out of place in the otherwise harmonious scene, truly an outsider, and one whose awkward placement at the far right of the planar field draws our attention and directs our gaze so that we, too, pause and cast an eye over the widely spread field. Exotic, multilayered, and implicitly individuated, the painting poses a simultaneity highly appropriate for the idea of "Kentucky," as the combined vignettes do not yield a cohesive narrative, unless it is that even in the midst of a fractured social construct humanity endures.

Johnson's painting was subsequently, and relentlessly, subjected to the same misinterpretations as Stowe's novel and Foster's song. Always one of Johnson's best-known works, two decades after the Civil War *Negro Life at the South* was still being displayed as a genre painting celebrating an easier time. As early as 1867 one critic wrote that the "details of the subject are prophetical," heralding "times that will never return again," for the "dilapidation unheeded and unchecked tells us that the end is near." Where "all was fun," now "the banjo is silent." This misappropriation attempts a desperate cover-up, perpetuating that "display of Southern paternalism toward the black members of the family as well as a manifestation of the romantic vogue" that Clement Eaton found inherent in the Old South mentality as it wrestled with the issue of slavery in the Reconstruction era.[37] The painting came to symbolize, for many white Americans, the effect of the lost cause of abolitionism, the belief that the end of slavery also exiled the freedman to the ghetto and the sharecropper farm. It is in fact, however, a far more challenging and wrenching work, demanding that the viewer face up to, if not resolve, the parallel existence of the black and white worlds, past, present, and yet to be seen.

War rages and photography displaces portraiture

The history of the Civil War has been well addressed elsewhere. When war erupted, the proximity of the two clashing cultures was personified by major players who emerged from the Ohio River Valley area. The country's previous vice president, John C. Breckinridge, now a Kentucky senator, walked out of the U.S. Senate chamber to join Confederate forces. A Kentuckian, Major Robert Anderson, defended Fort Sumter for the Union. Abraham Lincoln and Jefferson Davis, both native Kentuckians, faced off against each other (Fig. 55). The family of Francis Preston Blair, loyal civil servants of the Federal government, were Kentuckians. Ohio supplied its native sons Ulysses S. Grant, James Garfield, William McKinley, Rutherford B. Hayes, and Benjamin Harrison, all of whom would later be president. As hostilities in the aftermath of the firing on Sumter escalated, Kentucky's governor, Beriah Magoffin, called for a policy of neutrality. When Lincoln sent a request for four regiments of troops to assist in the defense of the Union, Magoffin was defiant. "I say, emphatically, Kentucky will furnish no troops for the wicked purpose of subduing her sister Southern States," the governor said, hoping that the commonwealth could "occupy the position of a friendly neutral and mediator between the belligerents."[38] While firmly in the Union, Kentucky partisans offered a fierce resistance to Federal forces. It is not surprising, therefore, that although Kentucky did not leave the Union, the Federal government later imposed Reconstruction on the state.

Following the war, several factors contributed to the demise of itinerant portrait traditions that had existed prior to 1861. On the socioeconomic level, disrupted trade relationships with the deep South and the economic decline of families that had been portrait patrons severely depressed the demand. Faced with a diminishing market in the South, trade competitions between the farmers of central Kentucky and the merchants of Louisville and Cincinnati escalated into a rivalry that reinforced a very narrow community. As the historian Thomas D. Clark wrote, "In conventions and mercantile gatherings, Louisville revived the question of sectional allegiance during the war, very much to Cincinnati's embarrassment."[39] The cultural synergy that had existed in the Ohio River Valley in the form of artists pursuing itinerancies between Cincinnati and Louisville all but disappeared. Louisville, as we shall see, became a destination for northeastern artists outside the avant-garde of New York and Philadelphia, whereas Cincinnati developed a native academic tradition that attracted national attention.

Developments in photography also influenced the

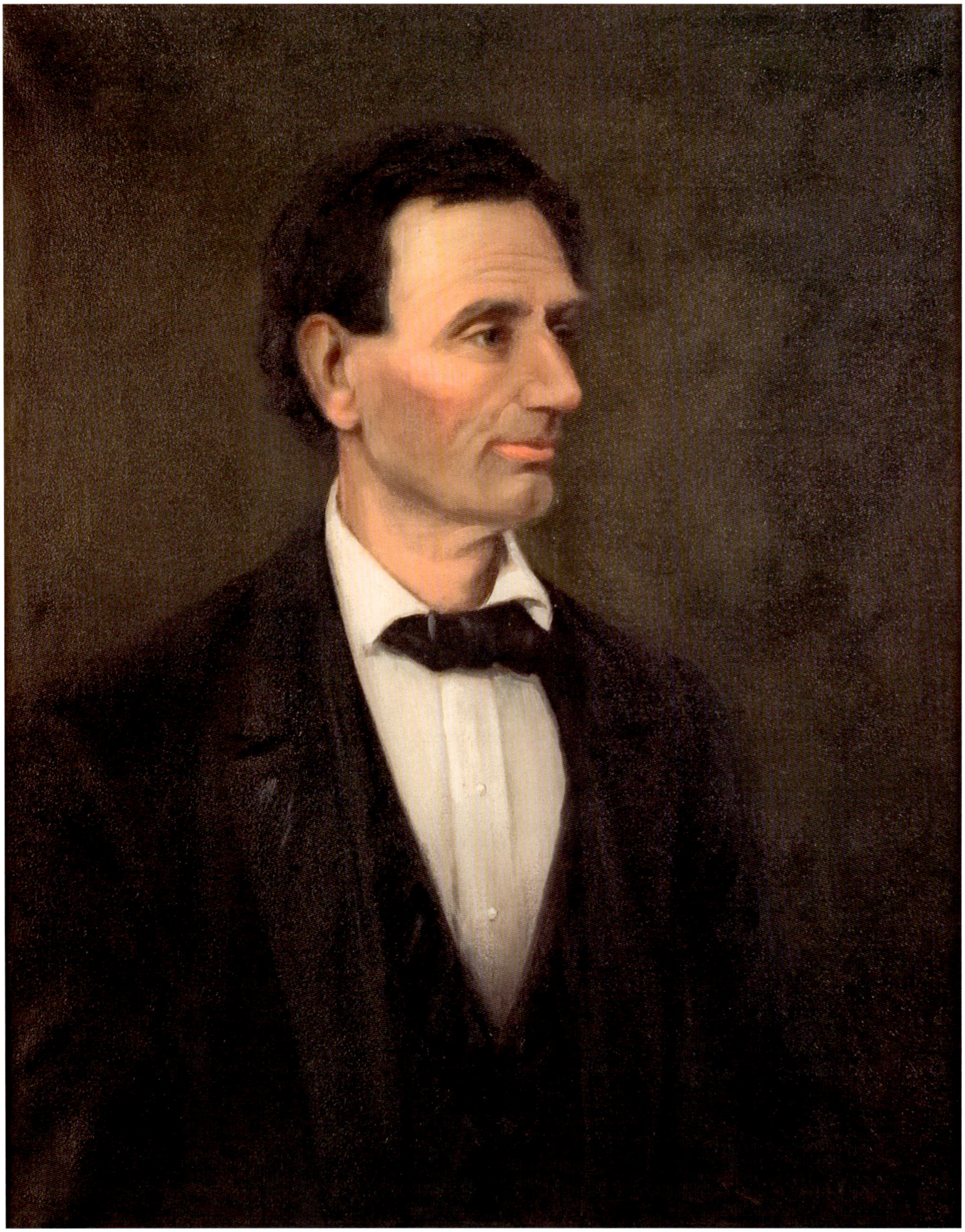

FIGURE 55. Ferdinand Graham Walker (1859–1927), *Abraham Lincoln* (1809–1865), ca. 1882, oil on canvas, 41½ × 34½″, The Filson Historical Society, 1993.10.

Walker's work was not painted from life, but is based on several noted photographic images of Lincoln, including one by Polycarp von Schneidau of Chicago in 1854, a profile by Alexander Hesler, made in Chicago in 1857, and a standing full length made during the Lincoln-Douglas debates and now in the Library of Congress. These earlier works all show Lincoln without a beard, which he began to grow in 1860. A full-length photograph of Lincoln standing, made by the Mathew Brady studio in 1863, is a possible source for the anatomical composition of Walker's portrait. Walker was frequently commissioned by late nineteenth-century Kentucky antiquarians to make copies of historical paintings, including one of George Washington after Charles Willson Peale, now in the Kentucky Historical Society collections.

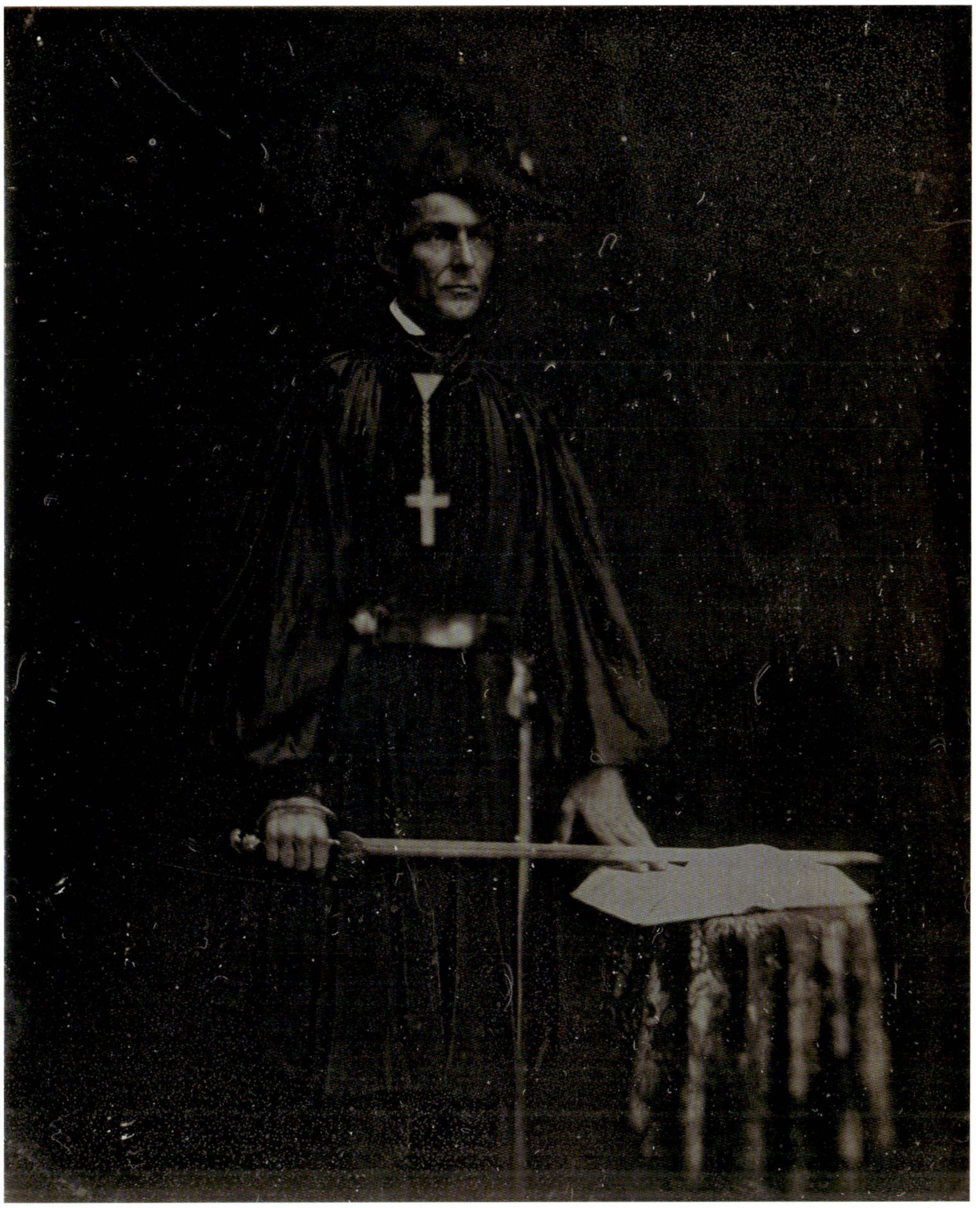

FIGURE 56. John Hewitt (active 1840–56), *Charles F. Willis,* daguerreotype, ca. 1843–1851, 3⅛ × 2⅝″, The Filson Historical Society, 986PC33X.1.

Charles F. Willis achieved the rank of Knight Templar in the Masonic Order, and he is shown here in full Masonic regalia. This is one is a series of eight daguerreotypes found in the cornerstone (laid 1851) of the Masonic Temple at Fourth and Green (now Liberty) Streets in Louisville.

portraitist. Cheaper and increasingly more available, photographic likeness was in the ascendancy, depressing the demand for portraiture among the middle class, a factor that would increasingly relegate the portrait artist of the late nineteenth century to the role of grand-manner interpreter for more prosperous and prominent patrons. Finally, the natural attrition that occurs with aging and death, as well as dislocation in the artistic community, reduced the roster. The popularity of photography also attracted many former portrait artists who made or contributed to hand-colored photographs.

In Kentucky, the photographer John Hewitt was well established in Louisville by 1842 (Fig. 56). In Lexington, the announcement of a branch of John Plumbe's National Daguerrin Gallery makes the competition clear, as Plumbe was "prepared to receive company, and sittings from all those who are desirous of obtaining, what heretofore has been difficult, a *beautiful daguerreotype picture,* with all the boldness and distinction of an oil painting, equaled by no painting in softness of tone, beauty of lights and shadows, and not to be rivaled in the perfection of its *likeness.*"[40]

Thomas LeClear's 1865 painting, *Interior with Portraits* (Fig. 57), is as important to our understanding of the effect of photography on portraiture as King's *Itinerant Artist* is to an understanding of portrait

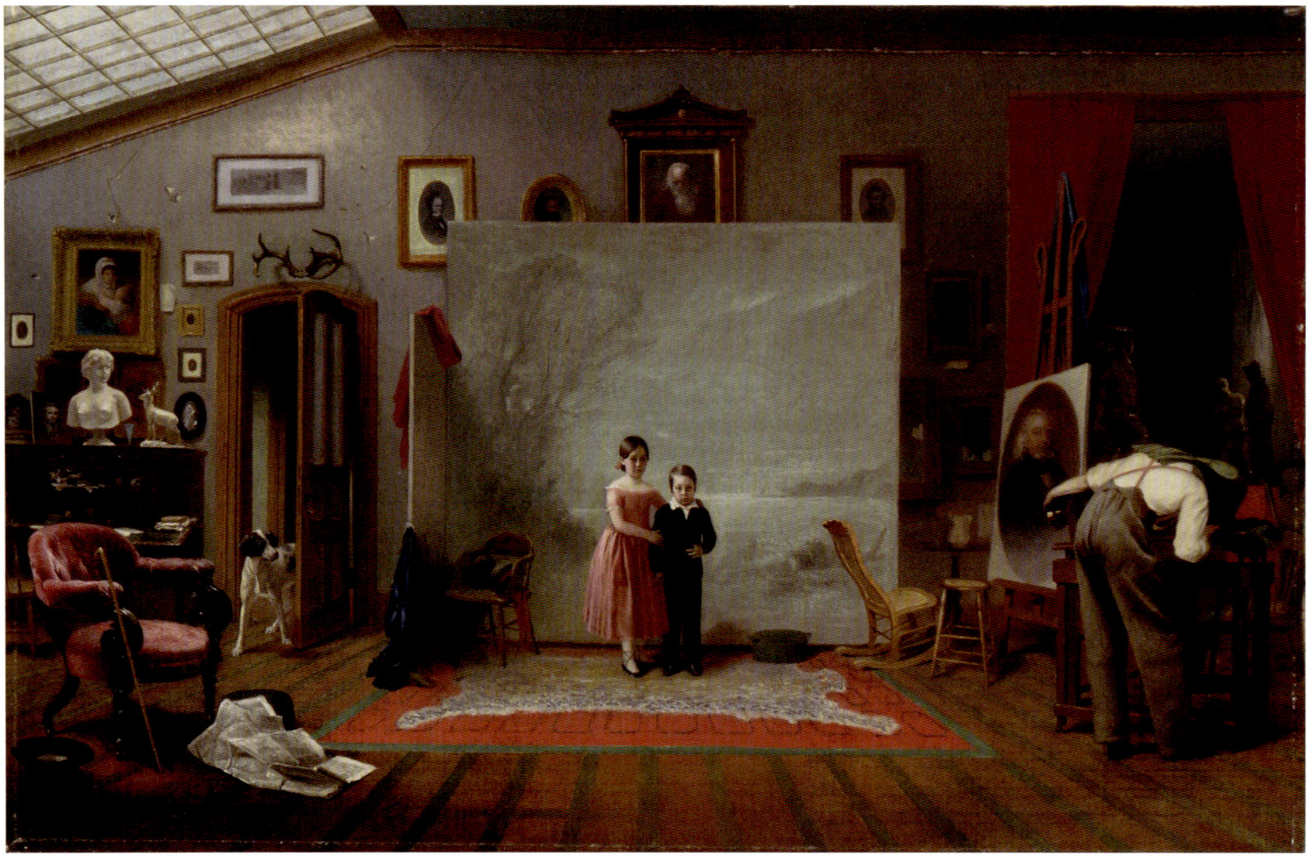

FIGURE 57. Thomas LeClear (1818–1882), *Interior with Portraits,* 1865, oil on canvas, 27⅞ × 40½″, Smithsonian American Art Museum, 1993.6.

composition in an earlier period. Painted in New York, the work has been described as a commission by an elder brother to create posthumous likenesses of two deceased siblings. But there are as many layers to the painting as there is clutter in the studio. Posing for a stagy photograph with a panoramic background are two children whose features had already been transferred to the canvas from extant, and dated, daguerreotypes. A photographer, making a photograph of two sitters whose previously photographed images provide verisimilitude of detail, offers a lot of embedding. The interior of the studio is an allegory of past and present. To the right stands an easel with a portrait in process, a reference to previous traditions enhanced by other paintings in the room, especially the bearded patriarch presiding above the panoramic backdrop. Of the backdrop Elizabeth Broun has written that "landscape painting now becomes merely a background foil for photography. This must have been a rude jibe at all the heroic Hudson River and western landscapes that were dominating the public exhibition rooms just then."[41] Perhaps, but it also serves as a very important spatial device. The orientation of the entire painting is horizontal, an expansion of the idea of the big picture within the big picture. The clutter, the bizarre juxtaposition of living and dead, the philosophic conflation of inherent art-historical reference with the spontaneity of new equipment and an intruding dog implies the artist's deep awareness of the simultaneity of approaches to the taking of likenesses. Even as the portraitist continues an older profession, a younger one offers a new challenge.

By 1865 there were few resident portraitists in Kentucky to face that challenge. In 1861 Joseph Henry Bush was the only portraitist listed in the Louisville city directory. He retired from painting, moved to the home of his brother Philip in Lexington, and died there in 1865. Oliver Frazer, whose eyesight had been failing throughout the 1850s, died in 1864. Samuel Woodson Price served with Union forces and received a wound at the Battle of Kennesaw, which would later cause his blindness. Appointed postmaster of Lexington, he painted in an upper floor of the post office, but he could not be said to have sustained the antebellum tradition of Jouett-Bush-Frazer. He was eventually fired by the Grant administration.[42]

During the war and the years just after, several portraitists from the North and the South took refuge in, or flight from, Kentucky. James Henry Beard moved to Covington in 1863 after a period of service as an ex-officio staffer for General Lew Wallace. In a prelude to his future career, he began an itinerancy in Woodford County, painting the family of Robert Alexander, a noted breeder of livestock. While with the family Beard painted a monumental canvas of their herd in the style of the Dutch painter Melchior d'Hondecoeter. This marked the beginning of a new career for Beard, who moved to New York in 1870, where he became a national academician best known for his animal paintings.[43]

William Browning Cooper moved to Henderson from Nashville in the early years of the war, and made intermittent itinerant visits to Louisville until 1877.[44] The mysterious Reson Crafft returned to Kentucky in 1863 after the fall of Vicksburg, Mississippi, where he had painted members of the Minerva Lane Hynes Cook family, according to her diary.[45] Reversing that trend, James T. Poindexter fled western Kentucky for the deep South, where he worked as a telegraph operator for the Confederacy, spending a period in New Orleans before returning to the area of Evansville, Indiana, in the 1870s.[46]

The art and literature created during the last forty years of the nineteenth century suggest that the end of the war heralded a shift in the cultural identity of Kentucky, leading to a disconnection from culture north of the Ohio River and the collapse of a healthy symbiotic socioeconomic relationship. Thenceforth, the binary definitions of urban and rural, agrarian and industrial, progressive and conservative would be well illustrated in the dreamy landscape painting and grand-manner portraits being produced south of the river, even as a more textured, observant, naturalistic style emerged from the academies of Cincinnati.

Previously, Kentucky's cultural profile personified the reasonable middle ground, reluctant to endorse either the perpetuation of slavery or radical abolitionism, eager for public funding of public works but suspicious of a distant central government. By 1865 it was also obvious that the western frontier had moved to a place far beyond the commonwealth. The younger Kentucky of Audubon, Jouett, and Bingham was a teeming jumping-off point for exploration and expansion most aptly characterized by jolly flatboatmen conveying goods on a river highway with verve and enthusiasm. For a stunned postbellum Kentucky, the "optimism that drove settlers to frontier Kentucky now seemed a rare commodity," noted the historians Lowell Harrison and James Klotter, as "one world was in fact ending, and a new, uncertain world built on the wreckage of war was replacing it."[47]

During the war many Kentuckians resented the actions of Federal forces, which brought trouble to loyalists as well as rebels. After the war, resentment of the Federal occupation and emancipation, concern over the status of newly freed blacks in society, and the determined efforts of conservative "Bourbon Democrats" to maintain a conservative status quo incited a much stronger identification with the South. As E. Merton Coulter wrote, Kentucky "now showed herself more Southern in habits of thought and sympathies, than, perhaps, any part of the former Confederacy itself. She posed as the champion of the states beset by the carpetbagger, and carried her proscription of Union men in her own borders so far as almost to bring down reconstruction on her own head. It was often remarked that she waited until after the war was over to secede from the Union."[48]

G. P. A. Healy paints "Lincoln's most intimate friend"

G. P. A. Healy spent the war years based in Chicago painting many of the leaders of the Union, including Ulysses S. Grant and William Tecumseh Sherman. Perhaps inspired by Healy's previous commission from Louis Philippe of France in 1845 to create a pantheon of American heroes for Versailles, Congress commissioned him to paint portraits of the presidents for the

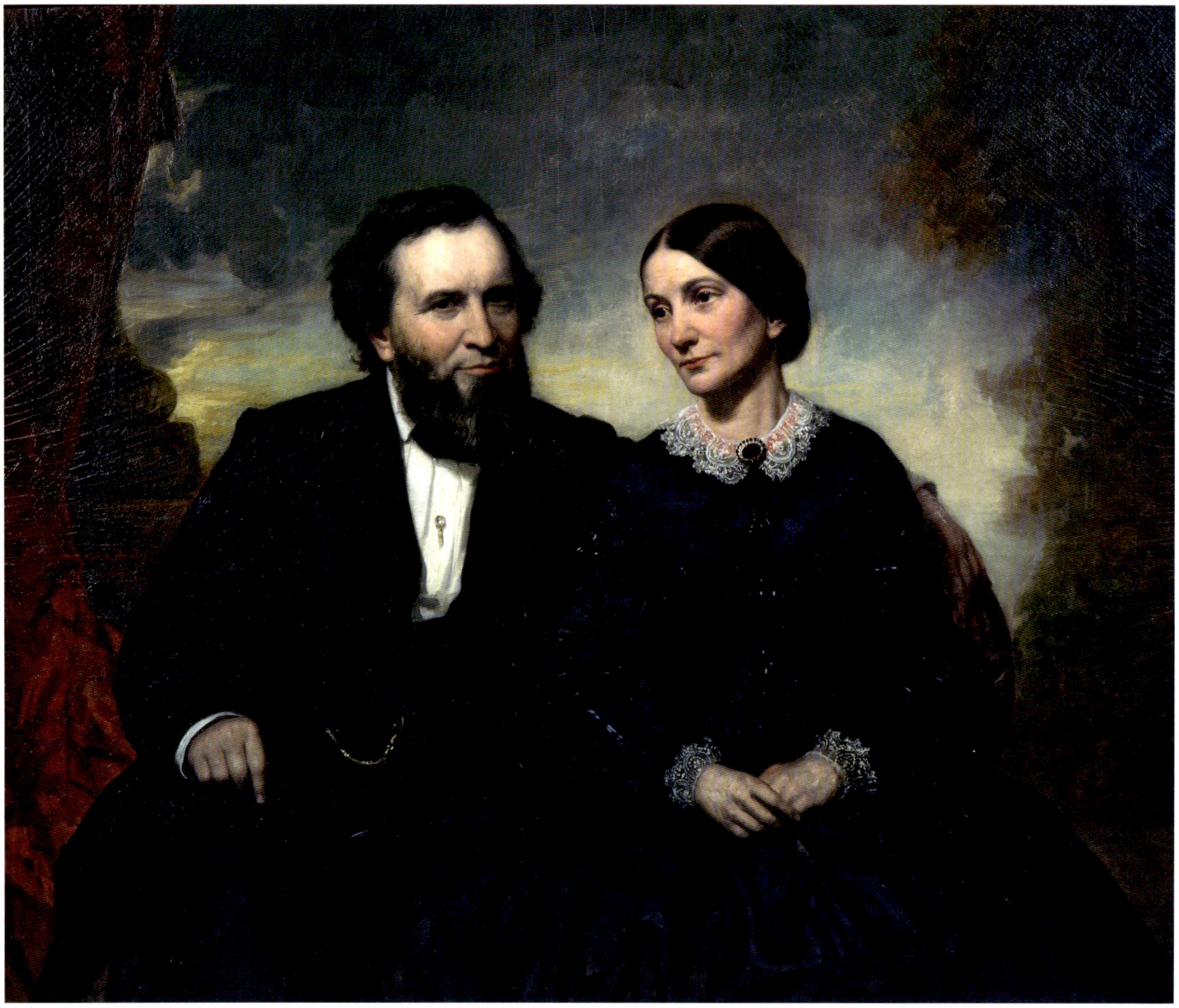

FIGURE 58. George Peter Alexander Healy (1813–1894), *Mr. & Mrs. Joshua Fry Speed* (Joshua Fry Speed, 1814–1882; Fanny Henning Speed, 1820–1902), 1864, oil on canvas, 45½ × 55½″, The Filson Historical Society, 1935.14.

White House. In 1864 Healy made sketches of Lincoln for a portrait painted at a much later date; it shows the president seated in a chair, leaning forward with a contemplative air. The later portrait is actually a detail from his *Peace Makers,* which depicts Grant, Sherman, Admiral David Porter, and Lincoln debating strategy on board the *River Queen* at City Point, Virginia.

Healy extended his connection to Lincoln when he painted the president's close friend Joshua Fry Speed and his wife, Fanny Henning, that same year (Fig. 58). Though the circumstances of the sitting are unclear, it would seem that Healy visited Louisville in 1864, as is evident by the date on the canvas. Kentucky had been an itinerant destination for the artist since his visit to Henry Clay in 1845, and many of his portraits are extant in the state. Joshua Fry Speed is often spoken of as "Lincoln's most intimate friend."[49] He was born in Kentucky at Farmington, the home of his parents, John and Lucy Fry Speed. Judge Speed was a prominent and wealthy local figure who provided Joshua with a good education at St. Joseph's College in Bardstown. Joshua "was a friendly, handsome, blue-eyed, medium sized, youth with the culture and bearing of a gentleman," according to one biographer.[50] After working as a clerk in the wholesale store of William Pope in Louisville, he set out on his own, moving in 1835 to Springfield,

Illinois, where he remained for the next six years. By 1837, when he met Lincoln, he was well established as a partner in the mercantile concern of James Bell and Company.[51]

Speed later recalled that the young lawyer Lincoln appeared in his store in need of a bed but lacked funds to pay for it. Humbly asking for credit until Christmas, Lincoln then confessed that if he failed as a local attorney, "I do not know that I can ever pay you." "As I looked up at him," recalled Speed, "I thought then and I think now that I never saw a sadder face." So moved, he made a generous offer. "I think I can suggest a plan by which you can avoid the debt and at the same time attain your bed. I have a large room with a double bed up stairs which you are very welcome to share with me." After Lincoln had bounded up and down the stairs to inspect the proffered accommodation, he returned, "beaming with pleasure," and said, "Well Speed, I am moved."[52] The arrangement lasted until Speed returned to Louisville in 1841.[53] After Speed's return to Louisville, Lincoln made an extended visit to Farmington in the late summer of 1841. They would remain friends, corresponding frequently, throughout Lincoln's life.

In February 1842 Speed married Fanny Henning, the ward of her uncle, John Williamson, who lived on a farm near Farmington. Fanny Henning attended the Science Hill School, which was run by the famous educator Julia Tevis and her husband, John. While there Fanny was chosen unanimously as Queen of the May for the school's spring exercises. In her autobiography, Julia Tevis wrote that Fanny "possessed a mind and a character as transparent as a clear brook. Her ingenuous face, her self-forgetting and amiable bearing towards her companions made her the most loved and cherished of them all."[54] Speed entered a partnership with his brother-in-law James Henning in 1851, and they became successful as real estate developers and property managers in the Louisville area. Speed was briefly active in politics as a representative in the state legislature for Jefferson County in 1848. He and Lincoln had chosen different parties after the decline of the Whigs in the 1850s, Lincoln becoming one of the new Republicans, and Speed a Democrat. They did not share the same perspective on slavery, either, Speed taking a pro-slavery, but also pro-Union, stance.[55]

When Lincoln was nominated for the presidency, Speed wrote to him on May 19, 1860: "You can hardly imagine, and I cannot describe my feelings when I saw by the papers this morning that you were a candidate for the Presidency. Allow a warm personal friend, though as you are perhaps aware, a political opponent, to congratulate you. Should you be elected and I think you have a fair chance for it . . . I am satisfied that you will honestly administer the government . . . and make a lasting reputation for yourself."[56] When Lincoln was elected he offered Speed the position of Secretary of the Treasury, which Speed declined, although his brother James Speed did become Attorney General in 1864. Throughout the war Joshua Speed kept in close touch with Lincoln regarding the shifting situation in Kentucky, and carried confidential communications between authorities in Kentucky and Washington.[57]

During the late 1860s the Speeds built a new house, Cold Spring, on a part of the Farmington estate, where the Healy portrait hung for nearly seventy years. The horizontal orientation of the work suggests that Healy was well aware of the effect of panoramic photographic sensibility. Speed's authority is affirmed by his direct gaze at the viewer, while Fanny inclines her head demurely toward him, perhaps in deference, perhaps in high Victorian devotion. Joshua Speed died in 1882. Fanny Henning lived on until 1902 and was buried, at some expense, in Cave Hill Cemetery, Louisville, with fourteen pallbearers, seventeen hired carriages, and one wagon for all the flowers.[58] As the couple had no children, Samuel Henning, a nephew, inherited the estate and the portrait. In September 1935 Samuel's daughter Julia Henning wrote to Rogers Clark Ballard Thruston, president of the Filson Club, that "now that the home of Mr. and Mrs. Speed has passed out of our hands" she hoped that "this picture might find its way to your distinguished institution."[59]

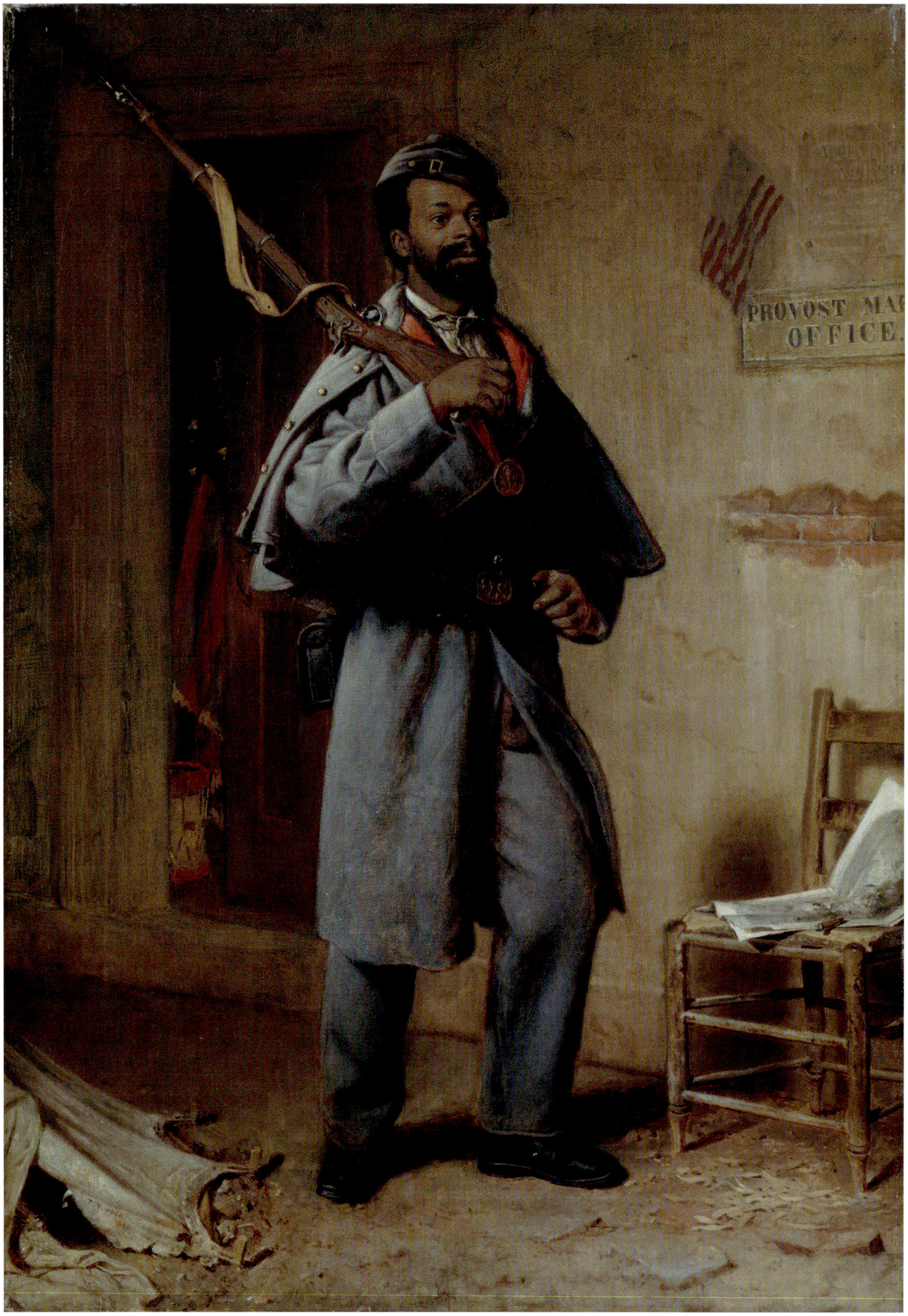
PROVOST MA
OFFICE.

1865–1920

Exhibitions, Collecting, and International Trends

A New England expatriate and a Confederate penitent address the newly freed slaves

In March 1865 Congress established the Freedmen's Bureau as a means of addressing the needs of African-Americans in the former slave states. In Kentucky, the Bureau established offices in Lexington, Louisville, and Paducah under General Clinton Fisk. Fisk reported to Congress that he had seen thirteen black soldiers whipped and two blinded in an attack in Lexington. There were reports of other assaults throughout the state. These episodes and the larger social issue of how the races could coexist in the postbellum world attracted the attention of two artists who had previously made their living by painting portraits but who became increasingly well known as painters of historical genre works.[1]

Thomas Waterman Wood was a native of Vermont who may have had studied with Chester Harding early in his career. Prior to moving to Nashville in 1859 Wood had studied in Europe and worked as an itinerant artist along the mid-Atlantic from Baltimore to New York. Wood remained in Nashville until 1863, when he moved to Louisville. Once in Louisville, he painted many highly detailed portraits of children. These most often featured the subject sitting in an allegorical meadow surrounded by an abundance of fruit, flowers, and foliage, embodiments of the lush Victorian sense of the Edenic nature of childhood. In 1865, in the midst of Kentucky's readjustment, Wood is said to have witnessed a one-legged African-American war veteran struggling across a street in Louisville, supported by a set of improvised crutches. This prompted a series of images of newly freed men called variously *War Episodes* and *A Bit of War History,* which the artist began in Louisville and first exhibited in New York in 1867, after having moved there. Many of these paintings feature the same architectural background detail: the wall of a provost marshall's office plastered with an announcement for volunteers, in which is set an open door through which we can see the Stars and Stripes of the Union. To the right a chair leans against the wall, and to the left the edge of a staked tent sprawls across the dirt.[2]

Two works, *A Bit of War History: The Recruit* and *A Bit of War History: The Veteran,* display powerful allegorical undercurrents (Figs. 59, 60). In *The Recruit* we

FIGURE 59 *(facing page).* Thomas Waterman Wood (1823–1903), *A Bit of War History: The Recruit,* 1866, oil on canvas, 28¼ × 20¼″, Metropolitan Museum of Art, New York, 84.12b.

FIGURE 60 *(overleaf).* Thomas Waterman Wood (1823–1903), *A Bit of War History: The Veteran,* 1866, oil on canvas, 28¼ × 20¼″, Metropolitan Museum of Art, New York, 84.12c.

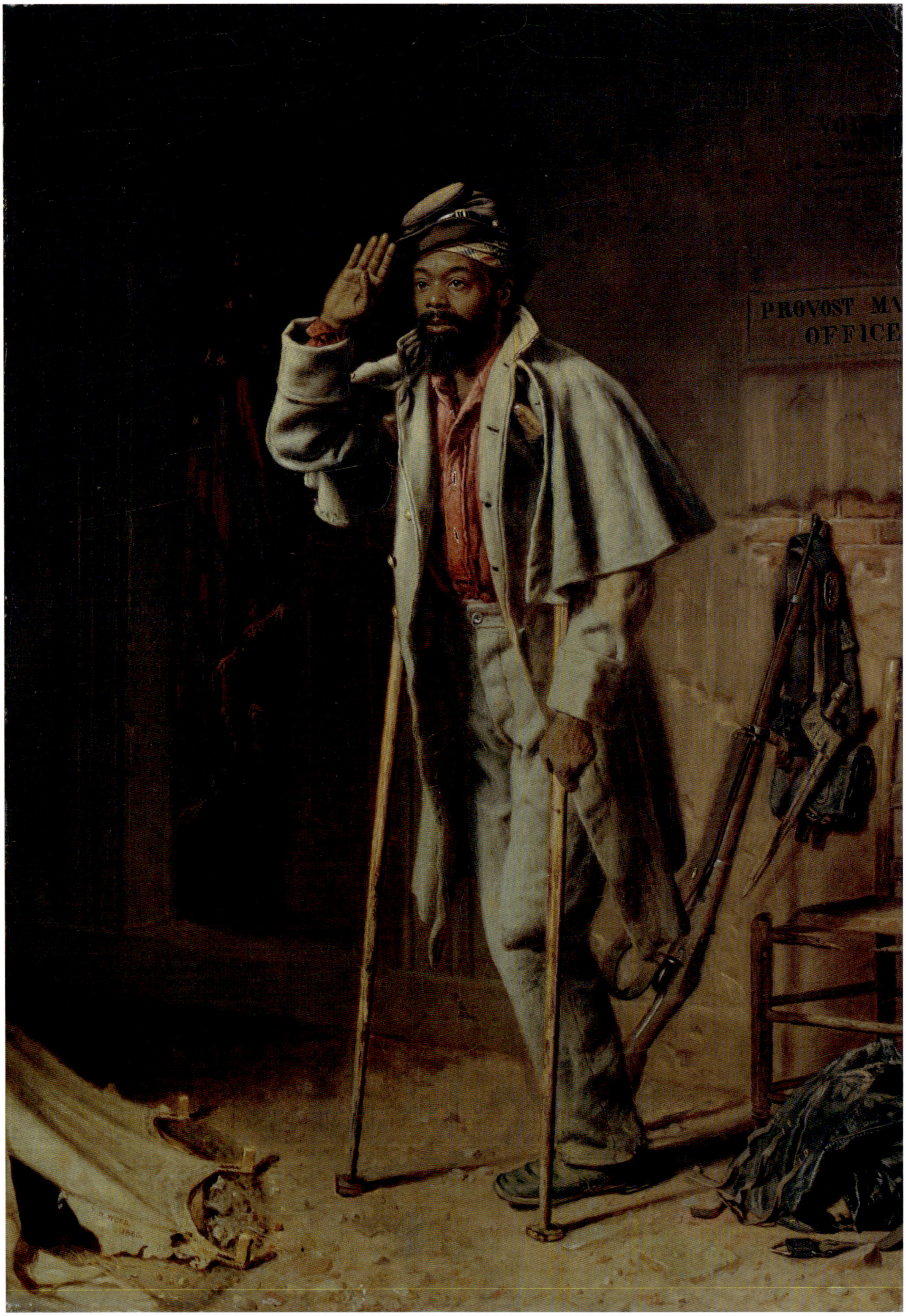
PROVOST
OFFICE

see a black soldier in full regalia as he prepares to march to war, gun slung over his shoulder, perhaps to the beat of the drum we can see through the doorway below the flag. Another, smaller flag is plastered to the wall above the office sign, while the chair is littered with newspapers. With his rakish cap and jaunty pose, this volunteer is not the cruel caricature of Currier and Ives's *Darktown* variety. Rather, a touching sense of sincerity colors the work. As a pendant, *The Veteran* tells a different story. War over, the drum is gone from the doorway and the wall shows signs of neglect and decay. Propped against that wall are the trappings of battle gear, a rifle from which dangles a bayonet and a powder pouch, and beneath the chair lies a rucksack. The veteran stands at attention, saluting left, held up by crude crutches, which support a leg that has been amputated below the knee. Again, a profound sense of sincerity underlies an intense allegory.

When the two paintings are hung as pendants, the recruit would be seen as marching toward the veteran, who is saluting him. Though the obvious message is that the price of volunteering is high, there are less obvious implications as well. As a pair, these works embody the willingness to go to war for the cause of freedom and the shabby circumstances that that freedom produces. The status of the African-American in Kentucky did not greatly improve after emancipation, as the state legislature enacted legislation to circumvent the Thirteenth and Fourteenth Amendments, which Kentucky did not ratify until 1976 in a rather belated tribute to the concept of independence and equality.

Whereas Wood's work made subtle allegorical references to the integration issue, Thomas Satterwhite Noble painted a series of full-blown melodramas that clarified his earlier ambiguity on the subject of abolition. Noble was born in Lexington to a prosperous family who kept ropewalks for the twisting of hemp into binding cords for southern cotton. He grew up in an environment of slaveholders and slave traders, witnessing the sales on Cheapside in Lexington and listening to slaves talking in the cabins behind his father's ropewalk. In the familiar scenario of creative-son-defies-prosperous-executive-father, Noble departed Lexington for art studies in Louisville with Samuel Woodson Price. Through Price, Oliver Frazer, and G. P. A. Healy, Noble learned of the atelier of Thomas Couture in Paris, France, for which he departed in 1856. In Couture's atelier he would have drawn from both plaster casts and life models. During his three years there Noble would also have absorbed the painterly trends of naturalism, which are apparent in his heavily glazed and textured surfaces.[3]

Couture was an artist with a social agenda. His most famous work, *Romans in the Decadence of the Empire,* defied the romance of neoclassicism by showing the citizens of Rome at their worst, indulging in orgiastic excess rather than as noble republicans fostering the civic virtue imagined by the Founding Fathers of Noble's country. The painting was also a thinly veiled attack on the bourgeois decadence of Louis Philippe's France. Couture painted this work in 1847, two years after Victor Hugo began his novel *Les Misérables,* about the plight of the French poor. During Noble's time in Paris the cultural milieu he experienced was rife with undercurrents he would have known from Kentucky. The intellectuals with whom he mingled regarded Napoleon III's Second Empire, which deposed a brief French republic, as a perpetuation of an entrenched aristocracy insensitive to the needs of the poor, symbolically if not actually enslaved.[4]

It would seem that the young Noble returned to America in 1858 with a heightened artistic and social consciousness. Upon his return, he joined his family in St. Louis, where his father had relocated his rope business. Though Noble may not have supported the institution of slavery, he enlisted in the Confederate army's corps of engineers and served three years, operating ropewalks and building pontoon bridges in Louisiana. When the war ended, he returned to St. Louis and began a series of paintings, which Albert Boime feels exposed "the injustice of slavery and the plight of black people in North America. Clearly the war and its aftermath influenced the production of these works, perhaps not without an underlying sense of guilt for his participation in the conflict and in remembrance of his childhood experiences."[5] Noble's motivation may well have been financial, considering the taste in northeastern urban areas for historical genre paintings depicting blacks in a positive light. Yet neither penitence nor profit explains the power of his work. Noble appropriated a complex social issue, which doubtless had a personal resonance, as a subject for narrative painting, a task to which he applied the richly textured style he had learned in France.

From 1866 to 1869 Noble painted five works dealing with slavery and abolition. *The Last Sale of Slaves* was painted in St. Louis in early 1866, not long after the adoption of the Thirteenth Amendment in December 1865. The central figure is a young woman of mixed race holding a baby in a Madonna-like pose as a rabid auctioneer seeks to incite the crowd. Groups both attend and ignore the sale, suggesting the variations of opinion on the issue itself. Noble took this work to New York when he moved there late in 1866, and it was the first work he exhibited at the National Academy.

John Brown's Blessing was painted in New York in 1867 and features the abolitionist insurrectionary being led from prison. He has paused to bless a young black child held up by his mother. Behind him a phalanx of armed guards, bayonets stiffly erect, establish a visual corridor, as though they were standing attention to the white-bearded old prophet figure before them instead of escorting him to his death. Of the entire series of works this one owes the greatest debt to the trends in European art Noble had witnessed in France. The bold figures are reminiscent of the work of Paul Delaroche, Couture's master. There is also an Orientalist feel to the turbaned mother kneeling with her baby.

Margaret Garner, also from 1867, depicts the tragic story of a slave who escaped across the Ohio River from Kentucky to Cincinnati in 1856 with her children, only to be tracked down by callous bounty hunters. Preferring to kill her children rather than return them to slavery, she has murdered one while two others lie unconscious at her feet and another clings to her skirts in terror. In this horrific picture the slave mother confronts her pursuers with the fury of a Medea as they gape in stunned amazement.[6] The empty space between them is a chasm, wide enough to suggest the symbolic distance between Ohio and Kentucky, free and slave.

The Price of Blood is the consummate work in this series (Fig. 61). In what appears to be an expensively furnished plantation office, three figures are grouped in precise triangularity, so that each is isolated in a mood of disconnection. The placid gentility of the mixed-race son on the left derives from the direct appropriation of the aristocratic stance of Gainsborough's *Blue Boy*. In the rear a slave trader, oblivious of the viewer, stands reading a document, presumably a bill of sale, his hand extended in a protective gesture over the pile of gold coins. To the right, the seated figure of the father-master is the most eerie of the group. Slippered and elegantly attired in a smoking jacket, he is the only figure to gaze out from the picture plane toward the viewer. Above his head, just barely discernable, is an old master print of the sacrifice of Isaac by his father, Abraham. The seller glares defiantly at the viewer as though he embodies the entire South challenging the nation to back off the slavery issue. A torn document that litters the floor could well be a previous promise of emancipation. As Albert Boime has pointed out, the pile of money on the table is an extended metaphor drawn from Harriet Beecher Stowe. In *Uncle Tom's Cabin* the character Cassy is shown the money obtained from the sale of her children by a cruel master. "He told me he had sold them; he showed me the money, the price of their blood."[7]

With this work Noble moved beyond allegorical references to prophets, patriarchs, and martyrs and into the steamy topic of miscegenation. Though sexual relations between master and slave were closeted, the fate of mixed race children was not. The sale of these children haunted antebellum Lexington, and Noble would have been aware of the heartrending efforts of local abolitionists to redeem them. *The Price of Blood* is Noble's clearest rejection of his Kentucky heritage. Boime points out that "during the aftermath of the Civil War" many former slave owners in Kentucky experienced the "pervasive sense of loss and the bitter reaction accompanying emancipation," an indication "that slavery had been indispensable to the self-identification and social status of slave owners. This realization would have made the psychological environment intolerable for progressives like Noble."[8]

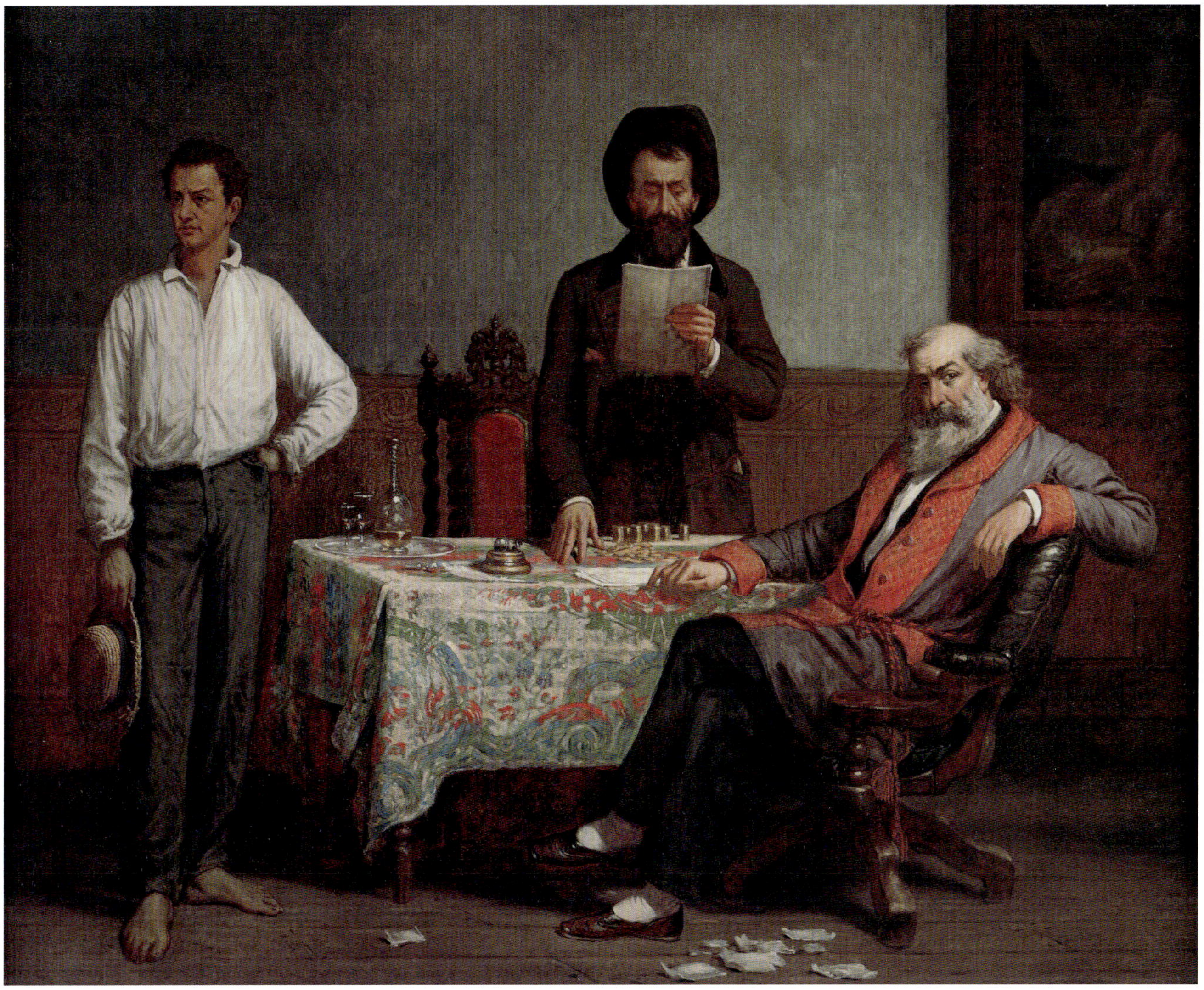

Noble painted one last painting in the series, *Fugitives in Flight,* in 1869, which combines references to the trans-Ohio flight of slaves with the mythic twilight crossing of the river Styx. In that same year Noble left New York for Cincinnati, where he became professor of art and the principal of the McMicken School of Design. Whether the proximity to Kentucky tempered his former zeal, he turned to other subject matter, history paintings that foreshadowed the colonial revival movement (Fig. 62). He also returned to portraiture and became increasingly rigid in his approach to the teaching of art. Late in his life one critic wrote of him that it was "easy to imagine that he felt at home" in the "rooms furnished with the silent and ghostly casts of antique sculpture" whose surfaces were "cold and rigid always."[9]

FIGURE 61. Thomas Satterwhite Noble (1835–1907), *The Price of Blood,* 1868, oil on canvas, 39¼ × 49½", Morris Museum of Art, Augusta, Georgia, 1989.03.237.

The immediate narrative concern of *The Price of Blood* had been the issue of slavery, but by the time it was painted the far more taboo subject of miscegenation could be read as a subtext. As early as 1863 a pamphlet published in New York, *Miscegenation: A Story of Racial Intimacy,* was a paranoid rant on the possibility of white women being wooed by black men. In a far more common scenario, many white men fathered children by slaves, and later by free black women. One of the responsibilities of the Freedmen's Bureau was to hold white southern men responsible for the support of any mixed-race child they fathered. Miscegenation continued to be regarded as an illicit form of human sexuality, and legal marriage between the races was prohibited by law until the Supreme Court case of *Loving v. Virginia* declared it legal in 1967.

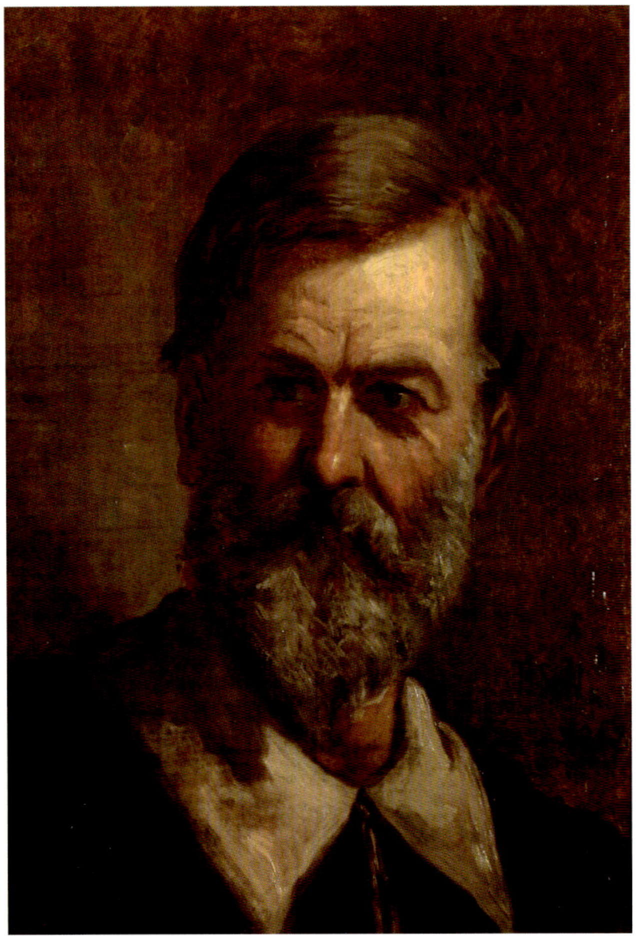

FIGURE 62. Thomas Satterwhite Noble (1835–1907), *Study for a Figure in Witch Hill* (possible self-portrait?), 1867, oil on canvas, 20 × 16″, The Filson Historical Society, 2005.4.

The fair years in Louisville

Between 1874 and 1888 presentations of European and American art in the galleries of the annual Louisville expositions offered the viewing public and the artistic community a rare opportunity to see works of art by masters old and new. As an index of the taste of the times, the catalogs of these exhibitions provide documentary evidence of the presence of a number of contemporary styles, both avant-garde and academic, the naturalistic strains of the Barbizon and Hague schools mingling with the academic style of the old Düsseldorf Academy, which had been so influential to the art of Bingham and Beard's generation.

The first Louisville Industrial Exposition opened in 1874 in buildings built specifically for the occasion.[10] This initial gathering of works of art was partially inspired by the collecting interests of Richard Jouett Menefee, who lent several works from his own collection, and of Horatio Victor Newcomb, who lent a bust of Napoleon by Antonio Canova. Several established European and American artists were invited to participate, and a notable collection of old master paintings, primarily Italian, belonging to Jonas Pickles of New Orleans was also installed. Some of the greatest names in art history were shown: works attributed to Luca Giordano, Sebastiano Ricci, Tintoretto, Anthony van Dyck, and others. Perhaps of greatest interest was a work attributed to Caravaggio, *Peter Denying Christ,* for sale at $10,000.[11] The display of these works would have been an opening preview for the old master–collecting mania that would ensue in the following decades.

Among the American works were several examples of the Hudson River School of luminist landscape painting, including works by J. F. Kensett, William S. Haseltine, Albert Bierstadt, and Thomas Cole. *Luminism* is the descriptive term subsequent art historians have given to those huge, dramatic renditions of the landscape lit by the transitional light at dawn and dusk that the late nineteenth-century public adored.[12] That they were also willing to pay big prices for them is made evident by the availability of Cole's allegorical *Cross and the World* series for sale at $5,000. Other landscape painters, from farther south, were also invited to show. Among them, Richard Clague, a landscape painter from New Orleans who was then little known but is now highly regarded, was represented by two works, an indication of the ongoing cultural ties between the two cities. Carl Christian Brenner, whose landscapes of local beech groves would be included in every subsequent exhibition, made his debut there as well.[13]

Several important portrait artists were well represented. Thomas LeClear of Buffalo and Brooklyn, whose association with the Newcomb family of Louisville brought him to the attention of the committee, was drawn to Louisville by these exhibitions. Portraits by the Ohio painter Joseph Oriel Eaton were shown as well. Works of the Kentucky portraitists Nicola Marschall and Samuel Woodson Price, who often depicted the leading political figures of the day, were to be seen. It was at this exposition that the first public showing of Victor Nehlig's *Scenes from the Life of*

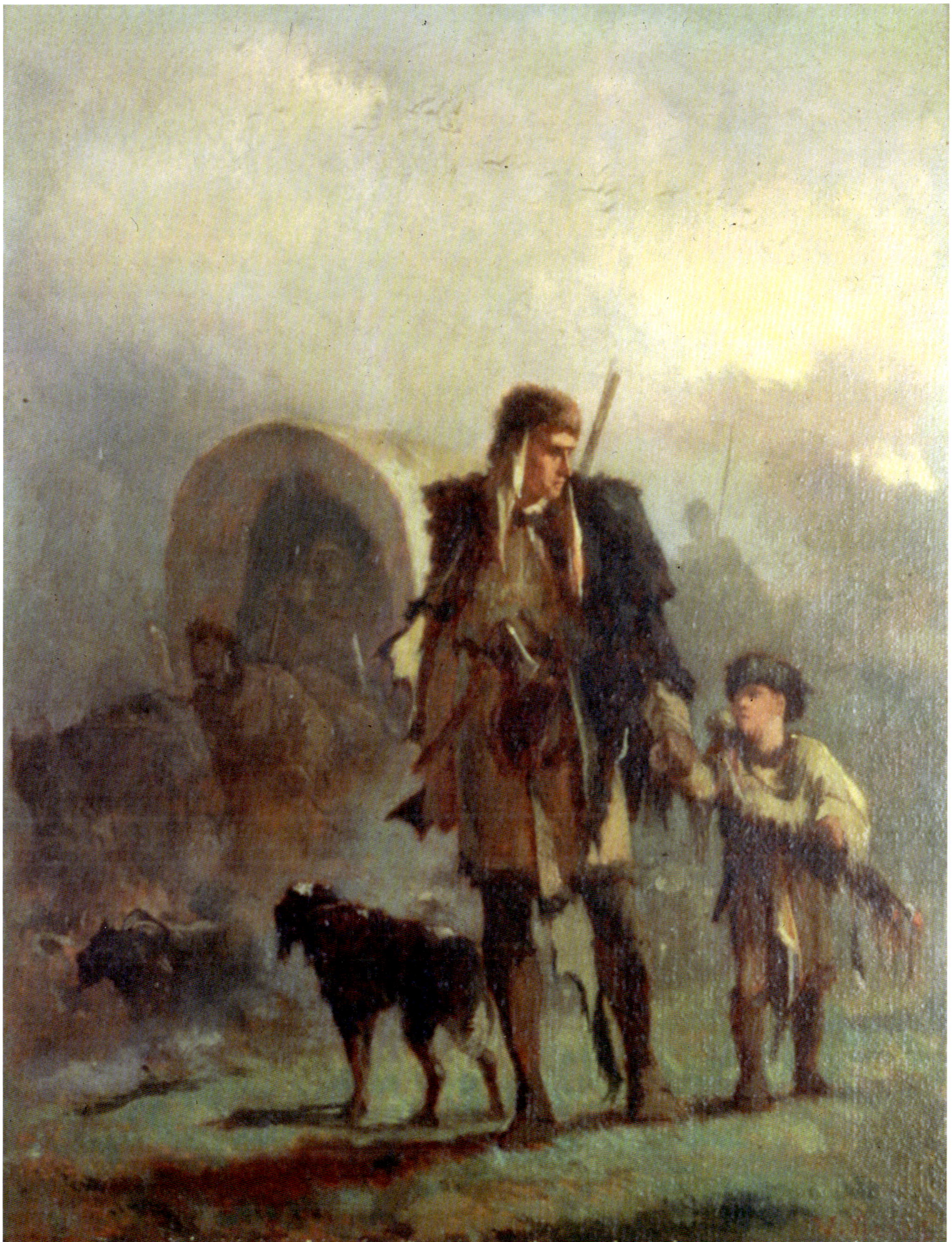

FIGURE 63. Victor Nehlig (1830–1909), detail from *Scenes from the Life of Daniel Boone (1734–1820)*, ca. 1870, oil on canvas, 31 × 66″, The Filson Historical Society, 1941.6.

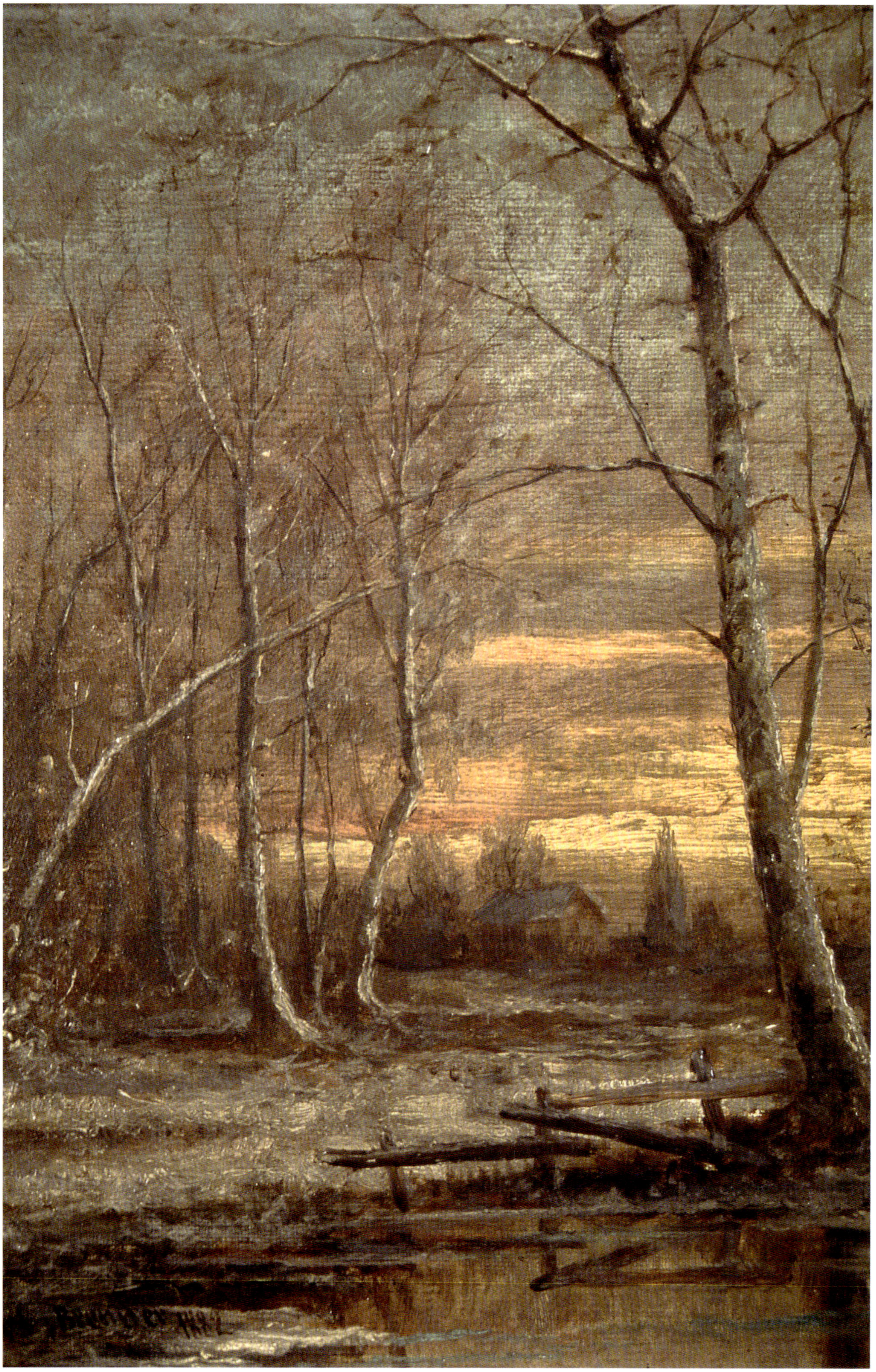

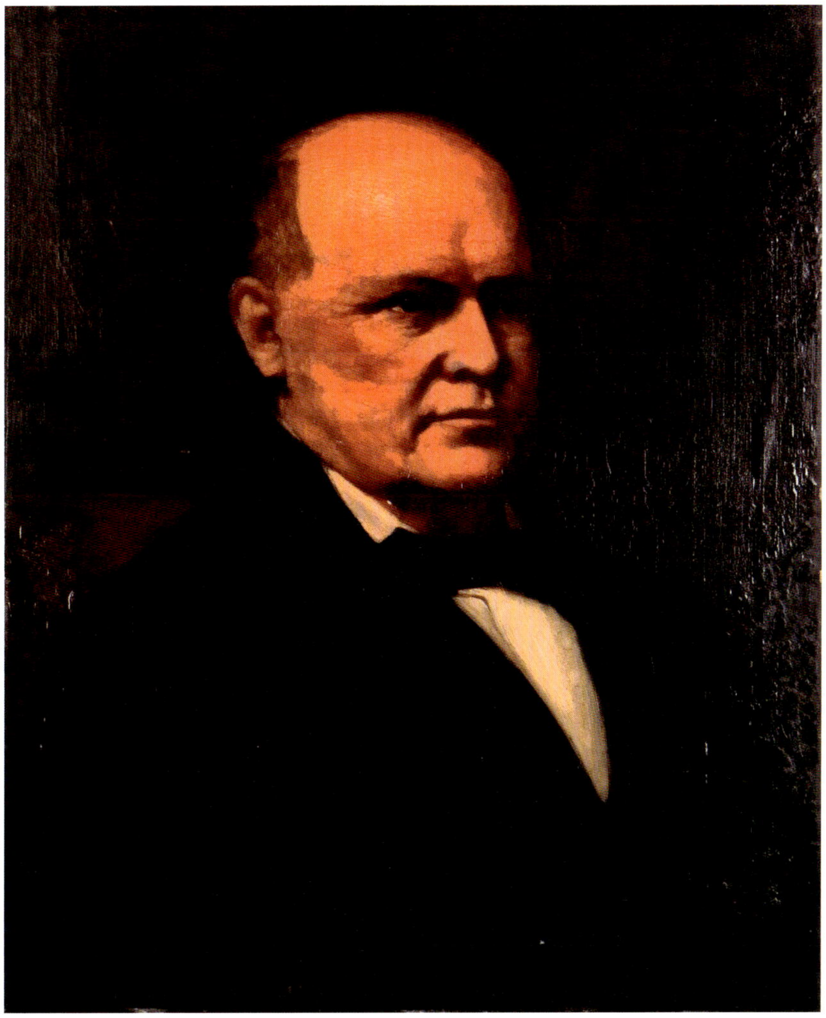

FIGURE 64 *(facing page)*. Carl Christian Brenner (1838–1888), *Landscape, Winter Scene,* 1882, oil on canvas, 11½ × 9¼″, The Filson Historical Society, 1975.24.1.

FIGURE 65. John Mulvany (1844–1906), *Dr. Stuart Robinson* (1814–1881), ca. 1874, oil on canvas, 44 × 41″, The Filson Historical Society, 1993.35.5.

Stuart Robinson, who was educated at the Princeton Seminary, was one of the leading lights of the Presbyterian Church in the South during his lengthy pastorate. His attitude that church and state should be decidedly separate, but that slavery had biblical justification, put him in the mainstream of Kentucky centrism. After sitting out the war in exile, leading an expatriate congregation in Toronto, he returned to Louisville. He was a founder of the Southern Presbyterian Church, which he served as moderator in 1869. This portrait may have been commissioned for the old Louisville Free Public Library, which housed a pantheon of local notables in the late nineteenth century; it was almost certainly painted during Mulvany's residency in the same building.

Daniel Boone, owned by Menefee, occurred (Fig. 63). Menefee, on first seeing this work, reportedly exclaimed to the artist, "You enchant me!"[14]

Inspired by the successful example of the Philadelphia Centennial Exhibition of 1876, the 1877 showing of art at the fairground structure built for this purpose at the corner of Chestnut and Fourth Streets was better organized and had a greater emphasis on American art. The Louisville exposition's Committee on Fine Arts included the collector Richard Jouett Menefee, mentioned earlier, and the antiquarian Reuben Thomas Durrett. Opening notes to the catalog indicate that several of the works on display "obtained medals at the Centennial last year."[15] Again, the Hudson River School was well represented, but so were the works of Kentucky artists, including Carl Christian Brenner (Fig. 64) and John B. Botto. Botto's work, darkly mysterious in the tonalist mood, was owned by George G. Moore of Louisville, then emerging as a noted collector. Moore's portrait, by John Mulvany, was shown together with Mulvany portraits of Judge Bland Ballard and Professor von Diederich of the Munich Academy. Mulvany, noted as resident in the Public Library Building, was an associate of Durrett. It was probably at this time that he painted the Presbyterian divine Dr. Stuart Robinson (Fig. 65). Nicola Marschall exhibited several portraits, including a pair he painted in Columbus, Mississippi, evidence of his ongoing relationship with the deep South, from which he came to Louisville. Lesser-known artists from Louisville included J. M. Eddy, H. G. Whipple, and Louisa Post.[16]

By 1883 the art galleries of the Southern Exposition, as it was now called, were lit by electrical light and organized by one of America's first museum professionals, Charles M. Kurtz (Fig. 66). Bennett Young was

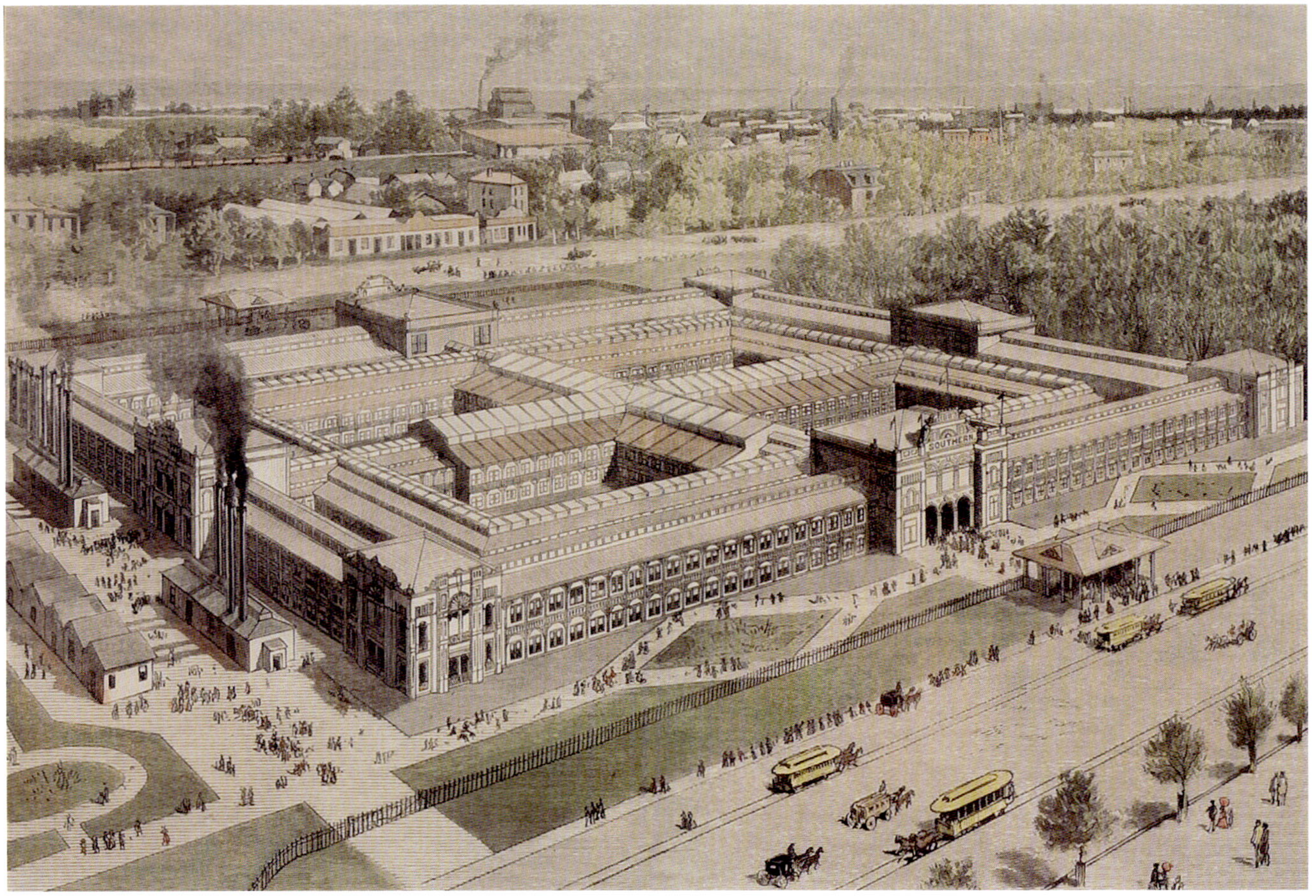

FIGURE 66. *The Southern Exposition,* 1883, lithograph, 21 × 28″, John P. Morton and Company, Louisville, The Filson Historical Society, 998PR6.1.

one of the directors of the event, and the art committee included Menefee and Henry Watterson, editor of the *Louisville Courier-Journal.* Young had asked Durrett to be a judge for several displays at the fairground and to chair the Pioneer Display Committee. The latter request was in recognition of Durrett's well-known interest in the history of Kentucky and an acknowledgment of the fine private library he had assembled on the topic. In a gracious nod to a fellow antiquarian's efforts, Durrett deferred the post to Richard Collins, who had revised and expanded *Historical Sketches of Kentucky,* first published by his father, Lewis Collins, in 1847.

Kurtz's opening notes for the catalog make clear the didactic intent of the affair: "It has been the aim of the Art Committee to secure, from the most prominent private galleries in the country, a collection of the best modern Works of Art obtainable—such a collection as may give the people of the South an opportunity to see, conveniently, under one roof, representations of the best works of the most distinguished artists of the time. The value of such a collection, even for a hundred days, from an educational standpoint alone, can not be overestimated. Here may be studied the methods of all the various schools, both foreign and American."[17]

Loans for the exhibition came from two sources, private collections and the American Art-Union; paintings from the latter were for sale, and Kurtz served as an agent for them. The American Art-Union, headed by Daniel Huntington and Thomas Waterman Wood, was then functioning as a cooperative through whose agencies "artists deal directly with their patrons, and can offer their pictures at prices considerably lower than they would be obliged to charge if art dealers' commissions had to be included."[18] Organizers claimed that this was "the first of the proposed series of special exhibitions" to make that happen. The 1883 Louisville exhibition, the most serious showing of art held in the Ohio River Valley since the end of the Civil War, occurred at a time when public art museums were being founded in important urban centers, notably in Cincinnati. One of the most celebrated works in the exhibition was not an American painting but a work by the British artist J. M. W. Turner for sale for $10,000. A Rembrandt lent by R. H. Wildberger of Memphis was, according to the exposition catalog, "supposed to be the original study" for *The Lesson in Anatomy* in the Royal Dutch Mauritshuis collection, painted by "one of the greatest portrait painters that ever lived," whose "marvelous richness of coloring" was "the admiration of the world."[19] This appreciation of Rembrandt was part of a revival of interest in seventeenth-century portraiture, strongly lit and richly brushed, which would soon captivate Frank Duveneck and other members of the Cincinnati School.

Standard Hudson River favorites were also present. One of Albert Bierstadt's monumental western landscape paintings was for sale at $25,000; it was noted that he had brought the highest prices of any living American artist. Works by Louis Comfort Tiffany, Gaines R. Donoho, and Eastman Johnson, and a Thomas Waterman Wood genre painting, *Let's Have a Smoke,* were shown as well. Concerning Johnson, the catalog notes that "among his earlier works were many representations of quaint domestic and Negro life, among which none is better known that his 'Old Kentucky Home' which has been lithographed, engraved, and 'chromoed' again and again."[20] As noted earlier, the painting has far more complexity than mere quaintness; the tribute in the exhibition catalog says more about the Lost Cause mentality in late nineteenth-century Kentucky than it does about Johnson's work.

A substantial group of artists from the French Barbizon School—Jean-François Millet, Jean-Baptiste-Camille Corot, Charles-François Daubigny, and Narcisse Díaz de la Peña—were considered the most important painters of the time. The notes to the catalog praise their ability to "harmonize manner of treatment with the love of nature," a comforting critical criterion for Kentuckians Carl Christian Brenner, Clarence Boyd, John B. Botto, and Robert Burns Wilson, who were then developing their skills as American painters in the Barbizon mood.[21] Nicola Marschall's postwar painting of former vice president John C. Breckinridge

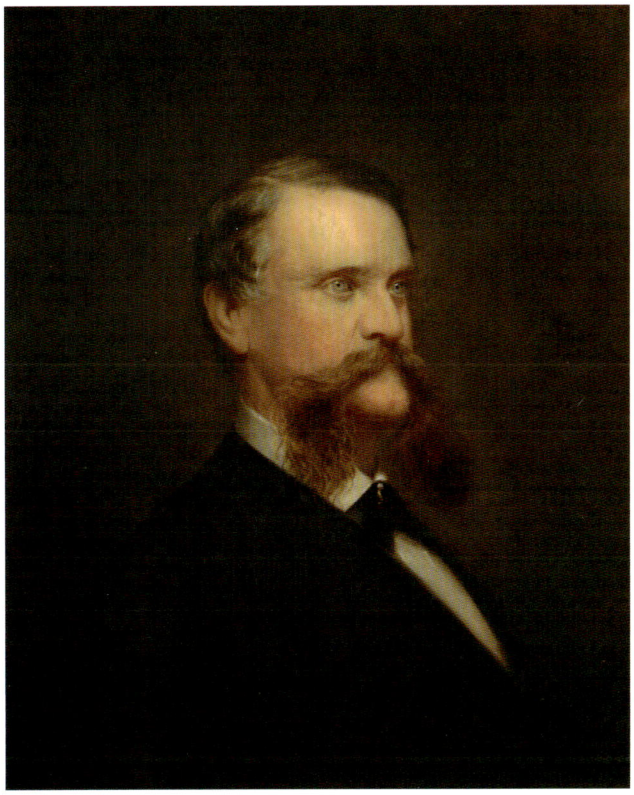

FIGURE 67. Nicola Marschall (1829–1917), *John Cabell Breckinridge* (1821–1875), 1881, oil on canvas, 29½ × 24½", The Filson Historical Society, 1913.1.334.

Breckinridge stands with Henry Clay as among the more prominent Kentuckians to command the national stage. Like his comrade General Robert E. Lee, he was left fatherless at an early age but achieved a law degree from Princeton. He was a boy wonder in politics, gaining his first seat in the Kentucky House at the age of twenty-eight and rising to the vice presidency of the United States at the age of thirty-six. Though not a secessionist, he was the most popular Democrat in the South and a leading presidential contender in the election of 1860. He continued to serve in the U.S. Senate after secession began, hoping to preserve the Union, but walked out of the chamber on December 4, 1861, and straight into a Confederate uniform. One of the Confederacy's most successful generals, Breckinridge served as its last secretary of war; he managed to escape Federal imprisonment by fleeing to Cuba. Pardoned in 1868, he returned to Kentucky, resumed his law practice, and became a voice of moderation, opposed to Ku Klux Klan extremism. James C. Klotter, his most sympathetic biographer, has called him a "man of unlimited promise" who, "like so many of his generation, never recovered from the Civil War."

was first shown at the 1883 exposition (Fig. 67). James W. Bachelor of Louisville lent a portrait of Mrs. Mary E. Bachelor by Nina Gordon Bachelor, who, the exhibition catalog states, was "born in Frankfort, Kentucky, pupil at the Pennsylvania Academy of Fine Arts, Philadelphia. [She] went to Paris, 1882, and studied for a time with Hensley, afterward becoming a pupil of St. Pierre, in whose studio she is painting at present."[22] No subsequent record of her activity exists. The local collector George H. Moore was again generous, this time with the loan of works by John George Brown, a noted genre painter from New York, as well as works by Brenner and Botto. John E. Green lent a portrait by Thomas LeClear, who was also represented by his portrait of President Ulysses S. Grant. LeClear's patron, H. Victor Newcomb, was also a generous lender. The Newcomb home was available to the public by appointment and was one of the few places in the area where noted artworks could be viewed.

The seminal event of the exposition may have been the first public showing of portraits by Matthew Harris Jouett in Kentucky since the artist's death. His grandson, Richard Jouett Menefee, already noted as a collector, lent two works he had inherited from his mother, Sarah, Jouett's daughter. *Mother and Child* depicts Peggy Allen Jouett and one of her children. A miniature of Peggy's mother, Mrs. Allen, was, according to the catalog, "painted with a brush hastily made from duck feathers, about 1811, when Mr. Jouett was a law student."[23] Other Jouett works shown included a portrait of Mrs. Daniel Weisiger, which was owned by A. J. Alexander of Woodford County; and portraits of a lady and a Colonel Morrison, both lent by Mrs. Henry Clay Pindell. Encouraged by the enthusiastic reception given his grandfather's paintings, Menefee was prompted to begin compiling a list of known Jouett works.

After 1884 the annual exhibition adopted a certain formula, based on the relationship among Kurtz, the local Louisville committee, and the American Art Union. Kurtz stated in the catalog for 1884, "In the selection of paintings for the Art Gallery of the Southern Exposition this year, the Art Committee kept in mind that this was to be an American Exhibition . . . , representing the American artists at their best."[24] The exhibition also represented the domineering presence of New York galleries, who were finally making inroads with the American public in their efforts to encourage the collecting of American art. Works by celebrated American artists, living and dead, notably Charles Robert Leslie, George Cochran Lambdin, Thomas Hicks, Thomas Sully, Albert Bierstadt, William Trost Richards, William Bradford, Thomas Moran, G. P. A. Healy, and Eastman Johnson, were for sale. The catalog is illustrated with many "quaint scenes from bygone eras," genre works in the colonial revival spirit, including examples of Enoch Wood Perry, Joseph Seymour Guy, and Edward Lamson Henry. This spectrum of artists, and their rather conservative, revivalist orientation, suggests that these fairs increasingly became commercial venues for the sale of art from northeastern galleries rather than a site for more avant-garde artists.[25]

The requisite old masters were "catalogued in all cases with deference to the attributions of their owners." These included *The Peddler* by Jan Steen, which was owned by Dr. J. R. Leaming of New York. *Victory of St. Michael* by Francesco Solimena was owned by Menefee, the authenticity of which, the catalog asserted, "is beyond question." Jouett Menefee, as he was called, had bought the work in 1871 in Naples from the family of the painter. It was on this same trip that Menefee encountered G. P. A. Healy in Italy and recorded the portraitist's recollections of earlier Kentucky painters. Several artists who became well established in the deep South were included in the 1884 exhibition. Johannes Oertel, a fledgling American symbolist who specialized in murky swamps and Christian iconography, settled in as the resident mystic painter at the University of the South in Sewanee, Tennessee. Though listed as living in Louisville, George W. Morrison, a native of Baltimore and a still-life painter, would become associated with New Orleans. Catalog notes indicated that Morrison "enjoyed studying Joseph Bonaparte's collection of paintings at Bordentown, New Jersey, in 1844, and has been a student of Nature ever since that time."[26] Carl Brandt, who would subsequently become the founding director of the Telfair Academy in Savannah, was represented.

Kentucky was well represented by artists both

historic and contemporary. A Jouett portrait of Henry Clay was lent by Mrs. J. M. Reed of Louisville, and another of Mrs. Robert S. Todd was lent by Mrs. M. P. Logan of Louisville. Most significant, Menefee lent Jouett's self-portrait and an unfinished sketch for a portrait of a gentleman. Miss H. B. Audubon, John J. Audubon's granddaughter, who was a teacher in Louisville, lent *Mud Swallows, Marsh Wren,* and a portrait of the naturalist by Henry Inman, copied by Nicola Marschall. Oliver Frazer, misidentified as "Olim" and mistakenly said to be a pupil of Jouett, was represented by *The Artist's Family,* painted in 1848 and owned by Miss Bessy Frazer of Lexington. There was also a special showing of sculpture by Joel Tanner Hart.[27]

Contemporary Louisville artists included Harvey Joiner, who was said to have "had no art instruction; and has been painting for about ten years"; and August Carl, who had been born in Hochspeyer, Bavaria, in 1856 and studied in Munich under Karl von Piloty. Not only Brenner senior, but also his son, Carolus Brenner, was represented in this year, as were Clarence Boyd and John B. Botto. Boyd's work incorporated languid portraits of young women in landscape settings reminiscent of Harvey Joiner's more formulaic work. Samuel Woodson Price sent two genre paintings, although the catalog notes that he was "now blind from a wound received in battle." Nicola Marschall included a portrait of General Nathan Bedford Forrest done shortly after the war. Several Kentucky women artists were also represented. Miss Minnie Milton sent *A Portrait from Life,* which was praised as "a portrait of a child rather broadly painted, with good drawing and characteristic expression." Other women painters included Eva B. Smith, Mattie Kirby, Sophie Gray, Lizzie Boyce, and Patty Thum, this being Thum's initial showing. Benoni Irwin, a native of Canada, was drawn to Louisville by the potential for commissions created by these fairs. In the 1884 exposition he showed a portrait of Albert Fink (Fig. 68) and a genre painting, *Lobster Boiling at New Bedford, Mass.* He also exhibited a portrait of the celebrated photographer of motion, Eadweard Muybridge.[28]

Though the exhibitions of 1885 and 1886 were well displayed and well organized, they reflected the commercial interests in the relationship between Charles Kurtz and the American Art Union. Clearly these exhibitions had moved beyond the calling to inform the southern public and to bring lesser-known collections and artists to a broader attention. Still, the selection of the paintings was well intended. "The paintings shown in this Exhibition," stated Kurtz in the 1885 catalog, "all the work of American artists . . . , comprise the pictures contributed to the first Prize Fund Exhibition of The American Art Association, held in New York." Prize money, to be awarded to four painters at $2,500 each, was raised from interested collectors in New York, Boston, Louisville, and St. Louis. Louisville contributors included Carl Christian Brenner, Richard Jouett Menefee, George H. Moore, and John B. Castleman. Henry Mosler's *The Last Sacraments* was one of the winners and was given to the Louisville Polytechnic Society.[29] Most of the artists shown were New York residents. Artists with Ohio River Valley connections included Brenner, Mosler, William Merritt Chase, Benoni Irwin, Patty Thum, and John Henry Twachtman.

In 1886 the Southern Exposition could claim "thirteen acres under roof," all of it lighted by "a system of arc and incandescent electric lights generated in seventeen dynamo machines," engines that "constitute the largest electric light single plant in the world." It was claimed that the Southern Exposition brought "within the area of its boundaries more electricity than has ever been generated and expended on any equal space in the world."[30] The art gallery was also "constructed within the main building," on the recommendation of several visiting artists, "to bring it closer to the other main attractions, with light supplied by skylights and side lights let into the walls above the hanging cornice." The catalog goes on to brag that the 1886 exhibition, "valued at over one-third of a million dollars," was the "best and most attractive collection of paintings to be found in this country." But although it had again been organized by Charles M. Kurtz, something had gone wrong. The exhibition was to have featured works from the second Prize Fund Exhibition of New York, but "owing to a breach of faith upon the part of the American Art Association . . . the Southern Exposition terminated its

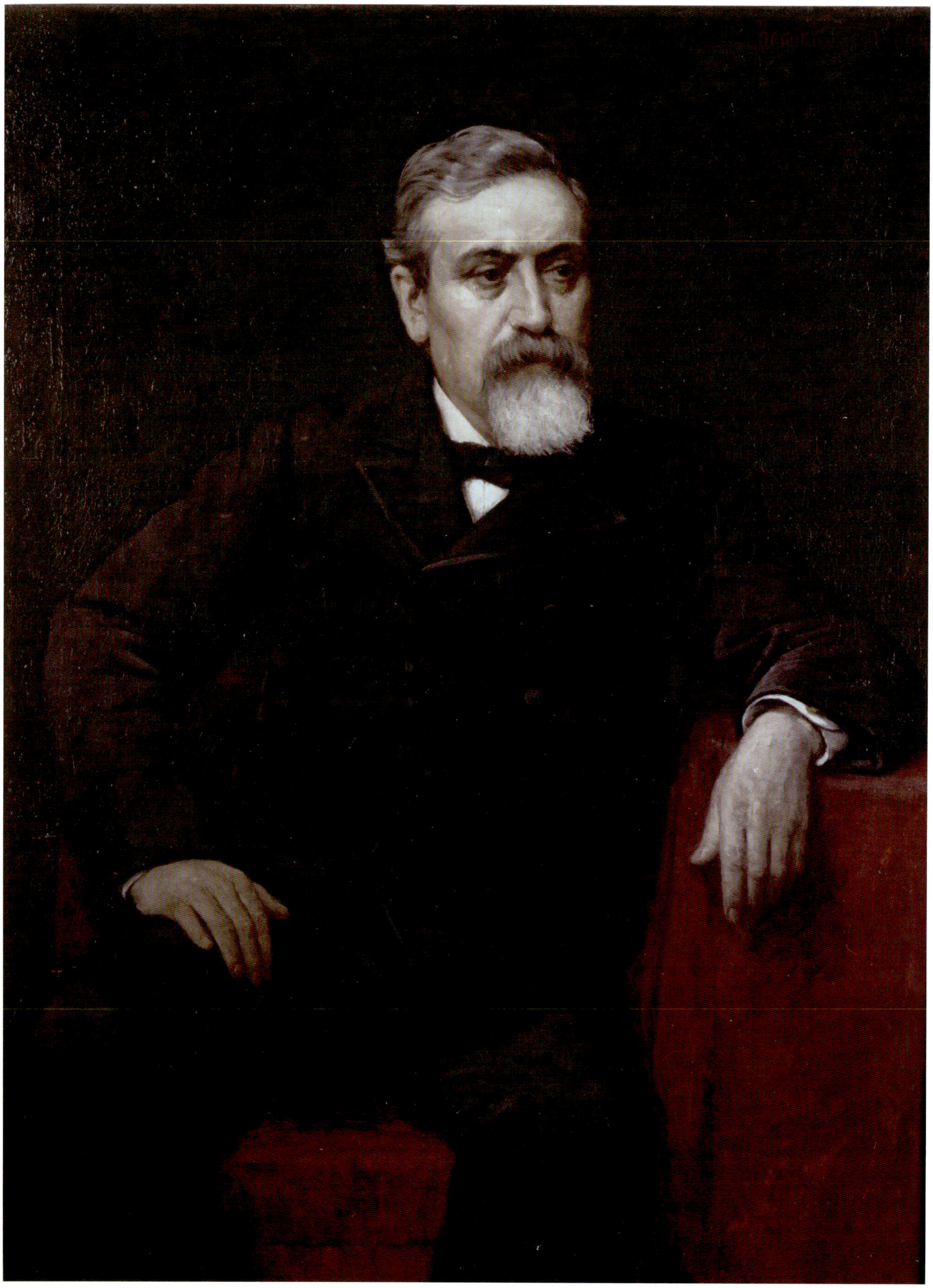

FIGURE 68 *(facing)*. Benoni Irwin (1840–1896), *Albert Fink* (1827–1897), 1884, oil on canvas, 47½ × 35½", The Filson Historical Society, 1959.16.

Born in Germany and trained as a civil engineer, Albert Fink immigrated to America in 1849, settling in Baltimore, where he worked for the B&O Railroad. His brilliant design for bridge trusses attracted the attention of the Louisville & Nashville (L&N) Railroad, which recruited him to expand their lines. During the Civil War it was his job to keep the L&N running, despite frequent attacks on the tracks. Fink also designed and constructed the first bridge across the Ohio to connect Louisville and Clarksville, Indiana, which opened in 1870. After a successful stint as L&N vice president, he undertook a series of executive positions for American rail line consortiums before retiring to Louisville in 1889.

negotiations in that quarter and exerted itself to obtain a collection of pictures which would even better satisfy the demands of a class of Exposition visitors which has enjoyed . . . the best collection of paintings publicly shown in America during that year."[31]

So, with the help of the National Academy of Design and the Buffalo Fine Arts Academy, 400 paintings, European and American, with a focus on grand-manner history painting, were assembled. Of note was *The French Revolution of 1848* by Felix Philippoteaux, ten feet high and twenty feet long. Robert Koehler's topical *The Strike* "shows a crowd of excited workingmen gathered in front of the residence of a wealthy iron-works owners. The story of the strike is well told in the unsympathetic face of the owner, the half-starved wife and children." There were also several monumental landscapes by Albert Bierstadt, as well as works by Thomas Moran and Jasper Cropsey. Thomas Eakins, dismissed from the Pennsylvania Academy for holding life classes, exhibited his "much-criticized but unmistakably powerful" *Ecce Homo,* the dead Christ on the cross. A small group of Kentuckians, including Brenner, Botto, and Thum, rounded out this important chapter in the history of art exhibitions in the region—exhibitions that attracted new artists, created an interest in artists from the past, and contributed to the eventual founding of the J. B. Speed Memorial Art Museum.[32]

Durrett's antiquarian interests result in the Filson Club

Reuben Thomas Durrett was born in Henry County, Kentucky. Well educated, he attended Georgetown College before graduating from Brown University in 1849. Returning to Kentucky, he took a law degree at the University of Louisville and set up a law practice in that city, which he continued for thirty years. After buying an interest in the *Louisville Daily Courier* in 1857, he served as an editor for two years. During the Civil War he was briefly interned for his well-known Southern sympathies before being transferred to Fort Lafayette, Indiana. In the aftermath of the war, many writers and amateur scholars explored Kentucky's frontier past—a past that looked much more comforting and energetic than the disconnected spirit of the postwar years. A child of his times, Durrett "grew to manhood," wrote the historian Thomas D. Clark, "in an era when the old pioneers had either just passed on or were in their closing years."[33] Durrett's interest in books seems to have come about in the years before the war; later he became one of the founders of the Louisville Free Library in 1870.

Durrett seems to have been, among his contemporaries, the one who was most concerned about the lamentable lack of a public interest in the preservation of historic materials. "Conflicting interests," he wrote in 1901, "have always been a curse to Kentucky in the march of public enterprises. We are behind nearly all of the other states in our literary means and I fear we shall continue so for years to come."[34] To address that concern Durrett invited ten friends from the antiquarian community, many of them lawyers like himself, to his home on Chestnut Street on May 15, 1884, the centennial of the publication of John Filson's *The Discovery, Settlement, and Present State of Kentucke.* At that meeting he proposed they band together as the Filson Club. The "purpose of the new organization was stated to be the collection and preservation of historical manuscripts, books, and other materials related to the old frontier, and to prepare and publish papers read at the meetings."[35] Although the initial group would expand, it continued to meet in Durrett's home until the year before his death in 1913.

A life of Filson by Durrett was the Filson Club's first publication, printed by the John P. Morton Company in 1884. The club's papers were printed in a quarto format on heavy, antique-finish white paper with large margins for notes. Ironically, subsequent historians have often faulted Durrett for the lack of credible documentation in his writings and his passion for writing colorful accounts rather than objective history. He greatly embellished the saga of Sieur de la Salle's exploration of the Ohio River, for example, including an account of la Salle's discovery of the falls of the Ohio, the future site of Louisville. It was Durrett who perpetuated the story that la Salle's hatchet was found embedded in the root system of an ancient sycamore tree, thus proving his presence in the area around 1670. The story has few takers today. Although the distinguished Kentucky historian Thomas D. Clark pointed out that Kentucky lacked a single professor of state history in Durrett's day, Clark's admiration for Durrett's efforts was tempered with objective academic criticism. "Colonel Durrett's *Centenary of Kentucky* (1892)," wrote Clark, "is too nebulous to be taken seriously. It is an astonishing fact that the avid collector of the fine library of early western Americana was so uncritical in his writings. He undoubtedly was acquainted with the contents of most of his collection, yet he seems to have made so little critical use of his knowledge or his sources. No one can say positively how many legends and popular anachronisms which plague modern historians seem to be attributable to Colonel Durrett."[36]

Many of Durrett's fellow Filsonians believed that the reputations of Confederate military figures, men they deemed gallant, could be salvaged from the ruin of war and provide exemplars of a new southern code of honor like the one in which the old South had taken pride. According to the historian Bertram Wyatt-Brown, "the traditional credo" of honor "lasted longer and in more pristine form in the slaveholding section than it did elsewhere in America. We cannot understand the roles assigned women in America, for instance, without reference to honor. Nor can we grasp the persistence of racism in American life generally without recognizing its intimate relationship to the code."[37]

This "traditional credo" was an idealistic social construct appropriated by the reactionary Bourbon Democrats in an effort to keep civil rights for African-Americans at bay. As Lowell Harrison and James Klotter note, many Kentuckians of Durrett's era could not "conceive of accepting the idea that blacks were their equals." They lived in a "world built on that set of racial values . . . under attack and in danger of being overturned, as political and social equality became the sought-after goal. In large part, white Kentuckians refused to replace the scheme of dominant and subordinate statuses with a system of equality."[38] Even Henry Watterson's admirable efforts to bridge "the bloody chasm" and create harmony between a New South and the Old Union did not prevent the violence, lawlessness, and episodes of lynching that haunted the history of the Commonwealth.[39]

Though Durrett remained an active author and leader of the Filson Club, his attention to his collection declined, as did his health, after 1901. He began to lament that his collection was no longer in good order, the result of rummagings in his extensive materials by himself and other gentlemen historians, including Theodore Roosevelt. After 1908 rumors began to circulate that Durrett might donate the materials to the public if the Commonwealth of Kentucky would build a fireproof building to house them. At the same time interest in the collection arose in Illinois. Durrett was well aware that there was not a single library in Kentucky capable of housing, cataloging, and preserving his collection.

Between 1908 and 1913 Reuben Durrett suffered several strokes, which resulted in his becoming increasingly isolated at his Chestnut Street home. In April 1913 Walter Lichtenstein, representing the University of Chicago, arranged to buy the entire collection, which was large enough as to fill several railway boxcars, for $22,500. Otto Rothert, who would be a leading figure in the Filson Club during the 1920s, felt that "Durrett sold his library because he feared that it might be dissipated and find its way into private hands" and that "he feared that any public library controlled by a city government might be at some time dominated by unscrupulous politicians."[40]

Contemporary descriptions of Durrett's holdings

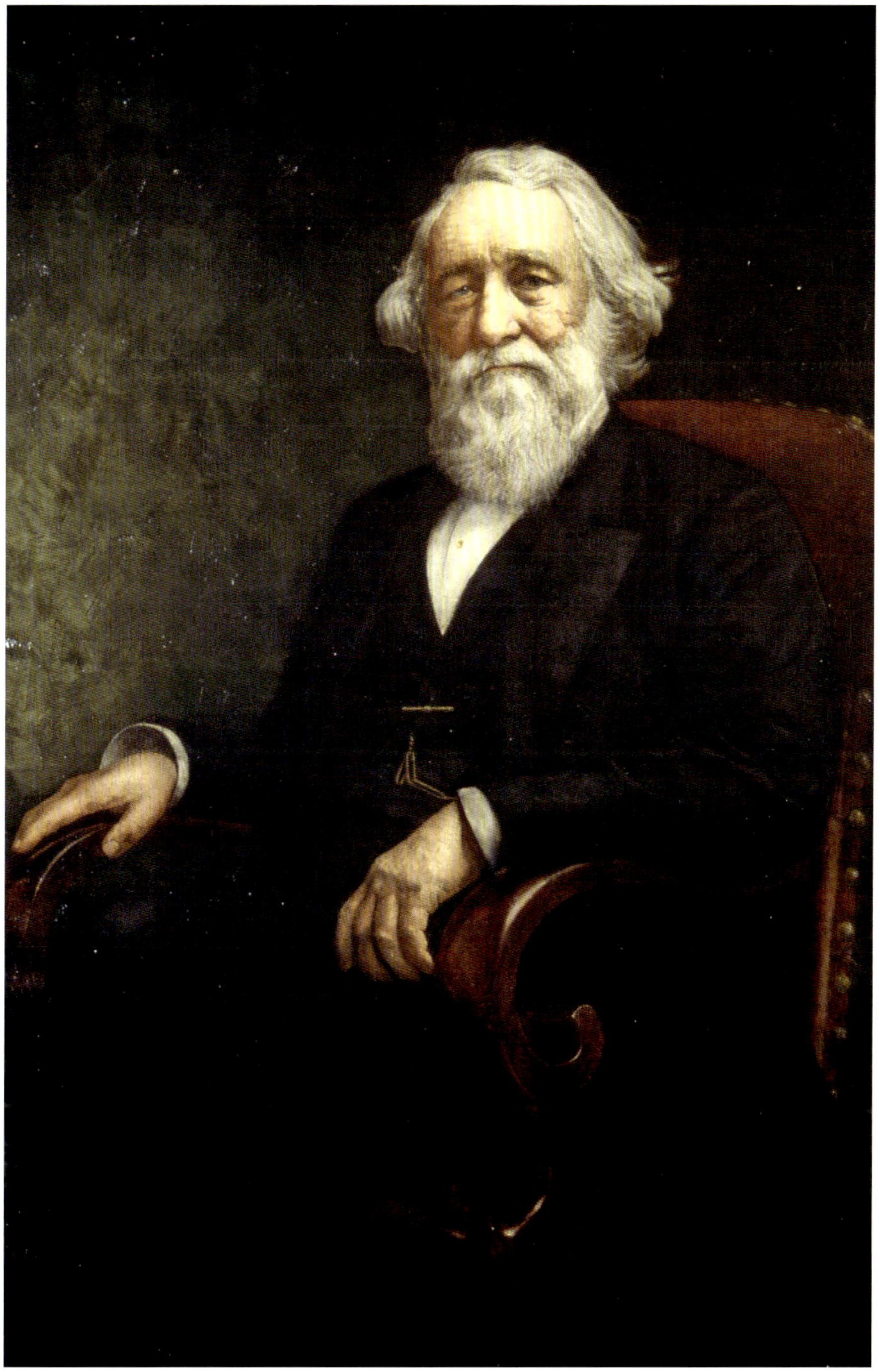

FIGURE 69. Aurelius Revenaugh (1840–1908), *Reuben Durrett* (1824–1913), n.d., oil on canvas, 52¾ × 37¾", The Filson Historical Society, 1909.1.

On May 16, 1909, the *Louisville Courier-Journal* reported that the silver anniversary of the Filson Club was "celebrated and Col. Durrett presented with a life-size portrait of himself, painted by his old departed friend, A. O. Revenaugh, whose work was a labor of love." The portrait was in the artist's studio at the time of his death, as he "had not expected a sale for this work of his brush. He considered it an honor and a privilege to have on the walls of his studio the likeness of the president of the Filson Club, the man who had done so much for Kentucky and for Kentucky history."

note that he owned portraits of George Rogers Clark and George Washington, although no specific works are mentioned. In the aftermath of the portrait enthusiasm generated by the reception of Matthew Harris Jouett at the Columbian Exposition in Chicago in 1893, Durrett gave several commissions to Rudolph Boccasini, Nicola Marschall, and Aurelius Revenaugh to copy historical prints or portraits for illustrative purposes. The first original work acquired by the Filson in 1892 was the portrait of General James Wilkinson by John Wesley Jarvis, from the estate of Richard Collins. From 1913 until the Filson acquired a permanent home on Breckinridge Street in 1928 there was a steady accumulation of works, largely by late nineteenth- and early twentieth-century portraitists. After 1928, sustained by prestige, visibility, and permanency, the Filson Club became one of the principal repositories of historic Kentucky portraiture (Fig. 69).

R. J. Menefee dies, Matthew Harris Jouett is re-interred, and the Jouett revival is created

In May 1899 Charles Henry Hart published an article entitled "Kentucky's Master-Painter Matthew Harris Jouett, 1788–1827" in *Harper's Magazine.* Hart was a frequent contributor to the popular journal, whose subscribers took particular interest in the antiquarian pursuits of the colonial revival sparked by the Philadelphia Centennial of 1876. Hart was also a leading expert on historical American portraiture and had published in several scholarly journals, including that of the American Historical Association. In undertaking Jouett, Hart departed from his usual subject matter—Gilbert Stuart and the Philadelphia portraitists—to generate interest in a painter from the South whose work was all but forgotten outside the Bluegrass. Jouett had been mentioned in William Dunlap's *History of the Rise and Progress of the Arts of Design in the United States* when it was published in 1834. Dunlap cited a letter from Henry Clay Jr., who felt that Jouett was "a man of taste and possessed a vein of humor copious and rich but unaffected and innocent in its tendency, which made him a charming companion, and which will perhaps greatly add to the interest of his biography."[41] As ever, Jouett's ability as a rambling raconteur was cited and admired.

As noted earlier, Jouett's works had returned to the local scene in the Southern Exposition years. At that time his grandson, the collector and antiquarian Richard Jouett Menefee, had begun an ambitious checklist of the artist's work. Menefee had Jouett's body exhumed from his grave in Fayette County and re-interred in Louisville's Cave Hill Cemetery, where he would join him in 1893. After Menefee's death, his widow, Sarah, donated Jouett portraits to the Metropolitan Museum (*John Grimes* in 1895) and to the Pennsylvania Academy of Fine Art (*Peter Grayson* in 1897) to further fulfill her husband's dedication to his grandfather. Jouett had yet to attract national attention, however, and his work was not included in the Philadelphia Centennial Exhibition of historical American art. Hart found it "passing strange" that the Centennial Exhibition "should have failed to bring to the front a knowledge of Jouett's art, and that it should have been left for its successor at Chicago" to do so. As curator of a portrait exhibition for the Chicago Columbian Exposition in 1893, Hart was in a position to correct the wrong, and did so. "The late lamented Jouett Menefee, Esq., of Louisville" offered the same portrait of John Grimes that had been exhibited in the Southern Exposition. Hart immediately accepted it, "without being seen, and the blind judgment thus exercised has been amply vindicated" (Fig. 70).[42] Hart was also given access to the documents that Menefee had gathered, including the original manuscript recounting Jouett's experience with Gilbert Stuart in Boston.

Marveling that Jouett, "an artist of the West," could have developed at all, Hart speculated that the "conditions of soil and service would seem to leave neither the opportunity nor possibility for the development of an art instinct." Hart's comments recall the old belief in the virtues of being self-taught. That native genius that Fanny Trollope so deeply distrusted Hart applauded, finding in Jouett's talent "evidence that genius will break all bounds." Echoing Samuel Woodson Price, he also thought the artist very fortunate not to have had "foreign influence and instruction."[43]

Hart generously allowed that "Stuart's influence over Jouett seems to have had only the effect of giving added versatility to his methods of work"; he found Jouett's portraits to be "so much like Stuart's that it is difficult to believe that they are the production by any other hand." This is hardly true. Hart's antiquarian observation is rife with the ponderous tones of high Victorian idealism. Jouett's appeal derives from his understanding of Stuart's technique and attitude toward the sitter, an understanding that he passed along to several antebellum Kentucky portraitists who practiced his style. As Hart phrased it, Jouett, following Stuart's instructions, gave to each sitter "the proper quality of its own time. Helplessness, purity, vitality, strength, and decadence were delineated by him with equal power and truth."[44]

Hart's 1899 article was followed by one he wrote for *Harper's* a year later, "Jouett's Kentucky Children." In this second piece, Hart carefully analyzes Jouett's portraits of children, focusing on composition and color,

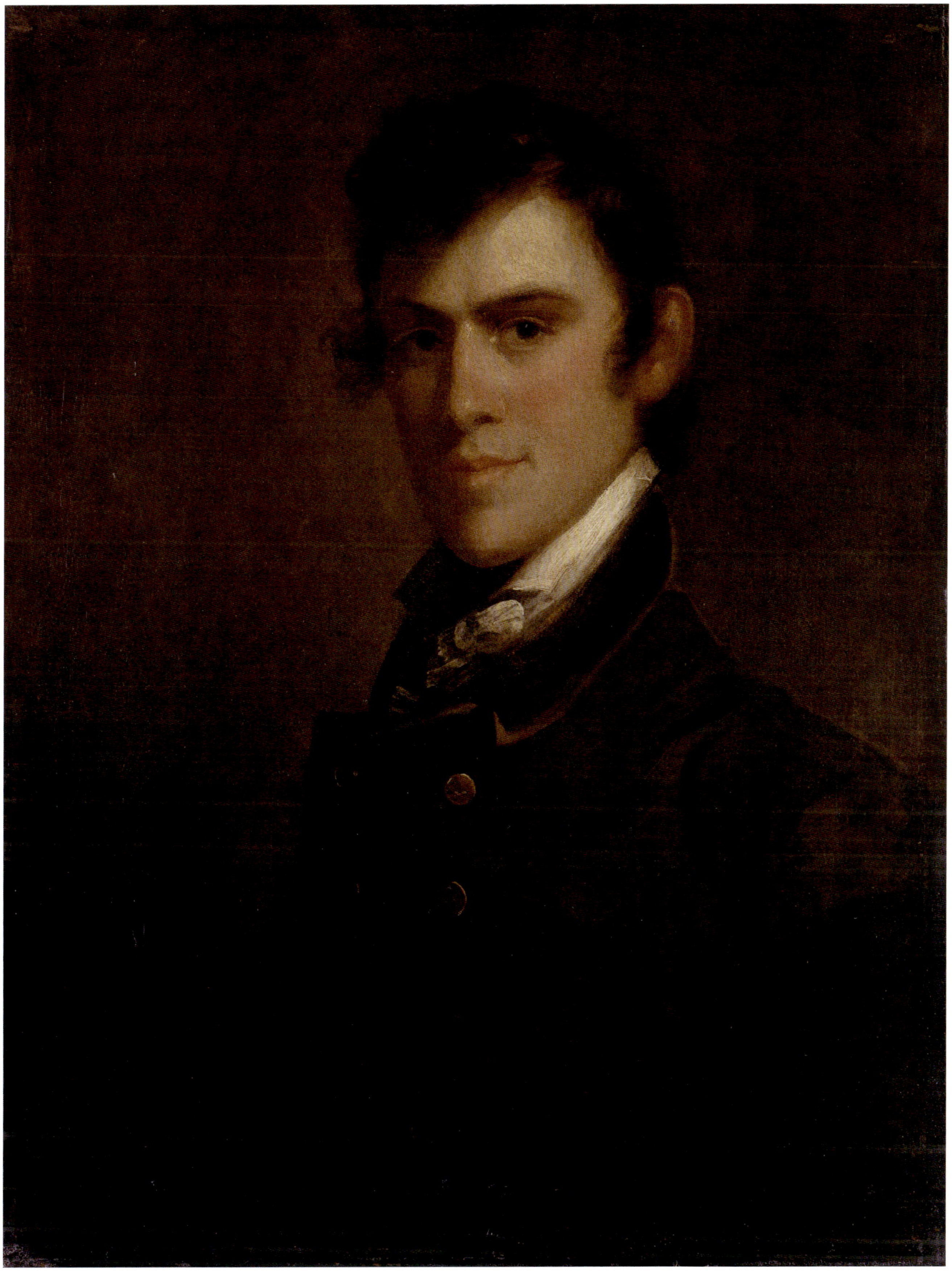

FIGURE 70. Matthew Harris Jouett (1788–1827), *John Grimes* (1799–1837), ca. 1824, oil on canvas, 28¼ × 21¾″, Metropolitan Museum of Art, 95.23.

Following her husband's death, Mrs. Richard Jouett Menefee gave this portrait to the Metropolitan Museum as a tribute to his successful efforts to restore his grandfather's reputation as Kentucky's premier portrait painter.

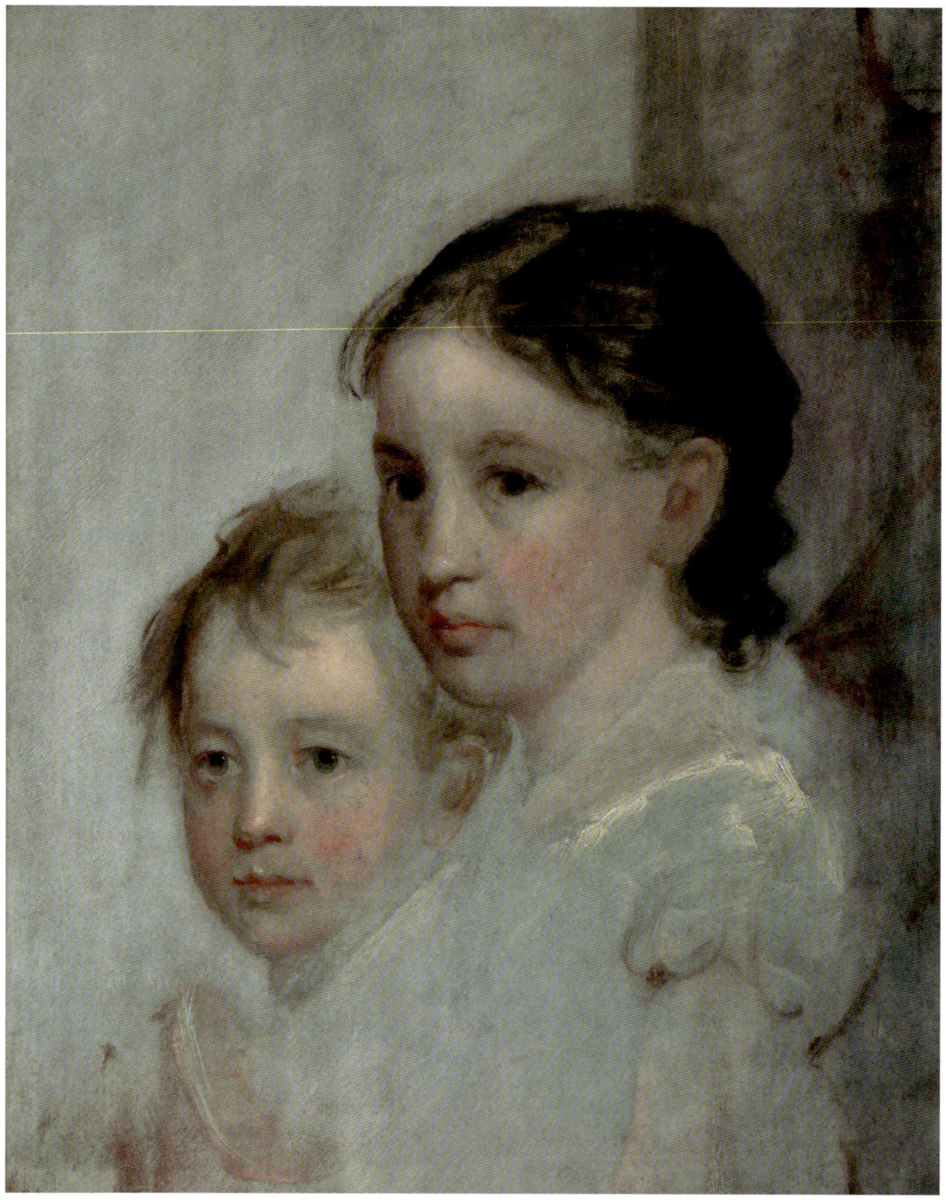

FIGURE 71. Matthew Harris Jouett (1788–1827), *Alexander John Mitchell Jr. and Martha Bell Mitchell,* oil on canvas, 20⅝ × 17″, collection of Michael and Louise Slaven, Louisville, Kentucky.

These children are the nephew and niece of Jouett's wife, Margaret Allen Jouett. Martha Bell Mitchell became the wife of the painter Oliver Frazer.

and makes interesting comparisons to the paintings of Anthony Van Dyke and Baron Greuze (Fig. 71). "Jouett did not paint children as diminutive men and women, or as young bodies with old heads, as most painters have done," he wrote. Instead, the old master of the Bluegrass pursued a "close observation and facility of expression."[45]

There may have been a hidden agenda in Hart's gushing admiration for genius rediscovered, for he was a discreet private dealer in prints and portraiture, and his writings supported a market he helped create. His interest also occurred in an era when the classic English portraits of Gainsborough, Reynolds, Romney, and others were beginning to attract the attention of robber-baron collectors, eager for the polish of age. Still, Hart deserves credit for the Jouett revival, and for bringing the portraiture of Kentucky to larger national attention. But there was a darker side to Jouett's renascence. After 1893 Jouett became so renowned among Kentuckians that many portrait owners assumed their works were by the master because the subjects appeared so notable, at least to them. This popularity accounts for the large number of works credited to Jouett and subsequently recorded as such by E. A. Jonas in his 1938 biography of Jouett and by Elizabeth Martin in her 1939 "complete catalog," both published by the Speed Art Museum. The two volumes perpetuated misattributions that confound the viewing public to this day.

Samuel Woodson Price recalls "old masters of the Bluegrass"

With the high Victorian flourish that characterizes his writings, Durrett introduced Samuel Woodson Price's *Old Masters of the Bluegrass* as the seventeenth publication of the Filson Club in 1902. Price had been blind since 1881 as a result of ill health and war wounds. Durrett admired him for "groping his way through eternal darkness to rescue his fellow-artists from oblivion." The artists Price recalled were the painters Matthew Harris Jouett, Joseph Henry Bush, John Grimes, Oliver Frazer, and Louis Morgan and the sculptor Joel Tanner Hart. Durrett announced that the "six biographic sketches which make up the book now under consideration were dictated by" Price and the "authorities used read to him without his seeing a word of either."[46] The only notes to the volume pinpoint the date when the individual biographies were given before the Filson Club. From that evidence we can conclude that the writings were dictated by Price between Richard Jouett Menefee's death in 1893 and the first reading in 1897 (Fig. 72).

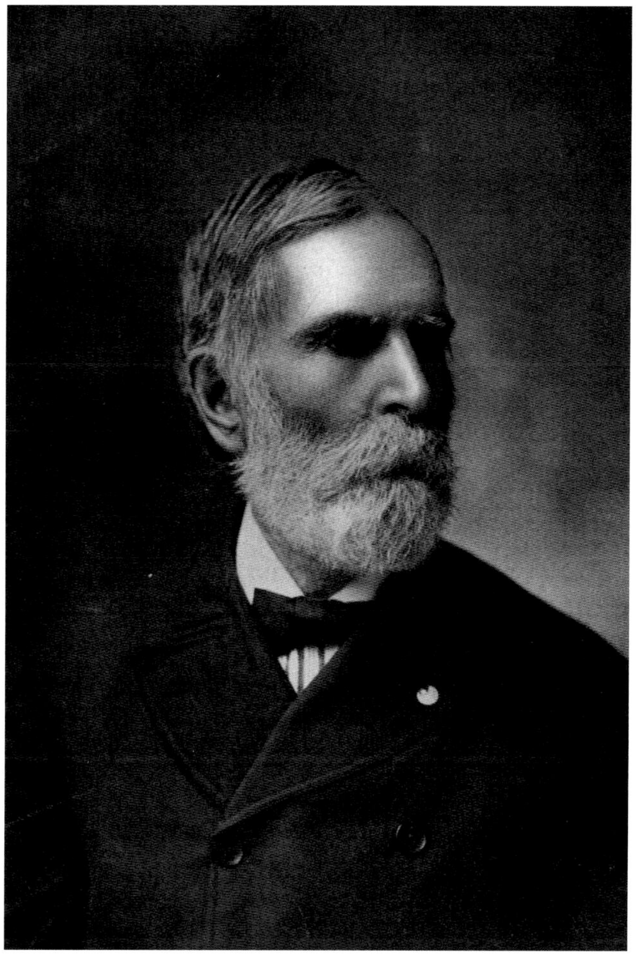

FIGURE 72. Samuel Woodson Price (1828–1918), from *Old Masters of the Bluegrass* (Louisville, Ky.: J. P. Morton and Co., 1902), frontispiece.

Price's book was the first serious attempt to address the issue of historical portraiture in Kentucky almost a century after its beginnings, and the information contained in the volume provided the foundation for much subsequent work. It is a combination of pious anecdotes and important information about actual portrait commissions and sittings, and its greatest value may be in Price's personal recollections of Bush, Frazer, Morgan, and Hart, whom he knew quite well. Regrettably, he was born after Jouett's death and was too young to have known Grimes. From the outset Price offers knowledge of portraiture in Kentucky that cannot be found elsewhere, although some of it was later disproved. It was Price who repeated the story that a William West came to Lexington in 1788 and that he was a brother to Edward West and uncle to young William Edward, born that same year. Research into the West family genealogy has discredited this by locating the entire generation of Edward West's family and their immediate predecessors.[47]

Information in Price's introduction, however, allows us to glimpse the efforts of some of Kentucky's earliest painters. Price makes a brief reference to Asa Park, who he says "attempted portraits," although "his best productions were fruit and flower pieces."[48] Though there are extant and well-regarded portraits, there is no evidence of Park's work as a still-life painter. Price also mentions the location of several portraits by George Beck, but the efforts of Edna Talbott Whitley and the Catalog of American Portraiture at the National Portrait Gallery have never located them.

Price's sketch of Jouett probably came from two primary sources, Menefee and Captain Alfred Pirtle. Menefee wrote a great many letters to an extended circle of family and friends seeking information for a catalogue raisonné of Jouett's works, which resulted in a list of 334 paintings attributed to him. Price could not have seen this list, but he would have had firsthand knowledge of its existence, and perhaps this was one of the documents read to him. He knew that Menefee "talked to those in the city and wrote to those outside who knew he owned paintings by Jouett for accurate information concerning others having such paintings." He also knew that Menefee's "main object was to write a monograph for The Filson Club . . . illustrated by steel engravings or half-tones of his principal works."[49] Menefee's complete list of works is printed at the end of Price's biographical sketch and subsequently became the source of several spurious attributions.

Price's second source for Jouett was a paper read before the Filson by Pirtle on Rear Admiral Edward Jouett, one of the painter's sons. While admitting that the "average reader cares but little for genealogy," Price includes an extended synopsis of Pirtle's findings on the Huguenot origins of the Jouett family and their arrival in Kentucky. With colonial revival enthusiasm for illustrious antecedents on the rise, Price connects the Jouett family to the French nobility, an "alliance with the blood royal of France."[50] The sketch concludes with the publication of several obituaries from the Lexington papers and a letter from G. P. A. Healy to Menefee dated October 12, 1878. Healy recalls having seen Menefee and his mother in Rome, where the Louisville collector was buying art. Healy writes that he first heard of Jouett during his student days in Paris with Oliver Frazer, who spoke "with pride and affection" of him. When Healy "saw the work of our gifted countryman . . . I fully understood . . . that we have great reason to feel proud of him."[51] As Menefee owned the portrait of John Grimes by Jouett, he is also the mostly likely source for Price's brief sketch of that artist. By publishing oral history, Price created the myth that Grimes was a penniless orphan who turned up in Lexington talented but in great need. In fact, Grimes was from a Dayton, Ohio, family; his elaborate will names many of them individually.[52]

Although Price never knew Jouett, Joseph Henry Bush was an acquaintance from Lexington and Louisville, where both had worked. From Bush he heard the legend that Louis-Philippe of France had stayed at the Bush family hotel in Frankfort and that the senior, German-born Bush had expelled the Duke of Orléans for his arrogance. Price is quite reliable in his account of Bush's itinerancy in the South, his residence at the Galt House Hotel in Louisville, and his financial acumen: "Unlike the majority of painters he had an eye to the value of money, and consequently judiciously invested his surplus, though not to his discomfort."[53]

Price arouses curiosity when he notes that Bush was "an indefatigable worker," whether "he painted directly from nature or from photographs." William Barrow Floyd, in his work on Bush, documents one example of Bush's copying from a daguerreotype, that of Cowles Green Meade.[54] Price recognized the opinion that although "the photograph is necessary to the accomplishment" of a portrait painted of a person deceased, it only "increases the desire of persons to have the faces of their loved ones perpetuated on canvas."[55] The only insight Price provides on the artist's life is related to his status as a bachelor throughout his life. "No artist was ever more wedded to his profession than was Bush. This may account, in a large measure, for his bachelorhood." He observed that Bush seemed to be fond of women, though "it is not positively known that he ever fell a victim to the gentler sex, though there was a rumor to the contrary." According to Price, Bush felt that marriage and commitment to a family retarded the growth of artists and that they were better off alone. That said, he does acknowledge Bush's abilities as a painter of children, especially his charming way of keeping them still during a sitting.[56]

Louis Morgan was also a personal acquaintance of Price. They often met in downtown Lexington, where both had studios. Morgan is sketched as a wildly passionate figure, a romantic in the mid-nineteenth-century style. Approaching Price one day with a handful of paintbrushes, he exclaimed, "Price, I hold in my hands instruments of immortal fame!"[57] It was Price who recounted Morgan's unfortunate infatuation with Letitia Dallam: her rejection of his suit led to his flight from Kentucky and his death "from a broken heart" at his brother's farm in Tennessee.[58]

Having studied, as a young man, in the studio of Oliver Frazer, with whom he remained in close contact throughout his life, Price was in a position to write in great detail about the life of that artist (Fig. 73). His

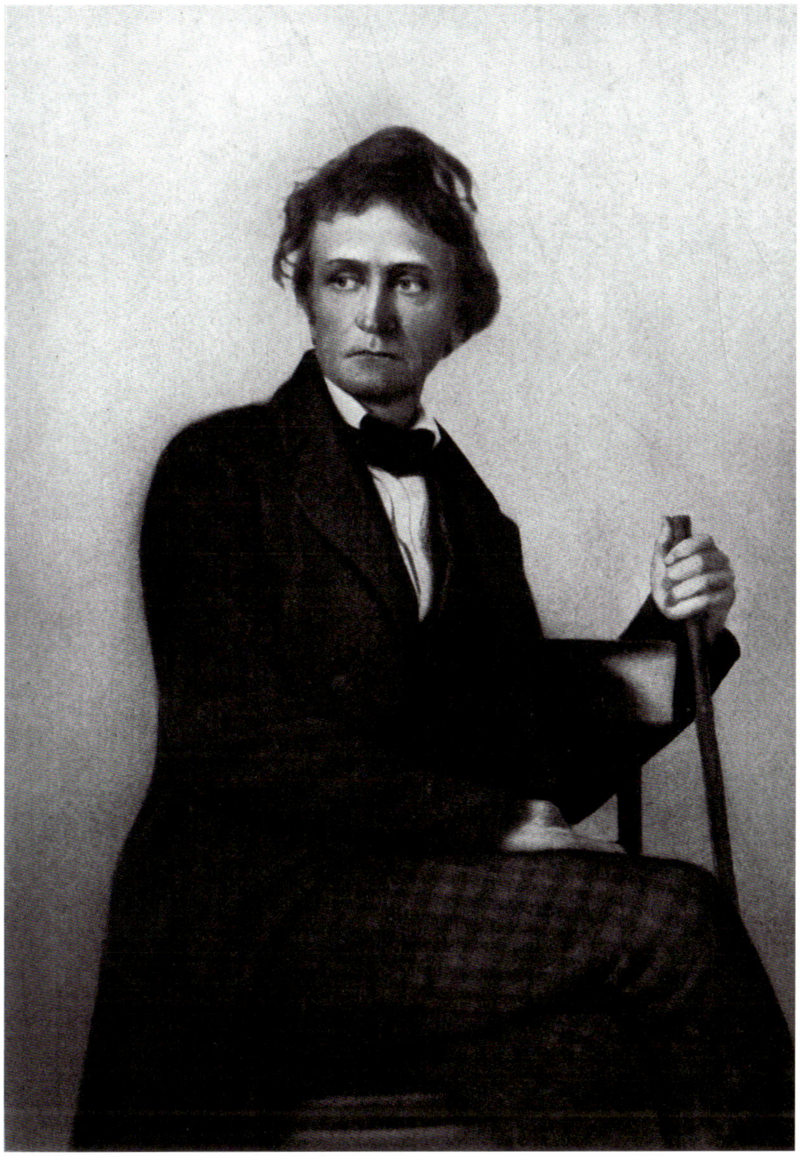

FIGURE 73. Oliver Frazer (1808–1864), from *Old Masters of the Bluegrass* (Louisville, Ky.: J. P. Morton and Co., 1902), 95.

sketch is full of anecdotes about Frazer's famous caustic sense of humor and his special friendship with G. P. A. Healy. These stories have the echo of the tall tales of the frontier days, featuring an artist larger than life who entranced all who came near him. Even Henry Clay "pronounced him one of the most entertaining persons he ever knew. When he sat to him for his portrait he was less restless than when being painted by any other artist."[59]

When *Old Masters of the Bluegrass* was published in 1902, it was the high tide of nostalgic writing in Kentucky, which William Ward has called "the genteel tradition." Several novelists, including James Lane Allen and John Fox Jr., whose novel *The Little Shepherd of Kingdom Come* was published the next year, sought to recall the "old Kentucky" of the antebellum period. They envisioned a "culture in which wealth, good breeding, quality and temper of mind, education, manners, and the cultivation of learning and the arts were of paramount importance."[60] It is that culture, and the artists painting portraits then, of which Price writes. His sketches imbue each of the artists he recalls with impressive native talent, great wit, bravado ability with brush and palette, and genius, which "to the art world . . . will be felt throughout all time."[61]

The aesthetics of the book, dictated by a blind man nearly seventy years of age, invite unfortunate comparisons with the more contemporary, realist, and naturalist strains to be seen in the art of Frank Duveneck in Cincinnati and the writings of Booth Tarkington. William Ward considers the spirit of the "genteel tradition" to be "too romantic, too idealistic, and the style . . . too heightened and too mannered" for modern tastes.[62] That may be, but the antiquarian and genealogical interests of this period spurred the recovery of art and artists now considered to be of interest on their own merits.

A Kentucky student of Frank Duveneck paints Louisville's idyllic poet, Madison Cawein

Frank Duveneck, who would become the most influential teacher of art in the history of the Ohio River Valley, was born in Covington, Kentucky. Although Duveneck was a Kentuckian, his life and art were shaped by the emigrant Catholic Germanic culture of his youth, a time when nearly 30 percent of the inhabitants of the Cincinnati area had origins in the Rhine Valley. There was a high demand for decorative painters in Cincinnati's Catholic community, the legacy of the floridly baroque churches of southern Germany. While young Duveneck was apprenticed to two locals, Johann Schmidt and Wilhelm Lamprecht, and working as an itinerant church painter, he learned of the art movement in Munich. Abandoning church painting, he traveled to Germany and sought the ateliers of William Leibl and Wilhelm von Diez, where he experienced the tremendous vitality of the art scene.

In a radical style shift, Duveneck abandoned the Germanic Ohio Biedermeier style derived from the Düsseldorf School, apparent in the works of James Henry Beard and Joseph Oriel Eaton, and pursued a highly secular realism. The Munich School, notes the art historian Julie Aronson, "favored realistic portrayals of unseemly characters with a rich, dark palette and paint-laden technique that referenced the baroque masters of the seventeenth century, particularly Franz Hals and Diego Velasquez."[63] Duveneck returned briefly to the Cincinnati area in late 1874 and taught for a year at the Mechanics' Institute. During that time he attracted a number of students who would be among the most famous painters of late nineteenth-century America, including Joseph Rodefer DeCamp, John Twachtman, Kenyon Cox, and Robert Frederick Blum. After a successful exhibition in Boston in 1875 he returned to Munich, taking a number of his students with him. They became known as the "Duveneck boys" and followed the artist when he moved on to Venice and Florence in the 1880s. It was in Florence that he proposed to Elizabeth Boott, whom he had met in Boston and whose father intended her to marry Henry James. They were married in 1886, in Paris.[64]

By the mid-1880s Duveneck had moved on from the darker hues of Munich School painterly portraits to a lighter style influenced by French impressionists and James Abbott McNeill Whistler, with whom he had worked in Venice. Following a trip to Paris in 1888, Elizabeth Duveneck died suddenly from pneumonia, leaving her husband the bereft father of a small son. When offered a teaching position at the Cincinnati Art Museum in 1890 by Maria Longworth Nichols Storer, he returned to America and took up residence in Covington, his base for the remainder of his life.[65]

Duveneck remained at the museum until 1895, and thereafter taught intermittently at the Cincinnati Art Club. He was not invited to teach at the Cincinnati Art Academy, which was directed by Thomas Satterwhite Noble, until 1900. Noble was an admirer neither of Duveneck's paintings nor of his approach to teaching, finding all that brushwork and enthusiasm a bit coarse. As noted earlier, Noble moved from being a progressive painter of historical genre works to a rather stiff academic.[66]

When Noble retired in 1903, Duveneck took his place as chairman of the faculty of the academy, a position he held until his death in 1919. The passion he once had for painting he transferred to teaching, becoming greatly admired by his students, who, according to Bruce Weber and Arthur Jones, felt he "was almost saintly in his devotion to them. A number of his former students commented upon his generous and sympathetic spirit."[67] Among the Kentuckians Duveneck taught were Dixie Selden and John Bernard Alberts Jr. Selden was often named as one of his favorite pupils, and at his request she painted a life portrait of him the year before his death (Fig. 74). Her image of the old

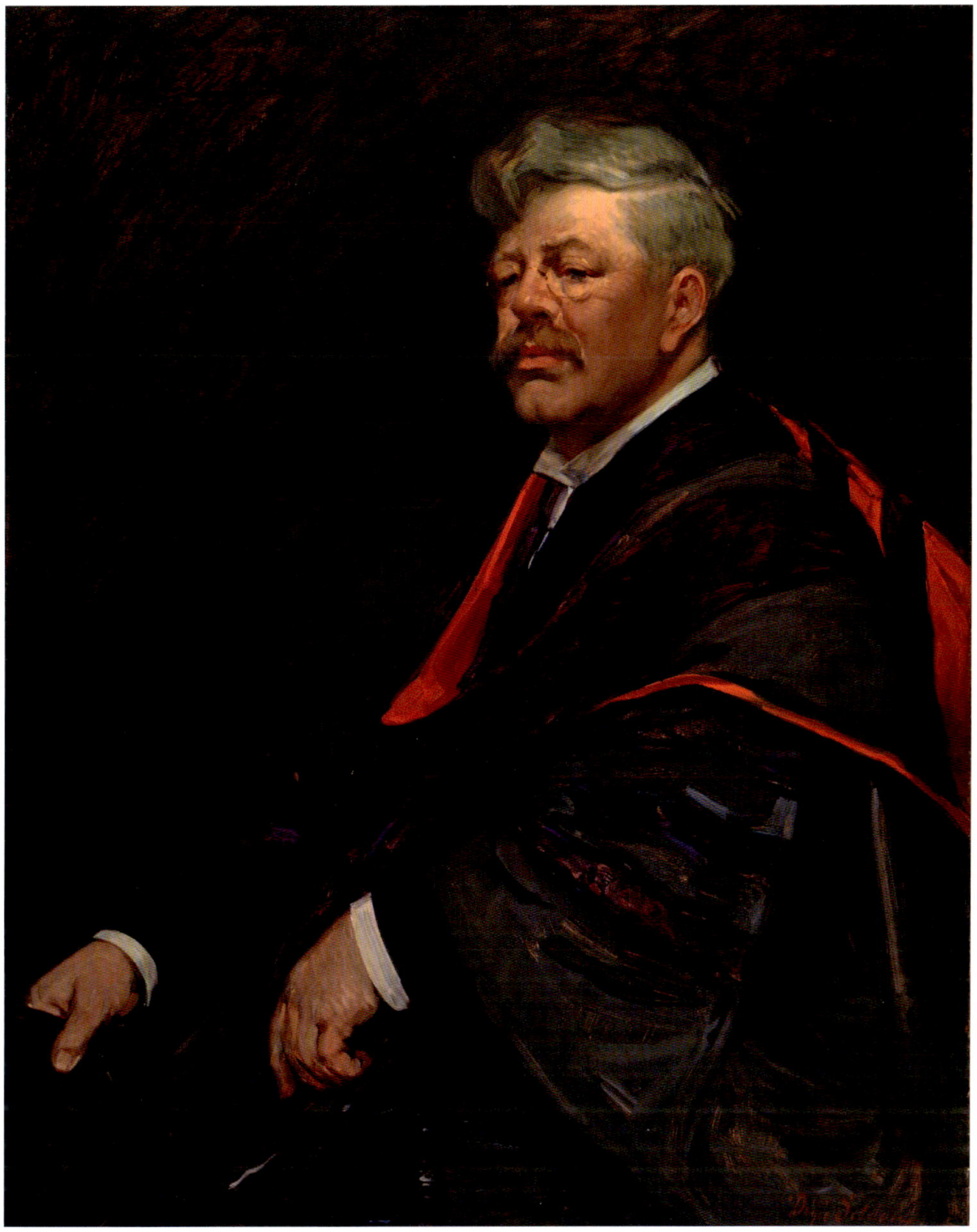

FIGURE 74. Dixie Selden (1868–1935), *Frank Duveneck* (1848–1919), n.d., oil on canvas, 51 × 43″, Cincinnati Art Museum, Gift of the Dixie Selden Estate, 1936.650.

artist, sitting in a slump and looking somewhat worn, is a tribute to both teacher and student.

John Bernard Alberts studied with Duveneck in Cincinnati from 1906 to 1909, prior to a period of study with Frank Weston Benson and Edmund Tarbell at the Boston Museum of Fine Arts. He then traveled in Europe and worked briefly in New York before returning to Louisville in 1914. Once home, he became part of the circle of writers, artists, and intellectuals surrounding the poet Madison Cawein. Cawein was the centerpiece of a group of men and women living on St. James Court, a tree-lined enclave that had been built by the Victoria Land Company on the site of the old Southern Exposition grounds. Other writers in this group included Alice Hegan Rice, the author of *Mrs. Wiggs of the Cabbage Patch,* and her husband, Cale Young Rice, also a talented amateur artist; Charles Neville Buck; Fannie Macaulay (who wrote under the name Frances Little); and Virginia Cary Hudson, who wrote a comic autobiography, *Oh Ye Jigs and Juleps.*

Cawein was an idyllic fantasist who perceived nature to be a haven for the subliminal longings and unseen forces that shape our lives and draw us ever back to a primeval, sensual state. Both his parents, "Doctor" William Cawein and Christina Stelsly Cawein, were rather otherworldly. William Cawein was a successful herbalist who concocted medications of the type that would today be called holistic. Christina Cawein claimed to be clairvoyant, possessed of a second sight that gave her a transcendental insight into the workings of nature unknown to more ordinary beings. Accordingly, young Madison was encouraged by his parents to write his dreamy, rambling poetry, which drew the attention of several important critics, including William Dean Howells and Edmund Gosse.[68]

Madison Cawein has been characterized as a poet who wrote "in a transitional period," who was not "consciously abandoning old ideas and conventions in order to find and adopt new techniques"; he was, rather, as the critic William Ward described him, "a poet dedicated to the past and trying to prove the validity of both his own writings and the tradition."[69] This is a modernist critique that endorses a polarity between the extremes of "reality" and "sentiment," as though only the dispassionate could distinguish an author or a painter. Like Samuel Woodson Price, Cawein is a part of that genteel tradition in late nineteenth- and early twentieth-century Kentucky culture that some have regarded as retarding more progressive ideas (Fig. 75).

Reading some of Cawein's poetry can reveal a much different persona. Despite the criticism of soppy sentiment, Cawein could be quite explicitly sensual. His poem "Dionysia" is a celebration of hedonist revelry as enacted by a mortal who glimpses a bacchante. He describes "her delicious body" and beholds her as "sweet of limb with breasts of musk." Becoming aroused, he seeks her.

> Wild my wine-stained hand
> O'er tumultuous hair is lifted;
> While the flushed and Phallic orgies
> Whirl around me; and the marges
> Of the wood are torn and rifted
> With lascivious laugh and shout,
> And barbarian there again—
> Shameless with the shameless rout,
>   Bacchus lusting in each vein,—
> With her pagan lips on mine,
> Like a God drunk with wine,
> On I reel.

Hardly the stuff of Sunday afternoon book groups assembled in gaslit parlors.[70]

Perhaps it is to be expected that Cawein did not have an easy life, nor did he come to a pleasant end. He married Gertrude McElvey in 1903, and they had a son the following year. Poetry is hardly the way to fortune, but at first Cawein was successful in using some family funds to speculate in real estate and the stock market. But family expenses, the costs of self-publication, and the maintenance of the mansion at 1436 St. James Court were high, and when he suffered losses from market reversals in 1912 he became destitute. By late 1914 he was exhausted; he died from a stroke that December. Although Cawein was much mourned in Louisville at the time of his death, he is now largely forgotten elsewhere.[71] In the last year of his life Cawein offered a challenge to John Alberts. According to Cawein's biographer Otto Rothert, the poet told the painter, "If you'll paint a picture showing a necklace of dew drops on a gossamer thread, I'll write a poem on it."[72] In the resulting picture a nude sprite weaves spiderwebs with dewdrops to form an ornament whose design would seem to be inspired by the same art nouveau trends that influenced Alberts's stained-glass designs.

Alberts's portraits of Madison Cawein and Otto Rothert are well-designed compositions with that air of drama one might associate with the St. James Court coterie. Cawein is captured in a jaunty mood, his entire body occupying the picture plane as he sits at his work. The portrait of Rothert, depicting a table and numerous books, contains many elements of a scholarly life (Fig. 76). Although one can see the influence of Duveneck's concern with lavish, painterly brushwork, there is also a discernable feel of the Boston School and the art of John Singer Sargent implicit in the personality of these paintings. When America joined the First World War in 1917, John Alberts volunteered. Though his goal was to be a painter of camouflage, he wound

FIGURE 75 *(facing)*. John Bernard Alberts Jr. (1886–1931), *Madison Cawein* (1865–1914), ca. 1910, oil on canvas, 55¾ × 41½", The Filson Historical Society, 1920.1.

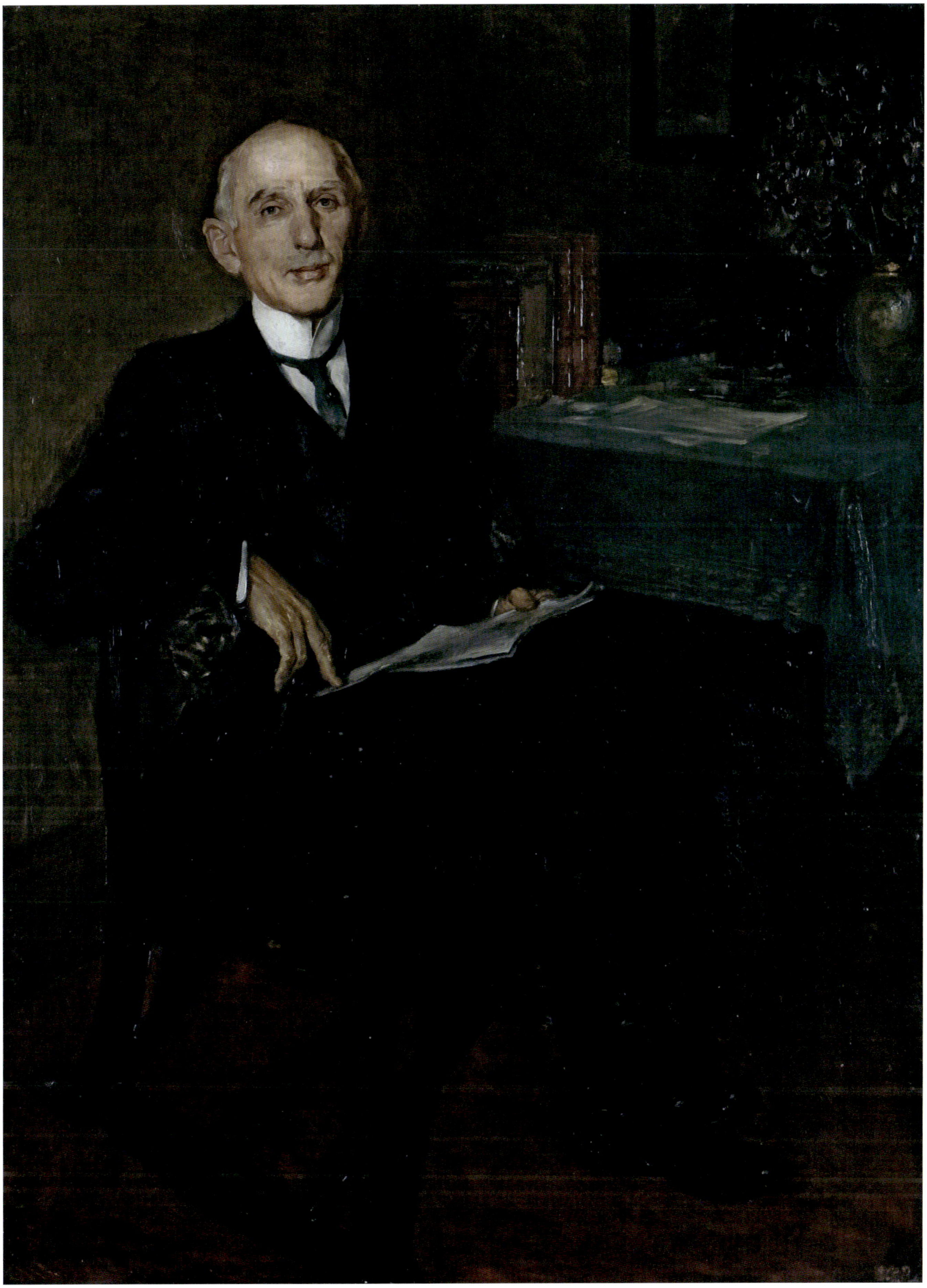

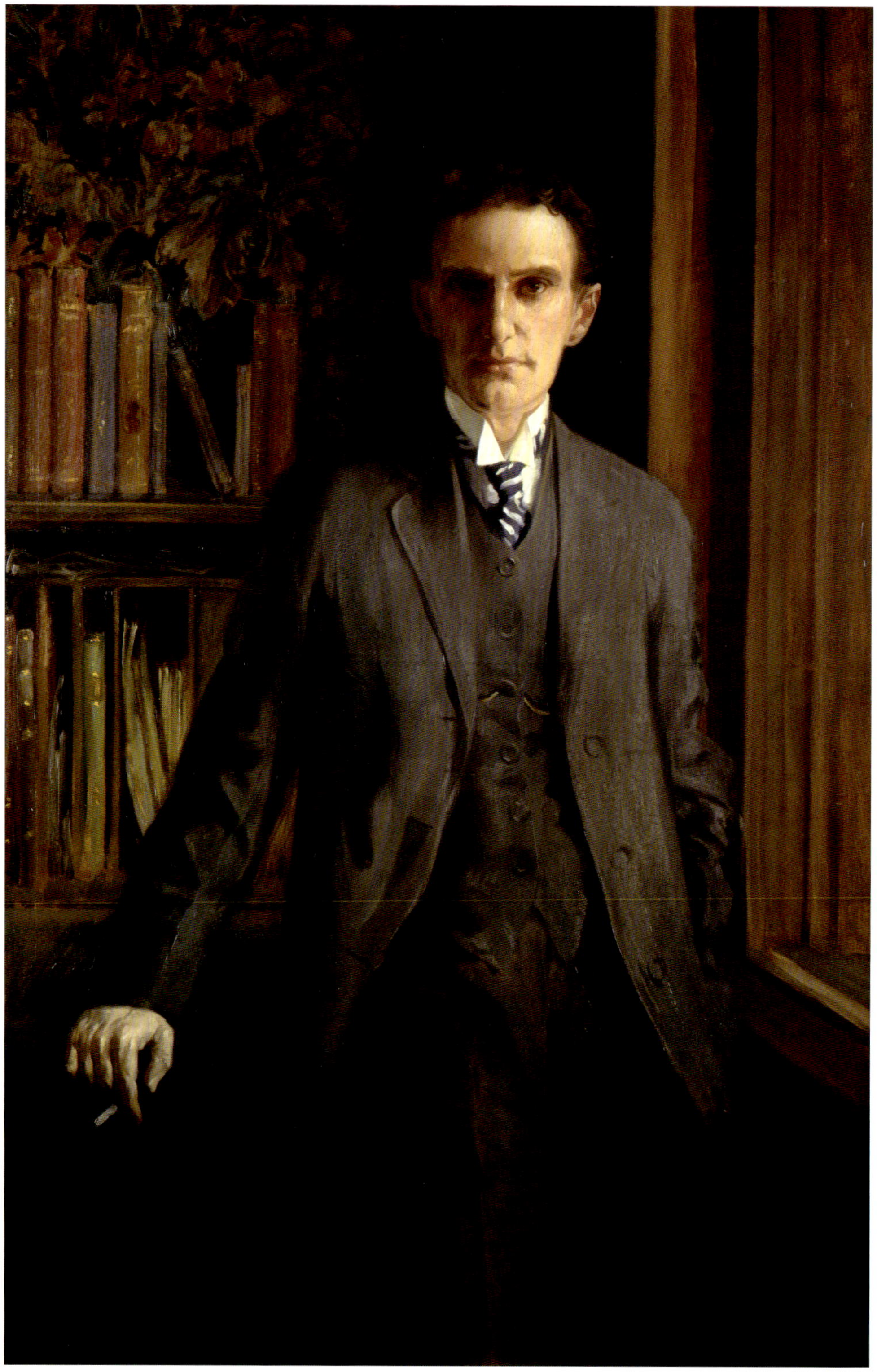

FIGURE 76. John Bernard Alberts Jr. (1886–1931), *Otto Rothert* (1871–1956), ca. 1916, oil on canvas, 58 × 41″, The Filson Historical Society, 1923.3.1.

up rendering scientific drawings at an army hospital. By late 1918 he was showing signs of multiple sclerosis and became unable to function on his own. He was cared for by his brother, Bruno, until his death in 1931. Bruno Alberts's family always felt that he sacrificed his own career to care for an ailing brother. This illness prevented John Alberts from becoming one of the last native Kentucky portraitists—and the best—capable of capturing the public imagination and reinvigorating an art form that was disappearing from the cultural terrain of the commonwealth.

Casting a backward glance

The portraits surveyed here can be seen as falling into two groups: those created before the introduction of photography and those created after. Artists before photography often went to great lengths to acquire the technical skills required to create what was then thought to be a reasonable likeness. Their efforts matched the spirit of their place and time. The first American frontier, the West that was the Ohio River Valley, was a place teeming with energy and ambition. Though the image of rustic heroes like Daniel Boone enjoyed great favor in popular culture, the portrait artists who painted him were not crude bumpkins with a brush. In most instances they were keenly aware of the currents of style circulating in the larger world, their knowledge having been acquired with considerable, and commendable, effort. Nor were they students in a classroom, having been taught a uniform, didactic lesson. Rather, they were observers of the richly fluid and dynamic act of painting, seeking to improve their technical skill and create a viable style and endeavoring to emulate, not copy, their old masters. Gilbert Stuart's recommendation that Matthew Harris Jouett gauge the character of his subject *before* he began to paint speaks clearly to the issue of gaze in that era. Before photography, a portraitist looked at a sitter with his own eyes and created a work of art based on the synergy of the interaction. Ponder the vocabulary. A *likeness* is something equivalent, not literal. A *portrait* is a portrayal in dramatic terms, a featured player. Extant portraits of that era are symbols from the past, subjects for discourse on the distinctions between artistic theories and practices.[73]

Once photography was introduced, an intervening lens was inserted between artist and sitter, transforming the artist's role into that of a mirror. Previously a sitter sought a likeness in keeping with the currencies of styles in representation. Photography transformed the previously relative concept of realism into actuality, as though the camera were, in the words of one critic, "an instrument of truth, a tool of romantic epistemology, and a scientific art-form which does unfailingly what only genius had been able to do earlier."[74] Confronted by the camera, some artists sought to alter their gaze in conformity with panoramic perspective—with mixed results. G. P. A. Healy's portrait of the Speeds (see Fig. 58) is a compromise, a painterly representation of the sitters in a studiolike setting. Late works by Patrick Henry Davenport and Phillip O. Jenkins have a stilted, flattened quality. Aurelius Revenaugh and Benoni Irwin managed to combine realistic depiction with a textured brushstroke and nuanced color field to achieve a magisterial effect. Other artists, notably Frank Duveneck and his followers Dixie Selden and John Alberts, continued to paint in a venerable high-art style, informed by seventeenth-century precedent and lit by impressionist innovation.

What truly illuminates this brief backward glance is the impressive array of artists working in Kentucky and the Ohio River Valley from whose work we may construct diverse aesthetic viewpoints. The quantity and quality of their work are also a tribute to the demands of an equally varied group of patrons, reflecting the complex relationship between sitter and subject. Samuel Woodson Price believed that the "desire of the pioneers to be reproduced on a flat surface, whether from vanity or not, was natural then as now, and for its gratification they would then as now make personal sacrifices."[75] Portraiture is at once memorial and mimetic, an artifact that offers a visual bridge between histories, oral and written, and the physical world they recount. As limners illumine, so this account of artistic activity is offered as a means of shedding light on the particular distinction of place and the tender concerns of its inhabitants. For though "death may deprive us of a beloved associate or a dear friend," as a writer in 1842 noted, "the painter cheats, in some measure, the fell destroyer" and preserves "a perfect presentment of those whom, living we so fondly loved, and whose memories, in death we so dearly cherish."[76]

PART TWO
Artists' Biographies

THE ARTISTS CHOSEN FOR INCLUSION in this section are those whose activity in Kentucky and the Ohio River Valley has been identified in previous art historical records and who have an identifiable body of work extant in sufficient quantity in public and private collections to assemble a checklist for comparative purposes. Each biography provides a brief but detailed life history; for each portrait shown, the identity of the sitter and a stylistic discussion of the work as it may relate to a certain moment in the artist's development; sources for further study from primary and secondary sources; and locations of works in public collections. A list of the abbreviations used at the end of each entry can be found in the Abbreviations of Archives and Collections section at the back of the book. Considering the currently limited scholarly activity in the field of historic southern portraiture, these entries seek to consolidate material culture (the portraits) with historical literature. It is hoped that these illustrations will provide prototypes to assist in the identification of artists of portraits that are not signed and whose oral history has been lost. The geographical area of study encompasses Kentucky and the neighboring areas of southern Ohio and southern Indiana, the valley through which the river runs.

WILLIAM APTHORP ADAMS

(1797–1878)

EDNA WHITLEY NOTES that the man announcing himself as R. A. Adams, a portrait painter, in the Paris, Kentucky, *Western Citizen* in 1848 is probably William Apthorp Adams. He was born in Boston, Massachusetts, to Seth and Elizabeth Apthorp Adams, kin of John Adams, one of America's Founding Fathers. The family migrated to Ohio around 1820. Adams began painting portraits in Zanesville, Ohio, in 1822 while reading law. During this time he became an itinerant portraitist and an associate of Thomas Cole (1801–1848), the noted landscape painter who was then in Steubenville, Ohio. Adams and Cole maintained their friendship through correspondence until Cole's death in 1848. Much of their correspondence was subsequently reproduced in Louis Legrand Noble's *Course of Empire, Voyage of Life, and Other Pictures of Thomas Cole, with Selections from His Letters and Miscellaneous Writings* (1853). These letters provide a firsthand account of artistic endeavors on the frontier of the Ohio River Valley. After practicing law in Zanesville, Adams moved to Cincinnati in 1840, where he was based for the rest of his life, becoming a familiar figure in the art community, well regarded as an amateur portraitist. His portrait was painted by James Henry Beard in 1859 and Frank Duveneck in 1874. Following retirement from public life in the late 1860s, Adams moved to Newport, Kentucky, where he died. His son, Cassily Adams (1843–1921), was also a painter. The Metropolitan Museum in New York has a drawing, *Hunter,* which is the only surviving figurative work of Adams's found to date.

Archives: AAA; literature: Hageman, Haverstock et al., Noble, Whitley.

BRUNO ALBERTS

(1888–1970)

FIGURE 77. Bruno Alberts, *Self-Portrait,* ca. 1938, oil on canvas, 29½ × 21½″, The Filson Historical Society, 1984.13.1.

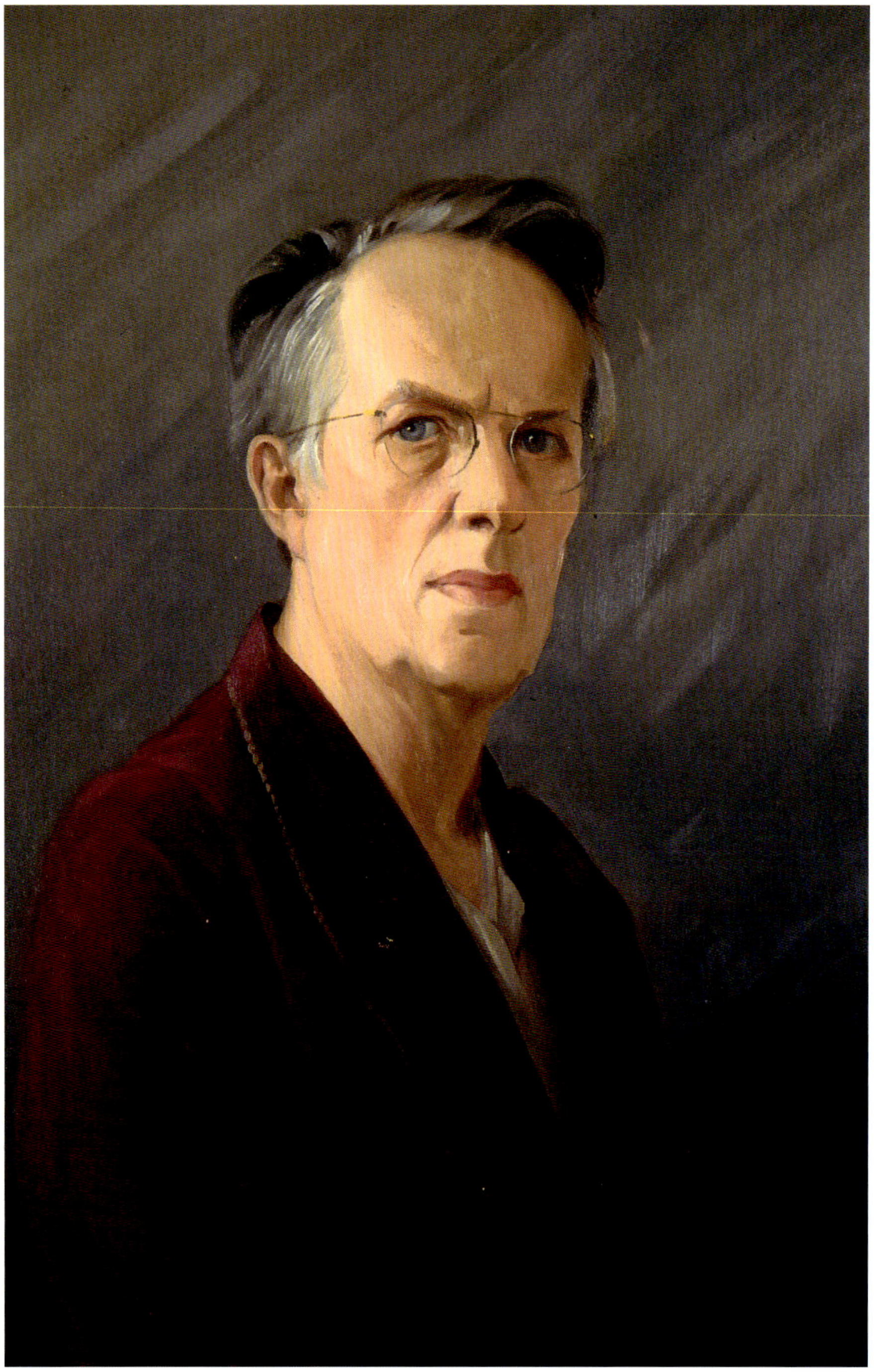

BRUNO ALBERTS, the younger brother of the artist John Alberts Jr., was born in Louisville, Kentucky. He studied with Frank Duveneck at the Cincinnati Art Academy from 1905 to 1908. He was active as a painter of landscape work in the local impressionist vernacular in Louisville, 1910–1935, where he was closely associated with the circle of Paul Plaschke. His painting *Paul Plaschke Painting Outdoors* was exhibited at the University of Kentucky Art Museum in 1981. When his brother became incapacitated in 1918, he became his principal caregiver. After John Alberts Jr. died in 1931, Bruno moved his family to Mandarin, Florida, where he developed a botanical business growing orchids. Arthur Jones and Bruce Weber speculate that his artistic career was overshadowed by the weight of his familial obligations. Following his retirement, Alberts began to paint again, returning with his wife to Louisville in 1964, where he exhibited his work at the First National Bank (Fig. 77). Following Alberts's death in Louisville, the Mandarin, Florida, Community Club held a memorial exhibition of his work.

Archives: FHS; collection: FHS; literature: Jones & Weber.

JOHN BERNARD ALBERTS JR.

(1886–1931)

JOHN ALBERTS JR.'S FATHER owned a glass shop on First Street between Green and Walnut (present Liberty and Muhammad Ali) in Louisville where he designed stained-glass windows, a craft his son began to practice while still a teenager. Alberts studied with Frank Duveneck at the Cincinnati Art Academy for three years (1906–1909), where he also acquired a love for Diego Velásquez's rich tonalities and painterly brush-work. Like other Duveneck pupils, he developed an artistically nurturing relationship with his master teacher, spending much time in Duveneck's Covington studio and corresponding with Duveneck frequently upon Alberts's return to Louisville. Alberts then studied in Boston (1909–1913) in the School of the Boston Museum of Fine Arts, where his teachers were Frank Weston Benson (1862–1951) and Edmund Charles Tarbell (1862–1938). Benson and Tarbell were the leading lights of the Boston School, American impressionists who favored broken brushwork, highly keyed color, and the placement of their portrait subjects in richly detailed settings. The Boston School's influence is especially apparent in Alberts's portraits of Madison Cawein (Fig. 75) and Otto Rothert (Fig. 76). Alberts next studied in various French ateliers, and upon his return to this country he worked briefly as a commercial artist in New York. When he returned to Louisville in 1914, his relation Gisbert Alberts introduced him to a circle of writers, artists, and antiquarians, many of whom lived on St. James Court and for whom he served as something of a court painter. From 1915 to 1917 Alberts divided his efforts among portraiture, stained-glass design, and symbolist paintings. In one sense his portrait of Maude Bonnie, looming large against a dark background, is a tribute to the lessons he learned from Duveneck (Fig. 78). But the haunting, insinuating gaze of the subject in this work is also a demonstration of his familiarity with European fin de siècle symbolist painting. With the start of the First World War he painted several intense allegories in the symbolist style, including *War* (1917). In that same year he painted *Paul Plaschke Drawing in His Studio.* Plaschke was only six years older than Alberts, and the two had recently established a studio together. The painting bears the inscription "to an alleged cartoonist from his alleged artist friend." John Alberts volunteered for service as a camouflage artist at Camp Zachary Taylor in Louisville late in 1917. While making scientific drawings at the base hospital in 1918 he was inoculated for the Spanish influenza pandemic with an experimental vaccine. His obituary in the *Louisville Courier-Journal,* August 25, 1931, notes that within six months of this inoculation "he was bedfast, and except for a few brief periods he never again left his bedroom," having been stricken with muscular sclerosis. He lived thirteen more years under the care of his devoted brother, Bruno. He was given a posthumous exhibition at the Speed Art Museum, Louisville, October 4–October 25, 1931.

Archives: FHS, Speed; collections: FHS, Greenville, JC; literature: Jones & Weber, Pennington (2008), Severns (1995), Speed.

FIGURE 78 *(overleaf).* John Bernard Alberts Jr., *Maude Johnson Williams Bonnie,* 1916, oil on canvas, 53½ × 34½″, The Filson Historical Society, 1984.5.

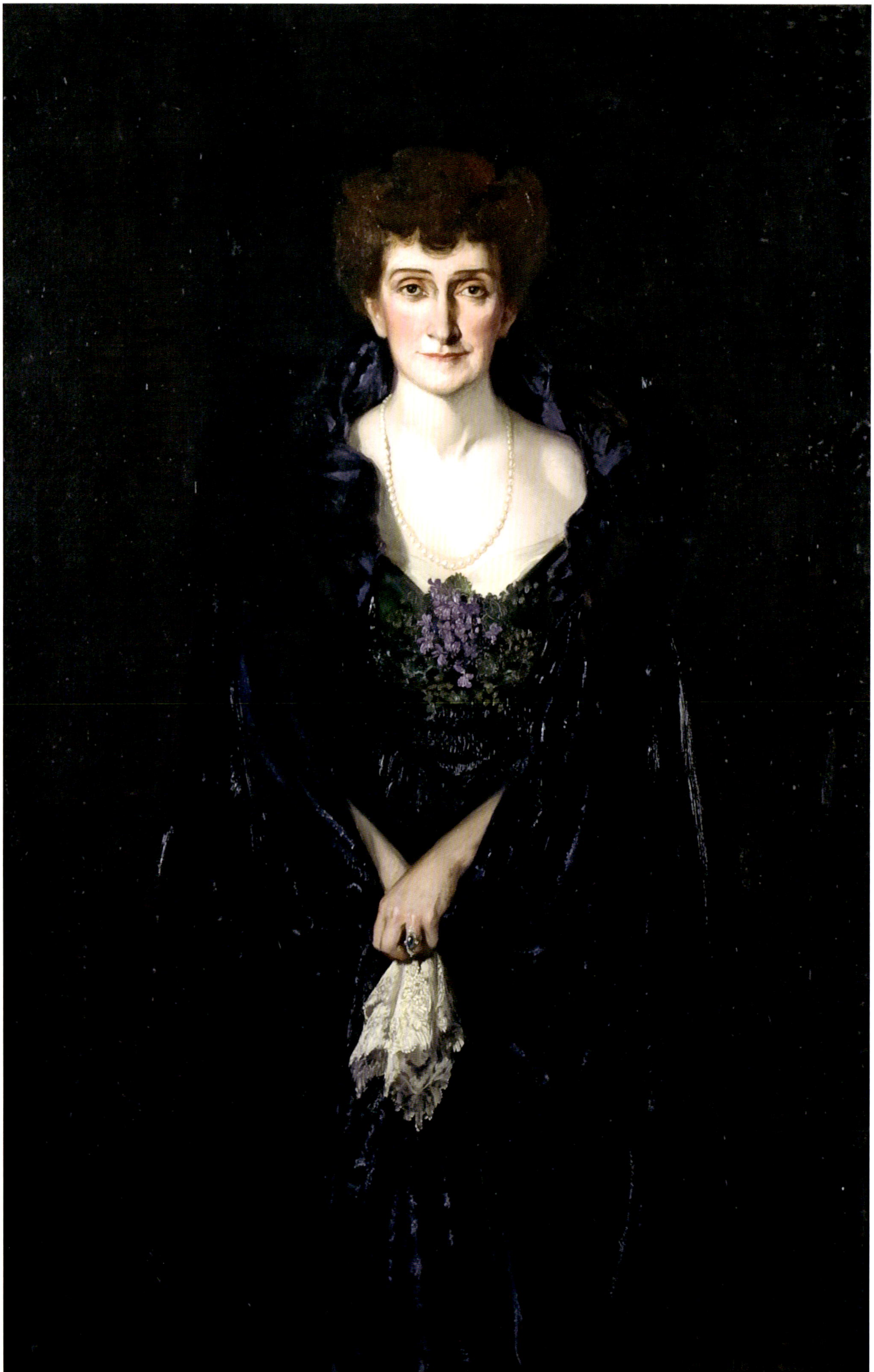

FRANCIS ALEXANDER

(1800–1881)

FRANCIS ALEXANDER WAS BORN in Killington, Connecticut, to Neil and Esther Smith Alexander, a prosperous farming family. A precocious talent, he began to paint when, according to Henry Tuckerman, "on account of a slight indisposition, he was struck with the beautiful colors of some fish he had caught, and attempted to reproduce them in water-color." Through the benefices of a local attorney, Prescott Hall, he pursued his studies in New York, 1820–1821, with Alexander Robinson. From 1821 to 1823 he was active in Providence, Rhode Island, where the patronage of Mrs. James B. Mason led to commissions to paint many of the families there. Between 1825 and 1831 he was active in Boston, where he received encouragement from the elderly Gilbert Stuart, whose head-and-shoulder portrait format he adopted (Fig. 79). He was active in Washington, D.C., 1830, where he painted Andrew Jackson and Andrew Jackson Donelson. Alexander then traveled to Italy, 1831–1833, where he worked in Florence and became involved in the American community, notably with sculptor Hiram Powers (1805–1873), from Cincinnati. It was this acquaintance that led to introductions in Kentucky, where he painted in 1843, as evidenced by an advertisement in the September 5, 1843, *Frankfort Intelligencer.* Alexander may also have pursued his connections to the Alexander family of Woodford County, the most prominent and successful stock breeders in Kentucky in the antebellum era. In 1836 he married a wealthy heiress, Lucia Grey Swett of Boston, despite her father's strong objections to his profession. From 1836 until his departure for Florence in 1853 Alexander was one of the most

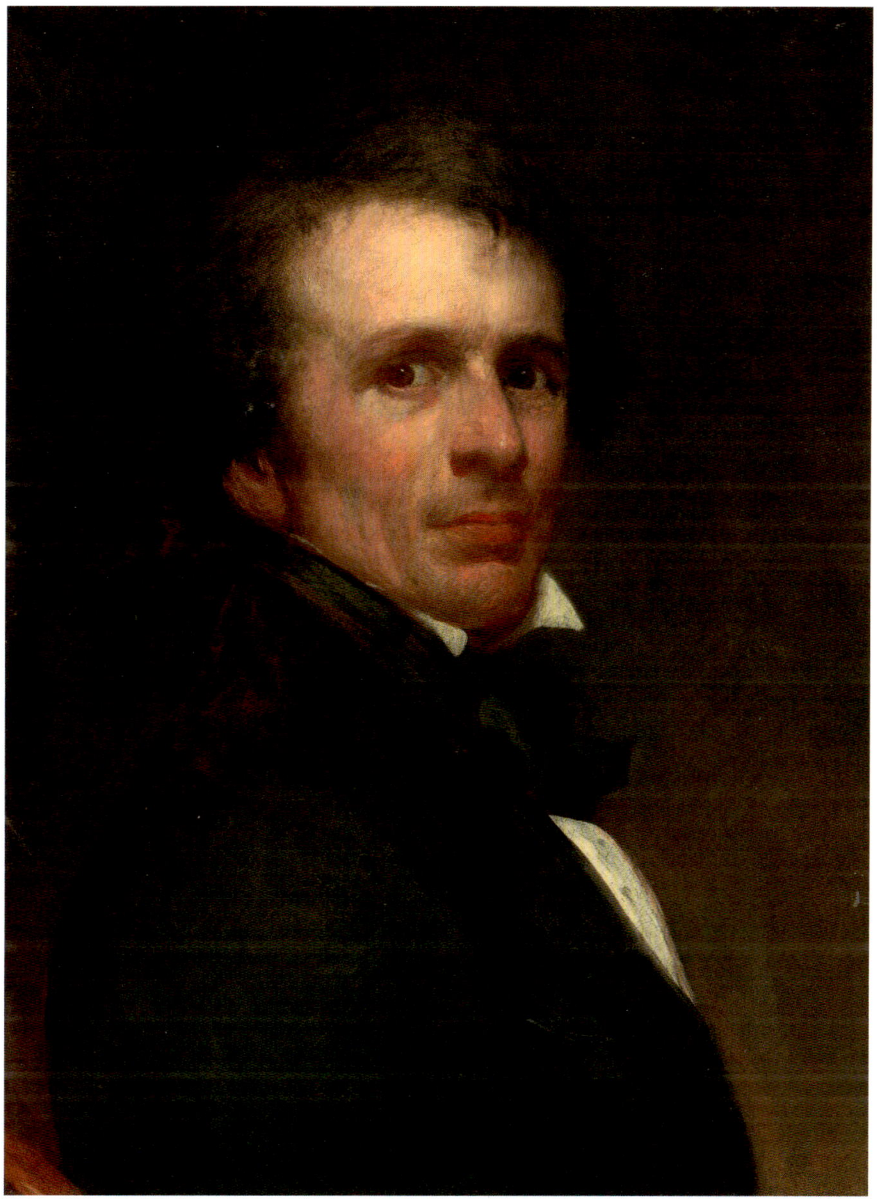

FIGURE 79. Francis Alexander, *Self-Portrait,* ca. 1830, oil on canvas, 24⅛ × 18⅛", Museum of Fine Arts, Boston, gift of Maxim Karolik for the M. and M. Karolik Collection of American Paintings, 1815–1865, 62.257.

popular portraitists in Boston. His most notable subject during his career in Boston as portraitist was Charles Dickens, whom he painted in 1845. Alexander met Dickens's steamer in the harbor and demanded a sitting. Stunned, Dickens is reported to have remarked that the "impertinence of the thing was without limit; but the enterprise was most astonishing." After 1853 Alexander and his wife lived in Florence, where his daughter, the painter and author Francesca Alexander, was born. The Kentucky sculptor Joel Tanner Hart was also part of the Florentine expatriate community, and through him Alexander again received invitations to Kentucky, where he was an itinerant in Fayette and Harrison Counties, 1867–1870. He died in Florence on March 27, 1880; his wife outlived him by twenty-five years, dying at the age of 105. It should be noted that his work is often confused with that of William Edward West's late period.

Archives: NPG; collections: BMFA, Met, NGA, NPG, RIHS, WH, Yale; literature: Dunlap, Groce & Wallace, Jeffrey Alan Gallery, J. Kelly, Pierce, Tuckerman, Whitley.

WILLIAM C. ALLEN

(ca. 1810–1854)

WILLIAM C. ALLEN'S ORIGINS are unknown, although he was probably in Kentucky because of the presence of the extended family of his sister, Mrs. William Burton. He was active in Louisville 1838–1845. Allen painted the portrait of Boone shown here (Fig. 80) in late 1839 and offered it to the state House of Representatives for the House's chamber; the offer was accepted in 1840. (A motion to pay Allen $500 for his efforts was tabled.) After exhibiting in Cincinnati in 1841, he went south to New Orleans. He advertised as a portraitist in the March 20, 1842, *New Orleans Daily Picayune,* with a studio on Royal Street, near the customhouse. Around that time he painted another monumental portrait, that of Zachary Taylor, for the Robert Q. Ward family. According to letters deposited by Allen's sister in the Kentucky Historical Society, the painter contracted yellow fever in Vicksburg and sought refuge in the home of Caroline Maker, where he died, leaving behind an unnamed woman "too young to have all her hopes of happiness blasted."

Archives: KHS; collection: KHS; literature: Mahé & McCaffrey, Whitley.

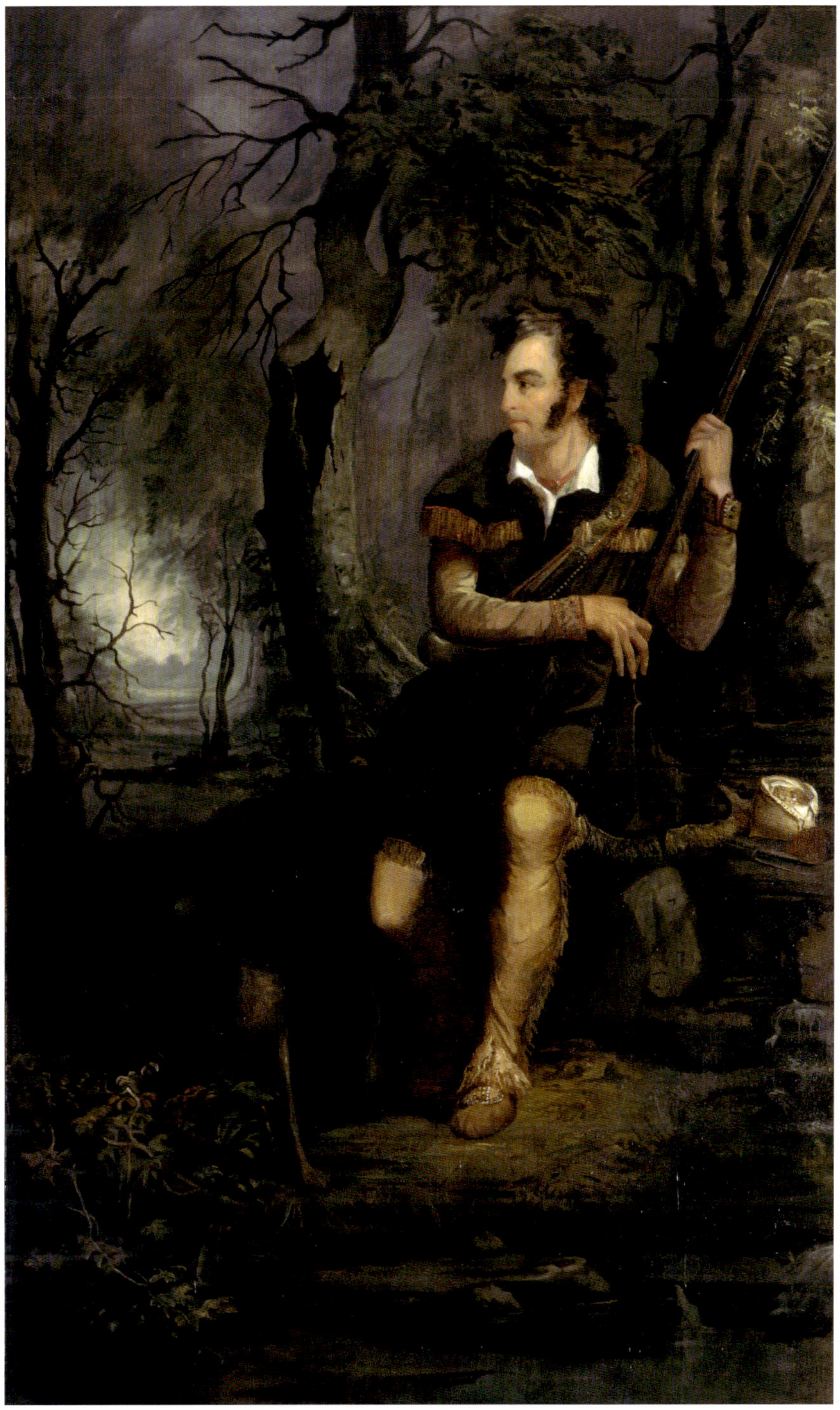

FIGURE 80. William C. Allen, *Daniel Boone,* 1839–1840, oil on canvas, 103 × 64½", Kentucky Historical Society, Frankfort.

JEAN AUBREY

(1810–1893)

JOHN AUBERG WAS BORN in Kassel, Germany, and subsequently active in Paris at the court of Louis Philippe, ca. 1838. While a resident of France, he took the French form of his name. He fled France during the revolutionary year of 1848 to work in Italy. Connections among the large German population of Cincinnati induced his migration to that city in 1853. Once there, he became known for his religious scenes, especially a large altarpiece he created for Holy Trinity Church, West Fifth at Mound Street, since destroyed. He advertised for portrait work in several locations between 1854 and 1869. Aubrey pursued an itinerancy in central Kentucky, especially in Bourbon County, between 1858 and 1869. He introduced Raphael Strauss, a fellow German painter, to the area. In later life he was known as "the ancient Aubrey," a figure much admired for his kindness and nurturing of younger artists in the "over the Rhine" community of Cincinnati. His most important extant work is a monumental portrait of Miles Greenwood (Fig. 81). Aubrey's activity as a painter declined after the Civil War. He died in Cincinnati and is buried in Spring Grove Cemetery.

Collections: CAM, CHM; literature: Cincinnati Art Museum (1979), Groce & Wallace, Haverstock et al., Knepper, Whitley.

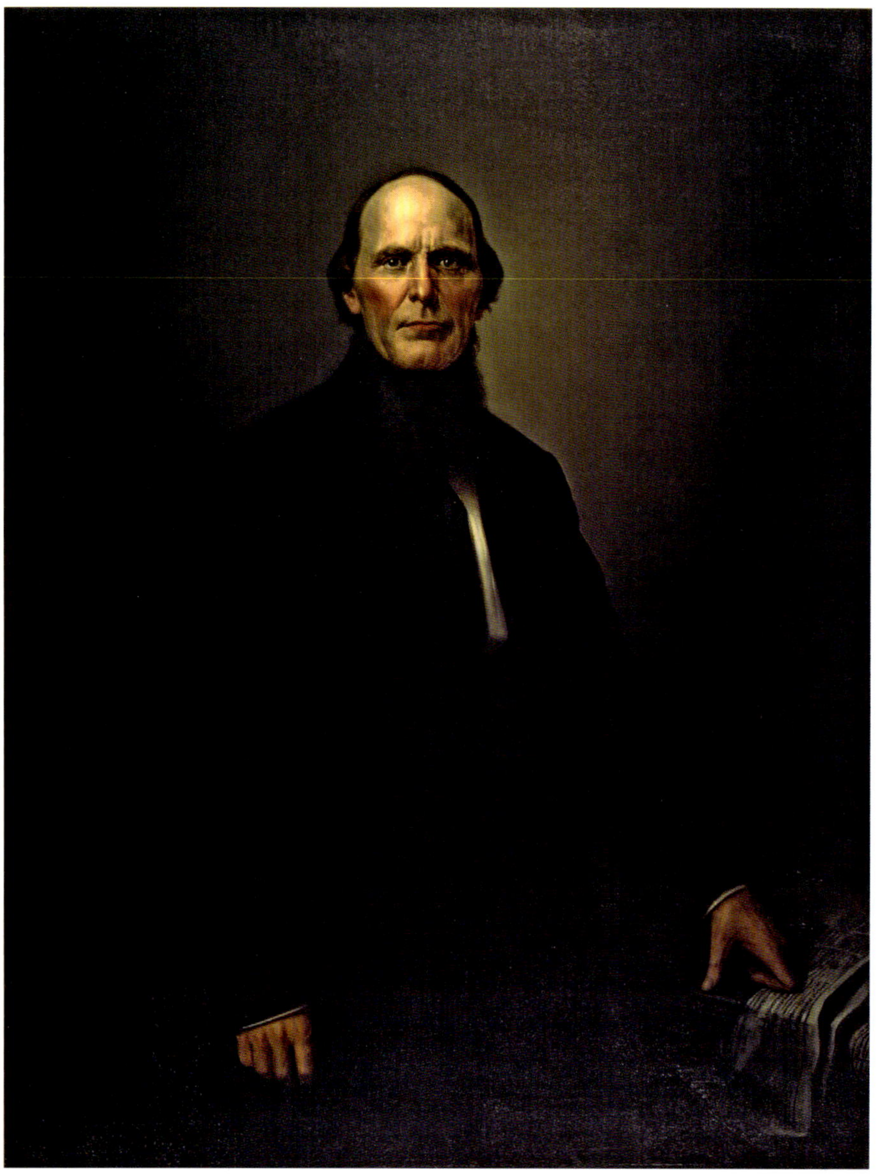

FIGURE 81. Jean Aubrey, *Miles Greenwood* (1807–1885), 1866, oil on canvas, $53\frac{9}{16} \times 41\frac{1}{8}$", Cincinnati Historical Society, 1971.11 CHS

Greenwood established the Eagle Ironworks on the Miami River near Cincinnati, a foundry that became the largest in the Midwest. An ardent abolitionist, he supplied a large quantity of armaments to Union forces during the Civil War. The Eagle Ironworks was the focus of arson by southern sympathizers three times during the war, its losses from those fires surpassing $100,000.

JOHN JAMES AUDUBON

(1785–1851)

JOHN JAMES AUDUBON was born in Les Cayes, Saint-Domingue (now Haiti), to Captain Jean Audubon and a young woman named Rabin to whom the captain was not married and who died soon after the infant's birth. His early years have been the subject of much speculation, including the mythic account that he was the lost Dauphin of France. Captain Audubon took the boy to France and legally adopted him in 1794. As to training, Audubon is said to have studied in Paris with Jacques-Louis David, ca. 1802; and to have worked with John Stein, an early Natchez, Mississippi, artist, ca. 1810, and with Thomas Sully in Philadelphia, ca. 1815. Audubon worked as an itinerant portraitist (profiles *en grisaile,* i.e., in monotone) in Louisville, Henderson, and Shippingport, Kentucky, 1808–1819. From Kentucky he launched his career as a naturalist artist in the lower Mississippi River Valley, especially in Louisiana, 1821–1837, which resulted in *The Birds of America,* published in England, 1827–1838. In later life he made visits to Kentucky on sketching and exploratory expeditions. He died, in a state of dementia, at his country place, Audubon Park, on the Hudson River near New York City. The complete set of original watercolor paintings for the bird series is in the possession of the New-York Historical Society.

Archives: FHS; collections: FHS, NYHS, Speed; select literature: Audubon (1832, 1926, 1929), Calo, Dwight (1963, 1965), Haverstock et al., Jones & Weber, Pennington (1989, 2008), Rhodes, Shelley, Whitley.

JAMES HENRY BEARD

(1812–1893)

FIGURE 82 *(facing page)*. James Henry Beard, *Portrait of Two Children*, n.d., oil on canvas, 53⅜ × 44$^{15}/_{16}$", Cincinnati Art Museum, gift of Mrs. A. G. Clarke (1898 loan converted to accession), 1977.12.

JAMES HENRY BEARD was born in Buffalo, New York, to Captain James and Harriet Wolcott Beard. He migrated west with his family to Ohio, ca. 1819, and lived in Lorain, Geauga, and Lake Counties prior to settling in Painesville, Ohio, in 1821. After his father's death in 1823 the eleven-year-old boy assumed support of his family by his craft, receiving instruction from a local schoolmaster, named Senter, before working with an itinerant limner, Jarvis Frary Hanks, ca. 1827. In the autumn of 1828 Beard began an itinerancy in the Western Reserve that ended in Pittsburgh in October 1829. While in Pittsburgh he met James Reid Lambdin and spent much time in that artist's museum of curiosities. Beard moved south in 1829, settling in Cincinnati, where he worked with Frederick Franks in 1830. From that base he pursued an itinerancy in Pittsburgh, Louisville, and New Orleans between 1831 and 1839. According to Henry Tuckerman, Beard received an appointment as "bearer of dispatches to the Court of St. James" from William Henry Harrison, the subject of one of his portraits; Harrison's early death after being elected president "dispelled his bright dreams" of becoming a diplomat. After 1840 he became increasingly active as a painter of genre and historical works, which attracted considerable attention from the American Art-Union in New York. He advertised his services as a portraitist at the Mansion House, Frankfort, Kentucky, in 1843, 1844, 1849, and 1855, and in Lexington, Kentucky, in 1844 and 1855. While in Baton Rouge, Louisiana, in 1848, he painted Zachary Taylor. At the outbreak of the Civil War Beard moved to Covington, Kentucky, with his family, serving on an ex-officio staff that provided support for the Union general Lew Wallace, author of *Ben-Hur.* He moved to New York in 1863, but he returned to work in Kentucky, 1863–1867, primarily in Woodford County, where he was associated with the family of the noted livestock breeder Colonel Robert A. Alexander, for whom he painted a monumental canvas in the manner of the Dutch naturalist Melchior d'Hondecoeter. In 1870 Beard made New York his permanent home and became a well-known animal painter and member of the National Academy of Design. He is noted especially for his portraits of children (Fig. 82) and for a style that departs from the strong color contrasts of the Germanic style practiced by his contemporaries in Cincinnati. A recently discovered painting, *The Illustrious Guest,* depicts Henry Clay stopping in a cavern during his 1844 campaign for the presidency, yet another in Beard's series of genre paintings of life on what was then the American frontier. In June 2009 *The Illustrious Guest* was placed on display at the Amon Carter Museum in Fort Worth, Texas. A self-portrait is recorded as being in the possession of the Lake County Historical Society, Mentor, Ohio. Beard died in Flushing, New York. His son, James Carter Beard, was an illustrator; his brother, William Holbrook Beard, was also a painter and married the daughter of portraitist Thomas LeClear.

Archives: CAM, LC, NPG, OHS; collections: BMFA, CAM, NAD, NPG, OHS; literature: Aronson (2003), Cincinnati Art Museum (1979), Hageman, Haverstock et al., HNOC, Tuckerman, Whitley.

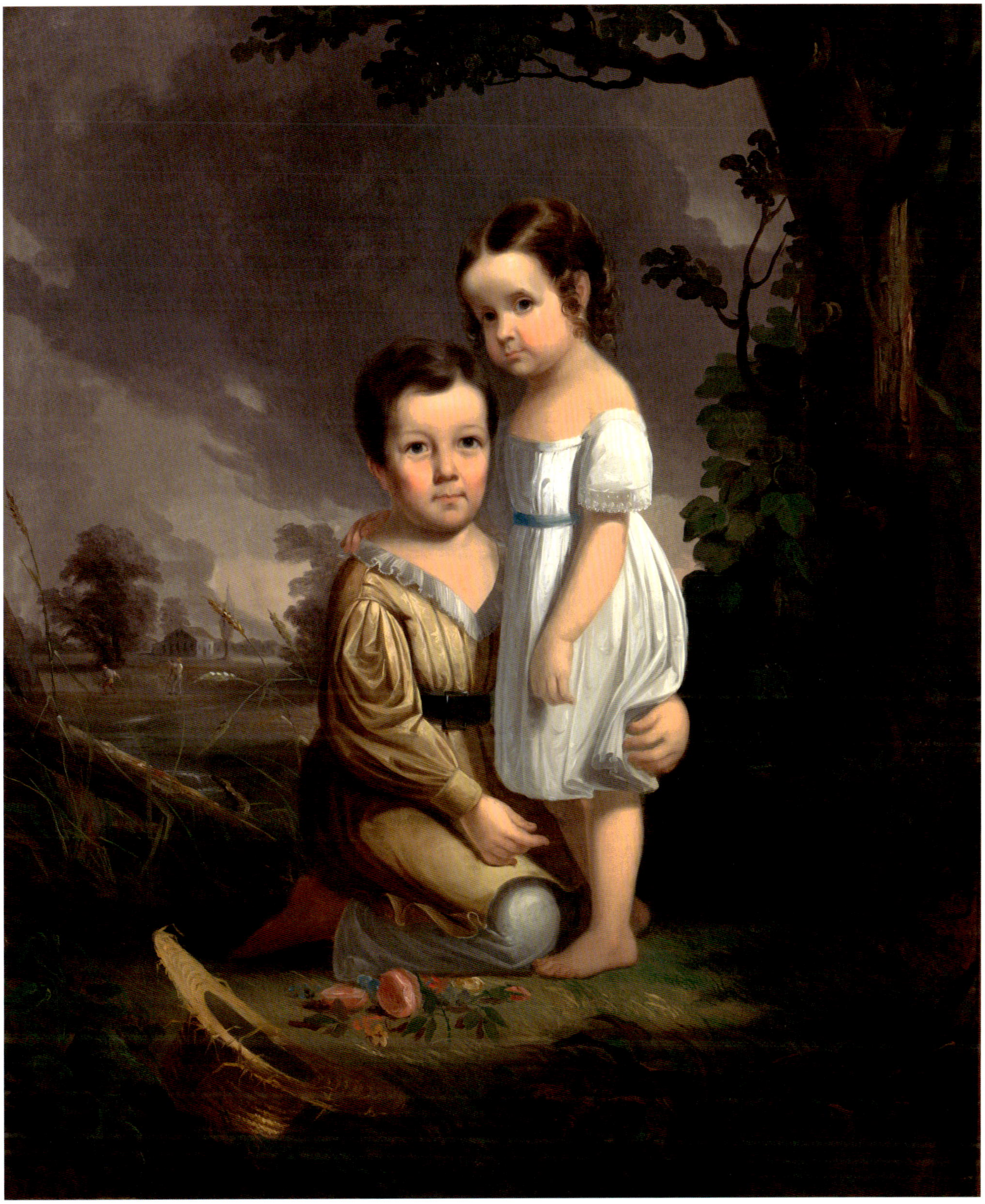

GEORGE CALEB BINGHAM

(1811–1879)

GEORGE CALEB BINGHAM was born in Augusta County, Virginia, to Henry Vest and Mary Amend Bingham, and migrated to Franklin, Missouri, with his parents in 1819. There his father opened a tavern; he eventually became a judge. Young Bingham became an apprentice to a cabinetmaker in 1827 but had already shown an interest in painting, copying engravings in a primitive manner with homemade pigments. He is claimed to have had some early instruction from Chester Harding when Harding was in Missouri to paint Daniel Boone. Bingham began to paint portraits in 1830, pursuing a Missouri itinerancy, during which time, ca. 1835, he became acquainted with the Rollins family. Dr. Anthony Wayne Rollins and his son James S. Rollins of Columbia, Missouri, became his first patrons, advancing him some $100 to pursue art lessons in St. Louis. Following his first success as a portraitist, he studied briefly at the Pennsylvania Academy of Fine Art, 1837. Returning to Missouri, he completed several portraits of the Rollins family in return for their patronage. It was during this early period in his career as a portraitist that he painted Samuel Bullitt Churchill (Fig. 83). Bingham was resident in Washington, D.C., 1841–1844, where he worked out of a tent set up near the Capitol and painted several important political figures, including Henry Clay and Daniel Webster. During that time he also spent six months in Petersburg, Virginia. He then returned to Missouri, where he began a series of genre paintings of frontiersmen and river men that culminated in *The Jolly Flatboatmen* of 1846, which was selected for engraving by the American Art-Union in New York. An ardent Whig, Bingham made his first run for political office in 1846 and was elected to the state legislature in 1848. In 1851 he turned from genre paintings of early settlers and entrepreneurs to works depicting the political struggles of the day, notably *County Election,* engraved in Philadelphia by John Sartain. He made visits to Kentucky in 1849, 1850, and 1853, selling subscriptions for prints of his work and seeking portrait commissions. He took his family abroad so that he could study at the Düsseldorf Academy in Germany, which specialized in genre and history painting, residing there 1856–1859. Bingham returned to Missouri on the eve of the Civil War, opposed secession, and served as state treasurer 1862–1865. As a protest against insurgent violence in neighboring Kansas following the war, he painted *Order No. 11* in 1868, an early acquisition of the Cincinnati Art Museum. He was made adjutant-general of Missouri in 1875 through the offices of Major James S. Rollins. Bingham died in Kansas City, Missouri, after a brief illness and was given a large funeral with a concluding oration by Rollins. At the time of his death Bingham was out of favor; Henry Tuckerman dismissed him with one small paragraph, in which he snipes that Bingham's "representations of border life and history" can boast no "special grasp or refinement in execution" and are appreciated only in "the West." Bingham returned to attention in the days of

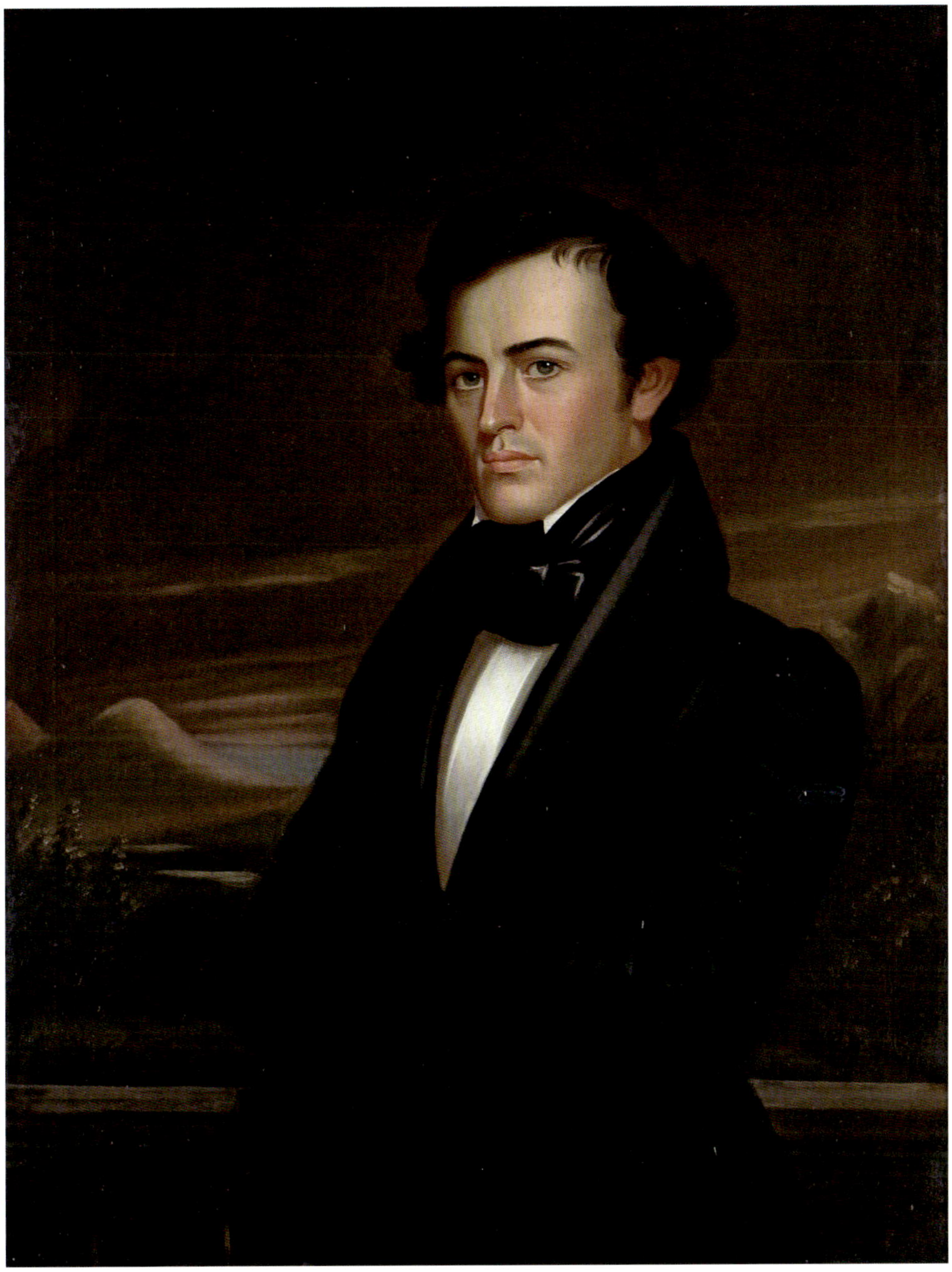

FIGURE 83. George Caleb Bingham, *Samuel Bullitt Churchill* (1812–1890), ca. 1838–1839, oil on canvas, 34½ × 26½″, The Filson Historical Society, 1986.9.1.

The son of Samuel and Abigail Oldham Churchill of Jefferson County, Kentucky, Churchill received a law degree from Transylvania University in Lexington in 1833 and moved to St. Louis in 1837, where his sister, Mrs. Meriwether Lewis Clark, was living. Churchill's portrait is one of the few early works in which Bingham sets the subject before a dark background in which there are glimpses of an atmospheric landscape reminiscent of continental portrait prints with romantic Sturm und Drang (storm and stress) elements.

American Scene painting; he was much admired by his fellow Missouri artist Thomas Hart Benton and many other painters employed by the Works Progress Administration during the Great Depression.

Archives: AAA, FHS, Getty; collections: FHS, Met, NGA, NPG, St. Louis; literature: Bloch (1967, 1986), Christ-Janer, McDermott (1959) , Pennington (2008), Rash, Rollins, Rusk, Shapiro, Tuckerman, Whitley.

CHARLES V. BOND

(ca. 1826–after 1864)

ACCORDING TO A PASSPORT application made in 1856, Charles V. Bond was born in Rutland, Vermont; his birth date is obscured by a ship's passenger list. He is identified by research at the National Gallery as having been twenty-two in 1848. He may have been the child of Eliel Bond, later identified in city directories as an innkeeper in Eaton County, Michigan, where the young Bond attracted attention in Detroit as a fledgling portraitist in 1840. The *Western Statesman* of Marshall, Michigan, July 16, 1840, praises him as a "precocious genius in portrait painting" at the age of fifteen, who "has the potential to rival Stuart, Harding and Copley." Local citizens, appreciative of his talents, raised funds that enabled him to travel to Italy for study. A painting subsequently exhibited as "*Fithian,* copied in 1841" would seem to indicate that Bond was in Europe in that year. Even when one takes into consideration the several discrepancies in his birth date, this trip abroad was made by a very young man, possibly only fifteen years old. He returned to America in 1844 and was active in Boston, 1844–1845, and again in 1848–1852 (Fig. 84). While in Boston he painted the abolitionist Wendell Phillips. Correspondence with Amos Lawrence of Boston in 1850–1851 indicates that he also worked in Brooklyn and New York. Bond informed Lawrence on August 25, 1851, that he was going abroad again. Advertisements in the 1852–1853 business directories for Detroit note his studio at 10 Fireman's Hall, where nineteen of his works were included in an 1853 exhibition, including images of former mayors, prominent citizens, and clergy. From 1855 to 1857 he is listed in Chicago directories, and it was while he was in that city that he painted a celebrated still life now in the collection of the National Gallery, Washington. He is recorded in

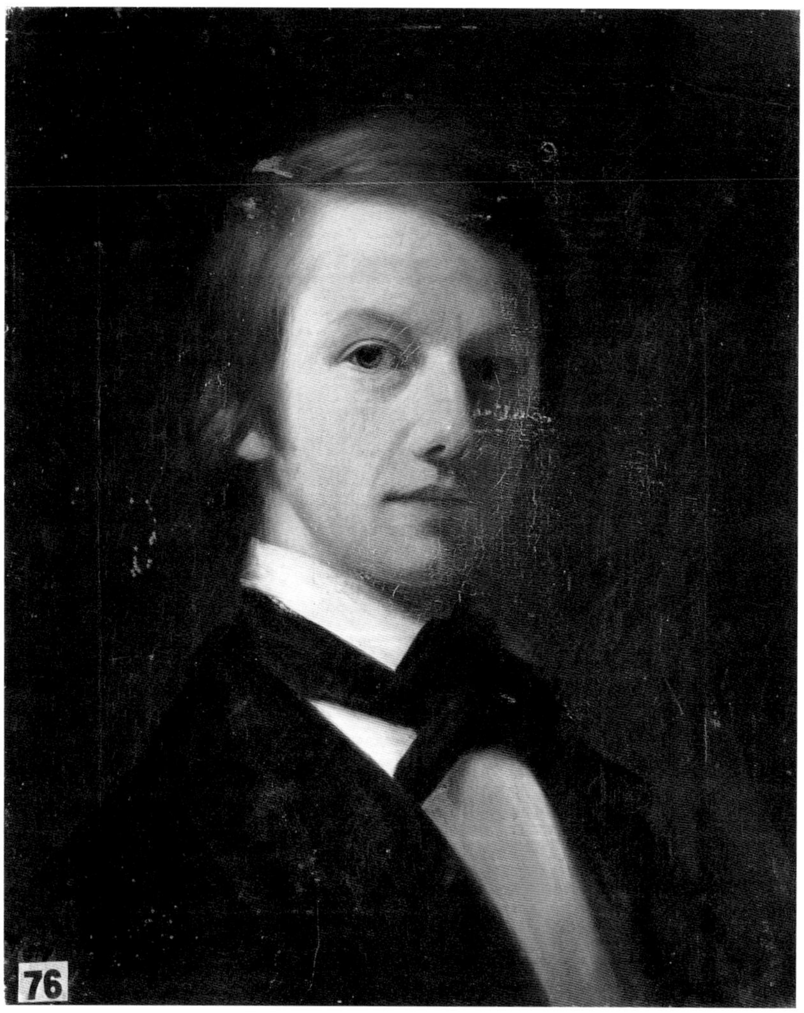

FIGURE 84. Charles V. Bond, *Self-Portrait,* 1847, gift of Henry Munson Utley, photograph © 1949 The Detroit Institute of Arts, 05.1.

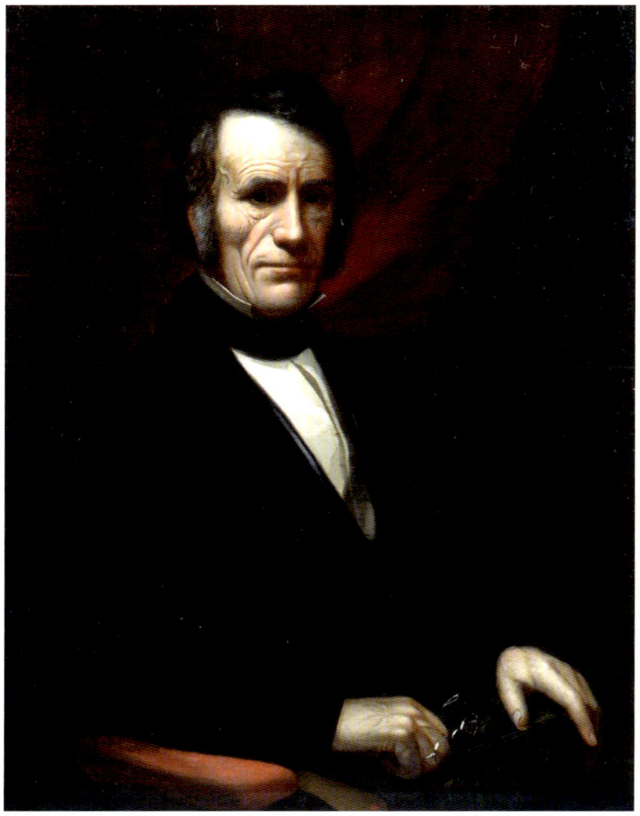

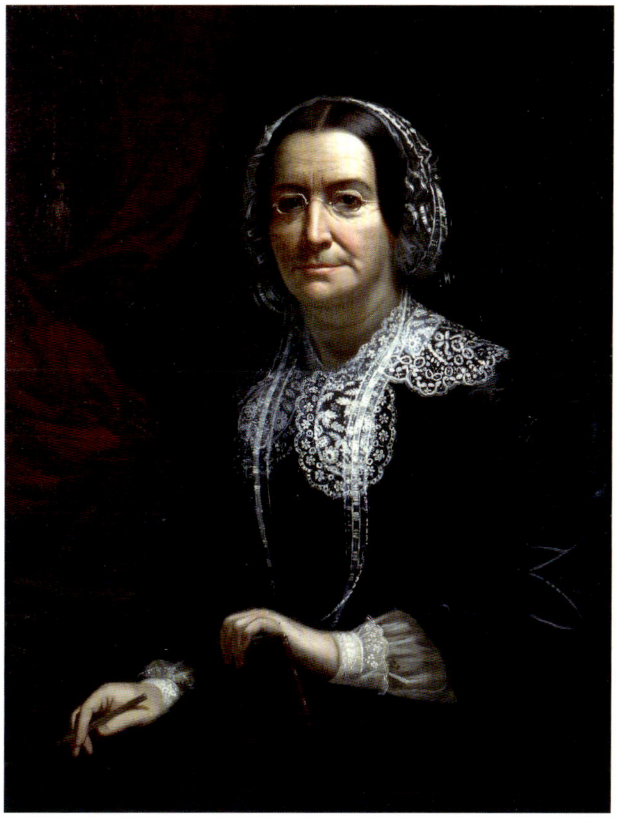

FIGURE 85. Charles V. Bond, *Reverend John Tevis* (1792–1861), ca. 1860, oil on canvas, 35 × 28″, The Filson Historical Society, 1974.12.1.

FIGURE 86. Charles V. Bond, *Julia Tevis* (1799–1880), ca. 1860, oil on canvas, 35 × 28″, The Filson Historical Society, 1974.12.2.

Julia Hieronymus married John Tevis, a Methodist minister, in 1824, and the following year they moved to Shelbyville, Kentucky, where Julia founded the Science Hill Female Academy. Julia Tevis ensured that hers was more than just a finishing school: mathematics, astronomy, languages, history, and chemistry were taught in a rigorous environment that won widespread admiration. A pioneer in women's education, she created one of the most respected schools in the country. The Tevis portraits, executed in a very grand manner, three-quarters-length style, are among the last works created by the artist known to survive.

Milwaukee, 1858–1859, and then in Louisville in 1860 and in 1864 at No. 85 Fourth Street. Considering the difficulties of traveling in 1864 because of the Civil War, it seems likely that Bond painted John and Julia Tevis during his first stay in Louisville (Figs. 85, 86). He was certainly peripatetic, thus rendering his biography little more than a trail of known works. Bond may have been one of those creative loners who haunt nineteenth-century studies. The National Gallery's systematic catalogue entry notes that "the artist lived in boarding houses in Milwaukee and elsewhere and moved frequently," which "may mean he was not married." He disappeared in 1864, though there has been speculation that he went abroad again, where he died in later years.

Archives: FHS; collections: FHS, NGA; literature: Chotner, Gibson, Groce & Wallace, Whitley.

ALEXANDER BRADFORD

(1791–1827)

ALEXANDER BRADFORD WAS BORN in Culpeper County, Virginia, to Austin and Elizabeth Hord Bradford, with whom he migrated to Newtown, Scott County, Kentucky, ca. 1807. He is listed as resident in Georgetown in the federal census for 1810 and 1820. His kinsman John Bradford ran the first printing press in Kentucky and served as chairman of the board of Transylvania University in Lexington. The Transylvania connection has caused speculation that Bradford may have been familiar with both George Beck and Matthew Harris Jouett, speculation enhanced by his clear appropriation of Jouett's neoclassical format. What little is known of his career stems from a commission he received from Martha Chandler Prewitt (1762–1833), a widow living on the Walnut Hill Road near the Clark–Fayette county line. When her husband, Robert, died in 1819 she was most distressed that she had no likeness of him. Upon receipt of a bequest from a relative in Virginia in 1825, she asked Bradford to paint her eight sons, a daughter, two daughters-in-law, and herself. The task took more than a year, during which time he lived with the Prewitt family. The portrait of Levi Prewitt (Fig. 36) has that bold presence, dominating the planar field and enhanced by a piercing sidelong glance, which gives many of the works in this series a riveting immediacy. Levi had settled in Scott County in 1818, where he served as an assistant to the county clerk until his marriage to Margaret Boyce, after which he took up farming at Cave Hill. Much of what is known of Bradford came from the oral history of the Prewitt family, as reported to Edna Talbott Whitley in the late 1930s. More recent information on the artist's life has been gathered by Nancy Katherine Evans Meng, a descendant of William Prewitt, whose portrait she owns. Her files and oral history were shared during a conversation with the author, May 2, 2008.

Literature: Jones & Weber, Pennington (2008), Whitley.

CARL CHRISTIAN BRENNER

(1838–1888)

CARL CHRISTIAN BRENNER was born in Lauterecken, in Bavaria, Germany, on August 10, 1838, the son of a wine merchant, Frederick Brenner. He studied in Germany with Philip Frolig, a minor German Romantic practitioner. Like many other craftsmen, he was displaced by the revolutions of 1848 in Germany; he migrated to New Orleans in 1853, where there was a strong German presence in the arts community. He journeyed upriver to Louisville in 1854, where he remained for the rest of his life. In 1864 Brenner married Ann Glass, with whom he had six children, including the artist Carolus Brenner. Carl Christian Brenner began painting landscapes in 1871, many based on his excursions into the woods near Louisville, especially in Oldham County. His work was exhibited at the Louisville Industrial Exposition in 1874, the Philadelphia Centennial Exposition in 1876, the National Academy of Design in New York 1878–1886, and at the Pennsylvania Academy of Fine Arts 1881–1885. After 1878 he became increasingly known for his landscapes in the tonalist mood. But there are records in the Smithsonian Index of American Painting of his work as a portraitist. Brenner's favorite topic as a landscape painter was the beech tree. Like his Louisville contemporary Harvey Joiner, he could be quite formulaic in his approach to subject matter, rendering masses of trees in dramatic colorations, registering deep shadows and glowing patches of sunlight. But Brenner was also known to have been a most enthusiastic artist *en plein air,* working out-of-doors in Cherokee Park and in nearby Pewee Valley. In an interview with the *Louisville Courier-Journal,* December 18, 1887, he observed, "Nature is not always in its most beautiful moods even in the same spot. The artist must be subjective as well as objective. He must draw from his memory and his heart experiences as well as from the scene before him." By adding a few personal touches of "slanting sunlight, mist, clouds and other circumstances," he believed the artist was capable of making "a hundred pictures" from one site. A portrait of Medora Griffin Miller credited to Brenner is reported in a private collection in Texas in the Smithsonian American Art Museum inventories. He died in Louisville in 1888.

Archives: FHS, Speed; collections: Cheekwood, Corcoran, FHS, JC, KHS, Midway, MMA, Ogden, Speed, St. Louis; literature: Bier, Jones, Jones & Weber, Pennington (1992, 1999, 2008).

CAROLUS BRENNER

(1865–1929)

FIGURE 87. Carolus Brenner, *Carl C. Brenner* (1838–1888), 1888, oil on canvas, 29 × 24½″, The Filson Historical Society, 1985.2.

CAROLUS BRENNER WAS BORN in Louisville, the eldest son of the painter Carl Christian Brenner (Fig. 87). His father sent him abroad to study in the mid-1880s. He was a student at the Munich Art Academy and then pursued sketching expeditions to Vienna, Paris, and the Dutch countryside. Brenner returned to Louisville after his father's death in 1888; there, in 1891, he painted a very striking three-quarter-length portrait of Captain William I. Hunt in military attire. That he was not terribly interested in portraiture may be ascertained from the extant numbers of still-life paintings in the sober Munich-school mood he produced. When his work did not attract substantial patronage in Louisville he sought exhibitions in St. Louis and Kansas City. He moved to Chicago in 1893, first working as a tour guide in the Fine Arts Building at the World's Columbian Exposition of 1893. Chicago became his permanent home in 1895, when he accepted his first position as an illustrator and commercial artist for the Mendel Brothers department store. He was responsible for their legendarily opulent windows, a success that led to his becoming head of Mendel's art department. He died in Chicago.

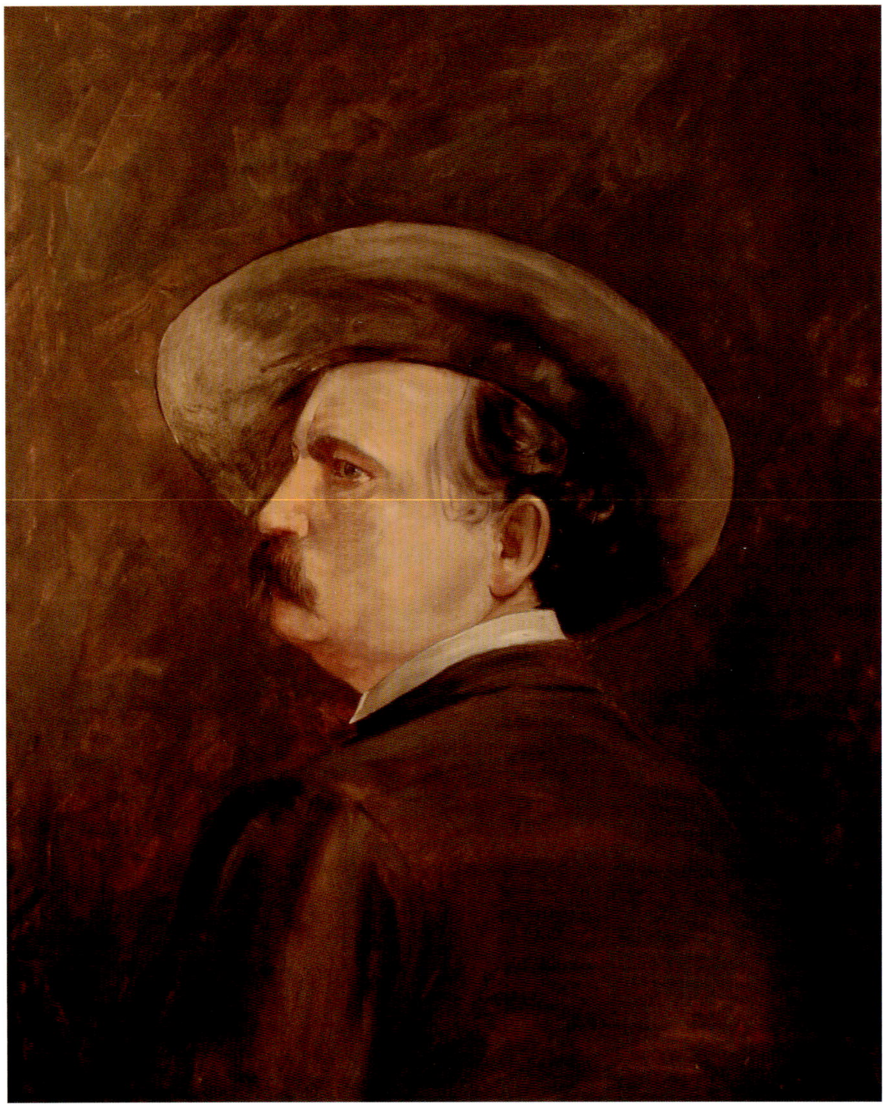

Archives: FHS, Speed; collection: FHS; literature: Jones & Weber, Pennington (2008).

JOSEPH HENRY BUSH

(1794–1865)

JOSEPH HENRY BUSH was born in Mercer County, Kentucky, but grew to maturity in Frankfort, Kentucky, where he worked with his father, Philip, a sign painter and innkeeper. Having attracted attention for his early abilities as a portrait painter, he was dispatched to Philadelphia in the company of his patron, Henry Clay, to work with Thomas Sully, 1814–1817. Bush remained in Philadelphia until 1817; that year he returned to Lexington and exhibited several works in Matthew Harris Jouett's premises that were based on old master precedents. William and George Rogers Clark were among Bush's most important early sitters in Kentucky. He is thought to

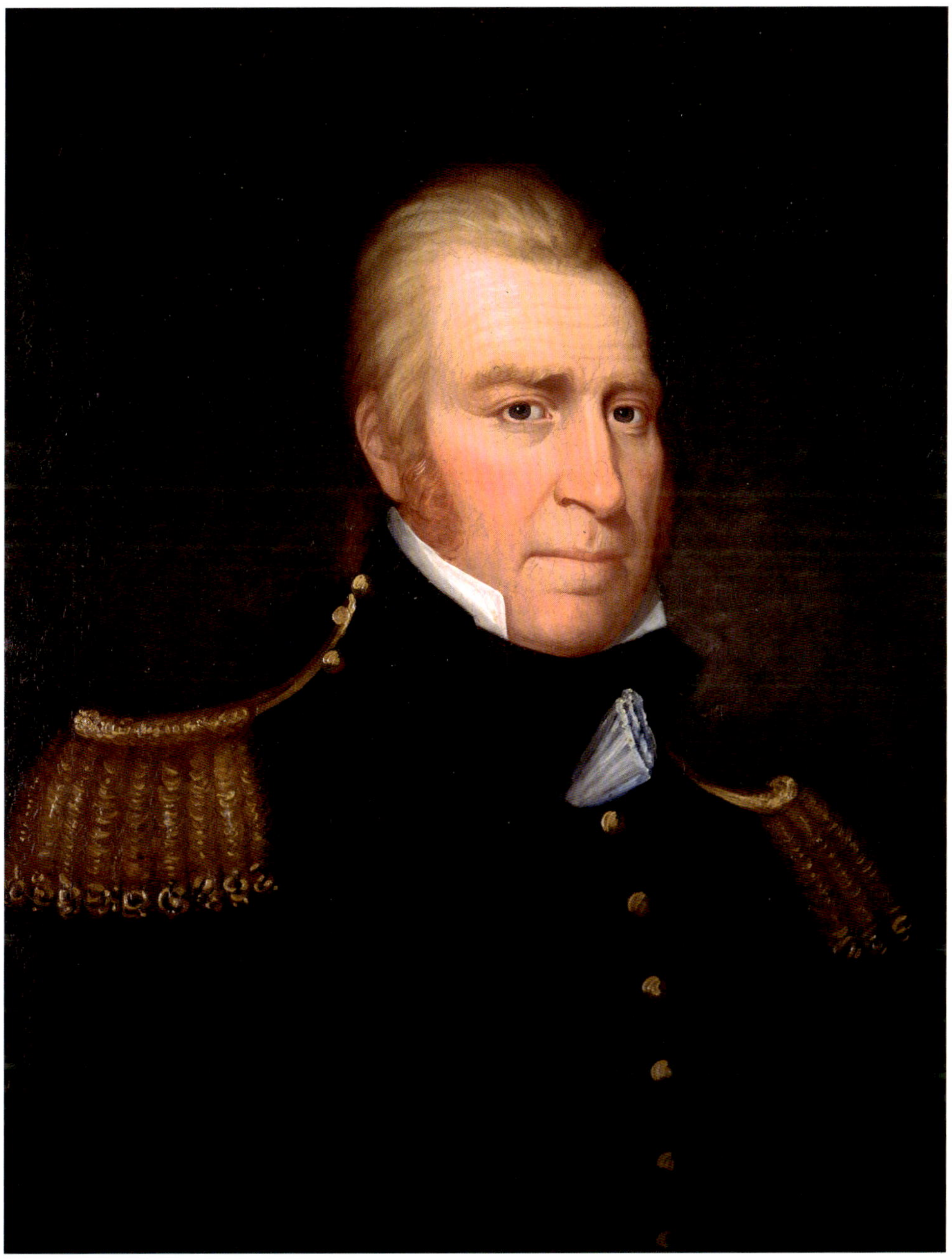

FIGURE 88. Joseph Henry Bush, *General William Clark* (1770–1838), ca. 1817, oil on canvas, 31½ × 26½″, The Filson Historical Society, 1939.11.1.

William Clark had moved with his family to Louisville in 1785. Although too young to have fought in the American Revolution, he joined the Kentucky militia while still in his teens, and became a lieutenant in the U.S. Army in 1792. When Thomas Jefferson asked Meriwether Lewis to lead an expedition west to explore beyond the Mississippi River in 1803, Lewis asked William Clark to be his co-commander. After the expedition Clark was made agent for Indian Affairs in the Louisiana Territory, brigadier general of the militia, and subsequently governor of the Missouri Territory. He later served as Superintendent of Indian Affairs, based in St. Louis, until his death in 1838. Bush's portrait of Clark is an ambitious attempt at high-style military portraiture and reveals some of the lessons he had learned in Philadelphia. The highly placed head, intense eyes, and prominent nose are modeled in a commanding way. The rendering of the uniform is a bit obtuse, attempting to suggest a broad-shouldered man turned slightly away from the planar field. The full epaulette on the left contrasts with the rather wispy one on the right, and the ruff is a bit small. These compositional quirks are more than compensated for by the depth of color, especially in the contrast between the subject's red hair and the blue of his uniform set against a dark background.

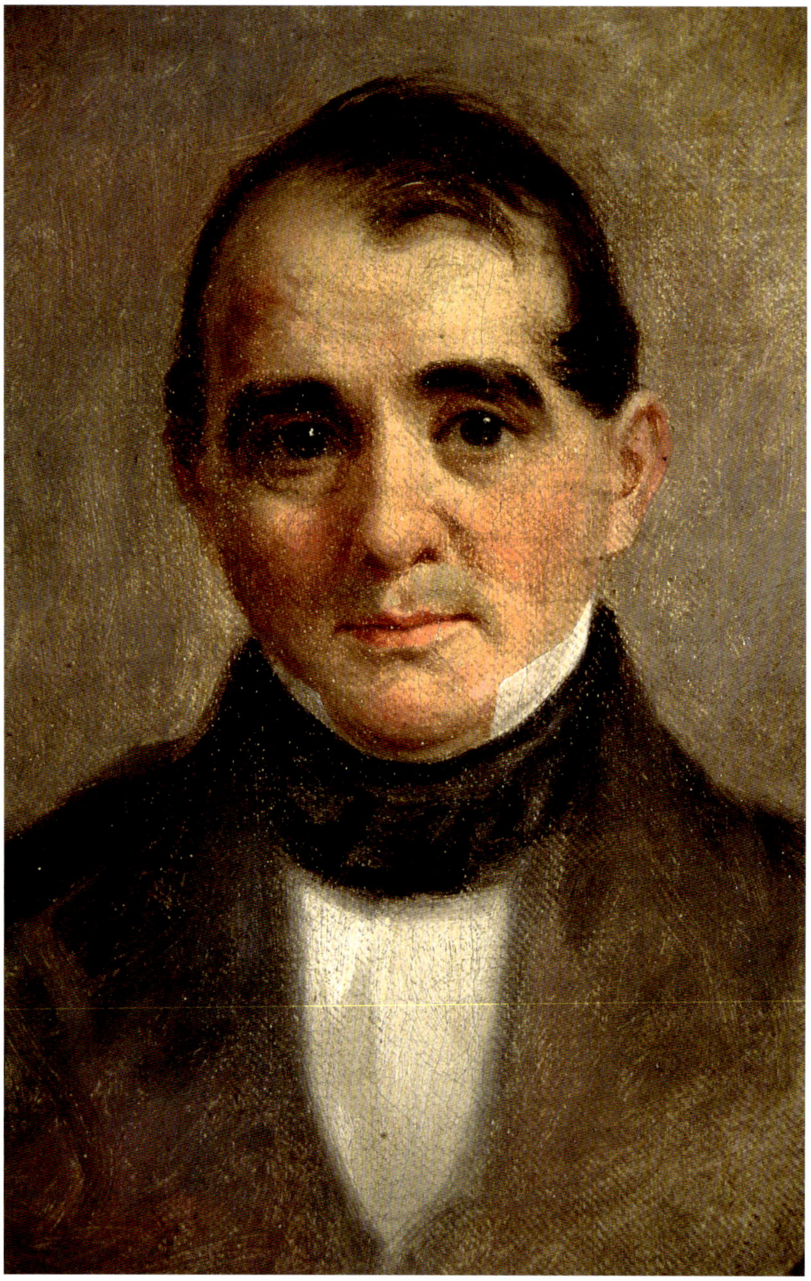

FIGURE 89. Joseph Henry Bush, *Self-portrait,* ca. 1835–1840, oil on canvas, 9½ × 7½", The Filson Historical Society, 1931.3.

have painted George Rogers Clark in 1813 with great frankness, showing his sitter's sad state of ill health, which had been brought about by strokes and a leg amputation. He painted William upon his return from Philadelphia (Fig. 88). While continuing to work in Lexington and Frankfort, he settled in Louisville in 1819, which served as his base for the rest of his professional life. He worked with Frederick Eckstein at the Cincinnati Academy of Fine Arts in 1826. Bush pursued a seasonal itinerancy between Louisville and New Orleans from 1819 to 1857, including several stays in Natchez (Fig. 89). Late in his career, during the 1850s, he began to paint portraits in an oval format. As this style progressed, his characteristic fullness of form and distinctive noses became more pronounced. He also moved toward a greater degree of realism than can be seen in his middle period, when the pouty-lipped children he painted in stacked formats of two over one or one over two seem a pale imitation of Sully at his best. The oval portraits were also motivated by a changing taste in frame fashions, as he began to offer more elaborate casings in the rococo revival style. The Dulaney portraits are excellent examples of that style (Figs. 90, 91). Bush remained in great demand until the outbreak of the Civil War, when he retired from painting and moved to the home of his brother, Dr. James M. Bush, in Lexington, where he was painted by G. P. A. Healy in May 1864. Bush died in Lexington and was buried in the Lexington Cemetery (section D, lot 99).

Archives: FHS; collections: CHM, Farmington, FHS, Locust Grove, LSM, Speed, Transylvania, UKAM, WH; literature: Floyd (1968), Haverstock et al., Jones & Weber, Pennington (Autumn 1986, 2008), Whitley.

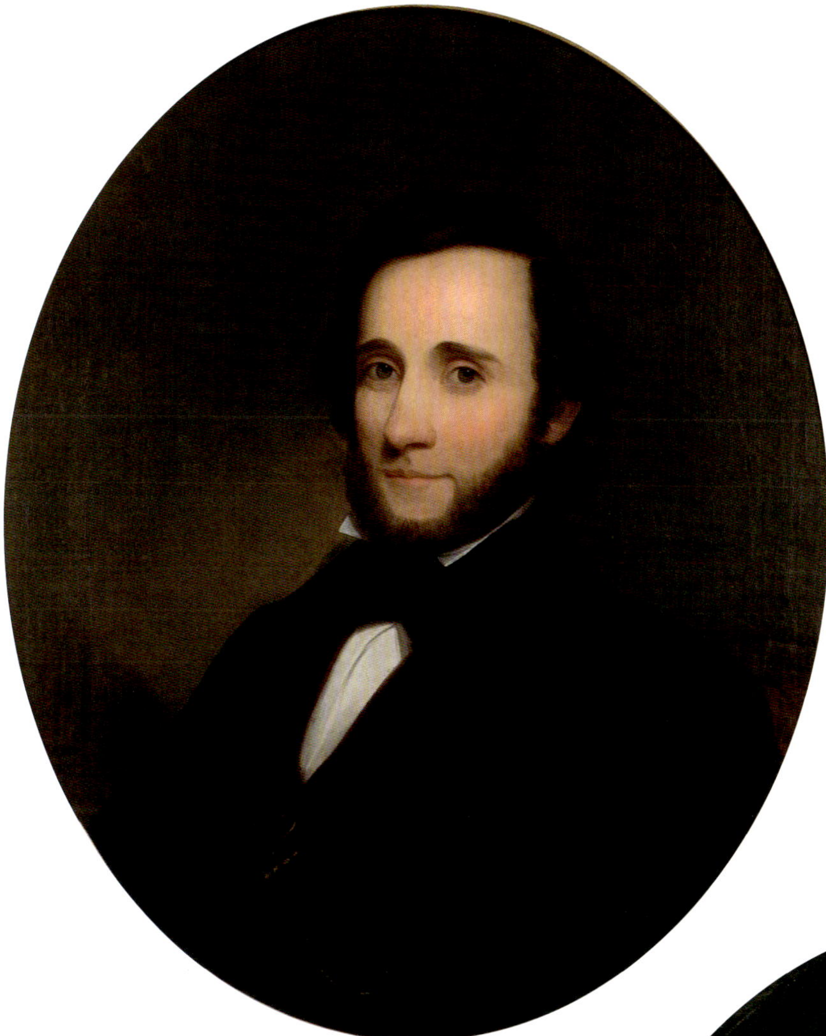

FIGURE 90 *(left)*. Joseph Henry Bush, *Woodford Hector Dulaney* (1822–1902), ca. 1855, oil on canvas, 29 × 24″, The Filson Historical Society, 1997.13.1.

FIGURE 91 *(below)*. Joseph Henry Bush, *Margaret Cawthon Dulaney* (1822–1901), ca. 1855, oil on canvas, 29 × 24″, The Filson Historical Society, 1997.13.2.

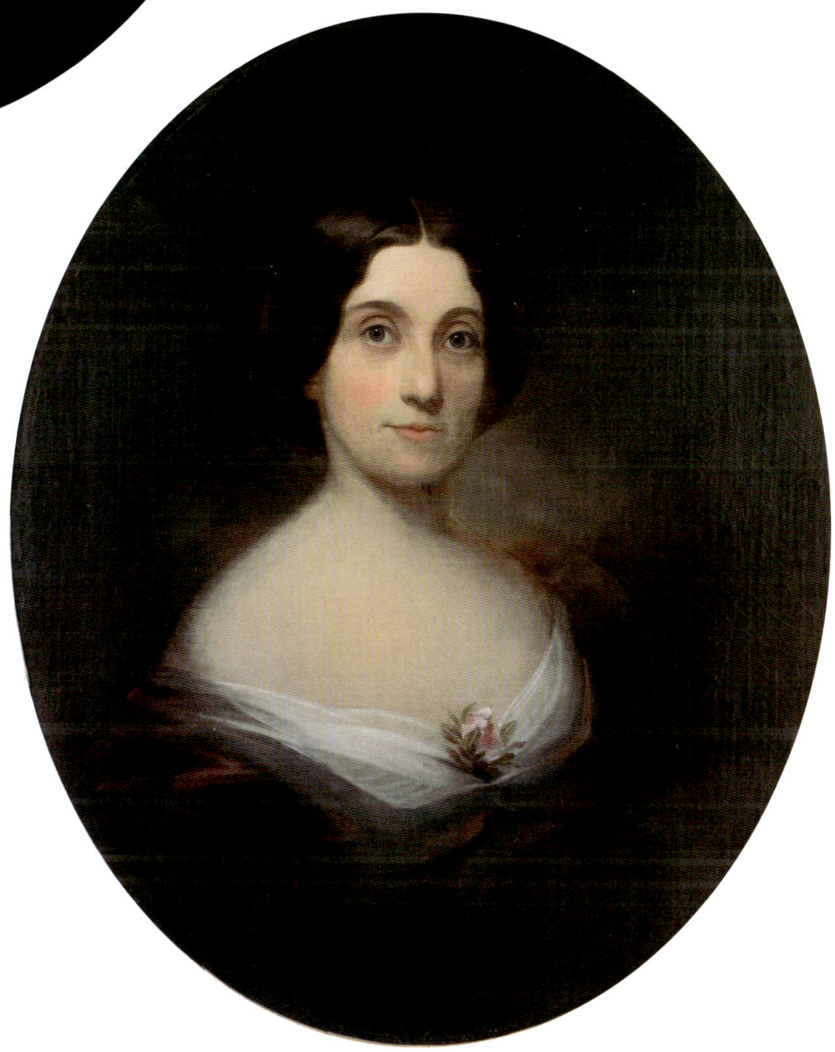

Woodford Dulaney was an Irish immigrant who came to America at an early age and is first noted as a clerk in a dry goods store in Waterford, Virginia, at the age of fourteen. He moved to Louisville in 1840, where he became a partner in the firm of Mark, Dulaney & Downs, the largest retail dry-goods store in Louisville at that time. In 1851 he married Margaret Cawthon, reputedly one of the richest women in Louisville, and together they had ten children. Dulaney served on the Louisville city council during the Civil War and was president of two railroads.

THOMAS CAMPBELL

(ca. 1790–ca. 1858)

THOMAS CAMPBELL IS SAID to have been born in Scotland, though his birth and death dates conflict in two critical sources. He is first noted in this country in Baltimore in 1832, announced by a local newspaper as having arrived from Edinburgh. Campbell joined the lithographer Colin Milne in a printing business in 1834, while also acting as an agent for medicinal products, notably Morrison's Hygeian Medicine. From 1835 to 1851 he moved between Louisville and Cincinnati and was one of the most peripatetic itinerant artists of the era. In his capacity as an agent for Morrison's, he visited Louisville in June 1835, where he settled. From a studio on Main Street between Fifth and Sixth Streets he launched a career as a miniaturist. Success in that

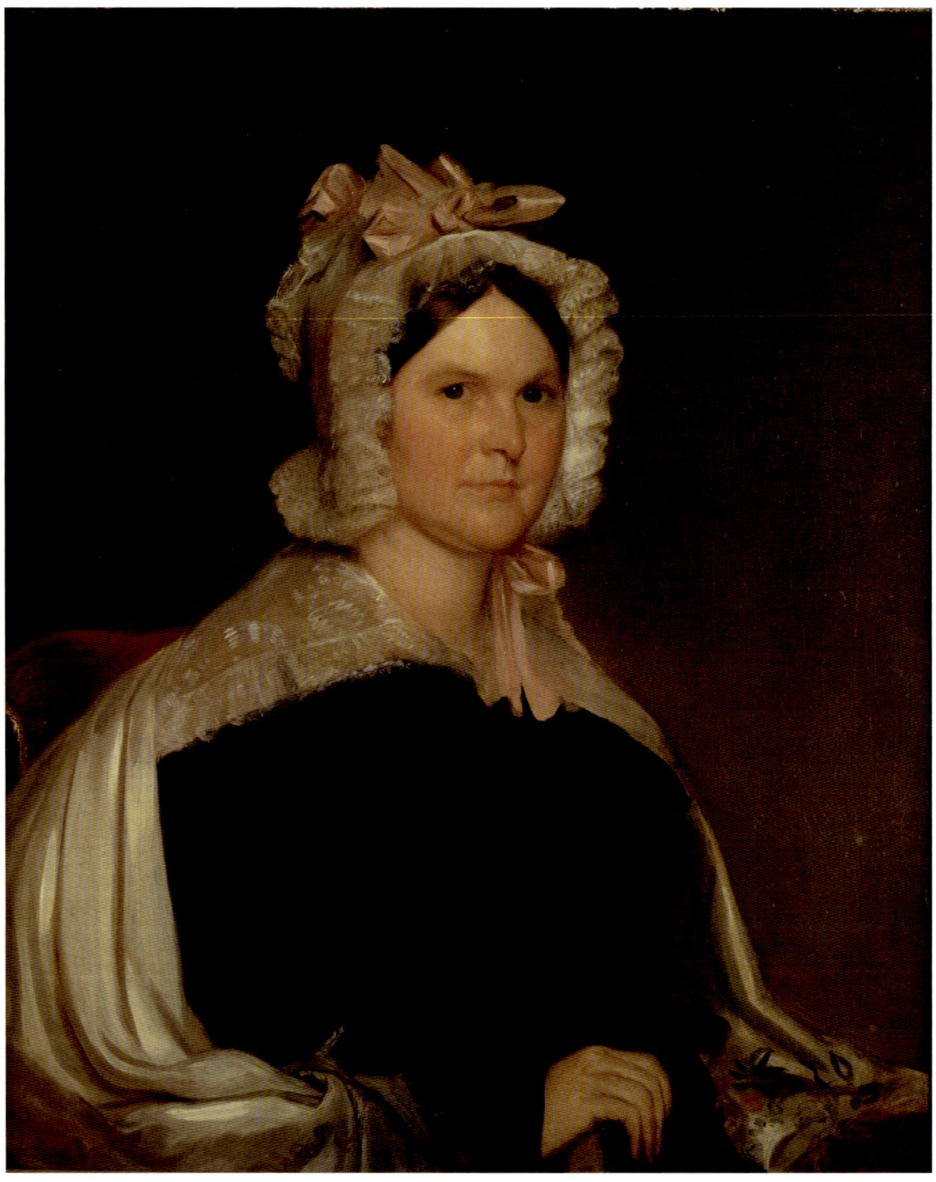

FIGURE 92. Thomas Campbell, *Abigail Oldham Churchill* (1789–1854), ca. 1845, oil on canvas, 30 × 25″, The Filson Historical Society, 1984.18.1.

practice led to an exhibition in Cincinnati in 1839, where he showed twenty-seven miniatures in a group exhibition of notable locals. He moved to Cincinnati in 1840, exhibiting work at the Cincinnati Academy of Fine Art as well as on the premises of the Society for the Promotion of Useful Knowledge. Campbell returned to Louisville in 1845, at which time he could have painted the Churchill portraits (Figs. 92, 93). Although Campbell kept a studio in Cincinnati between Race and Elm in 1846, most of his subsequent activity was in Louisville. Several of his lithographic works for sheet music, book illustrations, and a proposed "Kentucky Stock Book" have survived. Late in his career he advertised as a graphic artist, specializing in detailed woodcuts for commercial purposes. Although there is no record of Campbell after 1851, his two sons, Thomas E. and J. Alan, were listed as sculptors in the Louisville city directory for 1859, specializing in funereal monuments.

Collections: FHS, LAC; literature: Cist, Groce & Wallace, Hageman, Haverstock et al., Quick, Schmidt, Whitley.

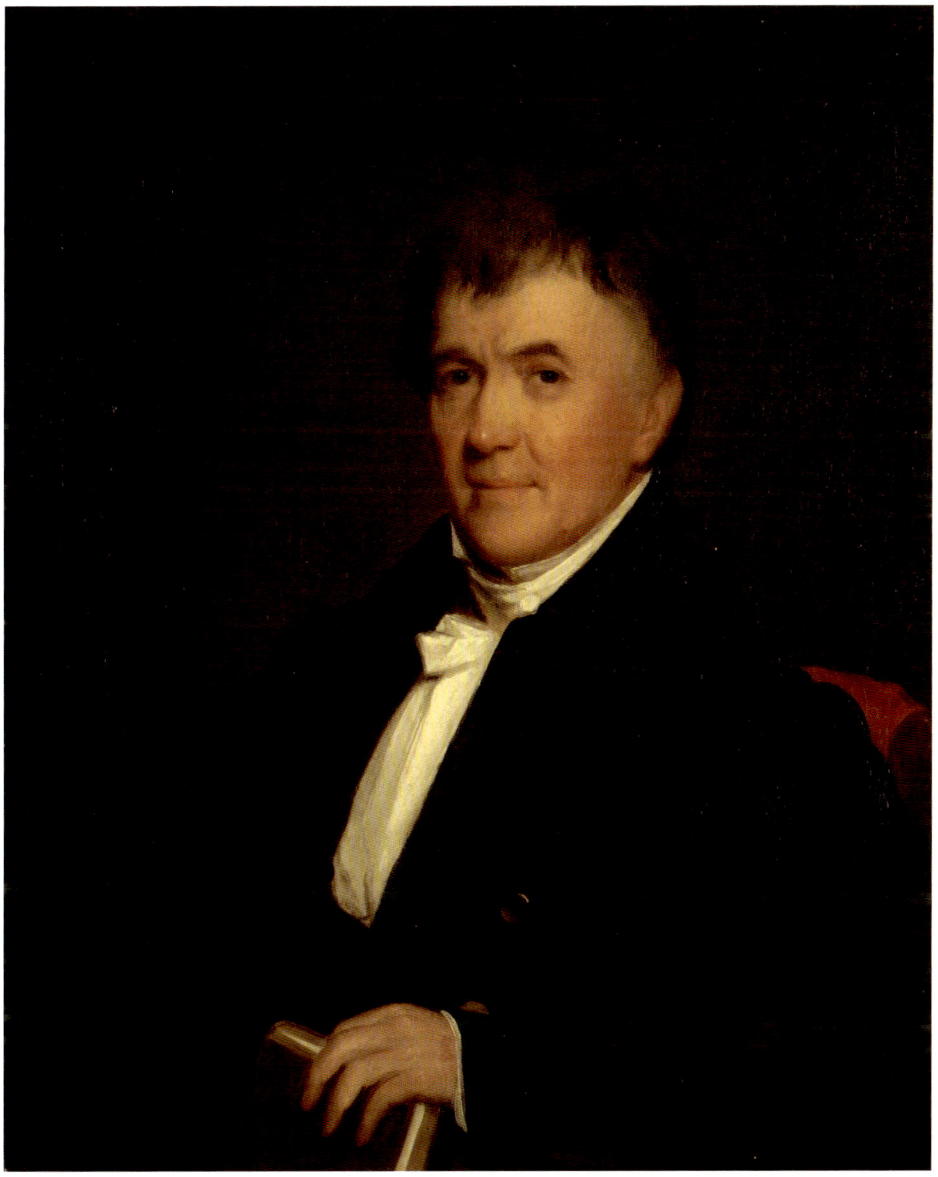

FIGURE 93. Thomas Campbell, *Samuel Churchill* (1779–1863), ca. 1845, oil on canvas, 30 × 25″, The Filson Historical Society, 1984.18.2.

Samuel Churchill was the son of Armistead Churchill, a Virginian who came to Kentucky around 1784. Samuel, his youngest son, was only sixteen when his father died in 1795. In 1803 he married Abigail Oldham, who was the daughter of Colonel William Oldham, for whom the Kentucky county was named, and who was also Churchill's step-niece. Two of his eleven children who grew to adulthood, John and Henry, leased their nephew Col. M. Lewis Clark land on which to establish a race track, named Churchill Downs in honor of their ancestor Armistead's original land grant. Samuel and Abigail were originally buried in the family cemetery but were re-interred at Cave Hill in 1910 by their descendant R. C. B. Thruston.

WASHINGTON BOGART COOPER

(1802–1889)

WASHINGTON BOGART COOPER was born near Jonesboro, Washington County, Tennessee, to James and Elizabeth Bogart Cooper, and raised in Carthage and Shelbyville, Tennessee. According to family lore, he studied with Ralph E. W. Earl, a portraitist and kinsman of Andrew Jackson, in Murfreesboro, 1822. He relocated to Nashville in 1830, where he was based for the remainder of his professional career. His younger brother, the artist William Browning Cooper, once reported him as having worked with Thomas Sully and Henry Inman during a trip east in 1831. Cooper kept a detailed account book of portrait commissions, of which the years 1837–1846 survive in the Tennessee State Library in Nashville. In these account books he lists the prices he charged for various sizes, rare information for the time. Cooper was also active as an itinerant in middle Tennessee, 1830–1885, and made several trips to Kentucky as well as to Cincinnati in 1842. Much in demand and highly productive, he is said to have painted thirty to thirty-five portraits a year, and thus became known as "the man of a thousand portraits." Among his most notable series of portraits were images of the governors of Tennessee before 1858, the early bishops of the Methodist Episcopal Church in Tennessee, and the Masonic Grand Masters of Nashville. Among his most famous clerical sitters was Alexander Campbell, a leading reformer of the 1840s (Fig. 94). Cooper married Ann Litton in 1839, with whom he had three sons. The artist died in Nashville and is buried in Mt. Olivet Cemetery.

Archives: TSL; collections: FHS, NPG, THS; literature: B. Bishop, Bruns, J. Kelly, Pennington (1993), Whitley.

FIGURE 94 *(facing page).* Washington Bogart Cooper, *Alexander Campbell* (1788–1866), ca. 1840–1845, oil on canvas, 29½ × 24½", The Filson Historical Society, 1993.35.1.

Campbell was born in Ireland, and the family moved to America in 1809 and settled in Pennsylvania. Having spent a year at the University of Glasgow seminary, he began preaching at the Brush Run, Pennsylvania, Disciples of Christ Church in 1810. He married Margaret Brown in 1811, and they made Bethany, Virginia (now West Virginia), their permanent home. Following the birth of his first child in 1812, Campbell was drawn to the Baptist Church owing to his doubts about infant baptism. In 1823 he founded the *Christian Baptist,* a journal that in 1830 became the *Millennial Harbinger,* a result of his increasing interest in the second coming of Christ. Campbell was often in Kentucky, where he was a very popular preacher. His tall and commanding presence attracted many admirers, and the Disciples Church became a major force in the ecclesiastical life of Kentucky. Cooper is most likely to have painted this portrait, previously in the collection of the Louisville Free Public Library and first cataloged by the Works Progress Administration, on one of his itinerant trips to Kentucky during the 1840s.

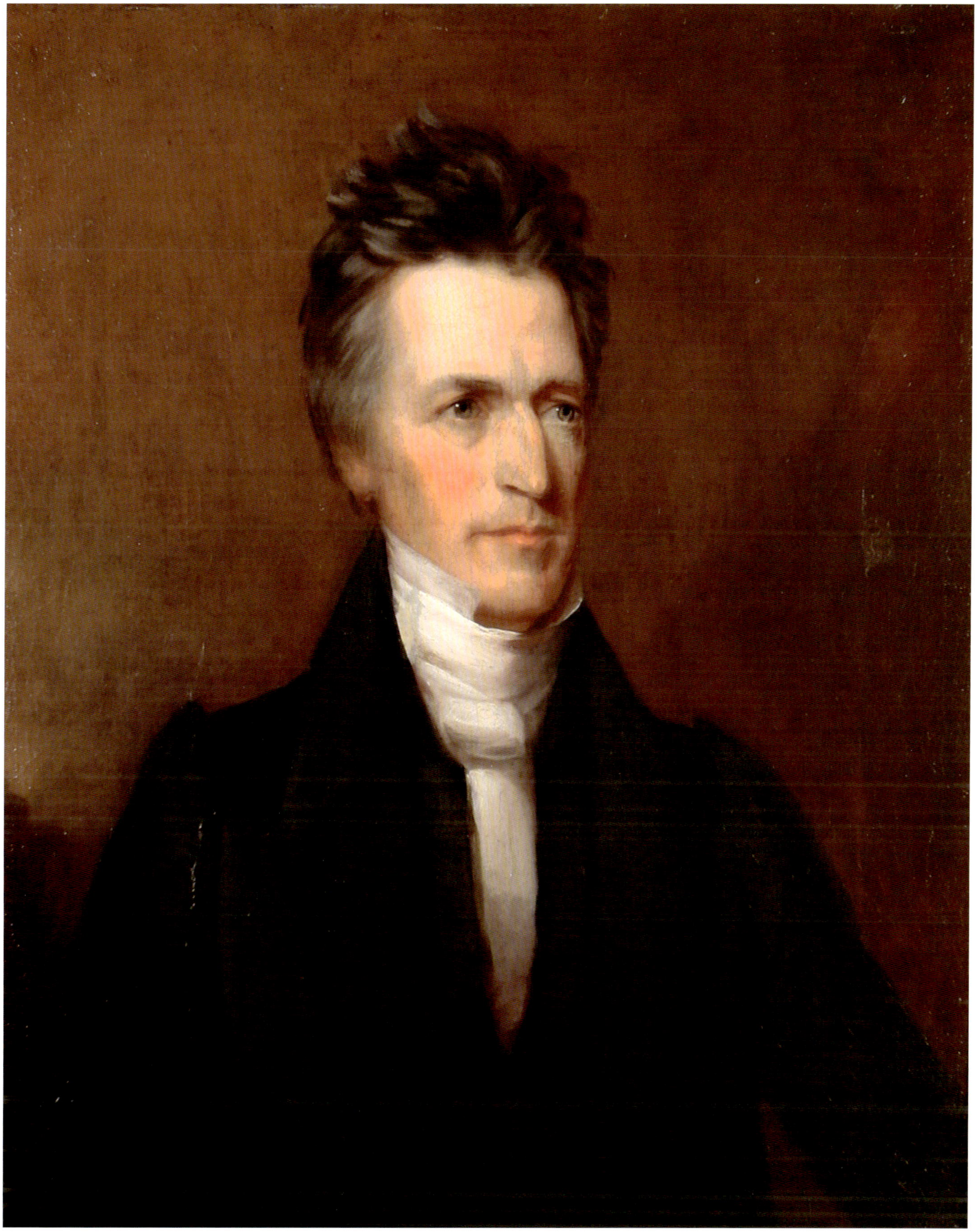

WILLIAM BROWNING COOPER

(1811–1900)

WILLIAM BROWNING COOPER was born near Carthage, Smith County, Tennessee, to James and Elizabeth Bogart Cooper. With the generous assistance of his brother, the painter Washington Bogart Cooper, he attended the National Academy of Design, 1832. Cooper returned to Nashville in 1832, moved to Memphis in 1834, then departed for Europe for a study tour, 1835–1838. Upon his return he worked as an itinerant based in Memphis from 1840 to 1853; he then moved back to Nashville in 1854, continuing an itinerancy that included Memphis, Columbia, Tennessee, and northern Alabama. He also worked in Washington, painting his fellow Tennesseans, presidents James Polk and Andrew Johnson. From 1854 to 1861 Cooper traveled a great deal, working in St. Louis, Chicago, New Orleans, and Little Rock. In the early years of the Civil War he moved to Henderson, Kentucky, and is listed in city directories as having a studio in Louisville in 1869–1870 and again in 1877. James Kelly disproves the oral history that both Cooper brothers signed their works "W. B. Cooper," making it difficult to distinguish between them. However, both artists developed a softer, more warmly colored style after the Civil War. William Cooper died in Chattanooga, Tennessee, and was buried in Macon, Georgia, near the home of his daughter.

Archives: AAA, TSL; collections: FHS, Speed, THS, TSM; Literature: Bruns, J. Kelly, Whitley.

AARON HOUGHTON CORWINE

(1802–1830)

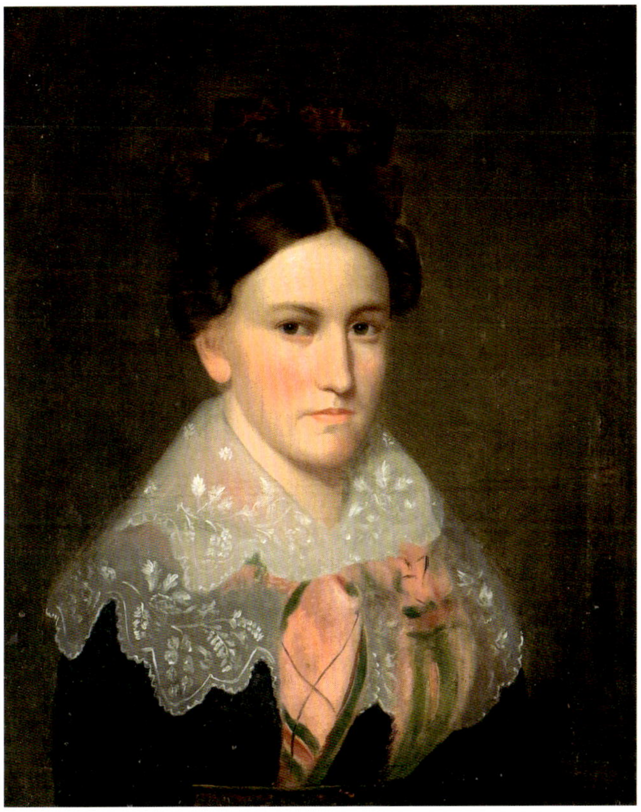

FIGURE 95. Aaron Houghton Corwine, *Dorothy Waltz Kerner* (d. 1885), 1828, oil on canvas, 27 × 21″, The Filson Historical Society, 2003.6.2.

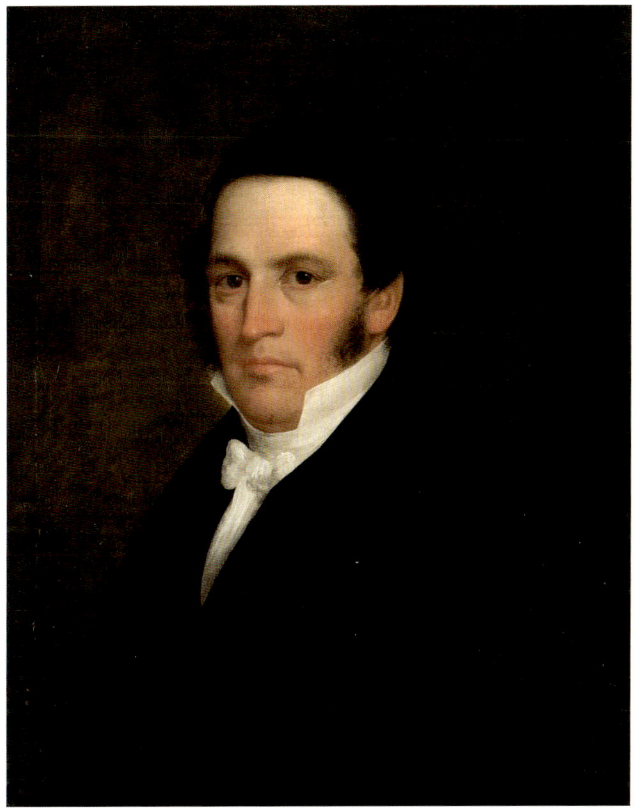

FIGURE 96. Aaron Houghton Corwine, *Lewis Kerner* (1800–1868), 1828, oil on canvas, 26 × 21″, The Filson Historical Society, 2003.6.1.

AARON HOUGHTON CORWINE was born in Mason County, Kentucky, to Amos Corwine and his wife. He was given some instruction by J. Turner, an itinerant working in Maysville, in 1817, and also studied with Thomas Sully in Philadelphia, 1819–1820. Corwine was resident in Cincinnati after 1820, while also active in northern Kentucky, 1818–1825. In 1825 he painted Andrew Jackson while Jackson was visiting Cincinnati. He exhibited at the Pennsylvania Academy, 1821–1822 and 1828–1829, and at the National Academy of Design in 1830. He traveled to England in 1829 for further study, but became ill and died from consumption in Philadelphia just after returning from his trip abroad. A portrait of Dr. Daniel Drake, attributed to Corwine by Whitley, once owned by the Fayette County Medical Society, seems indeed to be his work.

Archives: FHS; collections: CAM, FHS, Maysville; literature: Aronson (2003), Cincinnati Art Museum, Dwight (1955), Hageman, Haverstock et al., Jones & Weber, Pennington (2008), Whitley.

Lewis Kerner was born in Baden-Baden, Germany, to Lewis and Francesca Koerner, and he anglicized his name after he moved to America and settled in Cincinnati, in 1827. In Germany he had learned the trade of jeweler and clockmaker, which he followed once in Ohio. In 1828 he married Dorothy Waltz, also a native of Germany. According to Betty Bone Scheiss, a descendant, these portraits were painted to celebrate their marriage.

RESON B. CRAFFT

(ca. 1809–after 1877)

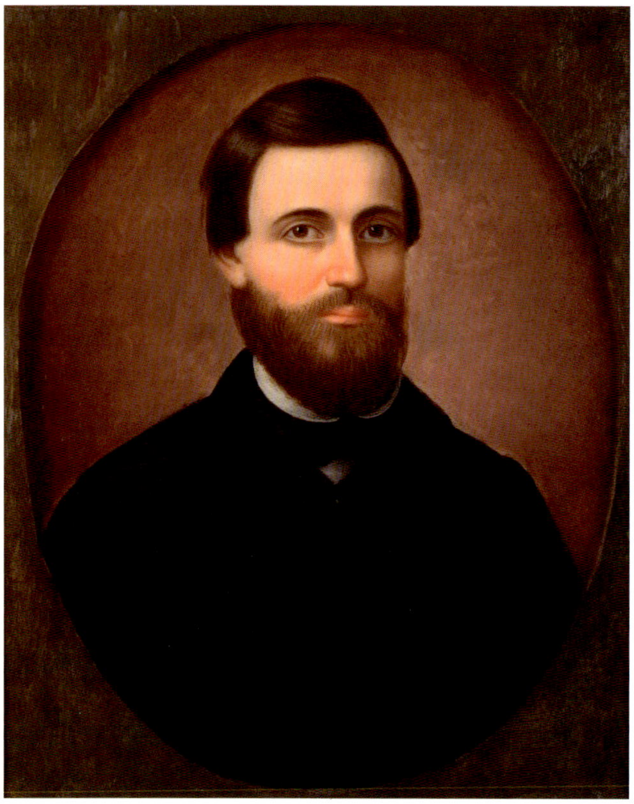

FIGURE 97. Reson B. Crafft, *George Martin Jessee* (1830–1896), dated February 16, 1864, oil on canvas, 30 × 24″, The Filson Historical Society, 1997.16.1.

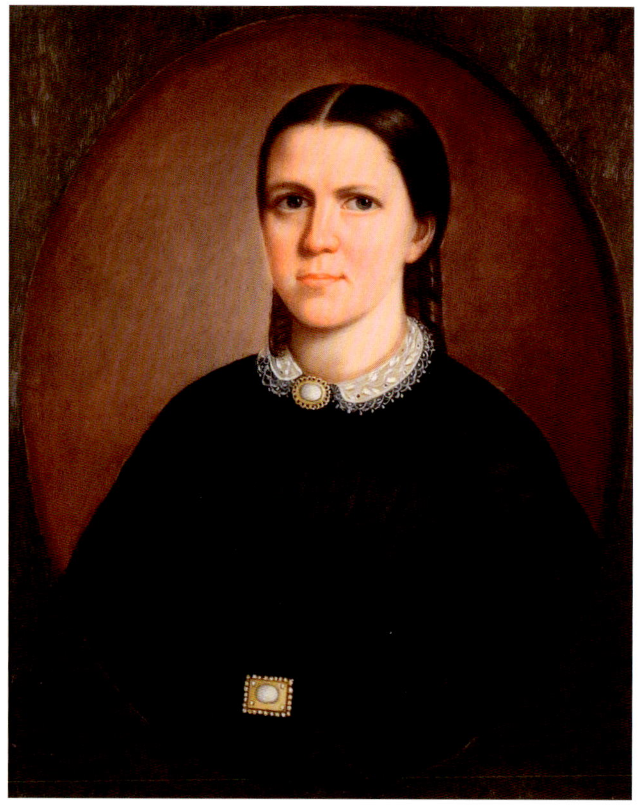

FIGURE 98. Reson B. Crafft, *Elizabeth Foree Jessee* (ca. 1830–1914), February 16, 1864, oil on canvas, 29½ × 24½″, The Filson Historical Society, 1997.16.2.

George Martin Jessee was the son of Thomas M. Jessee and Mary Bird McCracken Jessee. He married Elizabeth Foree, and they became the parents of ten children. During the Civil War George Jessee raised a Confederate force of volunteers known as Jessee's Battalion of Mounted Rifles. Apparently George and Elizabeth Jessee commissioned a portrait of three of their children from Crafft at the same time as the two of themselves, as all three are signed and dated February 16, 1864, on the back.

THERE IS MUCH confusing information about the self-taught itinerant variously known as Resin B. Craft, Reasoner Crafft, and R. B. Crofft. According to census records, he was born in Ohio. He is first reported as a portraitist in Fort Wayne, Indiana, 1836–1844, where he painted Robert Filson. Noted as working in Louisville and Madison County, Kentucky, 1845, Crafft later worked in Iowa, 1847, and in Ohio in the early 1850s. He returned to Louisville in 1853. An extant portrait of two children in the Valentine family, signed and dated on the rear "R B Crafft, 1864," may be a posthumous portrait taken from photographs. Together with the portraits of the Jessee family (Figs. 97–99), they indicate the artist was working in Henry County, Kentucky, in that year. Crafft is noted in Danville, Kentucky, in 1865, and may have been active in the deep South, especially Mississippi, where his work has been found. He settled permanently in Louisville, 1870, where, according to Jane Sikes Hageman, he later died.

Collection: FHS; literature: Burnet, Groce & Wallace, Hageman, Haverstock et al., Peat (1954), Pennington (2008), Rumford & Weekley, Speakes, Whitley.

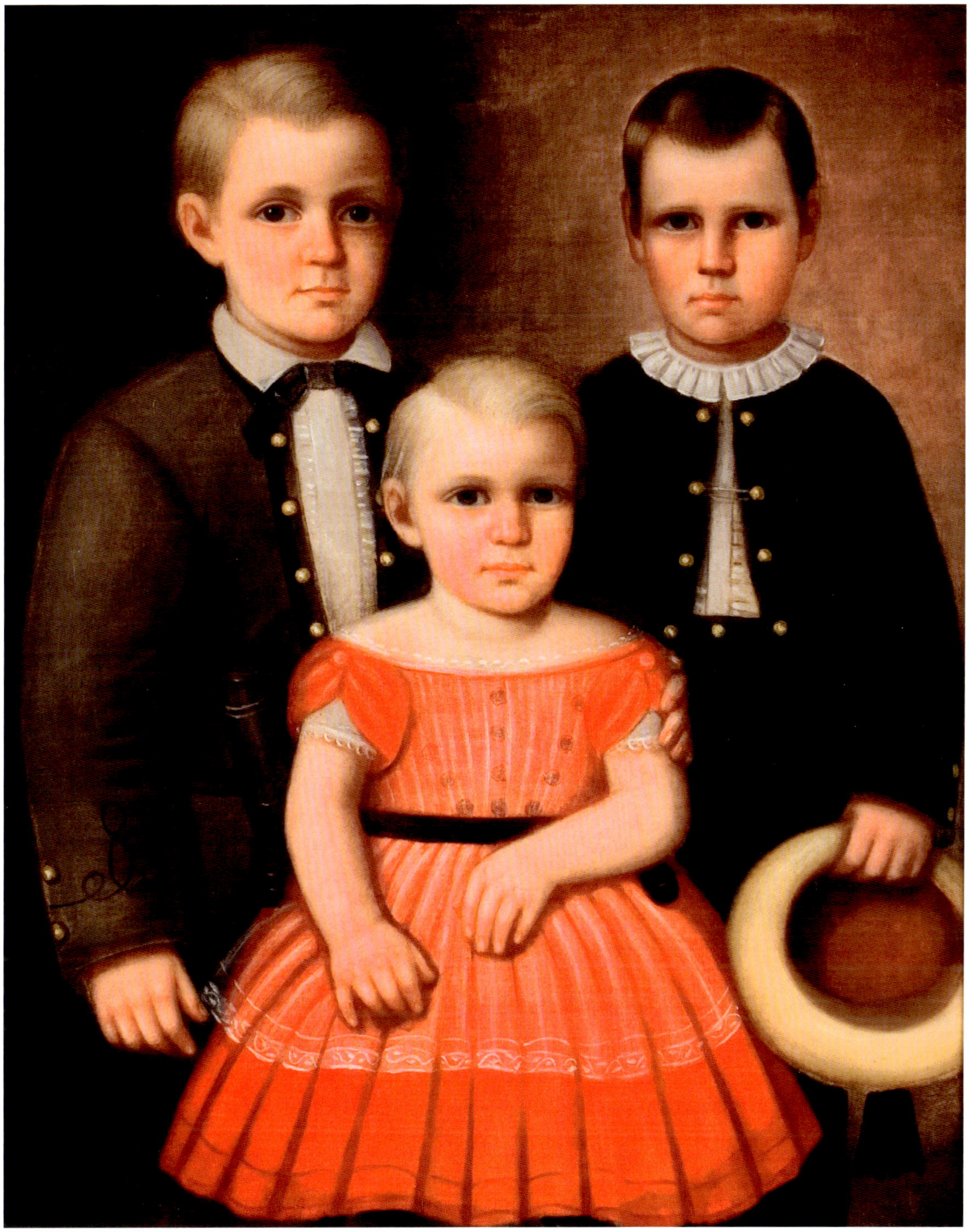

FIGURE 99. Reson B. Crafft, *Virgil McCracken Jessee, John Foree Jessee, William Jessee,* dated February 16, 1864, oil on canvas, 35½ × 29″, The Filson Historical Society, 1997.16.3.

Virgil McCracken Jessee, John Foree Jessee, and William Jessee were the three eldest of the Jessee children. The child who looks to be the eldest, on the left, is dressed in a gray uniform similar to that worn by Confederate forces, although his father is depicted in civilian clothing. Crafft is a classic plain painter, intrigued with costume detail and forthright in his use of color, which is applied to emphasize the contours of the figures standing against a neutral background. The intensity and immediacy of his work, as seen in the Jessee family group, makes him easy to identify and compounds the frustration at the lack of biographical information.

PATRICK HENRY DAVENPORT

(1803–1890)

PATRICK HENRY DAVENPORT was born in Danville, Kentucky, at the Indian Queen Tavern, which was operated by his parents, Richard and Elizabeth Tadlock Davenport. He was largely self-taught, although he may have had some experience working with Matthew Jouett and is reputed to have assisted Oliver Frazer in painting the full-length portrait of George Washington for the old State Capitol in 1838. Though there has been speculation that he began painting portraits at the age of fifteen, his first dated works are from the early 1820s. Davenport married Eliza Ann Bohannon in Vicksburg in 1827, and thereafter his presence and commissions reflect the strong family and socioeconomic ties between Kentucky and Mississippi during the antebellum period. Davenport was active as an itinerant in Kentucky—in Madison, Garrard, Boyle, Jefferson, and Nelson Counties—as well as in Cincinnati and rural Indiana and Illinois from 1820 to 1840. These were the years of his most intense period of activity as a portraitist, and he was particularly productive in Harrodsburg and Danville. Many works from this period repeat signature formulas: the subjects are placed high on the planar field, richly colored, and painted with strongly modeled features and highly detailed costumes, especially the women's lace caps. The subjects often seem to be glancing, as though surreptitiously, to the far right or left, making their abbreviated anatomies rather disengaged. In his own self-portrait Davenport gazes straight ahead with something of the same uneasy look. He also projected a highly architectonic hairstyle upon his female figures, often crowning them with a massive hair plait, adorned with combs of horn. His double portrait of the Hords is an unusual compositional departure for Davenport (Fig. 100). The Hord portrait was painted prior to Davenport's purchase, in 1839, of Crab Orchard Springs, a popular watering hole in Lincoln County, Kentucky. At five dollars a week, Crab Orchard was one of the most expensive and fashionable resorts in Kentucky, the "Saratoga of the South," according to J. Winston Coleman, who also reports it as being "the grand summer rallying-ground for Southern belles and beaux, and the realm of romance and flirtation." Davenport sold the resort in 1853 and invested the proceeds in a farm of two hundred acres near Sumner, Illinois. There is a marked difference, in the portraits that have been recorded, between his works done before and after the Civil War. The antebellum portraits, though charmingly awkward, all appear to be done from life. The later works, far fewer in number, have a clarity of feature and a flattened anatomical positioning that would seem to indicate they were done from photographs. He died in 1890 on his farm in Lawrence County, Illinois.

Collections: FHS, KHS; literature: J. Coleman (1955), Haverstock et al., Jones & Weber, Peat (1954), Pittenger & Perkins, Whitley.

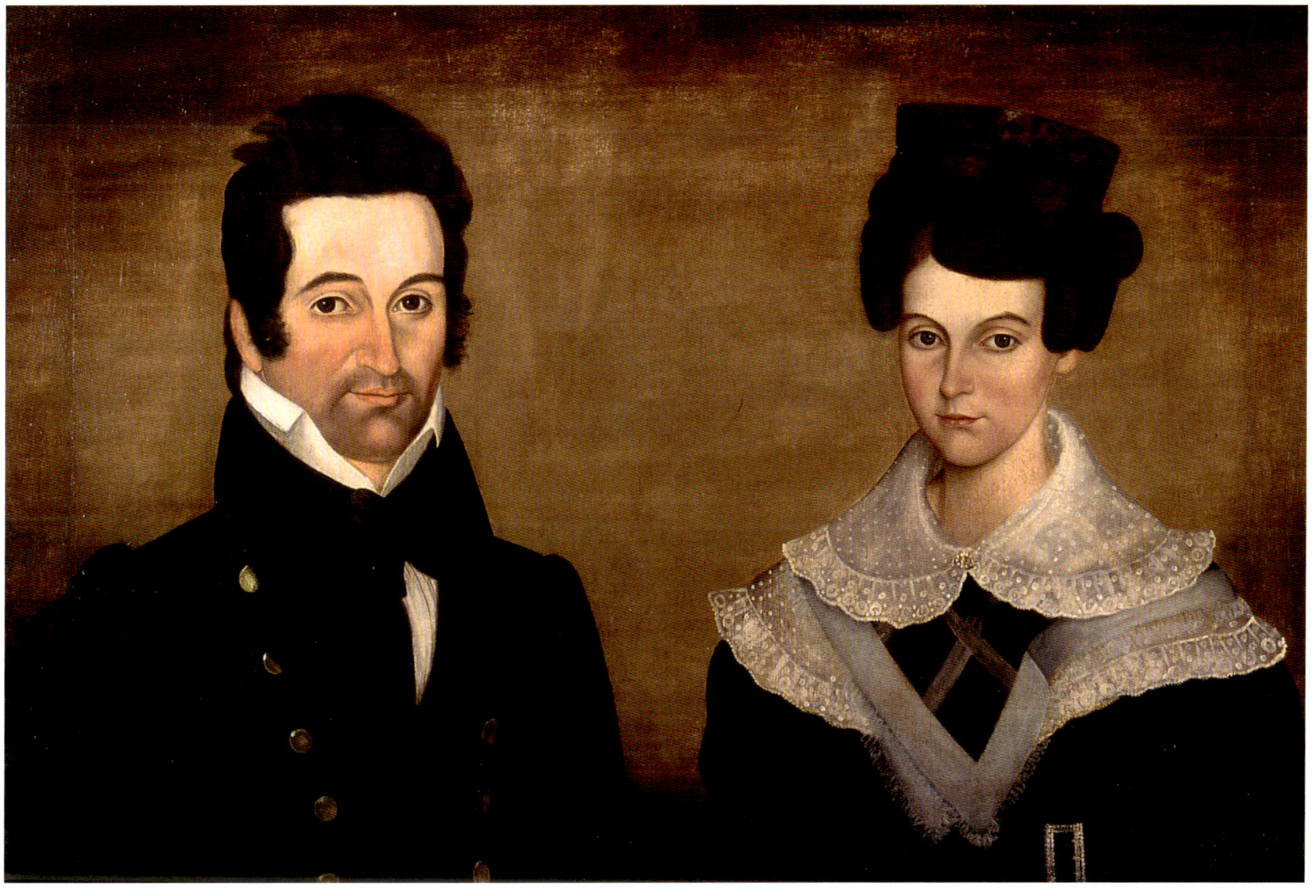

FIGURE 100. Patrick Henry Davenport, *Robert Craddock Hord* (1801–1848) *and Julia Ann Pickett Hord* (b. 1810), ca. 1835, oil on canvas, 26¾ × 41¼″, The Filson Historical Society, 1995.3.

Robert Craddock Hord, born in 1801, was the son of Willis and Polly Buckner Hord, natives of Port Royal, Virginia, who moved to Kentucky in 1793. Willis Hord was the first county clerk of Bracken County. In 1825 Robert married his first cousin Julia Pickett. She was only fifteen years old but had attended a finishing school for a year at her parent's request. They had seven children. By the early 1840s the Hords had settled in the Louisville area, where they built a Greek Revival–style home. There was sufficient property around the house for Hord to prosper as a planter and livestock breeder. Several items listed in his estate were used in making whiskey, which indicates he may have also been a distiller. He was killed in a runaway carriage accident in 1848.

SAMUEL H. DEARBORN

(ca. 1786–1852)

SAMUEL H. DEARBORN was born in Boston, the son of Benjamin Dearborn. He was apprenticed to a wood engraver, Abel Bowen of Boston, and then worked in Pittsburgh 1804–1805 as a miniaturist. Dearborn was active in northern Ohio, 1805–1809, before he appeared in Lexington, Kentucky, May 1, 1809, according to an advertisement in the *Kentucky Gazette.* During this time he was boarding in Frankfort with the

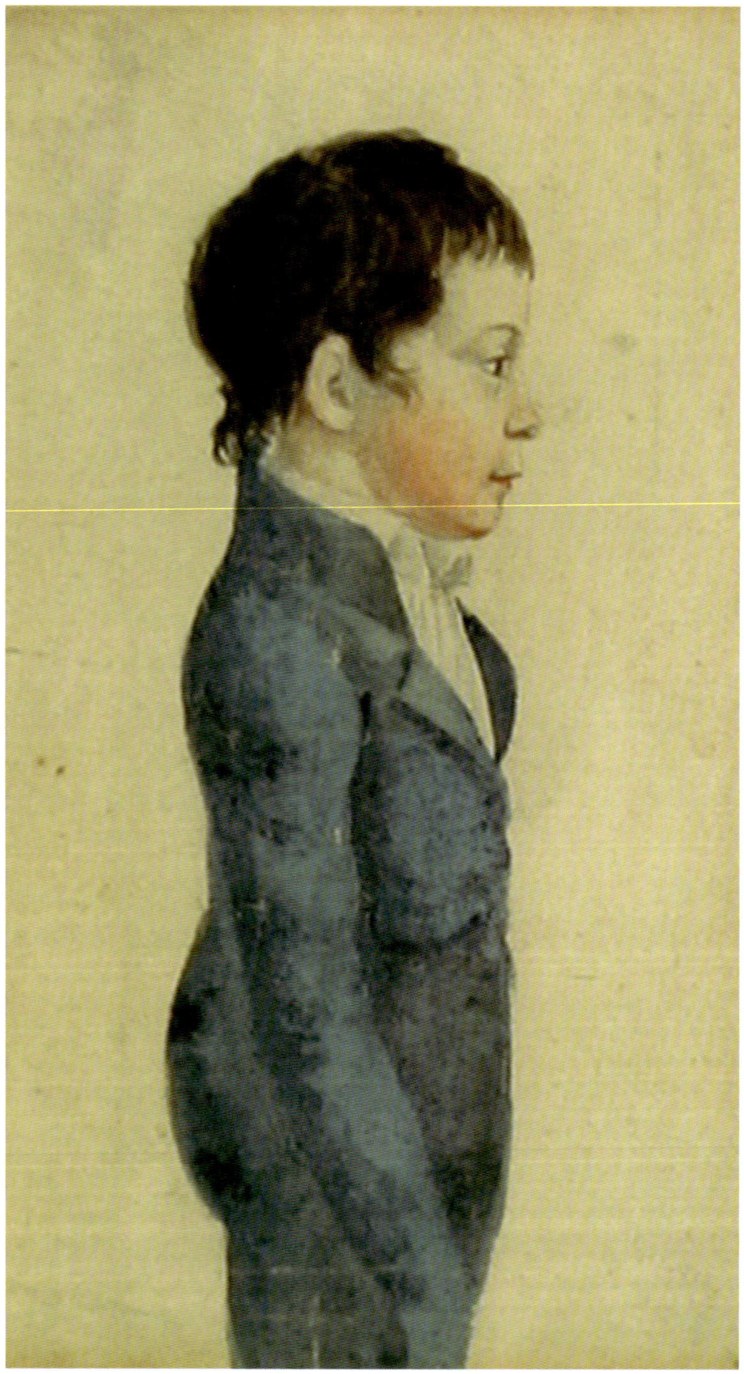

FIGURE 101. Samuel H. Dearborn, *James Love,* ca. 1810, watercolor or gouache on paper, 6½ × 4¼″ (detail; see Fig. 8), The Filson Historical Society, 1929.5.1.

James Love got caught up in the war fever that spread after the Battle of the River Raisin, a victory for the British and the Indians in the early days of the War of 1812. Though only fifteen, he volunteered and took part in the battle of Fort Meigs, fighting "as bravely and efficiently as the boldest man in the company," according to a report in the *Frankfort Commonwealth* of April 21, 1840. He would also prove to be Elizabeth Love's only surviving child, all the others having died by 1829.

widow of Thomas Love, Elizabeth Young Love, of whom he made two profile portraits, as well as portraits of all her children. He also made a rough watercolor sketch of a view of Frankfort as seen from a hilltop. That his regard for Elizabeth Love had a passionate aspect can be seen by the violent episode that followed a sharp criticism of her house's service by a fellow boarder, Isaac Robertson, an up-and-coming bureaucrat in the government of the commonwealth. According to accounts that accompanied the gift of the Love portrait to the Filson, Dearborn, on April 17, 1811, "having secured a dirk, made a cowardly attack upon Mr. Robertson, while he was seated in the garden . . . surrounded by his little children and entirely unarmed, and stabbed him savagely." Later that day Robertson died. Samuel Dearborn certainly stumbled into the right household for melodrama and romance. The Loves lived in a large log house that General James Wilkinson had built in 1786 when he laid out Frankfort. Thomas Love, who had been a major in the army, bought the house sometime around 1802. He died from a fever in 1809, leaving behind his wife and several small children, including a son named James (Fig. 101). Elizabeth Love was much admired in Frankfort for the fortitude she showed in turning her home into a boardinghouse to support her family. After Dearborn's murder of Robertson, Dearborn, enabled by some local friends, escaped jail and disappeared from Kentucky forever. Finding his way back to Boston, he changed his name to Nathaniel and produced some engraved "views of little merit," according to William Dunlap. He died in 1852, having gotten away with murder; he left behind a handful of the earliest documented profile portraits in Kentucky.

Collection: FHS; literature: Dunlap, Haverstock et al., Jones & Weber, Whitley.

MANUEL JOACHIM DE FRANCA

(1808–1865)

FIGURE 102 *(facing page).* Manuel Joachim de Franca, *Leo, Matilda, and Mary Churchill,* ca. 1848, oil on canvas, 39¼ × 37¾", The Filson Historical Society, 1986.9.3.

Leo died before the age of twelve. Matilda, the eldest, was born in 1841 and died, unmarried, in Frankfort in 1867. Mary Eliza was born in St. Louis in 1843 and married Richard Oswald Cowling in Frankfort in 1867.

MANUEL JOACHIM DE FRANCA was born in Oporto, Portugal, to a family of wine merchants. He is said to have been a student in Lisbon at the Royal Art Academy, but he fled civil unrest in Portugal in 1827, embarking for America and landing in Philadelphia. Once there he became an associate of Thomas Sully, ca. 1830, who admired his work and recommended him to the Pennsylvania Academy of Fine Arts. While in Philadelphia de Franca married Mahaloth Dawson, with whom he moved to Harrisburg, Pennsylvania, where he was active from 1830 to 1838 as a painter of Roman Catholic church interiors. The de Francas relocated to St. Louis in 1838. Once there, he came to the attention of James E. Yeatman, a local banker and philanthropist who founded the St. Louis Mercantile Library; Yeatman became de Franca's principal patron after 1840. For the next two decades he was the most sought-after resident painter in St. Louis. His portraits are very strongly colored and often feature dramatic background detail in the Continental style, as can be seen in his portrait of the astronomer James Roberts Jr. Connections he made through the Churchill family as well as a commission to paint a portrait of Henry Clay drew de Franca to Kentucky, where he was active as an itinerant in the decade before the Civil War. William Hyde wrote that his "portraits were painted with vigor and strength, were characterized by grace and refinement and by a lively appreciation of beauty and expression in his pictures of women and children." That praise certainly describes his portrait of three of the Churchill children (Fig. 102), the progeny of Samuel Bullitt Churchill (1812–1890) and his wife, Amelia Chouteau Walker Churchill (1819–1906), of St. Louis. De Franca also painted Mrs. Churchill as a serene beauty dressed in red and set against a moody, atmospheric background. De Franca died on August 22, 1865, in St. Louis. An exhibition of his portraits during the Louisiana Purchase Exhibition, St. Louis, in 1904, revived interest in his work.

Archives: StLPL; collections: Addison, Ashland, Brooklyn, CHM, Corcoran, FHS, MoHS, NPG, NYSHA, PAFA, Speed; literature: Bruns, Dunlap, Groce & Wallace, Hyde & Conard, Whitley.

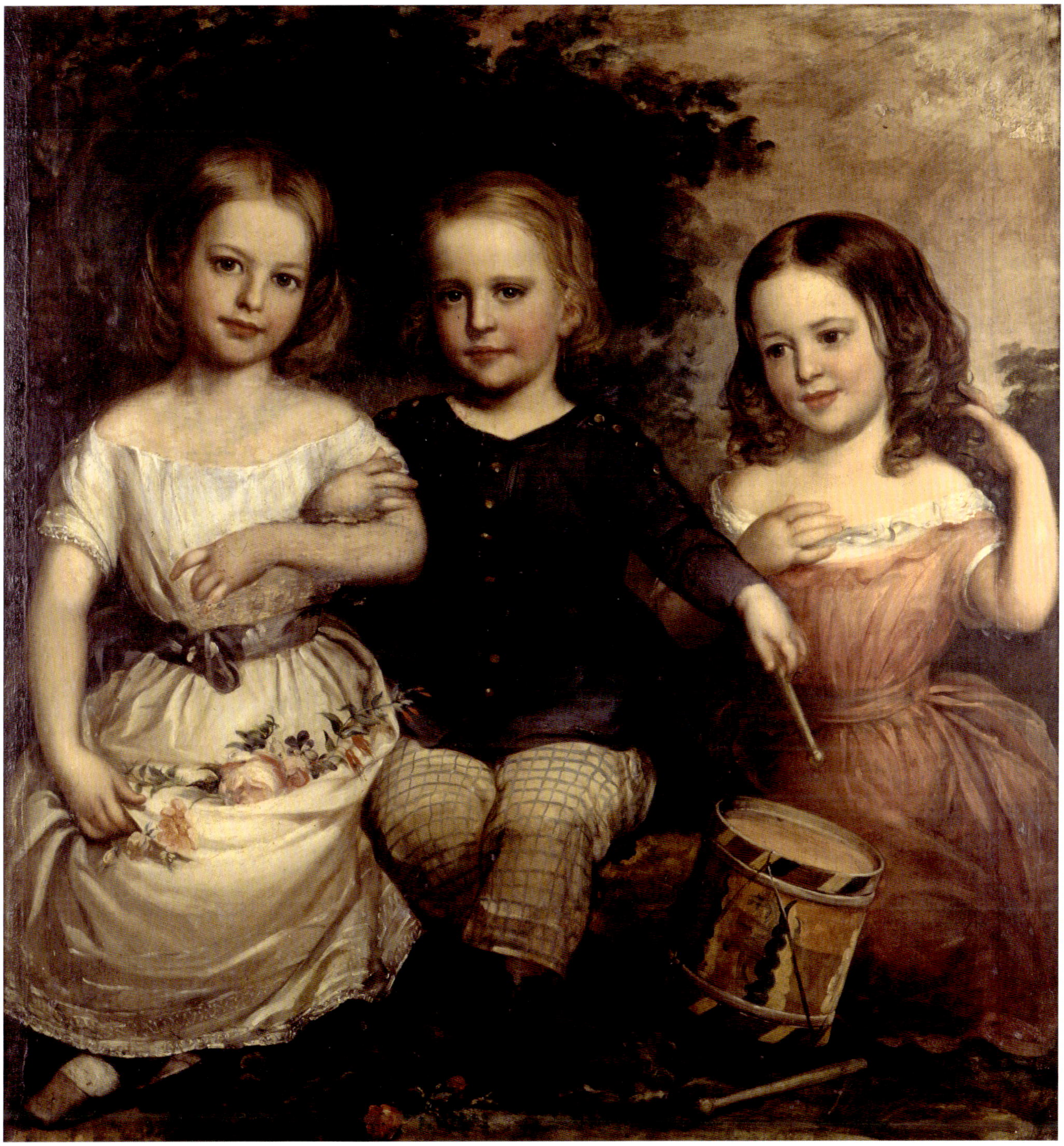

JOHN WOOD DODGE

(1807–1893)

BORN IN NEW YORK, John Wood Dodge was apprenticed to a sign painter, but he began to paint miniatures following study at the National Academy of Design, 1826–1827. Because of a respiratory ailment he moved south for the more moderate climate, arriving in Nashville in 1840. For the next ten years he used that base to launch a career as an itinerant. He worked in central Kentucky, 1839–1849, and wintered in New Orleans, 1848–1849. Although known primarily as a miniaturist, he painted several portraits "in small," including one of Henry Clay with his dog beneath a tree at Ashland, 1843. Dodge also painted one of the last life portraits of Andrew Jackson, a miniature, which he exhibited in his studio in New Orleans in 1848. During this same tenure in New Orleans he exhibited panoramas of New York and the interior of St. Peter's Church, Rome, in Armory Hall. Dodge purchased an apple orchard at Pomona, Tennessee, in 1845 as a consistent source of income and a place to which to retire. From 1849 to 1862 he was located in Huntsville, Alabama. During that time he painted a full-scale portrait of the infant Imogene Deloach, daughter of Claiborne Deloach of Nashville, which was reproduced in Bruns's *Louisiana Portraits.* Dodge returned to New York in 1862 but continued to work as an itinerant, this time in the Midwest. He visited Chicago frequently from 1869 to 1889 and served the local art academy there from 1874 to 1875. Two still-life paintings, *Gourmet's Delight: Roast Beef and Plum Pudding* and *Gourmet's Dessert: Fresh Fruit and Cake,* both oil on canvas, 16½ x 22, signed and dated lower right, 1887, were advertised in the Old Print Shop. They are unlike any other recorded works by this artist, indicative of a style from much earlier in the century. By 1889 Dodge had settled permanently in Pomona, where he died. A self-portrait was published in the August–September 1994 *American Art Review.*

Collections: Cheekwood, MMA, NPG, NYHS, UKAM; literature: Amyx (1988), Dunlap, J. Kelly, Mahé & McCaffrey, Poesch, Whitley.

ALONZO DOUGLASS

(ca. 1810–1886)

MARY SAYRE HAVERSTOCK et al. report that Alonzo Douglass was born in the District of Columbia, although Edna Talbott Whitley records it as someplace in Georgia, prompting the nickname "Georgia Coulas." He was in Cincinnati by 1829 and was intermittently active there until 1853. Douglass worked with Aaron Houghton Corwine in 1828, during which time he is likely to have painted a portrait of James Morsell (Fig. 103). This portrait is a stunning tribute to Corwine, as the large format and vivid coloration closely resemble that artist's work. It is interesting to consider (though it is mere speculation) whether the work was painted under Corwine's supervision or even with his assistance, as the verisimilitude of detail is so strong. Douglass was listed as a portraitist in the Cincinnati city directories for 1829, 1831, 1841, 1842, and 1844, and he resided, at least briefly, at Fourth and Walnut in that city. He painted Alexander Campbell in 1844. Census records also list him as living in Cincinnati in 1850 and 1860; both list him as a clerk, apparently living with his mother, Sarah W. Douglass, recorded as twenty-three years older than he. After 1860 he was resident in Louisville, where he died. The Catalog of American Portraiture at the National Portrait Gallery lists a self-portrait and a portrait of "Mrs. Douglass," both painted ca. 1840.

Collections: FHS, OHS; literature: Hageman, Haverstock et al., Whitley.

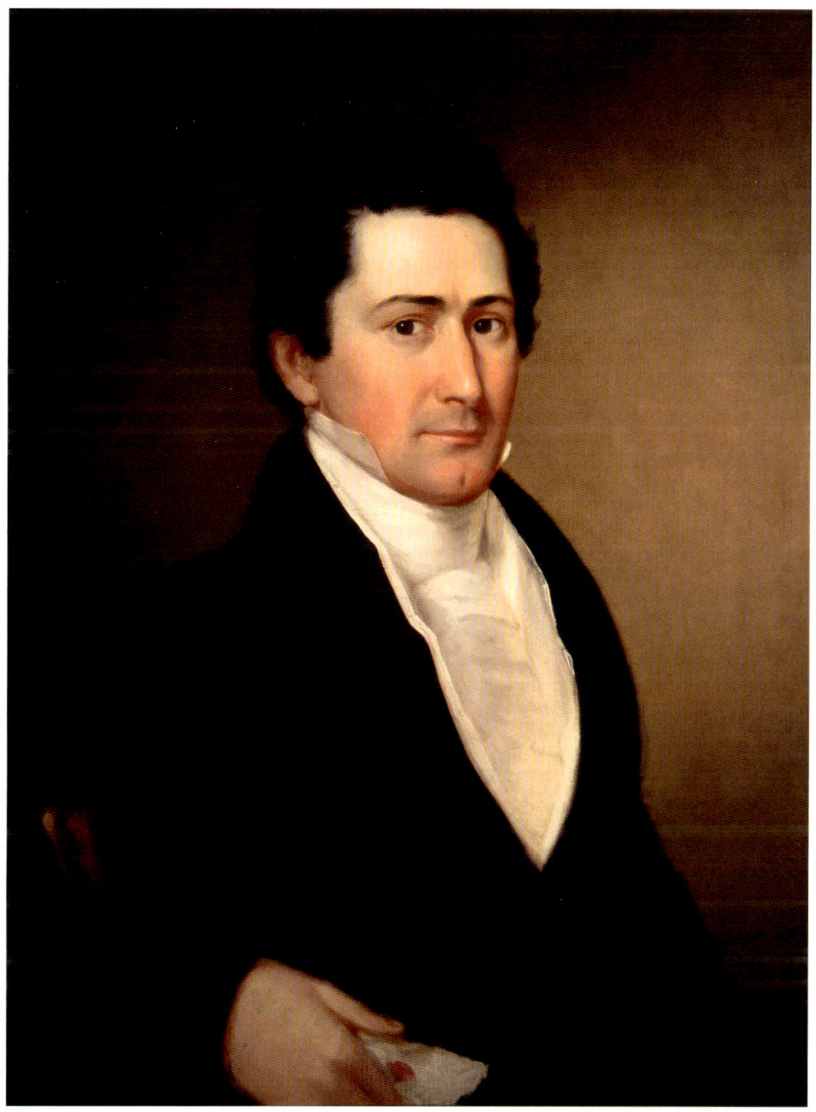

FIGURE 103. Alonzo Douglass, *James C. Morsell,* ca. 1829, oil on canvas, 27¾ × 22¾", The Filson Historical Society, 1989.20.

James C. Morsell was born in Calvert County, Maryland, to Benjamin and Hettie Cornwall Morsell, members of a large extended family who had been in Maryland since the seventeenth century. The city directory for Cincinnati lists him as an auctioneer in 1829. His grandmother was a first cousin to the artist.

ROBERT SCOTT DUNCANSON

(1821–1872)

FIGURE 104. Robert Scott Duncanson, *William Berthelet* (1841–1846), 1846, oil on canvas, 30 × 25″, Detroit Institute of Arts.

Berthelet was the grandson of Henri Berthelet, a successful merchant based in Detroit. Ketner speculates that Duncanson painted this child and his grandfather near the time of their death, commenting that the "stylized treatment of the human figure in these two works was typical of Duncanson's portraits and marked his figure painting throughout his career."

ROBERT SCOTT DUNCANSON was born in Fayette, New York, to Lucy and John Dean Duncanson, descendents of freed slaves from Virginia, according to Joseph Ketner. Previous oral history had assigned his birth to a Scotsman and a mulatto woman, as repeated by Rayford Logan and Michael Winston. Duncanson was reputed to have had some early education in Canada and was known to have worked with his father as a house and ornamental painter in Monroe, Michigan, until he moved in 1841 to Mt. Healthy, just outside Cincinnati. Once there, he began a career as a portraitist, although he also began to paint landscapes under the influence of William Louis

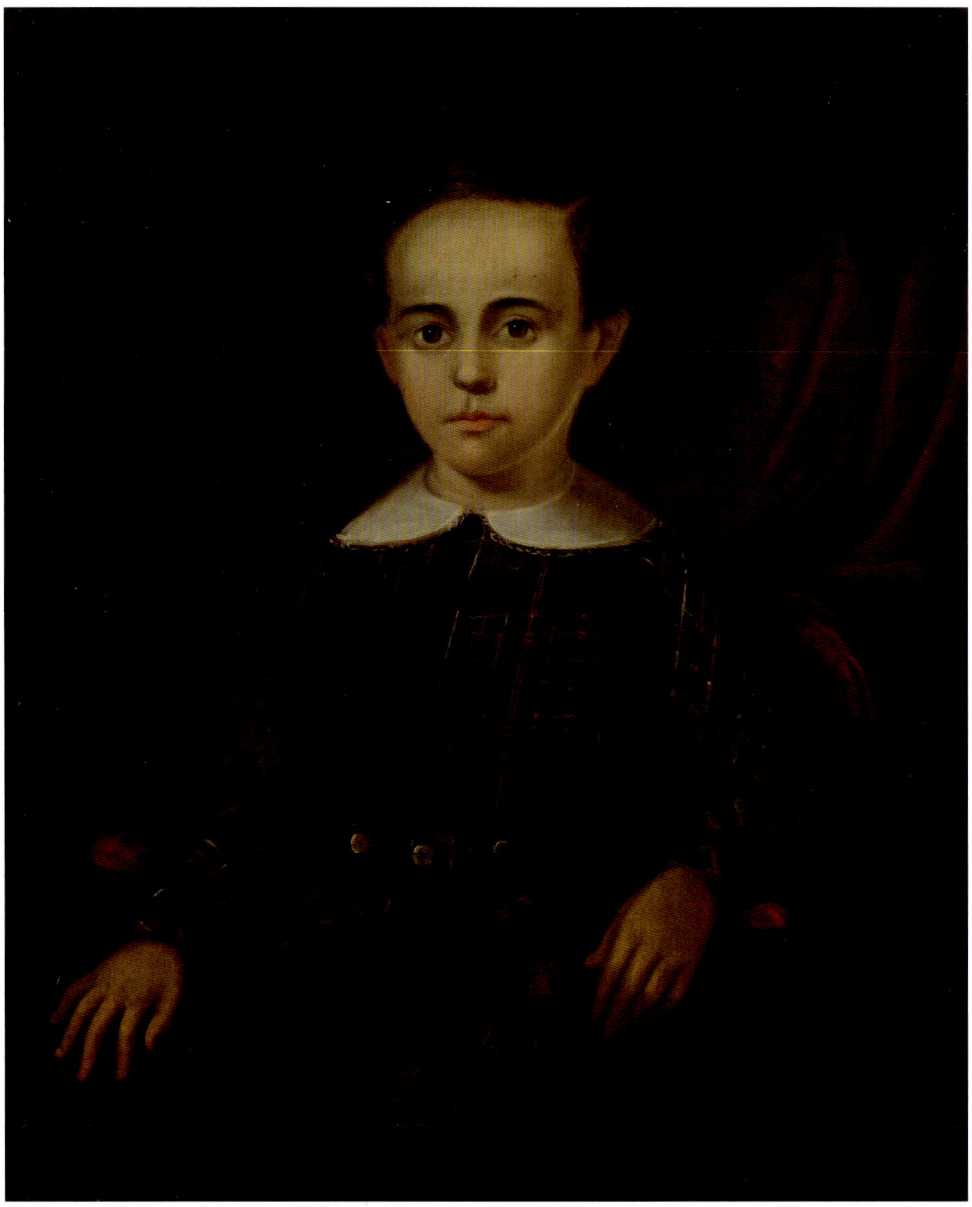

Sonntag. From 1845 to 1853 he was frequently in Detroit, where he painted portraits, notably that of young William Berthelet, a painting with the flatness and charm of a plain painting (Fig. 104). Though he is best remembered as a landscape painter, there are many portraits, still lifes, and history and genre paintings extant from this period. By 1850 he was resident in a studio in Cincinnati's Apollo Building with Sonntag, but he continued his travels to Michigan, North Carolina, western Pennsylvania, and New England. Duncanson journeyed to Europe with Sonntag in 1853 under the patronage of Nicholas Longworth, for whom he had painted murals at Longworth's home, Belmont, and whose portrait he painted in 1858. He studied art in London, Paris, and Florence, where he reconnected with Hiram Powers, a Cincinnati sculptor. After his return to America, Duncanson created a body of landscape art that reflects both his familiarity with ruins and intimate settings of the Old World and his awareness of mainstream American luminescent romanticism. He lived in Montreal during much of the Civil War, perhaps as a willing exile from the tensions in Cincinnati, where riots against free blacks occurred. After the war, in 1866, he visited England, where he had successfully shown his Scottish landscape work and his allegorical paintings since 1861. He returned to Cincinnati in 1867 and revisited Scotland in 1870–1871. His mental health declined steadily during the late 1860s, possibly as a result of exposure to lead paint, and he died in Detroit in 1872.

Collections: CAM, DIA, Howard, SAM, Taft; literature: Aronson (2003), Boyle & McElroy, Cederholm, Cincinnati Museum of Art (1979), Gibson, Groce & Wallace, Hageman, Haverstock et al., Ketner, Logan & Winston, McElroy, Porter, Whitley.

FRANK DUVENECK

(1848–1919)

FRANK DUVENECK WAS BORN in Covington, Kentucky, to Bernard and Katherine Siemers Decker, emigrants from Oldenburg, Westphalia, Germany. When his father died soon after Frank's birth, his mother married Joseph Duveneck, who adopted the child and gave him his name. Duveneck's mother was a devout Roman Catholic who had served as a maid in the home of the artist James Henry Beard. She attempted to direct her son's budding artistic talent to the church. Joe Duveneck was a prosperous grocer and brewer whose beer garden was one of the centers of German life in the transriver area. Frank was apprenticed to the Institute of Catholic Art in Covington in 1861 as a church decorator, in which field he worked in Covington, Kentucky; Latrobe, Pennsylvania; and Quebec, Canada, at times in association with the painter William Schmidt. While in New Jersey on a job he met a German Franciscan, Cosmo Wolff, who was knowledgeable about a group of painting monks in Munich and convinced Duveneck's parents that further study with them would enhance his skills for the church. While in Munich, 1869–1873, he studied with Wilhelm von Diez, Wilhelm Leibl, Ludwig Löfftz, and Wilhelm Trübner. Duveneck returned to Covington in 1873, where he painted religious works and portraits while teaching at the Ohio Mechanics Institute; he first exhibited his portraits in Cincinnati in 1874. Duveneck returned to Munich in 1875 after a successful exhibition in Boston that year, which secured his first financial success. After exhibiting in New York in 1877, he went back to Munich, where he remained until 1879. He moved to Florence that year and then on to Venice, working on an etching process with James A. M. Whistler, 1880–1881, while gathering an adoring group of students, "Duveneck's boys," about him. One of those "boys" was the painter John White Alexander, who met Duveneck in Munich and then moved on with him to Florence. It was during this period that Duveneck painted Alexander's portrait (Fig. 105). This is a dashing example of Duveneck's stylistic evolution, one in which the dark tonalities of the Munich School are richly enhanced by loose brushwork and florid facial coloration. In 1881 he returned to New York, where he became a successful portraitist in the grand manner and a noted muralist in the American Renaissance style. He returned briefly to Cincinnati, 1881, then went back to Italy. He moved to Paris, 1885, and while working there married Elizabeth Boott in 1886; his principal rival for her affections is reported to have been Henry James, who may have used her as a source for Isabel Archer in *A Portrait of a Lady.* Frank and Elizabeth had a son, Frank Boott Duveneck, while residing at Villa Castellani, outside Florence. After Elizabeth's death in 1888 he returned to Cincinnati, where he remained active as a teacher and painter for the rest of his life. He was made a member of the National Academy in 1906 and died in Cincinnati. In his will Duveneck left the personal work he had retained to the Cincinnati Art Museum, including his famous *Whistling Boy* and a model for the recumbent figure he sculpted for his wife's tomb in the American cemetery in Florence.

Archives: AAA, CAM; collections: CAM; literature: Aronson (2003), Ashbery, Cincinnati Museum of Art (1979), Duveneck, Haverstock et al., Sherman, Young.

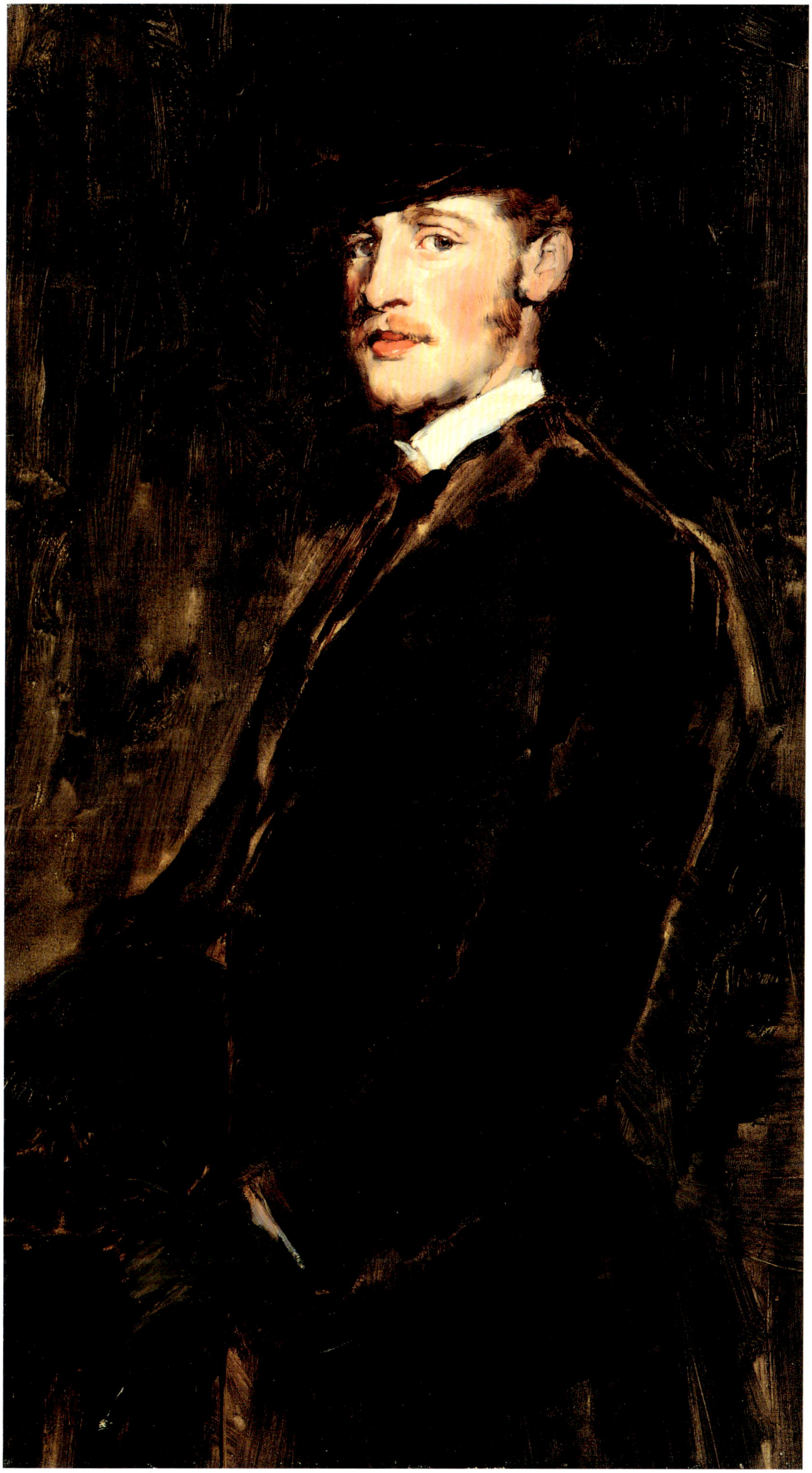

FIGURE 105. Frank Duveneck, *John White Alexander* (1856–1917), 1879, oil on canvas, 38 1/16 × 22 1/16″, Cincinnati Art Museum, 1908.1216 CAM.

JOSEPH ORIEL EATON

(1829–1875)

FIGURE 106. Joseph Oriel Eaton, *Commodore David Gibson* (1813–1897), ca. 1852, oil on canvas, 36 × 29″, Cincinnati Historical Society.

Gibson was born in Paisley, Scotland, emigrated to America in 1829, and was in Cincinnati by 1832. After a short stint as a miller he founded a highly successful distillery in New Richmond, Ohio. Gibson became one of the wealthiest men in America, reputedly worth as much as $6 million from his extensive investments in river shipping, railroads, fire insurance companies, and banks. He married Matilda Chessman in 1852 and lived in a large "marble mansion" in the Clifton section of Cincinnati. Eaton's portraits of the Gibsons have a very robust quality, each subject fully occupying the planar field, lushly modeled and contoured and strongly colored.

FIGURE 107 *(facing page)*. Joseph Oriel Eaton, *Matilda Chessman Gibson* (1839–1912), ca. 1852, oil on canvas, 36 × 29″, Cincinnati Historical Society.

JOSEPH ORIEL EATON was born in Newark, Ohio, to Orin and Mary Fidler Eaton. According to Wilbur Peat, Eaton ran away from home in 1845 with two early works he had painted, a portrait of George Washington and one of the local Methodist minister. The portrait of Washington he sold as a tavern sign. Making his way to Indianapolis on the proceeds, he set up as a portraitist, charging five dollars apiece, and attracted the patronage of Dr. Abner Pope, who introduced him to Jacob Cox. He became a pupil-assistant to Cox in Indianapolis, 1845, then moved on to Cincinnati in 1846, where he maintained a studio until 1864. With some encouragement from James Henry Beard, Eaton departed from the formulas of those artists who emulated Gilbert Stuart and later Thomas Sully and created works that are highly sensitive to the entrepreneurial Germanic spirit of the Ohio River Valley. His portraits of the Gibsons, from early in his tenure there, clearly demonstrate the attractions his work held for the local citizenry (Figs. 106, 107). Following his marriage in 1855 to Emma Jane

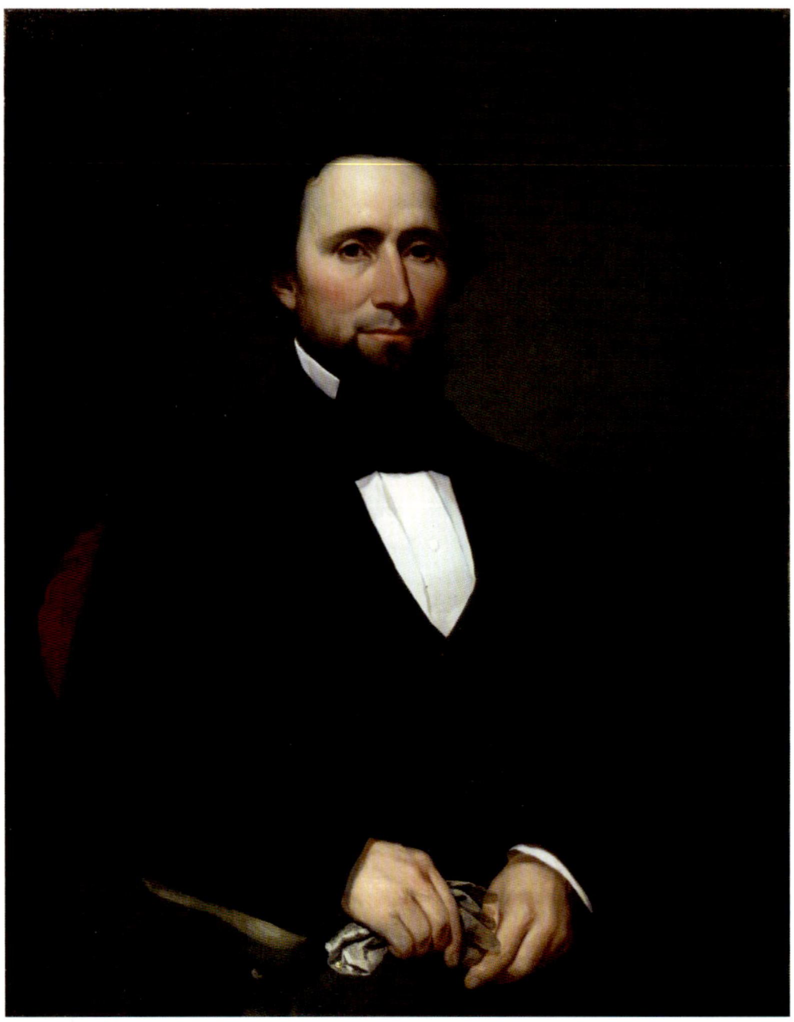

Goodman, Eaton lived in northern Kentucky. His activity as an itinerant included trips to New Orleans, 1853–1854 and 1857, and to Louisville, where he is recorded at the Exchange Hotel in 1860. That year he opened a studio on West Forth Street in Cincinnati with Charles T. Weber, making tinted photographs. Following a lengthy trip to Europe in 1869, Eaton settled in New York City, where he was an associate and frequent exhibiter at the National Academy of Design. While in New York, he painted Herman Melville in 1870, when the author of *Moby-Dick* was living in obscurity and working as a clerk in the New York Customs House. The portrait is now in the Houghton Library, Harvard University. According to the Reverend Charles Frederick Goss, Eaton "possessed fine social qualities and was personally acquainted with not only the leading artists of America but held the warm friendship of many prominent men and women," including William Merritt Chase, Bret Harte, and Sara Orne Jewett. Eaton is known to have painted landscapes, including *Farm at Yellow Springs, Ohio,* as well as several genre works based on his studies in Europe. Late in his career he was especially admired for his paintings of children. He died in Yonkers, New York.

Collections: CAM, CHM, DAI, Harvard, IMA, NAD, UC, UKAM, West Point; literature: Cincinnati Art Museum (1979), Goss, Haverstock et al., Peat (1954), Whitley.

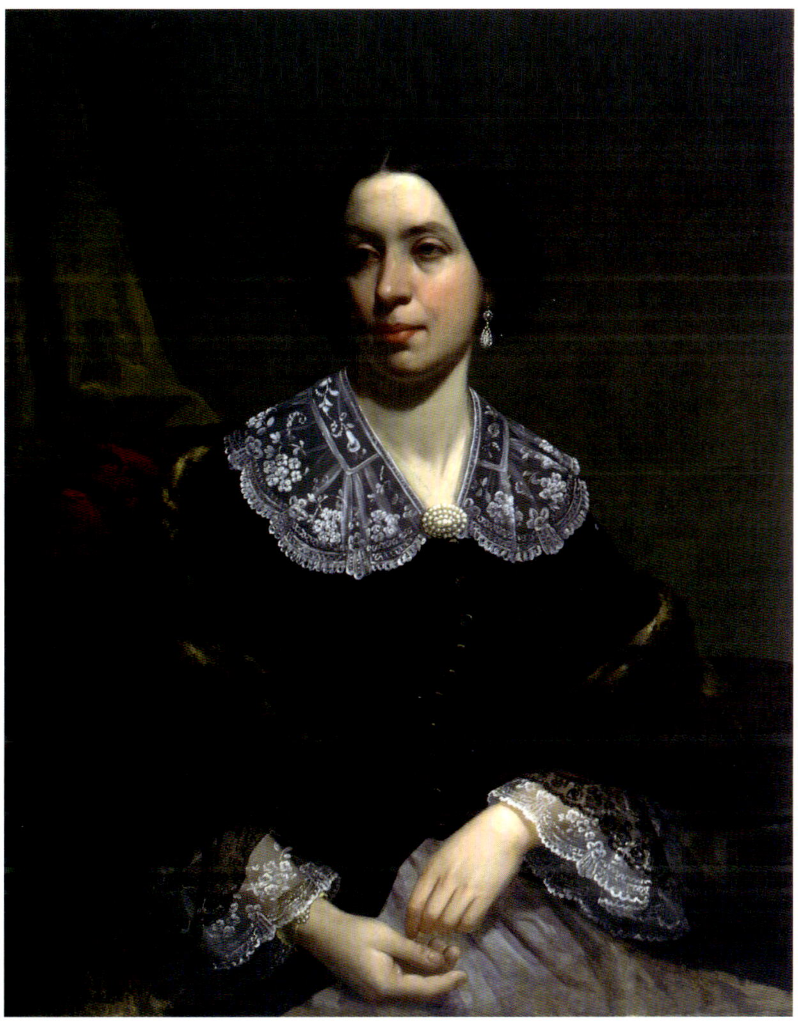

CLEMENT R. EDWARDS

(1820–1898)

FIGURE 108. Clement Reeves Edwards, *Self-Portrait,* ca. 1890, oil on board, 24 × 15¾", Kentucky Library and Museum, Western Kentucky University, 1979.2.5.

CLEMENT R. EDWARDS was born in Woodstown, New Jersey, and moved, with his family, to Cincinnati in 1830. After an apprenticeship as a sign painter in 1837, he opened a portrait studio there in 1840. In 1842 he pursued additional training in Philadelphia. Edwards joined the army in 1847 and, while serving in the Voltigeur Regiment during the Mexican War, he made sketches and studies for a subsequent painting of Chapultepec Castle, now in the Filson collection. Following the war he returned to Cincinnati, 1848, and resumed his portrait career there until 1856. He was active as an itinerant in Louisville, 1855, when he is said to have made a copy of the Jarvis portrait of General George Rogers Clark. In 1856 he relocated to Bowling Green, Kentucky, where his energies as a planter gradually overwhelmed his interest in art. He died in Bowling Green and is buried there, in Fairview Cemetery. The Kentucky Museum in Bowling Green has a large collection of his works (Fig. 108).

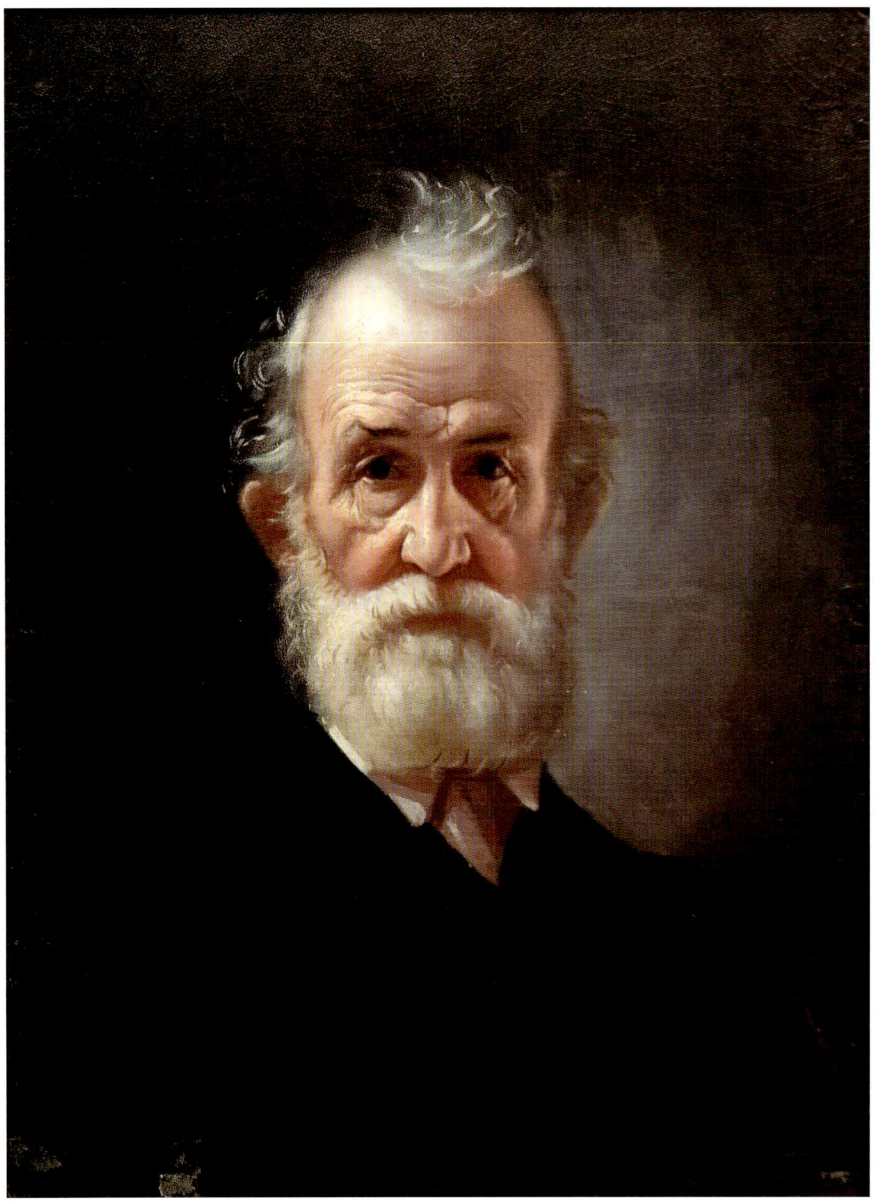

Archives: FHS; collections: FHS, KM; literature: Hageman, Haverstock et al., Whitley.

AARON C. ESHELMAN

(1826–1878)

AARON C. ESHELMAN was born in Lancaster, Pennsylvania, and was active as an itinerant in Bourbon, Fleming, Harrison, and Montgomery Counties, ca. 1845–1874 (Fig. 109). His only listing in the census records is from 1860, when he was recorded as living in Shawhan, northeast Bourbon County. There are many of his works extant in the area where he worked, and he was especially admired for his images of children. His portrait of Lena Benton, thought to have been painted in 1874, is reproduced in Arthur Jones and Bruce Weber's *Kentucky Painter,* who commented that Eshelman's "sitters appear awkward because of his inability to master the drawing of the full figure." The tiny little doll in this child's lap as well as her disproportionately large eyes suggest the artist continued to follow antebellum portrait conventions long after the war was over.

FIGURE 109. Aaron C. Eshelman, *John B. Richter,* ca. 1870, oil on canvas, 29 × 24″, The Filson Historical Society, 1964.4.

Collection: FHS, KHS; literature: Jones & Weber, Whitley.

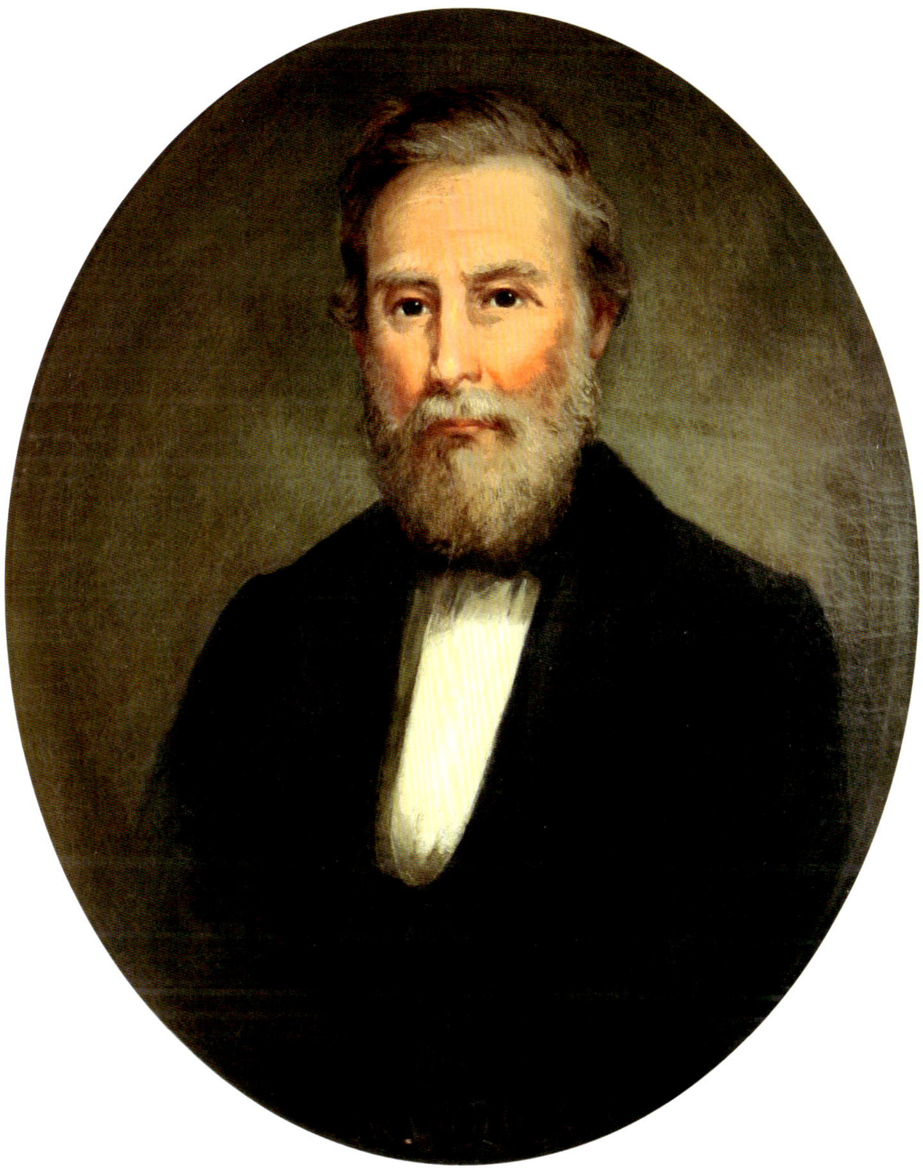

TREVOR THOMAS FOWLER

(1800–1871)

TREVOR THOMAS FOWLER was born in Dublin, Ireland. He studied at the Royal Academy, London, 1829, and at the Royal Hibernian Academy, Dublin, 1830. He made his first trip to America in 1830 and established a studio in New Orleans, at 10 St. Charles, which he would maintain for the rest of his life. He garnered considerable public notice in 1840 when he painted portraits of William Henry Harrison and Henry Clay, rivals in the presidential election of that year, as well as a portrait of Andrew Jackson. Active as an itinerant in the Mississippi River Valley, 1840–1854, with periods of residency in Cincinnati, 1846, 1850, and 1851, and Frankfort, 1842. During these years he often worked in partnership with Theodore Sidney Moïse, painting ambitious grand-manner portraits with still-life details and animal companions. The most outstanding example of their work in this style is the portrait of the sons of Orlando Brown, Mason and Orlando Jr., with their dog, Judge, which is still hanging in the Orlando Brown House, Frankfort. Fowler later painted Willina Robinson singly while on a visit to Frankfort in 1851 (Fig. 110). After 1854 Fowler divided his time between Philadelphia and New Orleans on a seasonal basis. He was also a painter of literary and genre works. He died in New Orleans.

Archives: HNOC, NOMA; collections: CHM, Maier, Marshall, MMA, NPG, NYHS, OBH, SAM, Speed, Waveland; literature: Bruns, Groce & Wallace, Hageman, Haverstock et al., Mahé & McCaffrey, Pennington (1992, 2008), Simon, Weber & Jones, Whitley.

FIGURE 110 *(facing page).* Trevor Thomas Fowler, *Willina Herndon Robinson,* 1851, oil on canvas, 36 × 29″, Morris Museum of Art, 1989.04.250.

Willina Robinson's husband, James, was governor of Kentucky during the turbulent years of 1862–1863. A graduate of Transylvania University and a prosperous farmer-attorney, he was elected to the state senate in 1851. Robinson supported Kentucky's neutrality and opposed the war. After his term as governor he returned to Scott County, where he and his wife were active in a number of eleemosynary concerns, most notably Georgetown College. The painting is signed on the small table and has Fowler's characteristic facial flush and diaphanous drapery.

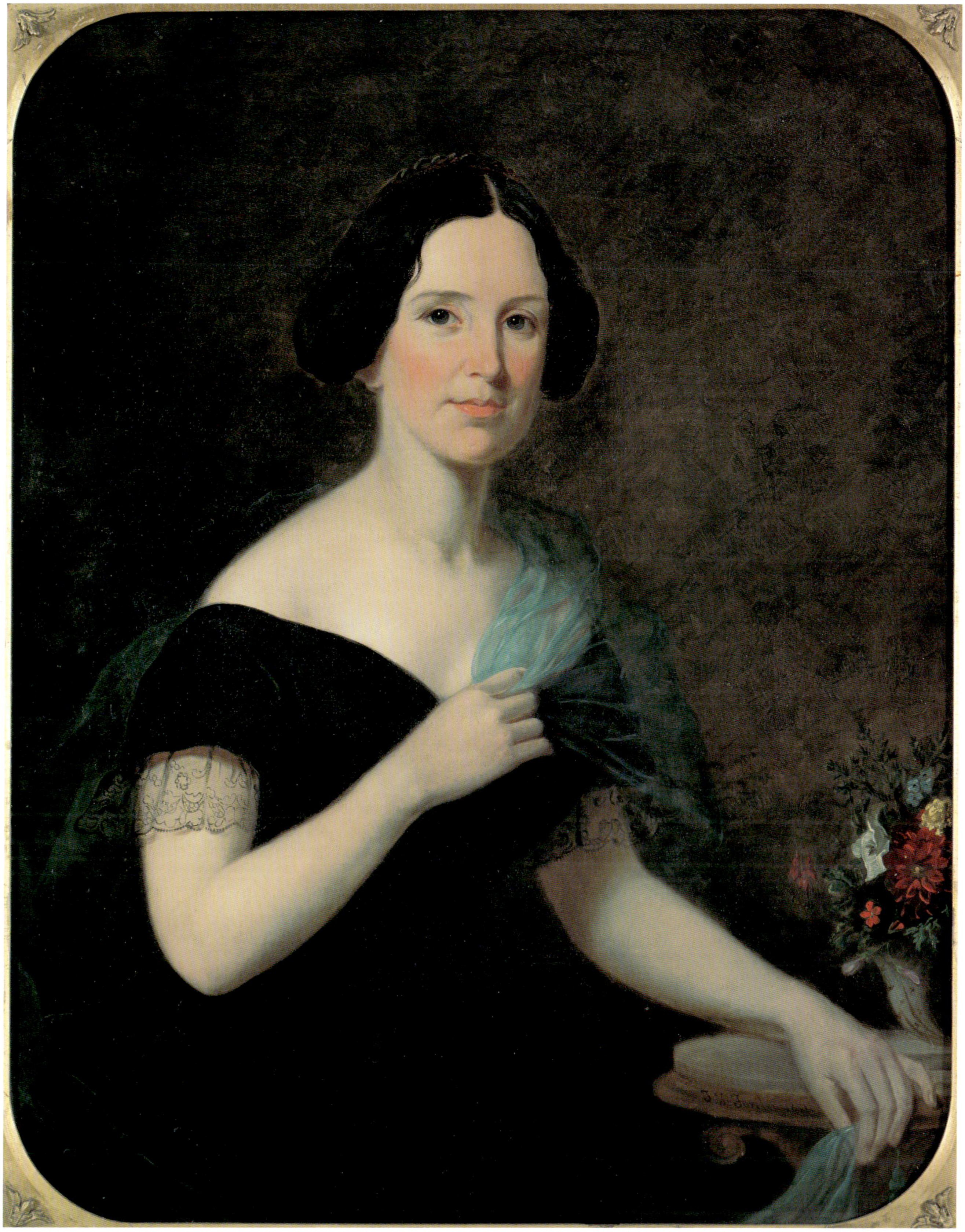

GODFREY NICHOLAS FRANKENSTEIN

(1820–1873)

GODFREY NICHOLAS FRANKENSTEIN was born in Darmstadt, Germany, the second son of John and Anna Dracht. He emigrated with his parents to Cincinnati in 1831, at which time his father changed the family name to Frankenstein, in accord with their German point of origin. He began his career as a self-taught portraitist in residence on Foote's Row, Cincinnati, 1838. It is likely he was painted by his brother John, who was then engaged in scholarly studies, not long after. Frankenstein made a study excursion to Niagara Falls in 1840, and the falls became one of the most frequently repeated scenes in his body of landscape works. He was the first president of the Academy of Fine Arts in Cincinnati, 1841. After 1849 he was based in Springfield, Ohio, where he shared a house with his unmarried sisters. He made a visit to Louisville in 1851, where he offered his services as a portraitist. His portrait of George Prentice almost certainly dates from that time (Fig. 111). Following his Louisville sojourn, Frankenstein returned to landscape painting. He completed a vast panoramic painting of Niagara Falls in 1853, which was exhibited extensively in America and Europe, 1853–1873. He is best known as a landscape painter, often composing works based on his sketches in Switzerland, where he lived 1867–1869. He died in Springfield.

Archives: CAM; collections: CAM, FHS; literature: Aronson (2003), Cincinnati Museum of Art (1979), Coyle, Dreppard, Hageman, Haverstock et al., Frankenstein (1853, 1864), MacKenzie, Whitley.

FIGURE 111 *(facing page)*. Godfrey Nicholas Frankenstein, *George D. Prentice* (1802–1870), ca. 1851, oil on canvas, 29 × 24¼″, The Filson Historical Society, 1929.8.54.

Prentice was one of those larger-than-life figures who personify the dynamic culture of antebellum Kentucky. He was born in Connecticut and studied at Brown University, where he was guided by the legendary Horace Mann. Journalism became his profession. He came to Kentucky in 1830 to write a campaign biography of Henry Clay, which sold well but yielded nothing for Prentice, as the printer went bankrupt. But Prentice stayed on, and in November 1830 he began publication of the *Louisville Journal*. His editorial writings were highly animated, and he had a morbid fascination with violence, including dueling, which he saw as theater rather than murder. In the 1850s he had a duel with Col. Reuben T. Durrett, the Kentucky historical writer and collector, which amounted to his most serious challenge. Like most ambiguous Whigs, Prentice remained loyal to the Union, although his son Courtland became a Confederate officer and lost his life in the battle of Augusta, Kentucky.

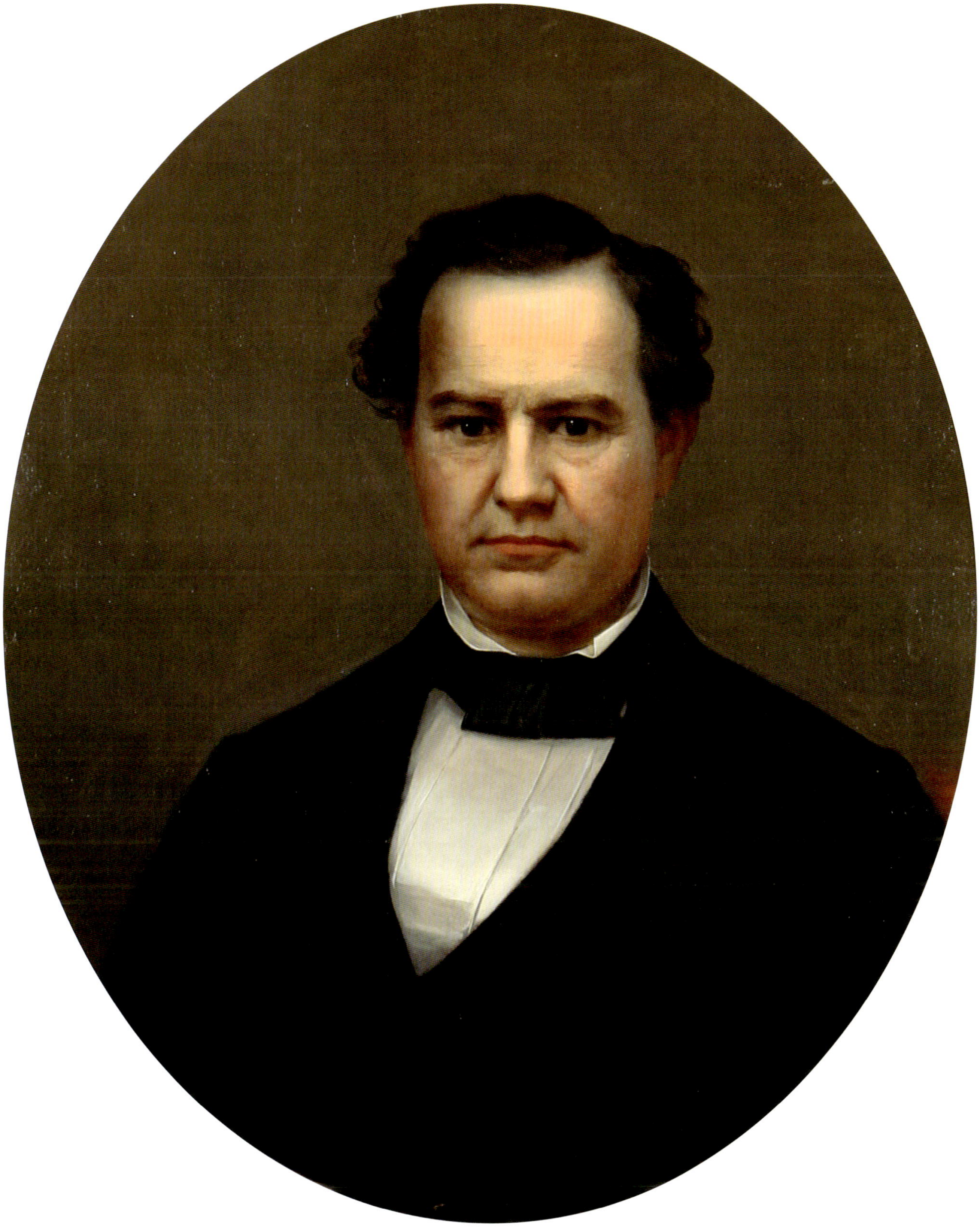

JOHN PETER FRANKENSTEIN

(1817–1881)

JOHN PETER FRANKENSTEIN was born in Darmstadt, Germany, the eldest son of John and Anna Dracht, with whom he emigrated to Cincinnati in 1831. Although briefly apprenticed as a copper engraver there in 1833, he, like his brother Godfrey, became a self-taught portraitist, active on Foote's Row in Cincinnati, 1836–1838. Between 1838 and 1843 he pursued an itinerancy in Boston, Albany, Philadelphia, and New York. At the same time, from 1839 to 1844, he was also active in Louisville, especially in 1839, painting members of the extended Rowan family. From 1849 to 1854 Frankenstein was based near his family, in Springfield, Ohio, with his wife, Laura Mather Brown, herself an artist, who later divorced him. From 1854 to 1864 Frankenstein was back in Cincinnati, with a studio at 14 East Fourth Street; he then moved to New York in 1875, where he died in 1881. A self-portrait in the possession of the antiquarian Victor Spark was noted by Hermann Warner Williams for the Catalog of American Portraiture in 1972.

Collections: CAM, OKH, SAM, Springfield; literature: Coyle, Jones & Weber, Frankenstein (1853, 1864), Hageman, Haverstock et al., MacKenzie, Taylor, Whitley.

OLIVER FRAZER

(1808–1864)

OLIVER FRAZER WAS BORN in Fayette County, Kentucky, to Alexander and Nancy Oliver Frazer. The Frazer brothers, Alexander and Robert, had emigrated from Ireland in the aftermath of Emmet's Rebellion of 1803. After landing in Philadelphia, they moved west to Paris, Kentucky, where they became established silversmiths. Alexander moved to Lexington and married on December 20, 1804, but died in 1810, leaving the care of his young son to his brother, Robert. Oliver Frazer had some exposure to Matthew Harris Jouett, 1826, and briefly studied with Thomas Sully (ca. 1828) in Philadelphia before traveling abroad in 1834 to study in Paris with Antoine-Jean Gros, during which time he also made the acquaintance of Thomas Couture and G. P. A. Healy. Prior to his departure for Europe he painted a copy of Gilbert Stuart's full-length portrait of George Washington for the old State Capitol in Frankfort. He returned to Lexington in 1838, where he opened a studio and married Martha Bell Mitchell, a niece of Mrs. Matthew H. Jouett. Not long after his return he painted a group portrait of the Anderson boys that is now in the Speed Art Museum, a loosely brushed work that demonstrates the vitality of the romantic style he learned abroad. Throughout his career Frazer tacked between two styles, one clear and resonant of neoclassic solidity and a more vague, romantic style that renders figures slightly elusive (Fig. 112). After 1840 he was the established portraitist of Lexington and central Kentucky, enjoying the patronage of several leading families, especially those of Henry Clay and Elisha Warfield, the renowned Thoroughbred breeder-trainer. His 1840 painting of Henry Clay Jr. became a cherished object at Ashland after Clay's death in the Mexican War. Frazer was well-off, relieved from the penurious existence of many of his fellow portrait artists by resources from his and his wife's families. That fact, combined with

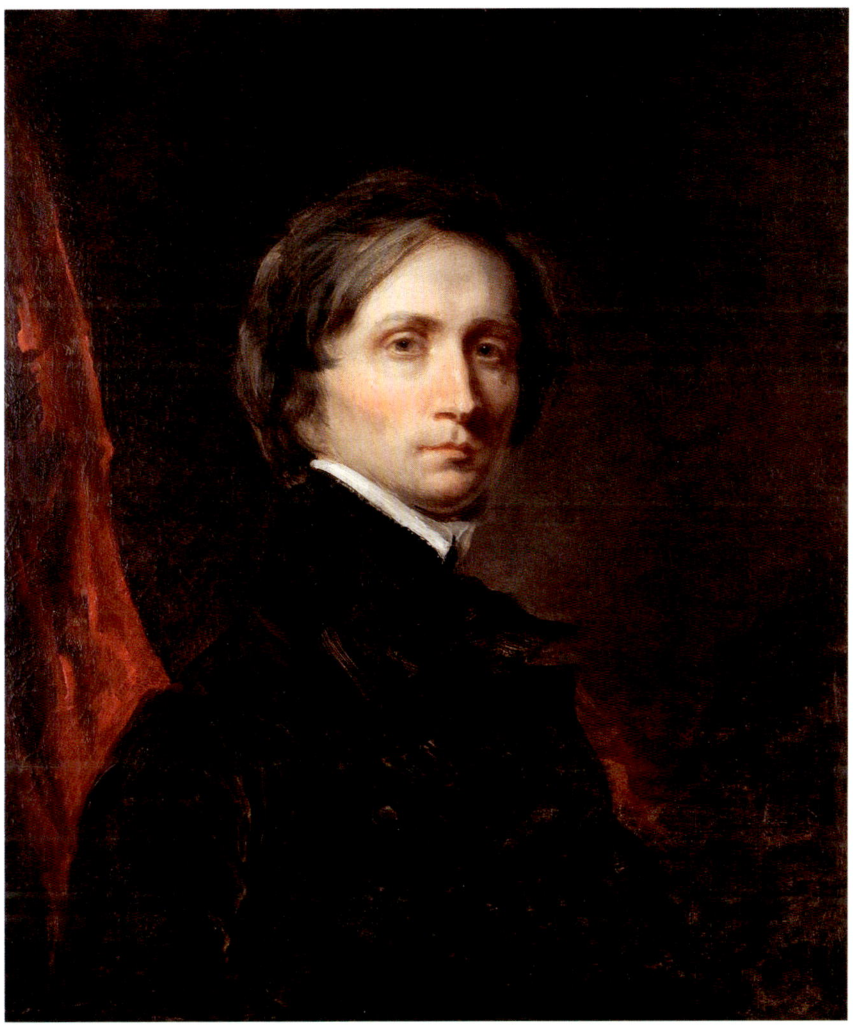

FIGURE 112. Oliver Frazer, *Self-Portrait,* ca. 1840, oil on canvas, 26 × 22¼″, The Filson Historical Society, 1995.2.1.

Frazer's declining eyesight after 1850, may account for the dwindling number of works he produced. He and his family lived at Eothen, built in 1798 by the Reverend James Moore and acquired by Frazer from his wife's aunt, Mrs. Waller Bullock Redd, in the early 1850s. He died there in 1864 and was buried in the Lexington Cemetery. The unevenness of Frazer's work has never dimmed the admiration he sustained in central Kentucky, where many, wrote William Floyd, felt his "drawing and coloring made him outstanding in the production of accurate and charming nineteenth century portraits."

Archives: FHS, UKSC; collections: Ashland, CAI, FHS, KHS, Speed; literature: Bridwell, Floyd (1968), Jones & Weber, Price, Simpson, Whitley.

WILLIAM FRYE (GEORGE WILHELM FREY)

(1812 or 1819–1872)

WILLIAM FRYE WAS BORN George Wilhelm Frey in Reslau, Germany, but he was reared in Vienna, where his father was a wholesale cloth manufacturer. He began his art studies in Prague, and while there, according to Minnie Frye Coleman, he "became fascinated with Fenimore Cooper's stories of the noble red man, and determined to journey to the new world to see them." Upon landing in New York, he appealed to his cousin Count Johan Schmidt for letters of introduction. Schmidt recommended him to George D. Prentice in Louisville, and Frye joined the German community there in 1845, becoming active as an itinerant in Kentucky, 1845–1849. Prentice subsequently recommended him to Clement Comer Clay of Huntsville, Alabama, whose portrait he painted. While in the area Frye met and married Virginia Catherine Hall in 1849, and he made Huntsville his home for the remainder of his life. Frye painted several portraits of the extended Clay family, and through their connections he launched an itinerancy in Canton, Jackson, and Natchez, Mississippi, as well as Memphis, Tennessee. He became a citizen of the United States in 1852, at which time he anglicized his name to "Frye," according to Coleman, "in order to get his mail in strange cities." By 1860, notices indicate that he was painting from daguerreotypes, which may account for the somewhat flat and stilted compositions of his later period. That he was willing to paint from existing images is apparent in the full-length portrait he painted of Henry Clay in 1866 (Fig. 113). A prolific artist, Frye went on to paint many leading figures in the government of the Confederacy, including Jefferson Davis and General Leroy Pope Walker. He is also known to have painted landscapes, including a view of the battle of Mobile Bay in 1864. He died in Huntsville in 1872.

Archives: Alabama, BMA, HNOC; collections: Alabama, ASC, BMA, CLS, FHS, HAM, HPL, IHS, MCM, Sturdivant, UA; literature: Adams, M. F. Coleman, Lay, Pennington (1993), Whitley.

FIGURE 113 *(overleaf).* William Frye, *Henry Clay,* 1866, oil on canvas, 152 × 84″, Kentucky Historical Society.

In late January 1865 the General Assembly of the Commonwealth of Kentucky passed a resolution authorizing a committee headed by J. J. Landram to "contract some competent artist for a life-size portrait of Henry Clay, to be placed in the Senate Chamber." Frye based his monumental painting on a memorial lithograph issued by William Pate in 1852 featuring Clay in a commanding pose, standing before neoclassical architectural elements meant to suggest the U.S. Senate Chamber. Frye's only competitor was Phineas Staunton (1817–1867), who painted Clay surrounded by several of his closest colleagues in the Senate. When Frye's painting was shown in Frankfort, the *Frankfort Commonwealth* for May 4, 1866, praised the work as one in which the "noble figure stands out in bold relief and animation, still charming and thrilling an audience with his golden and burning words."

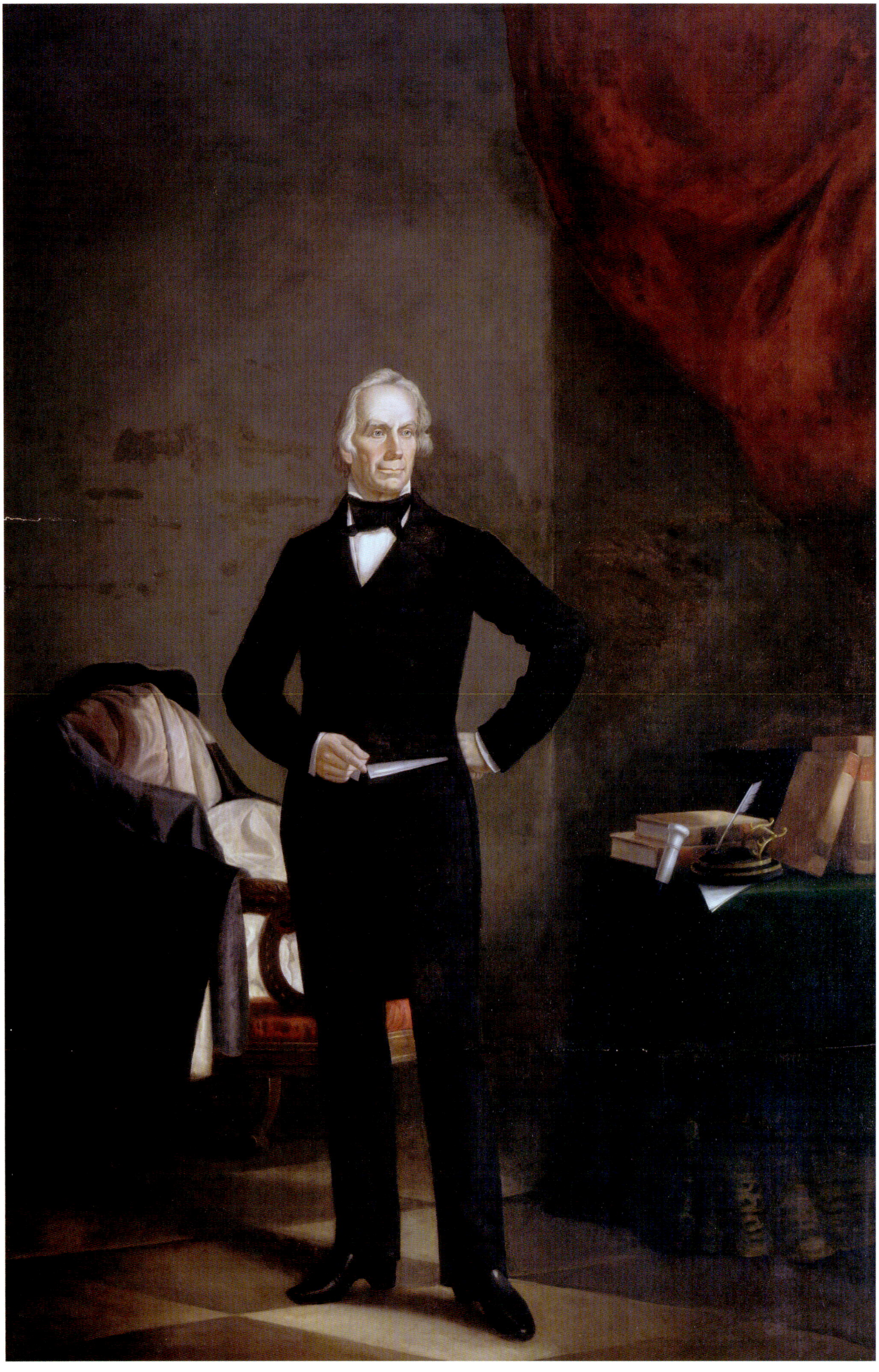

JACOB FRYMIRE

(1770–1820)

JACOB FRYMIRE was an itinerant portrait artist active in Winchester, Virginia, the tidewater and valley areas of Virginia, and in Woodford County, Kentucky, in 1806, where he painted members of the Marquis Calmes family. Fewer than thirty of his works are known to be extant.

Collections: CHM, MESDA; literature: Simmons, Virginia Museum of Fine Arts.

EDWIN F. GODDARD

(ca. 1815–1855)

FIGURE 114. Edwin F. Goddard, *Elizabeth Buckner Steele,* ca. 1855, oil on canvas, 38 × 32″, Buknore Farm, Bourbon County, Kentucky

EDWIN F. GODDARD was born in Massachusetts and was in Kentucky by 1839, working in Madison and Scott Counties, then in Bourbon County, ca. 1847–1855, painting members of the extended Ford, Spears, Clay, and Howard families. Goddard married Eleanor Lins of Sharpsburg, Kentucky, on April 11, 1836, with whom he had three daughters. His obituary from the September 7, 1855, *Western Citizen* notes that he died at his residence in Paris, Kentucky, "a man of rare genius and master of his profession as a portrait painter." Works attributed to him by Edna Talbott Whitley include a portrait of Mary Burch as a child, painted from memory after her death in 1849 while the artist was in residence with the family, and a group of portraits of the James Duncan family, now at Duncan Tavern. As the Duncan works are adhered to Masonite, and very dully colored, they are more likely to be later copies by Sudduth Goff (1887–1965) from photographs. Goddard's work is most readily identified by a very lush, warm coloration in the cheeks (Fig. 114), and by the wry manner in which his elderly subjects, notably Sally Clay Buckner and Noah Spears, gaze at the viewer.

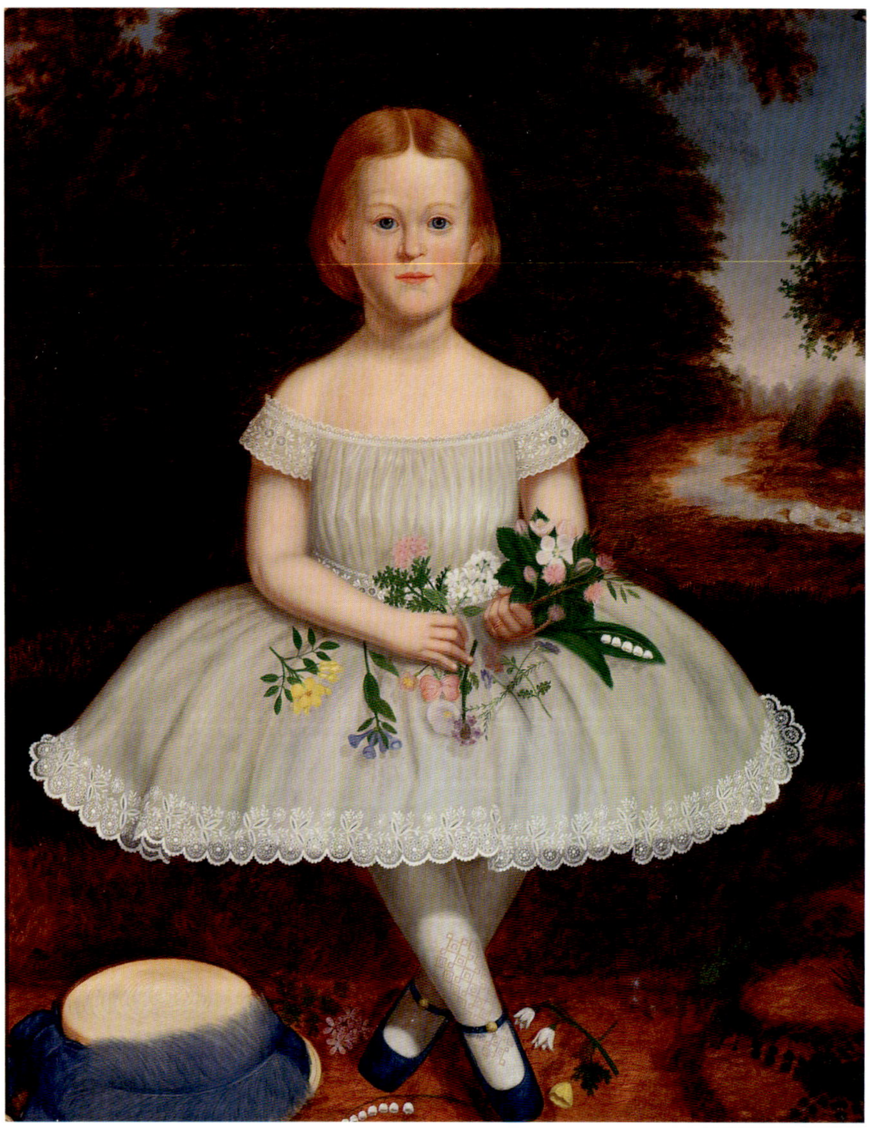

Collection: Duncan Tavern; literature: Whitley.

SOPHIE DEBUTTS GRAY

(1854–1942)

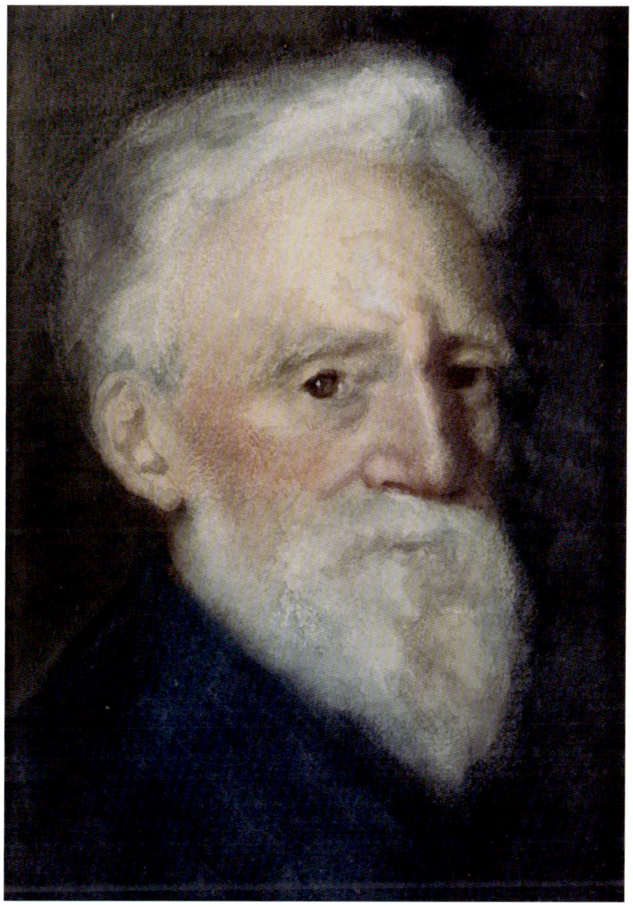

FIGURE 115. Sophie DeButts Gray, *John Thompson Gray Jr.* (1815–1902), ca. 1900, watercolor on paper, 6½ × 4¾", The Filson Historical Society, 1952.4.1.

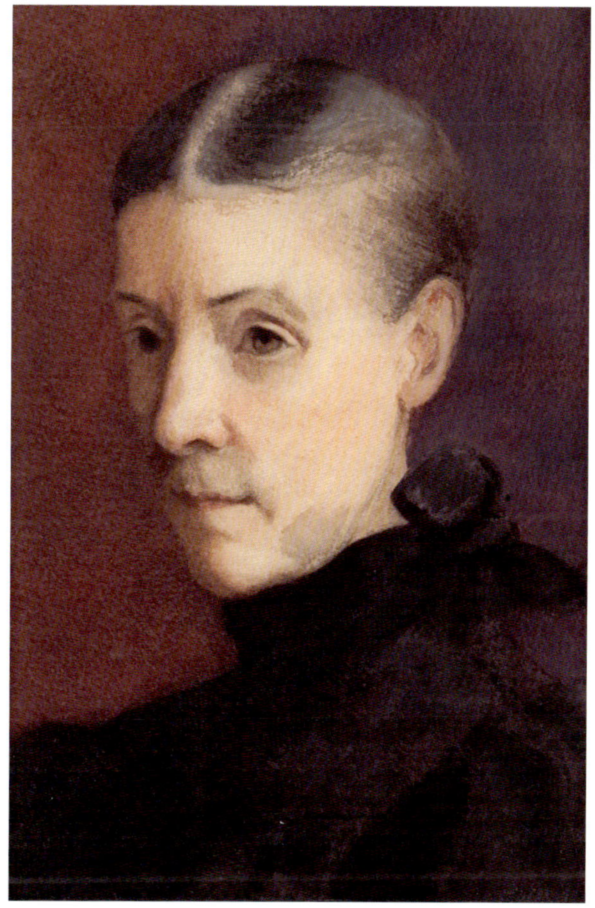

FIGURE 116. Sophie DeButts Gray, *Caroline DeButts Gray* (1829–1908), ca. 1900, watercolor on paper, 6½ × 4¾", The Filson Historical Society, 1952.4.2.

John Thompson Gray Jr. was a native of Louisville and a graduate of the Harvard University Law School. He practiced his profession in Louisville for some years after his graduation, but he later gave it up to manage the large estate he had inherited from his father. On June 14, 1849, he participated in one of the most famous duels in Kentucky history when he shot Henry C. Pope to death. The scandal attached to Gray was so strong that he left Louisville to live among relatives in Baltimore. While there he married Caroline DeButts; their daughter Sophie was born in Baltimore. Although John T. Gray Jr. returned to Louisville in the late 1850s, he never lived down his notoriety and spent a quiet life as a farmer and amateur author.

SOPHIE DEBUTTS GRAY was born in Baltimore, the daughter of John Thompson Gray Jr. and Caroline DeButts Gray of Baltimore, who had married in 1850. She studied in Baltimore with Benjamin West at the Maryland Mechanical Institute, and later in New York with Elliott Daingerfield. She exhibited work in Baltimore, Chicago, Washington (Corcoran Gallery), and New Orleans. She was a member of the Louisville Art League, whose gold medal she won at their first exhibition for her work *A Little Mountain Girl.* Though she was prolific and well known locally in her lifetime, works by her are now seldom seen, the portraits of her parents being the best-known examples of her work (Figs. 115, 116). Gray is listed as exhibiting portraits in the 1907 Southern Exposition from an address at 235 E. Jacob Street, Louisville, where she died in 1942. She is buried in Cave Hill Cemetery.

Collections: FHS, KHS; literature: Henry & Ray.

JOHN GRIMES

(1799–1837)

SAMUEL WOODSON PRICE wrote of John Grimes as a waif who just appeared in Lexington in the early 1820s; but his mother, Mary Sourbray, is known to have been part of a Pennsylvania family who had settled in Lexington in 1790. There is no mention of a father, and after 1801 Grimes's maternal family moved to Dayton, where his grandfather, George Sourbray, became a merchant under the name Sowerbright. When he died in 1811 his will directed that his grandsons, including Grimes, be apprenticed to tradesmen. Accordingly, the boy was apprenticed to Thomas Grant in Lexington, whose wife, Mary, was a Sourbray kinswoman. Grant was a partner in Deweese and Grant, a concern that sold tobacco products, manufactured oil paints for decorative purposes, imported wallpaper, and offered sign-painting services. Edna Talbott Whitley notes that this shop was "a gathering place for numbers of cultured men in the community," a place where young Grimes "heard discussions of literature, politics, philosophy, choice conversation that eventually led to a cultivated taste and to high intellectual attainments, which won him friends of value, wherever he went." There Grimes met Matthew Harris Jouett, who was so impressed by the young man's talent at drawing that he took him on as a student and painted his portrait. Grimes began an itinerancy in Huntsville, Alabama, in 1820, painting various connections of the Clement C. Clay family while in residence in an apartment above J. W. Tillford's store on the corner of Square and Eustis Streets. Grimes remained in Huntsville for some seven months. His portrait of Governor Thomas Bibb is composed in the same manner as Jouett's portrait of Justice Thomas Todd, continuing both artists' custom of basing portraits on prints of work by Gilbert Stuart. Grimes visited Huntsville again in 1823–1824. Also in 1824, Grimes assisted Jouett in an ambitious effort to paint a monumental copy of Annibale Carracci's *Three Marys;* this copy was unsold at the time of Jouett's death, although it subsequently came into the possession of the Roman Catholic Cathedral of the Assumption in Louisville. Grimes again returned to Huntsville and earned enough there to travel to Philadelphia in 1825 for further study with Thomas Sully. While in Philadelphia he exhibited portrait work at the Pennsylvania Academy. He was still in Philadelphia as late as June 1828, when Oliver Frazer wrote of him to his mother, speaking warmly of his work and good company. Grimes returned briefly to Lexington later in 1828 prior to moving on to Nashville, Tennessee, where he secured the patronage of Felix Grundy, the local congressman who had also served on the Kentucky Supreme Court. The large quantity of his extant work in Tennessee collections attests to his popularity there. He also taught painting and drawing to several young artists, including William Harrison Scarborough (1812–1871). Edward Patillo reports an 1831 portrait of Sam Houston "wearing nothing but 'a sash about his loins,'"which must have been painted after a print of John Vanderlyn's *Marius among the Ruins of Carthage.* Grimes was still in good health in January 1836, when he wrote a letter of recommendation for "D. Bacon" to Dr. Robert Bird of Philadelphia. Later that year he made a return visit to Huntsville, where he boarded with Mrs. Mary Mastin Irby at the corner of Freen and Gates Streets, painting Mr. and Mrs. Robert Frears as well as a self-portrait for his landlady in exchange for rent due. But while he was in Huntsville his health began to deteriorate, owing to tuberculosis, and he returned to Lexington to die in the home of his adoptive family, the Thomas Grants. He is buried in the old Episcopal Burying Ground on East Third Street in Lexington. John Grimes was a highly ambitious portrait artist whose "cultivated tastes" and "high intellectual attainments" are made quite clear in his coloration and compositional format. His Huntsville work, created while he was still a very young man, reveals his instinctive awareness of the uses of old-master print sources for compositional format, an insight he doubtless gleaned from Jouett's large collection. His portraits of mothers with their children in particular are often posed in "Madonna and Child" arrangements, the child invariably crawling toward the mother's lap. As his work matured following his time in Philadelphia, his style became much more expressively romantic, especially in the large, liquid eyes his gave his subjects. *The Morgan Boys,* reproduced in Jones & Weber and thought to have been painted on a visit to Lexington in 1833, is a fine example of his ability to interweave his full-length subjects in their elaborate costumes with the textured atmospheric background. His increasing use of strong color contrasts may be seen in the portrait of Anna Shelby Barrow, whose rosy cheeks and gently inclined head mark a final departure from the neoclassical format Jouett learned from Gilbert Stuart and passed on to his various followers.

Archives: AAA, TSM; collections: ASC, Speed, TSM, Weeden; literature: Barker, Jones & Weber, J. Kelly, Patillo, Price, Whitley.

CHESTER HARDING

(1792–1866)

CHESTER HARDING WAS BORN in Conway, Massachusetts, the fourth child of Abiel and Olive Smith Harding. In 1802 the family moved to New York state, where Harding and his brother Horace became cabinetmakers and decorative painters in Caledonia. He married Caroline Woodruff in 1815; and, though industrious, he failed in his efforts to support his family, incurred sufficient debt to face the threat of prison, and fled downriver on a flatboat to Pittsburgh and then on to Kentucky. The Harding family arrived in Paris, Kentucky, in 1818 at the invitation of his brother Horace, also an artist. Harding's daughter, Ophelia, was born in Paris, Kentucky. Chester Harding was resident in Paris until 1821, using this location as a base from which he made trips to Cincinnati in 1820 and to Missouri later in that year, at which time he painted Daniel Boone. He worked as an itinerant in Madison County, Kentucky, 1819, where he painted his monumental portrait of the Speed Smith family and other kin of General Green Clay. During this period in Kentucky he is thought to have become an acquaintance of Matthew Harris Jouett, with whom he exchanged works. Harding spent the winter of 1821–1822 in Washington, D.C., making important contacts, which led to a commission to paint members of the extended family of Senator E. H. Mills of Northampton, Massachusetts. His work there was so successful that he moved on to Boston, where he attracted favorable comments from Gilbert Stuart. In 1823 he sailed to England, where he painted the portrait of the Duke of Sussex, a brother of King George IV. He then moved on to Scotland, where his family joined him in 1825. They returned to Boston in 1826, settling in Springfield, Massachusetts, at 7 Chestnut Street, which became their permanent home. Harding also maintained a studio on School Street in Boston until 1846; thereafter he stayed in the Tremont House, a hotel. Harding became one of the most successful portraitists in America, painting several figures of note, including President James Monroe, Henry Clay, John C. Calhoun, Daniel Webster, Washington Allston, and Charles Carroll, the last surviving signer of the Declaration of Independence. Through extended family ties he continued to work as an itinerant in the South, with excursions to Richmond, Virginia, and New Orleans in 1841, as well as return trips to Kentucky in 1828 and 1833, and as the guest of Hugh Innes Brent of Paris, 1834, 1838, and 1842. During this last visit he most likely painted Frances Bibb Burnley (Fig. 117). His wife, Caroline, died in 1845. In mourning, Harding returned to London in 1846, where he stayed for nine months, during which time he painted Lord Aberdeen and the poet Samuel Rogers. Upon his return he spent the winter of 1848 in Washington, painting a full-length portrait of Henry Clay. After 1850 his activity as a portraitist slowed, although he did paint nearly all his children and grandchildren, some of his finest work. Harding's family was deeply divided by the Civil War. Two sons, Chester and Edward, fought for the Union, and two others, Horace and James, for the Confederacy. One of Harding's last portraits in the grand

FIGURE 117. Chester Harding, *Frances Bibb Burnley* (1810–1891), ca. 1842, oil on canvas, 26¼ × 21¼″, The Filson Historical Society, 1995.13.3.

Frances Bibb was the daughter of Judge George Bibb of Frankfort. In 1827 she married Albert T. Burnley, her father's law clerk. Burnley was variously a cotton factor with offices in Louisville and New Orleans, and a newspaper publisher in Washington during the administrations of Zachary Taylor and Millard Fillmore. After his death in 1861, Frances Burnley moved back to live in her father's home, Gray Gables.

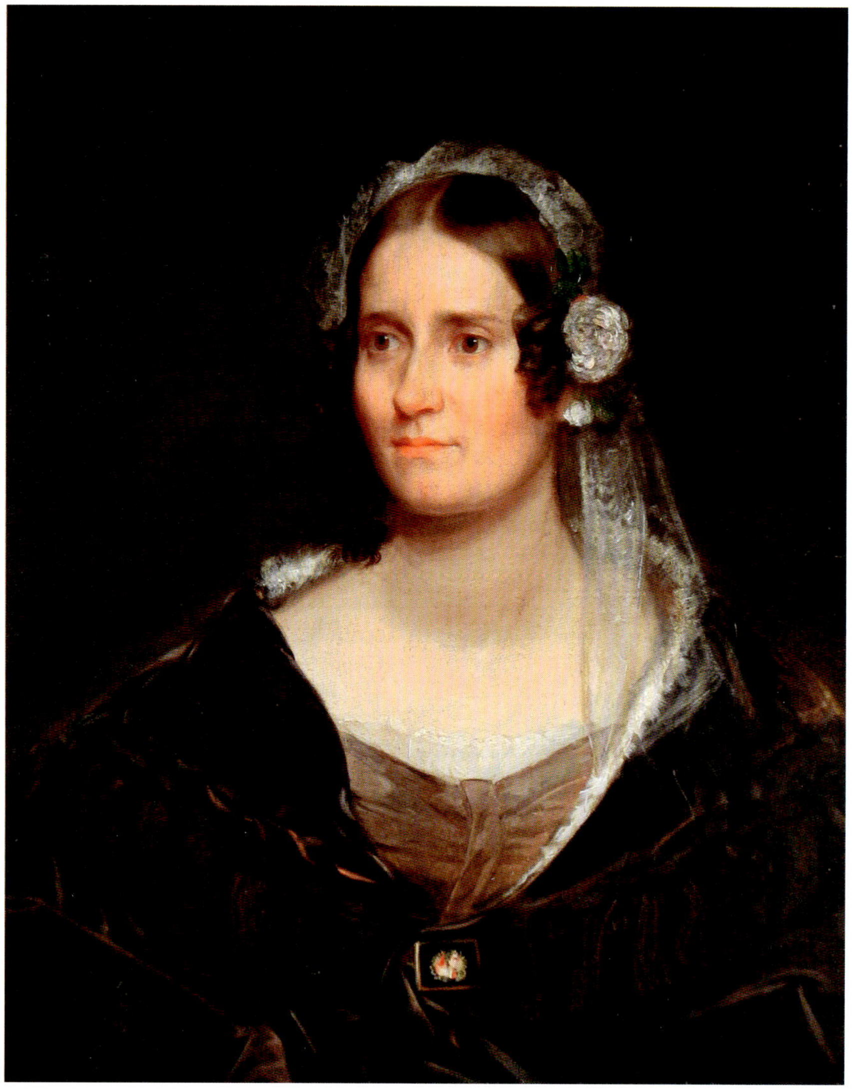

manner was of the Union general William Tecumseh Sherman. His health began to decline in 1865; he died the following year at the Tremont House and was buried in the Springfield Cemetery, the landscaping of which he had supervised. Henry Tuckerman wrote that the "massiveness and vigor of his body, his noble presence, and the mingled rusticity and courtliness of his manners, gave intimations of the stern and rough nursing of his earlier years, and kept the remembrance of the scenes and hardships through which he had made his way to the intimacy with the most distinguished men in his middle and later life."

Archives: AAA; select collections: FHS, NGA, NPG, OHS, Speed; literature: Burnley, Dunlap, Hageman, Harding (1866, 1890), Haverstock et al., Jones & Weber, Lipton (1984 "New Discoveries," 1985), Shackleton, Tuckerman, Vlach, Whitley.

HORACE HARDING

(1794–after 1857)

HORACE HARDING WAS BORN in Conway, Massachusetts, the fifth child of Abiel and Olive Smith Harding and brother of Chester Harding. He traveled west and established himself in Paris, Kentucky, in 1817 as a painter of portraits and fancy chairs. From his base in Paris he made itinerant excursions to Cincinnati, 1819, and Vincennes, Indiana, 1820. After his brother left Paris, Horace became a wandering itinerant, noted in Mobile, Alabama, 1822, and in southern Ohio until 1834, after which he was resident in Cincinnati until 1840, when he moved to New York. While in Cincinnati he made trips to New Orleans, 1835–1837, Versailles, Kentucky, 1837, and St. Louis, 1839. He was in New York until 1852, when he moved to Little Rock, Arkansas. Following a painting trip to New Orleans in 1857 he went to Woodville, Mississippi, where he died of cholera.

Collections: Duncan Tavern, OHS, St. Louis; literature: Hageman, Haverstock et al., Peat (1954), Whitley.

GEORGE PETER ALEXANDER HEALY

(1813–1894)

GEORGE PETER ALEXANDER HEALY was born in Boston to William Healy, a sea captain, and Mary Hicks Healy. After his father's early death he established a portrait studio in Boston at the age of eighteen and attracted the patronage of Mrs. Harrison Gray Otis, completing enough commissions to travel abroad for further study. He studied in Paris, 1834–1836, with Thomas Couture and Baron Gros; while there he became friends with the Kentuckian Oliver Frazer, of whom Healy said, "Of all my fellow students he is the one who lives most deeply in my affectionate remembrance." Healy was in London, 1838–1839, where he became an associate of the Royal Academy and married Louisa Phipps. He returned to Paris in 1840 and received numerous commissions from Louis Philippe, the French "Citizen King." Though based in Paris, Healy returned to America in 1840 and visited Louisville in 1840 and 1842. To fulfill a commission from Louis Philippe to create portraits of prominent Americans, he visited Lexington in 1845 to paint Henry Clay, using Frazer's studio, and painting Frazer and his wife as well as a self-portrait. On this same visit, he assisted Frazer in the completion of a portrait of Mrs. Samuel McKee, as Frazer's health and eyesight were already beginning to fail. Healy resettled his family in Chicago in 1855, and this city became his principal base for the rest of his life, although he continued to travel and paint abroad. He was very popular in the South, visiting New Orleans in 1857–1860 and Charleston in 1861. He was often in Kentucky, where he painted in Louisville, Lexington, and Bardstown in 1859, 1860, 1864, and 1865, creating a large body of work based on Kentucky sitters. He was always more popular in the South than in the North, where many of his contemporaries were put off by his aggressive pursuit of commissions and flagrantly bravura brushwork. "The vigor of execution in the best of Healy's work is not less remarkable than his facility and enterprise: his likenesses often want delicacy, but seldom lack emphasis," Henry Tuckerman wrote of him. He became active again in Europe after 1866, notably in Spain, 1871, and Romania, 1872. While he was abroad with his family the great Chicago fire of 1871 occurred, which damaged his home and studio. He was the first American artist to be asked to donate a self-portrait to the Uffizi Gallery in Florence. After the rise of Impressionism in France during the early 1870s, Healy began to feel isolated and spent more time in America, retiring to Chicago in 1892, where he died. His most famous work may well be the seated Lincoln portrait in the White House collection.

Archives: FHS, SAM, CHM; collections: CAI, Columbus, FHS, IMA, NGA, NPG, Speed, WH; literature: Ayers, Bigot, Carr, De Mare, Flexner, Healy, Holzer & Neely, Kloss et al., Quick, Tuckerman, Virginia Museum of Fine Arts, Whitley.

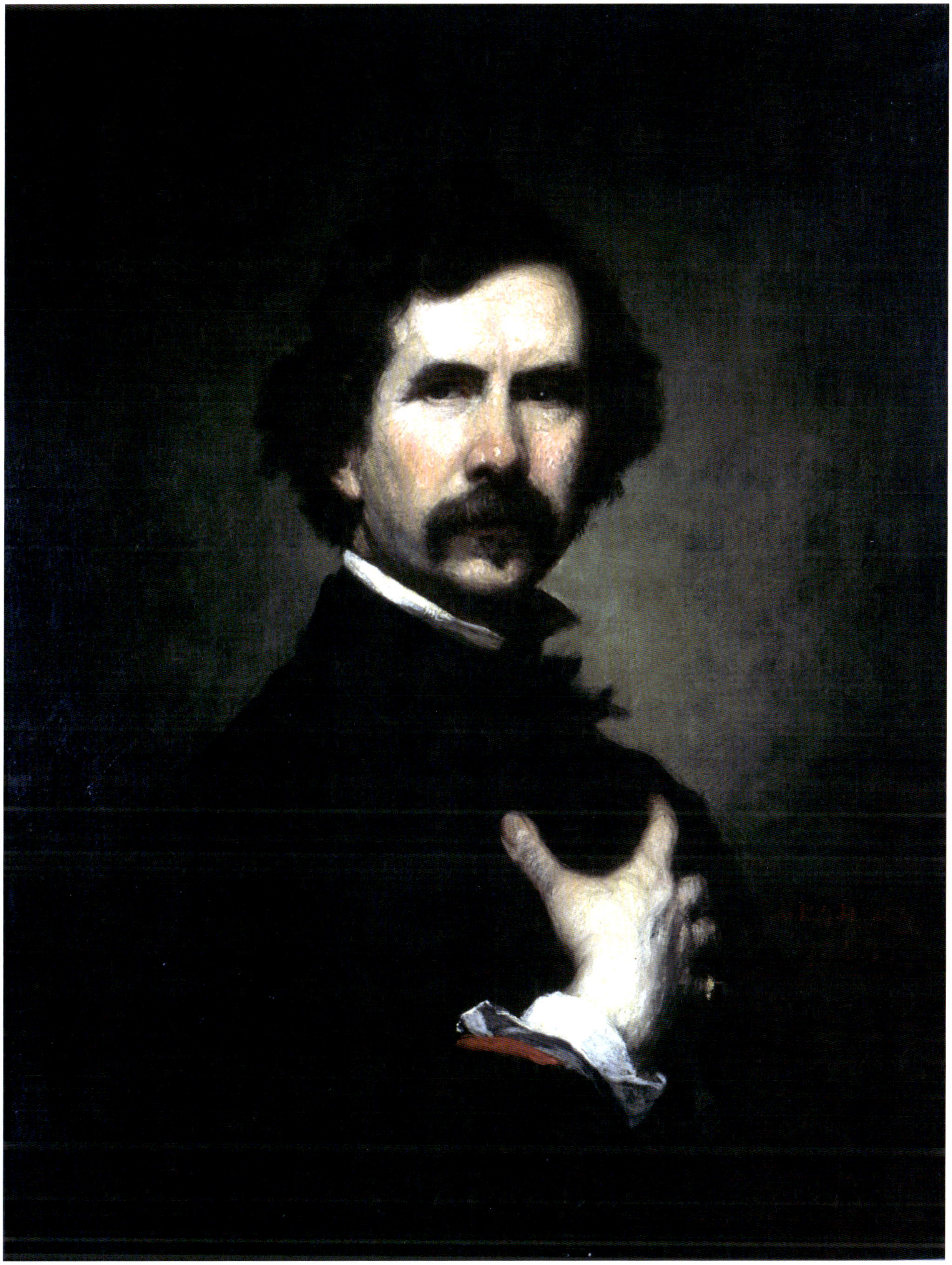

FIGURE 118. George Peter Alexander Healy, *Self-Portrait,* 1860, oil on canvas, 30⅛ × 24¼″, Speed Art Museum, gift of Miss Henrietta H. Henning, 1949.6.

ELLA SOPHONISBA HERGESHEIMER

(1873–1943)

FIGURE 119 *(facing page).* Ella Sophonisba Hergesheimer, *Self-Portrait,* 1931, oil on canvas, 48¾ × 32¾", collection of Cheekwood Museum of Art, Nashville, Tennessee, 1960.2.12.

ELLA HERGESHEIMER WAS BORN in Allentown, Pennsylvania, the daughter of Charles Potter and Elamanda Hergesheimer and the great-great-granddaughter of the distinguished American painter Charles Willson Peale (1741–1827), for whose daughter, her ancestor Sophonisba, she was named. Any natural ability Hergesheimer may have inherited was more than refined by her studies with two of the premier artists of their day, William Merrit Chase and Cecilia Beaux, at the Pennsylvania Academy of Fine Arts, 1900–1903. Beaux's work, especially her rather Whistlerian portraits, seem to have deeply impressed the young artist. Hergesheimer won the Cresson Traveling Scholarship in 1904, which enabled her to pursue further study in Europe, 1904–1907, including work at the Colarossi School in Paris. Hergesheimer was invited to Nashville, Tennessee, in 1907 by Bishop Holland McTyeire to undertake commissions for the Methodist Church and Vanderbilt University. The founding of Vanderbilt University inspired strong cultural ambitions in the city. Nashville was also the center for the hierarchy of the Methodist-Episcopal Church South, a fact that created a demand for portraiture of bishops and elders. Hergesheimer's portraits are quite well done, with subdued grand-manner echoes of Beaux and Sargent. She was also a still-life painter in the Peale tradition. Like her late portraits, these still lifes are solidly realistic representations, devoid of atmospherics and strongly colored in a manner that approaches the nuances of the art-deco style. Her watercolor work is much more freely expressive, as though, like Sargent, she could express herself in a more vivid manner outside the demands made by her portrait clientele. In a piece in the *Nashville Banner,* July 5, 1932, she professed a great admiration for the post-Impressionist artists in France, observing that "they have done something wonderful for us. They have given us design which in a great measure was lost by the impressionists, but which the great masters of the past always had." What we may be hearing here is an awareness of Cézanne's legacy of schematic composition enhanced by color gradation. Though based in Nashville after 1907, Hergesheimer was also active in southern Kentucky, in the Bowling Green area, where she taught classes and painted portraits for the faculty and staff of Western Kentucky State Teachers College (now Western Kentucky University). Among her students were the local artists Frances Fowler, Sarah Peyton, and Wickliffe Covington. She also worked in Lexington as early as 1918, offering classes and exhibiting her work at the public library. Her self-portrait (Fig. 119) displays the calm poise of one of those remarkably talented, well-educated women whose careers figure so prominently in the history of twentieth-century painting in the South. She died in Nashville.

Archives: UD; collections: Heckscher, KM, MMA, Reading, TSM, USC, USNA, Vanderbilt; literature: Burton, Chambers (1983), J. Kelly, Pennington (1992).

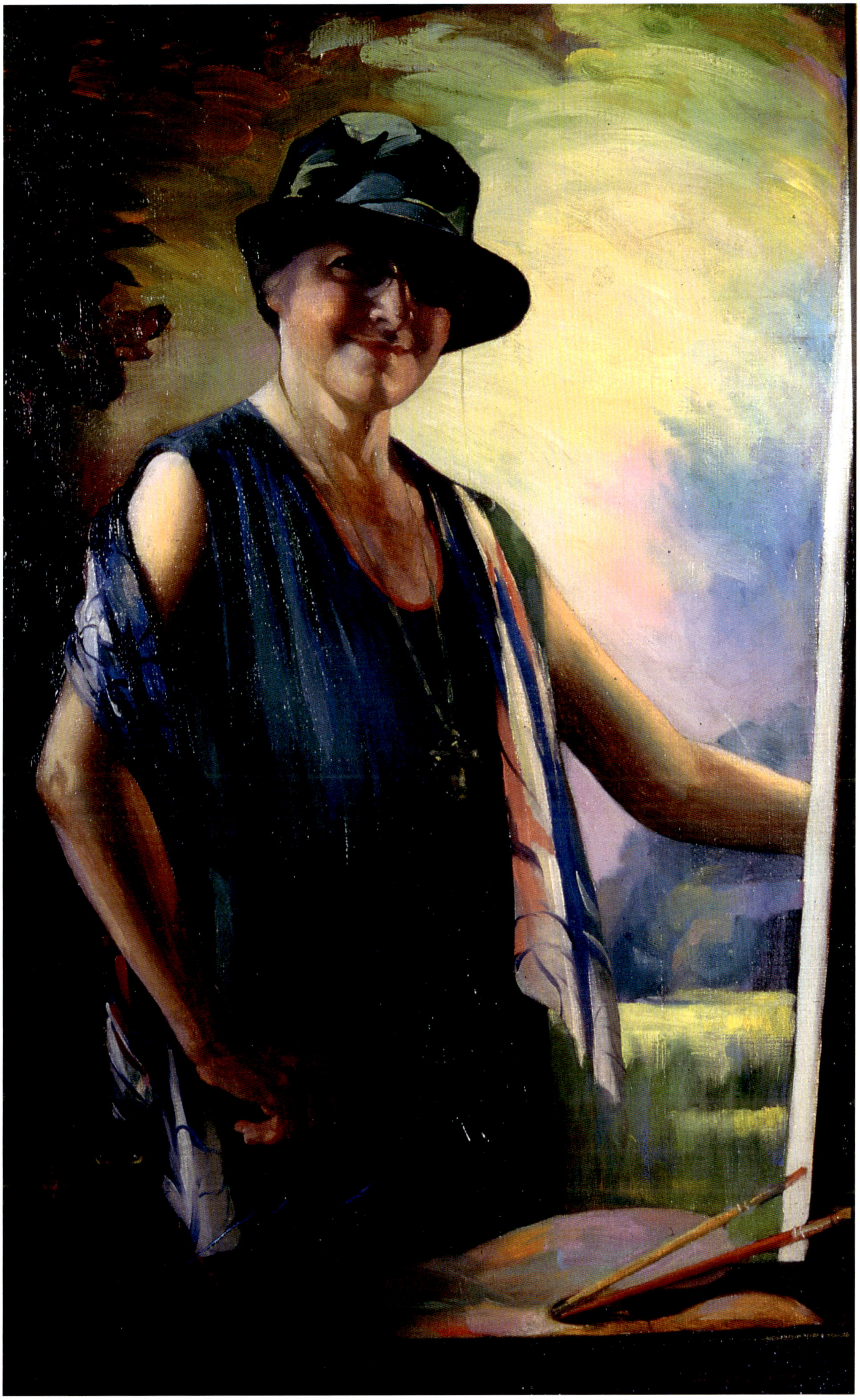

BENONI IRWIN

(1840–1896)

FIGURE 120. Benoni Irwin, *Silas Field Miller* (ca. 1829–1902), 1889, pastel on paper, 26¼ × 21¼", The Filson Historical Society, 1962.10.

BENONI IRWIN WAS BORN in Newmarket, Ontario, Canada, to Jared and Lydia Kennedy Irwin. While Lydia Irwin was pregnant, her husband was captured and imprisoned for his participation in the McKenzie Rebellion against the British. When their child was born, she named him Ben-Oni, from the Old Testament story of Jacob, the name meaning "son of my sorrows." Respecting his father's wishes, Irwin entered McGill University and graduated with an engineering degree. At around the same time he met and married Elizabeth de Bonheur, who bore him a daughter a year later and then died of consumption. After Elizabeth's death he continued his studies at the School of Practical Science in Toronto, but he increasingly became more interested in being a painter than an engineer. Irwin spent eight months traveling to California in 1862, working along the way, in order to place his daughter, Muriel, in the home

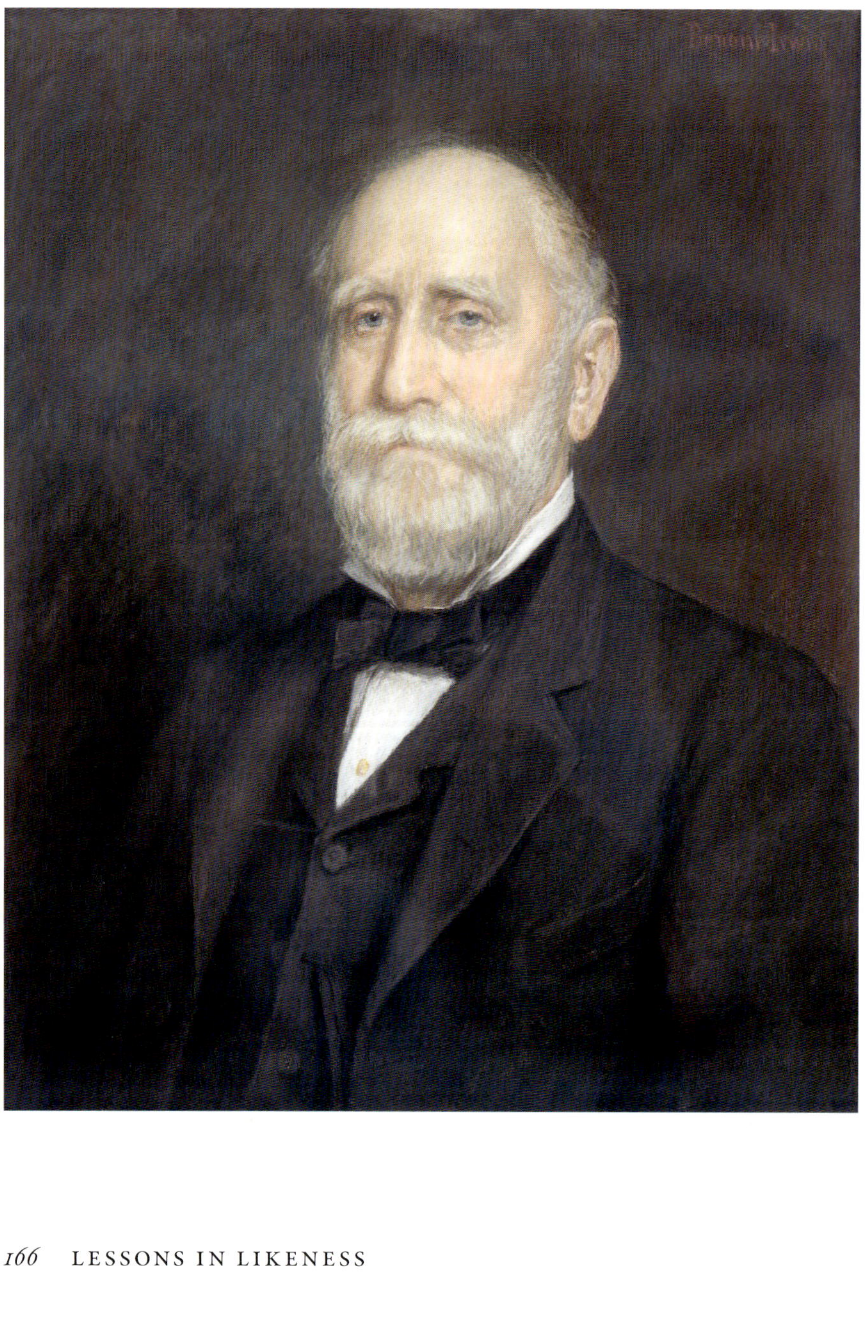

of his brother Edwin in the San Joaquin Valley. He returned east to New York and studied at the National Academy of Design, 1863–1865, with Asher B. Durand and Thomas Sier Cummings. Irwin remained in New York until 1867, when he again traveled the country from New York to Toronto to California, working in San Francisco in 1870. His first period of residence in Kentucky began in Louisville, 1870, when he moved into the home of his brother David, a prosperous merchant, and then into his own home and studio at 188 Third Street. From 1871 to 1877 he was again in San Francisco, painting portraits and fantasies from historical sources. Seeking to perfect his skills as a portraitist, he moved to Paris, France, where he studied with Carolus-Duran, the master teacher of John Singer Sargent, 1878–1879. Upon his return to America he spent nine months in Boston, 1879, before returning to California in 1880. He acquired a permanent residence in New York in 1882 but continued to visit California and Kentucky in pursuit of painting commissions until his death. During the time he was active in Louisville, exhibiting at the industrial expositions and painting portraits of members of the Watterson, Clay, McDowell, Speed, and Frazer families, he became the late nineteenth-century portrait artist of choice. His portrait of Silas Field Miller, proprietor of the Galt House Hotel in Louisville, demonstrates his luminous abilities as a pastel artist (Fig. 120). He was much admired by many of his contemporaries in New York; his portraits of the artists Frederick Remington, Hugh Bolton Jones, and Dwight Tryon are in the National Academy of Design collection. He drowned in a boating accident in 1896 while spending the summer with his family at South Coventry, Connecticut.

Archives: FHS, Nevada; collections: Ashland, Corcoran, Crocker, FHS, NAD, Oakland, Speed; literature: Bonura, Jones & Weber, Whitley.

JOHN WESLEY JARVIS

(1781–1840)

JOHN WESLEY JARVIS was born in South Shields, England, a kinsman of John Wesley, the Methodist reformer. He arrived in New York in 1785 and moved on to Philadelphia, ca. 1789; while in Philadelphia he became acquainted with Matthew Pratt, an important colonial sign and portrait painter. By 1800 he was back in New York, where he was apprenticed to David Edwin, a student of Edward Savage. Jarvis worked with Edward Malbone, creating eglomise (painted glass) miniatures heightened with gold before 1807, when he was in Philadelphia assisting Thomas Sully. He began regular periods of itinerancy in the South in 1810, with visits to Baltimore, Charleston, rural Maryland, New Orleans, and Washington, D.C. He was in Louisville in late 1820 at the invitation of the Croghan family, whose portraits he painted; during this time he was reputed to have painted a heroic portrait of George Rogers Clark that was based on life portraits either by J. Cook taken at Locust Grove in 1810–1811 at the request of Owen Gwathmey or by Joseph Henry Bush taken at Locust Grove in 1817. By several accounts, Jarvis's high spirits and abilities as a raconteur made him most welcome in rural southern settings. After his death many of his northern biographers took a critical view of his cavalier behavior and idiosyncratic approach to taking a likeness. Harry Wehle found his "mien . . . virile, solidly constructed, with a tendency toward coarsening of features." The high Victorians dismissed him. Henry Tuckerman wrote that for Jarvis, "vagabondage was intuitive," and "his labors as an artist, are among the most curious social phenomena of a period when conviviality was more sanctioned by fashion; and the deeper insight and more generalized experience of a scientific era had not yet quite dissipated the popular fallacy that genius is inevitably allied to recklessness . . . and a valid excuse for despising the wholesome discipline of social conformity." He was in Cincinnati, August 1828–April 1829. After 1830 he was based in New York, where he died in 1840. He is ably represented by Harold E. Dickson's entertaining biography, first published in 1949.

Archives: NYHS, SAM; collections: Ball State, CMA, FHS, MMA, NGA, NPG, Sheldon Swope, Snite, Toledo, WH; literature: Bolton & Groce, Dickson, Groce & Wallace, Holmberg, Quick, Tuckerman, Wehle, Whitley.

PHILIP OSKAR JENKINS

(ca. 1818?–after 1880)

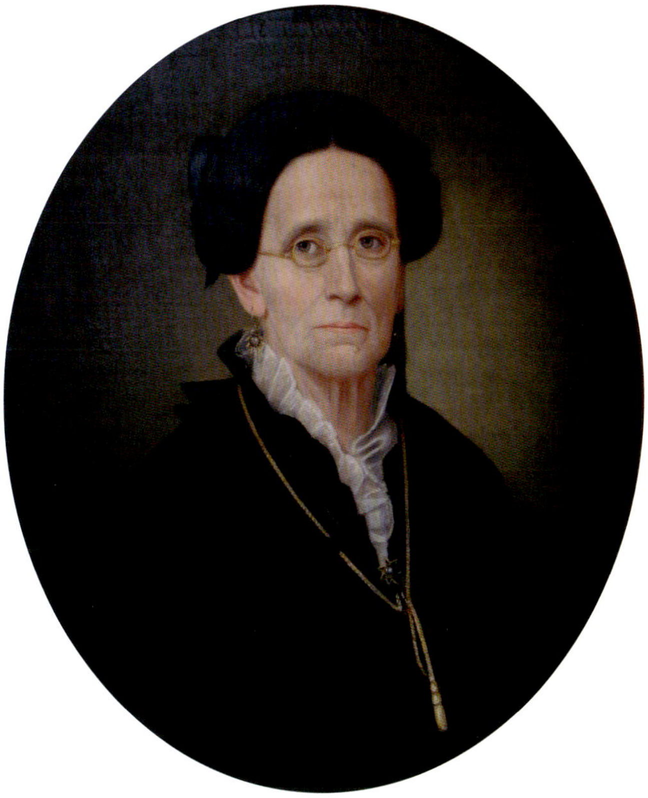

FIGURE 121. Philip Oskar Jenkins, *Sarah "Sallie" Rawlings Kennedy Read* (1816–1895), 1874, oil on canvas, 30 × 25″, The Filson Historical Society, 2000.11.2.

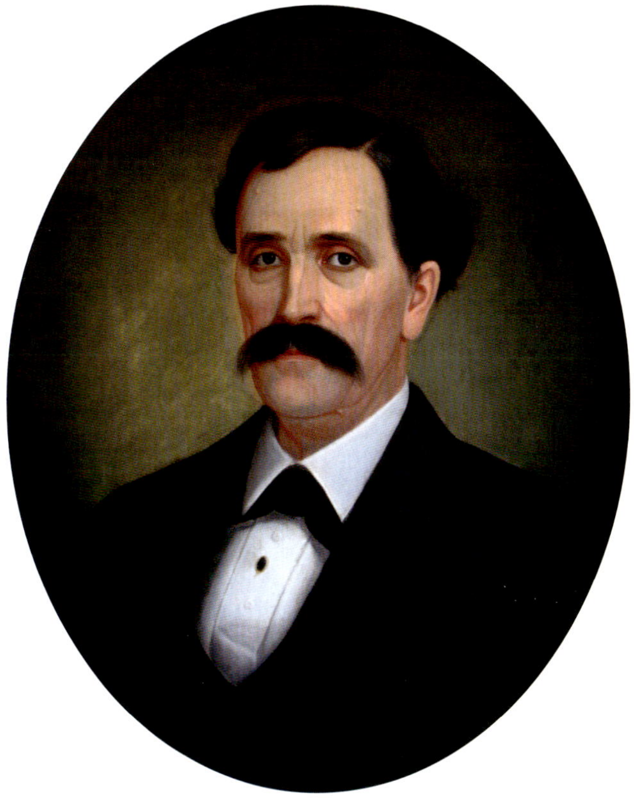

FIGURE 122. Philip Oskar Jenkins, *Congressman William B. Read* (1817–1880), 1874, oil on canvas, 30 × 25″, The Filson Historical Society, 2000.11.1.

PHILIP OSKAR JENKINS is thought to have been born in Kentucky, though precious little is known of his life. Census records identify him; his wife, Jemima Ingram; and his three children as living in Christian County, Kentucky, in 1860. He is noted as an itinerant working in Simpson County, Kentucky, 1860–1865. By 1870 he and his family were living in Washington, D.C., where his profession is listed as "portrait painter." He is last noted in the 1880 Washington, D.C., census. Though he may have known the William Reads from his days in western Kentucky, his signature on the back of his portraits of them indicates that they were painted in Washington, D.C., during Read's congressional tenure and therefore almost certainly at Read's invitation (Figs. 121, 122). Though painted in a very flat manner, anatomy pressed against the planar field, these portraits have a marvelous attention to detail, especially in the rendering of Mrs. Read's jewelry.

Collections: FHS, KM; literature: Whitley.

William Brown Read was a native of Hardin County, Kentucky, whose father, Louis Read, was active in local politics. He was admitted to the bar in 1849 and began to practice law in Hodgenville, the birthplace of Abraham Lincoln. He served in the state senate from 1857 to 1865. After the war Read practiced law in western Kentucky until 1870, when he was elected to congress as a Democrat in a very contentious election. He served two terms but was not renominated in 1874.

HARVEY JOINER

(1852–1932)

FIGURE 123. Harvey Joiner, *William Shakespeare Hays* (1837–1907), 1885, oil on canvas, 41½ × 36″, The Filson Historical Society, 1993.35.6.

Will Hays enjoyed a long career as a composer, wit, and local figure in Louisville, where he was born. His father, Hugh Hays, was a manufacturer of sufficient means to indulge his son's precocious interest in music. Hays was famous for his native genius, praised as someone who could play any instrument without instruction of any kind. Hays wrote, published, and sold an extraordinary number of songs. His best known, "Mollie Darling," is said to have sold more than 3 million copies during the 1870s. His opus is dominated by rousing hymns, such as "Save One Bright Crown for Me," and scores of nostalgic laments for the Old South, such as "My Sunny Southern Home." Apparently he became so caught up in his own mythic persona as the musical voice of the South that late in life he began to claim he had written "Dixie," the fight song of the Lost Cause.

HARVEY JOINER WAS BORN in Charlestown, Indiana, the son of Charles and Elizabeth Joiner, with whom he soon moved to Memphis, Indiana, where his father was a metalsmith. In 1868 he began working on boats in the bayous of Louisiana, where he is said to have made sketches of African-American workmen. Returning north to St. Louis in 1874, he made the acquaintance of a German portrait painter, David Hoffman, from whom he received some instruction and whom he assisted in making portraits. From 1875 to 1880 Joiner was active as an itinerant portraitist and church interior painter in southern Illinois and Utica, Indiana, where he painted *Ruth Gleaning in the Fields of Boaz* for the Christian Church. He established a studio in the Courier-Journal building in Louisville, 1880, where he worked for the rest of his career while living in Port Fulton, Indiana. His work was first publicly displayed at the 1884 Southern Exposition in Louisville. Although Joiner is much better known as a landscape painter, he, like many artists, depended on portrait commissions for steady income. One of his most noted subjects was William Shakespeare Hays (Fig. 123). Joiner's later portraits were more ambitious. His large, grand-manner pendant portraits of Russell M. Hughes and his wife, Lilly Bell Allen Hughes, may have been taken from photographs, but they are impressive nevertheless. His prodigious output of formulaic landscapes set in deep gold shadow boxes, featuring the eternally vanishing perspective of an obtuse allée of trees in Louisville's Cherokee Park, have made some suspect him of being a hack. Joiner is also the subject of an urban myth that is well worth repeating. According to legend, the spectral light that spreads across his forests' floors was created by parking his Model T just out of range on the edge of the picture plane and turning the headlamps on, directing the beams into the trees. Whether the tale is true or not, Joiner's paintings do indeed manifest a supernatural light that places them more in the symbolist school than with more earnest tonalists, such as Carl Brenner. His rich color gradations, often a harmonic progression from deep green to chartreuse, are most effective for enhancing depth and perspective. The absence of human presence also compounds the primeval atmosphere these works are intended to evoke. Late in life, he was reported by the *Louisville Times* of March 6, 1929, to have created over five thousand works. Joiner died in Port Fulton in 1932.

Collections: Allen Hite, FHS, InStateM, KHS, MMA, Speed; literature: Jones & Weber, Pennington (1992, 1999, 2008).

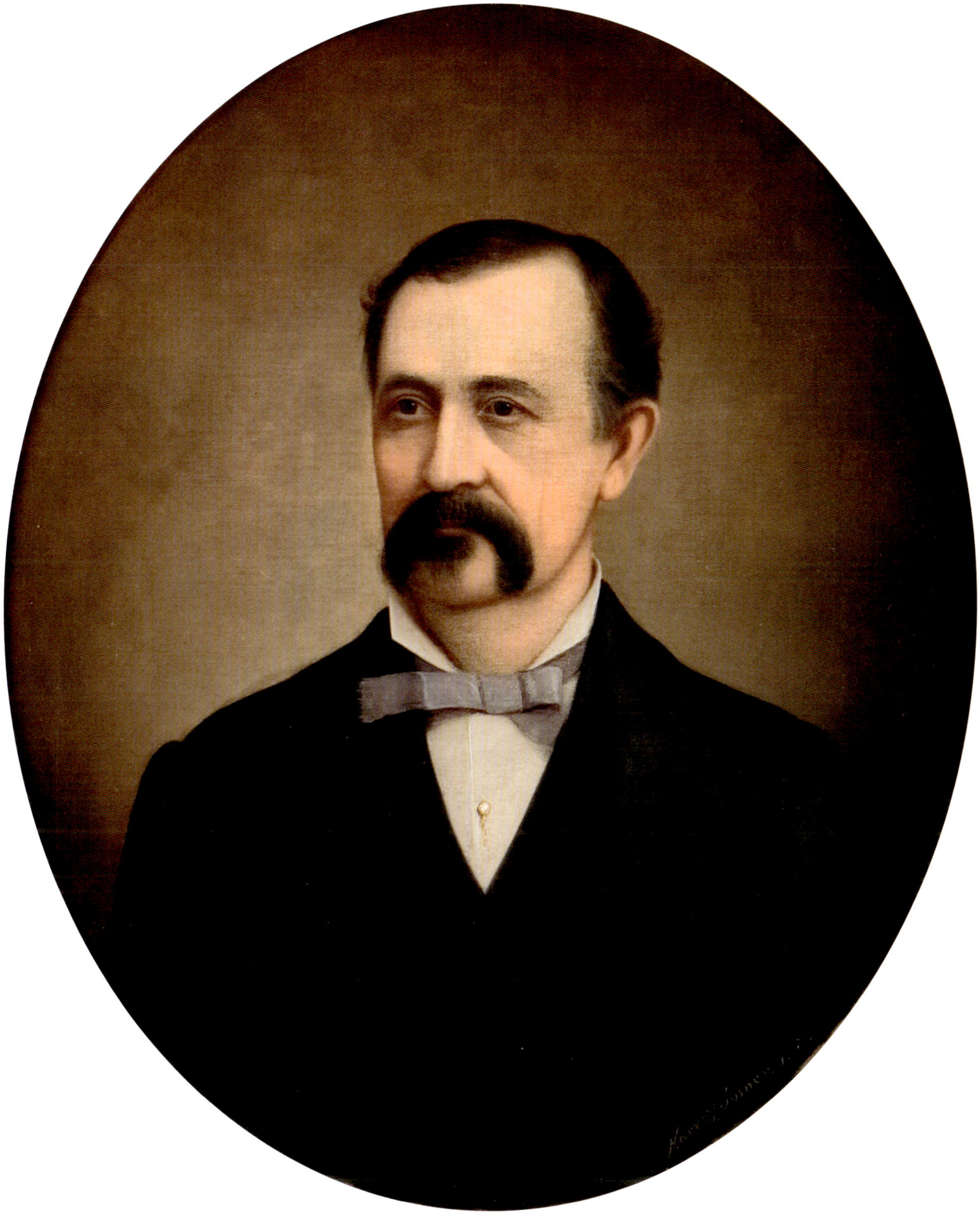

MATTHEW HARRIS JOUETT

(1788–1827)

MATTHEW HARRIS JOUETT was born in Harrodsburg, Kentucky, to Jack and Sally Robards Jouett. His father was a hero of the Revolution who alerted Charlottesville to Tarleton's raid. He studied law at Transylvania University, Lexington, 1804–1808, with George Bibb, and upon his graduation married Margaret Henderson Allen, May 25, 1812. He enlisted in the Third Mounted Regiment, Kentucky Volunteers, in the War of 1812. Jouett assumed the responsibility to replace $6,000 of his regiment's missing payroll funds lost in the Battle of River Raisin, a fact always noted as motivating him to become a portraitist. Jouett resigned from the army on January 20, 1815, and opened a studio in Lexington, painting portraits of some of his military compatriots from memory, including Colonel John Allen of Shelbyville, Captain Nathaniel Hart, and Captain Paschal Hickman. Seeking the sons of Edward West, his contemporary Lexington portraitists, he set out for Philadelphia; not finding them, he continued to Boston, where from July through October 1816 he worked with Gilbert Stuart, keeping an important record of his studies. Stuart is said to have painted Jouett's portrait, with the subject's hat in his hand, but the work is now lost. Upon Jouett's return to Kentucky, he established a studio in Lexington, 1816, initially charging $50 per portrait. He immediately attracted some of the most distinguished citizens of the commonwealth, notably Isaac Shelby (Fig. 124) and Henry Clay. An announcement in the *Lexington Kentucky Reporter* for June, 16, 1819, states that "Mr. Jouett has lately finished the Portraits of several of our distinguished fellow citizens," including the "full-length portrait of that eminent soldier, Col. Isaac Shelby." There is no evidence as to the fate of that later portrait of Shelby. Jouett began to work as an itinerant during the winters in Natchez and New Orleans, 1817–1827. He held an exhibition of his work at the Kentucky Hotel in Lexington, June 28, 1817, charging an admission fee of twenty-five cents. From 1817 to 1825 he occupied a studio in the Kentucky Hotel, opposite the Fayette Courthouse, on Short Street. He visited Thomas Sully in Philadelphia in 1823. From 1825 onward his studio was on North Upper Street in a building owned by Henry Clay; he also had a temporary studio in Louisville in 1826. In late July 1827 Jouett returned to his home near Lexington from Louisville, "indisposed by an attack of bilious fever," according to a fulsome obituary published by "a friend" in the *Kentucky Reporter,* August 1827. That "bilious fever" is likely to have been typhoid, and after suffering for ten days, the artist died, but not before taking great pains to put his estate in order, as the lists in E. A. Jonas indicate. His anonymous mourner identified him as a genius, who "as if inspired by heaven, seized the bright spark in the character of the victim, fanned it into a flame, and placed it in propitious contrast to the dark shade," an apt metaphor for the quality of his portraits. After his death in Fayette County, he was buried at his farm. Jouett was re-interred in Cave Hill Cemetery, Louisville, in 1893, at the time of the death of his grandson Richard Jouett Menefee.

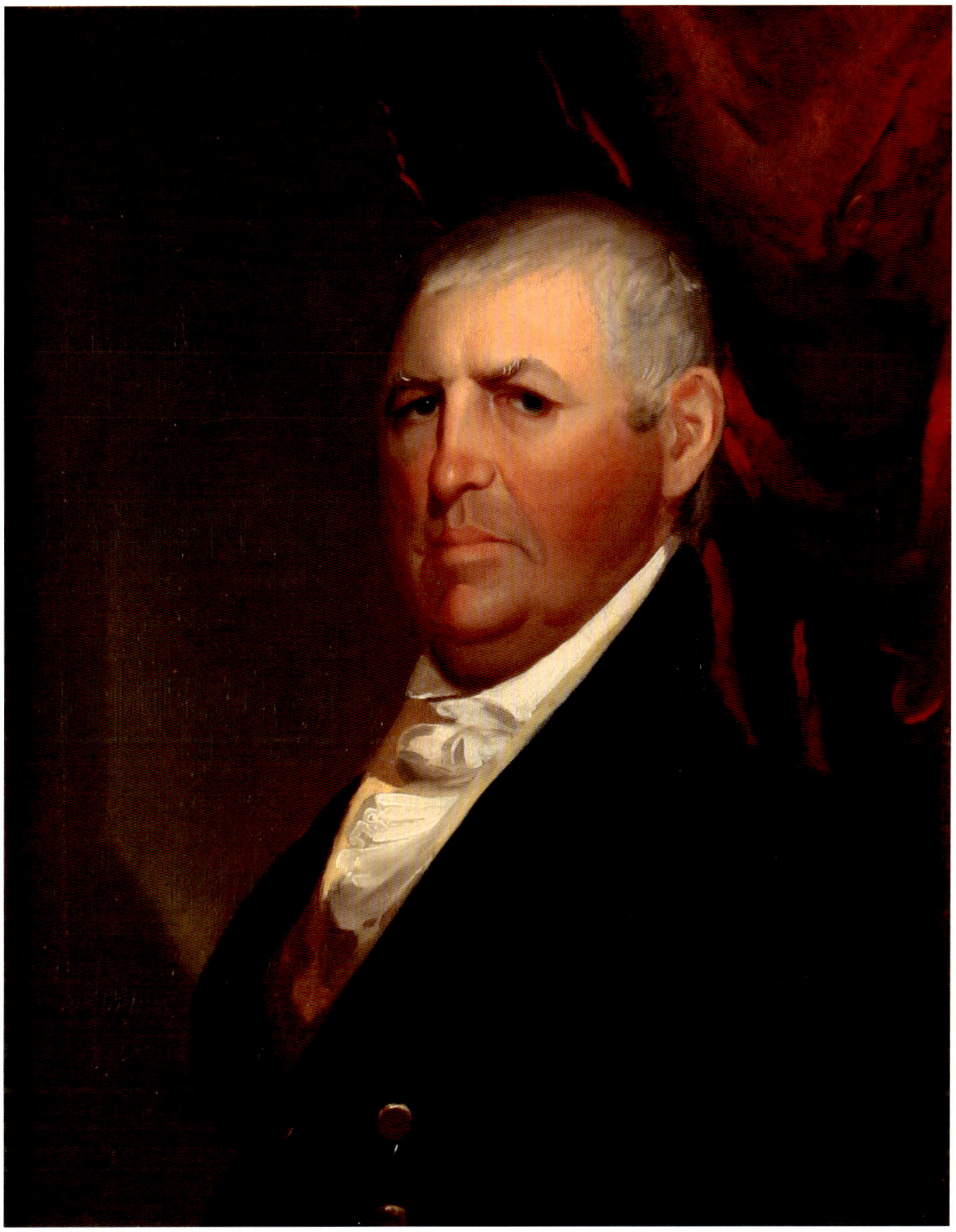

FIGURE 124. Matthew Harris Jouett, *Isaac Shelby* (1750–1826), ca. 1816, oil on canvas, 26½ × 21″, The Filson Historical Society, 1995.15.

Isaac Shelby, Kentucky's first governor, was born in Hagerstown, Maryland, to Evan and Letitia Cox Shelby. He fought in the Revolutionary War, and he was one of the principals in the Battle of King's Mountain in South Carolina. After his marriage to Susannah Hart in 1783, he moved to Knob Creek, Lincoln County, Kentucky. He was active in the early political conventions that led to statehood in 1792, and he was unanimously elected governor in May of that year. After his first term in office, he left public life and for sixteen years concentrated on building his farming operation at Traveler's Rest, in Boyle County. He became governor again on the eve of the War of 1812, and while in office served as a general at the Battle of the Thames. After this second term, he returned to his home, Traveler's Rest, where he spent his last years as a farmer.

To this date no accurate catalogue raisonné has been compiled, and a corrective essay on the errors of his early biographers is much needed. All accounts of him would seem to concur with William Dunlap's report that he "was a man of taste and possessed a vein of humor, copious and rich, but unaffected and innocent in its tendency, which made him a charming companion, and which will perhaps greatly add to the interest of his biography."

Archives: AAA, FHS; collections: FHS, KHS, MESDA, Met, NGA, NPG, OHS, PHS, Speed, State, WH; literature: Dunlap, Flexner, Floyd (1968), Hart (1899, 1900), Jonas, Jones & Weber, J. Kelly, Martin, Pennington (Autumn 1986, 1991, 1993, 2008), Price, Whitley, Wilson (1939, 1940).

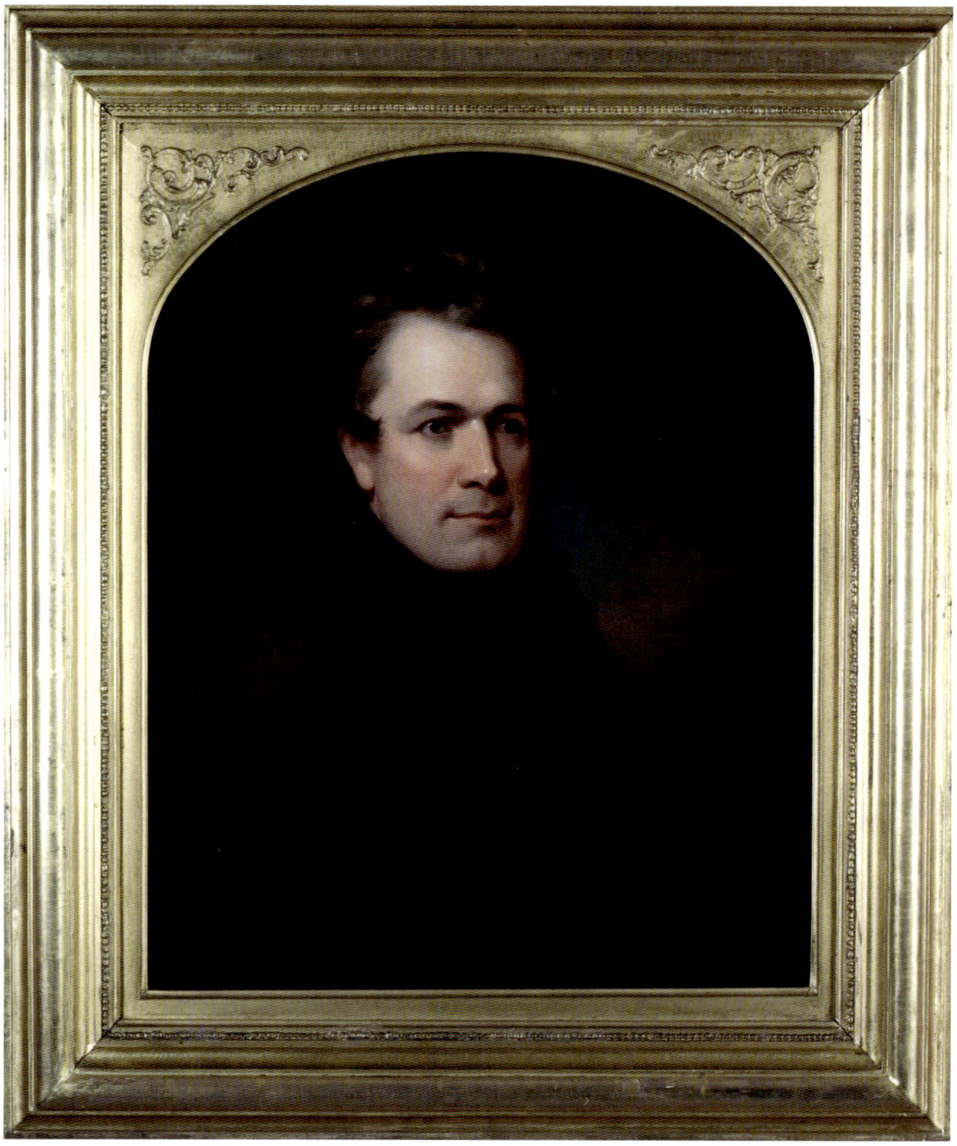

FIGURE 125. James Reid Lambdin, *Edward Dorsey Hobbs* (1810–1888), 1834, oil on canvas, 27½ × 22½", The Filson Historical Society, 1981.8.18.

Hobbs was a native of rural Jefferson County, but the family had moved to Louisville by 1820, where he was educated. At nineteen he established one of the first real estate offices in Louisville, an interest that led to his being elected city surveyor in 1831, and from that survey Hobbs published a set of maps of Louisville and the surrounding area. He then moved into finance, politics, and planting, founding the Louisville Savings Institution in 1835 and entering the Kentucky state legislature in 1843. He served as a representative until 1847, when he entered the state senate, a position he held until 1851, when he became the president of the Louisville and Frankfort Railroad Company. He resigned from the railroad in 1867 in order to devote full time to his farm, Evergreen, at Anchorage, Kentucky, where he managed Hobbs, Walker & Company, one of the largest nurseries in the South.

JAMES REID LAMBDIN

(1807–1889)

JAMES REID LAMBDIN was born in Pittsburgh to James and Prudence Lambdin. He was apprenticed to a sign painter and wood engraver, Edward Miles of Pittsburgh, ca. 1820, and then worked briefly with Thomas Sully in Philadelphia, 1823. He established a natural history museum, like that of Charles Willson Peale in Philadelphia, in Pittsburgh in 1823, remaining in that city until 1832, when he relocated, with the contents of his museum, to Louisville, Kentucky. While in Louisville he was in correspondence with William Dunlap, who acknowledged that for "much valuable information respecting the arts and artists of the west I am indebted to this amiable and enterprising gentleman." One of Lambdin's most notable sitters in Louisville was Edward Dorsey Hobbs (Fig. 125). Lambdin was active as an itinerant in the lower Mississippi River Valley from his Louisville base, 1832–1837, especially in Mobile and Natchez, where his brother, Samuel, resided at Mistletoe Plantation. He returned in 1838 to Philadelphia, where he spent the remainder of his career painting notable public figures, including each president from John Quincy Adams to James Garfield. Lambdin served as director of the Pennsylvania Academy of Fine Arts, 1845–1864, and taught at the University of Pennsylvania, 1861–1866. Lambdin is the father of the still-life artist George Cochran Lambdin. He died in Philadelphia in 1889.

Archives: AAA; collections: Corcoran, FHS, LSM, NGA, NYHS, Ogden, PAFA, WH; literature: Kleber (2001), Kloss et al., O'Connor, Pennington (Autumn 1986), Weidner, Whitley.

THOMAS LECLEAR

(1818–1882)

THOMAS LECLEAR WAS BORN in Oswego, New York. Largely self-taught, he had some studies in New York. He was first active in Oswego, then in New York City, 1845–1847, and in Buffalo, 1848–1861. While in Buffalo he became much sought after for his portraits of children, and he also painted several genre works on the theme of childhood. LeClear relocated to Brooklyn in 1861, but he continued his strong ties with the Buffalo art community, especially with the Buffalo Fine Arts Academy, which he helped found in 1862 using the proceeds from his successful art exhibition the year before. He was elected a National Academician in 1863 and made itinerant visits to Louisville in the late 1870s as a result of his association with the Newcomb family and his participation in the art exhibitions at the Expositions. His portrait of Warren Newcomb is most likely to have been painted in Brooklyn (Fig. 126). LeClear, ever attentive to the needs of the arts community in Buffalo, died there on a visit in 1882.

Archives: SAM; collections: Albright-Knox, Corcoran, FHS, Met, NYHS, SAM, Telfair; literature: Kleber (2001), Kloss et al., Krane, Newcomb, Viele, Williams.

FIGURE 126 *(facing page)*. Thomas LeClear, *Warren Newcomb* (1814–1866), ca. 1860–1866, oil on canvas, 24 × 20″, The Filson Historical Society, 1969.6.3.

Warren Newcomb and his brother, Horatio D. Newcomb (1809–1874), were natives of Springfield, Illinois, and became prosperous merchants in Louisville during the 1830s. In 1838 Horatio founded the wholesale grocery business H. D. Newcomb and Co., which specialized in molasses, sugar, and coffee. Warren represented the company on purchasing trips to New Orleans, where he met Josephine Le Monnier (1816–1901), whom he married in 1845. They later moved to New York, where their daughter Sophie Harriet (1855–1870) was born. Mindful of the prosperity he had achieved through his connections with the deep South, Newcomb wrote to Washington College in Virginia in March 1866, offering $10,000 to "be regarded as an expression of sympathy for the severe trials and afflictions and hopes my Southern friends have sustained in what they consider a just and patriotic cause." Robert E. Lee, president of the college, used the funds to create scholarships for a student body he hoped would succeed in reuniting North and South. Following Newcomb's death and that of his daughter, his widow founded Sophie Newcomb College in New Orleans in 1886, which, upon her death, received the remainder of his great fortune. By these acts the Newcombs provided one of the greatest philanthropic legacies to the postwar South.

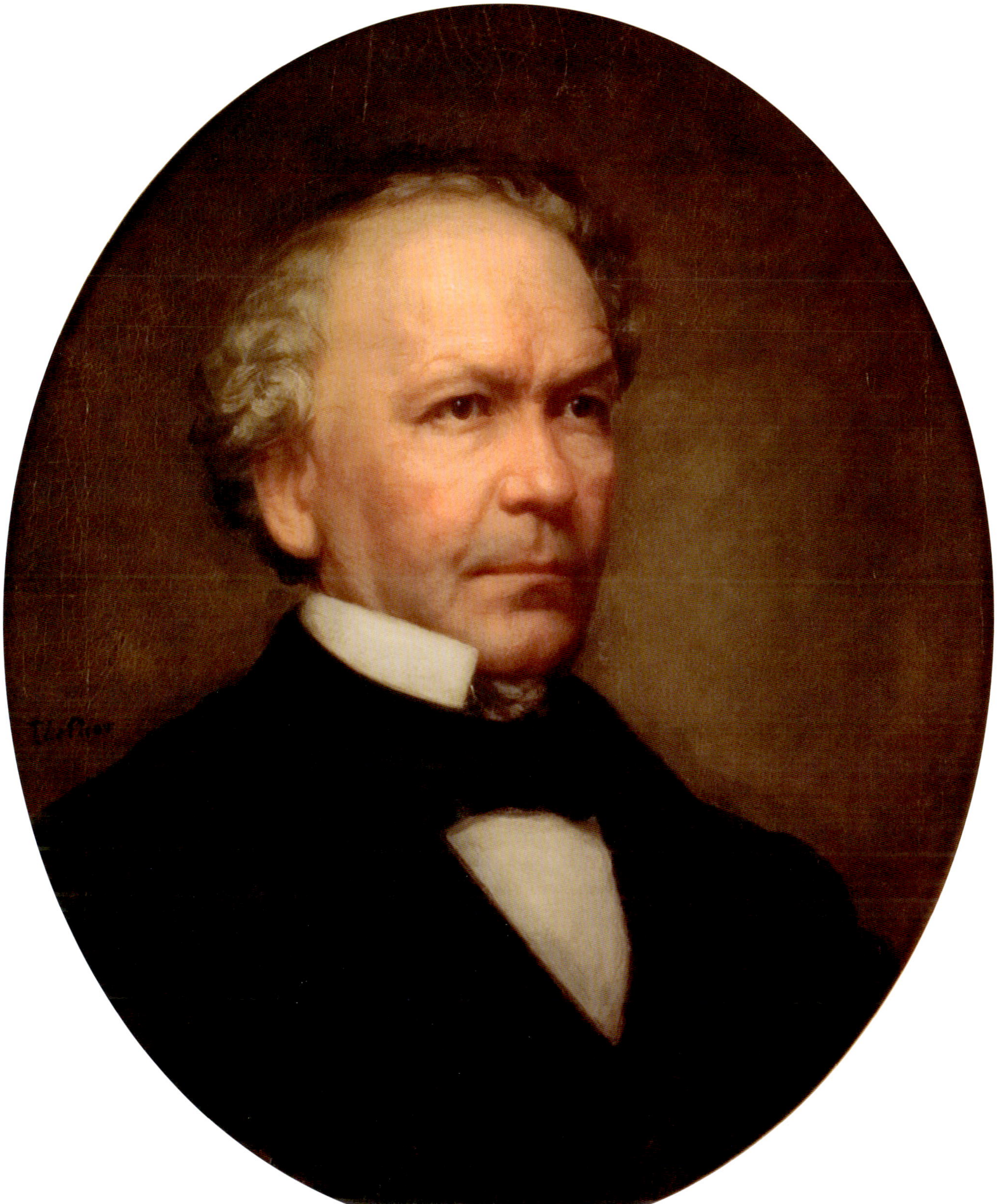

NICOLA MARSCHALL

(1829–1917)

NICOLA MARSCHALL WAS BORN in St. Wendel, Rhenish Prussia, to Emanuel Marschall, a prosperous tobacco and wine merchant, and his wife, Margaret Mohr. He was reputed to have had some training at the Düsseldorf Academy in Germany prior to his arrival in New Orleans in 1849. After a brief sojourn in Mobile, Alabama, Marschall settled in Marion, Alabama, where he taught art and music and worked as a portrait painter. By 1851 he was an art, music, and language (French and German) instructor at the Marion Female Seminary. He returned to Europe in 1857 for further studies at Düsseldorf and Munich, where he worked with Pieter C. Bernhard (1813–1880), a court painter to the Wittelsbach dynasty. Marschall came back to

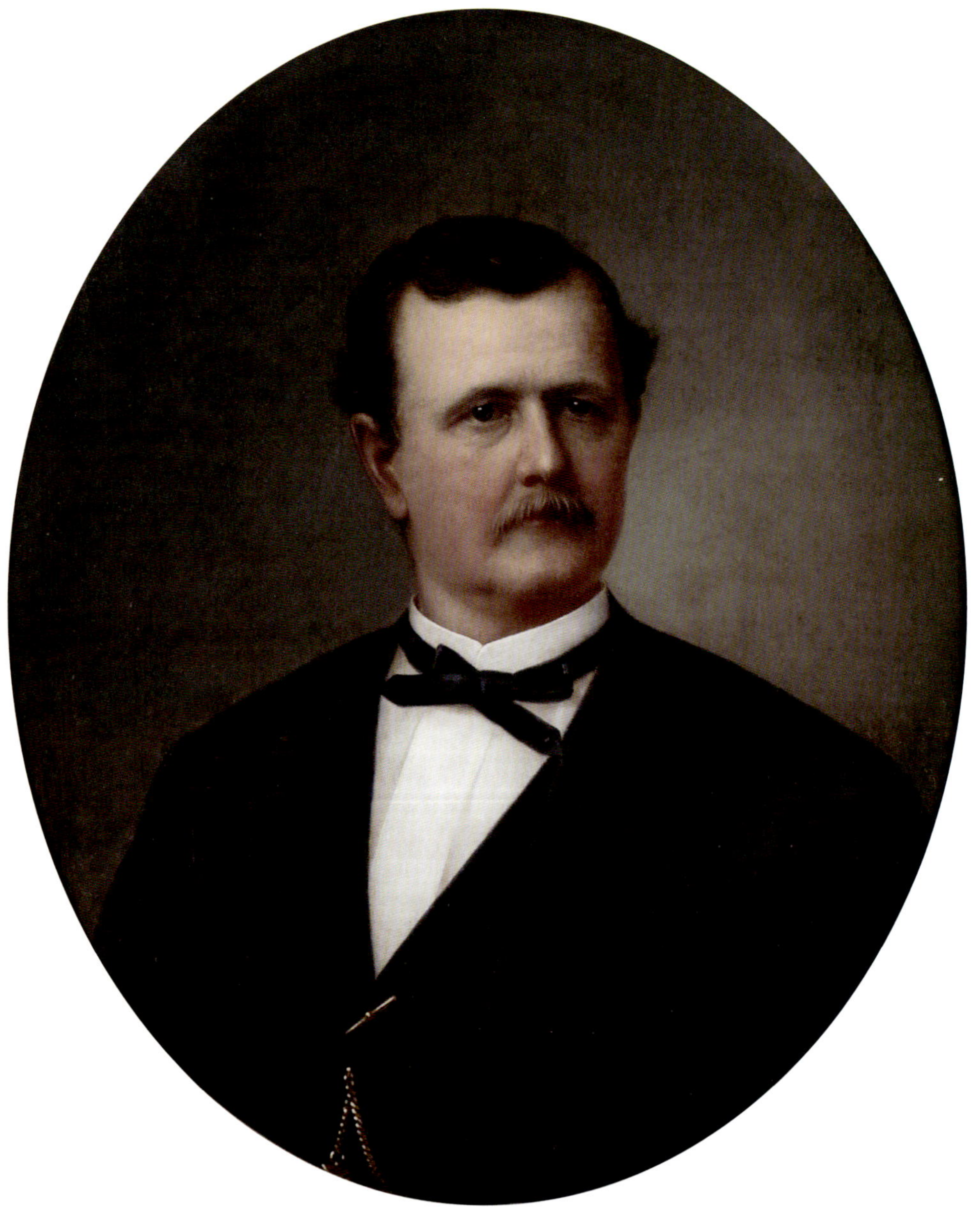

America in 1859, where he was again active in Marion and Mobile, Alabama, as well as in New Orleans. During that time he painted several highly imaginative portraits of children, which employed certain genre elements, including animals and allegorical landscape backgrounds. One of these works, *Girl with Cat,* in the Morris Museum of Art collection, is particularly accomplished. He served in the Confederate Army intermittently, including his service as a draftsman for the Second Alabama Engineers. At the request of Mrs. Napoleon Lockett, he designed what became the first Confederate flag, often called the Stars and Bars. He also designed the gray uniforms adopted by the Confederate Army. He was discharged at Meridian, Mississippi, May 1865, and married Mattie Eliza Marshall of Marion, a former student, in August 1865. Marschall moved to Louisville in 1873, where he had a studio at Fourth and Green (now Liberty) Streets until his retirement in 1908. During those years of the late nineteenth century he was the portraitist of choice for the city's Confederate veterans, an iconic participant in what Anne Marshall has termed "a strange conclusion to a triumphant war": the veterans' revisionist efforts to perpetuate the idea of Kentucky as a Confederate state. Among Marschall's sitters, few were more active in that cause than J. Stoddard Johnston (Fig. 127). Marschall was the last resident portrait artist of note to have ties with the antebellum portrait tradition. In his later years he created a large body of work, much of it drawn from photographic sources and lacking the animation of his earlier style. He died in Louisville and is buried in Cave Hill Cemetery, the final resting place of many Lost Cause fellow travelers.

Archives: FHS; collections: FHS, KHS, MMA, Mobile, Montgomery, OSC; literature: Alabama Department of Arhives and History, Cory, Costlow, Kleber (2001), Marshall, Pennington (1992), Whitley.

FIGURE 127 *(facing page).* Nicola Marschall, *Josiah Stoddard Johnston* (1833–1913), ca. 1890, oil on canvas, 29½ × 24½", The Filson Historical Society, 1998.9.

Johnston was born in New Orleans; but, orphaned before he was five, he grew up in Louisville with his maternal aunt, Mrs. George Hancock. He studied law at Yale, 1850–1853, and then returned to Louisville, where he married Eliza Johnson. They moved to Arkansas in 1854, where Johnston prospered as a cotton planter; they returned to Kentucky in 1859. He enlisted in the Army of the Confederacy in 1862 and served as a staff officer to Braxton Bragg, Simon Bolivar Buckner, and John C. Breckinridge, associates with whom he would long have political ties following the war. Although he returned to Arkansas for two years after the war, by 1867 he was back in Kentucky as the editor of the *Kentucky Yeoman,* and he became active in Kentucky politics. Johnston was either chairman or secretary of the state Democratic Party, 1868–1888, and served as adjutant general of Kentucky, 1871–1875, and secretary of state, 1875–1879. He was a conservative of the Bourbon Democrat type, who favored neither the Emancipation Proclamation nor an extended franchise. Johnston moved to Louisville in 1889 and entered the inner circle of the Filson Club, which suited the career he pursed in later life as a historian, publishing *Memorial History of Louisville* in 1896 and, not surprisingly, *Confederate History of Kentucky* in 1898. He died in Clayton, Missouri, but was returned to Louisville for burial in Cave Hill Cemetery.

JOSEPH MASON

(1802–1842)

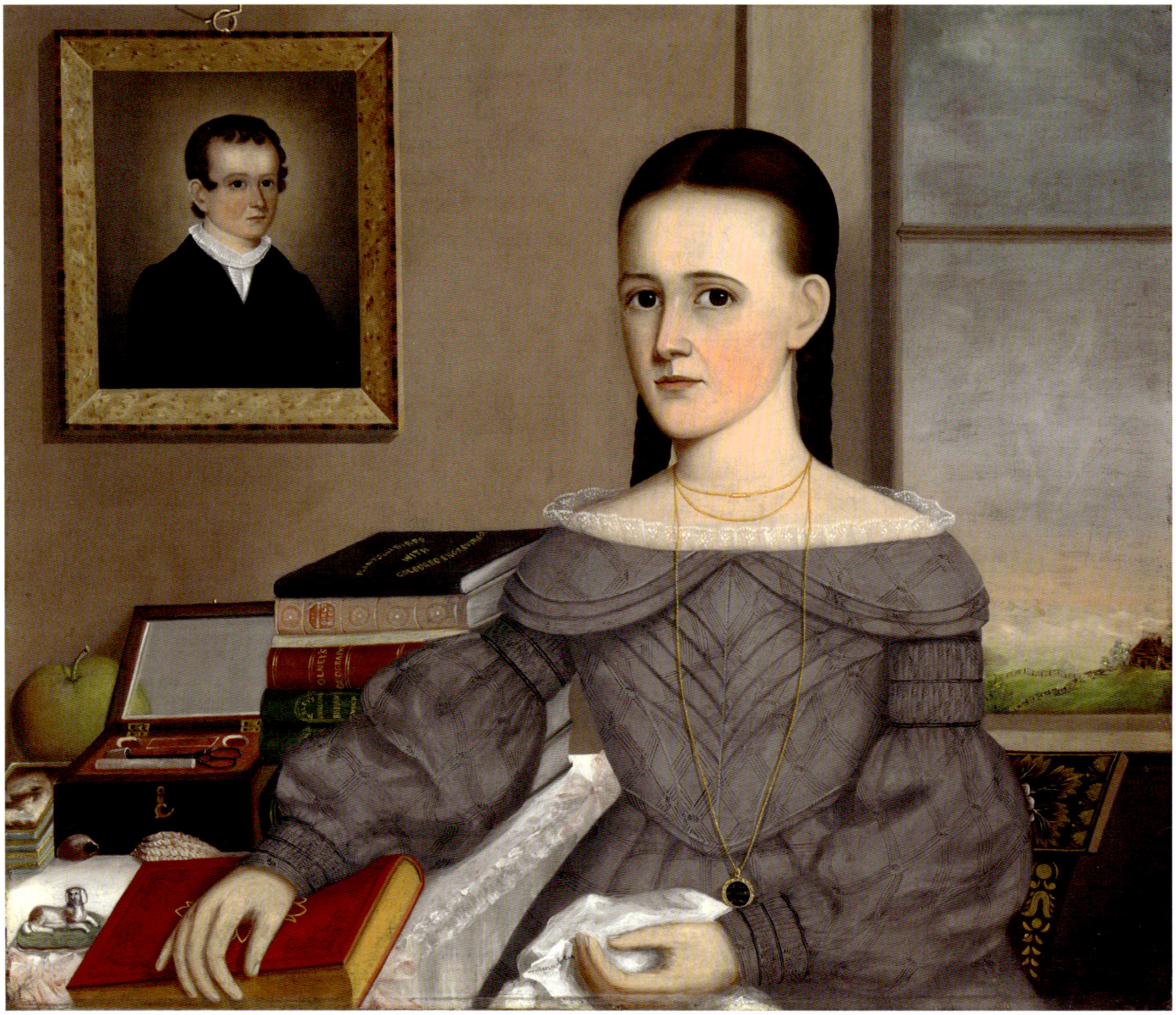

FIGURE 128. Joseph Mason, *Marie Jane Andrew,* 1841, oil on canvas, 26 × 30″, Indianapolis Museum of Art.

According to a letter from Charles F. Cochran on file in the Catalog of American Portraits, National Portrait Gallery, and dated 1855, La Porte, Indiana, this portrait was commissioned by Marie's distraught parents following her sudden death. Apparently Mason was in La Porte at the time, for he drew "sketches of the child from which he painted the portrait . . . the detail [is] extraordinary." Not only are the details extraordinary, but they also suggest autobiographical encryption. On the table to Marie's right is a stack of books, including C. B. Taylor's *Universal History of the United States,* 1831; Ramsey's *Universal History,* 1819; and Olney's *Geography,* 1828. Considering that Mason's father was a bookseller, the presence of these standard textbooks implies a dual role on the artist's part, that of traveling bookseller as well as painter. Note as well that the volume on the top of the stack is a book of "birds, with coloured engravings," a reference to Audubon. There is no mention in the Cochran letter identifying the young boy in the portrait on the wall.

JOSEPH MASON WAS BORN in Delaware, Ohio, son of Joseph Wilson Mason, a prosperous bookseller. (There has been some confusion about Mason's birth and death dates; Edna Talbott Whitley seems to have conflated the census records of Joseph Mason with Joseph R. Mason, 1807–1882, who also lived in southern Ohio.) He first studied with John James Audubon at the Western Academy in Cincinnati. Audubon was so impressed by Mason's skill as a draftsman that he invited the youth to accompany him to the lower Mississippi River Valley, drawing landscape and floral details for the bird pictures. In his notes on Audubon's collaborators, Douglas Lewis of the National Gallery credits Mason's drawings as having made the most significant contribution to the naturalist's published bird prints: Mason's eye for detail and accomplished understanding of perspective enhance the sense of scale and proportion of the ornithological subjects. At least fifty of his drawings were used for the completed prints, without credit, Audubon having signed his name in ink after having Mason sign in pencil. The pair parted in August 1822; Mason stayed behind in Natchez to paint portraits prior to returning to Cincinnati, where he opened a studio later that year. Mason was in Philadelphia, 1823–1829, where he exhibited a portrait at the Pennsylvania Academy of Fine Arts in 1823 and offered private art instruction. He returned to Cincinnati in 1832, where he was commissioned by the city council to paint a portrait of William Woodward, a local leather tanner who had donated land on Sycamore Street for a public school in 1827. He exhibited a portrait, *Cooper as Sir John Falstaff,* in the Cincinnati Academy Exhibition of 1841, organized by Godfrey Frankenstein. Douglas Lewis has suggested that Mason came from a family of means, which may account for the dearth of information on his career after 1832, when he lived quietly in the Cincinnati area, apparently unmotivated by the profit incentive. He may have pursued an itinerancy in New Orleans during this time, and certainly worked in rural Indiana, 1831–1841. He painted the portrait of Marie Jane Andrew on his last itinerant trip to Indiana and Michigan in 1841 (Fig. 128). Joseph Mason is one of the most intriguing artists in this study. Though much of his life is a mystery, his refined collaboration with Audubon and the stunning visual detail of this work imply a superb, though largely ignored, artistic ability. He died in his native Brown County, Ohio, in 1842, following a bout of pneumonia. That he was modest and understated can be discerned in Irving Richards's article, in which he quotes Mason as having professed, "I took no notes whilst I was with Audubon; and I was also at that time only a lad. Besides this I looked on him as my greatest friend; and it never once entered my mind that he would do me injustice when he came to publish his work."

Literature: Audubon (1926, 1929), Cist, Hageman, Haverstock et al., Lewis, MacKenzie, Mahé & McCaffrey, Peat (1954), Richards, Whitley.

MAGDALEN HARVIE MCDOWELL

(1829–1918)

MAGDALEN HARVIE MCDOWELL was born in Louisville, the daughter of Maria Hawkins Harvie and Dr. William Adair McDowell. She spent most of her life at Ashland, the Henry Clay home in Lexington, which had passed into the female line, of which she was a member. While few details are known of her biography, there are several extant paintings by her at Ashland, and there is also evidence that she collaborated in the design of several houses in the Aylesford area of Lexington. The paintings of her relations at Ashland would appear to be drawn from life, have an impressionistic coloration, and were created at a much later date than the Thruston portrait (Fig. 129). Her source for young Rogers's portrait seems to have been a *carte de visite* of one of Queen Victoria's children, painted at Balmoral Castle in Scotland by the German artist Karl Haag. McDowell's kinswoman Sophonisba Breckinridge remembered her as having "blazed the way for women's activities. When women were not admitted to the studios of the artists who taught, she learned to paint, and her pictures were thought worthy to hang even with the products of the masters of the craft. In a time when it was not thought possible that a woman might learn the intricacies of architecture, she designed buildings, small and large, private and public, that won the commendation of the artistic and the trained." McDowell died at Ashland in 1918.

Archives: UKSC; collections: Ashland, FHS; literature: S. P. Breckinridge, Jones & Weber, Pennington (2008), Whitley.

FIGURE 129 *(facing page)*. Magdalen Harvie McDowell, *Rogers Clark Ballard Thruston* (1858–1946), ca. 1864, oil on canvas, 32 × 27″, The Filson Historical Society, 1939.11.2.

R. C. B. Thruston's combined names represent the earliest families of Kentucky, a heritage nurtured by his parents, Frances Thruston and Andrew Jackson Ballard. As she had other sons, Frances Ballard asked Thruston to take her name, for the male line of the Thruston family had died out. Educated at Yale's Sheffield Scientific School, R. C. B. Thruston returned to Kentucky in 1882 to work for the state geological survey. He was a partner, with his brothers, in an investment concern that bought and sold properties in the Kentucky and Virginia mountains, 1887–1909. During this same time he made many photographs of mountain life in eastern Kentucky. After 1909 he devoted himself entirely to his antiquarian pursuits and photography, becoming an expert on and collector of American flags. He was president of the Filson Club, 1923–1946, and was responsible for acquiring a permanent home for the Filson's collections on Breckinridge Street in 1929. He died in Louisville and is buried in Cave Hill Cemetery.

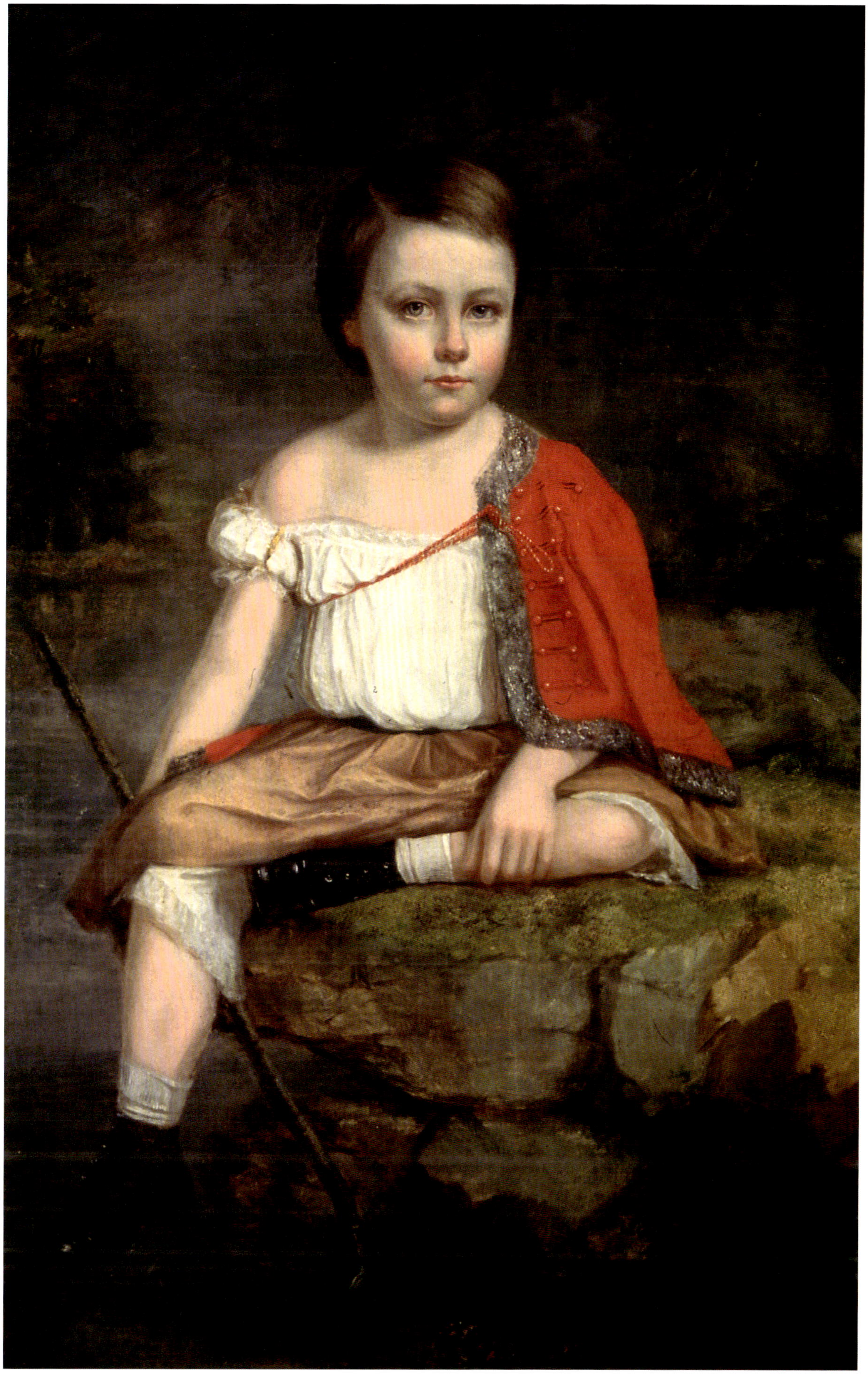

THEODORE SIDNEY MOÏSE

(1806–1883)

FIGURE 130. Theodore Sidney Moïse, *Lucinda Pope Wilson Selden* (ca. 1816–1890), ca. 1845, oil on canvas, 44½ × 38″, The Filson Historical Society, 1957.5.

Scant biographical information on Lucinda Wilson Selden is a reminder of the duality of portraiture as object and image, and the faded memory of those who leave few descendants. All that is known of her is that she was the daughter of Dr. Daniel and Henrietta Pope Wilson; her mother was a descendent of William Pope, scion of a pioneer family who settled Louisville and left a history of civic service; and she was married to William Selden in 1836. This information came with the painting, also indicating that it was inherited by a nephew, Thomas P. Jacob, son of Lucinda's sister Henrietta.

THEODORE SIDNEY MOÏSE was born in Charleston, South Carolina, to Abraham and Sarah Moïse, Jewish refugees from the slave revolt in Saint-Domingue. Self-taught, he began to paint portraits in Charleston while apprenticed to a cotton factor and opened a studio in Charleston in 1835. He then worked as an itinerant in Woodville, Mississippi, 1836–1841, prior to establishing a permanent base in New Orleans, 1841. Moïse pursued an itinerancy in Louisville and Frankfort, Kentucky, 1845–1850, often in partnership with Trevor Thomas Fowler. Their work is easily identified by

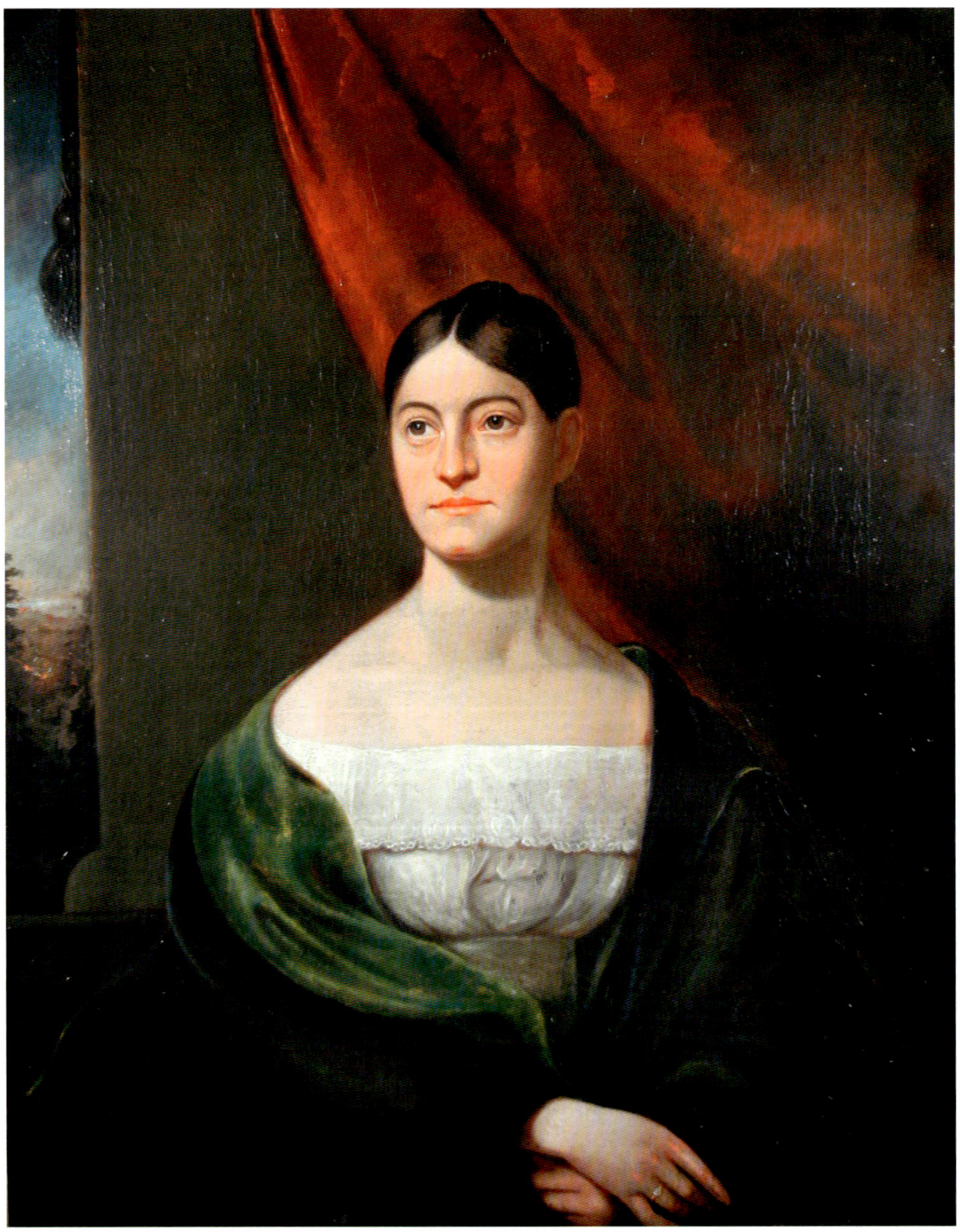

a standard compositional convention, the placement of a view of a moody landscape glimpsed through an open doorway with vaguely Doric details, a background detail enhancing depth and perspective and forcing the figure forward on the picture plane. This can be seen in their portraits of Betty Chinn Webb, Reuben Flournoy Ford, and Elizabeth Johnson Flournoy. The portraits of Lucinda Selden (Fig. 130) and Elizabeth Flournoy show their subjects posed in much the same manner, head slightly lifted, with just a faint air of distance, appropriate to the age's refined sense of self. Moïse and Fowler were involved in an intriguingly tangled case of mistaken identity perpetuated by a letter written and received but never answered. On his visit to Kentucky in 1842 to paint Henry Clay, the artist John Neagle met Orlando Brown, the editor of the *Kentucky Commonwealth,* in Frankfort. Brown's father had been Kentucky's first senator, and the family's political connections to Henry Clay provided the introduction. When the Clay portrait was shown in Kentucky, Brown wrote a very flattering article that appeared in the June 6, 1843, *Commonwealth.* Later that year, on December 10, 1843, Neagle wrote to Brown from Philadelphia. In the letter he wrote of his plan to return to Kentucky for the purpose of "executing certain portraits for which I have received commission," including "those of yourself and your children," adding that he hoped "the hair of little Orlando & Mason is again in picturesque order." But Neagle did not return to Kentucky, and the portrait now at the Orlando Brown House in Frankfort, previously attributed to Neagle, was painted by Moïse and Fowler. Moïse was in partnership with Benjamin Franklin Reinhart in New Orleans, 1859–1861, prior to enlisting in the Confederate Army, in which he attained the rank of major. He returned to New Orleans after the war, where he formed a partnership with Paul Poincy and became known as an excellent painter of horses and legendary panoramic group scenes at fairs and racetracks. He died at Natchitoches, Louisiana, in 1883.

Archives: HNOC, LSM, OBH; collections: FHS, HNOC, KHS, Met, OBH, Speed, TSM; literature: Bruns, Mahé & McCaffrey, Pennington (1991, 2008), Whitley.

LOUIS MORGAN

(1814–1852)

LOUIS MORGAN WAS BORN in Westmoreland County, Pennsylvania, in 1814 and moved with his family to Pittsburgh in 1830, where he was apprenticed to a chair painter. Although largely self-taught, he did meet William Wall, an English artist, in Pittsburgh, who offered him encouragement and gave him some instruction. Morgan was commissioned by James Barton Longacre and James Herring to paint Simon Kenton for their *National Portrait Gallery of Distinguished Americans* in late 1834, an accolade that signaled a revival of interest in figures of the first frontier. Morgan found Kenton in Zanesfield, living in obscurity in a squalid cabin. Although Morgan reported Kenton as being consumed by bitterness at his fate, he painted at least one portrait of him as a jolly old relic of fabled times, as hale and bluff as Shakespeare's

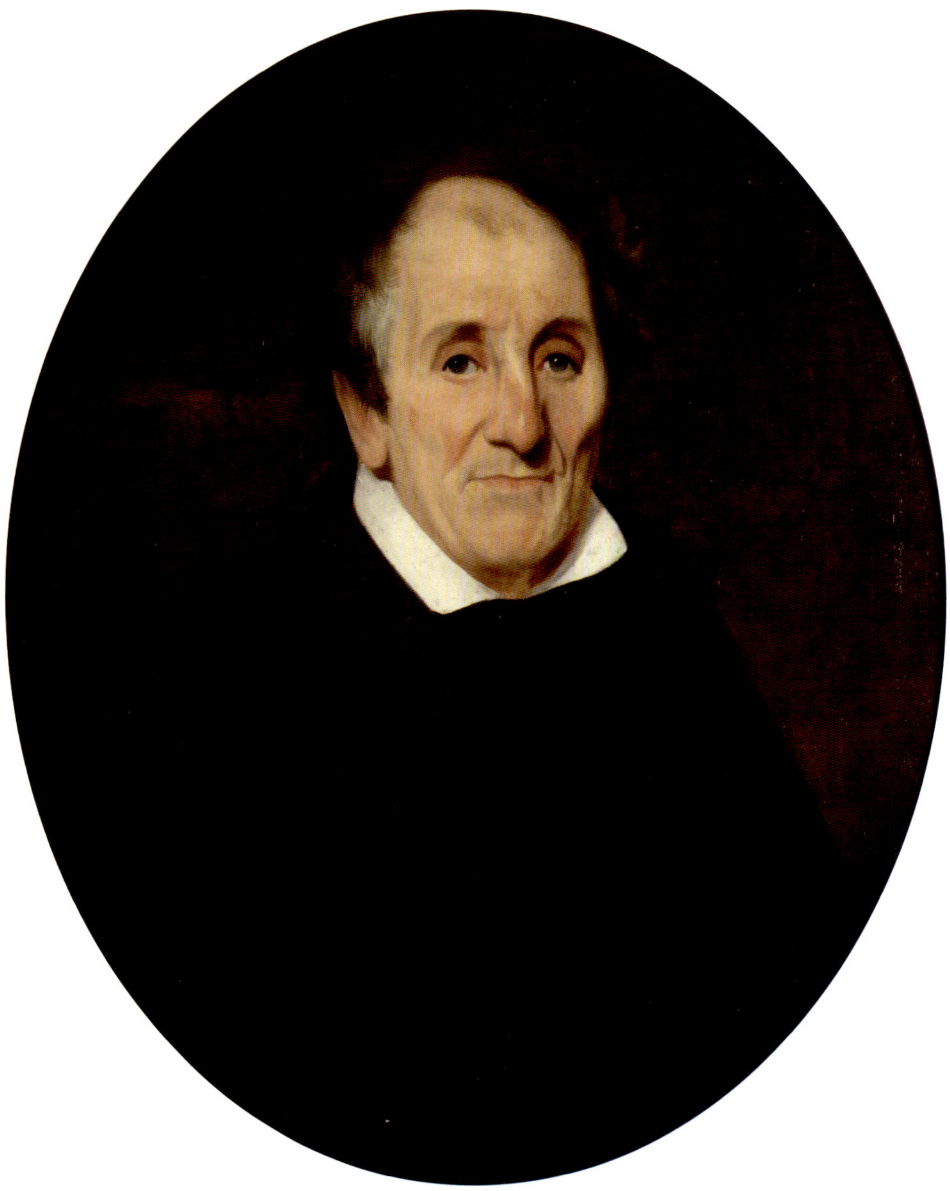

Falstaff or Dickens's Pickwick. That guise embodies a certain American romantic style, which invites a dialogue on the narrow space between historical fact and historical fiction. Another of his portraits, if less jovial, nevertheless depicts mild amusement (Fig. 131). Following the Kenton episode, Morgan advertised a studio on St. Clair Street, Frankfort, January 2, 1835, and remained active in the Louisville and Frankfort areas, 1835–1848, painting members of the Bullock, Joyes, Breckinridge, Johnson, and Castleman families. During those years Morgan also exhibited works in Cincinnati. He relocated to central Kentucky in 1848, where he worked from a studio at Winton Farm, Fayette County, and was associated with the Dallam and Peter families. It was at this time that he made the acquaintance of Samuel Woodson Price, who later wrote a firsthand account of his life. After an unfortunate infatuation with Letitia Dallam, Morgan moved to Montgomery County, Tennessee, where he died at the home of his brother, John L. Morgan.

Archives: OHS; collections: CHC, FHS, KHS, OHS; literature: Jones & Weber, Price, Speakes, Whitley.

FIGURE 131 *(facing page).* Louis Morgan, *Simon Kenton* (1755–1836), ca. 1834, oil on canvas, 29 × 24″, The Filson Historical Society, 1950.2.

Simon Kenton was a native of Fauquier County, Virginia, where he was known as a difficult child who refused to go to school and balked at reading, and he was once whipped at a wedding party for intruding on the nuptial couple's first night. In 1771, following a brawl with a neighbor whom he thought he had killed, Kenton fled westward, winding up in Pittsburgh, where he joined up with Simon Girty and some other shady frontier types, including George Yaeger and John Strader. In 1775 he and Thomas Williams, after a journey down the Ohio, landed at Limestone Creek and built a camp, the first settlement in northern Kentucky, from which Mason County grew. Kenton joined Daniel Boone at Boonesborough that fall. During the Revolution he served as a spy for George Rogers Clark, and he claimed to have saved Boone from an Indian attack in 1777. After the war he returned to his land claims in Mason County and married Martha Dowden in 1787, with whom he had five children. He also operated a store in Washington. Martha was burned in a house fire in 1796 and died from shock, after which Kenton married her cousin Elizabeth Jarboe, with whom he also had five children. Kenton's land transactions were always murky, and he was subject to speculators and claimants who challenged them; the result was financial failure. In 1798 he moved to the Zanesfield, Ohio, area in an attempt to recover, and was elected a brigadier general in the Ohio militia in 1805. After service with Isaac Shelby during the War of 1812, he passed into obscurity and declined into poverty. During a visit to Washington, Kentucky, in 1820 he was imprisoned for debt, an action that inspired the repeal of the Kentucky Debtor's Law in December 1821. He then returned to Zanesfield. Kenton was somewhat avenged when the state legislature named a new county, carved out of the western lands of Campbell County, in his honor in 1840. (There are variants of this portrait in the collections of the Ohio Historical Society and the Cincinnati Historical Society.)

GEORGE W. MORRISON

(1820–1893)

FIGURE 132. George W. Morrison, *Philip Lightfoot Lee* (1832–1875), ca. 1876, 39¼ × 34", The Filson Historical Society, 1992.23.1.

Lee was a native of Bullitt County who served two terms in the state legislature before the Civil War. His oft-quoted remark "I am for the Union, but if the Union is divided, I am for Kentucky" echoes the sentiment his kinsman Robert E. Lee held for Virginia. When war came Philip Lightfoot Lee joined the 2nd Kentucky Regiment, the "orphan brigade" that fought for the Confederacy. At the end of the war he returned to Kentucky, where he became the twice-elected Commonwealth Attorney in Louisville. His oratory was much admired, for in "denouncing murderers he was terrific, and he did more than all others to make murder unpopular in the city if not the state."

GEORGE W. MORRISON was born in Baltimore and is thought to have had some early art instruction with Rembrandt and Raphael Peale in the museum at 225 North Holiday Street that they opened in 1814. Morrison's obituary in the *New Albany Daily Ledger,* December 21, 1893, states that he went from "Baltimore to Connersville, Ind., while a youth." In Connersville he began painting portraits; and in 1843 he moved to New Albany, where "he established himself as an artist, and his life has been spent in this city and at Louisville where for a number of years he had art rooms." Morrison arrived in New Albany during the economic boom, propelled by steamboat building and trade with the South, that had made it the largest and most prosperous city in Indiana. Morrison painted many members of New Albany's founding family, the Scribners, including William and Abner, whose approval secured his place in the city's ambitious cultural scene. Soon after his arrival he married Lydia Maynard, a local, and they built a house on the Silver Hills, near New Albany. During the 1850s Morrison

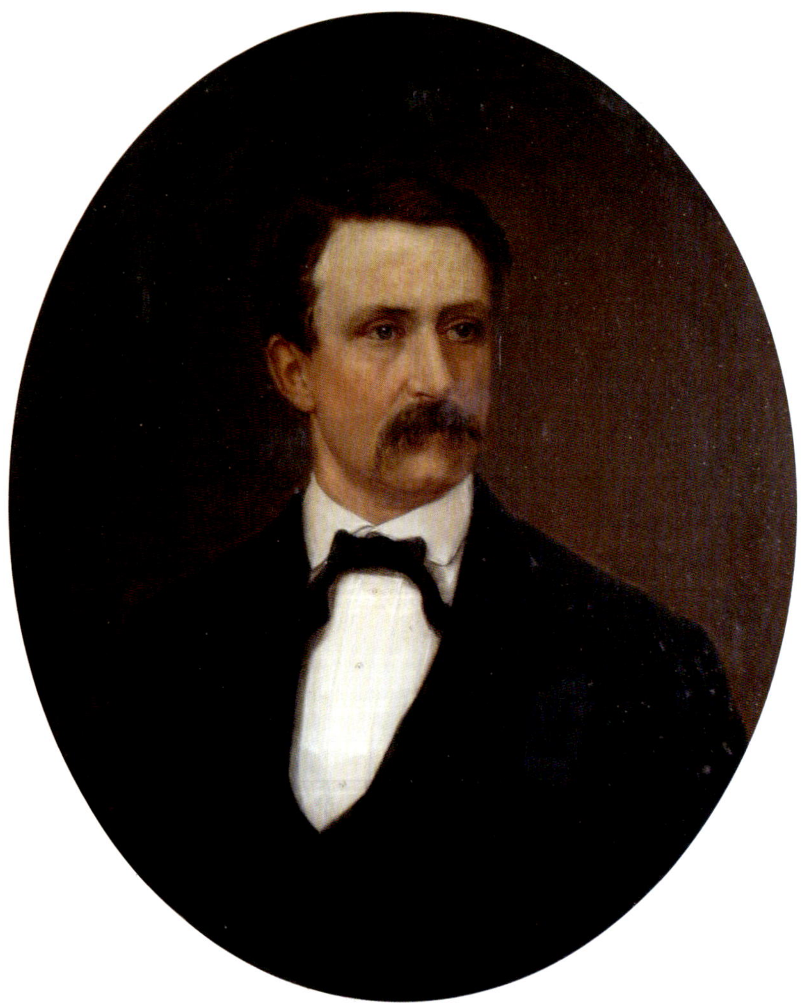

began to take advantage of the downriver trade with New Orleans, spending his winters painting there, although only the still-life painting dated 1854 in the Ogden collection documents his presence there. During his lifetime he was also well known as a landscape painter. His *View of New Albany* was lavishly praised in the March 1, 1853, *New Albany Ledger* as "invaluable—generations yet to be born will gaze with astonishment at the rapid growth of a city destined to become the great commercial emporium of the West." The painting was purchased by Harvey Scribner and is now in the New Albany Public Library. The October 29, 1867, *New Albany Daily Commercial* notes that it "may be interesting to know the whereabouts of some" of the landscape works Morrison painted, including a view of Harper's Ferry, a view from the Catskills, and several other works based on the local landscape. The same article also mentions several still-life paintings in local collections, including a large *Southern Fruit* composed in the lavish abundant style. Morrison's career as a portraitist reached its peak when he painted Ashbel P. Willard, governor of Indiana from 1857 to 1861. Following the Civil War, New Albany's economic boom ceased because of the decline in trade with the South. While Morrison's portrait commissions dwindled in the face of competition from photography, he continued to be an active landscape and still-life painter whose work was much in demand. Although his obituary in the *New Albany Daily Ledger* states that "hundreds of portraits painted by him adorn the homes of New Albany and many more are to be found in the homes of Louisville," few are extant at this time. Of those, his skills as a portrait artist may best be seen in his painting of George Henry Devol in the New Albany Public Library. In this work, as in other of his portraits of children, Morrison deployed a very elongated format, the height of the object often twice its width. Within this setting the figure dominates the scene, a clever device to enhance a child's presence in a much larger world. Like his contemporary Nicola Marschall, Morrison worked from photographs later in his career, often as a means of creating posthumous portraits, as in the case of Philip Lightfoot Lee (Fig. 132). Morrison remained in his home on Silver Hill for the rest of his life, cared for after his wife's death by his daughter Mary, also an artist. He died in 1893 and was buried on the grounds of his home, but was subsequently re-interred in Fairview Cemetery, New Albany. His obituary notes that he was "an artist who painted to life and who possessed the finest perception of his art" and that he was "quiet and retired in his manners . . . though well educated." A self-portrait is in the New Albany Public Library. (Some accounts have confused him with another George Morrison, an artist active in Wichita, Kansas, 1877–1934.)

Archives: NAPL; collections: FHS, ISH, NAPL, Ogden, Shelburne; literature: W. Davis, Kleber (2001), Peat (1954), Whitley.

JOHN MULVANY

(1844–1906)

JOHN MULVANY WAS BORN in Ireland and arrived, by some accounts, in New York in 1856 and had early training at the National Academy of Design, where he worked as a cleanup boy. Following action in the Civil War, he went to Europe and studied in Düsseldorf, Munich, and Antwerp. The historical genre paintings of Karl Piloty of Munich and the battle paintings of Nicaise de Keyser of Antwerp greatly influenced his work, as did the military portraiture of French painter Jean Meissonier. By 1871 Mulvany was back in the United States. He established a studio in Chicago, where he also did some photographic work, but his studio was burned in the fire of 1871. He is next noted as being resident in the Louisville Public Library Building in 1874; he exhibited portraiture at the Louisville Industrial Exposition of that year, when he is also reported to have painted John C. Breckinridge and Henry Watterson. Military history paintings by him were owned by Major W. H. Thomas of Louisville, his principal patron at that point, and were often lent to successive expositions. Mulvany then went west, drawn by the story of General George Armstrong Custer and the Battle of the Little Big Horn, and lived on the Iowa-Nebraska border, gathering material for a painting on the subject of the battle. He opened a studio in Kansas City in 1879, where for the next two years he worked on a monumental canvas, *Custer's Last Rally,* which was shown there in 1881 and then enjoyed a triumphal tour in the east. This work was subsequently purchased by H. K. Heinz of Pittsburgh. After 1881 Mulvany was active in Cincinnati, St. Louis, Chicago, Kansas City, and Louisville, primarily as a portraitist. He achieved considerable success as a painter of historical military scenes for museums and historical societies in the west in the 1880s and 1890s. In later years he lived in New York City and declined into alcoholism, drowning himself in the East River in 1906. The *New York Times* obituary notes that from "a fine physique of a man [with] handsome features and a kindly countenance, he had sunk to a ragged derelict, uncertain of a night's lodging or a day's food."

Archives: AAA; collections: DHS, FHS, IDHA, LDS; literature: Kurtz (1884), Taft, Weber-Scobie.

JOHN NEAGLE

(1796–1865)

JOHN NEAGLE WAS BORN in Boston to Maurice and Susannah Taylor Neagle. His father died when Neagle was four. He received some early instruction from Edward Petticolas and during grammar school took drawing lessons from a local Italian master, Pietro Ancora. He was then apprenticed to Thomas Wilson, a coach and ornamental painter, who was also working with the portraitist Bass Otis. While still a student Neagle came to the attention of Thomas Sully and Charles Willson Peale, who encouraged him. He began activity as an itinerant in Kentucky in 1818, but discouraged by Jouett's dominance as portraitist of choice, he moved on to New Orleans, where he stayed, with little success, until 1820. He returned to Philadelphia by ship, on which he suffered severe hardships that were compounded by meager funds, a situation he remedied at one point by the sale of a head of Washington—he had the canvas rolled up in his bag. Neagle, wrote William Dunlap, "was not the only American who has been extricated from difficulty by that same head." Once reestablished in Philadelphia, he attained great success and married Mary Chester Sully, the niece and stepdaughter of Thomas Sully, in 1826. Around this time he painted the Reverend Henry Bidleman Bascom (Fig. 133). In 1826 he painted his masterpiece, *Pat Lyon at the Forge,* a full-length portrait in the grand manner of a muscular craftsman in working attire posed as a triumphant warrior before his glowing forge. He also sought out Gilbert Stuart in Boston, painting the last portrait of the old artist. He returned

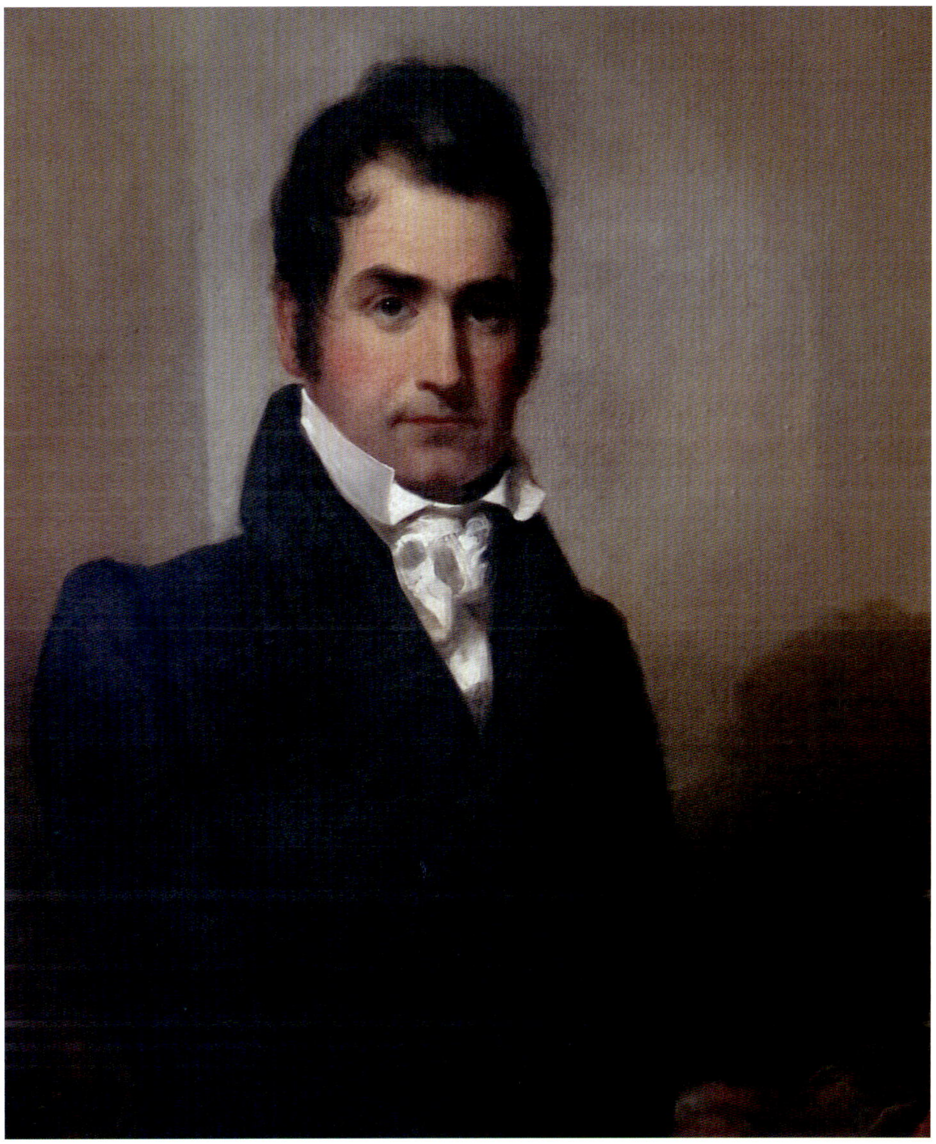

FIGURE 133. John Neagle, *Henry Bidleman Bascom* (1796–1850), ca. 1826, oil on canvas, 26 × 22″, Transylvania University, Lexington, Kentucky.

Bascom was one of the most popular pulpit orators of his day. He served as congressional chaplain 1824–1826, and as president of Transylvania University 1842–1849.

to Kentucky, 1842–1843, where he painted Henry Clay and others. Robert Torchia considers the Clay portrait to be "Neagle's last truly great work, and in many respects it should be considered the culmination of his career as a portraitist." Following the death of his wife in 1845, Neagle became increasingly withdrawn, although he painted a series of portraits of eminent physicians at the University of Pennsylvania. Among his most notable subjects during the decade of the 1850s were former vice president Richard Mentor Johnson and the artist William Rush. He suffered a stroke at the end of the decade and spent the remainder of his life in a paralytic state before dying in Philadelphia in 1865.

Archives: APS, FHS; collections: CAI, Corcoran, DIA, FHS, KHS, MHS, NGA, NPG, OHS, PAFA, St. Louis, Toledo, VHS, Yale; literature: Chambers (1976), Dunlap, Jones & Weber, Lynch, Pennsylvania Academy of the Fine Arts, Quick, Torchia, Whitley.

VICTOR NEHLIG

(1830–1909)

VICTOR NEHLIG WAS BORN in Paris, France, where he studied with Léon Cogniet. He opened a studio in New York in 1856 and made several painting trips to Cuba in the 1850s and 1860s. Nehlig visited Frankfort, Kentucky, in 1870 to obtain material on Daniel Boone with an eye toward public commissions. He, his wife, and their three children are listed in the 1870 New York census. He was made an associate of the National Academy of Design in 1870. In the decade of the Philadelphia Centennial of 1876 he was much admired as a history painter, often praised for his abilities to depict the "late eventful period of our country's history, a work for which his genius is admirably fitted," as Henry Tuckerman wrote. This praise was inspired by several works Nehlig painted on Civil War topics, notably the monumental *Battle of Antietam* and *Cavalry Charge of Lt. Henry B. Hidden.* Other history paintings he exhibited in New York include *The Artist's Dream, Armourer in the Olden Time,* and a landscape populated with departing Crusaders. Possibly financially satisfied by these successes, Nehlig returned to France in 1878, where he spent the rest of his life in rural retirement.

Collections: Butler, FHS, NAD, NYHS, SAM, Springfield; literature: Groce & Wallace, Haverstock et al., Jones & Weber, Louisville Industrial Exposition (1874, 1877), Tuckerman.

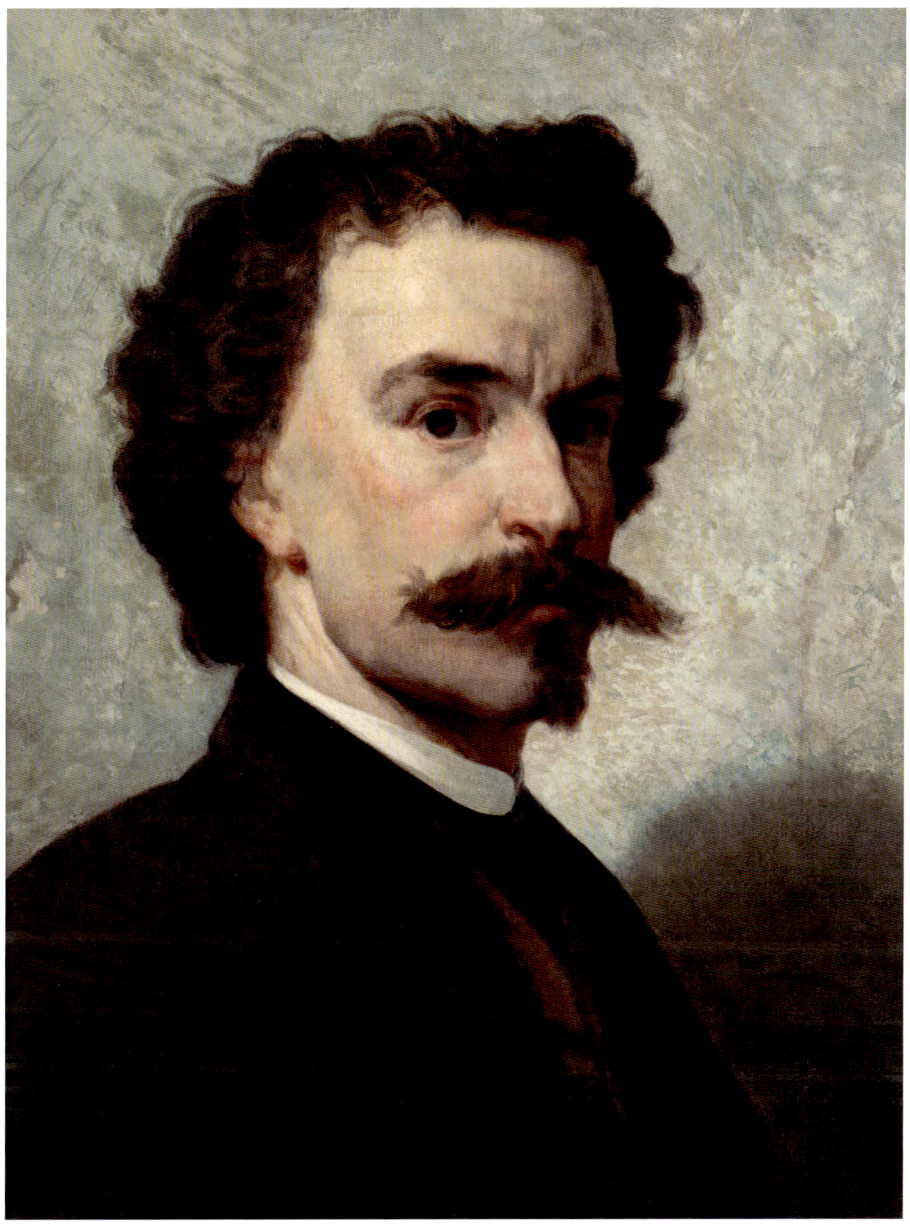

FIGURE 134. Victor Nehlig, *Self-Portrait,* n.d., oil on canvas, 20 × 16″, National Academy Museum, New York, 918-P.

THOMAS SATTERWHITE NOBLE

(1835–1907)

FIGURE 135. Thomas Satterwhite Noble, *Self-Portrait,* n.d., oil on canvas, 19⅞ × 16″, National Academy Museum, New York, 941-P.

THOMAS SATTERWHITE NOBLE was born in Lexington, Kentucky, to Thomas Hart and Rosamond Johnson Noble. After some juvenile studies with Samuel Woodson Price in Louisville in 1852, he went to Paris, France, in 1856, where he studied for three years with Thomas Couture. After returning to America in 1859 he was active as a portraitist in St. Louis, where his family had moved just before the outbreak of the Civil War. During the war he served with Confederate forces as an engineer building ropewalks, the family business, in the lower Mississippi Valley. After the war and a brief residency in St. Louis Noble moved to New York, where he attracted critical praise for his "immortalization of Margaret Garner" and a "beautiful incident in the life of John Brown," according to Henry Tuckerman. In 1869 he accepted an appointment as director of the McMicken School of Design, afterward the Art Academy of Cincinnati, which became the most noted setting for art training in the region. He spent two years on sabbatical in Munich, 1881–1883. After 1877 he also had a residence in New York City, where he became a member of the National Academy of Design. Noble retired from teaching in 1904 and moved full time to New York, where he died in 1907, his body being returned for burial to the Spring Grove Cemetery in Cincinnati.

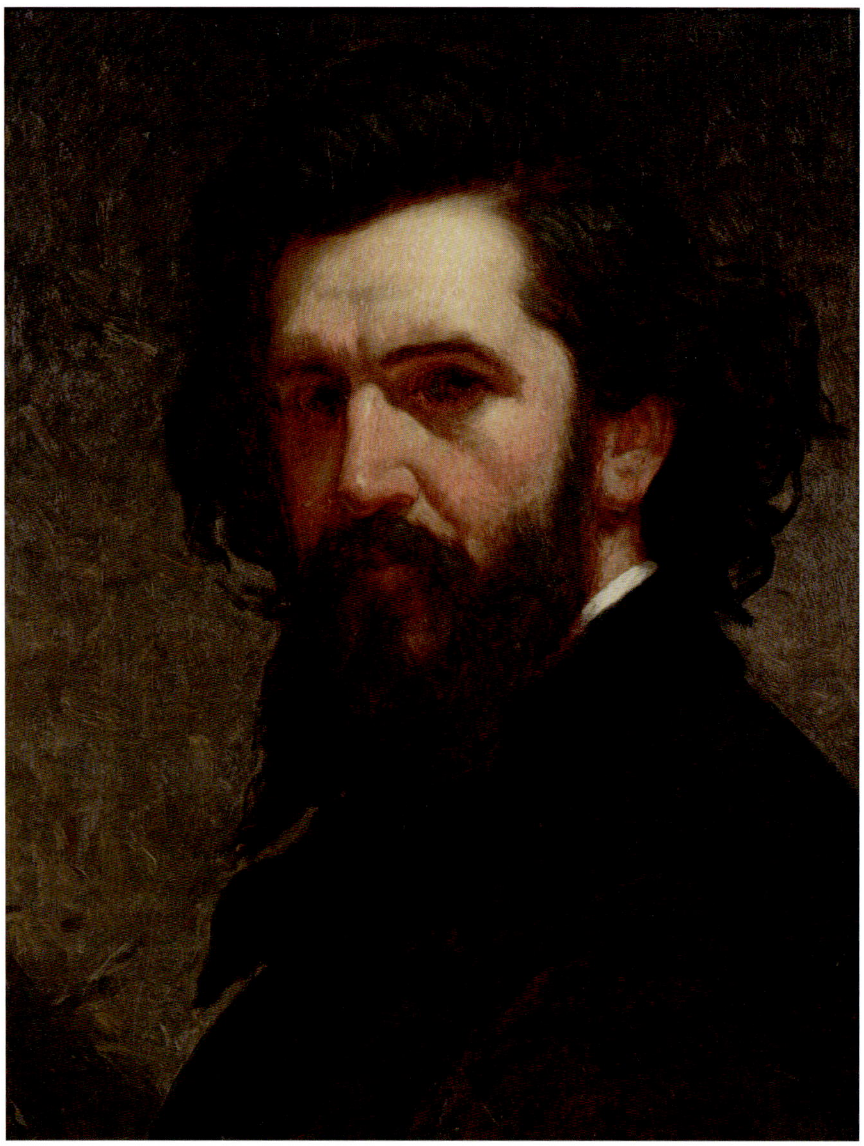

Archives: CAA, CAM; collections: CAM, FHS, Greenville, MHS, MMA, NAD, NYHS, OHS, Yale; literature: Aronson (2003), Birchfield et al., Boime, Cincinnati Art Museum (1979), Garretson, Haverstock et al., Jones & Weber, McElroy, Pennington (1992, 2008), Tuckerman, Whitley.

ASA PARK

(1790–1827)

ASA PARK WAS BORN in Newton, Massachusetts, on August 2, 1790, to Joshua and Lois Fuller Park, one of ten children. He first advertised himself in the *Lexington Reporter,* November 10, 1816, as being from "Boston under the patronage of the celebrated Stuart and Penniman." John Ritto Penniman was a sign and ornamental painter from whom Park would have learned the skills required to produce clear, semiotic images, broadly outlined and cast with that visual immediacy required of sign makers. Park may also have learned from Penniman the technique of placing

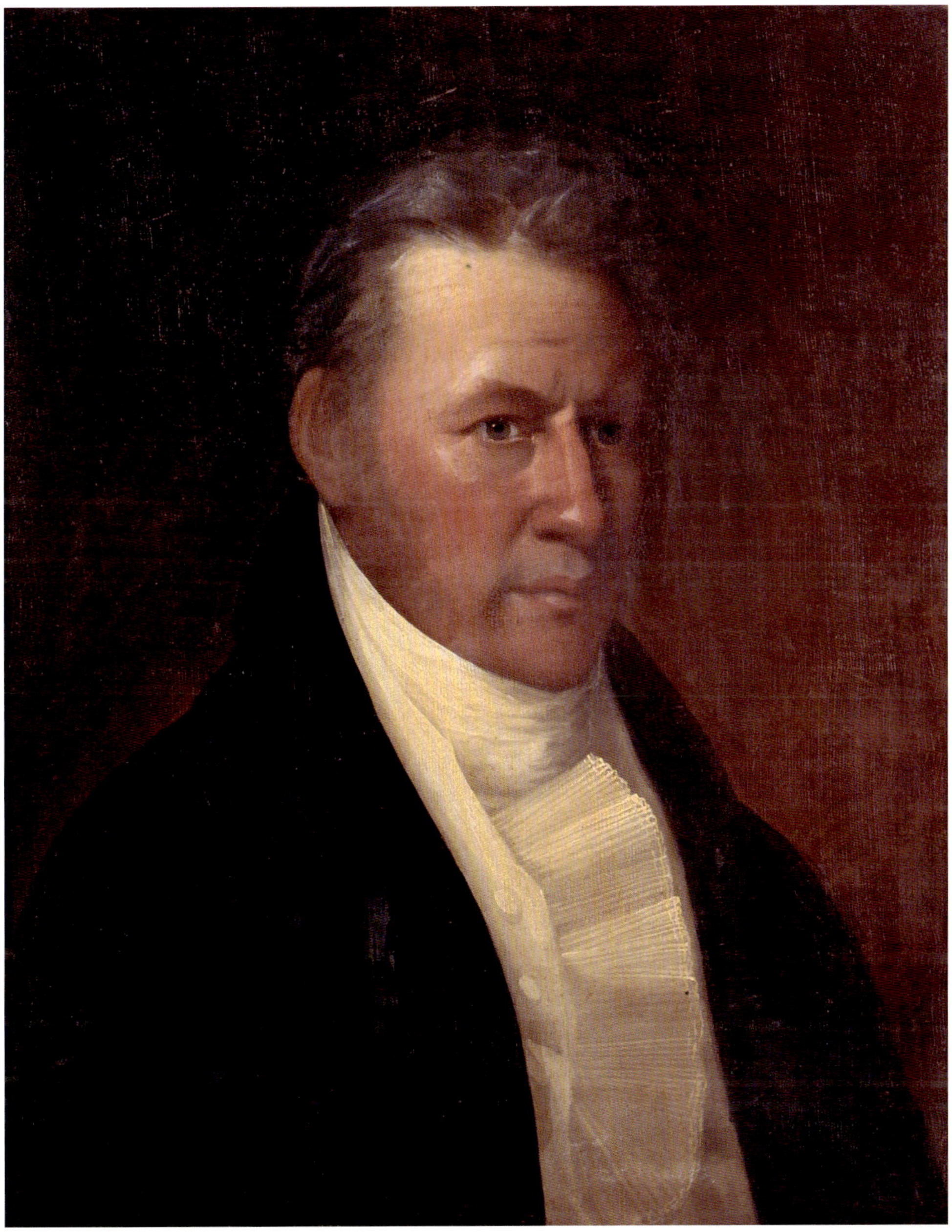

FIGURE 136. Asa Park, *James Birney,* 1818, oil on canvas, 33½ × 28″, Kentucky Historical Society, donated by Mrs. Virginia K. Birney IV, Frank Birney, and Janes Birney deLeeuw, 2007.17.

Birney was a native of Ireland who moved to Danville in 1792, where he became a prosperous merchant and farmer. His slaveholdings inspired his son, James G. Birney, to become an abolitionist and early member of the American Colonization Society.

the subject high on the planar field, usually in the upper left or right quadrant, and very forward toward the picture plane. Park's invocation of Gilbert Stuart is more likely incidental than pedagogic, although it certainly provided him a source for style, method, and composition similar to that practiced by Matthew Harris Jouett. Park's portraits differ from those works of Jouett, however, in two very distinct ways. Park's subjects are cast in an attenuated anatomical format separated by a large space between the arm or shoulder and the edge of the planar field. Jouett's subjects, by contrast, occupy the entire planar field in more careful proportions top to bottom and left to right. Furthermore, Jouett's sitters engage the viewer with their eyes. Park's sitters invariably have a rather glassy-eyed look about them; they seem to be gazing at a distant object off right, rather than at the viewer, a convention more in keeping with the semiotics of a well-versed sign painter than with an insightful portraitist striving to be true to Stuart's teachings on character and equal placement of light and shadow. Park's masterpiece is his full-length portrait of George Washington, which he may have brought from Boston—or painted in the spring of 1825, as part of the preparations for decorating the Grand Masonic Lodge in Lexington for the visit of the Marquis de Lafayette in May of that year, for which Park is known to have been the artist. From 1818 until 1826 Park kept various studios in Lexington, notably the one listed in the 1818 city directory at Mulberry and Main. During those years, Samuel Woodson Price notes, Park was often resident in the home of Edward West, by whose family he was "greatly beloved for years." From this base he was active in Danville and other central Kentucky locations as an itinerant. While in Danville he painted a portrait of James Birney (Fig. 136). Park moved to Cincinnati in 1820 in response to the severe downturn in Kentucky's economy, but he returned to Lexington in 1823. In 1825, according to James McCormick et al., he provided "a transparency of the spread eagle of the United States to adorn a large arch between the banquet hall and dancing room of the city's Masonic Hall, then under construction." In April 1826 he closed his studio in Lexington, and he died in January 1827. He was buried from the home of Thomas Studman on Short Street and interred in the garden of his surrogate father, Edward West, on High Street, with full Masonic honors. His grave was subsequently relocated to the Old Episcopal Cemetery on Third Street.

Archives: GC; collections: Duncan Tavern, GC, HSWP, KHS, NPG, Speed; literature: Floyd (1974), Jones & Weber, McCormick et al., Pennington (2008), Perrin, Price, Whitley.

PAUL PLASCHKE

(1880–1954)

PAUL PLASCHKE WAS BORN in Berlin, Germany, to Emil and Augusta Schnabel Plaschke, with whom he immigrated to New York in 1884. Emil Plaschke was a lithographer who came to this country to accept a position as foreman of the American Lithographic Company. An article in the *Kentucky Women's Journal* for April 1917 notes that Paul studied at "Steven's Institute, Hoboken, New Jersey, and was later a student of the Cooper Union Institute of Arts in New York." He joined the Art Students League in 1897, where he studied with George Luks, whose textured naturalism helped shape the realism of the American Ashcan School. Plaschke began to work as a cartoonist at the *New York World* in 1898, launching his career as an editorial cartoonist and illustrator, a craft he was soon to pursue. Plaschke married Ophelia Bennett of Louisville in 1899 and moved to the Louisville area, settling in New Albany, Indiana. He worked for the *Louisville Commercial* from 1899 to 1902, then the *Louisville Evening Post,* where he stayed until he began working for the *Courier-Journal* in 1913, where he would remain until 1937. During the waning days of World War I he created a series of drawings deeply critical of the Bolsheviks in postrevolutionary Russia. Cartooning was Plaschke's necessary vocation, but his true passion was landscape painting. He was a member of the Wonderland Way Art Club in New Albany. Between 1917 and 1949 he was a frequent exhibitor in Richmond, Indiana; Nashville, Tennessee; and at the Louisville Art Association, of which he was a founding member. He was also active from the beginning in the establishment of the J. B. Speed Art Museum. Hattie Speed greatly admired his work and bought it for the permanent collection from the outset. In 1937 he left the *Courier-Journal* to work for the *Chicago Herald-Examiner.* While in Chicago he exhibited at the John H. Vanderpoel Art Association. Plaschke retired from the *Herald-Examiner* in 1949 and returned to his home in New Albany, Indiana, where he died in 1954. He was buried in Cave Hill cemetery, Louisville.

Archives: FHS, Speed; collections: FHS, JC, Speed; literature: Jones & Weber, Payne & Payne, Pennington (2008).

JAMES THOMAS POINDEXTER

(1832–1891)

JAMES THOMAS POINDEXTER was born in Christian County, Kentucky. A self-taught artist, he began his career in Christian County, painting local residents in the Nelson and Davie families (Fig. 137). He married Nancy Marshall in 1852 and later moved to Evansville, where he was active as a painter until 1860. Newspaper accounts report him as having worked as a telegraph operator in the South during the Civil War. He advertised as a portrait painter, with a studio on Camp Street in New Orleans, 1870–1871, and his work has been found in Grenada, Mississippi. After this sojourn in the South he returned to Evansville, painting there and in western Kentucky, 1871–1882. The Evansville Museum has large holdings of his portraits of local citizens. He built a permanent residence in Eddyville, Kentucky, in 1882 and is listed as an artist in the 1889 Louisville City Directory. He died in Eddyville in 1891.

Archives: Evansville, HNOC; collections: Evansville, FHS, Speed; literature: Peat (1954), Speakes, Whitley.

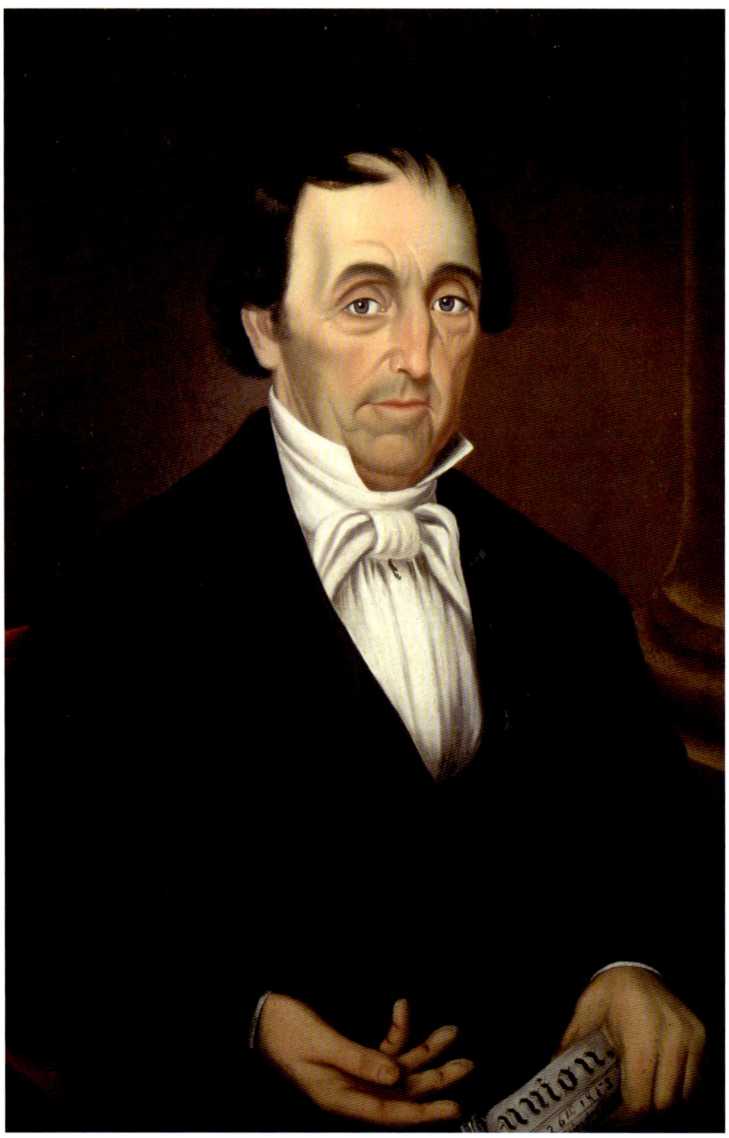

FIGURE 137. James Thomas Poindexter, *Ambrose Davie* (1787–1863), 1853, oil on canvas, 32¼ × 28¼", The Filson Historical Society, 1976.30.4.

Ambrose Davie was born in Person County, North Carolina, to William and Margaret Jones Davie. His father's first cousin was also a William (Richardson) Davie, a prominent North Carolina politician who looked after, and promoted the well-being of, his young kinsman Ambrose, seeing that he became a constable of his native county and was made an aide to the governor of North Carolina during the War of 1812. Ambrose Davie married Elizabeth Harleson, the widow of his cousin Ashburn Davie, in 1820, just prior to moving to Christian County, in western Kentucky. When Elizabeth and their two infant daughters died in 1823, Davie married another widow, Elizabeth Woodson West, by whom he had two sons, Winston and George Montgomery, who was a founder of the Filson. In 1839 he was again a widower, and the following year he married yet another widow, Anna Nicks Phillips, who outlived him. A successful planter with Southern sympathies, Davie supported the Union nonetheless. In this portrait he is seen holding a paper with the word "Union" written boldly at the top and the signature of the artist, and date, August 26, 1853, below.

SAMUEL WOODSON PRICE

(1828–1918)

SAMUEL WOODSON PRICE was born in Jessamine County, Kentucky, to Daniel and Eliza Crocket Price. He enrolled in the Kentucky Military Institute, 1846, and studied with William Redin, an English painter and architect active in central Kentucky, 1847. He also reported having had some lessons with Oliver Frazer. Price enrolled for further study in the Art Students League, New York, 1847–1849. He was active as a portraitist in Lexington, 1849–1851, and moved to Louisville, 1851, from

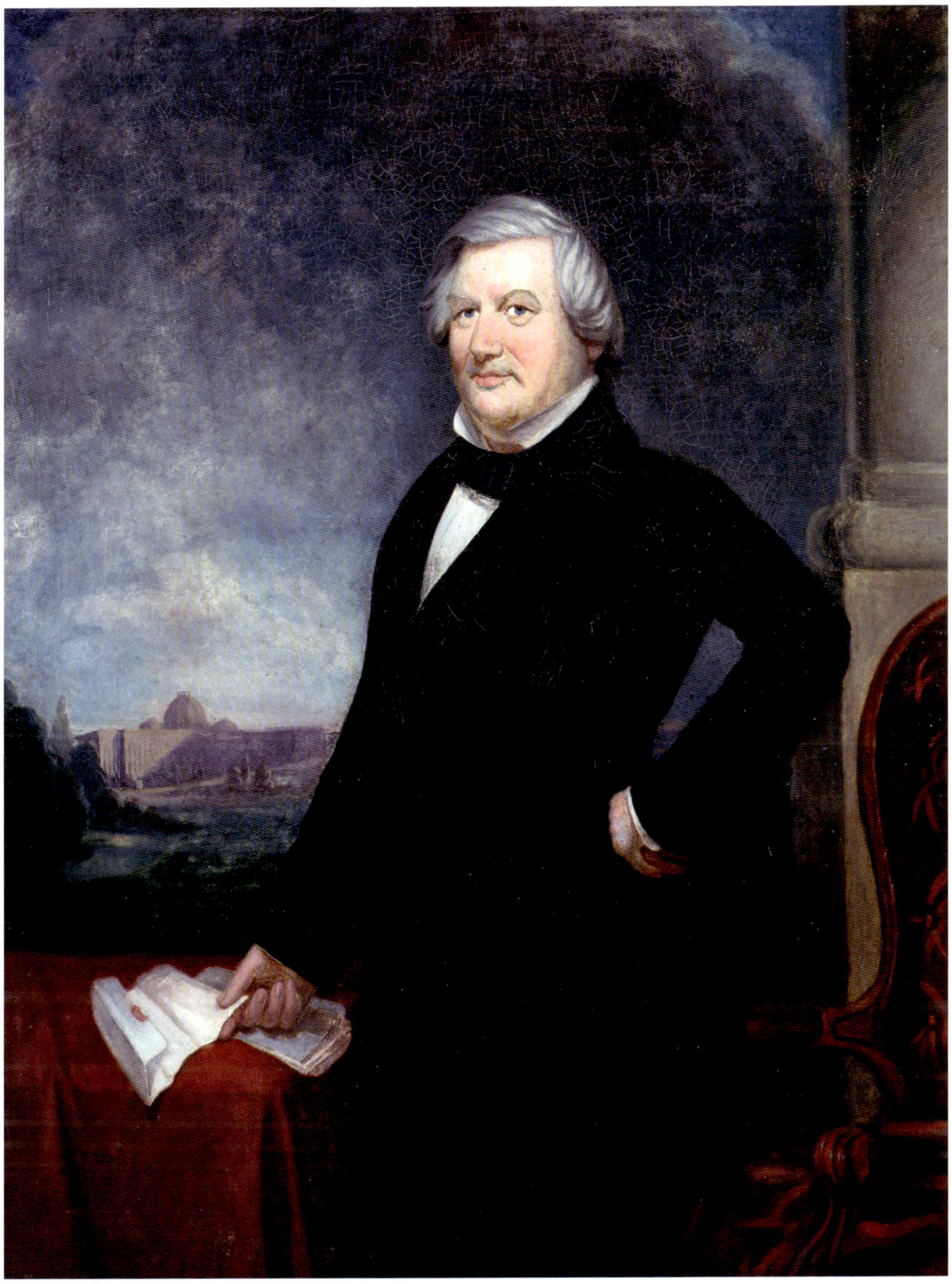

FIGURE 138. Samuel Woodson Price, *Millard Fillmore* (1800–1874), 1856, oil on canvas, 61 × 48″, The Filson Historical Society, 1946.4.1.

Fillmore was the last member of the Whig Party to hold the presidency.

which base he pursued an itinerancy in Tennessee and points south. Price was commissioned to paint Millard Fillmore's portrait for the Fillmore and Donelson Club in Clarksville, Indiana, at the time of the presidential campaign of 1856; the portrait was painted in Buffalo, New York. He has been praised for capturing the startling blue of Fillmore's eyes (Fig. 138). According to Julius Pratt, "While such of Fillmore's letters as survive make him seem singularly colorless, his contemporaries have left testimony to his impressive presence, kindly blue eyes, and gracious manner, all of which seem borne out by his portraits." Price returned to Lexington in 1859, and served in the Union Army during the Civil War, attaining the rank of brevet brigadier general in 1865. Afterward he was again active as a portraitist in Lexington, 1865–1878, while serving as postmaster, 1869–1876. Having been forced from office in the final days of the Grant administration, Price returned to Louisville in 1878. Injuries received in the war resulted in his becoming blind in 1881. At the invitation of Reuben Durrett, he dictated a series of reminiscences about the "old masters of the Bluegrass," which were presented to the Filson Club and then published in 1902. Price died in St. Louis at the home of his daughter, Mrs. Agnes Price Vogelgessing, and was initially buried in St. Louis, although he was re-interred in Arlington Cemetery in 1919 at the family's request.

Archives: FHS, UKSC; collections: FHS, NPG, Speed, TU, UKAM; literature: Jones & Weber, Pratt, Price, Whitley.

WILLIAM HENRY REDIN JR.

(1824–after 1872)

WILLIAM HENRY REDIN JR. was born in Suffolk County, England, to William Henry and Martha Eliza Young Redin. The family migrated to America, ca. 1826, and were resident in Louisville by 1834. He is noted as painting in Jessamine County, Kentucky, ca. 1840, and as having given some lessons to the young Samuel Woodson Price in Lexington, ca. 1847. He studied at the National Academy of Design in New York, 1843–1844, and then returned to Louisville, where he was active as a portraitist until 1860. Few of his portraits have been recorded, but of those the large-scale paintings of children from the Kennedy and Helm families are impressive in their attention to costume and atmospheric landscape illustrated with architectural detail (Fig. 139). Redin is primarily recalled as an architect. In that profession he brought the tenets of the English Oxford and Cambridge movements to the Gothic Revival style in Kentucky. He was responsible for the renovations to Christ Church Cathedral in Louisville, 1858–1860, and for churches in Pewee Valley and Anchorage, Kentucky. Considered his greatest achievement, the Cave Hill Cemetery gates in Louisville provide an impressive entrance to that private burial ground.

Literature: Kleber (2001), Whitley.

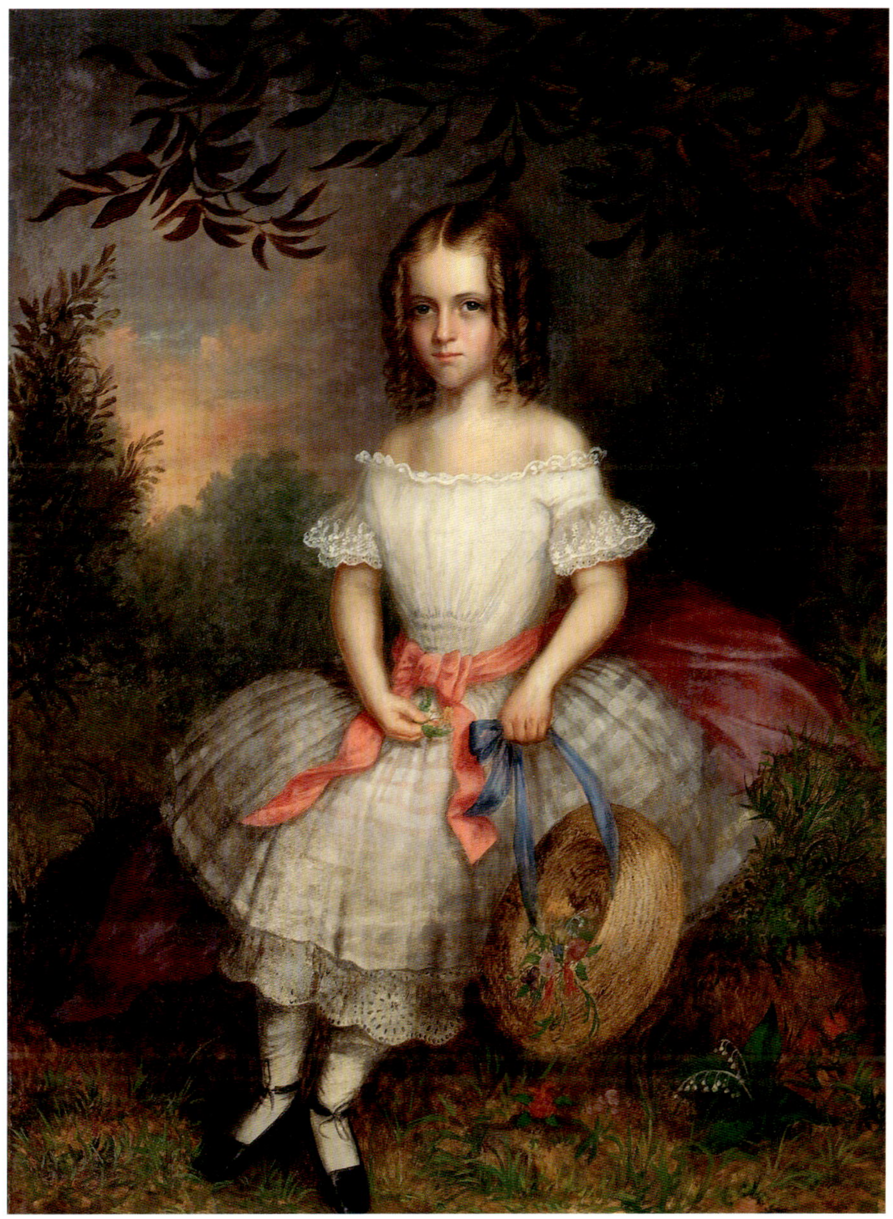

FIGURE 139. William Henry Redin Jr., *Margaret Helm* (1850–1936), ca. 1858, oil on canvas, 50 × 38″, Christ Church Cathedral, Lexington, Kentucky.

BENJAMIN FRANKLIN REINHART

(1829–1885)

FIGURE 140. Benjamin Franklin Reinhart, *James A. Smith,* ca. 1869, oil on canvas, 31½ × 24¼", The Filson Historical Society, 1931.2.1.

BENJAMIN FRANKLIN REINHART was born near Waynesburg, Pennsylvania. He studied at the National Academy of Design in 1847, and in Europe in Düsseldorf, Paris, and Rome, 1850–1853. He began itinerant activity in Ohio in the late 1840s and in the Mississippi Valley, 1853–1859, prior to setting up a studio in New Orleans, 1859–1862, notably in the "frame and picture shop of Hoffman." He was in Georgetown, Kentucky, 1858. During this period before the Civil War he created several history paintings of note, including *Halt on the Prairie.* Though reputed to have left New Orleans at the outbreak of the Civil War, he actually stayed there for some time and was apparently a staunch Confederate sympathizer, contributing money to Colonel

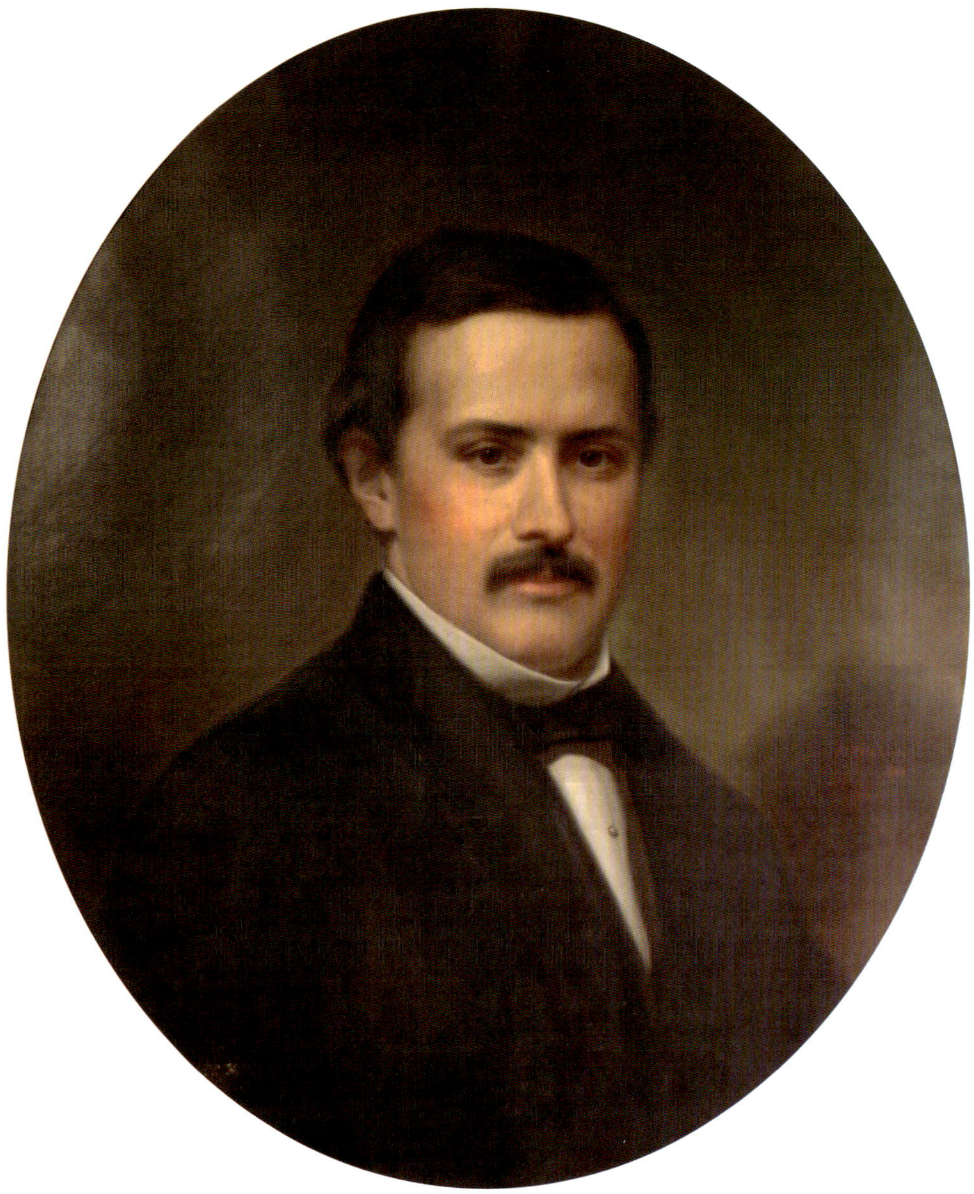

Frank Bartlett's regiment, who afterward called themselves "Reinhart's Guards." Reinhart painted Jefferson Davis and General P. G. T. Beauregard for the Soldier's Lottery in New Orleans in 1862, but he left New Orleans after the capitulation to Union forces in May 1862. He fled to England, where he remained until 1868, painting several notables, including Thomas Carlyle and Alfred, Lord Tennyson, as well as an image of Robert E. Lee drawn from a daguerreotype. He returned to America in 1868, setting up a studio in New York, from where he made periodic painting excursions into the South. He was again in New Orleans, 1868–1871, painting another life portrait of Jefferson Davis, and in Louisville in 1868 and 1869, painting John Hunt Morgan from a photograph. It was at this time that he may have also painted James A. Smith (Fig. 140), one of Morgan's confederates, from a photograph as well. He became an Associate of the National Academy of Design and died in Philadelphia in 1885.

Archives: FHS, HNOC; collections: Corcoran, FHS, LSM; literature: Bruns, Haverstock et al., Pennington (1991), Whitley.

AURELIUS O. REVENAUGH

(1840–1908)

FIGURE 141. Aurelius O. Revenaugh, *Mrs. Louisa Boehl* (1866–1901), ca. 1901, oil on canvas, 26½ × 21½", The Filson Historical Society, 1999.10.

AURELIUS O. REVENAUGH was born in Zanesville, Ohio, to John and Clarinda Blake Revenaugh. He studied medicine at the University of Michigan, Ann Arbor, before enlisting in the Union Army Signal Corps during the Civil War. At the end of the war he married Lavinia Mason of Elmira, New York, and returned to Ann Arbor. In Detroit, he studied with John Mix Stanley, ca. 1865–1866, and began his career as a painter in Jackson, Michigan. He appeared in Louisville, 1886, where he was known as "a maker of portraits and violins," resident in the *Courier-Journal* building. He was also active as an itinerant in Woodford, Fayette, and Madison Counties. During this time he painted a genre work of a newsboy in the snow, which enjoyed widespread distribution as a chromolithograph. Revenaugh was possibly a resident of Washington, D.C., in 1897, and was listed as exhibiting portraits of Andrew Carnegie and Reuben Durrett at the 1907 Southern Exposition from an address at the Wilkes Block in Louisville. His late portraits, such as that of Mrs. Louisa Boehl, have a highly finished surface reminiscent of the hand-colored photographs of the era against which he competed (Fig. 141). He died in Louisville in 1908 and was buried in Greenwood Cemetery, Vernon, Michigan.

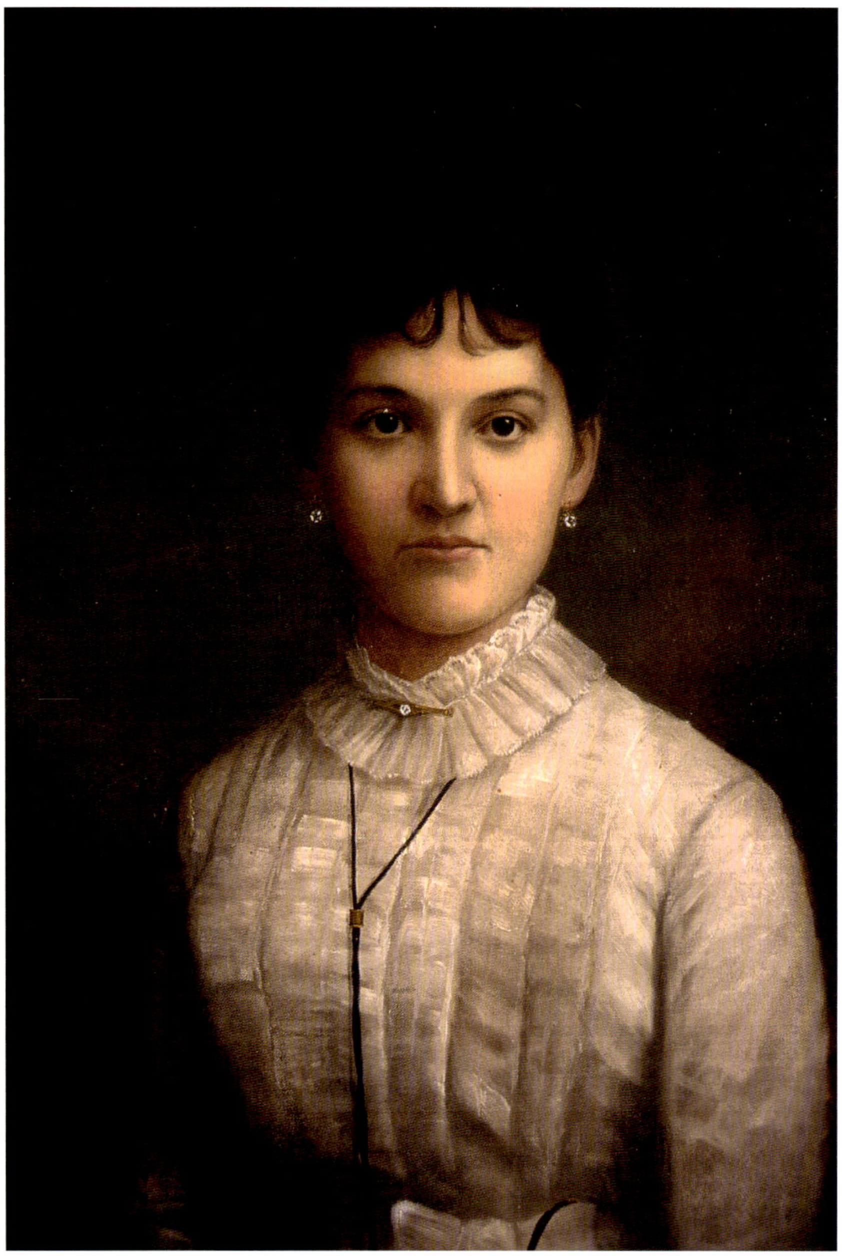

Collections: Brennan, FHS, Speed; literature: Haverstock et al., Jones & Weber, Pennington (2008).

DIXIE SELDEN

(1870–1935)

DIXIE SELDEN WAS BORN in Cincinnati to John and Martha Peyton McMillen Selden, with whom she soon moved to Covington, Kentucky, where she spent her childhood. Though northern by birth, and descended from Revolutionary War veterans in New York and Connecticut, both Selden parents were Southern in sympathy and named their daughter for D. D. Emmett's rousing song "Dixie Land." Southern sympathies and genealogical associations would remain lasting elements in Dixie Selden's life, and they proved especially important in her lifelong friendship with the McDowell and Breckinridge families at Ashland, the Henry Clay home in Lexington, Kentucky. Having lost both her siblings in infancy, Dixie became the focus of her parents' attention and traveled with them extensively in Europe in 1878 and again in 1882–1883. Genetta McLean reports that Selden's parents even went so far as to dress her in adult clothes and take her to casinos, where "she was the observed of all the observers." Selden's mother was an amateur painter who encouraged the young prodigy's talent. Accordingly, she was enrolled in the McMicken School of Design in Cincinnati in 1884, when she was just sixteen. She found her instructor there, Thomas S. Noble, to be uninspiring, and was delighted when the school merged with the Cincinnati Museum Association and she began taking classes with Frank Duveneck. Duveneck would remain a cherished teacher and champion, proposing Selden's work for male-dominated exhibitions and recommending her for important portrait commissions. In 1892 Selden became a founding member and officer of the Women's Art Club, Cincinnati. Having received additional instruction in illustration at the Art Academy of Cincinnati that year, she established herself as an illustrator and portraitist in 1894, based in Covington. In 1895 she began a tradition of yearly summer travels in both this country and abroad. Brittany and Normandy in France, and the New England seashore communities of Boothbay and Edgartown, figure prominently as subject matter for her impressionist landscapes and genre pictures. After both her parents died in 1908 she moved across the river to Cincinnati, where she maintained a series of studios and apartments for the rest of her life, notably on Race Street and at Cross Lane in Walnut Hills. Selden created two volumes of work: impressionist scenes of vivid color and warmth composed on, and from, her travels; and portraits with a gravitas familiar to the students of Duveneck. When that master teacher was given an honorary doctorate from the University of Cincinnati in 1917, Selden was asked to paint his portrait, which she finished in 1918 and which proved to be the last life sitting for Duveneck, who died in 1919 (see Fig. 74). After Selden's sudden death in 1935, a Memorial Exhibition was held at the Cincinnati Art Museum. In his eulogistic remarks, Herbert Green French commented, "Should her painting give to those who see it in the future some measure of the beauty of spirit which was hers, the world will be the better, even as those who knew her in the flesh were the better for that privilege."

Archives: Goldman; collections: Ashland, Butler, CAM, KHS, SAM, UC; literature: Aronson (2003), Cincinnati Art Museum (1979), McLean, Pennington (2008).

WILLIAM STAMMS SHACKLEFORD

(1815–after 1878)

FIGURE 142. William Stamms Shackleford, *Dr. John Coons,* ca. 1840, oil on canvas, 30 × 26½", Kentucky Historical Society, 721–1033.

WILLIAM STAMMS SHACKLEFORD was born most likely in Fleming County, Kentucky, to William S. and Sabina Metcalfe Shackleford, natives of Virginia, who were married in Bourbon County (which would have included Fleming County at that time) in February 1799. The legendary accounts of Shackleford's having some early training with Matthew Harris Jouett are in dispute, although he could have worked with the sculptor Joel Tanner Hart in 1826, after his parents moved to Lexington. Like several others, he assisted Oliver Frazer with the monumental portrait of Washington for the old State Capitol in 1833–1834, possibly painting draperies or other minor details. Shackleford began intermittent activity as an itinerant in Kentucky, 1838–1850, working in Flemingsburg, Winchester, Versailles, Cynthiana, and Danville. Many of his portraits from that era depict the subject high on the planar field, turned distinctly to the right and with startlingly penetrating glances. The portrait of Dr. John Coons of Woodford County is an example of that style (Fig. 142). Shackleford lived in Clarksville, Tennessee, ca. 1850–1860, where he painted a remarkable series of portraits of his brother James Shackelford's family sporting about in fanciful attire with their pets. His last known place of activity was Paris, Kentucky, in 1878, where he painted Fanny Shropshire and possibly copied a photograph of Congressman Brutus Junius Clay of Auvergne for a portrait commissioned by Ezekiel Field Clay at Runnymede. He died while visiting relatives in Missouri.

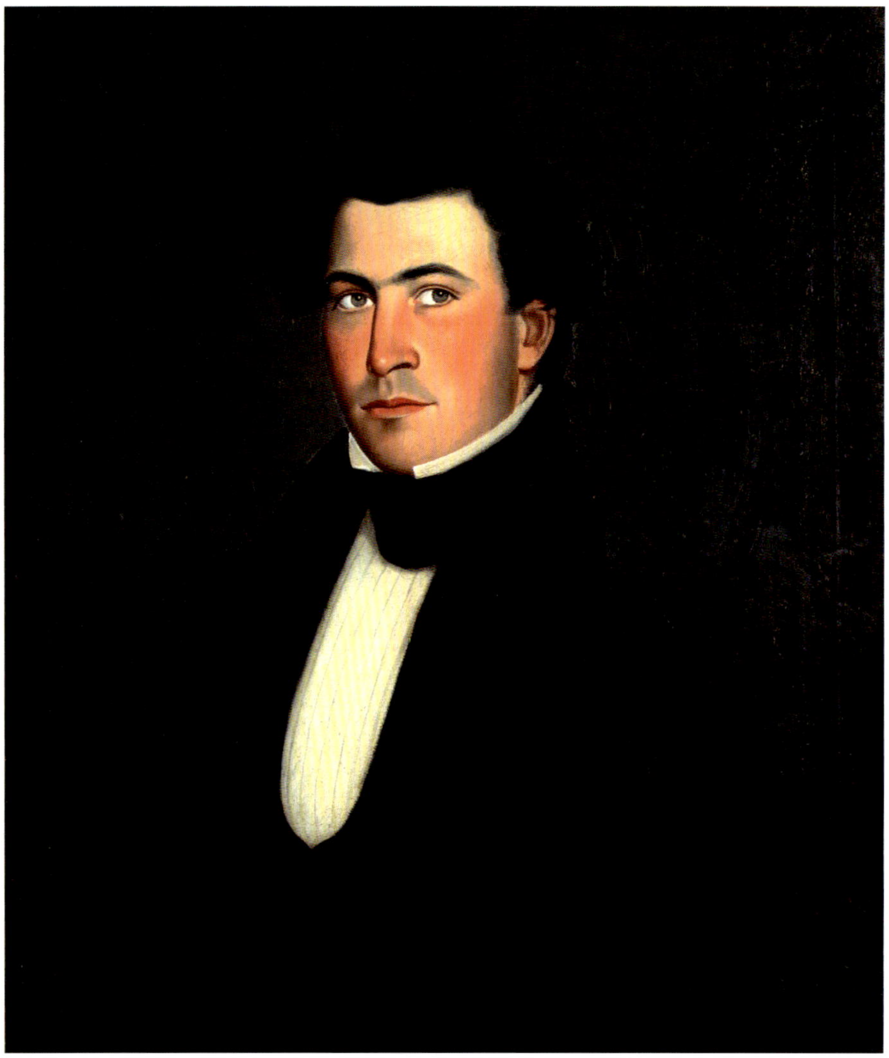

Collections: Clark County, KHS, THS; literature: J. Kelly, Whitley.

SOULE FAMILY

CHARLES SOULE SR. (1809–1869) was born in Freeport, Maine, but was orphaned at an early age and raised in Chillicothe, Ohio, by his maternal uncle, the painter Joseph Thoits Moore (1796–1854), to whom he was apprenticed as a sign and ornamental painter. Mary Sayre Haverstock et al. report that Soule's uncle Joseph "vehemently opposed his attempts at portrait painting" and that Soule "ran away from home in 1826." However, considering that Moore himself spent the years 1825–1826 in Philadelphia, he seems unlikely to have provoked his nephew's departure; instead, the move was more likely motivated by the young artist's ambitions. Soule set up shop in Dayton in 1826 as a carriage painter, but by 1833 he had established a studio there, offering portraits as well as fancy painting for homes and carriages. He then became active as an itinerant in the Mississippi River Valley, 1835–1841. Soule moved to Cincinnati in 1841, pursuing an itinerancy in Ohio and the Ohio River Valley as far west as St. Louis. Cincinnati was his base 1841–1853, during which time he continued to make itinerant excursions to Dayton. Charles T. Webber (1825–1911), a fellow artist, thought him "a disciple and imitator of Jarvis, [who] executed many beautiful and strongly characteristic portraits. Like Jarvis, he used the camera lucida to make his drawings; hence he never became the master in drawing that he was in color, merely from the want of practice." A camera lucida was an optical device that superimposed the subject being viewed upon the surface on which the artist painted. Webber's reference to this device being used in an Ohio River Valley setting is a rare manifestation of its utility and is subject to dispute. Although the January 25, 1851, *Cincinnati Enquirer* reported that the "greatest of our artists, Charley Soule, in the way of portrait painting, is hard at work in his studio," things would soon go terribly wrong. Soule had begun to drink heavily, and on a visit to Dayton in September 1851 he attempted suicide while in the grip of delirium tremens, hysterical over the idea that "he had murdered somebody, and was sentenced to be hung for it," to avoid which fate he cut his throat. Considering that he was visiting his wife, Elizabeth Mead Soule, and children at the time, a domestic dispute may have exacerbated his state of mind. In the aftermath of this episode his son, Charles Soule Jr., sought to prevent his father from further contact with the family, provoking an estrangement that lasted until the senior artist's death. Soule Sr. then moved to New York, where he is thought to have remained until 1858. He returned to Cincinnati in 1864 and died in Dayton in 1869. Four of his children were artists. Charles Soule Jr. (1835–1897) began his career as an ornamental painter under the tutelage of his father. Following their estrangement, Soule the younger remained in Dayton and began to paint portraits. Among those extant is a portrait of a young boy, thought to be Walter Gebhart, with his dog, richly colored with a glowing sunset in the background. A portrait of a young boy with a fishing pole in the Filson collection is painted with similar warmth and attention to atmospheric detail (Fig. 143).

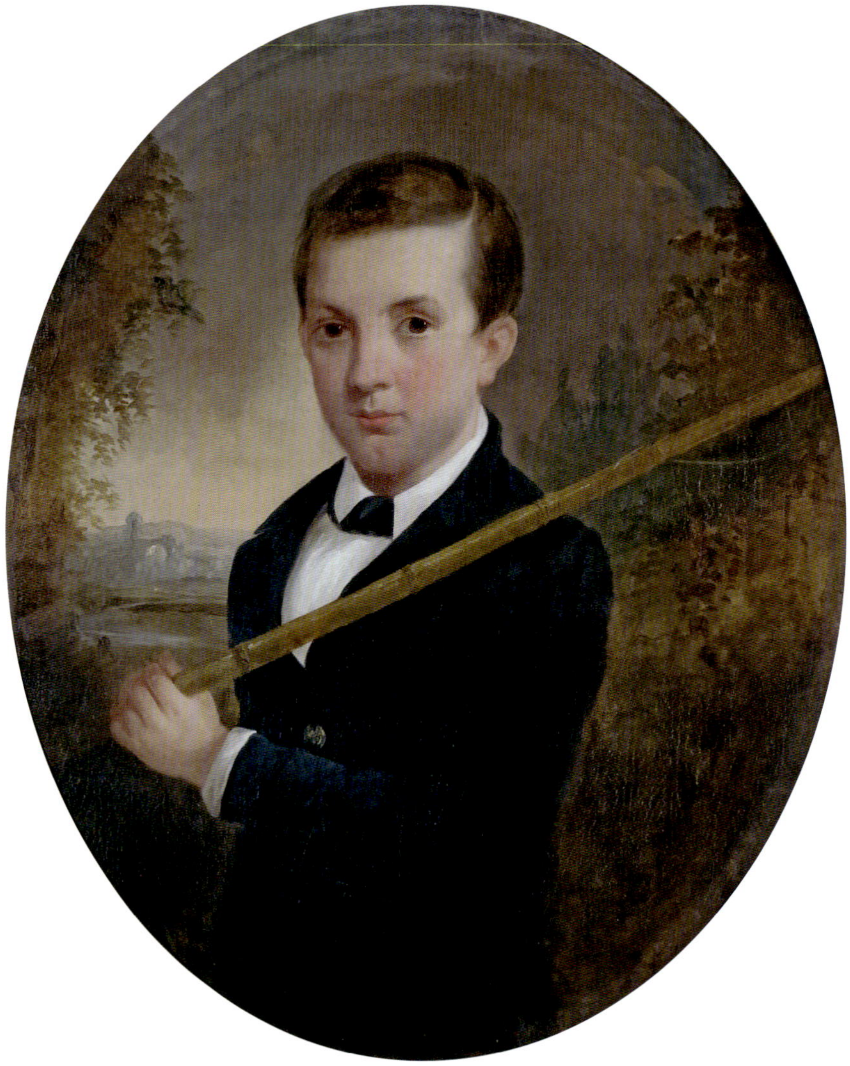

FIGURE 143. Charles Soule Jr., *William Norville Davies,* n.d., oil on linen, 29½ × 24½″, The Filson Historical Society, 1997.3.1.

Soule Jr. moved on to Portsmouth, Ohio, just before the Civil War and pursued an itinerancy across the Ohio River in northeastern Kentucky, notably in Maysville. During this time he also served as a lieutenant in the 56th Ohio Volunteer Infantry. After his father's death he returned to Dayton and painted *Civil War Widow,* a work much celebrated locally, though based on a print of Thomas Faed's *Evangeline.* Apart from painting trips to Cincinnati in 1877 and Portsmouth in 1885, he remained based in Dayton for the rest of his life. His sister Clara Soule (1834–ca. 1890), the eldest of his siblings, was also an artist and a teacher at the Cooper Female Seminary in Dayton. It was she who cared for their father during his last illness, after which she moved to Cincinnati, from which base she made itinerant visits to Lexington, Kentucky. Following her marriage to a man named Medlar, Clara moved to New York in the late 1880s. Octavia True Soule (1844–1908), the fourth of the Soule children, was also an art teacher in Dayton and well known locally for her still life work as well as for her abilities as a colorist of photographs. She married a local attorney, Oscar M. Gottschall, in 1869. Ella Soule (ca. 1848–?), the youngest of the Soule daughters, was known as a china painter in Dayton.

Archives: DAI; collections: DAI, FHS; literature: Hageman, Haverstock et al., "Soule Family of Dayton," Whitley.

RAPHAEL STRAUSS

(1830–1901)

RAPHAEL STRAUSS WAS BORN in Bavaria. According to Edna Talbott Whitley, "his father sent him to Munich to study with a famous court painter." He immigrated, with his wife, to Cincinnati in 1858, opening a studio in a building at the corner of John and Everett Streets, where he offered his services as a portraitist and as a tinter of photographs. As a tinter he entered a partnership with William Southgate Porter during the Civil War years. After the war Strauss began an itinerancy in central Kentucky. He was in Paris, Kentucky, several times between 1868 and 1873, painting the four children of Mr. and Mrs. Allen Bashford (Fig. 144). While in Cynthiana, Kentucky, he often worked from the home of the Howk (Hauch) family, associates from the German community in Cincinnati. Strauss was greatly admired in his own day for his attention to detail and the rather severe gravitas his subjects displayed, an admiration also derived from the close likeness they bore to the more expensive studio photographs of the day. His portraits were exhibited at important Cincinnati venues, including the Western Sanitary Fair, 1863; the Cincinnati Artists Association, 1866–1867; and the Cincinnati Industrial Expositions in 1871 and 1873. In the late 1880s he began to share a studio with the "ancient Aubrey" (Jean Aubrey) in the Pike Building at 152 West 4th Street. This studio became a much-beloved local salon, often noted in local papers as a gathering place for "art lovers." Strauss died in Cincinnati in 1901. His son, Joseph B. Strauss, was the civil engineer responsible for the construction of the Golden Gate Bridge in San Francisco.

Collections: CAM, Ft. Wayne; literature: Cincinnati Art Museum (1979), Haverstock et al., Whitley.

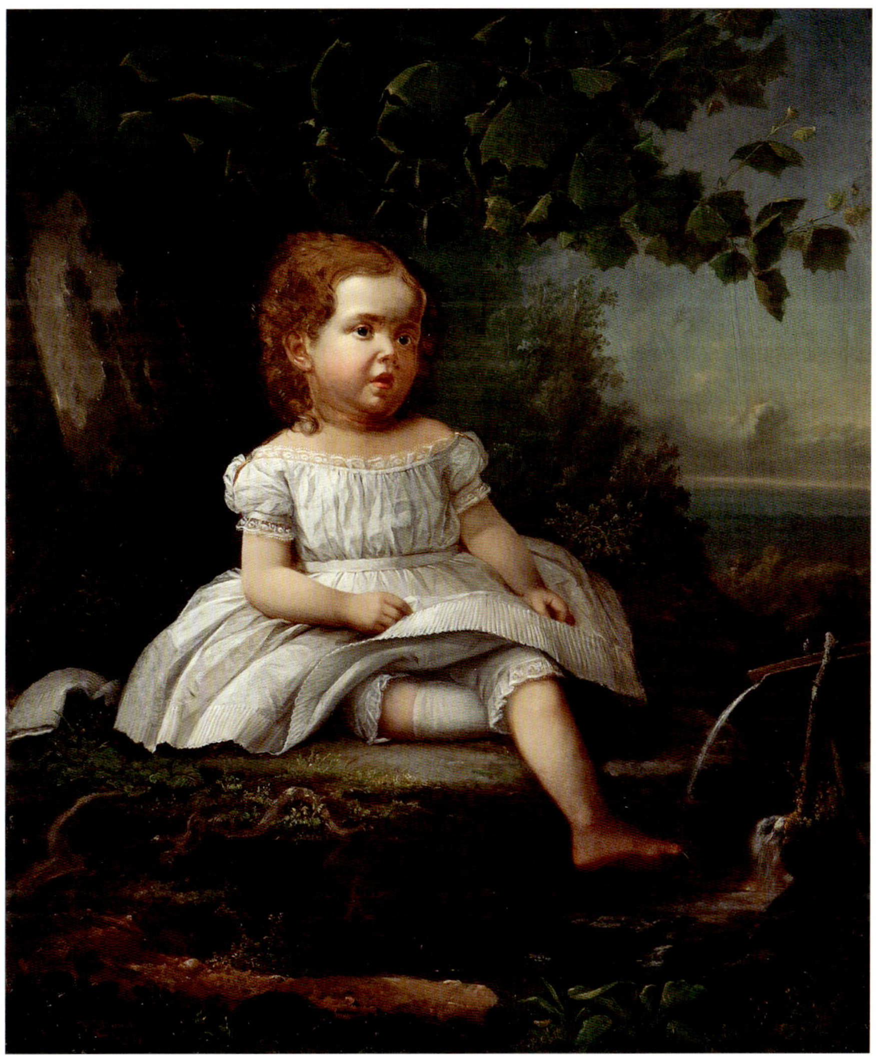

FIGURE 144. Raphael Strauss, *Janey Bashford* (b. 1868), 1873, oil on canvas, 42 × 36″, Mr. and Mrs. Louis Lanier Powell Prichard, Paris, Kentucky.

WILLIAM FRANCIS VER BRYCK

(1823–1899)

FIGURE 145. William Francis Ver Bryck, *Sue Downs Harding,* 1873, oil on canvas, 30 × 25″, Speed Art Museum, 1985.1.2, gift of the estate of Margaret M. Hughes.

WILLIAM FRANCIS VER BRYCK was born in New York City and studied at the National Academy of Design. He began making painting trips to Kentucky after 1851, including noted ones to Lexington, 1868; Louisville, 1869 and 1882; and Shelby County, 1873. While in Lexington in 1868 he worked from a studio at the Phoenix Hotel. George Washington Ranck notes that "no visiting artist ever met with as much success in Lexington as Mr. Ver Bryck." Ver Bryck's extant portraits in Kentucky offer an insight into the transition of styles in the postbellum era. His portrait of Sue Downs Harding dates from his visit to Shelby County in 1873 (Fig. 145). She is posed in a rather alluring manner, her hair down and falling across her bare shoulder, a pose reminiscent of that antebellum romantic style soon to be replaced by the more severe likenesses of the late nineteenth century. By comparison, his portrait of Governor Thomas Bramlette, painted in the same time frame, is far more severe, the subject stiffly placed before the planar field, head turned just slightly to the left, as though standing awkwardly before a camera making a photograph for documentary purposes. Ver Bryck subsequently moved to Madison, Wisconsin, where he died.

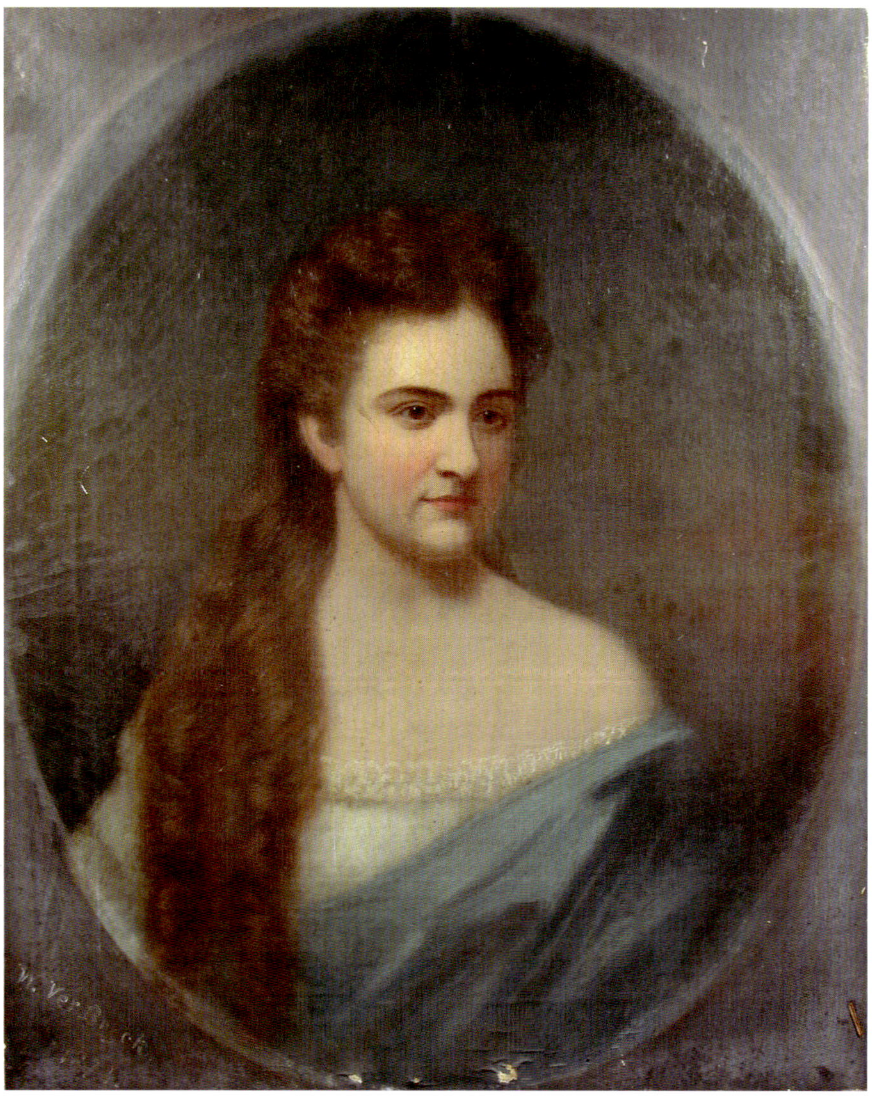

Collections: KHS, Speed, VHS, WHS; literature: Ranck, Whitley.

FERDINAND GRAHAM WALKER

(1859–1927)

FERDINAND GRAHAM WALKER was born in Mitchell, Indiana, near Louisville, the son of the Reverend Francis Walker and his wife, Elizabeth Graham Walker. He began his studies at DePauw College, Greenwood, Indiana. Reports that he also studied with Samuel Woodson Price are dubious, considering that Price was at that time the postmaster at Lexington. In 1883 Walker began his career as a portraitist by opening a studio in New Albany, Indiana, across the river from Louisville. With funds secured from those early commissions he traveled to Paris to study, 1885–1887. When he returned to America he worked in Washington, D.C., painting political figures and planning a cross-country expedition in search of gubernatorial commissions. When this ambition was not realized, Walker returned to New Albany, painting portraits and landscape work there and in Louisville. He went back to Paris in 1902, where he worked with Jacques-Emil Blanche (1861–1942). Upon his return he opened a studio in the Commercial Building at Fourth and Main Streets in downtown Louisville, where he was based for the remainder of his career. In that location he painted many portraits of prominent figures, including one of Walter N. Haldeman for the Jefferson Davis Memorial in Fairview, Kentucky, and a large portrait in the grand manner of Henry Watterson, seated at his *Courier-Journal* desk, pen in hand, looking thoughtfully at the viewer, a pedestal telephone just behind him. His portrait of General Bennett Young, beaming and bemedalled, may be his best work (Fig. 146). Walker has captured Young's sense of dash and bravura in his depiction of the subject's upright posture, ruddy cheeks, and sparkling blue eyes. Walker's portraiture is deeply indebted to photography. His subjects' gaze seems to be directed at a lens rather than a painter. Walker did work from photographs, notably in his portrait of the long-dead Lincoln, drawn from several sources, including Matthew Brady. During the First World War he advertised his willingness to make portraits from photographs of fallen soldiers. He copied several historical portraits for the Kentucky Historical Society, including a variant of Charles Willson Peale's image of George Washington. Walker was also a highly accomplished painter of landscape art in the American tonalist style based on French precedents from the Barbizon School. Many of these were exhibited in Louisville, including a scene near the American artist colony at Monnickendam, Holland, at the 1907 Southern Exposition. Walker retired from painting in 1925 and died in New Albany, Indiana, in 1927. He is buried, with his wife, Mary Watkins Walker, in the Fairview Cemetery in New Albany.

Archives: KHS, Speed; collections: FHS, KHS, MMA, NAPL, NCMA, Speed; literature: Kleber (2001), Jones & Weber.

FIGURE 146 *(overleaf)*. Ferdinand Graham Walker, *Bennett H. Young* (1843–1919), ca. 1915, oil on canvas, 47 × 35″, The Filson Historical Society, 1993.35.3.

Young was one of the towering figures in the civic and cultural life of late nineteenth-century Louisville. In 1863 he joined General John Hunt Morgan's cavalry, and later, as a Confederate agent, he participated in the raid on St. Albans, Vermont. Escaping extradition to the United States from Canada for that incursion, he then went to Great Britain, studying law in Belfast and Edinburgh. Upon his return to Louisville in 1868 he opened a practice as a trial lawyer while also masterminding the reorganization of the Louisville, New Albany and Chicago Railroad. He served as president of the Southern Exposition, 1884, and as president of the Kentucky School for the Blind. He was also active in the United Confederate Veterans, becoming their commander-in-chief in 1913. The following year he published *Confederate Wizards of the Saddle,* an account of his Confederate cavalry exploits.

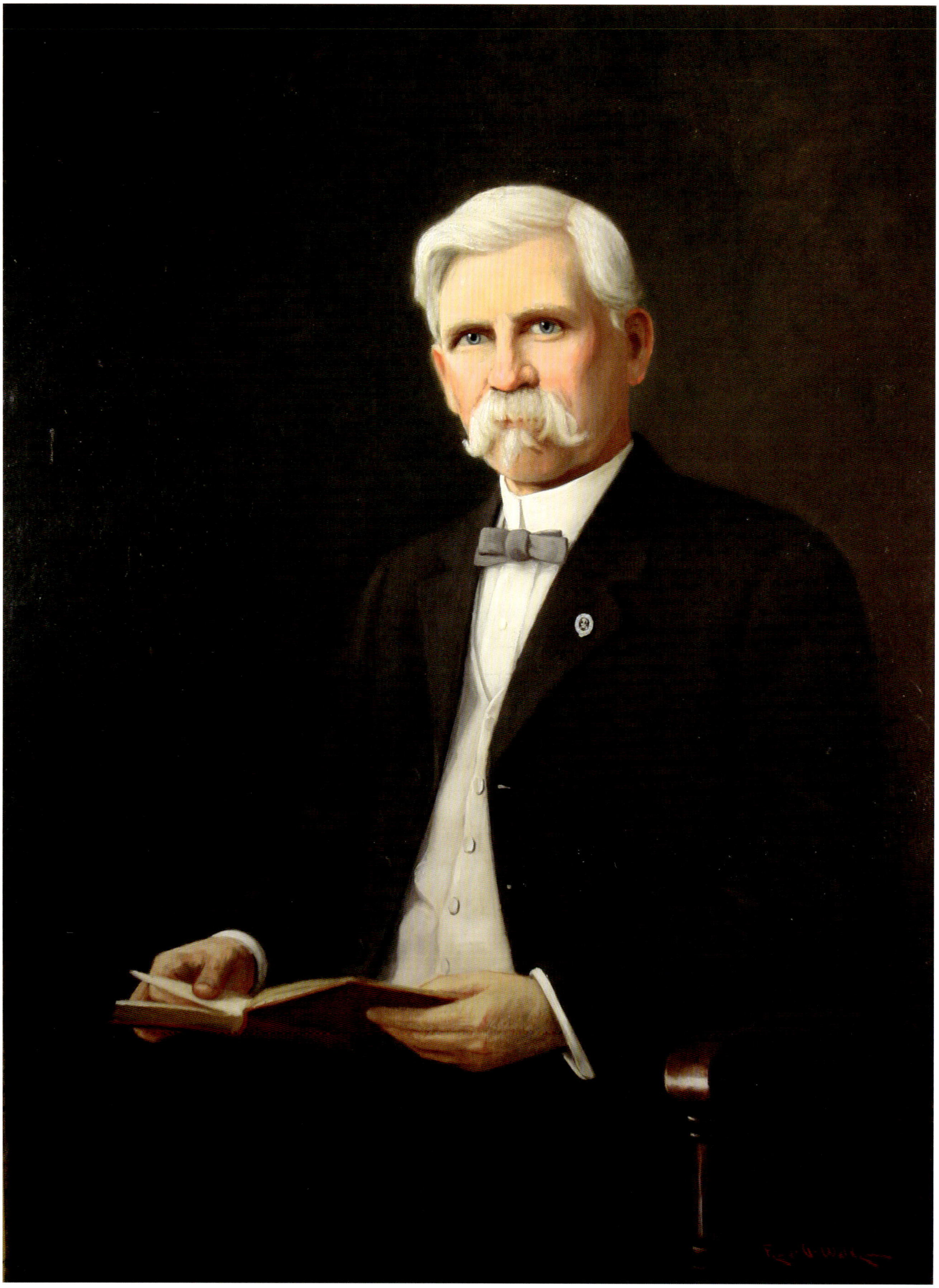

WILLIAM EDWARD WEST

(1788–1857)

WILLIAM EDWARD WEST was born in Lexington, Kentucky, to Sally Brown and Edward West, a silversmith, from whom he received early instruction. He kept a studio in Philadelphia, 1809–1817, during which time he worked with Thomas Sully. After 1817 he became active as an itinerant in the lower Mississippi River Valley, especially in Natchez and New Orleans, where a large body of his work is extant. One of his most notable works from this period is a refined painting of Joseph Emery Davis, eldest brother of Jefferson Davis, which is still at J. E. Davis's Rosemont Plantation in Woodville, Mississippi. A self-portrait painted prior to his departure for study in Italy,

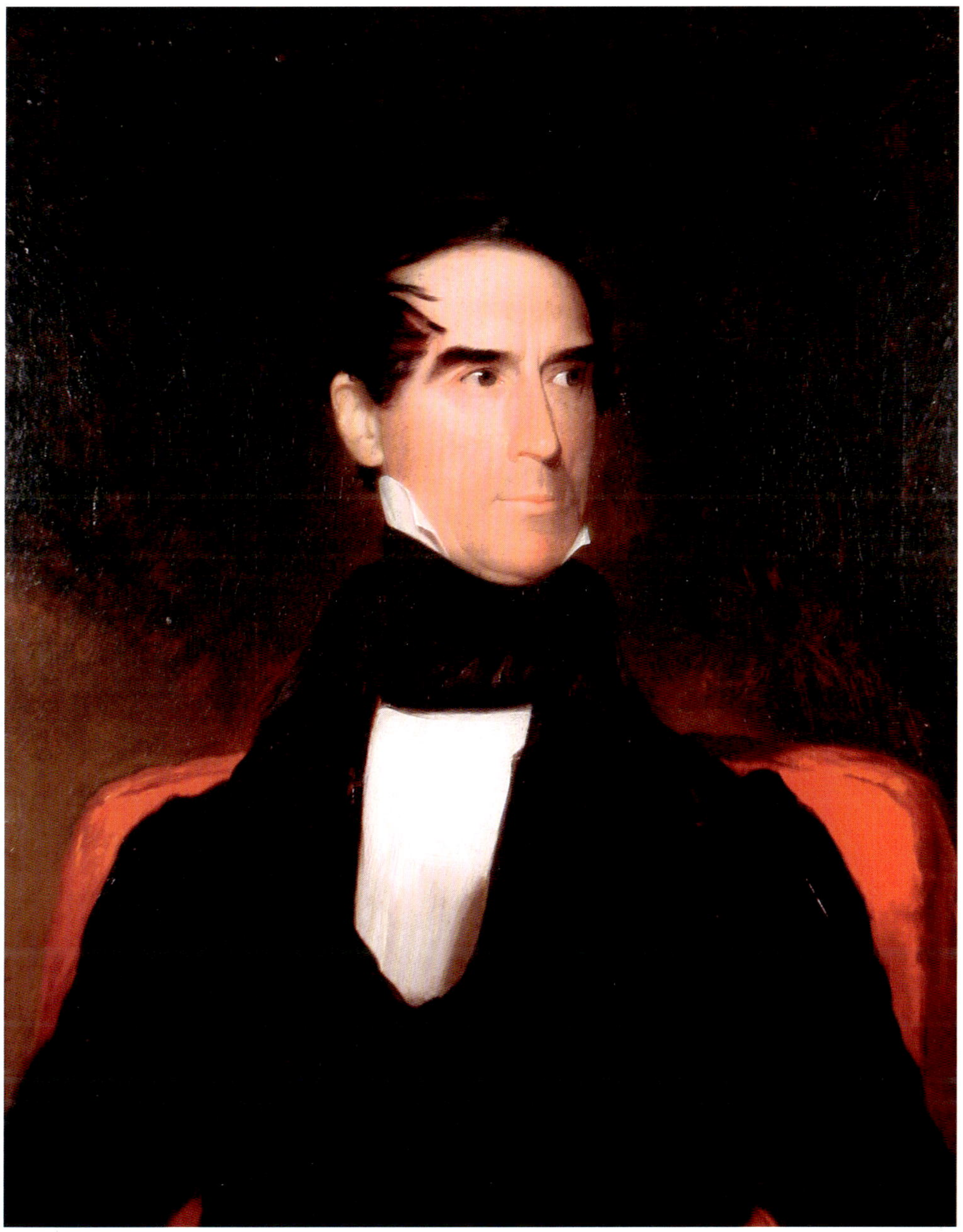

FIGURE 147. William Edward West, *John Spear Smith* (1804–1867), ca. 1840, oil on canvas, 29½ × 24¾″, The Filson Historical Society, 1997.19.1.

The Smith family were prominent in Maryland civic affairs, having served as congressmen and finance ministers for the state. John Spear Smith was also an antiquarian author and the founding president of the Maryland Historical Society. West painted several works for the extended Smith family, including a copy of Gilbert Stuart's portraits of Samuel Smith's parents, one of Smith's sister, and one of the sister's brother-in-law Edward Patterson. The bold anatomical massing, flashing eyes, and somewhat imperious glance are typical of West's Baltimore period.

ca. 1819, has recently been discovered in a Lexington, Kentucky, home. It was while living in Florence that he journeyed to paint Lord Byron in 1822. Following Byron's death in 1823, West moved to Paris, where he remained until 1825, when he moved to London. A personal investment failure forced his return to America. Well-connected, he worked out of a studio in Baltimore, 1837–1841, and with the help of the American consul in England repaid all his debts. Among his sitters was John Spear Smith, the son of Samuel and Margaret Spear Smith of Baltimore (Fig. 147). While abroad he had absorbed the English romantic coloration of Thomas Lawrence and the solidly intense composition of the later work of J. A. D. Ingres, evident in the large body of West's work extant from his Baltimore period. He resettled in New York in 1841, painting members of the Delano family and dabbling in spirituality. Two years before his death he made one last trip to Natchez, where he painted a haunting mourning portrait for the Young and Mercer families and revisited many of his early patrons. He died in 1857 in Nashville at the home of his sister, Jane West Woods, and is buried there in the old city cemetery.

Archives: AAA, LC, MHS, TSL; collections: Baltimore, Corcoran, FHS, MDHA, MMA, MHS, NPG, Speed; literature: Dunn, Flanary, Floyd (1968), Pennington (Autumn 1986, 1991, 2008), Tuckerman, Whitley.

CHARLES SNEED WILLIAMS

(1882–1964)

CHARLES SNEED WILLIAMS was born in Evansville, Indiana. He received his first recorded art instruction in Louisville, ca. 1905, from the Swiss painter Edward Biedermann (1864–1947). Biedermann specialized in landscape painting and was also a well-known illustrator of world fair sites, notably those in Chicago, 1893, and St. Louis, 1904. While in Louisville Williams learned of the Allan-Fraser Art School in Arboarth, Scotland, to which he applied for a scholarship. Patrick Allan-Fraser was a self-made Scottish millionaire who became an idealistic socialist, perhaps inspired by the late writings of John Ruskin and certainly by the Arts and Crafts aesthetic of William Morris. He turned his castellated residence, Hospitalfield, into a site for "a

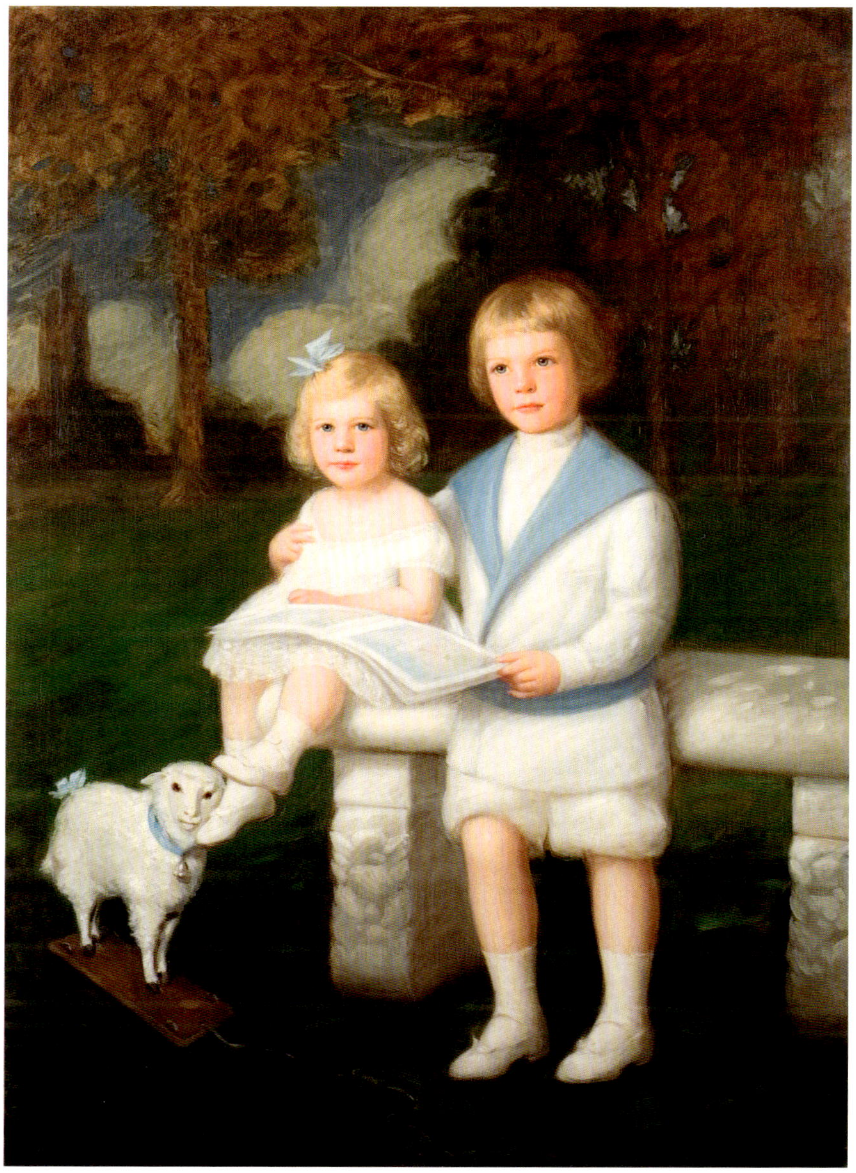

FIGURE 148. Charles Sneed Williams, *Jane* (1908–1988) *and Thruston Morton* (1907–1982), ca. 1914, oil on canvas, 60 × 43¾", The Filson Historical Society, 1988.32.

Jane and Thruston were the children of Mary Ballard and David Cummings Morton, whose families were present in Louisville from the pioneer period. Thruston Morton, educated at Woodbury Forest and Yale, became a prominent civil servant, holding office as a congressman, 1947–1953, assistant secretary of state for Dwight D. Eisenhower, 1953–1956, and senator, 1957–1969. He was also chairman of the Republican National Committee from 1959 to 1961. Jane Morton married George Washington Norton III, founder of WAVE-TV in Louisville. After his death and that of her son, Jane Norton became president of that broadcasting concern. Her charitable giving through the Norton Foundation greatly enhanced the programs of the Speed Art Museum, the Kentucky Center for the Arts, and Christ Church Cathedral. Painted on the eve of the First World War, this portrait makes more than a passing nod to two very disparate traditions. The scale of the children in relation to the background, as well as the diminutive toy lamb, recalls the grand ambitions of certain antebellum artists like Morrison and Frye, even as the vivid, pastel coloration echoes the Edwardian era in England, especially the work of John Singer Sargent and Philip de László, much admired by Louisville grandees.

highly considered program of social, architectural and agricultural improvements," which sought to construct "a micro-economy designed to harmonize culture once more with its traditions and aspirations." Williams received the scholarship and lived in the castle for four years, during which time he received instruction in life drawing, painting, and drawing from casts. The style Williams developed during his apprentice years in Scotland shows an awareness of certain international trends evident in the art of Sir John Lavery and William Orpen as well as the work of John Singer Sargent and J. A. M. Whistler. Williams's most personal characteristic was a fondness for setting his subjects, in highly colored relief, against a dark background, with a very deep glazing in the facial areas. After he left Arboarth Williams returned to Louisville for the first itinerant visit of a career that spanned the next forty years. It is likely that on that first visit he painted the extant portraits of Barry Bingham Sr. and the Morton children, Jane and Thruston (Fig. 148). These commissions led to Williams's becoming the society painter of choice in Louisville for the rest of his career. Williams returned to Scotland, opened a studio in Glasgow, and in 1912 married Elsie Luke, whose father was a wealthy shipbuilder for the John Brown & Company line. The couple eventually settled in London, where it is believed that her fortune underwrote his career as an artist. Williams's most noted English subject was Princess Marie Louise of Schleswig-Holstein, Queen Victoria's granddaughter. "Cousin Louie" was a great favorite in court circles and was helpful in securing Williams other commissions, notably that for the Duchesse de Rochefoucauld, a leading suffragette in France. For that portrait he earned membership in the Cercle de l'Union Artistique in Paris. From 1912 until his last recorded American visit in 1948, Williams pursued an itinerancy in Louisville and the Midwest, with extant work in Evansville, Indianapolis, and Chicago. He died in London, and his obituary was published in the October 17, 1964, *Louisville Times.* As an artist he is something more than a footnote in American society portraiture, and well deserving of future study.

Archives: Hospitalfield, Vanderpoel; FHS; collections: FHS, KHS, MOC, Speed, Vanderpoel; literature: Mallett.

ROBERT BURNS WILSON

(1851–1916)

ROBERT BURNS WILSON was born in Washington County, Pennsylvania, and orphaned at an early age. He began a career as an itinerant artist in 1869 prior to a journey by canoe to Union County, Kentucky, in 1871. Once in Kentucky, he became active as a landscape painter and portraitist in Lexington, Frankfort, and Louisville. Many of his landscape paintings follow a certain compositional formula, although he did experiment with various paint mediums for luminous effect. Wilson also experimented with portrait techniques. His watercolor portraits of the Brown girls, at the Orlando Brown House, seem to be cutout copies of photographs, hand-colored and superimposed over a detailed landscape sketch of their garden. He painted these subjects, and the children of Mayor E. H. Taylor, while living in Frankfort, and exhibited them in the art gallery of the 1884 Southern Exposition in Louisville. Wilson was also a writer who published several volumes of poems and a novel, *Until the Day Break,* 1900. His jingoist poem "Remember the Maine," published by William Randolph Hearst in the *New York Herald* of April 17, 1898, was used to incite the Spanish American war. Wilson and his wife, Anne, moved to New York in 1904 in the hopes of profiting from the attention that poem brought him. This was not to be, and he slowly slipped into obscurity and died in Brooklyn in 1916.

Collections: FHS, KHS, MMA, Speed, UKAM; literature: Coleman (1956), Pennington (2008).

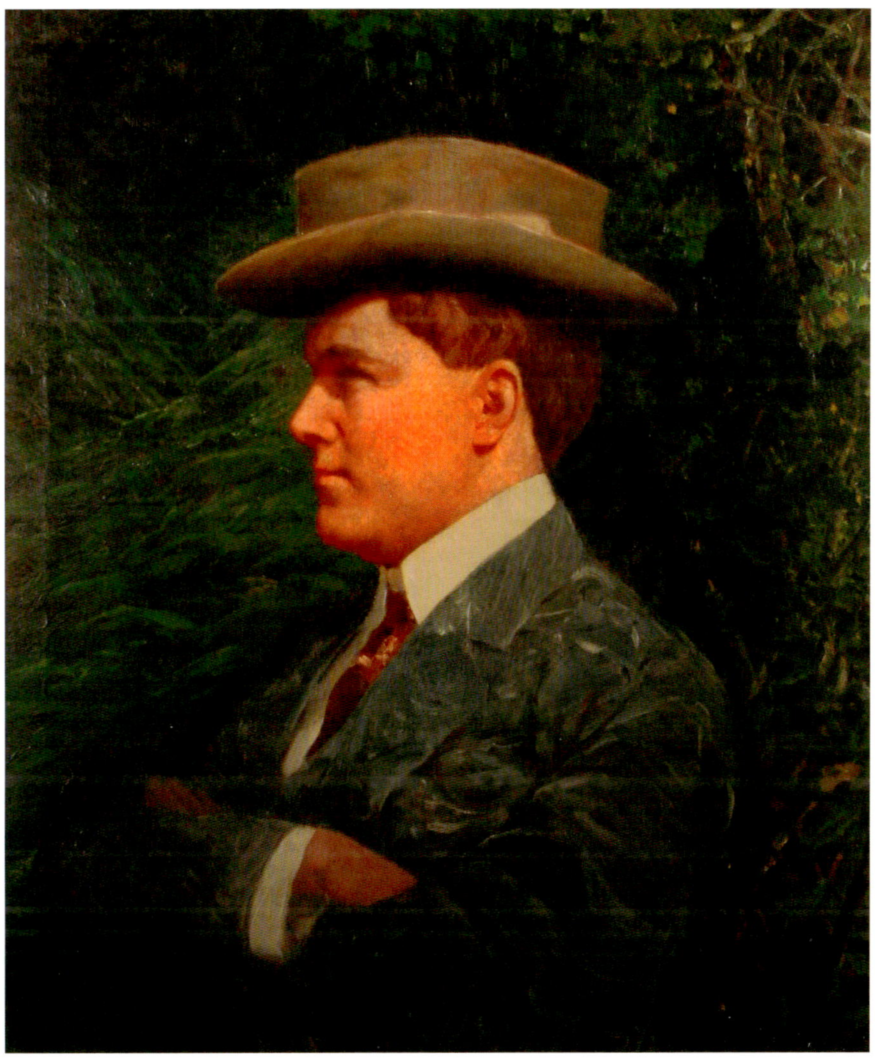

FIGURE 149. Robert Burns Wilson, *Leslie M. Mayo,* ca. 1905, oil on canvas, 30 × 25½″, The Filson Historical Society, 2008.9.1.

THOMAS WATERMAN WOOD

(1823–1903)

THOMAS WATERMAN WOOD was born in Montpelier, Vermont, and thought to have had some early studies with Chester Harding in Boston. He established a portrait studio in New York, 1853–1855, and was an itinerant, 1855–1858, working in Quebec, Washington, D.C., and Baltimore. He was in Paris, France, 1858–1859, copying old masters and studying art techniques. Wood relocated to Nashville, Tennessee, in 1861, where he painted lush children's portraits and began a career as a genre painter of

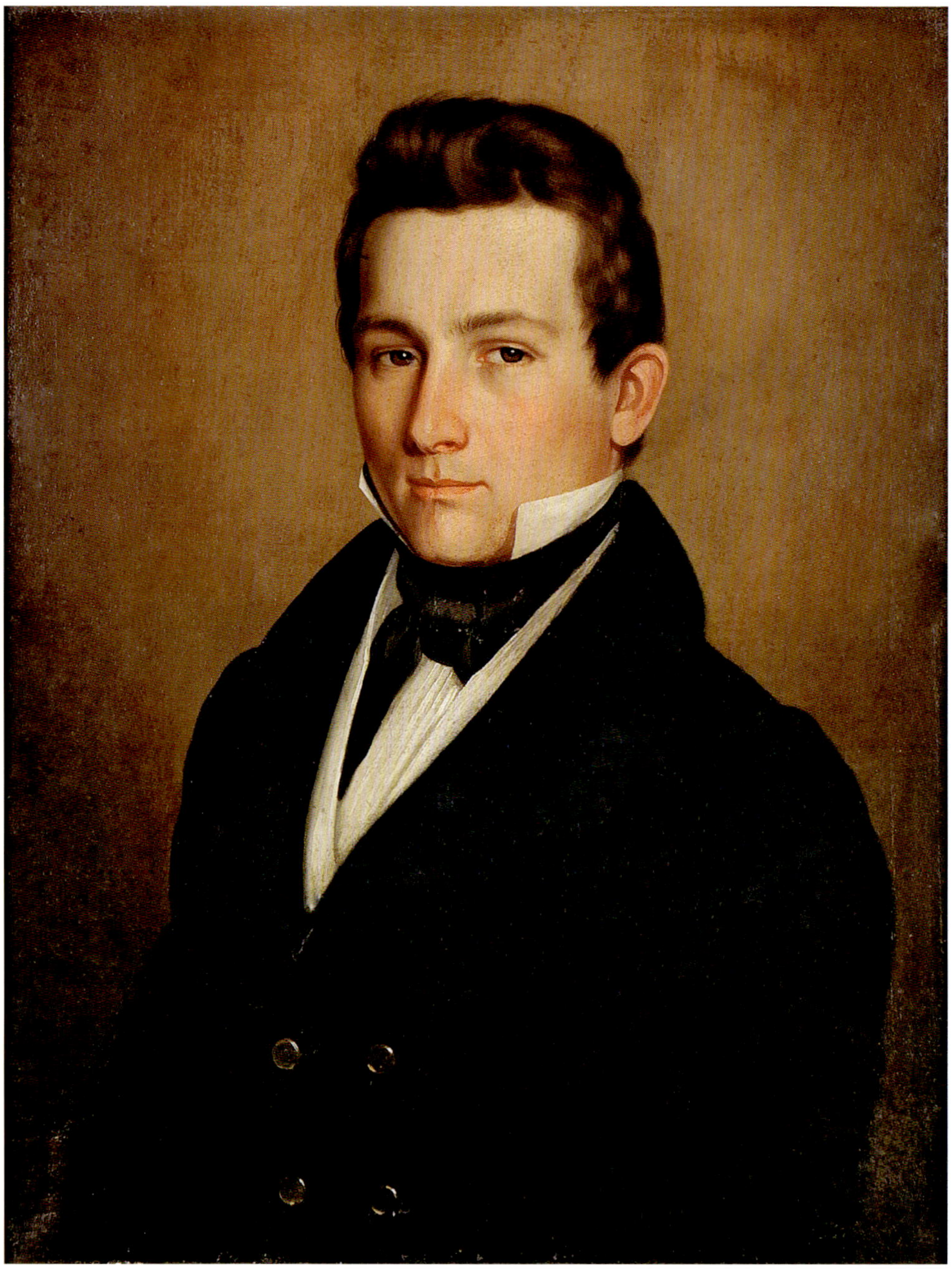

African-Americans. He departed Nashville in 1863 because of a threat to the city by Union forces, and moved to Louisville, where he began to paint a series of works based on African-American veterans of the Civil War. The Filson Historical Society suggests that he painted a posthumous portrait of John J. Hardin during that stay (Fig. 150). Wood moved to New York in 1866, where his genre paintings became successful and he was elected president of the National Academy of Design. He died in New York in 1903.

Archives: AAA; collections: FHS, KHS, Met, NAD, NGA, NPG, SAM, Speed, Wood, Yale; literature: Jones & Weber, J. Kelly, Whitley, T. W. Wood Art Gallery, L. Wright.

FIGURE 150 *(facing page).* Thomas Waterman Wood, *John J. Hardin* (1810–1847), ca. 1864, oil on canvas, 26 × 20½″, The Filson Historical Society, 1998.8.3.

Hardin was a native Kentuckian, born in Frankfort, the son of Senator Martin D. Hardin. He studied law at Transylvania University in Lexington before moving to Jacksonville, Illinois, in 1831. Once there he became a leading member of the Whig Party, winning election to the Illinois state House of Representatives, 1836–1842, and to the Twenty-eighth Congress, 1843–1845. In deference to Abraham Lincoln he declined to seek renomination in 1844, having previously prevented Lincoln from fighting a duel with James Shields in 1842. This portrait may be based on a daguerreotype that was made into a popular print and circulated during Hardin's 1842 campaign. He was killed at the Battle of Buena Vista during the Mexican War.

THOMAS JEFFERSON WRIGHT

(1798–1845)

FIGURE 151 *(facing page).* Thomas Jefferson Wright, *Cassandra Hukill Howard* (1790–1864), ca. 1830, oil on canvas, 29 × 24″, Clifton Anderson Collection.

Cassandra Howard was the wife of George Howard, a prosperous dry goods merchant in Montgomery County, Kentucky. She met him during a visit to Mt. Sterling from her native Delaware in 1806, at which time he was thirty and she sixteen. Cassandra and George had three children, Anne Sudduth and Elizabeth Barnes, and a son, Henry Clay Howard, named for the statesman.

THOMAS JEFFERSON WRIGHT was born in Montgomery County, Kentucky, to Israel Wright, a Welsh tailor, and his wife, Susannah Ferguson. His precocious talents came to the attention of the Howard family of Mt. Sterling, several of whom he was to paint. With their help he journeyed to Lexington in 1822 to meet Matthew Harris Jouett, at which time he asked for a letter of introduction to Thomas Sully in Philadelphia. Jouett obliged by writing to Sully that the "kindness with which you have heretofore honored my letters and commissions of every sort leaves but little ground to distrust the entire success of this application in favor of my young friend Jefferson Wright to whose acquaintance I hereby entreat you to be introduced. You will find Mr. W. amiable modest and entirely upon the reserve. He visits Phila with the view to avail himself of the helps, of the academy and the artists in portrait painting. Of his abilities I cannot speak decisively—They are reputed promising in this country and I believe them to be so. By his enthusiasm and industry he has become enabled to visit your city and with prospects of a tolerably long stay—Altho entirely devoid of the graces of early learning—you will find him by no means destitute of those lights characteristic of a good mind attentive to the object of its pursuit." Sully did not seem to have had the same effect on Wright as he did on Joseph Bush and Oliver Frazer. Yet he is hardly deserving of Pauline Pinckney's harsh critique that Wright's "portraiture is rather stiff and two-dimensional. If he actually studied under Sully there is no evidence of that training in his work." Wright often places his subjects in highly detailed settings, with elaborately swagged drapery, landscape views, and atmospheric cloud formations. His precise detail is also apparent in the use of a small baroque cartouche he painted at the bottom of his portrait of Thomas Gibson Howard to contain his signature. The Howard family gave Wright several commissions upon his return from Philadelphia. Of those, the portrait of Cassandra Howard displays many of his charming effects, seen in her bold gaze and diaphanous shawl posed before a curtain pulled back to the left (Fig. 151). After painting the Howards, Wright made an itinerant excursion to Virginia in 1832. His brother, Benjamin Franklin Wright, a cabinetmaker, had gone to Texas in the 1830s, where the artist had joined him by 1837. He advertised in the Houston paper that year and drew a commission from Sam Houston. His most notable Texas work is a portrait of Juan Seguín, a *Tejano* hero of the Texas Revolution with whom he was also one of the founders of the Masonic order in Texas. Wright saw action during the Mexican War as part of the Somervell expedition. He returned to Kentucky in 1845 to visit his family and contracted hepatitis in Louisville, where he died and is buried.

Archives: APS; collections: Duncan Tavern, MESDA, TexasSL, VMFA; Literature: Jones & Weber, Pennington (2008), Pinckney, Whitley.

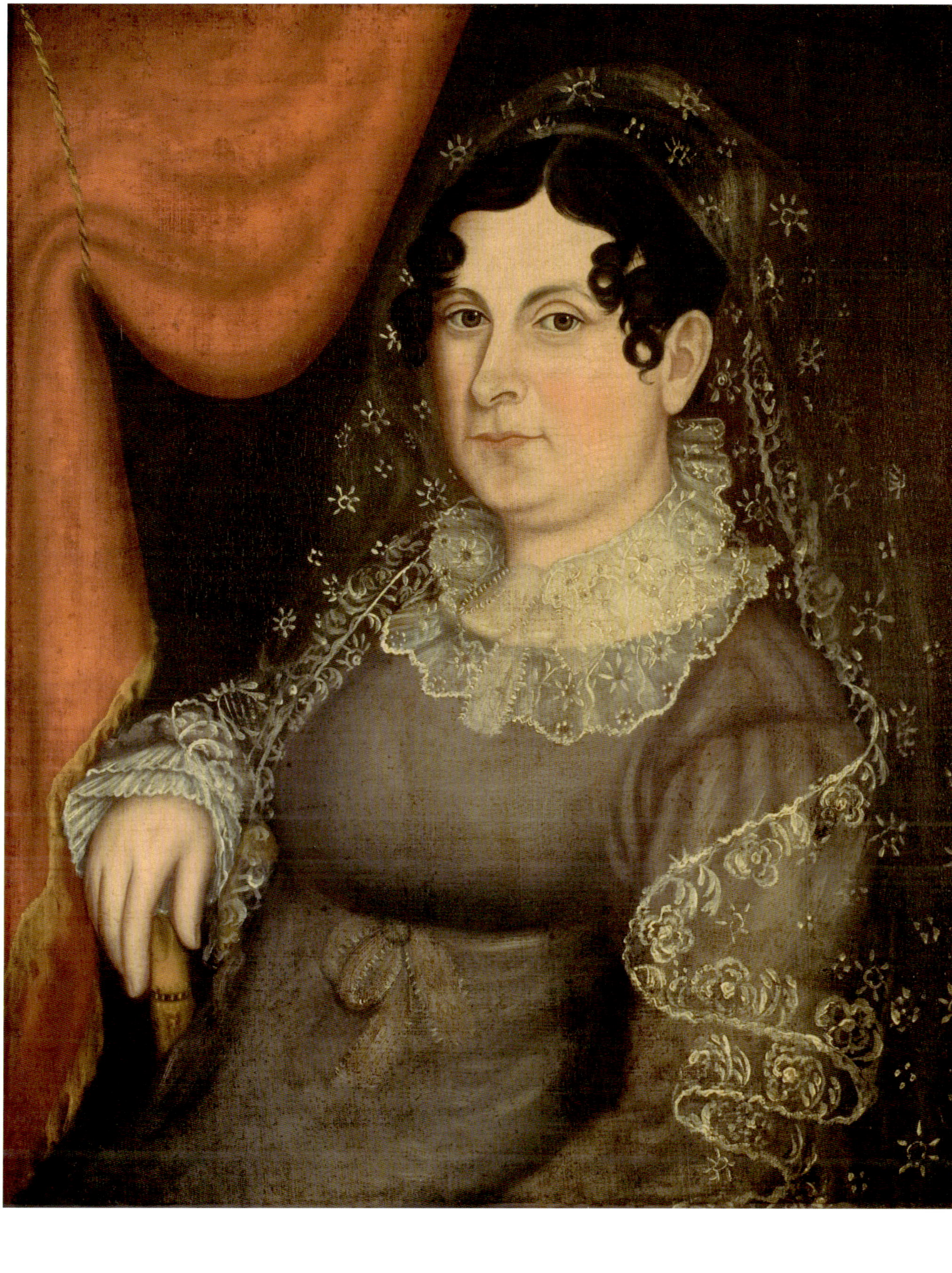

An Index of Artists in Edna Talbott Whitley's *Kentucky Ante-bellum Portraiture*

Although a large number of sources were consulted in the writing of this book, Edna Talbott Whitley's *Kentucky Ante-bellum Portraiture* needs to be singled out as pivotal to the study of portraiture in Kentucky and the Ohio River Valley. Whitley was born in Paris, Bourbon County, Kentucky, one of the oldest settlements in the Bluegrass. She was educated in the genteel tradition of home schools, which stressed the reading of classics, the practice of music and dance, and the acquisition of a strong moral, spiritual, and intellectual discipline. At the time of her birth, Bourbon County thought of itself as old, venerable, and resistant to change. The atmosphere in which she matured, married, and began her career as an amateur writer and antiquarian encouraged an almost religious devotion to the history of buildings, objects, and leading personalities from what was regarded as a golden era "before the war."

Her motivation may also be attributed to her mother, Sally Grimes Talbott, a founding member of the local Daughters of the American Revolution, whose aid Edna sought in rolling bandages for the Spanish-American War. Mrs. Talbott also collected antiques at a time when most locals thought of them as used furniture. In an interview with the *Lexington Herald Leader* in October 1972, Whitley said that "she bought back furniture that had been given to servants and from relatives who wanted golden oak. She collected five sideboards, one for each of her children, and stored them in the stable and basement" of her large Victorian house on Duncan Avenue.

Edna married a local attorney, Wade Hampton Whitley, whose family included several revered Confederate veterans. After his early death she taught piano and wrote various articles for local papers until she was inspired to undertake a project on Kentucky portraiture. In 1938 her friend and fellow Colonial Dame Katherine Stout Bradley of Georgetown, Kentucky, presented the historical activities committee of the state organization with a scrapbook of photographs of portraits. These photographs provided the basis for a much-needed and far more sweeping inventory of extant portraiture in the commonwealth than existed at the time.

In the preface to her book, Whitley stated that her goals were "threefold: the preservation of the known history of each painting, artist, portrait subject, which in the process of oral transmission, was in danger of becoming vaguer with successive generations; the preservation of photographs as insurance against complete loss, since most of the portraits were housed in private homes and thus subject to destruction by fire; the opportunity afforded for study of a number of works by known artists, at given periods of their productivity, as well as those of unknown painters who might be identified in the process" (vii). With this well-considered approach to artist, sitter, and object in mind, she began to collect information.

Although this process was driven by the genealogical interest in the sitters on the part of the Colonial Dames, who tracked down portraits and commissioned photographs, it soon became apparent that there was also a need for information on the artists themselves. To identify these portrait artists, their biographies, and their places of activity, Whitley consulted a vast range of sources. In downtown Paris she was able to read the complete record of the *Kentucky Citizen,* one of the first papers in the state, from whose pages she gleaned information from advertisements and notices of portrait services available. She also read all the published secondary sources, both national and regional, with particular attention to William Dunlap, Lewis Collins, and Charles Cist.

In the course of this study I also discovered that she had

access to the artist files of the Works Progress Administration, which were stored at the Louisville Public Library. During the depression the WPA hired people to abstract information from newspapers and write biographical accounts of local artists. It was from these files that she collected many of the anecdotes she reports as having been published in a certain paper on a certain day. While in Louisville she also worked at the Filson Club, reading archival material to enhance her biographies. In a letter to Mabel, the Filson librarian, on October 1, 1952, Whitley states that after nearly fifteen years she is "down to 'W' in my first draft, but of course there will be lots of revisions, corrections, etc. But I begin to feel some hope."

She worked at the Frick Art Reference Library in New York. Several times a year she would take the train north and stay at the Barbizon Hotel for Women so she could walk the few blocks to the Frick on Fifth Avenue. Helen Clay Frick and Dr. J. Hall Pleasants of Baltimore had been collecting photographs of southern portraits for more than twenty years, and these were carefully cataloged and stored on mounts with added information. Whitley's appreciation for the Frick was unbounded. "Without the pioneer work done in Kentucky by that Foundation," she told Justus Bier, the *Louisville Courier-Journal* art critic, "I doubt if the book would have been undertaken." Through the tedious method of verisimilitude of detail, Mrs. Whitley began to sort through the photographs, in search of likeness in like things. As a result of this work she was able to define and illustrate the work of more than 125 artists in Kentucky. At the back of the volume she published notes on over 600 portrait artists active in the region.

When *Kentucky Ante-bellum Portraiture* was published in an edition of one thousand volumes in 1956, Justus Bier, in the June 10 *Louisville Courier-Journal,* praised it as "a monumental work. It is a documentation of the most important phase in the early art life of a state where portraiture for a long time overshadowed all other types of art." After that publication, Edna Whitley continued to give lectures and write articles, and she published two directories of cabinetmakers in Kentucky, again gleaned from newspaper reading. At her eighty-fifth birthday celebration she said that "not having a purpose causes wrinkles in the soul."

On a personal note I can recall Edna Whitley as a fixture of my childhood, someone my grandmother would point out to me as a highly intelligent person who published books and whom I could call on and ask questions about Kentucky history if I would promise to be very nice and quiet (difficult for me). She was a very serious and formal person who was not especially fond of precocious children, as she made clear, but she did guide my reading and tolerated my enthusiasms. When I became a regional representative for the Archives of American Art in 1981, I went to Kentucky with the express purpose of doing an oral history with her. Being self-conscious about her amateur status, she was very reluctant to be taped, although she consented to let me sit with her in the afternoon and take notes on what she said. From those conversations came my first work on William Edward West and my increased appetite for portrait study.

It is now more than fifty years since the publication of *Kentucky Ante-bellum Portraiture,* and although there are no glaring errors in Whitley's work, there is more recent information to be incorporated into the biographical accounts. Furthermore, the efforts of the compilers of the Catalog of American Portraiture at the National Portrait Gallery have resulted in a much larger volume of visual material than Edna Whitley could ever have seen or consulted. It is to be hoped that building on her work only furthers her goal to perpetuate the lives and works of portrait artists who have given these lessons in likeness to illuminate an ever-receding past.

The following is a list of the artists she included in her biographical notes. Only those artists considered to be of note, as defined in my introduction, are included in the biographical section of the present study. In many instances Whitley included artists whose names turned up in city directories or newspaper advertisements, and for whom no extant works have been found. In the years since her publication several birth and death dates have been altered on the basis of new information. They are given here as published as yet another signpost for successive generations.

Alexander, Francis (1800–1881)
Allen, Thomas (in Louisville 1843/44)
Andrews, Eliphalet Fraser (1835–1915)
Armstrong, Arthur (1798–1851)
Aubrey, Jean (1810–1893)
Audubon, John James (1785–1851)
Audubon, John Woodhouse (1812–1862)
Bancroft, G. F. (ca. 1848)
Bancroft, Spencer T. (1828–1857)
Baumgardner, Peter (1834–post-1873)
Beard, James Henry (1812–1893)
Beck, George (1750–1815)
Bingham, George Caleb (1811–1879)
Boccasini, Rudolph (1885 receipt to Filson Club)
Bogle, James P. (1817–1873)
Boll, Nancy (Louisville, 1860)

Bradford, Alexander (1791–1827)
Bradford, John (177?–1824)
Brenner, C. C. (1838–1888)
Brown, Thomas (Louisville, 1860)
Brown, William Henry (1808–1882)
Buckley, Reuben H. (1814–ca. 1889)
Bush, Joseph Henry (1794–1865, in Louisville 1850s)
Campbell, Thomas (d. ca. 1851, in Louisville 1844–1851)
Carson, James (Louisville, 1844)
Clarke, Richard T. (1820–post-1867)
Cogswell, William F. (1819–1903)
Cooke, George (1793–1846)
Cooper, Washington Bogart (1802–1888)
Cooper, William Brown (1811–1890, in Louisville 1869–1870, 1877)
Copman, Pierce (Louisville, 1848)
Corwine, Aaron Houghton (1802–1830)
Craft, R. B. (pre-1839–post-1865)
Crump, Richard (Louisville, 1836–1841, 1844–1845, 1846–1852)
Curwin, J. (1837–post-1860, in Louisville 1860)
Davenport, Patrick Henry (1803–1890)
Dearborn, Samuel H. (pre-1800–post-1845)
Dodge, John Wood (1807–1893)
Douglas, Alonzo (ca. 1848)
Duncanson, Robert Scott (1821–1871)
Dury, George (1817–1894)
Duveneck, Frank (1848–1919)
Earle, Ralph Eleasar Whiteside (1788–1837)
Eaton, Joseph Oriel (1829–1875, Louisville, 1860)
Eckstein, F. J. (Louisville, 1851–1852)
Edwards, Clement R. (1820–1898)
Eichbaum, George Calder (1837–1919)
Elliott, Charles Loring (1812–1868)
Elrod, J. C. (ca. 1825–?, Louisville, 1860 dauguerreotypist)
Eshelman, A. (ca. 1826–post-1878)
Fahrenburg, Albert (Louisville, 1859–1860)
Falquet, Alexander (ca. 1856)
Farrer, Joseph (ca. 1821–post-1850)
Felt, John (Louisville, 1860)
Flagg, George Whiting (1816–1897)
Flagg, Jared B. (1920–1899)
Ford, Alexander (1820–post-1844)
Fourcade, Anarcharsis (1813–post-1860, Louisville, 1850s)
Fowler, Joseph (Louisville, 1850)
Fowler, Trevor Thomas (ca. 1829–post-1871)
Franca, Manuel Joaquim de (1808–1865)
Francis, John F. (1808–1888, Louisville, 1856)
Frankenstein, Godfrey Nikolaus (1820–1873)
Frankenstein, John Peter (1817–1881)
Frazer, Oliver (1808–1864)
Frye, George Wilhelm (1812–1872)
Funk, Francis (Louisville, 1860)
Fuqua, William J. (1839–1901)
Ganter, Daniel (ca. 1847)
Ganter, J. M. (ca. 1825–post-1857)
Garrett, John W. B. (ca. 1820–post-1857)
Gengembre, C. (1790–post-1850)
Goodard, Edwin F. (ca. 1800–1855)
Goodwin, J. B. (ca. 1845–1850)
Gorbut, William B. (Louisville, 1867–1868)
Gorham, John D. (ca. 1837–post-1865)
Goulding, Thomas (Louisville, 1843–1845)
Grimes, John (1799–1837)
Hankins, Cornelius (1863–1946)
Hansel, T. M. (Louisville, 1860)
Harding, Chester (1792–1866)
Hart, James M. (McDougall?) (1828–1901)
Haskins, Joseph (ca. 1818)
Heade, Martin Johnson (1819–1904)
Healey, George Peter Alexander (1813–1894)
Hervieu, Auguste (1814–1858)
Hicks, Thomas (1823–1890)
Hite, George Harrison (ca. 1835–1888)
Hobbs, J. W. (ca. 1860)
Hooper, Simon (ca. 1822)
Housel, T. M. (Louisville, 1860)
Huntington, Daniel (1816–1906)
Ingham, Charles Crowell (1796–1863)
Inman, Henry (1801–1846)
Irwine, Benoni (1840–1896)
Jackson, Moses (Louisville, 1844–1845)
Jarvis, Charles Wesley (1812–1868)
Jarvis, John Wesley (1780–1839)
Jenkins, P. O. (ca. 1818–post-1880)
Jenks, B. W. (Louisville, 1841–1842)
Jerome, Orien (Louisville, 1832)
Johnstone, William (ca. 1790–post-1860)
Jouett, Matthew Harris (1788–1827)
Kellogg, Miner Kilbourne (1814–1889)
King, Charles Bird (1785–1862)
Krementz, Joseph (Louisville, 1864–1865)
Kyle, Joseph (1815–1863)
Lambdin, George Cockran (1830–1896)
Lambdin, James Reid (1807–1889)
Leonard, S. (Louisville, 1842–1844)
Leonard, Samuel (ca. 1850)
Letton, John Wesley (ca. 1777–ca. 1845)

Letton, Ralph (1778–post-1840)
Locke, P. S. (ca. 1848)
Lockwood, Rembrandt (ca. 1840)
Lowery, H. (ca. 1860)
Lyon, Sidney S. (ca. 1806–post-1863)
Lyons, William (ca. 1826–1850)
Macey, Reuben J. A. (ca. 1830)
Marion, John C. (ca. 1822–ca. 1870)
Marrs, William R. (ca. 1859)
Marschall, Nicola (1829–1917)
Marsh, Peter (Louisville, 1840)
Marshall (? Montgomery Co.?)
Mason, Joseph R. (1807–1883)
Mayr, Christian (1805–1851)
McAbee, John W. (Louisville, 1848–1849)
McCann, William Penn (1830–1906)
McDowell, Magdalen Harvie (1829–1918)
McGarvey, John (ca. 1821–post-1850)
Mentelle, Waldemard (1769–1846)
Merine, J. C. (Louisville, 1848)
Merritt, John (ca. 1860)
Miller, Alfred Jacob (1810–1874)
Miller, Charles G. (ca. 1800–post-1852)
Moise, Theodore Sidney (1806–1883)
Moody, F. B. (ca. 1827–post-1870)
Moore, Rob? Bob? (ca. 1816–1869)
Morgan, Louis (1806–1851)
Morgan, Thomas W. (Louisville, 1838–1839)
Morton, Edmund (ca. 1861)
Mosler, Henry (1841–1920)
Moss, John (ca. 1860)
Myers, Daniel (Louisville, 1822)
Neagle, John (1796–1865)
Noble, Thomas Satterwhite (1835–1907)
Owen, David Dale (1807–1860)
Park, Asa (17?–1827)
Parker, C. R. (1799–1849)
Paul, Jeremiah, Jr. (Louisville, 1819)
Pering, Cornelius (1806–1881)
Perkins, S. (ca. 1860)
Peters, Alexander L. (1799–1835)
Phul, Anna Maria Von (1786–1823)
Poindexter, James Thomas (1832–1891)
Porter, W. S. (1824–post-1860)
Price, Samuel Woodson (1828–1918)
Rafinesque, Constantine Samuel (1783–1840)
Redin, William H., Jr. (1824–post-1865)
Reinhart, Benjamin Franklin (1829–1885)
Revenaugh, Aurelious O. (1840–1908)
Rive, Lean (Louisville, 1852–1853)
Robinson, Josiah (1805–post-1860)
Rogers, Williamson S. (1838–1864)
Rubel, Jessie (Louisville, 1866–1867)
St. Leger, Lewis (Louisville, 1845–1846)
Saunders, Xantippe (1837–1922)
Sawyer, Samuel T. (Louisville, 1841)
Shackelford, William (1815–post-1878)
Smith, A. C. (1815–post-1860)
Smith, Allan, Jr. (1810–1890)
Soule Family (Charles Sr., 1809–1869; Charles Jr., 1835–1897; Clara, 1834–1902; Olivia, 1844–1908)
Spence, Samuel S. (Louisville, 1840)
Starr, J. B. (Louisville, 1845–1846)
Strauss, Raphael (1830–1901)
Stuart, Charles P. (ca. 1870)
Stuart, James Reeve (1834–1915)
Tarbell, Ruth Shute (ca. 1803–1882)
Towell, T. (ca. 1834)
Troye, Edward C. De (1808–1874)
Turner, J. T. (ca. 1816–1817)
Vaughn, Charles A. (ca. 1844–1845)
Venable, John W. (ca. 1836–1851)
Ver Bryck, William Francis (1823–1899)
Vogel, M. (Louisville, 1845–1846)
Vorhees, James Paxton (1855–post-1900)
Warrell, James (ca. 1780–1854)
Webber, Charles T. (1825–1910)
West, John Brown (1786–post-1858)
West, William Edward (1788–1857)
West Family, including mythic "first portraitist"
Whipple, H. S. G. (Louisville, 1851–1852)
Whitelock, E. P. (Louisville, 1860)
Wise, James M. (Louisville, 1842)
Wright, Thoams Jefferson (1798–1845)
Wyant, Alexander Helwig (1836–1892)

NOTES

Introduction

1. Michael Quick, *American Portraiture in the Grand Manner: 1720–1920* (Los Angeles: Los Angeles County Museum of Art, 1981), 11.

2. Carrie Rebora Barratt and Ellen G. Miles, *Gilbert Stuart* (New York: Metropolitan Museum of Art, 2004), 9.

3. For a discussion of the duality of portraiture and family history, see Joanna Woodall, ed., *Portraiture: Facing the Subject* (Manchester: Manchester University Press, 1997).

4. Booth Tarkington, *Some Old Portraits: A Book about Art and Human Beings* (New York: Doubleday, 1939), 9.

5. Richard Brilliant, *Portraiture* (Cambridge, Mass.: Harvard University Press, 1991), 141.

6. Ibid.

7. Clay Lancaster, *Antebellum Architecture of Kentucky* (Lexington: University Press of Kentucky, 1991), 120–130.

8. For a discussion of the effect of the Romantic movement on painting style, see William Vaughan, *Romantic Art* (New York: Oxford University Press, 1978), 9–26.

9. Jean Lipman and Alice Winchester, *The Flowering of American Folk Art, 1776–1876* (New York: Viking in cooperation with the Whitney Museum of American Art, 1974), 8.

10. Oliver W. Larkin, *Art and Life in America,* rev. ed. (New York: Holt, Rinehart and Winston, 1960), 148.

1802–1835: Westward Movement, Eastern Instruction

1. Edna Talbott Whitley and Mary Spear Van Meter, interview by Estill Curtis Pennington, June 28–July 2, 1981, on file at the Archives of American Art, Smithsonian Institution, Washington, D.C. (hereafter cited as AAA).

2. For further information on Marquis Calmes, see John B. Winn Jr., "Biography of General Marquis Calmes and a Genealogy of the Calmes Family," unpublished typescript, microfilm, The Filson Historical Society, Louisville, Kentucky.

3. Linda Crocker Simmons, *Jacob Frymire: American Limner* (Washington, D.C.: Corcoran Gallery of Art, 1975), entries 22–24.

4. John James Audubon, *Ornithological Biography, or An Account of the Habits of the Birds of the United States of America* (Philadelphia: E. L. Carey and A. Hart, 1832), 30.

5. Richard Rhodes, *John James Audubon: The Making of an American* (New York: Knopf, 2004), 54.

6. Ibid., 140–143, 122; John James Audubon, *Delineations of American Scenery and Character* (New York: G. A. Baker & Co., 1926), 241.

7. Rhodes, *John James Audubon,* 144.

8. John Francis McDermott, "Likenesses by Audubon," *Antiques* 67 (June 1955): 499.

9. Ibid., 501. I have examined the drawing of Corwine included in McDermott's essay and now in a private collection in Anderson County, Kentucky. It appears to have been drawn on thick writing paper with two folds, left and right, indicating it may have been mailed at some point. There is a small portion of paper missing at the top right-hand corner.

10. John James Audubon, *The Journal of John James Audubon Made during His Trip to New Orleans, 1820–1821,* ed. Howard Corning (Boston: The Club of Odd Volumes, 1929), 12. Hereafter cited as *New Orleans Journal.*

11. Audubon, *Ornithological Biography,* 31.

12. Ibid., 239.

13. Ibid., 290–295; Audubon, *Delineations,* 241–245, quotation 241.

14. Audubon, *Ornithological Biography,* 503.

15. Audubon, *Delineations,* 117–123.

16. Quoted in Samuel Woodson Price, *Old Masters of the Bluegrass: Jouett, Bush, Grimes, Frazer, Morgan, Hart,* Filson Club Publications, no. 17 (Louisville, Ky.: J. P. Morton and Co., 1902), 20–21. The story of Jouett's father referring to him as a "damned sign painter" was told to Samuel Woodson Price by Richard Jouett Menefee, the artist's grandson.

17. Edna Talbott Whitley, *Kentucky Ante-bellum Portraiture* (Paris, Ky.: The National Society of the Colonial Dames of America in the Commonwealth of Kentucky, 1956), 703.

18. Matthew Harris Jouett, "Rude hints & observations, from repeated Conversations with Gilbert Stuart, Esqr. In the months of July, August, September, & Oct. 1816 under whose patronage and care I was for the time," in William Barrow Floyd, *Jouett-Bush-Frazer: Early Kentucky Artists* (Lexington, Ky.: privately printed, 1968), 170.

19. Nancy Snell Griffith, comp., *Humor of the Old Southwest: An Annotated Bibliography of Primary and Secondary Sources* (New York: Greenwood Press, 1989), n.p.

20. Jouett, "Rude hints," 169–177, quotations 169. In an interview I conducted on June 27, 1981, William Barrow Floyd stated that he had personal knowledge of the manuscript, which at one time was in the possession of the family with whose current generation he had contact, but that it was lost. This manuscript is one of the great missing treasures of primary material in American art studies, its actual fate a subject of considerable speculation. Here is the most likely scenario: Charles Henry Hart first reported the document's existence in an article he published on Jouett in *Harper's Magazine* in May 1899. Hart had been in contact with Richard Jouett Menefee, the keeper of his grandfather's heritage, to secure a Jouett work for the 1893 World's Columbian Exposition in Chicago, and Menefee is said to have lent Hart several documents, which were not returned after Menefee's death the same year. The document is next reported to have been in the possession of John Hill Morgan of New York, who published it as an appendix to his 1939 publication on Gilbert Stuart. Morgan states that Hart bought the manuscript from Mrs. Richard H. Menefee, the artist's daughter (which is open to question considering the veneration with which both she and her son held the portraitist), that Hart's widow sold it to the collector Harry MacNeil Bland of New York, and that it was Bland who allowed Morgan access to the manuscript. There is a typescript of Jouett's "Rude hints" in the Frick Art Reference Library. William Barrow Floyd, interview by Estill Curtis Pennington, June 27, 1981; Charles Henry Hart, "Kentucky's Master-Painter Matthew Harris Jouett, 1788–1827," *Harper's New Monthly Magazine* 98 (May 1899): 914–921; John Hill Morgan, *Gilbert Stuart and His Pupils* (New York: New-York Historical Society, 1939), 81–93.

21. Jouett, "Rude hints," 169, 170, 172.

22. Ibid., 175, 170, 177, 171, 169.

23. Ibid., 169, 173.

24. Ibid., 170, 171.

25. Ibid., 171,172, 177–178.

26. Ibid., 177.

27. Ibid.

28. James Thomas Flexner, *The Light of Distant Skies, 1760–1835* (New York: Harcourt, Brace, 1954), 204.

29. Floyd, *Jouett-Bush-Frazer,* 11.

30. Green Clay to Sidney Payne Clay, September 30, 1818, Filson Historical Society.

31. E. A. Jonas, *Matthew Harris Jouett, Kentucky Portrait Painter (1787–1827)* (Louisville, Ky.: J. B. Speed Memorial Art Museum, 1938), 69.

32. Lowell H. Harrison and James C. Klotter, *A New History of Kentucky* (Lexington: University Press of Kentucky, 1997), 129–130.

33. See Estill Curtis Pennington, *William Edward West, 1788–1857: Kentucky Painter* (Washington, D.C.: National Portrait Gallery, 1985), 54–55.

34. The original letter from Sophia Maria Michau Robinson to Dr. Antoine Saugraine was included in H. Fouré-Selter, trans., *L'Odyssée américaine d'une famille française [par] le docteur Antoine Saugraine; étude suivie de manuscrits inédits et de la correspondance de Sophie Michau Robinson* (Baltimore: Johns Hopkins Press, 1936). The quotation is taken from an English translation provided by Samuel Wilson, a distinguished New Orleans architect and antiquarian. Mrs. Wilson owned portraits of her Latrobe ancestors, and when they visited the exhibition William Edward West, Kentucky Painter at the Lauren Rogers Museum, Laurel, Mississippi, in July 1985, they brought me the translation of the letter and talked to me at length about West's career.

35. Matthew Harris Jouett to Lawrence Levy, February 1823, AAA.

36. Floyd, *Jouett-Bush-Frazer,* 83–124.

37. Estill Curtis Pennington, *Messengers of Style: Itinerancy and Taste in Southern Portraiture, 1784–1867* (Greenville, S.C.: Greenville County Museum of Art, 1993).

38. Leah Lipton, *A Truthful Likeness: Chester Harding and His Portraits* (Washington, D.C.: National Portrait Gallery, 1985).

39. Chester Harding, *My Egotistography* (Cambridge, Mass.: John Wilson and Son, 1866), 31–32.

40. Ibid., 32.

41. Ibid., 33–34.

42. Ibid., 34, 35.

43. Ibid., 36.

44. For an account of Bingham's encounter with Harding, see Leah Lipton, "Chester Harding and the Life Portraits of Daniel Boone," *American Art Journal* 16 (Summer 1984): 9–10; see also Leah Lipton, "New Discoveries in American Art: George Caleb Bingham in the Studio of Chester Harding, Franklin, Missouri, 1820," ed. Jayne A. Kuchna, *American Art Journal* 16 (Summer 1984): 90–91.

45. Lipton, *A Truthful Likeness,* 56.

46. Frances Trollope, *Domestic Manners of the Americans,* ed. Donald Smalley (New York: Knopf, 1949), 394.

47. Lewis Collins, *History of Kentucky,* 2 vols. (Louisville: John P. Morton and Co., 1924), 2:579; the *Inquisitor* is quoted in Mary Sayre Haverstock et al., comps. and eds., *Artists in Ohio, 1787–1900: A Biographical Dictionary* (Kent, Ohio: Kent State University Press, 2000), 185; Sully is quoted in Edward H. Dwight, "Aaron Houghton Corwine: Cincinnati Artist," *Antiques* 67 (June 1955): 503.

48. B. Drake and E. D. Mansfield, *Cincinnati in 1826* (Cincinnati: Morgan, Lodge and Fisher, 1827), 88.

49. Whitley, *Kentucky Ante-bellum Portraiture,* 646.

50. Jan Seidler Ramirez, "Hiram Powers," in Kathryn Greenthal, Paula M. Kozol, and Jan Seidler Ramirez, *American Figurative Sculpture in the Museum of Fine Arts, Boston* (Boston: The Museum, 1986), 31.

51. Dwight, "Aaron Houghton Corwine," 503.

52. Harold E. Dickson, *John Wesley Jarvis, American Painter, 1780–1840* (New York: New-York Historical Society, 1949), 223.

53. John Wesley Jarvis to Richea Etting, November 11, 1820, Historical Society of Pennsylvania, typescript copy in curatorial files of Filson Historical Society.

54. Ibid. The Panic of 1819 is discussed in Harrison and Klotter, *New History of Kentucky,* 97.

55. Audubon, *New Orleans Journal,* 112.

56. Audubon, *Ornithological Biography,* 410–414, quotations 410, 411.

57. Ibid., 410, 413; Audubon, *New Orleans Journal,* 152, 117, 118.

58. John Thornton Posey, "Rascality Revisited: In Defense of General James Wilkinson," *Filson Club Historical Quarterly* 74 (Fall 2000): 309–352, quotation 313.

59. James Wilkinson, *Memoirs of My Own Times,* 3 vols. (Philadelphia: Abraham Small, 1816), 1:821.

60. Posey, "Rascality Revisited."

61. West narrative, undated, William Edward West Papers, AAA. It was published, with annotations, in Estill Curtis Pennington, "Painting Lord Byron: An Account by William Edward West," *Archives of American Art Journal* 24 (1984): 16–21.

62. Pennington, "Painting Lord Byron," 19.

63. Ibid.

64. Ibid., 20.

65. See Washington Irving, *A History of New York from the Beginning of the World to the End of the Dutch Dynasty by Diedrich Knickerbocker,* rev. ed. (New York: G. P. Putnam's Sons, 1848); John Filson, *The Discovery, Settlement, and Present State of Kentucke* (Wilmington, Del.: James Adams, 1784). Irving's writings were the first by an American to enjoy great popularity in England.

66. Pennington, "Painting Lord Byron," 20. See also John Clubbe, *Byron's Natural Man: Daniel Boone and Kentucky* (Lexington, Ky.: King Library Press, 1982).

67. Pennington, "Painting Lord Byron," 20.

68. Pennington, *William Edward West,* 108.

69. John Neagle to John Sartain, November 15, 1842, John Neagle Miscellaneous Papers, FHS.

70. Carol Damon Andrews, "John Ritto Penniman (1782–1841), an Ingenious New England Artist," *Antiques* (July 1981): 147. Estill Curtis Pennington, "The Larger World of Asa Park," in James McCormick et al., *A Boston Painter in Kentucky: Asa Park (1790–1827)* (Georgetown, Ky.: Georgetown College Art Department and Georgetown & Scott County Museum, 2006), 14.

71. James McCormick, "Asa Park (1790–1827)," in McCormick et al., *A Boston Painter in Kentucky,* 20–35.

72. Whitley, *Kentucky Ante-bellum Portraiture,* 634. See also Estill Curtis Pennington, *Kentucky: The Master Painters from the Frontier Era to the Great Depression* ([Paris, Ky.:] Cane Ridge Publishing House, 2008), 15. Additional information on the artist's life was supplied by Nancy Katherine Evans Meng, a descendant of the Prewitt family, including the artist's relationship to the family, in correspondence and a conversation with me, May 2, 2008.

73. Price, *Old Masters of the Bluegrass,* 90.

74. Quoted ibid., 99. In his footnotes, Floyd quotes passages of Frazer's letters that were published in Price's *Old Masters of the Bluegrass* (1902), noting that Price had access to original material that was no longer available. However, several of Frazer's letters are included in the collections of FHS and the University of Kentucky Special Collections; Floyd, *Jouett-Bush-Frazer,* 194, n. 2.

75. Quoted in Price, *Old Masters of the Bluegrass,* 99, and Floyd, *Jouett-Bush-Frazer,* 126.

76. Quoted in Price, *Old Masters of the Bluegrass,* 102.

77. Floyd, *Jouett-Bush-Frazer,* 139.

78. Catherine Waller Carson to William and Catharine Waller, January 9, 1851, Carson Family Papers, FHS.

79. Drake and Mansfield, *Cincinnati in 1826,* 88–89.

80. Cincinnati Art Museum, *The Golden Age: Cincinnati Painters of the Nineteenth Century Represented in the Cincinnati Art Museum* (Cincinnati: Cincinnati Art Museum, 1979), 35–36.

81. H. A. Rattermann, ed., *The German Pioneer,* typescript translation from the German, originally published in Cincinnati, 1882–1883, in The Filson Historical Society Library.

82. John Frankenstein, *American Art: Its Awful Altitude: A Satire* (Cincinnati, 1864), n.p.

83. Rattermann, *The German Pioneer,* 53.

84. John Peter Frankenstein, "Niagara," *Harper's New Monthly Magazine* 7 (August 1853): 289–306.

85. Cincinnati Art Museum, *The Golden Age,* 73–74.

86. One of the most difficult aspects of portraiture for the nineteenth-century itinerant artist was the time required for drying. Accordingly, Sully spent a great deal of time discussing various macguilp (now more commonly spelled meglip) recipes for blending glazing mediums so that the finished portrait could easily be taken from the studio at the end of a session without damage. Thomas Sully, *Hints to Young Painters: A Historic Treatise on the Color, Expression, and Painting Techniques of American Artists of the Colonial and Federal Periods* (New York: Reinhold Publishing Corp., 1965), 21.

87. Ibid., 9.

88. Ibid., 6; Jesse Poesch, *The Art of the Old South: Painting, Sculpture, Architecture, and the Products of Craftsmen, 1560–1860* (New York: Knopf, 1983), 263.

89. Sully, *Hints to Young Painters,* 10.

90. Ibid., 31.

1835–1865: The Invention of Photography and the Coming of War

1. Andrew J. Cosentino, *The Paintings of Charles Bird King (1785–1862)* (Washington, D.C.: Smithsonian Institution Press for the National Collection of Fine Arts, 1977), 87.

2. William Dunlap, *A History of the Rise and Progress of the Arts of Design in the United States,* ed. Rita Weiss. 2 vols. (1834; rept., New York: Dover Publications, 1969), 2:262.

3. For an example of the use of mezzotints as anatomical sources in southern portraiture, see Martha Severns, "Jeremiah Theus of Charleston: Plagiarist or Pundit?" *Southern Quarterly* 24 (Fall–Winter 1985): 56–70.

4. E. A. Jonas, *Matthew Harris Jouett, Kentucky Portrait Painter (1787–1827)* (Louisville, Ky.: J. B. Speed Memorial Museum, 1938), 115–118.

5. This exchange can be found in the FHS curatorial files.

6. Robert Bishop, *Folk Painters of America* (1979; rept., New York: Greenwich House, 1983), 11.

7. John Michael Vlach, *Plain Painters: Making Sense of American Folk Art* (Washington, D.C.: Smithsonian Institution Press, 1988), xv.

8. For a discussion of the Whig Party in the larger context of American political history, see Richard Hofstadter, *Anti-Intellectualism in American Life* (New York: Knopf, 1963); see also Michael F. Holt, *The Rise and Fall of the American Whig Party* (New York: Oxford University Press, 1999).

9. Robert W. Torchia, *John Neagle: Philadelphia Portrait Painter* (Philadelphia: Historical Society of Pennsylvania, 1989), 100.

10. Quoted in Edna Talbott Whitley, *Kentucky Antebellum Portraiture* (Paris, Ky.: The National Society of the Colonial Dames of America in the Commonwealth of Kentucky, 1956), 655.

11. Clifford Amyx, "The Painters of Henry Clay as 'The Sage of Ashland,'" *Kentucky Review* 8 (Spring 1988): 74.

12. Quoted in Robert V. Remini, *Henry Clay: Statesman for the Union* (New York: Norton, 1991), 650.

13. Quoted in E. Merton Coulter, *The Civil War and Readjustment in Kentucky* (Chapel Hill: University of North Carolina Press, 1926), 178.

14. George P. A. Healy, *Reminiscences of a Portrait Painter* (Chicago: A. C. McClung and Co., 1894), 146–148.

15. Ibid., 149.

16. Marie Bigot, *Life of George P. A. Healy* (n.p., n.d.), 59.

17. Leah Lipton, *A Truthful Likeness: Chester Harding and His Portraits* (Washington, DC: National Portrait Gallery, 1985), 119.

18. Remini, *Henry Clay,* 780.

19. The most detailed account of Stowe's life and works is in Cindy Weinstein, *The Cambridge Companion to Harriet Beecher Stowe* (Cambridge: Cambridge University Press, 2004).

20. Harriet Beecher Stowe, *A Key to Uncle Tom's Cabin* (Boston: J. P. Jewett & Co., 1853), 22.

21. J. Winston Coleman, *Mrs. Stowe: Kentucky and Uncle Tom's Cabin* (Harrogate, Tenn.: Department of Lincolniana, Lincoln Memorial University, 1946), 5.

22. Joseph D. Ketner, *The Emergence of the African-American Artist: Robert S. Duncanson: 1821–1872* (Columbia: University of Missouri Press, 1993).

23. Ibid., 47.

24. Quoted ibid., 111.

25. E. Maurice Bloch, *The Paintings of George Caleb Bingham: A Catalogue Raisonné* (Columbia: University of Missouri Press, 1986), 133–134.

26. Nancy Rash, *The Paintings and Politics of George Caleb Bingham* (New Haven: Yale University Press, 1991), 1.

27. Hennig Cohen and William B. Dillingham, eds., *Humor of the Old Southwest,* 3rd ed. (Athens: University of Georgia Press, 1994), xvi–xvii.

28. Cohen and Dillingham, eds., *Humor of the Old Southwest,* 2nd ed. (Athens: University of Georgia Press, 1975), xiv.

29. John Filson, *The Discovery, Settlement, and Present State of Kentucke* (Wilmington, Del.: James Adams, 1784), 49–53.

30. E. Maurice Bloch, *George Caleb Bingham,* vol. 1, *The Evolution of an Artist* (Berkeley: University of California Press, 1967), 143.

31. George H. Genzmer, "George Caleb Bingham," in *Dictionary of American Biography,* ed. Allen Johnson (New York: Charles Scribner's Sons, 1929), 275.

32. George Caleb Bingham to J. S. Rollins, May 16, 1861, in "Letters of George Caleb Bingham to James S. Rollins, Part 4," ed. C. B. Rollins, *Missouri Historical Review* 32 (July 1938): 515.

33. Patricia Hills, "Painting Race: Eastman Johnson's Pictures of Slaves, Ex-Slaves, and Freedmen," in *Eastman Johnson: Painting America,* ed. Teresa A. Carbone (New York: Brooklyn Museum of Art, 1999); Linda Nochlin, *Realism* (Harmondsworth: Penguin, 1971), 34.

34. Hills, "Painting Race," 126.

35. See John Davis, "Eastman Johnson's 'Negro Life at the South' and Urban Slavery in Washington, D.C.," *Art Bulletin* 80 (March 1998): 67–92.

36. Hills, "Painting Race," 130.

37. Clement Eaton, *The Mind of the Old South* (Baton Rouge: Louisiana State University Press, 1964), 181.

38. Quoted in Coulter, *The Civil War and Readjustment in Kentucky,* 39.

39. Thomas D. Clark, *A History of Kentucky* (1937; rept., Ashland, Ky.: Jesse Stuart Foundation, 1992), 384.

40. Thomas M. House and Joe Nickell, "Guide to Nineteenth Century Lexington Photographers," manuscript, Margaret I. King Library, University of Kentucky, Lexington.

41. Elizabeth Broun, "Director's Choice: Interior with Portraits, Thomas LeClear," Smithsonian American Art Museum, http://americanart.si.edu/multimedia/tours/directors/leclear/index3.html.

42. William Barrow Floyd, *Jouett-Bush-Frazer: Early Kentucky Artists* (Lexington, Ky.: Privately printed, 1968), 119; R. T. Durrett, preface to Samuel Woodson Price, *Old Masters of the Bluegrass: Jouett, Bush, Grimes, Frazer, Morgan, Hart,* Filson Club Publications, no. 17 (Louisville, Ky.: J. P. Morton and Co., 1902), v–xiii.

43. Cincinnati Art Museum, *The Golden Age: Cincinnati Painters of the Nineteenth Century Represented in the Cincinnati Art Museum* (Cincinnati: Cincinnati Art Museum, 1979), 35.

44. James C. Kelly, "Portrait Painting in Tennessee," *Tennessee Historical Quarterly* 46 (Winter 1987): 193–285.

45. Minerva Cook diary, photocopy, Mississippi Department of History and Archives, Jackson, Mississippi.

46. Biographical information on James Thomas Poindexter comes from the curatorial files of the Evansville, Indiana, Museum of Art, and from conversations with Mary McNamee Bower, Curator of Art there.

47. Lowell H. Harrison and James C. Klotter, *A New History of Kentucky* (Lexington: University Press of Kentucky, 1997), 216, 215.

48. Coulter, *The Civil War and Readjustment in Kentucky,* 439.

49. Robert L. Kincaid, *Joshua Fry Speed, Lincoln's Most Intimate Friend* (Harrogate, Tenn.: Department of Lincolniana, Lincoln Memorial University, 1943), 33, n. 2.

50. Ibid., 10.

51. James J. Holmberg, "Joshua Fry Speed," in *The Encyclopedia of Louisville,* ed. John E. Kleber (Lexington: University Press of Kentucky, 2001), 843–844.

52. Kincaid, *Joshua Fry Speed,* 10.

53. In *The Intimate World of Abraham Lincoln* (New York: Free Press, 2005), 126, the clinical psychologist C. A. Tripp, an associate of the Kinsey Institute at Indiana University in Bloomington, speculated that Lincoln began "an intense and ongoing homosexual relationship" with Speed, a conjecture based upon Tripp's analysis of published letters and accounts. Though sharing beds during brief stays in homes and hostelries was common in the era, sharing a bed with the same man in a domestic arrangement for several years would have been most unusual. Tripp's use of the term "homosexual" should be considered anachronistic, a social construct devised in the late nineteenth century at the dawn of psychoanalysis. For a balanced perspective on the subject, see Byrne Fone, *Homophobia: A History* (New York: Metropolitan Books, 2000), 271–281.

54. Julia A. Tevis, *Sixty Years in a School-Room*

(Cincinnati: Western Methodist Book Concern, 1878), 454.

55. Holmberg, "Joshua Fry Speed."

56. Joshua Speed to Abraham Lincoln, May 19, 1860, as quoted and cited in David Herbert Donald, *"We Are Lincoln Men": Abraham Lincoln and His Friends* (New York: Simon and Schuster, 2003), 55.

57. Holmberg, "Joshua Fry Speed."

58. Curatorial files, Filson Historical Society.

59. Julia Henning to R. C. B. Thruston, curatorial files, FHS. For the Henning family genealogy, see Charles P. Stratton, "Henning and Duke Families of Louisville," photocopied typescript dated 1983 on file in the Kentucky Historical Society genealogical collection.

1865–1920: Exhibitions, Collecting, and International Trends

1. "Freedmen's Bureau" in *The Kentucky Encyclopedia,* ed. John E. Kleber (Lexington: University Press of Kentucky, 1992), 356–357.

2. Arthur F. Jones and Bruce Weber, *The Kentucky Painter: From the Frontier Era to the Great War: Exhibition, January 25–March 15, 1981* (Lexington: University of Kentucky Art Museum, 1981), p. 72.

3. Albert Boime, "Burgoo and Bourgeois: Thomas Noble's Images of Black People," in James D. Birchfield, Albert Boime, and William J. Hennessey, *Thomas Satterwhite Noble, 1835–1907* (Lexington: University of Kentucky Art Museum, 1988), 30.

4. Arnold Hauser, *The Social History of Art,* vol. 2 (New York: Knopf, 1952), 742–743.

5. Boime, "Burgoo and Bourgeois," 35; Martha Severns, *Greenville County Museum of Art: The Southern Collection* (New York: Hudson Hills Press, 1995), 76.

6. Toni Morrison's novel *Beloved* is based on this episode.

7. Boime, "Burgoo and Bourgeois," 55.

8. Ibid., 57.

9. Quoted in Cincinnati Art Museum, *The Golden Age: Cincinnati Painters of the Nineteenth Century Represented in the Cincinnati Art Museum* (Cincinnati: Cincinnati Art Museum, 1979), 25.

10. Louisville Industrial Exposition, *Catalogue of Paintings and Sculpture and of the Collections of the Department of Natural History* (Louisville, Ky.: John P. Morton and Co., 1874).

11. Ibid., 13, 22.

12. For luminism, see John Wilmerding, ed., *American Light: The Luminist Movement, 1850–1875; Paintings, Drawings, Photographs* (Washington, D.C.: National Gallery of Art, 1980).

13. Charles M. Kurtz, *Illustrated Catalog of the Art Gallery of the Southern Exposition, Louisville, Ky., August 16–October 25, 1884* (Louisville, Ky.: John P. Morton and Co, 1884), 2, 5.

14. Louisville Industrial Exposition, *Catalog of Paintings and Sculpture,* 5, 8.

15. Louisville Industrial Exposition, *Catalog of Paintings and Statuary* (Louisville, Ky.: John P. Morton & Co., 1877), 8.

16. Ibid.

17. Charles M. Kurtz, *Catalogue of Works of Art in the Art Building of the Southern Exposition at Louisville, Ky.* (Louisville, Ky.: John P. Morton & Co., 1883), 3. The holdings of the Archives of American Art, Smithsonian Institution, contain a large collection of Kurtz's personal papers, including a list of artists he chose for this exhibition.

18. Ibid., 38.

19. Ibid., 29.

20. Ibid., 51–52.

21. For a discussion of Brenner's work in the context of American tonalist painting, see Estill Curtis Pennington, *Subdued Hues: Mood and Scene in Southern Landscape Painting, 1865–1925* (Augusta, Ga.: Morris Museum of Art, 1999); and Peter Bermingham, *American Art in the Barbizon Mood* (Washington, D.C.: Smithsonian Press for the National Collection of Fine Arts, 1975).

22. Kurtz, *Catalogue of Works of Art,* 37.

23. Ibid., 77.

24. Kurtz, *Illustrated Catalogue* (1884), n.p.

25. For trends in the presentation of art at nineteenth-century expositions and world's fairs, see Tobin Andrews Sparling, *The Great Exhibition: A Question of Taste* (New Haven: Yale Center for British Art, 1982); and Carolyn Kinder Carr et al., *Revisiting the White City: American Art at the 1893 World's Fair* (Hanover, N.H.: University Press of New England, 1993).

26. Kurtz, *Illustrated Catalogue* (1884), "Introductory," 27, 35, 7, 8, 10, 13, 14, 18, 20, 23, 26, 27, 30, 32, 35, 93, 94.

27. Ibid., 64, 26, 32, 23, 93–99.

28. Ibid., 2, 49, 83, 82, 71, 48, 42, 19, 18, 34, 11, 28, 18.

29. Charles M. Kurtz, *Illustrated Catalogue of the Art Department of the Southern Exposition, Louisville, Ky., 1885* (Louisville, Ky.: John Morton & Co., 1885), 3, 4, 5.

30. Charles M. Kurtz, *Illustrated Catalogue of the Art Gallery of the Southern Exposition, Louisville, Ky., 1886* (Louisville: John Morton & Co., 1886) 20.

31. Ibid., 22.

32. For a history of the founding of the Speed Museum, see Ruth Cloudman, "A Brief History of the Collection" in Ruth Cloudman et al., *The Speed Art Museum: Highlights from the Collection* (New York: Merrell Publishers, 2007), 15–20.

33. Thomas D. Clark, "Reuben T. Durrett and His Kentuckiana Interest and Collection," *Filson Club History Quarterly* 56 (October 1982): 359.

34. Reuben Durrett to John J. Dickey, April 1, 1901, as cited ibid., 353.

35. Clark, "Durrett and His Kentuckiana Interest and Collection," 371.

36. Ibid., 365–366.

37. Bertram Wyatt-Brown, *Southern Honor: Ethics and Behavior in the Old South* (1982; rept., New York: Oxford University Press, 2008), xvi.

38. Harrison and Klotter, *A New History of Kentucky,* 217.

39. Ibid., 247.

40. Quoted in Edward M. Walters, "Reuben T. Durrett, the Durrett Collection, and the University of Chicago," *Filson Club History Quarterly* 56 (October 1982): 393.

41. William Dunlap, *A History of the Rise and Progress of the Arts of Design in the United States,* ed. Rita Weiss, 2 vols. (1834; rept., New York: Dover Publications, 1969), vol. 2, pt. 2, 319–320.

42. Charles Henry Hart, "Kentucky's Master-Painter Matthew Harris Jouett, 1788–1827," *Harper's New Monthly Magazine* 98 (May 1899): 914.

43. Ibid., 916–917.

44. Charles Henry Hart, "Jouett's Kentucky Children," *Harper's New Monthly Magazine* 101 (June 1900): 51.

45. Ibid., 53.

46. Reuben T. Durrett, preface to Samuel Woodson Price, *Old Masters of the Bluegrass: Jouett, Bush, Grimes, Frazer, Morgan, Hart,* Filson Club Publications, no. 17 (Louisville, Ky.: J. P. Morton and Co., 1902), xvii.

47. West family genealogy, typescript, William Edward West Papers, AAA.

48. Price, *Old Masters of the Bluegrass,* 4.

49. Ibid., 50.

50. Ibid., 8–9.

51. G. P. A. Healy to Richard J. Menefee, 12 October 1878, ibid., 42.

52. Edna Talbott Whitley, *Kentucky Ante-bellum Portraiture* (Paris, Ky.: The National Society of the Colonial Dames of America in the Commonwealth of Kentucky, 1956), 679.

53. Price, *Old Masters of the Bluegrass,* 77.

54. Ibid., 80; William Barrow Floyd, *Jouett-Bush-Frazer: Early Kentucky Artists* (Lexington, Ky.: privately printed, 1968), 113.

55. Price, *Old Masters of the Bluegrass,* 80, 79.

56. Ibid., 82.

57. Ibid., 137; quote from ibid, 139.

58. Ibid., 139.

59. Ibid., 118.

60. William S. Ward, *A Literary History of Kentucky* (Knoxville: University of Tennessee Press, 1988), 35.

61. Price, *Old Masters of the Bluegrass,* 92.

62. Ward, *A Literary History of Kentucky,* 36–37.

63. Julie Aronson, "American Impressionism and the Queen City," http://www.antiquesandfineart.com/articles/article.cfm?request=466.

64. Franklin Kelly, "Frank Duveneck, 1848–1919," in Franklin Kelly et al., *American Paintings of the Nineteeenth Century, Part I* (New York: Oxford University Press, 1996), 152.

65. Ibid.

66. Cincinnati Art Museum, *The Golden Age,* 25.

67. Bruce Weber and Arthur F. Jones, *The Kentucky Painter: From the Frontier Era to the Great War: Exhibition, January 25–March 15, 1981* (Lexington: University of Kentucky Art Museum, 1981), 38.

68. Ward, *A Literary History of Kentucky,* 97.

69. Ibid., 96.

70. Madison Cawein, *Myth and Romance; Being a Book of Verses* (New York: G. P. Putnam's Sons, 1899), 28.

71. Madeline C. Covi, "Madison Julius Cawein," in *The Encyclopedia of Louisville,* ed. John E. Kleber (Lexington: University Press of Kentucky, 2001), 167.

72. Quoted in Jones and Weber, *The Kentucky Painter,* 38.

73. Oliver Larkin, *Art and Life in America,* rev. ed. (New York: Holt, Rinehart and Winston, 1960), v.

74. Alfred H. Marks, "Hawthorne's Daguerreotypist: Scientist, Artist, Reformer," in Nathaniel Hawthorne, *The House of the Seven Gables,* ed. Seymour L. Gross (New York: Norton, 1967), 340.

75. Price, *Old Masters of the Bluegrass,* 3.

76. *New Orleans Times-Picayune,* February 13, 1842.

ABBREVIATIONS OF ARCHIVES AND COLLECTIONS

AAA: Archives of American Art, Smithsonian Institution, Washington, D.C.
Addison: Addison Gallery of American Art, Phillips Academy, Andover, Mass.
Alabama: Alabama Department of History and Archives, Montgomery.
Albright-Knox: Albright-Knox Art Gallery, Buffalo, N.Y.
Allen Hite: Allen R. Hite Art Institute, University of Louisville, Louisville, Ky.
APS: American Philosophical Society, Philadelphia.
ASC: Alabama Supreme Court, Montgomery.
Ashland: Ashland, the Henry Clay Home, Lexington, Ky.
Ball State: Ball State University, Muncie, Ind.
Baltimore: Baltimore Museum of Art, Baltimore.
BMA: Birmingham Museum of Art, Birmingham, Ala.
BMFA: Museum of Fine Arts, Boston.
Brennan: Brennan House, Louisville, Ky.
Brooklyn: Brooklyn Museum, Brooklyn, N.Y.
Butler: Butler Institute of American Art, Youngstown, Ohio.
CAA: Art Academy of Cincinnati, Cincinnati.
CAI: Chicago Art Institute, Chicago.
CAM: Cincinnati Art Museum, Cincinnati.
CHC: Cincinnati History Center, Cincinnati.
Cheekwood: Cheekwood Botanical Gardens and Museum of Art, Nashville.
CHM: Chicago Historical Museum, Chicago.
Clark County: Clark County Courthouse, Winchester, Ky.
CLS: Carnegie Library, Selma, Ala.
CMA: Cleveland Museum of Art, Cleveland.
Columbus: Columbus Museum of Art, Columbus, Ohio.
Corcoran: Corcoran Gallery of Art, Washington, D.C.
Crocker: Crocker Art Museum, Sacramento.
DAI: Dayton Art Institute, Dayton.
DHS: Detroit Historical Society, Detroit.
DIA: Detroit Institute of Art, Detroit.
Duncan Tavern: Duncan Tavern Historic Center, Paris, Ky.
Evansville: Evansville Museum of Art, History, and Science, Evansville, Ind.
Farmington: Farmington Historic Plantation, Louisville, Ky.
FHS: The Filson Historical Society, Louisville, Ky.
Ft. Wayne: Fort Wayne Museum of Art, Fort Wayne, Ind.
GC: Georgetown College, Georgetown, Ky.
Getty: J. Paul Getty Museum, Los Angeles.
Goldman: Goldman Archives, Cincinnati Art Gallery, Cincinnati.
Greenville: Greenville County Museum of Art, Greenville, S.C.
HAM: Historic Arkansas Museum, Little Rock.
Harvard: Houghton Library, Harvard University, Cambridge, Mass.
Heckscher: Heckscher Museum of Art, Huntington, N.Y.
HNOC: Historic New Orleans Collection, New Orleans.
Hospitalfield: The Patrick Allan Fraser of Hospitalfield Trust, Arboarth, Scotland
Howard: Howard University, Washington, D.C.
HPL: Huntsville Public Library, Huntsville, Ala.
HSWP: Historical Society of Western Pennsylvania, Pittsburgh
IDHA: Iowa Department of History and Archives, Des Moines
IHS: Indiana Historical Society, Indianapolis.
IMA: Indianapolis Museum of Art, Indianapolis.
InStateM: Indiana State Museum, Indianapolis.
ISH: Indiana State House, Indianapolis.
JC: Johnson Collection, Spartanburg, S.C.
KHS: Kentucky Historical Society, Frankfort.

KM: Kentucky Museum, Western Kentucky University, Bowling Green.

LAC: Los Angeles County Museum of Art, Los Angeles.

LC: Library of Congress, Washington, D.C.

LDS: Church of Jesus Christ of the Latter-Day Saints, Salt Lake City, Utah.

Locust Grove: Historic Locust Grove, Louisville, Ky.

LSM: Louisiana State Museum, New Orleans.

Maier: Maier Museum, Randolph Macon College, Lynchburg, Va.

Marshall: Marshall University, Huntington, W.Va.

Maysville: Kentucky Gateway Museum Center, Maysville, Ky.

MCM: Museum of the City of Mobile, Mobile, Ala.

MDHA: Mississippi Department of History and Archives, Jackson.

MESDA: Museum of Early Southern Decorative Arts, Winston-Salem, N.C.

Met: Metropolitan Museum of Art, New York.

MHS: Maryland Historical Society, Baltimore.

Midway: Midway College, Midway, Ky.

MMA: Morris Museum of Art, Augusta, Ga.

Mobile: Mobile Museum of Art, Mobile, Ala.

MOC: Museum of the Confederacy, Richmond, Va.

MoHS: Missouri Historical Society, Columbia.

Montgomery: Montgomery Museum of Fine Arts, Montgomery, Ala.

NAD: National Academy of Design, New York.

NAPL: New Albany Public Library, New Albany, Ind.

NCMA: North Carolina Museum of Art, Raleigh.

Nevada: Nevada Historical Society, Reno.

NGA: National Gallery of Art, Washington, D.C.

NOMA: New Orleans Museum of Art, New Orleans.

NPG: National Portrait Gallery, Washington, D.C.

NYHS: New-York Historical Society, New York.

NYSHA: New York State Historical Association, Cooperstown.

Oakland: Oakland Art Museum, Oakland, Calif.

OBH: Orlando Brown House, Frankfort, Ky.

Ogden: Ogden Museum of Southern Art, New Orleans.

OHS: Ohio Historical Society, Columbus.

OKH: My Old Kentucky Home State Park, Bardstown, Ky.

OSC: Old State Capitol, Jackson, Miss.

PAFA: Pennsylvania Academy of Fine Arts, Philadelphia.

PHS: Historical Society of Pennsylvania, Philadelphia.

Reading: Reading Public Museum, Reading, Pa.

RIHS: Rhode Island Historical Society, Providence.

SAM: Smithsonian American Art Museum, Washington, D.C.

Shelburne: Shelburne Museum, Shelburne, Vt.

Sheldon Swope: Sheldon Swope Museum of Art, Terra Haute, Ind.

Snite: Snite Museum, University of Notre Dame, Notre Dame, Ind.

Speed: Speed Art Museum, Louisville, Ky.

Springfield: Springfield Museum, Springfield, Ohio.

State: State Department, Washington, D.C.

St. Louis: St. Louis Museum of Art, St. Louis.

StLPL: St. Louis Public Library, St. Louis.

Sturdivant: Sturdivant Museum Association, Selma, Ala.

Taft: Taft Museum, Cincinnati.

Telfair: Telfair Museums, Savannah.

TexasSL: Texas State Library, Austin.

THS: Tennessee State Museum, Nashville.

Toledo: Toledo Museum of Art, Toledo.

Transylvania: Transylvania University, Lexington, Ky.

TSL: Tennessee State Library, Nashville.

TSM: Tennessee State Museum, Nashville.

TU: Tulane University, New Orleans.

UA: University of Alabama, Tuscaloosa.

UC: University of Cincinnati, Cincinnati.

UD: University of Delaware, Special Collections Library, Newark.

UKAM: University of Kentucky Art Museum, Lexington.

UKSC: University of Kentucky, Special Collections Library, Lexington.

USC: United States Capitol, Washington, D.C.

USNA: U.S. Naval Academy, Annapolis, Md.

Vanderbilt: Vanderbilt University, Nashville.

Vanderpoel: Vanderpoel Art Association, Chicago.

VHS: Virginia Historical Society, Richmond.

VMFA: Virginia Museum of Art, Richmond.

Waveland: Waveland State Historic Site, Lexington, Ky.

Weeden: Weeden House Museum, Selma, Ala.

West Point: U.S. Military Academy, West Point, N.Y.

WH: White House, Washington, D.C.

WHS: Wisconsin Historical Society, Madison.

Wood: Wood Art Gallery, Montpelier, Vt.

Yale: Yale University, New Haven, Conn.

BIBLIOGRAPHY

Primary Sources

Carson Family Papers, The Filson Historical Society.

Cooper, Washington Bogart. Accounts and Diary, 1837–1846. Manuscript, Tennessee State Library, Nashville.

Cooper, William. Monograph. Manuscript, Tennessee State Library, Nashville.

Harding, Chester. *My Egotistography.* Cambridge, Mass.: John Wilson and Son, 1866.

———. *A Sketch of Chester Harding, Artist: Drawn by His Own Hand.* Edited by Margaret E. White. Boston: Houghton, Mifflin, 1890.

Healy, George P. A. *Reminiscences of a Portrait Painter.* Chicago: A. C. McClung and Co., 1894.

Neagle, John, to John Sartain, November 15, 1842, John Neagle Miscellaneous Papers, The Filson Historical Society.

Newman, Willie Betty. Scrapbooks. Tennessee State Library, Nashville.

Tevis, Julia A. *Sixty Years in a School-Room.* Cincinnati: Western Methodist Book Concern, 1878.

Secondary Sources

Adams, E. Bryding, ed. *Made in Alabama: A State Legacy.* Birmingham: Birmingham Museum of Art, 1995.

Alabama Department of Archives and History. *Alabama Legislature Declares Nicola Marschall Designer First Confederate Flag.* Montgomery: Alabama Department of Archives and History, 1931.

Amyx, Clifford. "Henry Clay and the American State Portrait." *Kentucky Review* 10 (Fall 1990): 39–66.

———. "The Painters of Henry Clay as 'The Sage of Ashland.'" *Kentucky Review* 8 (Spring 1988): 69–80.

Andrews, Carol Damon. "John Ritto Penniman (1782–1841), an Ingenious New England Artist." *Antiques,* July 1981, 147.

Aron, Stephen. *American Confluence: The Missouri Frontier from Borderland to Border State.* Bloomington: Indiana University Press, 2006.

Aronson, Julie. "American Impressionism and the Queen City," http://www.antiquesandfineart.com/articles/article.cfm?request=466.

Aronson, Julie, ed., with contributions by Anita J. Ellis and Jennifer Howe. *The Cincinnati Wing: The Story of Art in the Queen City.* Cincinnati: Cincinnati Art Museum, 2003.

Ashbery, John. "The Indian Summer of Frank Duveneck." *Artnews* (April 1972): 27–29, 69–71.

Audubon, John James. *Delineations of American Scenery and Character.* New York: G. A. Baker & Co., 1926.

———. *The Journal of John James Audubon Made during His Trip to New Orleans, 1820–1821.* Edited by Howard Corning. Boston: The Club of Odd Volumes, 1929.

———. *Ornithological Biography, or An Account of the Habits of the Birds of the United States of America.* Philadelphia: E. L. Carey and A. Hart, 1832.

Ayres, William, ed. *Picturing History: American Painting, 1770–1930.* New York: Rizzoli in association with Fraunces Tavern Museum, 1993.

Barker, Virgil. *American Painting.* New York: Macmillan & Co., 1950.

Barratt, Carrie Rebora, and Ellen G. Miles. *Gilbert Stuart.* New York: Metropolitan Museum of Art, 2004.

Bermingham, Peter. *American Art in the Barbizon Mood.* Washington, D.C.: Smithsonian Institution Press for the National Collection of Fine Arts, 1975.

Berry-Hill Galleries. *John F. Francis, Not Just Desserts.* New York: Berry-Hill Galleries, 1990.
Bier, Justus. "Carl Christian Brenner: A German American Landscapist." *American German Review* 17 (August 1951): 20–33.
Bigot, Marie Healy. *Life of George P. A. Healy.* N.p., n.d.
The Biographical Encyclopedia of Kentucky of the Dead and Living Men of the Nineteenth Century. Cincinnati: J. M. Armstrong & Co., 1878.
Birchfield, James D., Albert Boime, and William J. Hennessey. *Thomas Satterwhite Noble, 1835–1907.* Lexington: University of Kentucky Art Museum, 1988.
Bishop, Budd H. "Samuel M. Shaver, Washington B. Cooper, and James Cameron." *Antiques* 100, no. 3 (September 1971): 432–437.
Bishop, Robert. *Folk Painters of America.* New York: E. P. Dutton, 1979. Reprint, New York: Greenwich House, 1983.
Bloch, E. Maurice. *George Caleb Bingham.* 2 vols. Berkeley: University of California Press, 1967.
———. *The Paintings of George Caleb Bingham: A Catalogue Raisonné.* Columbia: University of Missouri Press, 1986.
Boime, Albert. *Thomas Couture and the Eclectic Vision.* New Haven: Yale University Press, 1980.
Bolton, Theodore, and George C. Groce. "Catalog of Jarvis Works." *Arts Quarterly* 1 (Autumn 1938): 299–321.
Bonura, Carol. "Benoni Irwin." Manuscript, Speed Museum, Louisville, Kentucky.
Boyce, Annabel Schaefer. "The Artists Frankenstein." Master's thesis, Bryn Mawr College, 1981.
Boyle, Richard, and Guy McElroy. *Robert Scott Duncanson: A Centennial Exhibition.* Cincinnati: Cincinnati Art Museum, 1972.
Breckenridge, James D. *Likeness: A Conceptual History of Ancient Portraiture.* Evanston: Northwestern University Press, 1968.
Breckinridge, Sophonisba Preston. *Madeline McDowell Breckinridge: A Leader in the New South.* Chicago: University of Chicago Press, 1921.
Bridwell, Margaret M. "Oliver Frazer: Early Kentucky Portrait Painter." *Antiques* 92, no. 5 (November 1967): 718–721.
Brilliant, Richard. *Portraiture.* Cambridge, Mass.: Harvard University Press, 1991.
Broun, Elizabeth. "Director's Choice: Interior with Portraits, Thomas LeClear." Smithsonian American Art Museum. http://americanart.si.edu/multimedia/tours/directors/leclear/index3.html.
Bruns, Mrs. Thomas Nelson Carter, comp. *Louisiana Portraits.* New Orleans: National Society of the Colonial Dames of America in the State of Louisiana, 1975.
Burnet, Mary Q. *Art and Artists of Indiana.* New York: Century, 1921.
Burnley, Martha A. "Albert Triplett Burnley." *Southwestern Historical Quarterly* 14, no. 2 (1911): 150–154.
Burroughs, Alan. *Limners and Likenesses: Three Centuries of American Painting.* Cambridge, Mass: Harvard University Press, 1936.
Burton, Vincent. "Some Portraits by Ella S. Hergesheimer." *International Studio* 37 (March 1909): xxxii–xxxiii.
Calo, Mary Ann. *Critical Issues in American Art: A Book of Readings.* Boulder, Colo.: Westview Press, 1998.
Carr, Carolyn Kinder, et al. *Revisiting the White City: American Art at the 1893 World's Fair.* Hanover, N.H.: University Press of New England, 1993.
Cawein, Madison. *Myth and Romance: Being a Book of Verses.* New York: G. P. Putnam's Sons, 1899.
Cederholm, Theresa Dickason. *Afro-American Artists: A Bio-Bibliographical Directory.* Boston: Trustees of the Boston Public Library, 1973.
Chambers, Bruce. *Art and Artists of the South.* Columbia: University of South Carolina Press, 1984.
———. "David Gilmore Blythe (1815–1865): An Artist at Urbanization's Edge." PhD diss., University of Pennsylvania, 1974.
———. "Pythagorean Puzzle of Patrick Lyon." *Art Bulletin* 58 (June 1976): 225–233.
Childe, Cromwell. "A Painter of Pretty Women." *Quarterly Illustrator* 1 (December 1893): 279–282.
Chotner, Deborah, with contributions by Julie Aronson, Sarah D. Cash, and Laurie Weitzenkorn. *American Naïve Paintings.* Washington, D.C.: National Gallery of Art, 1992.
Christ-Janer, Albert. *George Caleb Bingham: Frontier Painter of Missouri.* New York: H. N. Abrams, 1975.
Cincinnati Art Museum. *Exhibition of Portraits of Early Cincinnatians.* Cincinnati: Cincinnati Art Museum, 1932.
———. *The Golden Age: Cincinnati Painters of the Nineteenth Century Represented in the Cincinnati Art Museum.* Cincinnati: Cincinnati Art Museum, 1979.
Cist, Charles. *Cincinnati in 1851.* Cincinnati: W. H. Moore & Co., 1851.
Clark, Thomas D. *A History of Kentucky.* 1937. Reprint, Ashland, Ky.: Jesse Stuart Foundation, 1992.
———. "Reuben T. Durrett and His Kentuckiana Interest

and Collection." *Filson Club History Quarterly* 56 (October 1982): 353–378.

Cloudman, Ruth, et al. *The Speed Art Museum: Highlights from the Collection.* New York: Merrell Publishers, 2007.

Clubbe, John. *Byron's Natural Man: Daniel Boone and Kentucky.* Lexington, Ky.: King Library Press, 1982.

Cohen, Hennig, and William B. Dillingham, eds. *Humor of the Old Southwest.* Boston: Houghton Mifflin, 1954 (2nd ed. 1975, 3rd ed. 1994, both Athens: University of Georgia Press).

Coleman, J. Winston. *Edward Troye: Animal and Portrait Painter.* Lexington, Ky.: Winburn Press, 1958.

———. *Famous Kentucky Duels.* Frankfort, Ky.: Roberts Print Co., 1953. Reprint, Lexington, Ky.: Henry Clay Press, 1969.

———. *Mrs. Stowe: Kentucky and Uncle Tom's Cabin.* Harrogate, Tenn.: Department of Lincolniana, Lincoln Memorial University, 1946.

———. *Robert Burns Wilson: Kentucky Painter, Novelist, and Poet.* Lexington, Ky.: Winburn Press, 1956.

———. *The Springs of Kentucky.* Lexington, Ky.: Winburn Press, 1955.

———. *Three Kentucky Artists: Hart, Price, Troye.* Lexington: University Press of Kentucky, 1974.

Coleman, Minnie Frye. "History of G. Wm. Frye, Artist." *Register of the Kentucky Historical Society* 13, no. 37 (January 1915): 41–42.

Collins, Lewis. *History of Kentucky.* 2 vols. Louisville, Ky.: John P. Morton & Co., 1924.

———. *Historical Sketches of Kentucky, Revised, Enlarged and Brought Down to the Year 1874 by His Son, Richard H. Collins.* 2 vols. Frankfort: Kentucky Historical Society, 1966.

Colton, Calvin. *The Private Correspondence of Henry Clay.* Cincinnati: H. W. Derby, 1856.

Cory, Mrs. Chapell. *The True Story of the First Confederate Flag.* Montgomery, Ala.: Department of History and Archives Publications Historical & Patriotic, 1931.

Cosentino, Andrew J. *The Paintings of Charles Bird King (1785–1862).* Washington, D.C.: Smithsonian Institution Press for the National Collection of Fine Arts, 1977.

Costlow, Owsley C. "The Life of Nicola Marschall." Manuscript, Center for the Study of Southern Painting, Morris Museum, Augusta, Georgia.

Coulter, E. Merton. *The Civil War and Readjustment in Kentucky.* Chapel Hill: University of North Carolina Press, 1926.

Coyle, William. *The Frankenstein Family in Springfield.* Springfield, Ohio: Clark County Historical Society, 1967.

Davis, John. "Eastman Johnson's 'Negro Life at the South' and Urban Slavery in Washington, D.C." *Art Bulletin* 80 (March 1998): 67–92.

Davis, William C. *The Orphan Brigade: The Kentucky Confederates Who Couldn't Go Home.* Mechanicsburg, Pa.: Stackpole Books, 1993.

De Mare, Marie. *G. P. A. Healy, American Artist: An Intimate Chronicle of the Nineteenth Century.* New York: McKay, 1954.

Dickson, Harold E. *John Wesley Jarvis, American Painter, 1780–1840.* New York: New-York Historical Society, 1949.

Donald, David Herbert. *"We Are Lincoln Men": Abraham Lincoln and His Friends* (New York: Simon and Schuster, 2003.

Drake, B., and E. D. Mansfield. *Cincinnati in 1826.* Cincinnati: Morgan, Lodge and Fisher, 1827.

Dreppard, Carl W. *American Pioneer Art and Artists.* Springfield, Mass.: Pond Eckberg Co., 1942.

Dunlap, William. *A History of the Rise and Progress of the Arts of Design in the United States.* Edited by Rita Weiss. 2 vols. 1834. Reprint, New York: Dover, 1969.

Dunn, David W. *A Suitable Likeness: The Paintings of John F. Francis, 1832–1879.* Lewisburg, Pa.: Packwood House Museum, 1986.

Dunn, Nellie Porterfield. "An Artist of the Past: William Edward West and His Friends at Home and Abroad." *Putnam's Monthly* (September 1907): 658–669.

Duveneck, Josephine W. *Frank Duveneck: Painter-Teacher.* San Francisco: John Howell-Books, 1970.

Dwight, Edward H. "Aaron Houghton Corwine: Cincinnati Artist." *Antiques* 67 (June 1955): 502–504.

———. "Audubon's Oils." *Art in America* 51 (April 1963): 77–79.

———. *Audubon Watercolors and Drawings.* Utica and New York: Munson-Williams-Proctor Institute and the Pierpont Morgan Library, 1965.

Eaton, Clement. *The Mind of the Old South.* Baton Rouge: Louisiana State University Press, 1964.

———. *The Waning of the Old South Civilization, 1860–1880s.* Athens: University of Georgia Press, 1968.

Filson, John. *The Discovery, Settlement, and Present State of Kentucke.* Wilmington, Del.: James Adams, 1784.

Flanary, Sarah. "William Edward West in New Orleans and Mississippi." *Antiques* 124 (November 1983): 1010–1015.

Flexner, James Thomas. *The Light of Distant Skies, 1760–1835.* New York: Harcourt, Brace, 1954.

Floyd, William Barrow. *Jouett-Bush-Frazer: Early Kentucky Artists.* Lexington, Ky.: Privately printed, 1968.

———. *Matthew Harris Jouett: Portrait Artist of the Old South.* Lexington, Ky.: Mitchell Fine Arts Center, Transylvania University, 1980.

———. "Portraits of Ante-bellum Kentuckians." *Antiques* 105 (April 1974): 808–816.

Fone, Byrne. *Homophobia: A History.* New York: Metropolitan Books, 2000.

Forsyth, William. *Art in Indiana.* Indianapolis: H. Lieber Co., 1916.

Fort, Ilene Susan, and Michael Quick. *American Art: A Catalogue of the Los Angeles County Museum of Art Collection.* Los Angeles: Los Angeles County Museum of Art, 1995.

Frankenstein, John. *American Art: Its Awful Altitude: A Satire.* Cincinnati: n.p., 1864.

Frankenstein, John Peter. "Niagara." *Harper's New Monthly Magazine* 7 (August 1853): 289–306.

Garretson, Mary Noble Welleck. "Thomas S. Noble and His Paintings." *New-York Historical Society Quarterly Bulletin* 24 (October 1940): 113–123.

Gibson, Arthur Hopkin, comp. *Artists of Early Michigan: A Biographical Dictionary of Artists Native to or Active in Michigan, 1701–1900.* Detroit: Wayne State University Press, 1975.

Gilbert, Barbara C. *Henry Mosler Rediscovered: A Nineteenth-Century Jewish-American Artist.* Los Angeles: Skirball Museum, Skirball Cultural Center, 1995.

Goodpasture, Ann. "Summary of Research to Date on W. S. Shackelford in Clarksville, Tennessee." Manuscript, Tennessee State Library, Nashville.

Goss, Rev. Charles Frederick. *Cincinnati, the Queen City, 1788–1912.* Cincinnati: S. J. Clark Publishing Co., 1912.

Greater Louisville Exposition. *Official Catalogue of Exhibits, Demonstrations, Concessions and Organizations of the Greater Louisville Exposition, First Regiment Armory, March 18–30, 1907.* Louisville: n.p., 1907.

Griffith, Nancy Snell, comp. *Humor of the Old Southwest: An Annotated Bibliography of Primary and Secondary Sources.* New York: Greenwood Press, 1989.

Groce, George C., and David H. Wallace. *The New-York Historical Society's Dictionary of Artists in America, 1564–1860.* New Haven: Yale University Press, 1957.

Hageman, Jane Sikes. *Ohio Pioneer Artists: A Pictorial Review.* Cincinnati: Ohio Furniture Makers, 1993.

Harrison, Lowell H., and James C. Klotter. *A New History of Kentucky.* Lexington: University Press of Kentucky, 1997.

Hart, Charles Henry. "Jouett's Kentucky Children." *Harpers' New Monthly Magazine* 101 (June 1900): 51–56.

———. "Kentucky's Master-Painter Matthew Harris Jouett, 1788–1827," *Harper's New Monthly Magazine* 98 (May 1899): 914–921.

Haverstock, Mary Sayre, Jeannette Mahoney Vance, and Brian L. Meggitt, comps. and eds. *Artists in Ohio, 1787–1900: A Biographical Dictionary.* Kent, Ohio: Kent State University Press, 2000.

Hauser, Arnold. *The Social History of Art.* 2 vols. New York: Knopf, 1952.

Henry, Bettie M., and Bess A. Ray. *Biographical Extracts Relating to Prominent Artists of Louisville and Kentucky.* Louisville, Ky.: Louisville Free Public Library, 1939.

Hills, Patricia. "The Genre Development of Eastman Johnson: The Sources and Development of His Styles and Themes." PhD diss., New York University, 1973.

———. "Painting Race: Eastman Johnson's Pictures of Slaves, Ex-Slaves, and Freedmen." In Teresa A. Carbone and Patricia Hills, with contributions by Jane Weiss, Sarah Burns, and Anne C. Rose, *Eastman Johnson, Painting America,* edited by Teresa A. Carbone. New York: Brooklyn Museum of Art, 1999.

Historical Activities Committee for the National Society of the Colonial Dames of America in the State of Alabama, comp. *Alabama Portraits prior to 1870.* Mobile: National Society of the Colonial Dames of America in the State of Alabama, 1969.

Hofstadter, Richard. *Anti-Intellectualism in American Life.* New York: Knopf, 1963.

Holmberg, James J. "John Wesley Jarvis's Portrait of George Rogers Clark." *Ohio Valley History* 6, no. 1 (Spring 2006): 65–67.

Holt, Michael F. *The Rise and Fall of the American Whig Party.* New York: Oxford University Press, 1999.

Holzer, Harold, and Mark E. Neely Jr. *Mine Eyes Have Seen the Glory: The Civil War in Art.* New York: Orion Books, 1993.

House, Thomas M., and Joe Nickell. "Guide to Nineteenth Century Lexington Photographers." Manuscript, Margaret I. King Library, University of Kentucky, Lexington.

Hyde, William, and Howard L. Conard. *Encyclopedia of the History of St. Louis.* 4 vols. Louisville, Ky.: Southern Publishing Co., 1899.

Irving, Washington. *A History of New York from the Beginning of the World to the End of the Dutch Dynasty by Diedrich Knickerbocker.* Rev. ed. New York: G. P. Putnam's Sons, 1848.

J. B. Speed Memorial Museum. *Centenary Exhibition of the Work of Matthew Harris Jouett; Supplemented by the Work of Gilbert Stuart, His Master, and Oliver Frazer and John Grimes, His Pupils; February 19–March 24, 1928.* Louisville, Ky.: J. B. Speed Memorial Museum, 1928.

Jacobs, James Ripley. *Tarnished Warrior: Major-General James Wilkinson.* New York: Macmillan Co., 1938.

Janson, Anthony F., and A. Ian Fraser. *Handbook of European and American Paintings to 1945: Indianapolis Museum of Art.* Indianapolis: Indianapolis Museum of Art, 1981.

Jeffrey Alan Gallery. *Francesca Alexander, 1837–1917: A Special Exhibition.* New York: Jeffrey Alan Gallery, 1983.

Jillson, Willard Rouse. *A Bibliography of Paul Sawyier, American Artist.* Frankfort, Ky.: State Journal Co., 1939.

John Herron Art Museum. *Wayman Adams, N.A.: Memorial Exhibition of Paintings, Dec. 6–Dec. 27, 1959, The John Herron Art Museum, Indianapolis, Indiana.* Indianapolis: John Herron Art Museum, 1959.

Johnson, Allen, ed. *Dictionary of American Biography.* New York: Charles Scribner's Sons, 1929.

Jonas, E. A. *Matthew Harris Jouett, Kentucky Portrait Painter (1787–1827).* Louisville, Ky.: J. B. Speed Memorial Museum, 1938.

Jones, Arthur. *The Art of Paul Sawyier.* Lexington: University Press of Kentucky, 1976.

———. *Dreaming over Woods and Hills: Kentucky Artists in the Humphrey Collection.* Lexington: University of Kentucky Art Museum, 1992.

Jones, Arthur, and Bruce Weber. *The Kentucky Painter: From the Frontier to the Great War: Exhibition, January 25–March 15, 1981.* Lexington: University of Kentucky Art Museum, 1981.

Katz, Wendy Jean. *Regionalism and Reform: Art and Class Formation in Antebellum Cincinnati.* Columbus: Ohio State University Press, 2002.

Keating, L. Clark. *Audubon: The Kentucky Years.* Lexington: University Press of Kentucky, 1976.

Kelly, Franklin, et al. *American Paintings of the Nineteenth Century, Part 1.* New York: Oxford University Press, 1996.

Kelly, James C. "Portrait Painting in Tennessee." *Tennessee Historical Quarterly* 46 (Winter 1987): 193–276.

Ketner, Joseph D. *The Emergence of an African-American Artist: Robert S. Duncanson, 1821–1872.* Columbia: University of Missouri Press, 1993.

Kincaid, Robert L. *Joshua Fry Speed, Lincoln's Most Intimate Friend.* Harrogate, Tenn.: Department of Lincolniana, Lincoln Memorial University, 1943.

Kleber, John E., ed. *The Encyclopedia of Louisville.* Lexington: University Press of Kentucky, 2001.

———. *The Kentucky Encyclopedia.* Lexington: University Press of Kentucky, 1992.

Kloss, William, et al. *A Nation's Pride: Art in the White House.* Washington, D.C.: White House Historical Association in cooperation with the National Geographic Society, 1992.

Klotter, James C. *The Breckinridges of Kentucky.* Lexington: University Press of Kentucky, 1986.

Knepper, George. *Ohio and Its People.* Kent, Ohio: Kent State University Press, 2003.

Koke, Richard, comp. *American Landscape and Genre Paintings in the New-York Historical Society: A Catalog of the Collection, Including Historical, Narrative, and Marine Art.* Boston: New-York Historical Society in association with G. K. Hall, 1982.

Krane, Susan. *The Wayward Muse: A Historical Survey of Painting in Buffalo.* Buffalo, N.Y.: Albright-Knox Gallery, 1987.

Kurtz, Charles M. *Catalogue of Works of Art in the Art Building of the Southern Exposition at Louisville, Ky.* Louisville, Ky.: John P. Morton & Co., 1883.

———. *Illustrated Catalogue of the Art Department of the Southern Exposition, Louisville, Ky., 1885: Including the Pictures in the American Art Association's Prize-Fund Exhibition, New York, 1885.* Louisville, Ky.: John P. Morton & Co., 1885.

———. *Illustrated Catalogue of the Art Gallery of the Southern Exposition, Louisville, Ky., August 16–October 25, 1884.* Louisville, Ky.: John P. Morton & Co., 1884.

———. *Illustrated Catalogue of the Art Gallery of the Southern Exposition, Louisville, Ky., 1886.* Louisville, Ky.: John P. Morton & Co., 1886.

Lancaster, Clay. *Antebellum Architecture of Kentucky.* Lexington: University Press of Kentucky, 1991.

Landgren, Marchal E. *Robert Loftin Newman, 1827–1912.* Washington, D.C.: National Collection of Fine Arts by the Smithsonian Institution Press, 1973.

Larkin, Oliver. *Art and Life in America.* Rev. ed. New York: Holt, Rinehart and Winston, 1960.

Lay, Mrs. Orville. *Alabama Portraits prior to 1870.* Mobile:

National Society of the Colonial Dames of America in the State of Alabama, 1969.
Lewis, Douglas. "Joseph Mason." Mansucript, National Gallery of Art Library, Washington, D.C.
Lipke, William C. *Thomas Waterman Wood, PNA, 1823–1903.* Montpelier, Vt.: T. W. Wood Art Gallery, 1972.
Lipman, Jean, and Alice Winchester. *The Flowering of American Folk Art, 1776–1876.* New York: Viking in cooperation with the Whitney Museum of American Art, 1974.
Lipton, Leah."Chester Harding and the Life Portraits of Daniel Boone." *American Art Journal* 16 (Summer 1984): 4–19.
———. "New Discoveries in American Art: George Caleb Bingham in the Studio of Chester Harding, Franklin, Missouri, 1820." Edited by Jayne A. Kuchna. *American Art Journal* 16 (Summer 1984): 90–91.
———. *A Truthful Likeness: Chester Harding and His Portraits.* Washington, D.C.: National Portrait Gallery, 1985.
Logan, Rayford W., and Michael R. Winston, eds. *Dictionary of American Negro Biography.* New York: Norton, 1982.
Louisville Industrial Exposition. *Catalogue of Paintings and Sculpture and of the Collections of the Department of Natural History.* Louisville, Ky.: John P. Morton and Co., 1874.
———. *Catalogue of Paintings and Statuary.* Louisville, Ky.: John P. Morton & Co., 1877.
Lynch, Marguerite. "John Neagle's Diary." *Art in America* 37 (April 1949): 79–99.
MacKenzie, Donald Ralph. *Painters in Ohio, 1788–1850: With a Bibliographic Index.* Columbus: Ohio State University Press, 1961.
Mahé, John A., II, and Rosanne McCaffrey, eds. *The Encyclopaedia of New Orleans Artists, 1718–1918.* New Orleans: Historic New Orleans Collection, 1987.
Mallett, Daniel Trowbridge. *Index of Artists, International-Biographical, Including Painters, Sculptors, Illustrators, Engravers, and Etchers of the Past and Present.* New York: R. R. Bowker, 1935.
Marks, Alfred H. "Hawthorne's Daguerreotypist: Scientist, Artist, Reformer." In Nathaniel Hawthorne, *The House of the Seven Gables.* Edited by Seymour L. Gross. New York: Norton, 1967.
Marshall, Anne E. "A Strange Conclusion to a Triumphant War: Memory, Identity, and the Creation of a Confederate Kentucky, 1865–1930." PhD diss., University of Georgia, 2004.
Martin, Mrs. William H. *Catalogue of All Known Paintings by Matthew Harris Jouett.* Louisville, Ky.: J. B. Speed Memorial Museum, 1939.
McCormick, James, et al. *A Boston Painter in Kentucky: Asa Park (1796–1827).* Georgetown, Ky.: Georgetown College Art Department and Georgetown & Scott County Museum, 2006.
McDermott, John Francis. *George Caleb Bingham, River Portraitist.* Norman: University of Oklahoma Press, 1959.
———. "Likenesses by Audubon." *Antiques* 67 (June 1955): 499–501.
McElroy, Guy C. *Facing History: The Black Image in American Art, 1710–1940.* San Francisco: Bedford Arts, 1990.
McLean, Genetta. *Dixie Selden: An American Impressionist.* Cincinnati: Cincinnati Art Gallery, 2001.
Meacham, Charles M. *A History of Christian County, Kentucky, from Oxcart to Airplane.* Nashville, Tenn.: Marshall & Bruce, 1930.
Morgan, John Hill. *Gilbert Stuart and His Pupils.* New York: New-York Historical Society, 1939.
Newcomb, John Bease. *Genealogical Memoir of the Newcomb Family.* Chicago: Knight & Leonard, 1874.
Noble, Louis Legrand. *The Course of Empire, Voyage of Life, and Other Pictures of Thomas Cole, with Selections from His Letters and Miscellaneous Writings Illustrative of His Life, Character and Genius.* New York: Cornish Lamport, 1853.
Nochlin, Linda. *Realism.* Harmondsworth: Penguin, 1971.
O'Connor, John, Jr. "Reviving a Forgotten Artist: Sketch of James Reid Lambdin, 1807–1884, the Pittsburgh Painter of American Statesmen." *Carnegie Magazine* 12 (1938): 115–118.
Patillo, Edward. "John C. Grimes, Alabama's First Portrait Artist." *Alabama Heritage* 63 (Winter 2002): 8–17.
Payne, Warren, and Julie Payne. *The Work of Paul Plaschke.* Jeffersonville, Ind.: Howard Steamboat Museum, 2008.
Peat, Wilbur D. *Chase Centennial Exhibition: Commemorating the Birth of William Merritt Chase, November 1, 1849.* Indianapolis: Art Association of Indianapolis, 1949.
———. *Pioneer Painters of Indiana.* Indianapolis: Art Association of Indianapolis, 1954.
———. *Portraits and Painters of the Governors of Indiana, 1800–1943.* Indianapolis: Indianapolis Historical Society, 1944.
Pennington, Estill Curtis. *Downriver: Currents of Style in Louisiana Painting, 1800–1950.* Gretna, La.: Pelican Publishing Co., 1991.

———. *Kentucky: The Master Painters from the Frontier Era to the Great Depression.* [Paris, Ky:] Cane Ridge Publishing, 2008.

———. "Kentucky-Mississippi Itinerancy." *Southern Quarterly* 25, no.1 (Autumn 1986): 3–21.

———. *Look Away: Reality and Sentiment in Southern Art.* Atlanta: Peachtree Publishers, 1989.

———. *Messengers of Style: Itinerancy and Taste in Southern Portraiture, 1784–1867.* Greenville, S.C.: Greenville County Museum of Art, 1993.

———. "Painting Lord Byron: An Account by William Edward West." *Archives of American Art Journal* 24 (1984): 16–21.

———. *A Southern Collection.* Augusta, Ga.: Morris Communications Group, 1992.

———. *Subdued Hues: Mood and Scene in Southern Landscape Painting, 1865–1925.* Augusta, Ga.: Morris Museum of Art, 1999.

———. *William Edward West, 1788–1857: Kentucky Painter.* Washington, D.C.: National Portrait Gallery, 1985.

Pennsylvania Academy of the Fine Arts. *Catalogue of an Exhibition of Portraits by John Neagle.* Philadelphia: Pennsylvania Academy of the Fine Arts, 1925.

Perrin, William Henry, ed. *History of Fayette County, Kentucky.* Easley, S.C.: Southern Historical Press, 1979.

Pierce, Catherine W. "W. Francis Alexander." Parts 1 and 2. *Old Time New England* 44 (October–December 1953): 29–46; 56 (October–December 1965): 35–44.

Pinckney, Pauline. *Painting in Texas: The Nineteenth Century.* Austin: University of Texas Press, 1967.

Pittenger, Charles, and Elizabeth A. Perkins. *Patrick Henry Davenport: Kentucky Portrait Maker.* Frankfort: Kentucky Historical Society, 1982.

Poesch, Jesse. *The Art of the Old South: Painting, Sculpture, Architecture, and the Products of Craftsmen, 1560–1860.* New York: Knopf, 1983.

Porter, James A. "Robert Scott Duncanson, Mid-Western Romantic Realist." *Art in America* 39 (October 1951): 98–154.

Posey, John Thorton. "Rascality Revisited: In Defense of General James Wilkinson." *Filson Club Historical Quarterly* 74 (Fall 2000): 309–326.

Pratt, Julius W. "Millard Fillmore." In *Dictionary of American Biography.* New York: Scribner, 1960.

Price, Samuel Woodson. *Old Masters of the Bluegrass: Jouett, Bush, Grimes, Frazer, Morgan, Hart.* Filson Club Publications, no. 17. Louisville, Ky.: J. P. Morton and Co., 1902.

Quick, Michael. *American Portraiture in the Grand Manner, 1720–1920.* Los Angeles: Los Angeles County Museum of Art, 1981.

Ramirez, Jan Seidler. "Hiram Powers." In Kathryn Greenthal, Paula M. Kozol, and Jan Seidler Ramirez, *American Figurative Sculpture in the Museum of Fine Arts, Boston,* 30–38. Boston: The Museum, 1986.

Ranck, George Washington. *History of Lexington, Kentucky: Its Annals and Recent Progress.* Cincinnati: Robert Clarke & Co., 1872.

Rash, Nancy. *The Paintings and Politics of George Caleb Bingham.* New Haven: Yale University Press, 1991.

Rattermann, H. A., ed. *The German Pioneer.* Typescript translation of the German original, published in Cincinnati, 1882–1883, in The Filson Historical Society Library.

Remini, Robert V. *Henry Clay: Statesman for the Union.* New York: Norton, 1991.

Rhodes, Richard. *John James Audubon: The Making of an American.* New York: Knopf, 2004.

Richards, Irving T. "Audubon, Joseph R. Mason, and John Neal." *American Literature* 6 (May 1934): 122–140.

Roark, Elisabeth. "John Frankenstein's 'Portrait of Godfrey Frankenstein' and the Aesthetics of Friedrich Schiller." *American Art* (Spring 2001): 74–83.

Rollins, C. B. "Letters of George Caleb Bingham to James S. Rollins." Parts 1–8. *Missouri Historical Review* 32 (October 1937): 3–34; 32 (January 1938): 162–202; 32 (April 1938): 340–377; 32 (July 1938): 484–522; 33 (October 1938): 45–78; 33 (January 1939): 203–229; 33 (April 1939): 349–384; 33 (July 1939): 499–526.

Roof, Katharine Metcalf. *The Life and Art of William Merritt Chase.* New York: C. Scribner's Sons, 1917.

Rothert, Otto A. *A Picturography of Madison Cawein.* Louisville, Ky.: J. P. Morton & Co., 1921.

———. *The Story of a Poet: Madison Cawein; His Intimate Life as Revealed by His Letters and Other Hitherto Unpublished Material, Including Reminiscences by His Closest Associates.* Filson Club Publications, no. 30. Louisville, Ky.: J. P. Morton & Co., 1921.

Rumford, Beatrix, and Carolyn J. Weekley. *Treasures from the Abby Aldrich Rockefeller Folk Art Center.* Boston: Little, Brown, 1989.

Rusk, Fern Helen. *George Caleb Bingham, the Missouri Artist.* Jefferson City, Mo.: Hugh Stephens Co., 1917.

Saugrain de Vigni, Antoine. *L'Odyssée américaine d'une famille française [par] le docteur Antoine Saugraine; étude suivie de manuscrits inédits et de la correspondance de Sophie Michau Robinson.* Trans. H. Fouré-Selter. Baltimore: Johns Hopkins Press, 1936.

Schmidt, Martin. "The Artist and the Artisan: Two Men of Early Louisville." *Filson Club Historical Quarterly* 62 (January 1988): 32–51.

Severns, Martha. *Greenville County Museum of Art: The Southern Collection.* New York: Hudson Hills Press, 1995.

———. "Jeremiah Theus of Charleston: Plagiarist or Pundit?" *Southern Quarterly* 24 (Fall–Winter 1985): 56–70.

Shackleton, Robert. "A Benvenuto of the Backwoods." *Harper's Magazine,* July 1916, 267–277.

Shapiro, Michael Edward. *George Caleb Bingham.* New York: Abrams, 1993.

Shelley, Donald A. "John James Audubon, Artist." *Magazine of Art* 39 (May 1946): 171–175.

Sherman, Frederick Fairchild. *Early American Portraiture.* New York: Privately printed, 1930. Reprint, New York: B. Blom, 1972.

Simmons, Linda Crocker. *Jacob Frymire: American Limner.* Washington, D.C.: Corcoran Gallery of Art, 1975.

Simon, Robin. *The Portrait in Britain and America.* Boston: G. K. Hall, 1987.

Simpson, Elizabeth Murphy. *Bluegrass Houses and Their Traditions.* Lexington, Ky.: Transylvania Press, 1932.

"Soule Family of Dayton." *Dayton Art Institute Bulletin* 35 (September 1976): n.p.

Sparling, Tobin Andrews. *The Great Exhibition: A Question of Taste.* New Haven: Yale Center for British Art, 1982.

Speakes, Vera Jacobs, comp. *Mississippi Portraiture.* Jackson: National Society of the Colonial Dames of America in the State of Mississippi, 1987.

Speed, Thomas. *Records and Memorials of the Speed Family.* Louisville, Ky.: Courier-Journal Job Printing Co., 1892.

Stowe, Harriet Beecher. *A Key to Uncle Tom's Cabin.* Boston: J. P. Jewett & Co., 1853.

Sully, Thomas. *Hints to Young Painters: A Historic Treatise on the Color, Expression, and Painting Techniques of American Artists of the Colonial and Federal Periods.* New York: Reinhold Publishing Corp., 1965.

T. W. Wood Art Gallery. *Catalog of Pictures in the Art Gallery.* Montpelier, Vt.: T. W. Wood Art Gallery, 1913.

Taft, Robert. "The Pictorial Record of the West, IV: Custer's Last Stand." In John Mulvany, "Cassily Adams and Otto Becker." *Kansas Historical Quarterly* (November 1946): 361–390.

Tarkington, Booth. *Some Old Portraits: A Book about Art and Human Beings.* New York: Doubleday, 1939.

Taylor, Joshua. *America as Art.* Washington, D.C.: National Collection of Fine Arts by the Smithsonian Institution Press, 1976.

Thompson, Rhodes, comp. *Voices from Cane Ridge.* St. Louis: Bethany Press, 1954.

Torchia, Robert W. *John Neagle: Philadelphia Portrait Painter.* Philadelphia: Historical Society of Pennsylvania, 1989.

Townsend, John Wilson. *Kentucky in American Letters, 1784–1912.* 2 vols. Cedar Rapids, Iowa: Torch Press, 1913.

———. "Paul Sawyier, Kentucky Artist: Some Recollections of Him." *Filson Club Historical Quarterly* 33 (October 1959): 310–313.

Tripp, C. A. *The Intimate World of Abraham Lincoln.* Edited by Lewis Gannett. New York: Free Press, 2005.

Trollope, Frances. *Domestic Manners of the Americans.* Edited by Donald Smalley. New York: Knopf, 1949.

Troye, Edward. *The Dead Sea, and the Ruins of Sodom and Gomorrah: Including also a Description of Troye's Painting of the Dead Sea, Now on Exhibition at the Apollo Rooms, 410 Broadway.* New York: W. A. Townsend, 1858.

———. *The Race Horses of America, 1832–1872.* 1867. Reprint, Saratoga Springs, N.Y.: National Museum of Racing, 1981.

Tuckerman, Henry T. *Book of the Artists. American Artist Life, Comprising Biographical and Critical Sketches of American Artists: Preceded by an Historical Account of the Rise and Progress of Art in America.* New York: G. P. Putnam & Sons, 1867.

Van Devanter, Ann C., and Alfred V. Frankenstein, with the assistance of Shirley S. Simpson. *American Self-Portraits, 1670–1973.* Washington, D.C.: International Exhibitions Foundation, 1974.

Vaughan, William. *Romantic Art.* New York: Oxford University Press, 1978.

Viele, Chase. "Four Artists of Mid-Nineteenth Century Buffalo." *New York History* 43 (January 1962): 49–78.

Virginia Museum of Fine Arts. *A Souvenir of the Exhibition Entitled Healy's Sitters; or, A Portrait Panorama of the Victorian Age, Being a Comprehensive Collection of the Likenesses of Some of the Most Important Personages of Europe & America, as Portrayed by George Peter Alexander Healy between the Years 1837 and 1899, Supplemented with Documents Relating to the Artist's Life and Furnishings of the Period, on View at the Virginia Museum of Fine Arts, 24 January–5 March 1950.* Richmond: Virginia Museum of Fine Arts, 1950.

Vitz, Robert C. *The Queen and the Arts: Cultural Life in Nineteenth-Century Cincinnati.* Kent, Ohio: Kent State University Press, 1989.

Vlach, John Michael. *Plain Painters: Making Sense of American Folk Art.* Washington, D.C.: Smithsonian Institution Press, 1988.

Walters, Edward M. "Reuben T. Durrett, the Durrett Collection, and the University of Chicago." *Filson Club History Quarterly* 56 (October 1982): 379–394.

Ward, William S. *A Literary History of Kentucky.* Knoxville: University of Tennessee Press, 1988.

Watson, E. W. "Wayman Adams Paints a Portrait." *Art Instruction* 3 (June 1939): 6–12.

Weber, Bruce, and Arthur F. Jones. *The Kentucky Painter: From the Frontier Era to the Great War: Exhibition, January 25–March 15, 1981.* Lexington: University of Kentucky Art Museum, 1981.

Weber-Scobie, Anne. *The Life and Work of Irish-American Artist John Mulvany (1839–1906).* Binghamton, N.Y.: the author, 1993.

Wehle, Harry B. *American Miniatures, 1730–1850.* 1927. Reprint, New York: Kennedy Galleries, 1970.

Weidner, Ruth Irwin. *The Lambdins of Philadelphia: Newly Discovered Works; The Lambdin Family Collection of Paintings by James Reid Lambdin and George Cochran Lambdin.* Philadelphia: Schwarz Gallery, 2002.

Weinstein, Cindy. *The Cambridge Companion to Harriet Beecher Stowe.* Cambridge: Cambridge University Press, 2004.

Whitley, Edna Talbott. *Kentucky Ante-bellum Portraiture.* Paris, Ky.: The National Society of the Colonial Dames of America in the Commonwealth of Kentucky, 1956.

Wilkinson, James. *Memoirs of My Own Times.* 3 vols. Philadelphia: Abraham Small, 1816.

Williams, Hermann Warner. *Mirror to the American Past: A Survey of American Genre Painting, 1750–1900.* Greenwich, Conn.: New York Graphic Society, 1973.

Wilmerding, John, ed. *American Light: The Luminist Movement, 1850–1875; Paintings, Drawings, Photographs.* Washington, D.C.: National Gallery of Art, 1980.

Wilson, Samuel M. "Additional Notes on Matthew Harris Jouett: Kentucky Portrait Painter." *Filson Club History Quarterly* 14 (January–April 1940): 65–102.

———. "Matthew Harris Jouett: Kentucky Portrait Painter." *Filson Club History Quarterly* 14 (April 1939): 75–96.

Woodall, Joanna, ed. *Portraiture: Facing the Subject.* Manchester: Manchester University Press, 1997.

Wright, Leslie Carol. "Men Making Meaning in Nineteenth-Century American Genre Painting, 1860–1900." PhD diss., Stanford University, 1993.

Wright, R. Lewis. *Artists in Virginia before 1900: An Annotated Checklist.* Charlottesville: University Press of Virginia, 1983.

Wyatt-Brown, Bertram. *Southern Honor: Ethics and Behavior in the Old South.* 1982. Reprint, New York: Oxford University Press, 2008.

Young, Mahonri Sharp. "The Two Worlds of Frank Duveneck." *American Art Journal* 1 (Spring 1969): 92–103.

INDEX

Page numbers in italics refer to an illustration or its caption.